THE KEY TO THE
SCIENCES OF MAN

THE KEY TO THE SCIENCES OF MAN

THE "IMPOSSIBLE" RELATIVITY OF VALUE REACTIONS

by

D. G. GARAN, Ph.D., J.U.D., LL.D.

•

Author of *The Paradox of Pleasure and Relativity,*
and *Relativity for Psychology*

•

PHILOSOPHICAL LIBRARY

New York

CONTENTS

Contents

Cholesterol. The Functional Causes of Cancer. Arthritis, Diabetes, Peptic Ulcer. Other Functional Disorders. Overweight. Longevity. The Medical Blunder of Our Age. Conclusion.

Education as an Art and as a Science. The Unseen Causal Sources in Adjustment and Motivation. Drug Addiction, and Juvenile Delinquency. Sexual Maladjustments, Social Complexes, Worries, Suicide. Work and Leisure. Conclusion.

Ideas, Ideologies, Doctrines, Symbols and Myths as Causes. The Illogic of Values, Reasons and Factual Conditions. Irrationality: More Confusion. Social Motivations, Intellect, Emotional "Improvements", and Restrictions. Compulsive Unwanted Reactions. Metaphysics of "Social" Causality. Cults and Customs as Fixations. The Compulsion of Social Disorders. The Paradoxical Course of History. The Contradictions of Political Movements. Science of Economic Adjustment. The Role of Capital, Consumption and Savings. Postmortem Economics of "Normal" Economy. Business Cycles. Savings vs. Consumption. Conclusion.

Matter and Field as Causal Opposites. Causal Explanations of the Dilemmas of Modern Physics. Mysteries of Light and Radiation. The Avowed Mystery of Gravitation. The Unseen Cause of Electromagnetism. The Mysteries of Cosmic Creation, Planets, Formation of Elements, Nuclear Reactions, Negative Matter. The Unseen Causes of the Living Process. Genetics: Half-

Contents

FOREWORD

The central idea of this book is contrary to the deepest value convictions by which we all live. Readers may therefore find completely unacceptable what the book tries to explain. But the only merit of this book — whatever its faults — is that it presents a generally important, though simple, causal truth which has remained unnoticed because it is humanly "impossible". The logic itself of the relativity, which is the central idea of the book, is contrary to the usual causal logic. This may make the reasoning in the book seem continuously distorted. We are therefore explaining the relative causal logic repeatedly throughout the book — which does not improve its style.

The unusualness of the central idea of the book creates other difficulties. We know it is graceful, in good writing, to understate one's own ideas and to emphasize the views of others. But the ideas in this book are so contrary to the generally held convictions that we had to oppose completely the present views. Moreover, we had to turn against the best authorities we could find in every field. The way to test a new idea is to check it against established facts. We have tried to confront our relativity concept with the most important facts discovered by the best minds in every field. Evidently, we had to end by opposing the foremost authorities; and had to do so in a grossly incomplete way due to lack of space. It may seem as if we are seeking to criticize, in a cursory, disrespectful way, what is best in our science and learning.

Against this, we are hopefully offering a causal insight which, though simple, could serve as the basis for the sciences of man. Everything man feels, thinks, knows or does is determined by organic value reactions; even abstract thought is a value process. The nature and causality of organic value reactions, as of all

ix

uniform natural phenomena, follow a simple causal law. This
law has not been discovered only because it is humanly "impossible".

Most sciences start with simple humanly unthinkable causal
truths. The roundness and movement of earth, the gravitational
force, or the evolution by selection are simple, obvious truths,
that were unthinkable or meaningless under the man-centered,
habitual value outlook. The direction in which such discoveries
have moved is toward the increasing rejection of the humanly
inveterate, nonrelative value convictions. The relativity of value
reactions or of values themselves is the furthest point on this
road and scientifically the most revealing, long hidden truth.

The relativity of value reactions means that a satisfaction,
pleasure release or inner value derives from equal need, nonsatisfaction, restriction or disvalue — as explained in the book.
The cause of this relativity is the most universal and most important fact of organic life: the maintenance by organism of its
sameness. No organism can become more than its normalcy,
statically or dynamically. Organic forces or motivations are satisfactions or pleasures as releases of the life flow itself. But satisfaction can arise only upon equal need as disturbance or nonsatisfaction; and any special motivational release of the life flow
requires its previous accumulation by restrictions.

In brief, within the inexorable organic limitedness or sameness,
any satisfaction, release of forces or use of reserves requires equal
nonsatisfaction or restriction, the opposite process. Since all
values are, at bottom, organic releases or satisfactions, they cannot arise without their equal opposites, the inner disvalues.

But the requirement of equal disvalue for every value is totally
unthinkable to man. All present thought and scientific logic
maintain that values derive from sources of similar, not opposite
nature, or that positive value reactions come from positive value
experiences. Since the values and value reactions determine all
human feelings, thought, knowledge or behavior, all fields dealing with man are presently governed by a causal logic contrary
to facts. Even the opposite, "negative" causal backgrounds of

man's "positive" physical reality, in the world of physics, are missed.

The relative insight reveals in all human experience and reality the "negative" causal side which is never seen or valued but actually determines, and exceeds in importance, the "positive" side men see, value and accept as decisive. The relative insight also makes possible a scientific or causally understood creation of human capacities and motivations. Needs as nonsatisfactions, and restrictions are the sources of satisfactions and releases, which constitute all motivations and capacities. These can be increased unlimitedly because nonsatisfactions and restrictions can be increased to any extent. Evidently, the relative insight can make the sciences of man causally understood or practically scientific, for the first time.

All humanistic thought and sciences proceed by the logic that values derive from sources of same nature or that positive value reactions come from positive experiences. Modern science is formally experimental, and experiments do show that immediate motivations or capacities improve upon increase in satisfactions or releases. Actually such direct increase in the strictly limited releases leads to their exhaustion, and to opposite reactions as the organism restores its inexorably limited sameness or normalcy.

Experimentally clear organic "improvements" thus lead to equal opposite reactions felt as worsening or disease. If such worsening is overcome by further direct increase in releases, the opposite reaction or "disease" becomes more intense. This vicious circle can deepen such overadjustments into functional impoverishment or disorders of any intensity. Drug use is the simplest example; but all overadjustments, mental or physiologic, obey the same law.

The result is that, in the modern, "scientific" atmosphere of the direct improvements or increased releases and freedoms, men are suffering from causally unexplained stresses, impoverishment and diseases, to an unprecedented extent, in spite of general progress. Modern man, encouraged to live by the improvements or pleasures alone, made possible by modern progress, is heading for self-destruction, through a causal or scientific misunderstanding. Only equal non-satisfactions or restrictions can provide the satisfactions or releases as the mental and physiologic enrichments and capacities. The relative insight offers the first scientific or causally understood defense of the moral restrictions and of our old restrictive cultural tradition.

The humanistic and scientific, direct causal logic is as general as it is absurd for the sciences of man. If the positive value reactions, the sources of the capacities, derived from positive value experiences, we would all be instant supermen. For we always strive to enjoy, and start with, the positive experiences alone. The modern human sciences become confusing alchemies in which the most precious human capacities are somehow expected to come with the ease of positive satisfactions or pleasures.

The relative insight shows that in the human sciences as well you do not get something for nothing. Our hedonistic and libertarian era has been created by causally confused, practically dangerous attitudes. The humanistic delusions about the noble sources of inner values, which are satisfactions or releases, should have been corrected by science. Instead, science has compounded the error by using a causal logic that is right in physical sciences but contrary to causal truths in the sciences of man. These sciences have to find their own, relative, causal logic, that we have tried to explain in this book.

D. G.

THE KEY TO THE
SCIENCES OF MAN

I

THE "IMPOSSIBLE" CAUSAL LAW

The central problem of our era of sciences is that the fields dealing with man are not yet scientific. The physical sciences and technology are advancing spectacularly and transforming our world, while there are only contradictions and conflicting views about the problems besetting man. We hear often that man now can travel to the moon but is unable to solve the human problems on the earth. The reason is that there can be no science without causal understanding, without the knowledge of what comes from what. In the technical sciences such understanding is clear and, ultimately, can be derived from the simplest natural laws. If we had such laws in the fields dealing with man, the controversies would cease and a science could begin.

Can there be simple causal laws for what man is or does? Man is a product of nature. He is an organism obeying most rigorous laws. Every organism maintains physiologically a state, normal for its species and itself, uniformly precise to the tiniest detail. And man's mental life must be obeying the same natural laws, since it is only an elaboration of the physiological self. But nature does not know complex causal laws. Therefore, the natural law or principle that governs man can be only elementarily simple. Let us not be confused by the multiplicity of effects or phenomena deriving from natural laws. The law of natural selection or of gravitation finds expression in endlessly numerous and varied forms, but remains one and simple.

Evidently the discovery of that simple law of the physiologic and mental behavior of man would be the most important event for man and science. Why has not the discovery been made? The reason is the contradiction of human existence. We shall explain this contradiction in detail later. Here, we may only

1

mention that man, as all living forms, exists by striving for release of the life flow, by the positively-felt drive for pleasure, but that restriction or opposition of this drive is what gives shape and evolutionary variation or enrichment to any living form or function. Without opposition or limitation, a drive or force, that is life, can only lose itself in formless dissipation.

Moreover, if this necessary opposition is to persist, the two sides in it should not become reconciled. Men should not re-signedly accept the inevitability of the opposing and limiting other side. As a normal and evolutionary living being man has to avoid all relativistic, degenerative attitudes, that a recognition of the two opposing sides in his existence, of its full causal truth, would bring.

The Law of Relative Causation

The simplest formulation of the law of relative causation is that *there can be no satisfaction, release, pleasure or inner value without equal need, nonsatisfaction, restriction or disvalue.* This is evident in the clearest form in the equivalence of a satisfaction, like eating or drinking, with the need or nonsatisfaction, like hunger or thirst. The most fundamental satisfactions like those of security or growth require as clearly their opposites, the in-security or restriction, if they are to be felt as values. Unchanging full security or growth is felt as little as unhindered breathing. Any satisfaction persisting in full gives no sense of satisfaction.

When we come to the more involved value processes like thinking, or the culturally conditioned value beliefs, the require-ment of the equal opposite may be less clear. One may only see that all cognition consists of differentiation and that for every value there is an equal disvalue or evil. But we can be sure that *all higher value processes and value feelings have to derive from the lower,* fundamental ones, therefore have to obey the same law or functional "design".

The all-inclusive fundamental natural purpose, "design" or *law of every living organism is to conserve its normalcy or same-ness.* This derives from the widest ultimate, therefore tautologically simple fact that everything exists by virtue of its capacity to persist, which amounts to existence for sake of existence. If this seems unconvincing, think of how every value loses meaning for man if his existence is in danger. Anything that does not have the capacity to persist is not there any more. But for an *organism*, its capacity to persist depends uniquely on its conservation of all the evolutionary acquired functions and forms, to the tiniest detail, in simple but total repetition of their sameness. This preservation of its identity or sameness by the organism is so universal or commonplace that it is not seen as anything worth knowing. But this very universality makes it the fundamental single law of organic life.

Every other function or form in the organism derives from this fundamental mechanism. Living forms can become extremely complex. But they always derive from a lower, fundamental mechanism, therefore cannot be different from it in their purpose and have to obey the same law. Organism, in all its functions, merely restores its normalcy upon disturbance — finds satisfactions upon experiencing needs. Naturally there can be only as much restoration as there was disturbance. All values for a person are embedded in the value of his existence, but without disturbance existence is meaningless. Only when threatened does the existence reveal its value.

It is obvious that there can be no value experience without organic change. Add this fact to that of the permanence of organic sameness, and you have the law of relative causation. If organism has to change in order to have experience but in the end has to remain the same, then every experience amounts to a change that requires equal, opposite change. Of course, an enormous amount of learning as permanent changes in release pathways is built up by the play of equal satisfactions and needs. But the pathways are not the force that moves or motivates organism. The releases or value reactions, using the pathways, are such forces and they can follow only the law of equal opposites.

Anyway, satisfaction, release, inner value or restoration of normalcy becomes possible only upon equal need, nonsatisfaction, restriction, disvalue or disturbance of normalcy. You can

add to an amount that has to remain the same only by previously subtracting from it. Fullest satisfaction, release or value
leads to no sense of satisfaction at all. If we were constantly
satisfied in our functions of eating, drinking or security, as we
now are in the function of breathing, we would not even know
what the satisfactions or pleasures of eating, drinking or security
are. Conversely, non-satisfaction, pain, restriction, inner disvalue,
or disturbance of normalcy is possible only to the extent there
was previous satisfaction, release, value, or restored normalcy.
But since we have here negative reactions, that go beyond the
normal simple scheme of the striving for positive normalcy, we
have to go into more detail.

Let us look at pain, as the prototype of negative reactions.
A person born with an organic defect that would make a normal
person feel excruciating pain feels nothing. Also experiments
with pain sensations from radiant heat show that the pain ceases
if the heat remains steady. All sensations decrease progressively
upon constant or even increasing stimulation, as the generally
recognized Weber-Fechner law shows. But experiments by psychologists can deal here only with sensations like vision, hearing
or touch. Real pain is neither experimented with nor can it be
experimentally measured. Statements by persons who have been
tortured confirm that pain ceases to increase upon reaching a
certain limit; and the torturers have to invent new means. All
this, however, does not provide full explanation. We know that
pain from real organic injury or disturbance does not cease upon
continuance, at least not completely.

Full explanation has to take into account the deep *interdependence of organic mechanisms.* An isolated mechanism, as in
the peripheral skin sensations, does react relatively. There a new
disturbance or pain is felt only after renewed restoration of normalcy. But when the skin on your fingers becomes senseless, in
cold, a deeper mechanism reacts with pain; and when the whole
finger becomes numb, still deeper mechanisms become subsequently involved. The fully relative insensitivity upon disturbance could be reached here, but *only after all the interdependent
mechanisms had run the full cycle of disturbance.* This would
require the full disturbance of the whole organism, amounting

to death. Thus for any disturbance, even a grave injury or hunger, the relative equalization of opposites is always reached, but only upon the final disturbance or loss of the whole previous organic growth. Something that has not grown cannot bring pain. But any growth, as the past wealth of positively-felt values, has to bring equal negative reactions, upon its decline and death.

The natural simple law of relativity produces involved effects where it applies to the endless variety of factors and conditions of organic existence. One of the main conditions is that organism has to accumulate vast reserves which become its normalcy. *By delaying or holding back the releases inherent in the force of life, organism accumulates sources of usable potentials.* Life is of cosmic strength, as we shall see later, but it would lose itself in formless dissipation if it were not restricted. By restriction this force is channeled to create complex forms of growth, and is held back as vast reserves of release potentials.

We shall use the concept "release" to designate the enjoyment of the flow of force and growth inherent in all life. The opposite concept "restriction" will be used to designate the "damming" up of the life force or the restraining of the growth rate, so that reserves or potentials of releases are accumulated for use as desired motivations and capacities.

Naturally the reserves of potentials of release or growth, that organism normally maintains, can be overspent, when the person is stimulated to enjoy himself, live faster or have stronger, more pleasant releases. We shall call it *overadjustment.* Then the organism has to restore the excessively spent release reserves. It does so by exactly opposite processes, restriction and slowed down life flow, which are felt as displeasures, anxiety or slow death. The overenjoyed pleasure or value feelings thus have to be "paid for" by exactly equal feelings of displeasure or disvalue. To maintain its normal status of potentials *organism has to respond to any excess in releases by an equal excess in restrictions.*

This is a very important unsuspected practical effect of the relative causation. All attempts by man and science to make direct improvements in organic potentials, without previous restrictions, will bring only more exhaustion, stress, anxiety and disorders. Increase in releases does yield positive feelings and satisfactions, which show as enrichment of psychological capacities or improvement of physical well-being. This is proved by experimental scientists, and basically believed by every man, since nobody is aware of the relative causal logic. But such *direct enrichments and improvements reverse into exactly opposite reactions,* incapacities and feelings of disease, in the end. Then to overcome these reactions the person has to increase the same means of stimulation, and ends by deepening the ill. The simplest illustration is offered by the use of drugs.

But it does not matter how such direct "improvements" in the releases are attained — by "positive thinking", transcendental meditation or coffee-and-beef diet. All addictions, functional diseases, hangovers upon overenjoyments, or depressions upon overstimulation are results of the same process. The *millions of all kinds of addicts,* including the smokers and coffee drinkers, are the living proofs, the *walking experiments,* in all their real-life completeness, of the relative causation.

The multiplicity of organic factors and levels of integration may produce all kinds of combinations and seeming inconsistencies of the relative effects. It is often pointed out that organism is endlessly adaptive, which seems contrary to the maintenance of organic sameness. In truth, *adaptation rather confirms* that organism preserves its sameness. Organism merely changes the adjustment under changed conditions so that the deeper organic sameness can be preserved. Exposed to heat, organism adapts, sweats, to preserve its normal temperature. The opposite effect follows later, when returned to normal temperature organism feels cold. Exposed to stimulation by nicotine or drug, organism develops counter-mechanisms, like the Nissl's granules, to conserve its normalcy. Then, if the drug or smoking is discontinued, these restrictive mechanisms produce the extremely strong opposite effect, before the organism has the time to remove them.

Organic growth is another confusing factor. Many theorists stress human growth as the source of never-ending increase in value experiences. But normal growth gives no particular sense of values. Any fully satisfied function, whether it is breathing or maintenance of an organ in its normal state, gives no sense of satisfaction, unless it has been previously disturbed. Moreover, normal growth is imperceptibly small in comparison with the other metabolic processes; and organism may level out any unevenness in growth to preserve the sameness of life. Also, if there is a small pleasure or value gain from the more vigorous growth in early youth, it is taken away by equal later decline and death. Even this oscillation is probably leveled out, greatly, by compensations within the range of whole life.

Certainly manipulations of the mechanisms of growth or increase of its rate can be a great source of release. But any increase above the normal rate of growth has to bring exactly equal decrease and restrictions in releases at the next phase. The same applies to all dynamic processes within the organism; which equally provide no experience as long as they proceed at their normal nondisturbed rate. Thus we can say that *dynamically as well as statically* organism obeys the law of relative causation.

The effects of the law are particularly clear-cut in the *psychological world*. There we do not have the difficulties that result from the deep organic involvements which require reaching the point of death before full relativity results. The psychological world is biologically so peripheral that it can operate without deeper involvements, even more so than the sensations of skin or vision do. In this world one reaches full completion of a value without delays. One can go from creation to extinction of a value — from "birth" to "death" — without the requirement that the organism undergo similar drastic changes. The whole purpose of mind is to create its own worlds, or destroy them, at every moment, as mere *"experiments" without actual, full bodily involvement.* These "experiments" obey the law of relativity, because the miniaturized experiences in them still are organic value processes; the experiences as changes derive their values or meanings from the permanence or standards of organic mechanisms. Even abstract thought is a value process, though the value experiences in it are infinitesimal and endlessly complex. Without conscious feeling, as value experience, there is no thought or knowledge. You can watch a TV scene and not know what you saw if you had no conscious feeling about it.

We may add some general reflections on the question of *natural laws.* A natural law is merely the result of men understanding something in nature with unerring completeness. All men understand perfectly, therefore simply and *uniformly,* what substance is, what causality means, how permanence of matter works or what force and movement are. The reason for this is that man exists along these lines exactly in the same way as nature does. Since thinking is a form of existence, man's thought and nature thus coincide here in full, automatic conformity. To different beings the above simple things would seem confusing complexities. Man as phenomenon of nature is an organism that exists as one, permanent, quantitative being. Because man as cognitive being exists and thinks in the same ways, the concepts of "one", "same", "more" and "less" are so universally and simply understood that they serve as the bases for the common "languages" of mathematics and logic. To a Martian insect-world consciousness such a term as "one" would be incomprehensible.

The *relative causation has the essence of natural law* because it derives from the organic sameness, in terms of which man exists as well as thinks. That is why all men understand with absolute uniformity the above term "same", as well as its opposite and derivative terms "different", "more" and "less". Also the categories of stableness and change derive from the terms of organic sameness; and as we shall see later, the most universal forms of thought, space and time, derive from these categories.

Of course the relative causation becomes dynamically meaningful through the fact that *opposition* of forces creates the organism with its permanent forms and reserves. As we saw, without opposition the force of life would dissipate formlessly. The opposition between the primordial drive for release and its restriction, by evolution and culture, is the source of most effects and phenomena of relative causation, as well as of the richness of forms of life.

A very important consequence of this *opposition* is that man has to remain inherently hostile to the causal truth of his existence or to the idea of relative causation. Man as a living organism has to strive for the pleasure release alone while the opposition or restrictions have to be supplied from outside, against his will. *If man became reconciled with the fact that the opposition is necessary, the very essence and force of the opposition would be lost.* Practically, any person or race of peoples accepting the idea of relativity, or of the inexorable organic limitation by its sameness, would see the futility of human strivings and lose all motivation. Consequently, struggle for survival and social selection let only those persons or peoples exist who have intense nonrelative attitudes. In other words, the idea of relativity is humanly degenerating, much like an unhealthy food that tastes and smells offensively because it is not to be consumed. Man had to become protected against all relativistic ideas. *The idea of relativity had to become impossible — ridiculous, boring and "logically" offensive.*

In itself, the relativity of value experiences is almost self-evident. In the abstract or practically unimportant fields, it has been recognized as a fact. *In philosophy,* it has been established directly or indirectly. The polarity of values and interdependence of opposites in thought was perceived already by the Greek philosophers — Pythagoras, Socrates, Plato or Aristotle. Typically, Plato saw that a pleasant state follows an unpleasant one, and vice versa. Later, the stoicism accepted the insight that all pleasures bring equal pain. Of course the real relativists, the sophists and cynics had to be branded forever as ridiculous degenerates, though the skepticism they introduced characterized the Greek philosophy for its last three centuries, after Aristotle.[1]

This skepticism corresponds to our most modern philosophical trends. The positivists, pragmatists and analytic philosophers recognize that in knowledge, in their main area of study, answers are possible only upon practical or meaningful questions — which is what the satisfaction and need correspondence requires. Contrasts or comparison as the method of cognition was clear to Medieval philosophers, notably St. Thomas and Cusa. So was the requirement of evil for discernment of good; this was made particularly clear in the philosophies of St. Augustine and Leibniz. The full meaning of the relativity was accepted by the early modernists, Hobbes and Spinoza, as well as by the later relativists Spencer and Hamilton, and also to a great extent by Whitehead.[2]

Particularly the dialectic method of Hegel, which has found such important applications, confirms the relative causation. Thesis and antithesis — actually value and disvalue — fit everything men can think of or do; the various syntheses that Hegel added, for more logical coherence, have been found to be rather arbitrary.[5] The dialectic use of opposites can certainly explain everything, and Hegelianism has been one of the strongest philosophical movements. Fichte and Schelling also used the dialectic method of opposites, and Nietzsche held that nothing can be known otherwise than by being related.[1,4] Oriental philosophies have recognized the futility of pleasures, which is the practical effect of relative causation. The now so popular Zen originated from the Mahayana Buddhism which accepts complete relativism.[6] All religions have stressed similar futility of pleasures. Ascetics, flagellants, yoga and shamans, as well as practitioners of Zen, have used suffering or restrictions for inducement of opposite emotions of ecstasy.

In psychology the relativity has been recognized in various ways, where it does not relate to practical adjustment. In the field of perception, the relativity and relative dependence of values have been long established (E. G. Boring, R. S. Woodworth).[21] One finds it repeatedly demonstrated how a gray figure appears dark on a light background, and light on a dark one. The illusions discovered by the Gestaltists are all due to the relativity, as we shall see later. The Gestaltists, notably Koffka, have explained aftereffects of perception as opposite processes during reconstitution by brain mechanisms of their normal state.[21] But in more practical matters the relativity is never taken seriously; a textbook may mention as a humorous aside the fact that a student used to poor food or bad treatment finds it satisfactory.

We have to mention the *Weber-Fechner law,* which has been generally accepted as a "landmark".[3] It shows how effects of stimulation diminish with its increase. Psychologists, beginning with Wundt, have recognized that this law establishes the general psychological relativity.[3] The determining importance of such relativity has been noticed in many fields, from maze learning to stock market analysis and the economic utility theory, as well as in aesthetic judgments.[3] But the relativity idea is inherently unacceptable in modern psychology, and not only because it is "ridiculous."

The relativity works by a *logic that is exactly contrary* to the logic of the present exact sciences. Adding more of a psychological value, like satisfaction, decreases it; and subtracting from it or adding the opposite value, like need, increases it. But psychologists, aspiring to the now authoritative scientism, use only the logic and methods of physical sciences. Every experiment, recording of observations, method of procedure, logical correlation, use of mathematics, and reaching of conclusions or theories is effected under the ordinary, "scientific", nonrelative logic.

Even in the clearest cases psychologists are misled by the "scientific" logic. For instance, everybody knows that a hard period in one's life, like a difficult school term or a heavy work week, makes the vacation or weekend so much more pleasant. Yet all psychologists, as scientists, have blamed the difficulties or frustrations in a person's past for his later negative reactions. It should be noted that a frustration may lead to negative effects, but only if it was compensated for by unwarranted inner satisfactions, which then as overadjustments lead to the opposite reactions.

Of course psychology and science in general recognize, indirectly, the facts which make the relative causation inevitable. The *maintenance by organism of its sameness* is recognized as the central principle of organic existence (E. Nagel).[7] The "dynamic stability" that conserves the "morphological identity" of organism is seen as the universal property of life (R. Dubos).[8] Psychologists recognize that organism compensates for changes or disturbances (N. L. Munn)[9] and keeps its conditions within its normal limits (C. T. Morgan).[10] Such homeostatic tendencies are now found to be more prevalent than was previously believed (A. H. Maslow).[11] The law of homeostasis is seen as one of the generally recognized principles in psychology (B. B. Wolman).[12] But if the conservation of the organic sameness is the universal principle, then *the relative or opposite causation be-comes self-evident.* Then, as we saw, one only has to add the fact that all value experience derives from organic change, which is clear to every scientist. The conservation of organic sameness requires that every organic change is met with equal opposite processes. Also the interpretation of all behavior in terms of needs and satisfactions is fairly accepted in psychology. But the reversed causal logic, that the opposite causation or the satisfaction-need interdependence implies, makes the law of relativity unthinkable for psychologists or scientists.

We may add that theories on homeostasis in itself can explain little and may rather mislead. They imply that organism remains static, by adapting itself to change. Just the reverse is ultimately true. The organism reacts with opposite processes to functional changes, particularly to overadjustments. This is what explains the most important mental and physiologic phenomena, like disorders, functional diseases or vicious-circle worsening through experimentally clear improvements. Only the relative or opposite causation, with its "impossible" causal logic, can explain these virtual mysteries in every field of modern science dealing with man.

The relativity is least acceptable *in the general humanistic thought* that dominates our education and learning. Inner values are extolled and seen as causal essences of everything positive, though their real causal sources are their opposites, the negatively felt nonsatisfactions and harrowing restrictions. Values like love or interest are shown, in endless "discoveries", to be satisfactions — as they certainly are — that the theorists want to increase directly. Why not let everybody enjoy such satisfactions? Just show how pleasant they are, and fight the reactionary, restrictive establishment that suppresses pleasures. It is never even mentioned that such satisfactions grow from their hard, negatively-felt opposites. Further, the world and man's place in it are explained in terms of values, like harmony, order or providence, whereas our very sense that these are values arises from our continuous need for them, from their scarcity or absence in the world. Or sublime philosophies are expounded about aesthetic and emotionally deep experiences, often not different from those induced by mind-expanding drugs. It is not understood that such experiences can only derive from, or lead to, their opposites, equally deep needs, nonsatisfactions, restrictions or displeasures.

But men follow the law of relative causation, without knowing it, in their *practical adjustment*. For if they do not, they fail. In result, cultural selection — as continuation of the evolutionary selection — lets only those forms of adjustment continue which embody the relative wisdoms of enrichment of potentials through *restrictions*. All culture, education and morals are systems of *restrictions*, that create needs, obligations, stresses, guilt or conscience, so that equally rich satisfaction and release potentials become available.

Naturally, man strives only for the positive experiences. Therefore pleasure has always to be used as the drive. But it has to be, gradually, turned around, against itself, by conditioning of satisfactions, and by promises of reward, of future success or of happiness in this world and the other. That is why all cultural and moral adjustment is so complex and contradictory. Endless philosophies, preachings, moralizations, superstitions and supranatural fears have been used, in all cultures, to explain and justify the restrictions. The modern liberal men are proving clearly and easily how wrong, superstitious, hypocritical and backward the restrictive traditions are. *Scientific* understanding of the requirement of restrictions would be the modern solution.

The Phenomena of Relativity

Now we may look at the main phenomena of the relativity of value experiences. These experiences determine everything man feels, thinks or does. But they are governed by the relativity, that is presently not even suspected and is contrary to the generally accepted causal logic. Consequently the phenomena of relativity can explain various mysteries and contradictions that presently extend to virtually everything in the sciences dealing with man.

The Opposite Causation. An overenjoyment, induced by drugs, alcohol, or psychological self-stimulation, leads to exactly as deep suffering, hangover or depression. Any organic mechanism driven above its normalcy has to reverse by equal opposite readjustments. All organic value causation proceeds by opposites, as organism restores its normalcy, upon change, by opposite processes. In this sense all relative causation is opposite causation, and we shall often use the two terms synonymously. The opposite causation becomes particularly interesting where strong, unwanted negative reactions break out because of previous enjoyment of strong positive emotions. Such enjoyment may seem as best adjustment and experimentally always shows as a clear improvement.

We shall use the term **overadjustment** to explain how such "improvements", eagerly enjoyed by man at first opportunity, lead to impoverishment of the same psychological and physical functions that were overenjoyed. Modern man is helped enormously in attainment of such "improvements", by the affluence of modern life and by the liberal, or typically "scientific" medical attitudes, expounded by all kinds of experts. The progressively increasing modern functional diseases, of mind or body, are the results of overadjustments, of constant "improvements" that deepen into cumulative worsening. Because excessive enjoyments of *any experience* have to lead to as excessive opposite reactions, man *ends by reacting in ways he wants least* to the extent he has been enabled to enjoy his experiences in ways he likes best. An additional fact here has to be considered.

A **vicious circle** of increased worsening through increased "improvements" is set in motion when upon each reversal or worsening the enjoyment of the feeling of well-being is intensified, by additions in the positively-felt stimulation. This requires a neurotic or enjoyment-seeking personality. A mere compensation of the worsening with just sufficient "improvement" would not lead to a progressive deepening of the overadjustment syndrome. But if the person is inclined to seek increased enjoyment of his feelings of well-being, or is encouraged and enabled to do so, the vicious circle becomes inevitable. As the impoverishment deepens upon every added enjoyment, *the unwanted reaction, exhaustion or disease can reach any, rationally inconceivable degree, through* *nothing more than continuously added, experimentally clear, direct improvements.*

Since the person uses all his ingenuity in attaining such enjoyments, the aftereffects follow, point-by-point, with the same "ingenuity". Hence the appearance, and even clinical proofs, that an *ingenious unconscious* is acting against the person's obvious intents. The opposite reactions are never connected with the previous enjoyment, because as its opposites they seem to have nothing in common with it in any way. Moreover, due to the organic complexity the opposite reactions may come through completely different mechanisms. Thus strong food is enjoyed through the stomach but its effects may be dealt with by the liver. Of course all organs serve the integrated function of life or growth, and in this overall function the opposite reactions take place, at deepest levels and with determining effects for every organ or experience.

We may mention another curious consequence of the fact that man never recognizes the real causes of his disorder. The person *forcibly tries to explain his negative reactions by rational*, factual reasons. Suffering from phobia or paranoia, he will go to any length in arranging scarcest evidence so that the fear is proved to be factually justified. This may become his main, compulsive preoccupation. Apparently the brain mechanisms always require — as they normally should — that emotion be connected with facts, even if the facts have to be invented. Unfortunately psychologists as well concentrate on the ideational contents, revealed in analyses. They have vast theories on how to interpret the ideas the patient has. Still it all is bound to be irrelevant, because the real causes of disorders never are any ideas. Such causes are, rather, the organic release problems, arising in ways exactly contrary to the intents and ideas of the patient or to the reasoning of psychologists.

Overadjustments are always difficult to recognize. Continuous increase in releases is not particularly noticed, because it is felt as very satisfactory or normal, and the person gets used to it. When the overadjustment deepens into a grave exhaustion it is again difficult to see the opposites at work. In its latest stages the overadjustment becomes a mere struggle with the deepening impoverishment which has become overwhelmingly more apparent than the constantly added "improvements" that are losing their effect. But *though the overadjustment becomes only a torture it cannot be abandoned.* The drug addiction is the simplest example, but the same rule applies whatever the means used.

If the psychotic derives his overadjustment by mere snapping of his fingers or avoidance of unlucky numbers, he still suffers full aftereffects. Exactly because he derives real overenjoyment with such ease, he drives himself into strong negative reactions in this easy way, as if without real, equal cause. Moreover, the psychotic cannot abandon the mere sign or "idea". For him it is just as real a means of release as is heroin for the addict. He can only add to it, which he does eagerly, thus creating a complex system of ideas or mannerisms. If he has built himself up into a more and more powerful Napoleon, he cannot abandon the idea even if it now brings him only negative reactions. Every step in such build-up brought him real, physiologic releases; that is why he pursued the idea. Consequently, every step down, back to his pre-Napoleon level would require equally real, physiologic deflation or restriction.

Contrast. No value can be experienced without previous or subsequent disvalue, and vice versa. Everything is known or evaluated through differentiation, which ultimately means through contrasting of opposites. If the world around an object had become a hundred times larger, the object would be seen as a hundred times smaller and nothing else would seem to have changed. Every value can be changed, or reversed, in the same way, by changing what it is compared with.

The only limitations to doing so are our difficulties in manipulating total environments, or to amplify our limits of perception or of other sensations. If we could distort everything in one way, e.g., make it curved to one side, then normal shapes, like straight lines, would appear distorted in the opposite way. In experiments, subjects saw straight forms as curved, after they had worn glasses that curved everything in the opposite way. The same was observed with tactile distortions. We could make zero degree cold appear as warm and 100 degree heat as cold, in similar ways, if our range for experiencing temperatures was hundreds of degrees above and below zero.

No such limitations apply in the psychological world. There we can build, change or distort value objects to any size or degree, and amplify, or decrease the value of any experience. One can live in a world of complete unreality, of perfect security or self-superiority — and then feel, without reason, insecure or inferior when facing normal conditions. People suffer, as "irrationally", from all kinds of distorted feelings and delusions, particularly the negative, unwanted ones, because the opposite, highly wanted, positive feelings are exaggerated most. Hence the seeming irrationality and "self-destructive" drives that the behavioral scientists now stress as causal factors. Further, the brain processes must be even more flexible and extensive in possibilities of comparisons than is vision, which already permits a wide range of relative effects. An object can be made to appear light or dark, yellow or green, depending on the opposite value of the background. There are no colors in themselves. In a room where everything is red, one finds no red but only shades of gray. On the other hand, gray shadow appears red in a room lighted by a green-shaded lamp.

If the rule of contrast is clear enough in simpler cases, it is the last thing theorists would use for wider, involved, and more important insights. For it works by the reverse logic of getting less value by addition. Since contrast or differentiation by opposition rules all cognition, the result is that neither scientists nor philosophers are aware of the most universal causal backgrounds and of the real causal factors that determine what is felt as value or known as reality. The most universal and therefore most important causal sources are felt or known least. We do not feel or "know" the atmospheric pressure or gravitation. Conversely, what is exceptionally rare, therefore causally least important, is felt or known as glaringly clear, incisive or important.

The *reversed logic* of values in cognition, through contrast, renders untrue the most important beliefs in every field. Since human behavior and reactions depend on value experiences deriving from their opposites, most theories in human sciences are bound to be wrong, because the usual like-comes-from-like logic is contrary to value causation. The fallacies are widest in the humanistic theorization and philosophy. Their domain is values and ultimate truths or essences. But no value has meaning without its opposite and there can be no final truths, as everything derives only from differentiation against something else, different or *opposite. Because every value, or value "essence" derives from its opposites, the humanistic value outlook and philosophies show as true the exact reverse of what is causally true.*

We may add that even in the fundamental theory of physics the absolutely universal causal source has not yet been recognized because it is far less noticeable or even registrable by instruments than is the atmospheric pressure. We shall discuss this later, when we shall also see how the discovery of the universal physical causal source provides new fundamental insights for other natural sciences

In brief, the direct human nonrelative view is bound to be most erroneous exactly in matters which are most important for man. Where human values are strongest, they derive from their strongest opposites; and where the causal sources of values or reality are most universal they are not even noticed.

Fixation. A very important phenomenon of the relativity, particularly in the cultural and social life, is fixation. Because no one thing has a definite value, there is no limit to which people can get disoriented and lost in their value world. The value of a thing depends on the background it is compared with or on previously established channels of satisfactions. Therefore, *the past experience alone may determine whether a thing has or does not have value.* We value only what we "know", from past experience, as satisfactory to our own needs or what we have happened to find as pleasant; the converse is true of the unpleasant. Something we know little, may it be ever so valuable, we do not seek or value. Of course biologically men "know" or have satisfaction backgrounds for many values, therefore do not become disoriented by the value relativity.

But culturally and socially man has created his own value environments, with no criteria or control beyond himself. Only his own backgrounds of satisfaction or "knowledge" become determining. A *vicious circle* of self-deepening of values is the result. *As a thing known or appreciated is enjoyed it is known or evaluated even better and therefore enjoyed even more.* Thus a value that has come to a people's attention first, by accident, may become boundlessly significant. It may absorb the attention of the people and exclude other values that may be, objectively, really important. Negative values or avoidances deepen in the same way into incomprehensibly frightening taboos.

The vicious circle of opposite causation also becomes part of the fixation. As the value is overenjoyed, impoverishment of releases results, and remedy is sought in further enjoyment of the same, known and therefore easier or readier source. Similarly a vicious-circle enjoyment of avoidance of an object accumulates into an incredibly frightening phobia. Or a moral objection may deepen into a witch-hunt, through overenjoyment of self-righteousness, which has no meaning without the wickedness of others. In fixations, as in mental disorders, a decisive factor is the person's inability to bear restrictions or delay enjoyments. Potentials for satisfaction, interest or value can be created only through previous painful accumulation of restrictions and needs or non-satisfactions. Without them, the person develops no new interests and his only values remain those enjoyed in the easy, previous, fixational ways.

Of course such values become exhausted and have to be endlessly improved, by more elaboration, at each vicious-circle worsening. That is why the fixational values and customs of peoples resemble the mannerisms or ritualism of neuroses and psychoses. What usually saves a culture from complete fixational disorientation is difficulties of life. These force the people to seek new ways and accept restrictions, which then provides new backgrounds and wider resourcefulness in selecting values. The modern era with its greater ease, absence of difficulties and aversion to restrictions is particularly conducive to fixations.

The proofs of fixation are as many as there are rationally

unexplainable strong customs, sacred values, cultural and religious "treasures", political symbols, peculiar styles and ways of life, fashions, particular forms of entertainment, customary rituals, dogmas, scriptures, holy beliefs, status symbols and social musts. All fixational values become absolutely certain, reasonable and convincing to the people. For it is the deepened value itself that determines what seems or does not seem reasonable and right, in every respect. Thus people become unsuspecting victims of accidental fixations — slaves of their self-created ghosts.

Moreover, our cultural leaders and theorists become the most zealous guardians of the senseless fixations, much like priests of cults. For they are the enthusiastic defenders of our deepest, most certain values, and fixations are such values, more than is anything else. Thus the humanistic theorists try to discover the very soul of a people in its meaningless, accidentally evolving customs and rituals. Or they may become awed adorers of masterpieces and celebrated artists that have become famous by mere fixations. The result is religious adoration of one painting, and disgusted rejection of a similar or better one merely because experts found it not to be a famous original. Mere accidental blobs of paint are treated as revealing highest genius if they are believed to come from a famous artist.

Unlimitedness of Mental Potentials. Because inner values have no strict limits, you can do anything with them — turn the tiniest value into a weighty force or create value out of nothing by creating an opposite background source for it. And all our motivations, interests or behavior is determined by our feelings of values. For instance, in education, through restriction of the grosser natural pleasures the slighter pleasures offered by the things to be learned are turned into dominant forces controlling the whole behavior. Or, by conditioned imposition of new restrictions or nonsatisfactions as needs, new potentials of releases or satisfactions are created.

The unlimited potentials of man, and his ultimate destiny of limitless progress, are inherent in the evolutionary force of life itself. As we mentioned, the force of life is of unlimited, cosmic strength. As such it can create new endless forms and effects —

but only to the extent it is opposed. Dynamite can move a mountain when packed in, that is, opposed tightly enough; it dissipates itself without effect if let to react freely. The chain-reaction process of life is an explosion or negative fire, though it acts slowly, as we shall explain later. It expands through endless forms of life which become enriched under opposition. The universal law of evolution by selection illustrates this progress through opposition. A new enriched form evolves when a new difficulty or opposition is encountered.

For the already evolved organisms, persisting normally by conserving their sameness, the opposition as the creative factor has to come by way of restrictions or hindrances on the life flow that strives to reach its normal limits. This life flow, in its inherently unquenchable strength, always finds new, circuitous, more elaborate ways when opposed. Finding new ways around obstacles imposed on satisfactions is the universal law of conditioning or learning, as individual "evolution". Also, the *accumulation of organic reserves is, in final analysis, an accumulation of restraints or delays on the normal life flow to be released as a force when and where necessary.* Thus the releases of the force of life, ultimately of growth, are the sources of all fulfillment, but restriction is the way such releases are made available as motivations and abilities. These can be increased unlimitedly by equal increase in the restrictions.

Here we have the decisive difference between the causal logic that now dominates in all theory as well as science, and the logic of relative causation that is true for the economy of human potentials. Neither man nor humanistic thought can accept that satisfactions or values derive from their opposites. Moreover, the modern science builds on the experimental observations that increase in release or satisfactions improves performance. It certainly does. But only previous restrictions can make the releases available.

Without the restrictions or the opposition the increase of releases or satisfactions has to result in exhaustion of release potentials. This is what happens in overadjustment, the cause of all mental and physical impoverishment, disorders and functional diseases. These problems are becoming the increasing scourge of modern man, as he rejects the restrictive traditions and follows the logically positive, liberal and "scientific" attitudes. Real sciences of man, based on the presently unthinkable insight in the relative or opposite causation, are becoming necessary more than ever.

The Contradictions of Human Existence

Perhaps the best evidence of the seemingly paradoxical logic of the relative or opposite causation are the contradictions of human existence. They are revealed in the paradox of the central human drive. Man lives only for happiness or pleasure. But pleasure, as the most direct, natural happiness, is the last thing man is to be permitted to enjoy if he is to be saved from degenerative self-destruction. Pleasure is, ultimately, the only drive of human nature. But its truest, most pleasant fulfillment, through use of drugs or other means of functional enjoyment, brings the impoverishment, disorder, disease and every reaction man wants least. The opposite causation is the simple mechanistic explanation of this paradox, as we have seen. But men can never accept its logic. They only know intuitively that the sellers of the logically fail-proof formulas for happiness are cranks.

Thus men know least, and never seriously want to learn anything, about the very first thing they are living for. Attainment of happiness belongs in fairy tales. It is amazing how little has been written on happiness. A library that may have a whole wing filled with volumes on a subject like religion may have only a small shelf of books on happiness.[13] Thus while the restrictions on natural happiness, that religion deals with, are subjects of vast discussion, the happiness itself is something people are reluctant to hear about.

It may seem as if a curse has been put on man so that he fails and defeats himself while striving for what is in his very nature and what clearly appears to be the best way to success. Satisfaction is all that one needs to succeed in everything he does. Love is the panacea for all ills, offering the best capacities, will power, mental abilities, practical success and even physical health, as theorists constantly prove. And love is a satisfaction, a deeply pleasant feeling, extending to other men and the world. Similarly, interest is a pleasant satisfaction with work or things to be done, and can ensure highest mental power as well as success. Hope, confidence and other such satisfactions can equally bring enrichment of capacities, success and pleasure.

Every man wants these pleasant feelings and the success they clearly bring. But man's lot is not to have them — unless he "earns" them by equal hardships. This is what the relative causation can explain, while the theorists and moralists can offer only endless, contradictory sophistications. These are not much better than the explanation that man has to toil hard because of his original sin.

Furthermore, man seems to bring on himself deliberately all the negative reactions, hate, ill feelings, defeat, disorder and functional diseases. Men everywhere seem to refuse to accept the joy of life, pleasure, or satisfaction with world and fellow men, which could lift them to new heights of fulfillment and success. In an often-quoted statement by Bertrand Russell, he explains how all our difficulties arise from our refusal to open our hearts to joy. He finds that men could have all their problems solved if only they could be reasonable and would turn away from their negative feelings and toward readiness for enjoyment. No wonder that the logically free-thinking and "scientifically" minded modern men accept the theories about self-punishment, death instinct, and the unconscious world of horrible conflicts. Why else should men drive themselves in all the misery — from anxiety of alienation to disorders and war — with such intensity?

Here the relative or opposite causation provides a simple mechanistic explanation of *how the strongest human drive, the striving for pleasure, leads to the negative reactions.* Every human motivation or effort requires a release of pleasure as the life flow itself. Trouble becomes inevitable when the person draws such release in the easy, direct way by simply increasing it, without its previous accumulation through restrictions. Such direct increase as an excess spending of life reserves has to lead to exactly opposite, excessive restriction on the release of pleasures, on satisfactions or flow of life. Hence the exaggerated negative feelings and behavior contrary, in every value aspect, to the desired, positive feelings and motivations. But because the reversed logic of opposite causation is never even suspected or mentioned, we find here only endless contradictions and confusion, in philosophical or scientific theories.

The best modern philosopher may sound like a moralizing preacher. Thus we are told that "there is no costless comfort to be had in this world" and that "where love is made cheap there is cheapness of the civilization's soul" (W. E. Hocking).[14] The "paradox" that happiness can be won only by indirect attack and that it grows from "apprehension" or "liability" may be noted (R. B. Perry).[16] So may be the fact that there can be no good without evil, no success without failure, no righteousness without sin, no pleasure without pain, and no truth without error.[16] According to William James, "beauty and hideousness, love and cruelty, life and death keep house together in indispensable partnership"; and the good must be menaced or lost to be felt as such.[15]

Explanations may be more consistent causally if the view is adopted that "the tension of the opposites is the mainspring of the Cosmos" and that "in absence of resistance energy has no power, and vanishes", as W. Macneile Dixon explains.[17] He finds that there can be no good without evil; that it is sickness which makes health desirable, or fatigue which gives sweetness to rest; and that "as you experience happiness, in like proportion you are exposed to the experience of suffering". He concludes that without opposition or tension there can be no logic or consciousness; "in a word, no opposition, no world".[17]

In all philosophies, the presence of evil in the world has remained a perennial unresolved problem. If the negative is not recognized as the causal condition of the positive, then the negative has to remain logically unnecessary. Older philosophies thus tried to explain evil in terms of nonexistence or of absence of good. Such sophistry is not good enough for modern minds. Existentialism, as the most typical modern movement, has turned the negativity of existence into the very essence of reality. Actually existentialism itself is a proof of how the overprotection or excessive positive expectations of modern man result in the excessive negative reactions.

In science — psychology, psychiatry, or social sciences — the contradictions in human adjustment are the reason why the claimed *irrationality* of man has become the basis of most theories. The Freudianism is generally accepted, in spite of its obvious prescientific personifications, because it permits unlimited "explanations" of irrationality and inner conflicts. The only alternatives to it are the assumptions that faulty learning or conditioning turns man away from real satisfactions; or that he yields to irrational instincts; or that his misconceptions, wrong ideas and lack of understanding become the causes of his negative reactions or deeply unsatisfactory adjustments. In short, all scientists see that positive reactions or satisfactions are the sources of positive adjustment, but they argue that unconscious, erroneous and unreasonable attitudes of man prevent him from enjoying the satisfactions.

This is clearly contrary to facts. Men live and act by *reasonable and intelligent planning* in everything they do. They are not so stupid as to learn or become conditioned to torment themselves. Nor are they misled by wrong ideas or lack of understanding. Acceptance of the *positively felt satisfactions is the simplest thing* in the world. Particularly on the unconscious level the striving for satisfactions alone dominates. The simple fact is that men have built by reason and intelligence stupendous systems of adjustment with every imaginable satisfaction in them. It is argued that modern man has turned to purely material or technological enjoyments and away from the true, deeper, or basic satisfactions of his real nature. But every man knows perfectly what is truly, deeply and basically satisfactory for him, and its attainment is the very drive that determines his nature. The material enjoyments only serve, most directly, this drive.

Man lives and builds by reason and intelligence. Particularly the modern man has attained a gigantic progress with every rationally perfect satisfaction in it. It is because of the relative

or opposite causation that modern man, so successfully enjoying all the satisfactions or releases, suffers from all the exhaustion, shallowness of feeling, negativity, excessive restriction, mental and physical impoverishment or functional and social disorders.

A typical form of adjustment that reveals the paradox of
satisfactions and the contradiction of human existence is the
Sin. In all cultures sins have been branded as the ugliest things.
But this is a joke, particularly for the liberal modern man. Sins
are beautiful. They are pleasures men strive for: adventurous
sex as the source of the most genuine interest and beauty;
physical superiority, often expressed in violence and crime that
enliven every manly TV show; or the most invigorating enjoyments of one's natural gratifications. Positive satisfactions become
sins exactly when they are natural, liberated, enjoyable and
stimulating. The moralists and philosophers who pretend that
sins are ugly are hypocrites. Modern science clearly proves that
increase in releases, which every sin serves, is best for direct
improvements of adjustment.

Because the nature of sin is not causally understood, the ethics
has become an endless confusion. Moralists may condemn the
traditional sins, many of which have become irrelevant. The
real modern "sins" as excesses in releases bring impoverishment
in every field, from psychology to economics. But moralists do
not see them as sins, and the "scientific" theories foist them on
us as improvements of adjustment.

All *morals and religions* are a general proof of the contradiction of human existence. They are the universal guides of human
adjustment but are so difficult to live with that strong, superstitious teachings about punishments and rewards have always
been necessary. That is why enlightenment and science have
turned against religions and the restrictive cultural traditions. We
are to be liberated from the superstitions, as well as from the
repressions and guilt, now scientifically proven as damaging, that
religions and moral education impose. It is deplored that we
have suffered here a degradation as unique as was the Fall
of Man.[19] Actually culture here is only continuing to do, selec-

tively, on a higher level, what natural evolution has done by way of difficulties or opposition, which has brought all the enrichment in adjustment.

Man is the *most restricted of all animals.* He is an "infant ape", because he is stunted by the evolutionary opposition at deepest levels of growth or releases. He has "climbed back on the evolutionary tree", in logical scientific terms.[18] Consciousness itself is a product of restriction. It is a life, in miniaturized forms, added above the purely biological life. As such it requires its own additional reserves of living energy. These are created by the restrictions on the normal growth, which is thus "dammed" up as a reservoir of potentials. Naturally, the way this works is complex beyond human understanding because of the astronomic multiplicity of interactions. But it all follows the natural, simple principle of restriction, by which all evolution creates higher forms.

By the way, man is *the only animal that laughs.* This is so because he is the only one that bears within himself surplus restrictions, which can be released by the laughter. It is clear, even from the way laughter goes off, like a pricked balloon, that laughter is a release. Obviously, the release is possible only if there was tension or restriction. It is also clear that laughter is caused by realization of unseriousness. Laughter is a relief from the tension of seriousness, i.e., from the restrictions on the full life flow, that underlie all our normal or "serious" adjustment. The very universality of these restrictions, and of the inherent seriousness of all adjustment, makes them unnoticed. Hence the general inability of theorists to discover the natural simple cause of laughter. They realize that it bears on unseriousness, and is a release — from something they have not discovered. In a wide survey of the theories on laughter, D. H. Monro concludes that it has remained unexplained. The best known theorists — Bergson, Schopenhauer, Freud — have emphasized the contrast or conflict, in various forms. Surely there is plenty of contrast; but contrast is the method of all experience. We may add that the unseriousness in laughter has to be of a specially original, previously unsuspected kind, and we have to be led, by a trick, into logically accepting it. We cannot laugh all the time (though we may laugh continuously when intoxicated). Therefore all the usual and not logically inevitable realization of unseriousness has long been counteracted by one's universal need to uphold the seriousness or the restrictions.

Generally, if you look at the *whole cultural and historical development* of man, the contradiction of his existence is so evident that it hardly needs discussion. Anything worthwhile that man has attained, he has had to pay for painfully in toil and self-denial, through long effort and countless errors. Looking back in history one is astounded by the stubborn resistance of men to what is good for them, which they have accepted only by being forced into it. We can be sure that future men will have as much reason to be astounded by our apparent stupidity.

Actually it is not any stupidity but the incompatibility of what man is by nature with what he has to do in order to enrich his adjustment. He can live and act only by striving for releases or satisfactions, but these can be created or enriched only by opposition, restrictions, or needs as nonsatisfactions. Once such enrichment is attained everything else becomes possible, individually or socially. Men never lack perfect intentions, and all the logical utopias could be made real, if only men had the motivational potentials. Political and economic success clearly depends on restrictive enrichment and accumulation of motivations and resources, as we shall see later.

Without the opposition or restrictions man would drive himself into degeneration. If we were able to stimulate ourselves into obtaining stronger pleasure releases we would do so irresistibly. The end-result would be the same as from use of drugs — an organic exhaustion and disaster. Of course, due to natural selection only those species survive which embody organic restrictions on the releases. The brain, the organ of higher evolution, is a system of restrictions. That is why numbing or incapacitating of it, by alcohol or narcotics, brings pleasure. The same happens in cases of illness of the brain, like a syphilitic paresis, or upon debilitating brain operations (G. K. Yacorzynski).[22] Lobotomy is a form of such operations. Normally organism guards well its restrictive mechanisms and reacts with pain against interference with them.

But as man becomes more capable of outsmarting nature, he comes closer to increasing the pleasure releases at will by all kinds of means, biological, chemical or psychological. It should be realized that increase in releases has the same effect whether it is obtained by heroin, self-stimulation, transactional therapy or "positive thinking". The difference is only in the degree of immediate effectiveness. Nor is there a difference, in nature, between taking an aspirin for headache and a separation of a pain-carrying nerve, though we know that upon losing sensations of pain our body would not survive for long. We also know that we could prevent most of our ills if we avoided the indulgences we are too weak to resist. One can think here of smoking, overweight, rich foods, coffee, alcohol or other things people cannot miss noticing as being bad for them. But the same causal logic is missed in regard to all the other pleasures man strives for and finds as *immediate improvements* in his feeling of well-being.

What is more, scientists, doctors and do-it-yourself experts help modern man to enjoy *such improvements*. Every experiment and logical observation shows increase in the releases, mental or somatic, as clear improvement, though it leads to their exhaustion. The modern life, science, medicine and progress are enabling man enormously to enjoy every pleasurable improvement in his feeling of well-being, and to cover up by further release improvements the resulting worsening or feeling of ill. Modern man is made the master of his own reactions of pleasure. No wonder that the unexplainable functional disorders and diseases are becoming the scourge of modern man.

In brief, man lives only for pleasure release, but his higher evolutionary and cultural adjustment is attained through restrictions or opposition of his primordial pleasure drive. His striving for the pleasure or happiness is his very nature, yet it has to be denied if his capacities are to be enriched and he is not to drive himself into the degeneration and impoverishment, that are the causes of the increasing mental, physical and social disorders and ills of modern life. Moreover, the contradiction of human existence is not to be resolved. The two sides in the opposition, which creates the variety and enrichment of life, have to remain unreconciled; otherwise there would not be the opposition. Man should not recognize, emotionally or motivationally, the inevitable necessity of the opposite, restrictive side. To do so would amount to accepting a relativistic, resigned attitude of life, with which no people can survive for long or succeed in social selection.

Relativity and Pleasure

Pleasure is the driving force behind all behavior, but *it makes causally no sense unless the relative causation is understood.* In fact, without such understanding the pleasure drive appears to be exactly contrary to normal human motivation. Everybody knows that the person who lives by pleasures most fully has the least of motivation or will power. At the same time it is clear that all motivations and capacities are pleasures or satisfactions, and that even the highest motivations are conditioned elaborations of the basic natural pleasures. We do not need to repeat the explanation of the paradox that pleasure release is the sole source of potentials but that only its opposition or restriction can create its reserves or enrich it.

Psychologists, particularly the Freudians, have tried to account for the paradox by claiming conflict, struggle, jealousy and scheming between agencies inside the psyche. They have observed that people often suffer disorders upon reaching fullest satisfactions, or are "unable to bear success", as was, apparently, Freud himself.[20] Moreover, it is generally known that a real trouble cures neuroses. Supposedly the vengeful Superego wrecks the person enjoying the success, or is satisfied only after the person has paid by suffering. All theories on unconscious conflicts and self-punishment, including those of Freud, Alexander and Menninger, use such explanations.[22] Typically Freud started with the assumption that pleasure is the determining factor, but changed his theory, in his book *Beyond the Pleasure Principle,* admitting that the way pleasure works is not yet known and that a neurosis is rather a pleasure turned into displeasure.[20,22]

No other psychologist or scientist has tried to build a theory on the pleasure concept.

It is truly unbelievable that the pleasure, as *the clear and simple mechanism that makes man tick,* is disregarded in psychology and behavioral sciences. Pleasure is clearly the dominant force that controls all behavior, and it is so simple or clear but causally so all-inclusive in accounting for everything that goes on inside the organism that it is the only complete, mechanistic causal concept the scientist could use.

We clearly act according to what we find pleasant, in ninety per cent of cases, if we consider that for man a future pleasure also becomes a present pleasure, determining the choice of action. By following the pleasure we choose what we do in our eating, drinking, sleeping, reading, work, entertainment, play, hobbies, interests, planning of our life, marriage, career or striving for anything we want. In perhaps ten per cent of cases we may do what is unpleasant. But we do so because we are conditioned to gain pleasure from doing it. We know that fulfilling one's duty or following the "voice of conscience" gives satisfaction. These conditioned pleasures can derive only from the natural pleasures or satisfactions, like those of survival or superiority.

Pleasure is the universal principle of living nature. Seeing it as merely a feeling is missing the most important insight. Animals, or all living forms and tissues, do not feel pleasure, but they strive to do only that which we know is pleasant. And by doing so they are finding, out of millions of possible choices, only what is best for their normal existence. Thus what we know as pleasure is the ultimate, self-explanatory principle of existence by virtue of survival, realizing itself in living nature. It is identical with the life force itself that creates and controls everything in the organism. In man as a conscious living being, controlled by conscious reactions, it had to become consciously felt, as the pleasure, to serve as such a determining causal principle. *Pleasure is thus a conscious representation of the very force of life realizing itself through endless, otherwise ungraspable living processes.* We shall use the concept "pleasure release" or simply "release" for such realization of the life force; and "restriction" for the accumulation of this force.

The living forms do nothing more, or less, than striving for the pleasure, which thus becomes causally synonymous with the integrated living processes of the organism. The higher, more complex and refined processes, the evolutionary and cultural adjustments, can derive only from the lower ones, from the same sources that are controlled by the pleasure. Conditioning of pleasure is the method by which evolution and all learning, including cultural education, proceeds. Every trainer as well as teacher, and most psychologists, knows that pleasure offered under the desired, changed conditions produces the learning. Without the pleasure there can be no learning, nor any action.

Pleasure is the only driving force for the organism. But all learning or conditioning aims at modifying the pleasure so that it becomes a moving force behind new, different behavior. The pleasure flow may be finally turned, by continuous conditioning or curbing, to run against the natural pleasures, or to "dam" them up, in the creation of the release reserves. Such use of pleasure, as the only force, for opposition of lower pleasures becomes endlessly varied and subtle in all cultural and educational adjustment. The natural, more direct "pleasure" becomes sin, in traditional morals, as it is being identified with the clearer, lower, unconditioned pleasures. Or, in the liberal education, all pleasures are, logically, to be set free — though they can be enriched or refined only by their restriction.

The dominance of all behavior by pleasure has been demonstrated experimentally. Stimulation of pleasure centers in the brain, in the limbic area, induces animals to forget everything else and to seek only such stimulation. If the stimulation is being released upon pressing a bar, the "animal goes into an orgy of bar pressing."[21] Of course the most impressive "experiment" is the life itself in showing how people lose every sense of value or morals once they become dominated by pleasure drive stronger than the conditioned pleasures. Drug addicts, even the users of minor narcotics, like the smokers, as well as people in the grip of central natural drives, like the passionate lovers, may forget all moral restraints, even dangers to life, just to obtain the pleasure. In brief, the pleasure, direct or conditioned, dominates all behavior — the natural functions as well as their most refined elaborations in cultural conduct.

Equally important is the fact that the sense of pleasure, as the source of all feelings, is *miraculously precise and mechanistic in providing us with causal "information"* about the organic processes involved. The feeling of pleasure guides the organism, as well as every tissue or process inside it, in all its adjustment, to the tiniest detail or reaction. It has to be precise without exception. If it fails, the organism perishes. If an animal loses precision in evaluating or tasting which food is pleasant, he will eat the wrong food and die. The same happens at every, minutest level of organic integration, under the same guidance by the pleasure.

In other words, through the feeling of pleasure we "know" what and how causally happens in all the myriads of processes that determine what the organism does. Of course the feeling itself reduces it all to the simple yes and no of pleasure and displeasure. But this exactly proves that the knowledge here is uniquely complete, that our knowing here totally coincides with the natural process. All universal, most revealing causal laws are simple for the same reason. The knowledge provided by the feeling is totally mechanistic because it precisely relates all the environmental and biochemical factors and gives their precise causal meanings — as no experiment in the world could do.

Take the simplest feeling of the taste, the pleasantness and unpleasantness, of food. By finding a piece of food tasteful you have established that the varied elements in the food correspond to the varied requirements of your body and will meet them after passing through as varied organic processes. Thus by a simple act of tasting the food, in a few seconds, you have established what hundreds of scientists experimenting for years would not be able to do.

In effect, the feelings of pleasure and displeasure contain the precise historical *"knowledge" of the whole million-year evolution* of the organism, of every causal factor and meaning in it.

For if the pleasure feeling did not guide the animal in precisely interpreting and following the causal evolutionary meanings, the animal would be unable to comply with the evolutionary, purposeful adaptation and would not live for a day. We shall explain later why nature can be so miraculously superior to human mind.

To take the next simplest feeling, the sexual pleasure, it provides one with ungraspably wide, precise and mechanistic causal insights. They all are revealed to him through the mere feeling of beauty of the opposite sex, its organs or mechanisms. For instance, a few-seconds look at a beautiful woman reveals to a man vast and precise information about her suitability for reproduction through all the processes of intercourse, conception, gestation, birth or feeding of the progenies, as well as for endowing them with the best qualities. Other feelings, like those of security, fear, aggression, body comforts, pain, and general beauty, which result from evaluation of numerous advantages in nature, may be even more complex, providing even greater wealth of the mechanistically precise causal "information".

By rejecting the concepts of pleasure the scientists reject *the only way living processes can be causally understood.* For instance, when a doctor receives biochemical data from analyses, they really show only the reactions of the life flow or pleasure, from various organs and tissues. Stimulation of an organ or tissue provides more of the general releases of the life force or pleasure. This shows in the analysis as an improvement of the organ or its functions. But actually such improvement ends as worsening, to the extent the release reserves were being exhausted by the stimulation. The doctor using the results of the analyses thus may arrive at causally completely wrong conclusions, under his "scientific" assumptions.

The point is that every scientist or experimenter, unwittingly, deals only with the pleasure or release reactions of organism through its organs, tissues or cells, but these reactions obey *the reversed relative causal logic* of value reactions. That is why all functional diseases have remained frankly admitted mysteries in medicine and psychiatry. The doctor can never reach beyond the integrated reactions or deal directly with the biochemical causes obeying the direct, nonrelative or usual causal logic. He could do so if he could see how the myriads of elements or molecules interact at each point and instant, or how the physical elements become life. No genius in the world can do this, because it goes beyond the ways mind works.

The same is true of all mental, instinctual, psychological, social or other reactions. They are all organically integrated value reactions, unanalyzable in their myriad elements and obeying the relative, reversed logic of the general releases or pleasure reactions. As we shall see later, a single, crudely simple drug or hormone can improve or cure, temporarily, almost the whole series of the main mental and physiologic reactions and disorders. Apparently, the general releases of life or pleasure flow determine everything in the organism and behavior.

In brief, the *miraculously revealing but paradoxical pleasure mechanisms explain and determine all human reactions,* motivations and abilities, whether it is behavior or health. The paradoxes of restriction and overadjustment become decisive. The simple restriction in the pleasure or life flow can provide enrichment of any potential, even extension of life. But modern science with its direct logic and its method of analyzing everything in its elements proceeds exactly contrary to these causal truths.

That is why no real sciences of man have evolved. None of the behavior problems, or of the main modern, functional, disorders and diseases is causally understood; no single rule is certain in education, adjustment or motivation; and not one accepted law has been discovered for human behavior, whether individual or social. At the same time it is clear that each kind of problem, disorder or disease has some one common cause, which as a natural principle can be only elementarily simple. The pleasure as the life flow, with its restrictions or lack of them, in various forms, is such cause or principle. Search for causes and explanations by analyzing living processes in their endless elements is preposterous, because the myriad factors, from million-year evolution, are decisive but are left out in analysis or experiment. All causal factors are accounted for, in every detail, by the simple feelings of pleasure.

Even the *evolution itself* of the virtual miracles of life can be explained by the simple principle of pleasure as the life flow. Presently the best scientists may be, rightly, mystified by the miracles of life and may see closer explanations in vitalism or in metaphysical philosophies, like that of Bergson, than in modern science.[8] Viewed in the "scientific" terms of the interaction of separate units any living process is unfathomably complex, yet purposeful. The purposefulness here corresponds to the better realization of the life flow, which is known to man, in all its details, as the pleasure. We may note that learning, as the adaptation to conditions, is found even in experimental psychology to be a self-deepening of pathways of conditioned pleasure. This is clear from the Law of Effect, established by Pavlov and Thorndike. Actually all evolution is such learning as automatic self-deepening of those forms of pleasure flow which find more favorable outlet: the better the flow, the stronger the channels or forms it automatically creates. We shall explain, in discussing genetics, how such evolutionary learning can be inherited.

Another principle, namely subordination, has to be added to explain how the conditioned better life flow automatically establishes stronger forms. If each living molecule or cell strived only for its own self-strengthening, organism would disintegrate. Each element must expand only on condition that the whole is favored first. Such a principle is not hard to imagine. Even the simplest model can serve to illustrate it. Imagine a bunch of pieces of expanding, say, spongelike material, "striving" to pass through a narrow opening as they are carried by a stream. Each one will compress itself, contrary to its individual tendency to expand, in order to permit the whole to pass through the opening.

You can think of various, better models, but the principle of favoring the whole first by its parts is simple and mechanistically feasible. It is all that is needed to ensure that organism will automatically find the most favorable or purposeful life flow, which man knows as pleasure. This principle merely has to be obeyed in each process and at every level within the organism. We shall see later, in explaining the Inner Selection, how the selective evolution, that promotes the "learned" better life flow, works in the same way at every tiniest level inside the organism. Of course the primary determining factor is the selection by survival which favors those forms that integrate more elements and become more complex, under the conditioning opposition that produces the "learning".

But what is simple when viewed under the above principles applying to few elements, becomes a virtual mystery when we try to imagine how it works in experimental detail, with the uncountable elements and levels involved. Here science should realize that mind is inherently incapable of grasping multiplicity. Scientists trying to explain living processes by isolated elements, as the experimentally "scientific" methods require, can only perpetuate the mystery. The multiplicity of causal, evolutionary factors, left out by experimental methods — but accounted for by the pleasure concepts — is so overwhelming, that the mystery and confusion can be only increased by "scientific" approaches. Even where clear detailed experimental data are obtained, *similar* behavioral or biochemical processes may show, objectively, for totally *dissimilar* causal conditions: when the animal or tissue is overactive in stress or in enjoyment; being harmed or recovering; under threat or most favorable condition.

Nature all around us is unfathomably miraculous in its multiplicity. Think of the mysterious instincts that turn a beehive into a complex purposeful society, or of the biochemistry of an organism that produces thousands of ingenious compounds that no scientist can duplicate. Here we have to stress the fact that *nature is not metaphysically superior to mind but merely works in a different way.*

Mind has to generalize, to reduce everything to "ones" before it can grasp it. In abstract thought man as a unified organic "one" relates to the world in the one-to-one way, as it creates the miniaturized inner "experiments". That is why nobody can think of more than one thing at the same time, and why generalization, the reduction to "ones", is the very nature of abstract thought. In contrast, living nature proceeds by interrelated myriads of elements at every point and instant. The only bridge between the two worlds is the mechanism of feeling or pleasure, which as a living process follows the endless multiplicity but reduces it, for mind, to the simple terms of yes and no or positive and negative.

Scientists ignoring this fact are wasting their talents in what amounts to naive efforts. For instance, migratory birds, salmon, eels, and other animals travel unerringly over thousands of miles. The mud wasp performs ingenious surgery on other insects to conserve them as food for its larvae. Societies of animals and insects work like superhuman organizations dealing purposefully with uncountable ecological factors. Monkeys, whales, dolphins and, actually, all animals communicate and cooperate in ways often more efficient than communication by language could produce. Scientists then try to find some one term, as the abstract understanding requires, to explain such miracles. Supposedly, the birds are guided by the North Star; salmon by the temperature difference in water; or the socially cooperating insects by some particular scent. The communication by animals is analyzed in terms of words and signs, as the abstract "ones" that mind uses.

In reality, the bird, salmon, ant or monkey is guided by *uncountable* stimuli and responses, producing the endlessly complex precise behavior. Acts of the above kind may seem to be examples of high intelligence, because they are comparable to human intelligent acts, but actually are far less miraculous than the performance of a simple cell or any organic agent. If one persists in thinking in terms of human intelligence, he has to regard the production of any of the billions of cells in the organism as a creation by chemical geniuses more intelligent than any man could ever be. Think of how every one of the reproductive cells is created so that it will determine the next organism to every purposeful detail for all its life.

Man is as superhumanly capable when he reacts by feeling — finding beauty in sex or pleasantness in food, as we saw. Scientists should not disregard this unique factor, the pleasure, that provides man with superhuman insights into the virtual miracles of nature, and is the equally superhuman source of all organic causation, in simplest ways. No doubt, abstract mind has an advantage over the way nature and pleasure or feeling work. It has foresight and can act by planning. If this could be combined with the way nature works, real miracles would be possible.

If man could understand and deal with the myriads of elements at once as nature does, he could see at once what a living process is, as he now sees how a wheel turns; he could construct new living forms, animals of every kind, as he now creates tools; he could shape himself into any form he wanted, as he now shapes his clothes; or he could diagnose and cure any disease by simply reacting to it. Such a combination is not possible, and should be left for speculation to philosophers of science. But scientists should at least understand that pleasure, as a natural process, supplies man with insights that no science in the world can offer to him. For the same reasons, by dealing with pleasure, in the simplest ways, we can determine our unfathomably complex organic processes. Almost every capacity, mental or physical, can be created by enrichment of the release potentials, through restriction of pleasure releases.

But in modern science the pleasure concepts have no place. In experimentally scientific terms pleasure is "mentalistic" or unreal. It cannot be dealt with experimentally. This is so because pleasure covers endlessly many factors, while experiment deals with isolated few. Every phenomenon of life or living is, experimentally or "scientifically", mentalistic or physically ungraspable. Modern science, as imitation of the authoritative physical sciences, has no methods for dealing with what seems so unreal only because it results from experimentally unmanageable multiplicity.

Moreover, the very logic of sciences, as we have seen, is contrary to the pleasure or value causation that determines all organic adjustment. Therefore no idea or discovery in science ever fits or points to the pleasure concepts. Also, pleasure with its single positive-or-negative answer is for scientists meaninglessly simple. Of course this very simplicity shows how total are the insights pleasure reveals. But in all immature sciences "inventiveness" or complexity is regarded as the mark of scientism, until the simple cause is discovered and complexity becomes necessary only in application of the causal law to endless details.

Other objections are that feelings or pleasure is unmeasurable and vague. Surely pleasure cannot be measured by physical terms. But it measures perfectly in the terms of its own domain and where it matters. Measuring is nothing but a relating, and pleasure or any organic value is exactly equal to its opposite. Practically, measurement of pleasure can never be a problem. If one knows that he has to accumulate pleasure potentials always as much as he can, by the hard restrictions, he does not need measurements. These may appear interesting to the experimental scientists, the modern "alchemists" in human sciences, searching for formulas of increase in releases without the equal opposite effort. Nor is pleasure a vague factor, in its proper domain. It is the clearest, most dominant value sought and precisely measured by everybody at every moment.

The great *universal fact is that men live for and by pleasure.* This is so common, and clear to everybody that only exceptions to it seem remarkable and worth noticing. Every organism as well as any process inside it is guided by what is consciously known as pleasure. Certainly it would not matter to call it by some other name — basic drive, central instinct, will of existence or élan vital. We chose the term "pleasure" because it expresses best how the natural drives, branching off into more refined elaborations, become the values man lives by. All values have the same nature, characterized by what is desired, wished, wanted, enjoyed, valuable, good, satisfactory, or simply pleasant.

Pleasure concept can *serve as a natural law* in a real science of man. All natural laws result from co-incidence of man's ways of existing, and thinking, with those of nature: along such lines our understanding of nature is totally complete and simple. Pleasure is such simple and total co-incidental understanding of the otherwise ungraspable living processes. Pleasure thus provides the only, miraculous causal insights into living processes and living nature. For the same reasons it is *the only factor by which we can control or determine,* as miraculously, all human capacities, mental, physiologic, motivational and social. The simple restriction of pleasures enriches and creates the release reserves, from which all other capacities derive or are conditioned.

The human sciences cannot become scientific or causally understood without the concepts of pleasure, by which we all live and all organisms are governed. Unfortunately, for the modern, experimental scientists pleasure is ungraspable or "mentalistic" as well as too commonplace to seem worth scientific attention. The main obstacle, however, is the lack of insight in the relativity of value reactions. Without such insight, pleasure appears the last possible source of capacities, because enjoyment of pleasure leads to exhaustion of potentials. Only the relative insight can explain the paradox of enrichment of pleasure potentials through their restriction.

Relativity, Science and the Modern Alchemy

The relative insight explains the never-suspected causation of value experiences, which determine what man feels, thinks and does. Even abstract thought consists of tiny value experiences. And the physiologic, integrated processes follow the causal logic of value reactions. In fields such as psychology, psychiatry, medicine, education, behavioral and social sciences, as well as in aesthetics, philosophy or cultural theories, the relative insights can reveal, for the first time, the unsuspected, negative *causal sources* of the positive reactions accepted as the determining factors. The very logic or way of thinking in these fields is presently contrary to causal truths or to the fact that value reactions or inner values, which practically means all "values", originate from their opposites. That is why none of these fields is really scientific at present. Sciences are born from discovery of simple, though often unthinkable, causal truths. The law of relative causation is such a truth for the sciences of man.

We may look first at some of the fields where the value reactions are more directly evident as causal factors. *Psychology* is the key science, because everything in the world depends on what man wants and is capable of doing: on his motivations or value feelings and his refined enrichment of pleasure releases. Both are governed by the paradoxical causal logic of increase or enrichment of releases through their restriction.

In *psychiatry* this insight would make the treatment, and particularly the prevention, of mental disorders a scientifically exact engineering. It would be difficult to carry out only because of unwillingness of people to bear restrictions. Nobody suffers a mental disorder as long as he has available plenty of positive release potentials, which are accumulated by previous restrictions.

In *medicine*, the functional diseases would become causally understood and thus scientifically controllable, for the first time. These "diseases of civilization" are caused by physiologic over-enjoyments or overadjustments, malignantly deepening through the vicious-circle effect. They are not causally understood because their causal logic of *worsening through experimentally apparent improvements* is contrary to every method and way of thinking of modern science. The lack of causal understanding of these diseases is frankly admitted in modern medicine, and is recognized as the main obstacle in dealing with them. These diseases have become almost the only unvanquished, increasing killers in the field of modern medicine. Even the infectious diseases, or other medical problems become fatal difficulties mostly because of functional impairments of the patients.

In the fields dealing with *education,* adjustment and motivation, we presently find nothing but controversies. Those who want to uphold the restrictive cultural tradition have to resort to the old superstitious and hypocritical sophistry, preaching and metaphysics. Every "scientific" proof shows the restrictions to be the main evils. For, experimentally, direct increase in releases shows as clear enrichment of motivations — though it brings their exhaustion in the end. Consequently the science in these fields can help only if it is counteracted by the good common sense of the scientists, or is turned against its own logic through vast, confusing sophistications.

The same is true for the fields of *social sciences.* There as well the value reactions and release potentials are the only determining factors for what people want and are able to do. The alchemistic sophistry there becomes even richer. Positive, pleasant value experiences are claimed to be the sources of all positive reactions. Or mere ideas, ideologies, reasons and logical factors are accepted as determining causes. Social or political theories and philosophies are almost as many as there are concerned citizens, leaders, thinkers and philosophers. Socially, as individually, "maladjustments" or frustrations are blamed for every ill though they serve the accumulation of needs or nonsatisfactions and thus are the real sources of satisfaction or motivation potentials. A perfect adjustment, felt as such, has to lead to immobility. This becomes unbearable and people resort to overadjustments, which end as motivational and functional impoverishment, disorders and diseases.

In the fields of *humanistic thought,* philosophy, aesthetics or cultural theories, the relative insight is, evidently, contrary to everything always held as true. These fields are dominated by value beliefs and the noble assumptions that positive values derive from value essences of the same, never opposite, nature. Thus the value delusions here rule supreme. That is why the theories or philosophies in these fields are so endlessly controversial that nobody even expects coherent answers. Scientifically or rationally these fields have ceased to be taken seriously. They continue to be cultivated, inertially, as our educational Learning, with the usual extreme strength of fixations. The theorists themselves in these fields are abandoning their philosophical positions and trying to become scientific.

They are doing so in the worst way — by imitating the rejection of the restrictive cultural tradition. The wisdom of restrictions had remained the underlying spirit in these fields, in spite of the confusing, logical theories about freedoms. The relative insight can vindicate these underlying restrictive wisdoms. But it has to expose the value delusion and thus the final reason why these fields are inherently futile. Thought itself is a relative value process, and if relativity is true, philosophy is impossible — which is amply proven by the modern history of philosophy itself.

In *physical sciences* the insight in the relativity of value reactions is not practically necessary. Yet even here the relative insight can reveal the unsuspected, clearly missing causal sources, of the physical reality as the ultimate "value" of man. Physicists from Newton to Einstein have postulated the necessity of a universal causal medium, ether, fields or structural space. But only a relative view can explain how such medium as the opposite of matter can be millions of times stronger or denser than any substance and still is not felt, known or even measurable by instruments. The comparison with the atmospheric pressure may be thought of, though the effects there are far less absolute than here. Movement is free in such medium because it is the medium itself that causes the movement, or any other effect of matter. An object moved by a stream of densest medium experiences no friction or drag. We see clearly through such medium because seeing is receiving of waves, and wave is nonsensical without a medium. All effects of matter are such movements between the medium and matter, and consist mostly of waves.

Above all, no new assumptions but only a relative view is necessary to see that the "nothingness" or space as the opposite against which matter exists is as real as matter. If there was only matter, without nothingness, we could not know matter; it would not exist. Under the relative view the above medium is as necessary as is sand for seeing footprints in it. The recognition of the space as a reality solves all the mystifying dilemmas in physics, as we shall see later. Thus by mere abandonment of the one-sided, nonrelative view, of the natural human blindness, physicists could explain, for the first time, the seemingly unexplainable causality of physical phenomena, which is the central problem of the modern theoretical physics.

Once the fundamental causal source or causal laws of the physical world are established, the other physical sciences, like astrophysics or cosmography, can become thoroughly scientific and free of mysteries. Even the natural sciences like biology or genetics can become fully scientific only after the fundamental causality of matter and thus of the living matter is understood. The unsuspected causal principle of living process — which as a natural principle has to be simple — offers new explanations of the working of living forms, as well as of the gradual and purposeful inheritance of traits acquired through evolutionary conditioning, particularly through the inner selection. This covers the fundamental causal factors on which all sciences of living nature are built.

The relative view amounts to a world outlook that *reveals the unseen, opposite, determining causal side of the world of mind* as well as of matter. This unseen causal side is far more important than the side of the positive effects or values which alone man knows or sees as decisive. For the causal side is the source of such effects. Thus the relative view reveals to man the fundamentally decisive vast universe he does not see because of his one-track view focused on the narrow world of his values, or on his positive reality. Men have lived before with a narrowed view, believing the earth to be the center of creation, because of similar nonobjective focusing on their "reality" and values. The relative insight is the last step in liberating man from his narrowness of outlook. It leads beyond the values themselves as the sources of all, inveterate and delusory, truths and reality.

True science has always advanced in the direction of relativism, of dispelling man's beliefs about his world of values as the center of the universe or as the preferred point of reference. The relativity of all values in themselves is the last disillusionment, that man or scientist will resist by his very nature, by everything he inherently feels or knows. Value beliefs are stronger than clearest abstract truths. Even the founder of exact science, Francis Bacon, found the theory of Copernicus unacceptable, as contrary to "common sense". The relativity of all values is *more "impossible" than any one of the unthinkable ideas scientists have finally accepted.* Intelligence and erudition of scientists is no help when it comes to really new ideas. Scientists and philosophers of the past had far more knowledge or observations than would have been necessary for seeing the earth as a round planet or natural creation as evolution by survival. The more learned the scientists are, the more difficult it is for them to accept simple "impossible" new ideas, which have to appear nonscientific and absurd.

Particularly the relative causation is seemingly ridiculous, as well as simple. A modern scientist would, therefore, appear not only a ridiculous crank but also a simpleton by accepting such an idea. And he would appear so under the very standards he as scientist has learned and lived for all his life; or in the eyes of the very people, the other scientists, for whose esteem he lives. All great badly needed breakthroughs in science come from utterly unthinkable ideas. The basic scientific truths are simple, and if an idea is not unthinkable some scientist will have discovered it already, even before it is needed. It is clear that in the fields of sciences of man the unthinkable, simple breakthrough is long overdue.

The nonrelative view in the human sciences is becoming unbearable. It not only precludes all causal insights but perpetuates a dangerous modern alchemy. Under the nonrelative, "scientific" logic positive reactions or potentials are expected from positive value experiences. Men are urged by the modern science to have more of positive experiences, that is, pleasure releases — which experimentally do show as immediate sources of capacities. This logic is the only certainty all scientists accept. Of course proceeding by it has led to the confusion and controversy, as well as to the increase of functional disorders and diseases, in the fields of modern science and medicine.

The direct logic of experimental scientism here turns it into a *modern alchemy* in which one expects to obtain the release potential, the most precious capital for man, not only for nothing but even with the premium of the pleasant positive experience. Innumerable experts are eager to explain how to do it, what to avoid or where to look for hidden, unconscious reasons of failure. The theories offered are as many as there are scientists, and as inventively arcane as were the formulas of the alchemists.

The only thing that really matters, the difficult unpleasant accumulation of the release potentials through restrictions, is completely missed. If a person has such potentials, as the satisfactions with whatever he does, everything is easy. But the theorists never even mention the equally hard, opposite, effort that the creation of such satisfaction potentials requires. They have offered, instead, every possible combination of formulistic factors, irrelevant in terms of the equivalence of restrictions and releases. This is what makes the modern theories resemble formulas of alchemists trying every possible combination of causally irrelevant factors. Such factors are costless or easy exactly because they are irrelevant.

In any real causation the equivalence of cause and effect is inexorable. The *law of equivalence* or permanence of matter was the basis for physical sciences. It would have appeared, though, pointless to the alchemists, for it permitted no "scientific", inventive, profitable or complex procedures worthy of learned men. Now our scientists have to realize that in the human sciences as well the acceptance of the simple but hard law of the equivalence of release and restriction can be the basis for these sciences. The potentials as releases or satisfactions require equally weighty, hard and unpleasant restrictions or needs which are nonsatisfactions. No amount of inventiveness can circumvent this rule, and no formulistic complexity is needed. The inventive formulas of costless gains seem possible in the present theory because they are built on ways of thinking of physical sciences, which are inherently irrelevant for the human sciences. The formulas of alchemists were as irrelevantly built on assumptions of philosophy, which then was the authoritative learning.

What is more, the modern alchemy becomes the most *dangerous fallacy* ever foisted on man by any system of beliefs or learning. As we saw, the primordial drive in man is the striving for pleasure releases, for their increase, in every possible way. If man was really permitted and given the means to attain all the pleasures he wants, he would exhaust his every potential, mental or physiologic, and would end, through the vicious-circle of overadjustments, by suffering every functional disorder and disease. Use of drugs, and their aftereffects are only narrow examples of what can happen with every function enjoyed or "improved" with scientific effectiveness.

We always have to keep in mind that the restrictive and, necessarily, superstitious cultural tradition is being destroyed by the modern scientific and rationally liberal attitudes. Experimental scientists always prove the restrictions to be the main evils, and increase in releases the cause of increased capacities. This is also what the directly logical observation of every man shows. The blunder of the modern age is the rejection of the contradictory traditions of *restrictions* by which men have always lived. The modern experimental scientism and rational liberalism are systems of dangerous half truths. Real science built on causal understanding showing the necessity of restrictions is the way out of the disaster in which modern man is sinking.

If modern science and medicine continue providing man with increasingly improved subtle means for managing his pleasure releases, the result will be a progressively increasing scourge of the modern disorders and diseases. Moreover, it will come about as a continuous *seeming improvement*. As a conscious planner man could avoid feeling any pain or ill, by increasing releases or removing restrictions, through the thousands of means and skills he invents to get such "improvements". Of course the real cause of the pain or ill is not removed in this way and more release becomes necessary to uphold the "improvement" against the inevitable worsening — until final collapse.

Particularly dangerous is the fact that man feels he is really getting better in every way while he is obtaining the "improvements" which deepen into the disaster, in the vicious-circle way. Furthermore, the modern doctor, psychiatrist or scientist proceeds by the same direct logic of immediate improvements. Only the opposite causation could explain what ultimately happens, but it has never been even mentioned, in any form.

This applies to all organic functions, even to their most complex elaborations that constitute our mental life, motivations, values and sources of our behavior. *In all of them the artifically heightened improvements end as malignantly deepening vicious-circle worsening.* And for all of them the modern life, science and medicine are inventing the most ingenious means and skills. Equally "ingenious" and intense disturbances and incapacities follow such artificial improvements which exhaust the release reserves, inexorably limited by the organic sameness.

The *greatest danger for man as a conscious being* is his ability to "improve" artificially, in the way he wants, his deepest functions and releases. No genius in the world can constructively reorganize or really improve these astronomically complex organic processes. In the end the organism has to return to its normalcy by opposite ways after such improvements. The result is the opposite reactions and the vicious-circle disaster of over-adjustments. Modern scientism helps man, with enormous efficiency, on this road of increasing functional modern diseases or deepening exhaustion of potentials.

The essence of this scientism is the virtually alchemistic logic according to which you can obtain the positive capacities without equal effort or expenditure — by deriving your positive reactions from similar positive experiences in the past. This like-comes-from-like logic, of physical sciences, is the only one known to modern scientists and theorists. It also corresponds to what every man believes. But the practical, contradictory life proves such alchemy as flagrantly wrong. If we could obtain the positive capacities, which are satisfactions or pleasure releases, from equal pleasant satisfactions in the past, we would all be supermen and the world would be an instant utopia. The miracle could not fail. For we all start, in everything we do, with the greatest possible positive enjoyment. Therefore we would automatically gravitate into more and more positive reactions and capacities. Not to do so would require effort.

The modern scientism in the field of human sciences amounts to an alchemy. It becomes a menace, because it not only is flagrantly wrong but encourages man to increase and manage, the way he wants, his pleasure releases. This is the greatest danger for man as a conscious planning being. That is why the modern, functional diseases are alarmingly increasing together with the progress of modern science and medicine, which are admittedly mystified by their causes.

Conclusion

The law of relative causation is simple, almost self-evident. Satisfaction, release or value requires equal need as nonsatisfaction, restriction or disvalue. Organism maintains its sameness and cannot become more than or different from its normalcy. Value reactions determine everything man feels, thinks, knows or does. But any value experience can result only from organic change. Consequently, due to the maintenance by the organism of its sameness, every value experience requires, or leads to, equal opposite experience. Satisfaction or release is possible only to the extent there was nonsatisfaction or restriction. If organic "reserves" are used up, through excessive releases, equal restriction results as organism restores its normalcy.

But no person or culture could survive for long with a relativistic attitude. Therefore the relativity concept is offensive, like a food that tastes or smells bad, to every man or trend of thought. Moreover, in the relative causation, through the opposites, more value is obtained by subtraction, that is, addition of opposite value and less by addition of the same value. Adding satisfaction precludes possibility of further satisfaction. This reversed logic is contrary to everything the modern scientist does, thinks, looks for or assumes as certain. Experiment always shows an increase in releases, in all their forms, as immediate source of capacities, though actually it leads to their exhaustion and opposite, restrictive, negative reactions.

Though utterly unacceptable to man and contrary to everything held as true in human thought and science, the relative insight is the precondition for making the fields dealing with man scientific, for the first time. No science is possible without causal understanding, or with beliefs contrary to what is causally true. All human motivations, abilities and behavior derive from value reactions or releases, governed by the relative causation. Higher, more refined, cultural, or spiritual reactions are elaborations of the lower ones. Even abstract thought is a value process, a differentiation in values, however minute and complex.

But for all value experiences, the positive value is presently never connected with the negative backgrounds or disvalues that are its causes. As a result, in all fields dealing with man, with his physical, mental, cultural or social performance and capacities, the real causes are never suspected. Even in man's knowledge of physical reality, of his primordial "positive value", the negative causal source is missed.

Thus in every field of human behavior, health, values or knowledge the relative insight reveals the unseen causal side which is wider and more decisive than the positive-value side now solely recognized, by man, theorist or scientist. The relative insight becomes a world view revealing the vast "negative" universe that is the source of the narrow subjective, positive value world which alone is presently seen. One immediate practical result of this insight is that it shows how the present "scientism" helps modern man to drive himself into the increasing impoverishment, functional diseases and disorders he suffers from. He does so because he strives for the positive releases or satisfactions alone without previous accumulation of restrictions, nonsatisfactions or needs — the causal sources and value opposites of the satisfactions.

II

THE HUMANISTIC VALUE DELUSIONS

The nonrelative humanistic value outlook, deriving from the natural human belief in value gain, becomes a source of causal delusions in everything man feels, knows or does. Every human experience, even abstract thought, is at its basis a value process, of needs and satisfactions, or disturbances of normalcy and its restoration. Thus all capacities, reality and knowledge of man derive from value opposites. But the humanistic thought proceeds by the logic that values come from value sources of the same, not opposite, nature. The result is that everything in the world of man — except the secondary physical realities — is seen as true in ways exactly contrary to causal facts.

This belief that values, as the positive reactions or capacities, derive from sources of same nature becomes a practical danger when progress enables man to carry out his theoretical convictions. Why not make everybody enjoy to the fullest the values, satisfactions or releases, which are so beneficial and pleasant? This has become the most repeated truth, expounded by numerous modern human scientists, in every possible area and aspect. The danger is that this progressive, liberal world outlook nurtures at their very roots the modern tendencies of enjoyment, freedom or increase in releases, which threaten men's health, normalcy and progress. The results of this fallacy are found everywhere in modern life, from the violent student riots to the alarming increase in mental and functional diseases.

Ironically, the humanists deplore most the boredom or shallowness of modern life, and blame it on technology. Actually boredom and emotional exhaustion are caused by overenjoyment of inner values, crude or refined; and the humanistic emphasis on

53

deeper value enjoyments is here most to blame. It may sound convincing to contrast the materialistic, "quantitative" technology with spiritual "qualitative" value experiences. But the qualitatively superb, seemingly most spiritual experience, whether from use of LSD or other intense overenjoyment, is the surest way to emotional exhaustion and negative reactions. Above all, the humanistic theories become obstacles in every field of human sciences, behavior or knowledge, because their value outlook prevents the discovery of the real causal sources, the negative backgrounds or disvalues, which determine man's world of values and reality.

Missing the Causal Insights

The real causal sources of values, their opposite backgrounds or disvalues, are the last things to be recognized as such in the humanistic thinking. We do not need to repeat that all experience, even knowledge, is a value process. Humanists themselves stress the value nature of all experience and reality. Moreover, values are always viewed as the inner values, the value reactions, whatever the object they are attached to. Value is what is desired, felt as good, satisfactory, pleasant, interesting, positive, or simply valuable. Evidently values are conditioned, refined satisfactions or releases, deriving from lower organic satisfactions. But there can be no organic satisfaction without equal need, nor release without equal restriction, its value opposite. This is true of satisfaction in itself, or as a quality enjoyed in an object. The food, that is needed or lacking, has great satisfaction value, while the air, which is even more essential but not lacking, has no value.

Conditioned value systems obey the same logic. Morals are highly valued because they are so lacking in man or contrary to his nature, therefore difficult to acquire. Sex and natural appetites have no value because they are never lacking, though they are equally important for normal human existence. Because men have to struggle incessantly to evolve morals, they finally see them as the essence of their lives or of human nature and as the highest value given to man by his Creator.

We have to emphasize that the relative view *does not imply rejection of values,* like morals or love. Morality is the most valuable way to impose restrictions, and love is the richest source of capacities. In fact, the insight in the relative causation is to serve the promotion of such values, in a causally or scientifically understood way. This makes a great difference. Morals then are understood as the necessary hard system of restrictions that make releases available, and not as a value or satisfaction inherent in man's nature, which evidently would break out by itself without effort. Or, love then is recognized as the satisfaction potential created by restrictions or by hard pressures of survival, exactly contrary to the resulting release-rich, gratifying love. Thus love does not come *logically, by just being enjoyed.* If it did, men would create a paradise at once. The heavenly love by child grows from the infernal, conditioned anxieties of survival, that the parents impose on him because they live under the same, necessary conditioning and treat the child as part of themselves — which is the highest possible, natural love.

Sometimes the word "value" is used to designate the external, objective attainments, like the moral practice or the unselfish works of love, rather than the inner values. Such external phenomena are, evidently, not governed by the relative causation. We do not hold that increase in the moral practice or in the unselfish love leads to opposite effects. On the contrary, such increase should be the highest goal. But to attain it, the inner values as release potentials have to be created in the above paradoxical way, by increasing *their opposites,* the restrictions. In the simplest case, an attempt to create the gratifying feeling of love in a child by lavishing gratifications on him produces the spoilt child who has least of love.

The young generation is taught the great truths of freedoms and unconditioned love, but has to be brought up under restrictions and conditioned pressures. Revolt against hypocrisy, lies and seemingly unnecessary, evil repressions is then inevitable. Our scientific age requires a *scientific* recognition of the negatively felt restrictions as sources of values. Otherwise the modern attitudes of satisfactions and freedom will bring more of the cultural degradation, alienation, mental disorders, functional diseases and loss of capacities.

Now we may look at the main values extolled in humanistic thought, to see in detail the fallacy of its causal logic.

Love is the value that has been praised and glorified in every kind of theory, from the behaviorism of Watson to the religious philosophies of Tillich or Buber. There is even a research center on altruistic love, at the University of Harvard, once directed by its distinguished creator P. A. Sorokin. Love is found to be a force that can accomplish anything and have every possible value. This shows that love is merely a general organic state of highest motivation. People know this instinctively. In any language "love" is used to designate highest motivation, for sin as well as virtue. One can "love" a drink, or his fellow men. People may even "love" to hurt each other. Evidently, love is *a general organic satisfaction, and as such is governed by the opposite causation.*

The natural, organic essence of love is particularly evident from its strongest, clearest form, the sexual love, which has been often assumed to be the natural basis of all love.[1,3] And sexual love is one of the most egoistic, instinctive motivations of men. Jealousy is the measure of such love and it has brought more cruelty than any other human drive. Even the parental love is naturally egoistic. It derives from the need of parent to have and treat the children as part of himself. A parent may hurt his children if they resist his love or do not follow him. Parents committing suicide often kill their children first. All basal mechanisms of love are natural, organic satisfactions or releases, that can derive only from their opposites, needs or restrictions.

Conditioned restriction is the way the highest, unselfish love is created. It is self-evident that such love is the *opposite* of the only fundamental natural motivation of man, his selfish drive. This is very significant. It shows that our richest motivations or usable releases result from *opposition or conditioned restriction of our strongest release source.* One may think here of releases being "dammed" up and then used through desired release channels. That is why the relieving and satisfying unselfish love requires the restrictive, difficult conditioning.

The unselfish love is a restrictively conditioned satisfaction mostly of the need for security or survival, which is the highest, selfish, organic need. The child conforms his behavior the way parents want it, in order to have their fullest favor, their love. He instinctively knows he cannot survive if the parents are not close to him or if he does not follow them. As this love is being perfectly enjoyed, a need for more perfection in it increases due to value relativity. The conditioning is reinforced throughout the person's life as other people replace the parents, and the conditioned survival reactions deepen by fixation, much like taboos. The important fact is that the beautiful, warm feeling of love derives from the never recognized ugly, terrifying tensions of survival. There is nothing more dreadful for the individual than his incapacity to ensure self-survival. This dread is conditioned, in the child, into the need for love which then is a satisfaction *as powerful as such need or dread.* In all love, primitive or sublime, the satisfaction or value is as great as the need or disvalue.

Trained animals really love their master, but this love is created by conditioning the animals' fears, deprivations and needs. If the trainer applied real love, satisfying what the animals really want, they would remain wild beasts. Similarly, men love God to the extent they suffer threats or needs. Disasters and afflictions are the surest ways of making people turn to their "loving" gods, with feelings of love and gratitude. Peoples have gods only where they have needs, values depending on needs, threats to survival, dangers, failures of crops, sickness, or fears of death. The more civilized peoples have a God as Love itself because they feel how needed or lacking everywhere love is. Of course the love for God is deeply genuine — because the needs are direly real.

In brief, *love is a satisfaction, as intense as is the need,* its value opposite, from which it derives. But for a humanistic theorist it would be horrible to think of the tormenting, infernal needs and threats as the sources of the beautiful, heavenly love. For the theorists the love is a pure value in itself, emanating from an as sublime value source. As Sorokin states, love is energy that "flows spontaneously, neither hindered by any internal friction nor demanding any special effort."[2] Any requirement of hard, unpleasant value opposites is never considered. Rather, mere identification with the Superconscious, and use of positively felt, ecstatic techniques is recommended. Or it should be merely demonstrated to people how beneficial love is; and men should merely "direct" their energy of hate against their real enemies.[2]

Love is viewed as the greatest satisfaction or self-fulfillment of man. Most great thinkers, from Empedocles or Plato to Julian Huxley or Unamuno have extolled love as such satisfaction and fulfillment, often as having the depth and nature of sexual love.[4] Expectedly, love has been demonstrated to be a panacea for almost every ill.[3] This has been proven in modern therapy, by authorities like Menninger or Reik.[3] There can be no doubt that love, as the state of highest motivations or enrichment of organic releases, can make you well and resourceful in every way. But such release enrichment or reserves can be created only by the above opposition or "damming" up. After that the release may seem like the expression of the richest potency of man, comparable to the exalted emotions of orgasm.[3]

If such potency was a natural part of man we would be endlessly powerful, happy enjoyers of it, having not one difficulty in the world. Still, in the humanistic thought, love as the highest value has to have a source of the same noble essence, of the fullest satisfaction. Then, logically, man has merely to try to enjoy it. If the humanistic theorists really had it their way — as they are beginning to have — they would destroy the practical, contradictory, restrictive system by which love is created. They would try to flood life with love as satisfaction and thus end the very possibility of such satisfaction.

What we saw in regard to Love as inner value applies to all other values. We may look briefly at *Beauty* as the second most extolled value in the humanistic thought. Beauty and art are considered the highest goals of our culture and deeply revealing sources for all knowledge (J. Huxley).[1] They are accepted as solutions for the difficulties of modern life and science (J. Barzun).[5] Beauty, together with Truth and Goodness, is part of the ultimate trilogy of values (R. B. Perry).[6] Even our moral, altruistic growth supposedly has its basis in the aesthetic experience (H. M. Jones, F. S. C. Northrop).[7,8] Beauty is the very

you are
what you read

use your library

prototype of sublime, spiritual value, in philosophy and literature.

It is fairly evident, however, that beauty is merely a feeling of satisfaction or pleasure. There is hardly a difference between enjoying the beauty of nature and finding satisfaction in sexual admiration, tasty food or physical comfort. Whatever the pleasure release that constitutes the enjoyment of beauty, it is *organic*, therefore governed by the *relative or opposite causation*. Naturally, endless detailed elaborations, the mental contents, can be worked into each change of releases and restrictions. That is why an organic release may carry the conviction that intricate, ultimate problems have been solved, as drug experiences often show. However, the humanistic thinkers are concerned about the deepening of a value experience, not about its detailed intellectual elaborations which have to be as shallow, in emotional values, as they are vast.

Mystery about the feelings of beauty is inevitable also because they are as incomprehensible as are all processes of life, in their myriad multiplicity. In such general integrated reaction as a deep feeling of beauty, every function, every "cell" in the organism takes part, under countless evolutionary purposes. But in the terms of mind, one only knows, while experiencing deep pleasure of beauty, that he is attaining goodness, value, satisfaction or ultimate mental answers and insights. A person can derive a deeply convincing discovery of God and of all solutions from a release-inducing drug like LSD. Since the source of beauty thus remains a mystery, men attribute it to the highest, supernatural world.

The opposite causation of the feelings of beauty is evident. You could create any feeling of beauty by first imposing as strong deprivations. Think of the ecstatic balm of water for the desert traveler who was dying of thirst; or of the beauty of the world sublime beyond words for the man doomed to death permitted to live. Of course you cannot impose experimentally such deprivations. But "experiments" in which the positive opposite is induced first are easy, and are being performed by the thousands of drug users every day. The feelings created by drugs are as sublime and genuine as the most spiritual experiences. This has been confirmed by scientists, philosophers and writers, from William James and Bergson to Aldous Huxley and Maugham. But the final reactions from drugs are equally negative, base and primitive feelings. This proves that even the sublimest experiences of beauty are governed by the opposite causation, as all organic value reactions are.

In a word, the feeling of beauty must derive from, or lead to, its value opposites, base, distressing restrictions, nonsatisfactions, needs or feelings of dread. This may be inconceivable to the humanistic philosophers thinking of the sublime sources of beauty; but they should have learned by now from the stark and ugly modern drug experience how different is the causal reality.

Aesthetics has gained a high place in modern philosophy because it is one of the remaining fields of mystery. But practical life shows degeneration growing from the confusion in aesthetics and art. The more sober observers find the development of modern art abhorent and hard to believe. It looks like a treason, in which "the modern artist finds himself doing the work of dehumanizing he abhors" (J. Barzun).[5] Artists seem to have "taken the characteristics of the enemy they sought to destroy."[5] Actually, similar "treason" and confusion reign in all fields of modern creation. The modern man enjoys more opportunity for talent and leisure than men ever did, but he suffers from alienation, insecurity and anxiety so much more (H. J. Muller).[9]

We may mention briefly the inner value of *Truth,* which is often listed as the third greatest value. Evidently, truth has meaning only as a satisfaction of the need to know, whatever the object may be. Such satisfaction or inner value cannot be greater than was the tension, nonsatisfaction or inner disvalue that constituted the need. Increase of value here clearly destroys the value. Total understanding of something, like one's own existence, gives no sense of truth. Our great Truths are our invented answers to the main uncertainties of our world — about afterlife, gods, values, or purpose of human existence. Such Truths are as great to us as is the absence of their factual, objective understanding

Another great value is the *Intelligence, Order* or *Harmony* man discovers in the world. Again, the value feeling about the order in the universe is directly proportional to actual disorder in it. If everything in the world was in perfect harmony with man, like his normal adjustments to atmospheric pressures or to ordinary elements of earth, man would not know that there is any harmony. Order in nature is valued by man because it is rare and requires great effort in being established or discovered, as a necessary guide. Laws in nature are few, while the rest of it is endlessly irregular or chaotic. As men work painstakingly, throughout their lives, to discover and establish laws and order, they finally see the order or harmony as the very essence of their world.

The highest value in social life is *Freedom*. Everybody, from the hippies to the President, sees freedom as the primary noble goal. In itself, without restrictions as its opposites, freedom has no meaning. A man alone on an island, enjoying perfect freedom, would not know what freedom is. Freedom has become the highest value, repeated in constitutions, revolutionary movements, and everyday social aspirations as people have met with tightening social restrictions. Since the more advanced people have established more of the necessary social restrictions, they have also richer theories, monuments and ideas about the value of freedom. Moreover, a highly advanced people living in the atmosphere of continuous social restrictions do not notice them particularly and rather praise the rare, few freedoms they enjoy or aspire to.

It then may look as if the more advanced peoples have progressed because of their pursuit of the value of freedom. This is what our humanistic theorists are teaching as scientific truths. It seems as if people should just gain more freedoms — which is certainly pleasant — to reach higher progress. The great truths of freedom then are brought to the less advanced emerging nations, by their educated leaders, though their people need social restrictions more than anything else. The civilized nations have become possible because their people have built the tradition of hard restrictions through hundreds of years.

Happiness is the universal practical value men live for though as we saw it is unattainable to man. Those who have written on happiness have either found it paradoxical or failed to see the role of the opposite causal value backgrounds they themselves describe. R. M. MacIver states that paradoxically we find happiness by looking for something else or forgetting about it.[10] A. W. Watts emphasizes that the "balance of opposites" should not be upset and that total acceptance of the opposite, fear or unhappiness, is necessary.[11] H. M. Jones starts with Russell's motto that a rational pursuit of happiness would suffice to regenerate the world, but concludes that limitations and hardships are part of it.[12] Happiness could certainly cure every ill in the world and enable men to attain their highest capacities. Moreover, men want happiness more than anything else, and it is the easiest thing for them to understand or enjoy. The real, opposite causal sources of happiness are never connected with it.

It is amazing how the experts on happiness fail to connect it, in their writings, with its opposite causal backgrounds they themselves describe. G. Brochmann tells, in his book on happiness, how his highest experience of bliss occurred after living through the most painful day in his life, in an "inexplicable almost insane way." Another author on happiness, A. E. Wiggam, writes that happiness can be learned in the way he did — after very unhappy years which he describes but does not causally connect with his later happy state of mind. A. Whitman writes about several instances of experiencing unique bliss, in all of which the incidentally described background experiences are as unique despair, threat, boredom or fatigue.[39] E. G. Vining tells in her book *The World in Tune* about experience of ecstasy after "long months of sorrow had clamped tight my heart". E. Byrd, writing on the delights of life, illustrates them with the bliss she experienced after weeks of near fatal illness.[39] C. Moustakas tells of unique moments of ecstatic joy and beauty, just after an "awesome" blizzard experience. G. P. Morrill, writing about the miracles of bliss does not notice the opposite nature of the backgrounds he himself describes: dread, frustrations, exhaustion, "black moods", tension, sickness or threat of death. Colin Wilson gives an interesting description of how, after a very unpleasant journey, he found himself feeling "a great burst of elation" and saying "this is absurd". He derived an important theory from analysis of such experiences, without recognizing their clear opposite causality. A. H. Maslow, in his explanations of "peak experiences", uses examples which reveal the opposite backgrounds: housewife scurrying during her most hectic hour, man on a war-time convoy at night, or he himself recovering from illness.[13]

The emergence of feelings of happiness or bliss from painful torment or exhaustion has been always known in practice. Savages and primitive peoples have practiced tormenting, exhaustive rituals for inducement of ecstatic release experiences. Similar methods of self-torture have been used by shamans, flagellants, penitents, ascetics and yoga. The satori of yoga and Zen is induced by practices that are made painful to extremes. Daisetz Suzuki tells that a week he spent at a Zen monastery "was the most severe week physically, and I would say mentally too that I have known" — after which he had an as unique experience of a blissful satori.

Before we conclude we have to say more about the general moral and cultural values. Morals are held in high value because they are difficult for man to attain. Natural drives and appetites, which are as important as morals for normal human conduct but come easily by themselves, have no value and are rather viewed as sinful. Morals become a genuine satisfaction after we have invested so much continuous effort to have them. Any value or interest becomes a genuine gratification or release after its opposites, the restrictions, needs, nonsatisfactions or inner disvalues have been accumulated. Then it can be shown that the morals or cultural values are satisfactions or fulfillment of "human nature" emanating from a higher source of morals and values.

All cultural values are similarly deceptive. Social cooperation is a supreme need, requiring desperate effort. The result is the philosophical "discovery", since Aristotle, that man is a social animal. In truth, social cooperation, beyond family, is forced on man by needs of survival. Men of nature know only to kill or enslave other men not protected by a tribe as extended family. If men had any inkling of social nature, they would simply let social cooperation grow and bring them the enormous benefits it has brought in the past and, we know, will bring in the future.

But men have always resisted closer, "anthill" social integration and extolled the ideal of individual freedoms.

In the end we may stress the total preclusion in the humanistic thought of the insight in the real, opposite causation of values. Positive values are assumed to originate from positive value sources. Thus the naturally necessary human value delusion is perpetuated, particularly since it agrees with the usual, and "scientific" logic of physical causality. Satisfactions, releases or values are certainly the direct sources of every human capacity. They are also the most pleasant things for man. Yet we do not attain our capacities by enjoying ourselves. The humanistic world is one in which *all the real, opposite causes of values are missed or viewed contrary to causal facts.* Since values constitute everything we feel or even know — which determines what we do — the humanistic world becomes causally a total fallacy.

We do not doubt that the humanistic value convictions are noble and genuine. But in our scientific age the humanistic theorists are abandoning the old humanistic, *restrictive,* necessarily superstitious tradition and are trying to be scientific. The result is the worst of dangers: causal errors advocated by nobly motivated learned men in the name of highest values and science. The modern attitudes of satisfactions and freedoms, permissiveness and libertarianism are practically dangerous outgrowths from the delusions of humanistic enlightenment.

Why not Enjoy the Positive Values?

The values are satisfactions, either as our positive emotions, like love and freedom, or as satisfying feelings about what we do and experience, like our compliance with our moral "nature" or enjoyment of beauty. Furthermore, the inner values as releases make all our desired motivations and capacities possible. If you have love you can achieve anything. Love for knowledge or for what you have to do is interest, which makes everything easy. Similarly if you are happy, follow the satisfactions of moral will, have enthusiasm, faith, confidence or sense of freedom and beauty, you can reach every success with pleasure and vigor. Thus the richness of inner values, as satisfaction or release potentials, enables us to carry out all our good, perfectly reasonable intents, which we always have in abundance. Even our physical health depends on release potentials; love can indeed cure all ills. The only problem is how to create the inner values.

As long as the relative or opposite causation is not understood, the creation of the inner values must seem to be a matter of *accepting or recognizing what is good and pleasant.* Only the opposites of the positive values could make their attainment hard or unpleasant; and humanistic theorists would abhor the idea of values deriving from their opposites. Consequently, the learned authorities are stressing the need to explain how beneficial the values are and what are the direct, satisfying ways of attaining them.

Thus love is to be promoted through explanation of its benefits as well as of the deeply gratifying ways of attaining it, according to Sorokin.[2] His suggested identification with the Superconscious, its "acceptance", the "transfiguration", religious rituals, meditation, absolution from guilt, and catharsis, are near ecstatic experiences.[2] The recommended techniques, like "habituation", "precipitation" and reflex conditioning or the learning of insights, do not involve hard restrictions.[2] Of course a thinker like Sorokin has to notice that love is often too clearly born from suffering, frustration or calamity. But he explains this as a process of clarification of insights, through "polarization" of values. Another authority, Rollo May, sees love as a "sharing of pleasure and delight" with others, or as ecstatic acceptance of the universe, that men miss because of philosophical misunderstandings about the "daimonic" principle, lack of "intentionality", misunderstood nature of love and will or failure to expand consciousness.[13]

Whatever the nonrelative theories about it, love has to appear as a deeply *gratifying fulfillment,* that people fail to enjoy only because of some misunderstanding. Even our physical well-being can be, medically, proven to depend on acceptance of enjoyment of love. As Dr. S. Blanton shows, "we fall ill emotionally and physically if we do not love".[14] He finds that "once we accept the ways of love, there is no end to opportunities that lie before us for joyful living". Supposedly we miss our resources of "power, strength and courage hardly imagined" only because we reject love or fail to use the channels of love for discharge of such resources.[14] Refusal to accept love, or fear of falling in love has been blamed by many authorities.[15,16] People do refuse rushing into enjoyments of love, because they know intuitively that over-enjoyments bring hangovers. But this is not clear in logical scientism.

Scientists urge us *not to fear love*. We should learn to please ourselves, to enjoy and express our feelings, to live spontaneously, to prefer stimulating experiences and to love or accept ourselves (M. B. Hodge).[16] We are urged to yield to the positive feeling of love, through which world becomes "friendly, warm, exciting and plastic" (R. Harper).[15] According to Lewis Mumford we have to live so that "not a day pass without some more smiling expression of the delights of love . . . the linements of satisfied desire".[17] He finds that "to make ourselves capable of loving and ready to receive love is the paramount problem". The joyful fulfillment through love, much as in sexual love, is generally accepted as a goal.[4] Evidently, only ignorance of the benefits of love seems to prevent men from enjoying it.

We are, similarly, urged to enjoy the other great values. Sir Julian Huxley stresses enjoyment of the "qualitative" values, of beauty, pure wonder and delight, or inner peace and harmony.[1] More spontaneous, emotionally richer life, freer naturally genuine human experiences, even "erotic exuberance" are urged by Jacques Barzun as ways out of the emotional degradation of modern life.[5] The author of *The Greening of America*, Charles Reich, expects the new expanded Consciousness to come through freer enjoyments of everything, from clothes or hippie styles to music and drugs.[18] We are to enjoy beauty, "sunsets and stars, lying in the grass, humor and play", the "state of wonder and awe", or "breathless sense of wonder", as well as more varied sex.[18]

Modern technology, material progress or enjoyments of mere "things" are, of course, blamed for the impoverishment of the sense of values in modern life (P. A. Sorokin, E. Fromm).[20] But the theorists themselves have to recognize that modern man can enjoy everything, even art, more than men ever could before. Our "culture is permeated as never before by products and emanations of art" (J. Barzun).[5] We are defeating ourselves, as "we aspire for happiness, and prepare wretchedness of ourselves. The more we try to improve our well-being, the more we lose our peace of mind, perpetuate dissatisfaction and restlessness".[19] It is the "paradox of our age that its pleasures are often negated by concomitant anxiety" (J. Henry).

Actually the cause is not any enslavement to the "techne". As Daniel Bell points out, the "obverse side of the coin" shows that modern man enjoys unprecedented freedom, personal choice, opportunity for wider interests, artistic enjoyments and individualism.[19] Only, our experiences and enjoyments have become immediate or instantaneous, as in "hallucinogenic or Zen experiences, poetry without rules or art that has turned . . . to chance, shock and junk".[19] Modern art is found to be "bloodless, insecure, devitalized, neurotic . . . something nongenuine, counterfeit and mechanical" (A. Moravia).[31] Man seems to have deliberately abandoned "all inwardness and sense of value in veiled preparation for death" (K. Jaspers).[30]

Everything clearly points to *emotional impoverishment and exhaustion, through modern overenjoyments.* The technical and material progress, or the preoccupation with mere "things" could be blamed least, because it never brings deep emotional enjoyment, according to humanistic scientists themselves. If there is no real emotional involvement or overenjoyment, there can be no grave emotional aftereffects or impoverishment. Actually the material progress is used by modern man to attain what he really, deeply wants and enjoys. Man is too intelligent to work for what might not bring him genuine satisfaction, pleasure or the desired value. Surely the more "natural", rugged, old-style country life provided a deeper sense of values (L. Mumford, W. E. Hocking).[17,23] But the appreciation of the world comes exactly because of lesser previous enjoyments. Luxuries of life that man seeks are also the enjoyments that directly or naturally are of the highest value to him, and enable him to enjoy all other values, most directly.

It does not help to argue that the satisfaction of some deeper inner needs has been neglected in the rush for the material improvements. Man's order of preferences of deeper needs is as miraculously perfect as is the ungraspable integration of pleasure mechanisms. A deeper, more "basic" value gets attention before other values in ways that no scientist can understand. Surely there are basic cultural "values" that are dangerously neglected, namely, the real sources of values — the restrictions or negatively felt needs that make the release or values possible. But the exact opposite of such restrictions or nonsatisfactions is the passionate goal of the theorists who clamor most about impoverishment of deeper basic values.

Erich Fromm has been a foremost critic of the shallowness of modern values.[20] He rightly blames the overconsumption of everything, "drinking in of music, screenplays, fun, sex, liquor and cigarettes". But Fromm has been a particularly zealous advocate of intense, spontaneous, ecstatic experiences, fullness of living, and enjoyment of deepest values.[20] Similarly, Lewis Mumford is a great critic of the poverty of values in our life. But he urges us to strive for experiences of "such poignancy, intensity and fullness" that they may outweigh one's whole lifetime.[17] Herbert Marcuse, the philosophical leader of the "greening" generation, deplores the one-dimensional shallowness of life in the industrial society and of merely "quantitative" satisfactions.[21] The main appeal of his theory is the call for liberation or desublimation of our natural and sexual enjoyments, deepening of aesthetic pleasures and new imaginative expansion of joy and happiness.[21]

In truth, if we really followed the advice of such authorities and lived with the ecstatic, poignant or imaginatively expanded enjoyments, we would be suffering from emotional overenjoyment and exhaustion or impoverishment of inner values, to the point of psychotic disorders. The final basis of all values is the organic release, and it cannot be increased without equal previous or later restriction. Whether the excess of releases is induced by idealistic self-suggestion, transcendental meditation or psychedelic drug, the result is the same, because organism still has to return to its inexorably limited normalcy.

The humanistic philosophy has always stressed the pursuit of happiness inherent in human nature, freedom and reason, while rejecting the superstitious, negatively felt, seemingly unnecessary traditional restrictions (C. Lamont).[22] Liberal, enlightened believers in human nature have maintained that satisfaction of our truly natural needs is the solution for our problems (P. J. Tillich, J. W. Krutch). The humanistic philosophy finds support in the "scientific" modern approaches, particularly of the modern psychology, which stress the natural satisfactions, and dangers of repressions. This is also true of the recent anti-progress and human-nature approaches. The now popular humanistic psychology is founded on the belief in the powers inherent in human nature, to be released through the "peak experiences" that are "absolute delights" (A. H. Maslow). The recent advances in drugs aroused great enthusiasm and hopes among the varied believers in the resources hidden in human psyche, as we shall discuss later. Of course the final results from the drugs have been disastrous.

Confusion has been inevitable. The necessity of "restriction of impulses" or of "discipline" may be recognized, while satisfaction of natural instincts and all natural drives may still be stressed (W. E. Hocking).[23] We are to "find such a mode of satisfying any wish that all other wishes may also be satisfied." The "disagreeable after-clap of an agreeable indulgence" may be explained by the assertion that such indulgence could not have been a really satisfactory one [23] Actually even drug effects can be as "true" as a religious experience, if they are strong enough. The necessity of restrictions has never been understood even by the best theorists. William James argued that "the capacity of the strenuous mood lies so deep down among our natural human possibilities that even if there were no metaphysical grounds for believing in God, men would postulate one simply as a pretext for living hard". Thus men seem to impose the hard restrictions or displeasures on themselves without a real need, by a misunderstanding.

Our Constitution, inspired by the doctrines of enlightenment, proclaims the pursuit of happiness as the universal goal of men. But these were only "glittering generalities" of theory (H. M. Jones).[12] Theoretical truths were not expected to be carried out in practice. Deep enjoyments as fulfillment of life, hailed by Emerson, became practical concerns in the new era, initiated by the genius of William James.[12] The preoccupation with satisfactions has become since a serious business, of grave general and medical concern, exploited by advertising agencies, vast industries and mass media. Best authorities have been dealing with the problem of how to increase the enjoyment of satisfactions in their various forms of happiness, joy of life, interest, enthusiasm, peace of mind, relaxation, freedom of gratifications and avoidance of "conflicts" or restrictions.[12]

We hardly need to go into demonstrating the vastness of modern theory and do-it-yourself literature on attainment of more satisfactions or releases. Every theorist seems to have made the sure discovery that satisfactions or positive reactions bring us the capacities and benefits as well as the "fulfillment" we want. This discovery is being made in regard to every problem, in every field. The experts include psychologists and scientists, as well as the general prophets, from Norman Vincent Peale to Charles Reich. You can find in every *Reader's Digest* a condensation of some new exciting discovery, by some important author, of how to enrich your capacities prodigiously by increasing some positive emotion or value feeling.

Each one of such "discoveries" should have provided utopian solutions, with no inherent difficulty involved. Also, each theory advocating the increase in positive emotions can be experimentally proved to work, as long as the opposite effects can be delayed or disregarded. Various "positive" movements have been enthusiastically started everywhere, from healing to franchise business, with clearly great successes — to collapse and be forgotten. The failure can still be blamed on abandonment by the person of the strong positive attitudes, which are causally never connected with the opposite reactions, that inevitably follow.

In sum, the humanistic thought with its directly logical belief in values, has perpetuated the *alchemistic fallacy* that inner values or capacities can be enriched by direct increase of such values, which are satisfactions or releases. It amounts to expecting *enrichment of capacities through positive enjoyments.* The result is confusion and practical danger. Inner values are, in the end, organic releases or pleasures. And the greatest danger for man mentally, physically or socially, is his now enormously improved drive to increase *directly* his pleasure releases, which leads to their equal impoverishment.

Thus the unique modern progress and plenty are becoming the sources of equal human impoverishment, anxiety, mental or social disorders and functional diseases. Explanations are sought in assumed nonsatisfaction of the real human nature. But anything required by such nature could be only pleasant and simple to attain. Whatever the arguments, the usual, humanly necessary, direct value logic is bound to mislead. If values came from sources of same value, there would be no contradiction, variety, effort, richness of adjustment or vast cultural elaborations.

The Gullible Victims

The humanistic fallacy of seeing the causation of inner values in the insidiously dangerous ways contrary to causal facts has its disturbing consequences wherever humanistic thought has enough influence. Humanistic education and enlightenment have produced the constantly recurring cultural revolts, riots and revolutionary movements by radical intellectuals, particularly by young students who have not yet acquired the contradictory traditional wisdoms of practical life and culture. It is inevitable that by stressing constant *enjoyment* of values the humanistic education turns its pupils into negatively reacting "psychopaths" who have to hate or destroy.

The prime victims of the fallacy are the liberal thinkers and intellectuals, as well as the students, who live by the humanistic, "learned" truths. That is why centers of education and learning turn into nests of disruption and practical cultural demoralization. The indirect victims of the fallacy are theorists in all fields of human sciences — education, psychology, psychiatry, medicine, personal and social adjustment, philosophy, aesthetics or theory of cultural progress. Inner values, as organic release reactions, determine everything men feel or do; even knowledge is a value process. Thus the whole causal world of man becomes distorted by the logic of value delusions — in the fields dealing with man, or even in the theories about the fundamental causes of physics. The learned liberal men are fighting for more freedoms and satisfactions everywhere, in education or health care, thus fostering overadjustments and unintendedly promoting the exhaustion, disorders and diseases modern men suffer from.

We may as well look first at the *student riots*, particularly of the late 60s, as the most typical expression of the permanent problem of our education and generation "gap". As a study by John Fischer showed, the rioters were generally the undergraduates of liberal arts, almost never the students of engineering, medicine, law, or physical sciences. They were the pure, pampered idealists formed by the humanistic education and not yet "corrupted" by hypocrisies and contradictions of practical life. The conflict between fathers and sons has been a typical result of humanistic education since the great period of enlightenment. Every generation returns to the restrictive tradition. But before it does it confronts the old hypocrites who continue repeating the humanistic doctrines of freedoms and satisfaction but have already learned the practical requirements of restrictions and non-satisfactions. Presently the conflicts due to the "generation gap", and the revolt against the "establishment" are more intense than ever, because in our age of efficiency and plenty the ideals or theories are carried further to their fulfillment.

A significant fact is that the recent student riots, in this country and elsewhere, were almost *self-evidently irrational, compulsive reactions,* which can originate only from emotional, opposite exaggerations. The only definite ideas and flag the rioters could follow were those of anarchists. Of course nobody has ever lacked plausible reasons for his irrational acts. The students rioted for all kinds of reasons, that accidentally came their way or were fashionable, emotionally exciting or catchy enough for idealistic sloganeering. The demonstrators never even tried to formulate practical programs (G. F. Kennan).[24] Everybody knew that if the students did not have a "cause", like the war, they would invent one. Their inventiveness became a standard theme for cartoonists. The revolt in itself was the goal.

The causes of demonstrators could be quite convincing, because cultural conditioning and human adjustment are "hypocritical" and contradictory. But the real cause of the riots was psychological stress, as any psychiatrist could see. Even such a progressive psychiatrist as Bruno Bettelheim had to recognize that the students' "occasional on-target attacks on real evils have misled many well-meaning people into overlooking their true motif; this is hate, not desire for a better world". Political ideologies became mere pretexts for revolt. Rightist demonstrators, like those of the Free Campus Movement, acted in the same anarchistic way as the leftist students.

The student riots simply spread from university to university, at certain seasons, or from country to country, as fashions or mass movements do, however unrelated their reasons or factual conditions. They also waned in the way mass movements exhaust themselves or fashions fade. Then the radical students turned out to be least interested in practical political work. It would have been ridiculous to ask the demonstrators rational questions. For instance, why should they deny democratic equality and freedom to others? Even a million rioting students would represent only a small percentage of the population. The very purpose of riots or demonstrations was to impose the will of the demonstrators by force, not by rightful representation. Those who created and led the riots loved the use of physical force and destruction. Or why did the young demonstrators try to impose their solutions for the complex problems, while they never even tried to study them and completely lacked the vast, hard experience or mature wisdom needed, and possessed by the authorities they so violently opposed.

Some people claimed, convincingly, that the students were misled by political conspiracy. Actually the students acted with "conspiratory" irrationality for the same reasons that make the compulsive neurotic act against good sense with intense ingenuity.

Those who tried to blame the student revolts on conspiracy were as wrong as those who sought for justifiable reasons or grievances to explain them. The student riots were excessive negative emotional reactions and as such could originate only in the least suspected, opposite emotional excesses or overenjoyments.

Modern educators have been using all kinds of value enjoyments as inducements for learning. For instance, the student is grandly promised that knowledge will make him free. Or his learning and discovery of values is to bring him deep satisfactions. The whole learning process is promoted as a way of enjoying what the student is doing or learning. This has to become a system of overenjoyments or exaggerations that do not correspond to reality. The expected freedoms or satisfactions do not come or are not true. Then somebody has to be blamed and hated in justification. The enjoyed exaggerated feelings of freedom or satisfactions reverse into the feeling of repression and harrassment by others. The continuous enjoyment of increased self-superiority through learned values leads to embittered disappointments when such superiority is not recognized.

The student demonstrations became easy and intense because of the *crowd effect.* Most of our conduct is conditioned on the consideration of what others will think. Because such emotional conditioning is accumulated every day of our lives, it becomes a strong, irrational force we hardly know ourselves. Consequently, people derive intense, easy satisfactions from a crowd dominated by the same attitudes they hold. Modern conditions make formation of crowds easy. The result is the phenomenon of students and other groups forming massive crowds for intense common enjoyments, like the rock festivals as well as mass demonstrations.

The student riots were *only the more typical examples of what is happening all the time* in the conflict between generations, that has come with the humanistic enlightenment and reformed education. The "counterculture" and youth revolution are its modern forms. Typically, the great apostles of *counterculture* are Marcuse, Norman Brown, Ginsberg, Alan Watts, Leary, or Paul Goodman.[25] They are the advocates of increased, deep value enjoyments, attained by every possible means, including drugs and sexual freedom. They are proving, logically, how such enjoyments could increase all our potentials as well as enrich our lives, opening utopian possibilities men have failed to recognize. The most concrete realization of the counterculture has been the culture of hippies and beatniks.[25] It shows what happens in practice with the utopian ideals. Hardly any movement has been so clearly degenerating and culturally disruptive. It has left behind mental disorders, crime, spiritual as well as material poverty and cultural desolation.

But when the culture of *hippies or beatniks* first appeared it was hailed as the new Christianity. The beatniks and hippies were compared to the early Christians who overthrew the sophisticated Alexandrians.[5] Their culture was seen as a return to the pastoral romance.[33] It was hoped that "love may become once again, as in the past, a frolic and amusement",[1] or comparable to the "lovemaking in a meadow".[21] This agrees with the humanistic, logical belief in human nature, value enjoyments and freedom. One may think here of the Brethren of Free Spirit, of the fourteenth century, or the Ranters, of the sixteenth. The Brethren stressed the primeval innocence of sex and ended by practicing love making in their churches. The result was degeneration of spiritual and practical life, much as in our counterculture.

Yet all our radical liberals, not only the hippies, are fighting for similar "free spirit", for life based on enjoyment of love and genuine freedom, with the free use of drugs and liberated sex.[22,26,27] The new Consciousness of the "greening America" is to be brought by the hippie type culture offering every form of sensuous pleasures.[18]

The result is the *"uncommitted" or alienated youth*. Their own opinions and attitudes, reported by K. Keniston,[28] are revealing. What they want is increased "awareness, passion, pleasure and immediacy" of feelings, or "zest, exuberance and passion", that would give life immediacy of experience, spontaneity, wholeness and fulfillment.[28] It is a clear, logical effort to have the enriching positive emotions or potentials directly and fully, without the seemingly unnecessary enslaving restrictions. The practical limitations are blamed on technology, with its cold efficiency, control, materialism, competitiveness, "upwardly mobile striving", and insensitivity.[28] The recurrent arguments about the nonhumanity of technology may sound logical, but they imply the absurdity that man does not know how to enjoy the pleasant enriching reactions; that he serves the cold, efficient technology because of such miscalculation.

A good example of the logical advocacy of more enjoyments and freedoms is the teachings of Paul Goodman, the recognized first apostle of the *counterculture*.[25] He blames the anxiety, dissatisfaction and weakness of our young people on lack of real satisfactions and freedoms — though he recognizes that they enjoy more prosperity and permissiveness than youth ever did.[29] He sees solutions in enjoyment of the stronger natural pleasures practiced by the beats who "are achieving a simpler fraternity, animality and sexuality than we have had".[29] Goodman finds that the beats are more logical and real than the others, who are "idiotic". He argues that youth should be permitted real enjoyments, including free sex and drugs. Supposedly, education becomes irrelevant to youth because sex is shunned or restricted in our schools. More and better sex as well as drugs should be made available; if heroin is to be prohibited, then something like alcohol should be permitted.[29]

In fact, the reformist leaders like Goodman only want to see realized in practice what the humanistic theorists have been teaching about freedoms and humanly real satisfaction. It is highly revealing that the less radical, *practical* humanists are easily proven to be hypocrites who have betrayed their ideas. That is why teachers like Marcuse are acclaimed as leaders by the radicals. He shows how the liberals insidiously mutilate the liberties and deny the satisfactions that they themselves have been professing.[21] He calls for a radical revolt to shake the seemingly liberal society out of its self-deceptive "state of amnesia". All radicals are *outraged about the practical liberalism,* which supposedly has "substituted empty rhetoric for significant content".[26]

Our whole professedly liberal modern society appears hypocritical under enlightened rational view.[27] That is why the more educated groups have more radicals among them, as the study by Goodwin Watson has shown. The phoniness of our culture of corporate state is seen as its weak point that will make it yield to the "greening" generation bringing genuine freedoms and happiness.[18] The radicals do not realize how conditioned, "brainwashed" and restricted they themselves are and have to be as cultural beings; or that restrictions are not felt to the extent they are general.

The *"alienation" and anxiety,* amidst highest prosperity and progress, are the paradoxical, unsuspected results of our liberal, hedonistic way of life. The theories offered to explain the anxiety and alienation become philosophical mystifications. Theorists are invoking arcane concepts about Identity, Self, Loss of Identity, or Discovery of Self and of deep values within it.[30] Solutions through the formula "Know and Trust Thyself" are recommended by modern theorists as they were by the Delphi oracle.[30]

Practically the finding of Self or Identity becomes only a more complex term for increase of releases, just as Alienation becomes a similar term for their impoverishment. It is always the positive, *pleasant experience that is viewed as the discovery of self.* For ultimately one's ego or self is the source of all releases or values; one finds them always inside himself. Conversely, in case of release impoverishment one tries to avoid his "self" or the demands of his organism for restoration of normalcy through restrictions. This looks like an alienation from self; and from the reality, which is distorted to avoid such return to normalcy.

Of course the direct increase of releases through the easy enjoyment of Identity or Self can only bring release exhaustion or degradation of capacities. And the negative reactions during "alienation", as the pressures back to normalcy, are the ways to restore the potentials. Just the reverse logic is followed by modern scientists, in their abstruse theories. Gaining of Identity is viewed as attainment of freedoms from "superego" restrictions.[30] Satisfactions, rewards and enjoyment of success are seen as requirements of positive development of Self. Anxiety or Alienation, supposedly, comes from renunciation of instinctual

gratifications.[30] The attainment of Identity is, in general, expected to be the *logically direct, positively felt* way of avoiding
the anxiety.[30] Besides, the theories of Identity, Self, or loss of
Self become contradictory in themselves. The loss of self is, in
fact, found to be a highly positive experience, comparable to
the "release from the self in Zen"[31] which is generally recommended by the modern experts. According to Freud the loss of
self brings an "oceanic feeling of oneness with the universe".
It is a nonanxious state of neutralized drives, free of all anxiety
and conflict.[30]

In art and literature, the "tendency toward non-identity" is
traced from Byron and romanticists to Beckett and existentialists,
as well as to the creations by artists like Dubuffet, Pollock or
Mondrian.[31] Alienation and anxiety are the main subjects of
the most typical works of modern literature. Writers and artists
love to dwell on the experiences of loss of self or existential
doom and futility, that they pretend to decry in deep despair.
This is a modern version of the romantic weeping, by poets and
writers, about death and futility of life. Liberation from life
or Self, from our everyday anxieties and worries, is indeed an
enjoyment, if it is all conceived poetically, in absence of real
threats to self or dangers of death. It becomes a kind of nirvana.
For the followers of counterculture the most popular writer is
Hermann Hesse, who equally sought the nirvana while dwelling
on existential "despair" together with exalted search for self;
significantly, he suffered from psychotic disorders.

In religion the old tradition of imposing restrictions, necessarily through fear and guilt, is being rejected. Religion is now
expected to "encourage the positive emotional responses that
build health", and to "grant release from damaging sense of
guilt."[33] Rational, enlightened thinkers, from Nietzsche to Moravia
have blamed Christianity for degeneration of men. They do not
see how the restrictions, in their various forms of seeming weakness, become the sources of potentials. The Nietzschean Super-
man, boundlessly enjoying every release, logically could not fail;
but practically would suffer from psychosis.

Interesting questions for the humanistic philosophy of religion arise from the modern experience with drugs. If depth or genuineness of value feelings is to be accepted as criterion, then drugs, like LSD, are clearly sources of religious revelations. As W. Braden explains, in his book on drugs and religion,[32] a person under influence of drugs "feels he knows essentially everything there is to know" and reaches a transcendental union with God. Braden has every logical reason to contend that this should create a revolution in the Western religions and in our fundamental beliefs. Philosophers as well as scientists have observed the genuineness and depth of religious experiences from drugs. But the end result of the exalted feelings is opposite degradation and limitation of value experiences.

The practically most important "victims" of the value delusions are the *scientists in the fields dealing with man.* There can be no science without causal understanding. But the usual value logic is exactly contrary to the causal truths. Since values are the basis of everything we feel, do or know, the whole causal world of man remains unseen, and reality is viewed in ways contrary to facts, because the opposite causality of values remains unthinkable. We shall explain this later, repeatedly, for all human sciences, from psychology and medicine to history and economics, or even for the fundamental causal knowledge in physics and natural sciences. No wonder that all of science is now often viewed as an aberration. The confusion is, understandably, deepened by intensified absorption of the humanistic and "scientific" learning.

That is why the more educated people are more confused when it comes to practical as well as truly scientific insights about ourselves. The "free" educators or the liberal cultural leaders are typical examples. They have created the permissive and hedonistic atmosphere, of freedoms and "fulfillment", that has led to more anxiety and stress, violence and disorders. A world of unrestrained satisfactions is "scientifically" perfect and easy, but practically leads to opposite results. It is regrettable that modern learning has become the source of support for enjoyments and freedoms, which man is seeking too much already. In the past the learning was used to sustain the restrictive moral and cultural traditions. Today one wanting to appear educated has to profess the liberal fashions.

In this atmosphere the modern "enlightened" educators and parents have brought up a generation that is hateful and stress-ridden to the same unprecedented degree in which love and prosperity have been lavished on it. The hate and stress have become so excessive that meaningful communication across the "generation gap" has become impossible. What is lacking is, simply, love. But love is a satisfaction that can arise only from a need which has to be accumulated by nonsatisfactions or restrictive conditioning, always negatively felt.

Naturally, the nonsatisfactions and restrictions have to be imposed in the name of satisfactions and freedoms. Even the efforts to "understand" the rioting students was practically advisable, just as it is better to "reason" with a spiteful child. Also the difficulties that the student riots created brought progress, in the way all difficulties men create for themselves make them evolve new ways. But it was as inane to try to find rational causes or reasons for the clearly excessive student reactions as it is for the radicals and liberals to cry about the "brainwashing" and deceitful restrictive conditioning in the system. All men, including the radicals, are "brainwashed" and conditioned to the extent they are cultural beings.

In the end, we may repeat the insidious fact that *the most learned, leading groups are the prime victims* of the humanistic delusions. The radical liberals are people with higher general, humanistic education. Under a logical, idealistic view it does seem absurd that the clearly positive, truly valued and directly beneficial satisfactions should be denied. The deep value enjoyment is the inevitably logical goal for all theorists — from William James to Charles Reich — who seek solutions in value experiences. Hippies were the most logical pursuers of the humanistic value beliefs. In the notorious murder trial of Charles Manson and his hippie gang, its members, former college students, testified that he was the only person who showed in life what they had been taught about values.

Heavenly ecstasy is followed by infernal debasement, and full freedom in releases or inner values leads to psychotic restriction, in the world of value experiences or feelings. But a logic contrary to this causal truth governs humanistic thought and educational theory, which accept the positive feeling, fulfillment and freedom as the goals. If we lived totally in accordance with the humanistic value theories we would all be disturbed, stress-ridden and hateful psychopaths.

The Fallacies of Value Outlook Become Obstacles

The humanistic causal logic is identical with the natural human *value outlook* which precludes the insight that value experiences derive from their value opposites. Man may see that satisfactions come from needs or even that releases require previous restrictions. But he can never accept that the real source of the values he lives for is their opposites which he constantly avoids. The natural human value outlook is good enough for unplanned adjustment, through evolution and selective, nonscientific cultural progress. There the restrictions are imposed by natural difficulties, or by cultural tradition evolved through blind selection. But the modern, scientific man is becoming capable of planning or directing his own organic adjustment. And he is beginning to destroy himself, because he does not yet understand the requirement of restriction, nonsatisfaction or inner disvalue in higher adjustment, creation of capacities or avoidance of their impoverishment.

Modern men die exceedingly from functional diseases, caused by overadjustment, therefore not causally understood, as doctors have to admit. Man enabled to increase his pleasure releases tries to live with pleasures alone, by eliminating the negatively-felt organic restrictions. The result is malignant abnormalcy and functional impoverishment, deepening under the vicious circle of the overadjustment into grave diseases. We have to emphasize that the same is happening in the psychological, cultural and social adjustment of modern man. He is suffering increasingly from functional impoverishment, mental disorders, anxiety and stress, as he prodigiously improves his enjoyments, sense of security and freedom from stress. Here as well every direct improvement deepens, through the vicious circle, into its unrecognizable opposite.

Particularly the freedom from anxiety and stress has become *the most wanted value, overenjoyed* through the unprecedented improvements perfected in our culture, education and social life. The result is the equally increasing, unexplainable, malignant anxiety and stress, found at the roots of all modern disorders and diseases. Science rather worsens the various kinds of malignant impoverishment of our adjustment as it proceeds by the same causal logic of direct increase in positively felt experiences or enjoyments. No wonder that the fields dealing with mental, cultural or social behavior can be characterized as a "vast confusion that has lately taken the name of Behavioral Sciences" (J. Barzun).[5]

Besides the reversedly wrong causal logic, the value outlook perpetuates another general delusion: *value appears important when it is rare, therefore factually least important.* The remarkable, interesting records and legends of a given culture dwell on what is exceptional. The philosophers prove the higher nature of man by adducing his remarkable efforts in upholding his values, that are hard for him exactly because they are exceptions from his general nature. Literature and art record what is interesting or striking, as a contrast to the usual or general background. In psychology or anthropology the scientists try to find explanations in legends and folklore, that often center on horrendous, even incestuous or parricidal themes, because these are dramatically interesting by being extraordinary. As such they, evidently, reveal a general absence of happenings or intents of this kind.

Whether it is the analysis of a patient or of a whole culture, the scientists are observing and accepting as important what is striking, "characteristic", or remarkable, therefore in fact least important generally or causally. Scientists undoubtedly can distinguish the exceptional from the general. But the cause of confusion here is inherent in the paradox of value reactions. The person or nation may indeed feel or behave in the extraordinary ways contrary to the usual or generally accepted feelings and behavior. The neurotic may even be obsessed with the horrendous ideas of incest or parricide. The reason is the opposite causation. In all cases of excesses, the person feels, therefore behaves, in ways exactly contrary to the feelings that he wants most or that he cultivates as the normal experiences. By wanting and cultivating them intensely he overenjoys them and ends by suffering the least wanted, strangely abnormal opposite reactions.

Just as the rare or unusual values seem to be causally important, *the universal or general, really important causal backgrounds remain unnoticed.* Something that is always there, like the atmospheric pressure or gravitation, is not felt or known. Even a child can see the gravitation at work, but it remained nonexistent for the learned men and philosophers seeking ingenious explanations of the forces of nature for thousands of years. Moreover, the universal truths, potentially evident to everybody, are also too usual or commonplace to appear scientific, though science has to be founded on the universal causal truths. Man could have discovered that the earth is round by looking at the horizon; or that it rotates, by thinking about the rising sun, in a way not centered on his small world. But these facts were too universal or common, and the habit of viewing the world as man-centered was too general, to be noticed.

In sciences dealing with man the universal, commonplace facts have equally not yet been noticed. The pleasure — in its conditioned forms — governs everything man does or lives for. But it has remained a commonplace fact of no scientific interest. Similarly, scientists have not yet noticed the unique universal capacity of pleasure or feelings to reveal to mind the causal meanings of one's myriad organic processes which mind can never grasp directly.

The most universal fact, that determines all organic existence, is the preservation by organism of its evolutionary sameness, to its minutest details. This fact is so general or commonplace that it "scientifically" appears meaningless, though it can, evidently, serve as the basis for explaining all causality of organisms including men. Similarly unnoticed is the existence of organism as a permanent one entity, that is at bottom the source of the universal human notions like "same", "one" or permanence, from which derive our logic, mathematics, and the human way of thinking, reflected in language. Every language in the world has the same parts of speech, due to the categories of space and time deriving ultimately from the permanence of organic existence, as we shall see in discussing philosophy.

The inherent contradiction of human existence itself remains unnoticed because of its universality. The main fact of this contradiction is that man gains happiness, satisfaction or release only through its equal denial, the hard efforts or conditioned restrictions, which create the rich and varied adjustment, the complex civilization. But nobody particularly notices this contradiction of existence, because it is so universal — because things just are this way.

For similar reasons men hardly notice the conditioning or "brainwashing", by which the pleasure, as the universal force of life, is turned into desired motivations. Further, the basal needs, of growth and security, that are conditioned, are never noticed, because they are omnipresent in the organic existence. Scientists talk about conditioning through external reflexes or activities, like the child's responses to feeding or cuddling, much as in animal reflex conditioning. The humanistic opponents to ideas of conditioning then can convincingly expound how silly the scientific assumptions of conditioning are. Psychologists seek for all kinds of remarkable incidents in childhood, while the real drives and their conditioning remain unnoticed because they are as general as an atmosphere.

In brief, all the decisive, causal facts of human existence, including its driving force, the pleasure, and its basic needs, as well as their use and transformation, have remained scientifically and theoretically unnoticed, exactly because they are so universal.

Of course the main fallacy of the value outlook is its total exclusion of the causal truth that values derive from their opposites and that reality as known to us is ruled by the *principle of opposition*. Reality without opposition is nonsensical. Everything is known through relation to something different, ultimately opposite. The nature of physical reality is force, but a force without opposition is a meaningless dissipation. The laws of the universe, and of the living nature, result from the opposition, between the Field and matter. A free force or event, evidently, obeys no law, no determined order. In the living processes the same opposition works in myriad forcible ways, thus inexorably governing or predetermining tiniest living phenomena, to exquisite perfection. The most evident creation through opposition is the evolution of living forms. New, richer, more complex and resourceful forms are evolved as the old ways of satisfaction or release are opposed and new, circuitous ways are found.

The discovery by Darwin, though surprisingly simple, genially explains vast phenomena that had remained mysterious miracles of purposive creation. This discovery amounts to recognition of the opposition as the creator, though only in a limited area. Similar vast explanations would become possible in all fields if the principle of opposition, inherent in all reality, was more widely recognized. The insight that opposition or restriction enriches all human capacities could turn the sciences of man into scientific engineering potentially more successful than even the tremendously fruitful technical sciences.

The resistance to the idea of evolution was inherent in the value outlook. Because man is animal to a very great extent, he has to struggle against this part in his nature continuously. As a result, he values his non-animality above everything else, and finally sees it as the essence of his being. So the strong animality in man, as disvalue, created the equally strong opposite value conviction that precluded scientific causal insight. In all areas that are essentially important for man, where he evolves his strongest value convictions, the values originate from equally strong needs or factual presence of disvalues. *Thus the value outlook perpetuates convictions contrary to causal truths particularly in those matters that are most decisive* for dealing with man or understanding his world and his place in the universe.

The practically important fields where the principle of creation through opposition conflicts with the value outlook are the *human sciences*. The central problem here is the enrichment of human capacities, which, as we saw, comes from opposition or restriction. We do not need to repeat how dangerous becomes the logic that positive reactions originate from positive background experiences. The increased, *vicious-circle "improvements"* in satisfactions or releases have led to the increase in mental and physical disorders, psychopathy and functional diseases. Encouragement to have more satisfactions or pleasures is the last thing man needs.

In our scientific era, having more values results in having more pleasures, because inner values are, factually, satisfactions or releases. Modern man is permitted and enabled to try to live by pleasures alone. This is evidently bound to destroy his normality. The behavioral, psychological, educational and social sciences become virtual alchemies, as positive capacities are expected from positive satisfactions which are the easiest things for man. The result is endless confusion and complexity, as well as the encouragement of overadjustments, the sources of the increasing afflictions of modern man.

Even in the fields serving the humanistic interests themselves, the value outlook has brought confusing defeat. *Philosophy,* the very embodiment of the value outlook, has become for the more precise modern mind "something that cannot be done", as we shall see later. In *aesthetics,* the causal confusions, particularly about contrast and fixation, have turned art into the travesty of smears or junk being adored as sacred objects and "paintings" by chimpanzees not being distinguishable from art. The worst consequence of the value outlook is the deepening of *cultural fixations.* The emphasis on the direct verity of value feelings permits mere fixations to grow into sacred values of our culture and way of life. Thus abnormal outgrowths comparable to neurotic reactions, which fixations are, become the highest ideals and values we are urged to accept and further cultivate as treasures of insights and progress.

The value outlook confines man to a curiously primitive stage of scientific development and of human progress. Man has attained spectacular successes in the physical or technical sciences. There the causal logic of direct increase in values, or of like-comes-from-like, is fully sufficient. But the paradox of value deriving from its *opposite* applies to the higher living, organic world. There the primordial, "physical" striving for release has to be opposed by restrictions, in order to attain the enrichment of organic capacities. But man is not yet aware of this necessity of the opposition. He still proceeds by the *primitive, "physical" inertia alone,* leaving the task of opposition to the blind evolutionary and cultural, selectively growing restrictive mechanisms and traditions. It can be said that man is still enslaved by his merely "physical" impulses, and has not yet reached the stage of consciousness that would enable him to become his own creator.

A delusion that has particularly kept man from recognizing the principle of evolutionary opposition is his nonrelative view of the harmony and purposefulness in the world. This delusion is compounded by the tendency of humanistic thinkers to view the world in its *last stage of adaptation,* where it does appear harmonious. If one looks for value essences he necessarily grasps a phenomenon in this last stage revealing such harmony or value. The historical or evolutionary aspects of adaptation, that would reveal the conflicting, opposing forces creating it, are excluded because they can be only disturbing and are unnecessary under the value outlook.

Actually, the adaptive "harmony" is as impressive, strong or extensive as is the opposition of forces creating it. The ocean beach is truly "ingeniously" and impressively built, of strongest rock, or in forms that cleverly resist the waves. The living nature is so endlessly harmonious because the opposition of forces there has worked at endless points and levels, through the selective evolution.

Let us take the simplest example, "creation" of a river by the opposition between the flow of water and the resistance of ground. The river seems to be ingeniously planned to flow, through hundreds of miles, toward the sea in such a way that every valley or advantage of terrain has been used in a seeming calculation to produce the shortest, most effective route. The river bed seems to be built with similar ingeniousness and calculated economy. Where the ground is too hard or steep it is circum-

vented, or the softer layers in it are attacked first, and the circuitous channel is built precisely so that no more effort is ex-
pended in curbing the water flow than would be required for
digging through the resistant ground. If there is no choice, a steep
narrow channel is formed so that the river can rush through
faster. Provision is made, in forming the channel, even for the
seasonal excess water, to be contained and conducted in equally
economical ways. Moreover, everything connected with the river
is purposefully taken care of. Where plants and fish in the river
require softer flow, deeper water, or special soil, it is provided
in exactly the right amounts. Where animals have their watering
tracks, the banks are made more accessible; and where a big
city needs a port, the river is deep enough to provide it.

This may be sufficient to show that any final adjustment,
through struggle of opposing forces or blind eliminative selection
and adaptation, appears to be purposefully and ingeniously
created, when it is viewed in its last stage. Obviously, the example
of the "creation" of a river is too transparently simple to deceive. But the living world is always a mystery to human minds,
because of its unfathomable multiplicity. Even in the physical
world the final causes are still mysteries. In result, the delusion
of purposefulness and harmony in the world remains general,
under the natural human value outlook. This delusion is being
dispelled every time science makes a new discovery or scientists
gain causal understanding.

Here we may mention the much discussed *schism between
humanities and sciences.* It has become one of the main problems of our scientific and cultural world. It is dividing the learned
men into hostile camps of two separate cultures.[33] In the words
of C. P. Snow, who has prominently exposed the problem, the
"misunderstandings are growing worse rather than better" as the
two groups have "almost ceased to communicate at all."[34] Re-
conciliation has been diligently sought, but mostly in favor of
philosophical approaches, particularly since the physical sciences
are now also only "hypothetical".[35] It is pointed out that the
great scientists, Einstein, Bohr, Pauli, Born, Schroedinger or
Heisenberg, are "bilingual", speaking in the languages both of

philosophy and science[33] — which they have to do as long as the real, opposite causes are missed in sciences, including physics.

Thus it is argued that "the Romantic doctrine is as tenable as that of latest physics" and that the world views of Wordsworth, Thoreau or Novalis should be taken seriously (J. Barzun).[5] Even the abandonment, by science, of the anthropocentrism, as the more human view, is deplored (G. J. Holton).[33] Intuition and value insights are held to be more revealing than bare facts; heart better than head. One supposedly gains by leaving a lecture on astronomy and going outside to look at the stars, as Walt Whitman suggested. Restoration of the "repressed intuition" is urged, and myth, poetry or music is placed on equal level with science.[5] Such attitudes are stressed in the perennially recurring anti-science movements.

Literature, art and philosophy have been invested with powers of science; and such works as the *Golden Bough* by Frazer, writings by Freud or even explanations by Einstein and Planck are referred to as examples.[5] Assumedly a "work of art like a discovery or generalization in science may be epoch-making" (R. B. Perry).[6] The famous dictum "Beauty is truth, truth beauty" is repeated by best authorities.[36] It is claimed that "Eddington or Einstein arrived at the truths in the same way as did Shakespeare or Rembrandt" (J. Bronowski). The "integralist" cognition derived from intuition, idealistic insights and sense of values is shown to be auspiciously replacing the positivistic empirical thinking (P. A. Sorokin). One may note "the typical hostile attitude toward science and scientists" by the most articulate modern defenders of humanistic thought like Miguel de Unamuno or Jose Ortega (R. Dubos). "In the words of Jacques Maritain", who should be considered a foremost authority, "the 'deadly disease' that science set off in society is 'the denial of eternal truths and absolute values' ".[33]

Particularly the now popular most advanced "humanistic" and "counterculture" theorists, from Arthur Koestler or Abraham Maslow to Theodore Roszak and Carlos Castaneda, have turned against rational scientism in favor of deeply human, even transcendental and mystical value experiences. Thus the mystifying

absence of causal certainties in sciences is substituted by systems
of the deepest emotional or *value convictions.*

We saw how the value convictions perpetuate *causal beliefs
contrary to facts* and lead, logically, to the emphasis on satisfactions and freedoms, which makes human sciences impossible
and encourages overadjustments, the causes of impoverishment
and diseases. The humanists themselves are noticing that the
humanities do not help, that "when the tradition falters and
dies, teaching and preaching the humanities is futile" (J. Barzun).[5] Confusion is inevitable because the humanistic theory has
to be contradicted by practice. Then it may seem that the humanism has fought "unnecessary battles [and] opposed itself to science,
to humanitarianism, to democracy, to romanticism and to modern-
ism" which are seen as the natural allies of humanism converted into enemies by humanism's disloyalty to itself (R. B.
Perry).[36]

The value outlook is bound to diverge from the barren positivism of real sciences. Best humanists may tolerate acceptance
of supernatural phenomena, clairvoyance, telepathy, spiritism, or
possibility of miracles.[5] Also, arcane symbolic and philosophical
interpretations are favored, however unreal they may become.
Assumedly, working "hard" stone brought to man the hard reality principle; "grinding" of grain taught man to bear the daily
"grind"; and ornamentation of body "was an effort to establish
a human identity, a human significance, a human purpose" (L.
Mumford).[17] The presently popular existential philosophizing may
become more important than reality. A convict and pervert is
elevated into a saint by Sartre in his book *Saint Genet,* because
Genet had, supposedly, asserted his authentic existential identity
by choosing the crime and perversion.[4] The causal explanations
are specious. Genet is a pervert because "having been caught
stealing from behind, his back opens when he steals; it is with
his back that he awaits human gazes and catastrophies".[4] Pages
and pages of such grand philosophy are offered by Sartre. The
mystery and sophistry grow from the value outlook.

The value outlook shows as important the *rare, striking, gran-
diosely original thoughts and ideas — which are causally least*

important. For man his grand ideas are greater than reality, and the humanist thinkers readily accept that "ideas are the most real things in the universe", or that "intellect is the master of passions".[36] The theory of ethics has been always dominated by the "notion that our moral judgments arise from impartial reflective acts".[38] Ideas as sources of values are accepted in most value theories[37] — which makes the alchemy of creating human capacities out of nothing, complete.

Above all, *values are mysteries even to the humanists themselves* for whom they are the basis of everything. There is no accepted theory or science of values. It is hoped that science of values will evolve upon discoveries comparable to those of Newton or Einstein, and that such science will offer solutions for the rest of human problems (R. S. Hartman).[33] One of the main arguments why science of values is not possible is that values are different from facts. It is argued, for instance, that "goodness cannot be defined; it is simple, like yellowness or sweetness" (G. E. Moore).[38] In truth, these as other values and feelings can be perfectly understood, predicted and controlled, as science requires, if their relative causality is understood.

Goodness or yellowness can be defined, by differentiation against opposites. Yellowness can be predicted and controlled. A grey object will appear yellow against a background or previous experience of opposite, complementary color. Conversely a yellow object loses its color in an environment where everything is yellow. Goodness is a satisfaction, that derives from need which is a nonsatisfaction. If we were ready or able to inflict universal badness on the world we could produce goodness much as we can make the world sublimely beautiful for a prisoner by letting him out of a dungeon. The usual "scientific" efforts are of course bound to fail. For instance, an "empirical procedure for ascertaining values" has been suggested: individual value experiences would be analyzed under improved conditions, as in all experimental research.[38] Actually, the result would be an added confusion, because improvement or increase of value leads to satisfaction or satiation, which extinguishes the feeling of value.

The "scientism" can mislead even the best theorist. In his

excellent general theory of value, R. B. Perry tries to conform his notion of value with the scientific concepts of learning, habit, reflexes, instinct or unconscious reactions.[6] But these factors are causally weightless in human adjustment, which is determined by pleasure or releases and their conscious pursuit. Yet Perry excludes the pleasure concept and rather accepts cognitive factors, generalizations, beliefs, habits of thought or the "cognitive environment".[6] The Interest, as the source of all value in his theory, then becomes almost an abstract factor. Thus "interest may be founded on truth and error."[6] Consequently it does not matter if reality is or is not there. It matters decisively in real life, where exaggerated expectations or overenjoyed values bring the inner disvalues or disorders. But in most value theories idea, not drive, is the basis of value,[37] while in reality only the pleasure drive and its economy matter.

In general, under the humanistic value outlook the goal of human existence and progress is the *attainment of deeper inner values.* The humanistic spokesmen have made it particularly clear that the quality of experience as opposed to its mere quantity is the goal. This general attitude is *self-defeating as well as dangerous.* No quality of experience can be increased without exactly equal opposite, negative quality. There is no way around this law, however absurd this may seem to man. Only the quantity of detailed value-disvalue differentiations and of the learning pathways left by them can be increased. The quantitative experience or dreary, scientific knowledge, and the quantitative, technical material world that corresponds to it, are the only possible objects of increase or progress. Knowledge, learning or abstract thought have always to be made as dreary or "shallow" as possible, so that more of such content can be formed out of the limited releases or inner values.

The general humanistic efforts to deepen value experiences become insidious dangers because they lead to overadjustments. They are aimed at increasing the most general or fundamental inner values, the satisfactions of security, fulfillment and growth or acceleration of releases, through values like love, "identity", beauty or freedom. These satisfactions are nonspecific enough not to be noticed as sources of overenjoyments. Specific oversatisfactions, like overeating or use of narcotics, are more easily noticed as dangers.

But a general satisfaction, like security or release of growth, *controls the secondary satisfactions and depends on specific enjoyments.* Under the sense of security, fulfillment or freedom, one feels free to overenjoy everything else. Further, overenjoyment of the general values leads to the opposite feelings, like insecurity, emptiness, displeasure or sense of repression. Then the secondary specific enjoyments are resorted to as badly needed compensations or supports for the value feelings. Such specific, concrete enjoyments may include excessive indulgences in foods, idleness or narcotics as well as in emotional releases through psychic overenjoyments, aggression, hate and violence. The end results are physical, mental and social diseases and disorders, caused by the vicious-circle, malignant overadjustments.

Conclusion

The humanistic thought, that dominates our learning and culture, is based on the direct, logical belief in values. Moreover, the values are viewed as the inner values or positive feelings, experienced directly or as evaluations of value objects. Such feelings can be, ultimately, only organic satisfactions or releases. But an organic satisfaction, value or release cannot exist without equal need as nonsatisfaction, disvalue or restriction. Men have their greatest values where they have their greatest needs or factual disvalues. A value that comes without difficulty or restriction, like the breathing or undisturbed existence, has no value meaning.

The causal source of every value as feeling, or as results of cognitive differentiation, is its value opposite. Yet this simple truth, of the relative or opposite causation, is contrary to the very logic of the humanistic thought, as well as to the natural human attitudes. Values are believed to derive from sources of the same nature. This delusion, exactly contrary to causal facts, prevents man from seeing the most important, causal side of his existence and reality.

Value reactions determine all human behavior and capacities, everything men feel, want to do, or are able to do. And the sources of the value reactions, physical or mental, are their unsuspected opposites. That is why there are no sciences of man. In fact, even the ultimate sources of the physical reality, of the first value of man, is its never suspected opposite. Hence the mystery about the fundamental causes in physics, or in the living process and genetic mechanisms. Man sees and extols only the values, never their unrecognizable opposites, the real sources of his world.

If values or satisfactions are to derive from sources of the same nature, then all one has to do is to proceed from a satisfaction to more satisfactions. This would be perfectly easy for man. He always starts with a satisfaction and never wants anything but satisfactions. Since satisfactions or releases are also the direct sources of all capacities, the theorists are bound to arrive at easy solutions. Sure enough, nine tenths of the humanistic thought are dominated by the emphasis that people should just adopt the positively felt values, like the warm and deeply gratifying love, in order to attain all capacities and genuine satisfactions. The necessity of the equal negatively felt, infernal nonsatisfactions as needs or restrictions has never yet been mentioned. Of course even animals "know" or "understand" satisfactions perfectly and adopt them without hesitation.

This virtual alchemy becomes a danger because it encourages overenjoyments of the most general inner values, like security or growth releases, which control all secondary, specific gratifications. The victims of the resulting overadjustments are increasing in the modern life which makes the enjoyments prodigiously effective. Functional diseases, physical and mental, caused by overadjustments and admittedly not understood causally, are the scourge of modern man.

Because of similar overenjoyments we are plagued by disorders, violence, generation strife, drug addiction and "alienation". The student riots clearly revealed the irrational negative aftereffects of the positive value overenjoyments cultivated in the learning of humanities. The humanistic enlightenment is liberating man so that he can enjoy all inner values, which become concrete gratifications and radical "improvements" in our logically scientific and efficient age. By trying to live with satisfactions or releases alone men will exhaust their limited organic normalcy and drive themselves deeper into functional impoverishment, stress, anxiety and alienation.

Such self-destructive liberalism and permissiveness are particularly dangerous because they are promoted by our most learned groups, who control the modern life. The learned people, brought up on the humanistic belief in enjoyment of inner values or fulfillment of one's individual nature, now want to see these verities brought to life. They are supported by the experimental scientism which equally shows that increase in satisfactions or releases brings immediate improvement in capacities. Thus the liberalism in its various behavioral, educational, cultural and political forms has, absurdly, become the mark and goal of learnedness and scientific progress. If man needed more freedom, permissiveness or satisfaction in order to advance, he would long ago have reached the highest possible progress.

A dominant humanistic attitude is that the technological or material progress has degraded our lives, through impoverishment of our inner value experiences. Actually the impoverishment is caused by overadjustments or overenjoyments which become inevitable in the atmosphere created by the humanistic emphasis on value enjoyments. The technological progress is merely used as a means in attainment of such overenjoyments. It is untenable to assume that man is somehow misled in his choices of his deepest, most significant value enjoyments. He is far too intelligent for that. He knows with absolute perfection what the fundamental, natural, "true" or most genuine and satisfactory inner values are. That is why he overenjoys them, and ends by suffering their impoverishment.

III

PSYCHOLOGY, THE KEY SCIENCE STILL AN ALCHEMY

Psychology is the key science because everything in man's world depends on the way the human mind works. Psychology can supply the principles for the engineering of human motivations and capacities, for their enrichment and refinement, through restrictive accumulation and channeling of releases. If man has the power of motivations and the capacities to implement them, he can achieve anything in fulfillment of his best intents, which he never lacks. But psychology has not become a science, because it proceeds by a causal logic contrary to psychological causality.

In simplest terms, it proceeds by the general human belief and "scientific" logic that positive potentials, which are enrichments in releases, come from similar positively felt past experiences. The contrary is causally true, as releases or satisfactions can be enriched only by previous accumulation of restrictions or needs which are nonsatisfactions (we defined before the concepts of release and restriction). Every motivation or positive capacity, as release or satisfaction, has to be paid for by exactly equal humanly most difficult, restrictive, negatively felt effort.

In contrast, not effort but satisfaction is expected in modern psychology to create the positive potentials, the most valuable capital in human adjustment. This is what turns modern psychology into a virtual modern alchemy. According to the endless and complex modern psychological theories one attains the positive capacities not only by having been free of restrictions or frustrations and needs or nonsatisfactions, but by having lived through more satisfactory, positively felt experiences. Of course if this was true men would attain the most positive adjustments automatically, by enjoying themselves.

In reality the central problem in psychology is why does man bring on himself all the negative reactions and disorders, that afflict or threaten everybody. Due to the opposite causation and its vicious-circle effects a person overenjoying positive experiences or pleasure releases ends by suffering the exactly opposite negative reactions. If the person uses all his powers and ingenuity to extend the overenjoyment, the opposite reactions emerge with equal intensity and "ingenuity", against his will.

As long as the opposite or relative causation is not understood, the only explanation seems to be that the person ingeniously acts against himself without knowing it. The Freudian Unconscious is so widely accepted because there is no other way to explain the mystery. Actually the Freudian theory is an alchemistic system of prescientific personifications, of modern demons that, certainly, can explain everything. But this remains in modern psychology the only, desperately needed, explanation of why people react and feel, therefore behave, in ways they want least.

The advance of modern psychology becomes an advance in confusion. Because of its reversedly wrong, "scientific" causal logic, psychology progresses, with colossal effort, away from everything that could reveal the simple causal principles it needs to become a science. The fundamental causal laws are simple, but psychology is becoming vast and complex beyond bounds, with no simple causal principles in sight. The newest additions to the confusion come from humanistic and philosophical orientation,[5] expounded in all kinds of humanistic, existential "human potential", "sensitivity", "encounter" or transcendental meditation approaches. Thus the whole system of the humanistic and philosophical, inherently alchemistic, value delusions is being added on top of the confusion growing from the adherence to the "scientific" logic and to the theories about the unconscious.

The Alchemistic Causal Logic of Psychology

Naturally, if it is not understood that every release potential requires equal hard opposite effort, then *the alchemy of getting this most precious psychic capital by easy know-how* becomes the highest priority. Then it is a unique opportunity for psychologists to teach people the easiest techniques or formulas of how to enjoy the positive capacities. For under the "scientific" experimental observation the *exercise of such capacities shows to be only pleasant* — because they are satisfactions or releases. That they require exactly opposite, experimentally negative experiences of restrictions, needs or nonsatisfaction as their causal sources, is the last thing modern psychologists would recognize.

The clear unfailing way to have the positive experiences then seems to be to want them, to strive for them directly. Here the psychologists have as vast and varied theories, sophisticated and simple, as have the humanistic experts in advocating "positive thinking", acceptance of deeply gratifying higher values or rejection of hate and fear. Menninger has enough authority to state simply how beneficial to mind and health are the positive emotions, particularly love and hope.[1] This theory is logically simple. The direct sources of the strongest emotions of love are the natural sexual satisfactions or releases. Accordingly, the restriction of such releases or of the natural sexual love is a blunder, perpetuated by our culture, religion and education,[1] which suppress enjoyments and natural pleasures. Other authorities similarly deplore our cultural restrictions as a "massive system of manacles and fetters which man has forged for himself";[2] or point out that our education at home, school and church does not make the slightest effort for developing our capacities of enjoyment.[3]

In other theories the enjoyment of satisfactions may be stressed in more recondite ways. Maslow sees satisfaction of the basic needs as the precondition for development of higher mental and cultural motivations. He also sees "peak experiences" as sources of harmonious personality integration.[4,28] Modern psychologists may find even the satisfaction with self — which is the easiest, egoistic gratification — as a way to improvement of mental life (C. Rogers).[4,37] Logically it may, indeed, seem that greater satisfaction with oneself, with what one is doing, is all that is needed for satisfactory motivations.

The easiest way to have positive reactions is to *use some stimulation,* chemical, physical or psychological. When the first effects of the mind-expanding drugs, particularly of LSD were reported, serious scientists predicted a beginning of a great era. Testifying before a Senate committee, Dr. R. H. Felix, then Director of the Institute of Mental Health, said that upon discovery of the right chemical or electric means for alteration of emotional states the possibilities will be unlimited and "wildest dreams are likely to be ultra conservative". Dr. Glenn T. Seaborg stated that discovery of such pharmaceuticals which emotionally change human personality would rank as one among the fifteen most revolutionary discoveries ever made.[5]

The belief in the use of drugs, or similar direct means, for increase of human potentials has always been widely accepted and remains strong.[5] Among its most famous apostles are Freud, William James, Bergson and Aldous Huxley. Various modern researches on use of chemical electric and other stimulants are rather expanding and constitute the main concrete efforts of the "behavioral engineering".[5] Of course all such efforts fail as disastrously in the end as they seem experimentally clearly promising at the beginning; the story of LSD is a good example. All artificially induced changes lead to opposite reactions, as organism restores its limited normal rate of releases or growth.

Learning theories are prominent examples of the more involved modern alchemistic thinking in psychology. Such theories are vast and varied. In fact, they remain, besides the psychoanalytic theory, almost the only other general system of explanations of behavior. However varied, all learning theories rest on the assumption that by learning of insights and skills human capacities and behavior can be improved. It is never recognized that the painful accumulation of the negatively felt backgrounds, restrictions and nonsatisfactions, is the only source of release enrichment, which determines whether any behavior, including learning, is possible or impossible, easy or insurmountably difficult. Learning is viewed in its usual sense: if one learns to do something, he can do it with *continuous ease and pleasure*, by doing it right. To proceed by this logic in dealing with psychic capacities, evidently, amounts to an alchemy. All this equally applies to all conditioning that is held, by psychologists, to be the same as the conditioning *by which animals learn.*

The mystery of why people drive themselves into feeling and behaving in ways they clearly do not want is the central problem in learning theories as well. It looks as if the person has learned his behavior in wrong ways, contrary to good reasons, or is failing to learn the right ways. There are various *theories about behavior disorders induced by learning or conditioning.* In their preference for experimental proof, psychologists like to refer to experiments on conditioning or learning of anxiety reactions or "neuroses" in animals. The best known such experiments are by Pavlov, N. R. F. Maier and Lidell.

Actually, it is danger or punishment here that the animals learn to expect, as they are put through confusing punishing conditioning. Lidell himself recognized that the reaction is not anxiety but learned expectancy of danger.[37] In fact, such experimental "neuroses" can be induced by simple scaring of animals, with air blasts or high-pitched sounds.[8] But learned fear of danger, in animal or man, is never a behavior disorder or self-deepening neurosis. Not even the dumbest animal can learn or be conditioned to increase his negative reactions by himself as man does in his behavior disorders. Obviously animals can behave only in one, preset way. If a punishing condition is met on that way, the animal learns to avoid and fear it.

In contrast, man has thousands of ways he chooses from at every moment, and he takes the one with least danger or most pleasure. *Exactly because he can choose the most pleasant ways,* he overenjoys the satisfactions and suffers the anxiety or neuroses as aftereffects. Of course there are conditions in which man also has no choice and has to face dangers. But behavior disorders disappear under such conditions — under dangers of war, bombings or even concentration camps.[37] Men can never *learn* behavior disorders, neuroses and emotional or functional impoverishment, which cause all the difficulties of life and health. Such disorders are unpleasant throughout, in their effects as well as in their immediate causes, which are forms of the release impoverishment. Thus everything in these disorders is contrary to the pleasure drive which is the only force behind learning.

Understandably, psychologists seek explanations in all kinds of more complex, secondary mechanisms of learning. Faulty generalization is often blamed. It is argued that by generalization from a negative past experience the negative reaction is extended further and further. A person may be one day afraid to go on the subway, the next unable to take the surface car and later even become afraid to walk under a bridge (R. W. White).[7] Similarly, psychologists may seek explanations in more complex concepts such as learning cues, signs, verbalizations or labelings, and their assumed displacements.[11] Theories by best authorities, Mowrer, Dollard and Miller, offer extensive, involved explanations by such mechanisms.[12] Also frequent is the argument that an initial negative effect or fright prevents the person from relearning. Further, habit has been often accepted as explanation, particularly in the theories of Allport, Murphy and Woodworth. Other authorities have blamed incapacity to learn, "emotional stupidity", reluctance to learn because of lack of positive experiences, and faulty learning due to fear, ignorance or superstitious attitudes.[37]

All such explanations, sophisticated as they may be, are untenable for the simple reason that man always knows perfectly and seeks eagerly what is pleasant; and the positive reactions are as pleasant as the disorders are not. Nobody in the world will use a generalization, cue, sign, label or habit to frighten himself or to create for himself the unpleasant negative or disordered reactions. On the contrary, *all such mechanisms are used to increase the positive reactions at every opportunity.* Exactly because the positive reactions are thus overenjoyed the opposite negative, disorder reactions become inevitable.

Habits become traps, as pursuit of nearer, easier enjoyments and values bring opposite aftereffects which are compensated for and deepened by further desperate fixational recourse to the same enjoyments or values. The person becomes a victim of his habitual overenjoyed values, much as in neuroses, and the habit may seem to have acquired the "functional autonomy" explained in the theory of Allport. As to the avoidance of relearning because of negative past experience, the relearning or defenses are most intense and perfect in behavior disorders and neuroses.[7] Moreover *the pleasant positive emotions are absolutely easy to learn.* There can never be any incapacity to learn, faulty learning, stupidity, or superstitious obstacles in acquiring the positive reactions. These, when available, are always automatically and eagerly found and enjoyed, whatever the past experience.

Theories of learning or conditioning dominate all except the Freudian psychology. But learning or conditioning to have positive reactions directly as indicated by the "scientific" logic is bound to lead to overenjoyments and their negative aftereffects. In the practical cultural tradition, "learning" is the hard, subtle ways of conditioning — different from the conditioning by which animals learn — that impose restrictions or frustrations and needs or nonsatisfactions. The logical "scientific" approaches are destroying this tradition. This is happening in all fields, from education to medicine, and is helped by most approaches, from behaviorist advocacy of easy, satisfying mass conditioning, explained by Skinner,[6] to the liberalism of modern humanistic reformers.

The same alchemistic causal logic governs *theories about reason, ideas and techniques* as means of adjustment. Since the techniques used in exact sciences are so successful, their use in analyzing and controlling behavior is often recommended. The person is to gain information, make analysis, reach rational evaluations about his behavior, then carry out the reached decisions.[8,9] Understanding, insight, knowledge, personal skills, and information are seen as decisive factors.[9] Use of involved, formulistic techniques is the basis of the most popular recent modern approaches, like the Human Potential Movement, group encounter, transaction analysis and sensitivity training. Here the human potentials are expected to be created by mere ritualistic or directly satisfying performances, having symbolic or release functions.

This amounts to pure alchemy, but it rests on the most authoritative psychological theories, particularly of Gestalt psychology, Field theories and Behaviorism, as well as the Humanistic psychology. Gestalt psychologists and therapists have always maintained that new, greater causal wholes can be created by mere combination of forms. The Field theories share the Gestaltist beliefs in the creative function of configuration or mere direction of forces. But even Behaviorism, which remains the central theory in psychology, is supporting the belief in mere techniques. It is not the emotional or release weight but merely the techniques of conditioning that are expected to create and control behavior.[6] The great advocates of practical behaviorism, Eysenck or Skinner, offer only the best, most operant forms of conditioning, without any regard to the "mentalistic" emotional or release weight and to economy of releases.[6,25]

Mere cognitive factors are accepted as decisive in various theories, particularly those about Self, Identity and Alienation. From a collection of authoritative views on *The Self in Social Interaction*[4] it is apparent that the *"self" is a cognitive product,* evolving through knowledge of self, differentiation of meanings of self, self-image, interpretation of information about self, translation of "reflexive meanings", and "self-conception".[4] The very popular modern concepts of Identity and Alienation are of the same cognitive and ideational nature. Alienation results from loss of Identity or Self through the same cognitive or ideational processes.[4] It is noted that "the theories of cognitive consistency now dominate the literature".[4] Identification is probably the most frequently used concept in explaining all kinds of adjustment problems, and it is similarly a cognitive process.

Even philosophical, particularly existential concerns are viewed as important psychological factors. In the celebrated logotherapy of Victor E. Frankl, search for meaning of life and existential insights are considered as determining factors. The expanding existential psychology claims that concerns about being and non-being are causes of psychological problems.[10] Even love and will become matters of conceptual interpretations about Eros, Daimonic principle, Intentionality, Meaning and Consciousness (R. May).[10]

All theories about *ideas and cognitive factors as psychological causes are alchemistic*. Ideas are easy and inexpensive psychologically. Everybody knows how our ideas may change completely with our feelings. But feelings or pleasure, governed by the paradox of opposite causation, makes no sense "scientifically". Psychologists are left only with the ideational contents, the ideas they find in the minds of the people. Actually, such ideas grow from the compulsive need of men to find "reasons" for what they feel, which they causally understand as little as psychologists do.

Yet most of the practical psychological work centers on exchange of reasons and ideas between psychologists and the persons they want to help. The gist of every discussion or book on adjustment becomes providing the insights of how rationally desirable and satisfactory it is to adopt the positive behavior. All the analyses, counseling and group discussions are aimed at creation of new insights for avoiding the irrational, and unpleasant, negative behavior.

Conflicts as causes, of disorders and stress, are assumed to arise from difficulties of choice or from opposition between "approach" and "avoidance" in facing decisions (N. E. Miller).[11] Here the choice, evaluation or decision making cannot possibly amount to weighty emotional experiences, since it is a cognitive, short-lasting decision, preceding the behavior or the course of experiences. All such conflicts can be only processes of reasoning. Surely, "conflict" is part of disorder, but it is not a difficulty of choosing or deciding. The person knows perfectly which course of behavior he wants and what is pleasant, satisfactory or normal. *Exactly because he eliminates conflicts with anything unpleasant* or nonsatisfactory, the resulting overenjoyment deepens into a disorder. This is the real and continuous, self-deepening "conflict".

Abnormal behavior is also seen as resulting from foolish assumptions or *miscalculations*. Thus in the classic theories of Alfred Adler disorders are explained as incapacities that a person contracts to excuse himself for not attaining the superiority he wants more than anything else. According to other authorities, the person foolishly assumes that a failure "adds to the fascination of neurosis"; or he "clings to his fear or other malad-justment in spite of its inconvenience . . . because it means something for his personality" (A. H. Maslow, R. S. Wood-worth).[37] There are many theories about people clinging to their maladjustive habits because of misconceptions. In truth, neuroses and fixations become traps because negative reactions, resulting from overenjoyments, are compensated for by the same, nearest, easiest enjoyments.

Reasons, insights, understanding, learning and discovery of truths are psychologically as weightless as rationalizations. So are rational faults, miscalculations or lack of reason. The posi-tive behavior depends on availability of *satisfactions or releases, which man always understands perfectly.* The alternative to rea-sons as causes is the unconscious causation, in modern psychology. We shall see later the purely alchemistic nature of the psychology of the Unconscious. But even in the ordinary, conscious causa-tion, psychologists find that "life may be built on foundation of a few significant events" (G. Murphy).[37] Psychologists accept what analyses of the minds of people reveal. People always ex-plain their motivations by some singular ideationally grand or "significant" reason, while the simple but paradoxical release causation is not suspected. *If reasons or insights were decisive, the world could be reformed by a good lecture.*

In sum, everything shows modern psychology to be alchemistic in the sense that the weightiest potentials are expected to derive from easy, positively felt experiences; or from mere learning and conditioning without regard to any emotional opposite equivalent; or from ideas, reason and insights; as well as from the totally weightless unconscious causes.

Imitation of "Scientism", the New Scholasticism

A few centuries ago men were as intelligent as we are and as eager to be scientific. They followed the authoritative science of their time, the philosophical learning, and built complex, scien-tifically sophisticated disciplines. But philosophy disdained the simple facts of physical reality and was not restricted by con-sideration of physical laws. Similarly, modern psychology rejects the "mentalistic" world of feelings or pleasure, by which men live; and is not restricted by the realization of the simple law that every organic capacity or release requires equal effort or restriction. This law is self-evident from the limitations of organism to its sameness, as well as from the simplest common-sense insight that you never succeed without equal effort.

But the presently authoritative scientism, of physical sciences, precludes recognition of the equal-restriction or opposite causation, as well as of the really determining, "mental", emotional life. Modern psychologists are like the learned men of the scholastic era who *refused to look at reality or be practically scientific, in the name of science.*

Of course modern scientists are particularly careful to avoid the stupidities of the past. Hence the emphasis on experimentalism. But merely avoiding past mistakes has never helped where completely new discoveries or breakthroughs are required. Typically, modern psychologists think they are on a sure way to scientism by avoiding the old scholastic method. According to a story,[31] a group of medieval scholars wanting to know how many teeth there are in a horse's mouth decided that the question could not be answered because no book of learning contained such information and it was incompatible with learned methods to look in the horse's mouth. Actually, the modern psychologists are repeating the same mistake of refusing to look in the "horse's mouth". They refuse to accept the "mentalistic", emotional factors or plainly the pleasure, that determines everything men do; or to see the "scientifically" impossible, relative causal law that governs the emotions, pleasures or simply what men feel and live by.

Experimentalism. The experimental logic and methods of physical sciences, that provide a direct look at the physical causal factors and their understanding, preclude such insights when applied to value reactions, which determine all behavior. It is ridiculous to think that an experimenter could account for the determining factors in the living, value reactions. An organism has acquired, during millions of years and through uncountable life experiences, myriads of ways of value reactions. When you deal with them in terms of feelings or pleasure you account for all of them in the virtually miraculous integrated way pleasure works. In contrast, *experiments neither could nor are intended to take into account such myriad factors.* But an experiment that does not account for most of the determining factors involved is useless, to say the least.

Even a more critical fallacy of experimentalism is *the direct causal logic* which is right for physical sciences but completely misleading for behavior, determined by value reactions. Every experiment proves that directly added release or satisfaction increases motivations and capacities, whereas in fact it exhausts them and if continued leads to abnormality. Conversely, experiments or clinical observations show that restriction is the direct cause of negative reactions, release impoverishment or disorders, while actually it counteracts them by accumulating the release potentials. The forms of causal dependence of releases or satisfactions on their opposites, restrictions and needs or nonsatisfactions, are endlessly varied. Still, they determine all behavior or values, and the experimenter has to deal with them in one way or another — under the wrong logic and methods.

The more complex it all becomes, the more strictly the experimenter holds to the direct "scientific" logic. And it does become increasingly more complex as the wrong causal logic is perpetuated. The experimenter uses the direct causal logic and mathematics in everything he observes, registers, calculates, verifies, correlates or makes conclusions about. But in value reactions *adding the same value, like satisfaction, decreases it,* and subtracting from it, by adding the opposite value, like need or nonsatisfaction, increases it. The highest total of satisfactions extinguishes their potential.

An overall result is that truly scientific experimenters have to limit their work to studying simplified physiologic and animal reactions. These have nothing to do with the myriad reality of value experiences, but are so repetitively automatic that the endlessly multiple value causation and its disturbing reverse logic do not come up. Most studies turn into narrow, method-centered experimentation with "itty-bitty facts", or an "addiction to machines, rats and infants", in words of Allport.[13] Thus to have a real experimental science, free of the unknowable and inconsistent value factors, the experimentalists *disregard all value experiences, the whole conscious life,* which consists of value experiences. The subjects might as well be unconscious or act without consciousness as animals do.

Since psychological life is nothing if it is not conscious, scientists may find that modern psychology ends where real psychology should begin.[34,35] Experiments remain consistent as long as they are not extended beyond the automatic, constant physiologic and animal reactions. Actually such reactions have also evolved through value processes, but these have been so long and permanently established, during evolution of the species, that no temporary value influences can change them. The experimentalist can safely play with such automatic responses, much like one can operate a machine by pushing buttons without regard to the forces and mechanisms that make it work. If the experimentalist intends to deal with behavior in this way, he is like a man expecting to reconstruct a machine by merely changing around the buttons and switches. It is not the external responses that determine behavior, but inner values that determine the responses.

Only through concepts of the inner value causation can behavior be dealt with causally or scientifically. Whether it is the mouse fearing the cat, the deer responding to musk or man following the human pleasure drives, the causal factors are past-determined inner value processes, perfectly "understood" through feeling, but neither graspable nor accepted as relevant in experiments. The causal past value experiences explain why an animal, a lion, does not even "see" a man approaching in a car. The experimenter himself uses introspective value notions wherever causal understanding is gained. Purely experimentally, a rat may respond with the same agitation whether it is expecting a threat or a gratification.

Causally completely different reactions may appear experimentally to consist of the same movements, responses, mechanisms, or most detailed reactions, even the same brain waves. At every stage of a study of behavior the causal understanding is supplied by insights about the value reactions, while the pure experiment in itself can add only meaningless bits of information. The strict experimenter is like the reporter who, in his assignment to cover a complex political conference, refuses to go into the conference room and gathers his information from noises he hears outside.

The paramount fact is that psychological life is a conscious activity and that consciousness consists of value experiences, *obeying their paradoxical causal logic and graspable, in their myriad complexity, through simple feelings, but never through experiments.* The scientific experimentalism is adopted from physical sciences. If physicists could see what goes on inside matter they would never use experiments. But in the psychological world, of conscious values, a person cannot help seeing what goes inside him, even when he badly wants to ignore it. In physical sciences experimentation leads to successes because the causal connections there are perfectly clear, and not subject to an unthinkable causal logic. The reverse is true in psychology.

Yet because experiments have led to success in physical sciences, psychologists assume that through mere continuation with the experimentation, even without a causal theory, a psychological science will be established. But as J. B. Conant shows, the emphasis on mere "empiricism" leads modern psychology deeper into the jungle of wrong leads and confusion.[34] The amount of experimentation is colossal; and the laws of psychology, as natural laws, must be simple. Yet the discovery of such universal simple laws in psychology is more remote than ever. Strict experimenters do not even intend to establish general psychological theory.[15] But without a theory the experimentalism can only add to the confusion — because the reversedly wrong causal logic is compounded.

The experimentalism, with its "scientific" logic, invoked by all kinds of theorists, has in fact become here a *dangerous blunder* of our age. In general, it has perpetuated the human and "scientific" fallacy that direct increase in releases is the way to improve reactions or potentials. Modern men suffer from overadjustive "improvements" that malignantly turn into self-deepening exhaustion and functional impoverishment or diseases, in every field of adjustment and health. But all kinds of theorists and experts prove by experiments and experimental observations the positive immediate improvement effects and build theories thereon.

Since the real causation, the dependence of satisfaction or release on equal need or restriction, is not recognized, there are no scientific criteria to disprove any theory. Endlessly numerous, varied and conflicting theories are therefore increasingly advanced and proved. The more erroneous they become, *by condemning restrictions,* the better are the experimental proofs to support them. Even the Freudian theories can be clinically proved. It is clearly erroneous to condemn the whole, restrictive, cultural tradition, but that is what the experimental modern scientism is implicitly doing.

Now we may look briefly at the unquestioning "scientific" imitation — comparable to the former scholasticism — in the main schools of psychology.

Behaviorism. The most clearly "scientific" psychological school is behaviorism; and most psychologists are behaviorists, though now psychologists do not like to be considered as members of psychological schools,[15] discredited by failures and controversies. Behaviorism started by emphasis on the experimental methods — with their logic of physical sciences — as the very basis of scientism in psychology.[36] Consequently, only the units of behavior that can be separated out or effectively isolated, as required in experiment, notably the stimuli and responses, become the relevant factors in psychology. The endless interactions that constitute the living reactions as integrated wholes of feelings or of "mental" experiences are excluded. The result is atomism and physicalism, useful in physical sciences but completely crippling in psychology, where *only the living, mental wholes, the conscious feelings and values* are causally relevant. As we saw, physically the same form of behavior, response, activity or even galvanic skin response may have completely different, even opposite causal significance.

Equally crippling is the behaviorist use of the direct experimental logic and mathematics which give more value upon addition and less upon subtraction, or addition of opposite value. The *exactly reverse logic applies to value reactions,* which determine all behavior. The goal of behaviorism as a true experimental scientism is to establish the experimentally logical relationships between stimuli and responses and thus to arrive at empirical laws. As Waston, the founder of behaviorism stated, even the behavior of a nation could be predicted by finding out the stimuli it has been exposed to.

In truth, a people or an individual exposed to strong stimulation ceases to respond to it, so that when the stimulation has reached the fullest extent or become omnipresent it psychologically does not even exist any more. Behaviorists had to resort increasingly to a new concept, the intervening variable.[37] But it had to be left deliberately undefined, to permit "explanations" of the unpredictable, actually paradoxical, background causation. It is recognized that "the intervening variables do not explain the behavior but merely name it";[8] that they have no factual content and only serve to summarize;[13] or that they cannot be directly observed.[14]

Behaviorism seems, logically, to be a clear and simple scientific approach that could not fail. All exact sciences are founded on causal laws discovered from observations of relations of causes and effects. Behaviorists proposed the methods of just such observation of causes and effects, specifically, of the stimuli and responses. The logically clear scientism has attracted most psychologists to behaviorism. The task seemed so simple, yet the truly gigantic effort invested in this scientism has produced only an endless complexity, without even a hope of reaching the simple, natural causal laws. All kinds of logically failproof behavioristic approaches have been tried, like the "uniformity theory" of Hull aiming at average laws; the probability and objective relation theory of Brunswick; the descriptive behaviorism; various methods of operational and factor analyses; as well as mathematical, vectorial and topological theories.[37] Every one of such clearly "scientific" behaviorist approaches *should have logically given the simple answers.* But the only result has been an added complexity.

We may mention the main imitations of scientism by behaviorists that make them comparable to the former schoolmen
not daring to "look into the horse's mouth". Behaviorists could
not recognize mental images, feelings, consciousness, or *any value
experiences, by which we simple mortals live.* They had to
construe emotions as visceral reflexes, and thought as a form of
speech consisting of movements of larynx. The reason is that
the endlessly multiple processes of organic and brain responses
are experimentally ungraspable — as are all our conscious and
all living experiences.

On the central problem of *learning or conditioning* behaviorists could not recognize satisfaction or pleasure as the force behind learning, though it is accepted as such by the greatest
psychologists, like Pavlov or Thorndike, and is used as such
force by every animal trainer as well as educator. Mere frequency of behavior was accepted as determining by behaviorists,
instead of the satisfaction, though nothing extinguishes learning
better than frequency of behavior that is not rewarded by satisfaction or pleasure.

Further, the educational conditioning was conceived by behaviorists as a conditioning of mere reflexes, and not of the
experimentally ungraspable yet organically simple values we
live by. In the "epoch-making" experiment by Watson, he showed
that infants could be conditioned to fear objects by being frightened with noise. He proclaimed that by such conditioning children could be brought up to become anything — doctors and
lawyers, or beggars and thieves.[15] In truth, this kind of conditioning would be a self-defeating farce. As the vast complex
values take over during the child's growth he would evolve rather
particularly strong adjustments for counteracting such silly interferences as the "frightening" noise. But behaviorists had to
refuse to look at the world of values, mental life, feelings or
pleasure, which are the determining realities, and the real objects
of conditioning.

Gestalt Psychology. The growth of Gestalt psychology, the
second most important psychological school, is easily under-

standable. The logical scientific and behaviorist assumptions collapse upon the Gestaltist proofs that no object or stimulus has a logical constancy and that its meaning or value depends on the whole of which it is part. In effect, the Gestaltist proofs are *unintended discoveries of the relativity* of values and meanings, of their dependence on the surrounding values they are related with. Gestalt means configuration, and relation is recognized as its determining characteristic.[15,37]

The main discoveries of Gestaltists are the visual illusions. Actually these are due to the relativity of perceived values. A line appears shorter when placed along a much longer line. A circle seems smaller amidst great circles; or an angle narrower between broader angles. A line drawn through a stretch of lines slanted in one direction appears slanted in the opposite direction. Any form seems distorted in a way opposite to the distortions of the background. In a room uniformly slanted in one way, people find their bodies curiously slanted in the opposite way. As to other sensory values, colorless gray appears green in spatial or temporal vicinity of red, its opposite. After touching objects uniformly distorted in one direction, people find straight objects to be distorted in the opposite direction. A note in a melody, right in one key, appears high if other notes have been sounded in a lower key. One smells fragrance stronger after he has been in musty air; finds a food sweeter after bitter food; or feels warmth stronger when coming in from cold. Gestaltists have not gone beyond the illusions of sensory perception. They have not realized that similar "illusions", due to the same opposite causation, in the fields of various strong feelings, become psychological disorders.

Anyway, there is not one illusion discovered by the Gestaltists that cannot be *explained by the relative causation*.[37] The rule that evaluations are arrived at by relating has to be added; it is part of relative causation. Thus in the Mueller-Lyer illusion, prongs extended at the ends of a line make the line seem longer, because the relating proceeds in the direction of its prolongation. The relative causation also explains the afterimages and oscillations in perception, pointed out by Gestaltists together with the illusions. Afterimage is, evidently, the opposite aftereffect of an excessive or "exaggerated" sensory experience.

The oscillation of perception reveals the important fact that even ideational meanings are subject to aftereffects — that they ultimately consist of value processes. A drawing that could be seen equally well as a rabbit's head turned left or as a duck's head turned right, oscillates in your perception. While you continue viewing it as a rabbit's head it forcibly turns into the duck's head. Here the "exaggeration" consists of the attribution of only one meaning to something that has an equally good other meaning. This "exaggeration" is inevitable because we can perceive only one thing at a time.

Other discoveries of Gestaltists, like the principles of "pregnance", familiarity, proximity, similarity, symmetry or perceptual self-organization can be explained by the fact that all experiences are relations dominated by value "prejudices", biological and cultural.[37] All Gestaltist discoveries can be explained by value phenomena and their simple relative causation. But the Gestaltists had to formulate hundreds of laws, even in the narrow field of perception they studied. Moreover, every Gestalt, whether it is that of Renaissance or of an apple, becomes a law in itself or an essence irreducible to any other simpler laws. A Gestalt is any "individual and characteristic entity" and "its essence is the reason of its existence" (K. Koffka, W. Koehler).[16]

Obviously a system that has hundreds of laws and numberless "essences" can not be scientific, and rather requires a humanlike purposeful creator. Sure enough, the main theorists of Gestalt psychology have espoused metaphysical idealism. K. Koffka holds that the Gestalt "cannot be explained by mere chaos"; and he turns against positivism as a "dogma that all events are equally unintelligible, irrational, meaningless, purely factual."[37] W. Koehler expounds, in his book *The Place of Value in a World of Facts,* a transcendental theory on values and meanings inherent in the physical world that are to be of the same nature as our mental experiences. Koehler has to admit that such views go against the whole mechanistic thinking of sciences, which therefore "should be turned around".[16]

This reveals the central fallacy of Gestalt psychology. The Gestaltists have discovered the strange, relative phenomena of perception but, failing to recognize the simple law of value relativity that explains them, have to postulate principles, laws and Gestalt essences for each one of them. This evidently requires a Mind operating behind the phenomena. The point is that every one of the Gestalts or Gestalt principles — actually phenomena of relativity — presents its own peculiar meaning, sense or value. There is an explanation of how this can happen without a Mind behind the perceived world. The explanation is the mind of the perceiver with its strange relative, varied value reactions. This requires thinking in terms of the endless living, adaptive and evolutionary value world, still explainable mechanistically by the organic persistence or preservation of sameness, from which the law of relative causality derives.

The Gestaltists, however, could not deign to think in such seemingly unscientific, nonexperimental, "mentalistic" terms. *They wanted to be scientific in the sense of experimental physical sciences* which exclude concepts of values or mind, as well as all the infinite, living processes, governed by the historical or relative causation. In physics, the gravity of water does not change because it has or has not flown yesterday. Gestaltists have been expressly strict in holding to purely physical explanations and excluding the historical causation. They have sought explanations in concepts of fields, like those of electric currents, and in isomorphism that requires purely physical constructs similar in the brain and in the perceived physical world.[16,36]

In brief, Gestalt psychology, in its unquestioning imitation of scientism, excluded all mental or value concepts, therefore *had to refer to the traditional metaphysical idealism to explain the distinct basic meaningfulness or value effects* of every Gestalt and of countless Gestalt principles. The simple law of relative value causation that explains all the strange Gestalt phenomena could never be thought of by Gestaltists as strict "scientists".

Field theories are part of the Gestalt psychology; Field and Gestalt are interchangeable concepts. Kurt Lewin, the best Field theorist, was a Gestaltist[15] and strong opponent of the view of historical causality,[14] though such causality underlies his main experiments.[37] In general, the Gestalt psychology is a *very convenient theory*. It permits easy explanations, because anything can be construed as a Gestalt; and by its very terms a Gestalt cannot be further explained or reduced to other causal determinants. Since a Gestalt can produce values different or greater than its constituting elements, the Gestalt psychology is one of the main sources of support for the modern alchemists.

In the *Gestalt therapy* changes in capacities are expected from formulistic acts, like chewing and swallowing a bit of food, concentrating on an object, or tightening of chest muscles. The increasing practices in the vein of the Esalen treatment are based on beliefs in formulistic, symbolic and ritualistic performances supported by the theory of Gestalt psychology.

Other Schools. The older schools of psychology — structuralism, functionalism, introspectionism, parallelism or associationism — proceeded in the naturally sensible way of looking at the psychological phenomena directly. They did not exclude the conscious "mentalistic" experiences, which constitute the psychological life.[36] For them "it was unthinkable that psychology should be unconcerned about inner human experiences".[13] The best early psychologists saw the conscious sensations, feelings, thoughts, impressions or the conscious behavior as the fields of their study.[37] The nonconscious behavior was, properly, viewed as belonging in biology.[13] But the early psychologists failed, to such an extent that everything they did was rejected. The reverse approach was adopted, to exclude the conscious phenomena and to deal with behavior only in the experimentally scientific ways of the exact, physical sciences.[18] The new approaches did not make conspicuous mistakes, because they did not deal with psychologically relevant matters.

The mistakes that the older schools made were important and led to unsolvable contradictions. The unsuspected reasons were the use of the wrong causal logic and the failure to see the most important causal factors. The early schools as well *imitated without questioning the scientism* of their time by adopting the "scientific" causal *logic of like-comes-from-like* or of positive reactions originating from positive experiences. This was easy because the humanistic thought was also turning scientific and rejecting the old restrictive beliefs. Anyway, the theories of the old schools, including those of associationism and parallelism, were based on the assumptions that all experiences, ideas and reactions originate from similar or kindred experiences and backgrounds.[15,17]

But a closer look and experimentation showed that there was no such causal relation of kindred or similar experiences. Such experimental results were obtained: by Binet on solving of problems; by Kuelpe on the process of volition; by Marbe on forming of judgements; by Ach on making of decisions; by Watt and Messer on preparing for response; by Thorndike, Mueller, and Schumann on "the will to learn"; and by Woodworth on the "perceptual reactions."[17] Some of these, and other psychologists, belonging to the Wuerzburg school, showed that solutions, answers, or motivations came easily almost automatically, after the difficult and different preparation, "set" or "task" had been built up.[17] Satisfactions always come easily after the corresponding needs, however detailed, have been accumulated. Of course explanations implying the opposite or relative causality were not thought of. Rather the mystifications of the Freudian theory on the Unconscious and of the Gestalt psychology are tied in with the discoveries of the Wuerzburg school.[37] In any event, the usual, direct, associational causal logic, by which the old schools were trying to explain the psychological, conscious life, was proven to be untrue. As Flugel says in his history of early psychology, a little careful experimentation was enough to shatter the beliefs of centuries.

The early psychologists not only proceeded with the wrong, "scientific" causal logic but *missed all the important causal factors* in psychological life. Under the nonrelative view, the real causal sources of positive reactions, their negative value opposites, were never suspected. The most important, universal causal factors, like the pleasure or its conditioning, were missed exactly because they are so universal or ordinary as to appear nonexistent or meaningless. The most fundamental satisfactions and needs, of growth, security, competition or survival, and their conditioning, were overlooked because of their similar universality.

Thus the early schools of psychology had to fail. The turn toward pure scientism of physical sciences then led to physicalism and atomism. This has, naturally, only deepened the fallacies and rather set back psychology as a science of living reactions. Opposition to this imitation of physical sciences has been equally strong and extensive; modern psychology offers only endless controversies on its basic insights.

The *"dynamic" psychologies* have adopted inner drives and purposes as determinants of behavior. The theories of Freud, the claimed founder of dynamic psychology, will be discussed later. The Hormic School, stressing purpose in behavior, was founded by McDougall who wanted to make psychology more than experimentation with reflexes of mice. Human purposes were seen as determined by instincts, though McDougall recognized that the driving forces behind instincts are their "cores" governed by pleasantness and unpleasantness.[15]

But the hormists too *wanted to be "scientific"*, therefore could not accept pleasantness as cause. They chose the instincts, because these can be conceived in terms of physical mechanisms. Thus they adopted such instincts as sneezing, coughing or laughing which can be almost mechanically construed. Then, to cover all human behavior, hormists postulated such instincts as acquisitiveness, constructiveness or gregariousness. But such "instincts" rather explain how the culturally conditioned psychologist thinks, not how nature works. Nature's instincts as purposes are brutally simple and few. In fact, the organism has only one purpose, to conserve its sameness. On the other hand, nature's instincts as mechanisms are endlessly many even for the tiniest function. When a cat stalks a mouse, countless mechanisms of sense perception, muscles, organs, tissues, glands and nerves take part. The hormic psychology and theories of instincts thus become useless tributes to "scientism" and can explain nothing of the psychological, organic causation.

All "dynamic" theories become grossly, even dangerously erroneous because they deal with drives, growth or releases, which have the effect of leading to exhaustion and impoverishment upon direct increase or improvement.

The atomism and physicalism of psychological scientism has been particularly opposed by the *organismic* and *personalistic* theories which have turned back to what is relevant and important in psychological life. But again this has led only to more important mistakes. For instance, the organismic approach of Adolf Meyer has had lasting influence on modern psychiatry,[17] and has contributed more than any other to the perpetuation of the logic that negative reactions originate from negatively felt backgrounds. The organismic psychology has been a great support for psychosomatics, which has extended to the fields of physical health the dangerous fallacy of the direct release improvement logic. The personalistic psychology has played a similar role. It stresses what is characteristic or "salient" in personality. But the most salient traits in one's behavior derive from exact opposites in his causal makeup. The person with the most salient traits of insecurity is the one whose personality has been formed under greatest security or overprotection.

Finally the most recent, *humanistic trends* in psychology represent a strong opposition to the imitation of physical sciences. Their main emphasis is on values, human nature, personal value experiences and the broader humanistic, existential and phenomenological insights. This humanistic orientation, originally supported by foremost psychologists — G. W. Allport, J. F. T. Bugental, A. H. Maslow, H. A. Murray, and C. R. Rogers[18] — is now gaining influence. But emphasis on humanistic viewpoints and values is more misleading than physicalism if the relative or opposite causation of values is not understood. Then all the humanistic value delusions, that are the gravest permanent obstacles to all causal understanding, become dominant.

The Freudian Lore: The Only Explanation and Pure Alchemy

The central, most interesting problem in psychology is *why does a person bring on himself the negative feelings and reactions he wants least.* If the relative or opposite causation is understood it is clear that any overenjoyment, whether by use of drugs or by psychological stimulation, has to bring equal opposite feelings, which determine all reactions and behavior. As a person with neurotic or overenjoyment tendencies tries to avoid such aftereffects, by further overenjoyment, he deepens the negative aftereffects in a vicious-circle way which can intensify them to any degree. Thus as the efforts to extend the overenjoyment become more intense and ingenious, the opposite feelings and reactions emerge *with equal intensity and ingenuity.* It may seem as if a skillful scheming agency inside the person is acting against him. Then the Freudian Unconscious, acting within the person against him, seems to be the only explanation.

Actually the Freudian Unconscious is a prescientific personification, as were gods and devils, that naturally can explain anything. Moreover, Freudianism becomes a dangerous belief because it exacerbates the rejection of restrictions which always appear as direct causes of impoverishment and disorder, under the usual causal logic. Above all, Freudianism is a pure alchemy. It is built on the assumption that gravest psychic effects, emotions and potentials derive from unconscious experiences, which by their very definition are never felt; for to the extent something is felt it has to be conscious.

Let us make it clear, at the beginning, that unconscious behavior is frequent and important. We always tend to do what is pleasant, often without being or wanting to be conscious about it. We rather rationalize or invent our reasons. In extreme cases, as in the "hysteric" reactions, one may exclude the consciousness to the point of sinking into amnesia or paralysis. But all this is as different from the Freudian explanations as day is from night.

In all such behavior it is always the person himself, not any separate agency inside him, who drifts toward the pleasures, which are always conscious, or excludes the unpleasant realizations for the sake of what is consciously pleasant. Without exception *such unconscious behavior is directed toward continuance of satisfactions, releases or pleasures,* that are consciously enjoyed. In contrast, the Freudian Unconscious is a separate agency inside the person, working against him and *bringing him the most unpleasant, horrible or tormenting* realizations and conflicts. Moreover, this is supposedly happening on the unconscious, deeper natural level, which is dominated by pleasure alone, and to which we drift in the usual unconscious behavior in order to have more unhindered, conflict-free pleasant experiences.

The fallacy of Freud of not distinguishing between pleasure and torment — between black and white — is clear from the very case with which the psychoanalysis started. The girl treated by Breuer and Freud was induced through hypnosis to recall the tormenting realizations she had repressed or refused to live through. After she was thus forced to live them through fully, with corresponding tormenting emotional upheaval[7] or "catharsis", her hysteria reactions disappeared. In all disorders the cause is the distortions resulting from excessive striving for pleasure or avoidance of displeasure. When the distortion is corrected, as by forcing the avoided tormenting experiences on the hysteric, the disorder is gone; restriction of pleasure releases has the same effect.

But the Freudian theory accepts the exact reverse as true. The deepest natural instinctive *pleasures are assumed to be repressed, and release of pleasure or removal of restrictions, becomes the goal* of therapy. We shall explain later how Freud landed in this blunder by taking the hysteric reactions as examples for all disorders. The end result was the absurdity of people wanting to torment, harm or kill themselves against their clear will as well as against the deepest natural unconscious drives for pleasure, release and self-preservation. Further, the Freudianism leads to the most dangerous attitudes and beliefs that restrictions of natural pleasures are causes of insanity or disease and that free uninhibited gratifications should be the goals of healthy, normal life.

The *personification of the Unconscious* is the central invention and the greatest attraction of the Freudian theory, since it permits every explanation — when explanations are so desperately needed. In all prescientific systems, where the simple cause of endlessly various effects is missed, a personified agent, god or spirit, offers complete explanations. The Freudian Unconscious is always an agent who *reflects, reasons, remembers and draws con-clusions, as well as plots and controls* their execution. Take the most important psychoanalytic concept, the Oedipus complex. It requires that the Unconscious self realize how he desires the mother, but is ashamed or afraid to have her; and that he there-fore hates the father and wants to harm him but by projection starts fearing him, therefore resorts to the various elaborations, maneuvers or adjustments of behavior, while the person has not the slightest idea about this weird world.

The same applies to all unconscious mechanisms, death in-stinct or Thanatos, Eros, castration complex, libido attachments, erotization, sublimation or any unconscious process. Under the death instinct the Unconscious seeks all kinds self-punishment or "suicides" in ways so ingenious that it outwits the person in his most careful efforts to avoid death.[19] Under the mechanism of sublimation and symbolization the Unconscious makes the person work for money as substitute for the play with feces, or turns him into a spendthrift in compensation for suppressed excretion.[22] Any effort or life goal of the person may be only a substitution skillfully directed by the Unconscious for some sexual desire, phallic wish, or natural function repressed in childhood.[23]

The endless symptoms in disorders are accepted as elaborate reactions or readjustments meaningfully carried out by the Unconscious, or as expression of intricate conflicts lived through the Unconscious.[23] Moreover, the Unconscious uses dozens of disguises, distortions, reversions, twistings, transformations, ab-surdities and symbolizations, to hide its intents, to make them pass as legitimate efforts or to find involved outlets.[20] Coal miners may suffer disorders because of an unconscious conflict from using the "phallic pick on mother earth"; or a chess player may become paranoiac because he "castrates" his father by winning his games.[37]

The very purpose and practice of psychoanalysis consists of unraveling, interpreting and making conscious the skillfully hid-den and disguised meanings of the memories, conflicts, symbolic elaborations and intricate purposes of the Unconscious.[23] It makes no difference whether the Unconscious is constituted by Superego, Id, Censor, Eros, Libido, Thanatos or other unconscious agencies. They *all require the same capacities of reasoning, evaluating, conceiving, plotting and carrying out* the complex mental acts, ideas, intents, reactions and intricate behavior. The invention of the various agencies merely confirms that the explanations had to become complex.

It cannot be overemphasized that without such personifications of the Unconscious the psychoanalysis can explain nothing, and that *the personified acts of the Unconscious are the only and unreducible explanations given.* In the often mentioned case analyzed by Freud, Johnny is afraid of horses because he unconsciously fears castration by his father, and has displaced this fear on horses, which he can avoid, while he cannot avoid father. Thus the personified causes are clearly given and no other explanation or a reduction of the causes is either intended or possible, because this is the only way to explain the complex mental and strangely compulsive, unrational fears of Johnny. That the Unconscious inside him must be reasoning, evaluating, planning and carrying out its scheme was the very gist of his analysis by Freud.

Of course an existence of *a separately thinking or experiencing being inside the person is an absurdity.* It would require a separate, fully integrated conscious organism, with its own brain, inside the person. All mental experience consists of reactions by the organism as a totally integrated whole. That is why no genius can think of two things at the same time. Particularly anything as basic, painful or threatening as the decisive conflicts, say, the death wish or Oedipus complex, would be reacted to by the organism with fullest awareness. In the truly unconscious, hysteric reactions all mental processes in the area of conflict are totally blocked, even if this involves paralysis of adjacent areas. For as soon as there is any mental experience it is conscious and only one for the whole organism.

Freud realized the impossibility of the separate personified agencies inside the person. But he argued that these concepts are derived from clinically observed realities and should not be rejected on formal scientific grounds.[20] Certainly, all the ingenuity and skillful persistence of the negative reactions against the person's will can be observed clinically, or otherwise. But they are the effects of the *simple and mechanistic* relative or opposite causation.

We can mention only briefly *the rich Freudian lore of mystery, horror, sex, dreams and magic* that became a necessary part of Freud's theory. The anxiety, obsessions, fears or depression reaches extremes in mental disorders. The reason is the vicious-circle effect, which acts like a noose that tightens upon every improvement sought by the neurotic to avoid the negative feelings. But without the insight into the opposite causation, horrible hidden, ingenious forces had to be assumed as the causes of such extreme, uncannily persisting reactions and fears.

Freud sought explanations in the strong taboos or customary fears and revulsions all people have.[20] Actually, such taboos grow through mere fixations, therefore can never reveal essential, non-accidental causation. It was *typical of Freud to accept as decisive what is dramatic, salient, shocking or glaringly noticeable* — therefore exceptional or rare and *causally least important*. Legends and folklore, often used by Freud, the same as stories created by writers, dwell on matters which are remarkable or interesting exactly because they are opposite to the general, causally determining backgrounds. Similarly we use shocking notions in our swearing because they are the unusual contraries of our general values by which we live. This applies to all psychological phenomena, and Freud accepted their salient or shocking aspects as causally determining — contrary to what is causally true.

Thus Freud arrived at postulating *the culturally most fixational and shocking* concepts as causes: shameful or unusual aspects of sex, incest, Oedipus complex, masochism, castration fear, penis envy, or the fixationally shocking defecation, urination and feces. In truth, such fixational matters are outrageous only for the civilized grownups, not for the person in early childhood — when the conflicts are assumed to generate — and not for any deeply unconscious instinctive self. Moreover, if fundamental drives like that of incest in Oedipus complex existed, they would be found most normal. Then lack of incestuous desires or of wish to kill father would be considered shameful. Also the whole complex would be openly and extensively used as force or basis for culturally laudable institutions, like marriage or family authority.

Of course psychiatrists discover similar culturally shocking or shameful ideas to be part of mental disorders. But this again confirms that their *opposites*, the usual or normal, culturally praised and urged values are particularly strong. As such they become objects of neurotic overenjoyments, which then lead to the opposite, least wanted, shameful abnormal reactions and ideas.

The *Oedipus complex* is the basis of most of the Freudian and Neo-Freudian theories, applied to all fields, from infant care to political sciences. The extent to which the Oedipus complex is accepted is amazing — but predictable. Modern scientists discover the Oedipal ideas abundantly in legends, literature, mental reactions, swearing, expressions of speech, taboos and fixations. Logically, they accept them as causally important, though the very salience or sensational nature of such ideas proves that *they are opposites of universal, strongest values*. Also, the hate of father, or of parents is observed everywhere — in the manifestations of the generation gap as well as in behavior disorders.

In truth, such hate as an excessive feeling is the result of exaggerated enjoyment of love from parents: the love is overenjoyed while there is little of true feeling for it. The normal source of love for parents is the child's dependence or survival need and its thorough impression on him by restrictive conditioning. This is lacking in modern education, while the enjoyment of love as satisfaction, without need, is intensified. Hence the exaggeration and opposite reactions. Without such love there would be none of the emotionally involved hate but only indifferent calculation of danger or adjustment to hostility from parents as antagonists.

Castration fear is a typical Freudian invention, viewed by many theorists as an important cause.[21] Something like it had to be invented to explain the strangling anxiety or negative emotions, actually caused by the noose of the vicious-circle causation. *Cannibalism* is the next best thing for a horror story, and Freudians have claimed discovery of urges, fears and fantasies of cannibalism in various forms.[20] Supposedly we have memories of the prehistoric Oedipal cannibalistic sacrifices. This, as well as Freud's explanation of the whole Oedipal complex, would require inheritance of memory traces, which was recognized as unscientific even by the great follower of Freud, Ernest Jones. Of course all people are fascinated by the same humanly sensational ideas — killing of father, human sacrifice, or eating of human flesh — as Freud was. Therefore similarities between the Freudian concepts and the ideas in various religions, myths or rituals can be easily found.

Sex, more than anything else, offers rich variety of unspeakably shameful, shocking aspects — to the culturally conditioned adults having lived for years under the same fixations or taboos. Sex does dominate our lives. One can imagine how weirdly different would be a world peopled by eunuchs. Whether we go to a concert, sing in church, beautify our homes, plan cities, improve environment or bear sacrifice for our beloved country, sex is a determining factor. But these drives of sex are so fundamentally omnipresent that we do not even notice them.

Freudians, viewing as important only what is salient or remarkable, have *concentrated on the exciting, or culturally shameful genital aspects of sex*. These are the objects of the conscious cultural fixations or taboos, but would have no shameful, prohibitive or specific meaning for the unconscious self or during the early years of development. Sex as the strongest source of enjoyment inevitably leads to disorders if it is not restricted. Normal satisfaction requires here, as elsewhere, accumulation of its opposite, the nonsatisfaction or hunger. One gets sick if he eats without being hungry. But for the people steeped in the Freudian beliefs sexual hunger is a dreadful, diseased condition.

In all areas of sex Freudians are dealing only with what is *remarkable or exceptional*, therefore causally unimportant; or with the sharply noticed sexual acts, like coitus — which is only

a short release phase in the continuous unnoticed and causally determining sexual life. Hence the Freudian emphasis on the fixationally shocking or dramatic concepts of genitals, phallus, coitus,
vagina or womb, as well as the sexual deviations. The rare,
therefore particularly sensational sadism and masochism have
been accepted as general mechanisms for explaining anything,
from a migraine to causes of wars.[20] We do not have space to
repeat all the shocking discoveries, of infants wanting to "suck
out father's genital", girls developing totally under the penis envy,
boys wanting to destroy with penis, or children acquiring traumas
for life upon seeing naked body of opposite sex or parents' intercourse.[37] In reality children have none of the "traumatic"
fixations about nakedness or intercourse; and Freud at least
admitted that the stories about traumas from seeing parents'
intercourse or about similar traumatic early sexual events are
invented by patients during analysis.[20]

Similarly, because ideas about *feces, defecation* or *urination*
are so shocking — to a civilized person having lived for years
with the cultural fixations — Freudians have claimed such things
to be determining factors in early childhood. Thus sublimated
playing with feces becomes the later motivation behind cook-
ing, metal welding, building, carpentry, engraving, sculpture and
architecture.[37] Urethral eroticism is the motivation behind engineering and other occupations having to do with pipes, conductors and channels.[23] Sublimations connected with defecation
and toilet training are assumed as causes of one's later generosity
or stinginess, financial success or failure in life.[22] Even stam-
mering is sublimation of defecation, because of resemblance of
noises, according to Freud.

Magic and mystery were, evidently, needed in such strange
causation, and Freud added them in plenty through his theory
of *symbolism and dreams*. This is fully in character with his
predilection for the sensational or dramatic. Magicians and dream
interpreters of all times have used symbolism. According to
Freudians a person may even drown himself just because he
symbolically associates water with mother's lap and the sinking
with entering woman's body.[23] The Freudian symbolism is end-

lessly expansive. Anything seen in a dream can be shown to have symbolic sexual meaning. Thus anything elongated, standing up, or "working", even a machine, means male genitals; or anything "containing" something, even a room or landscape, the female organs. Moreover, it can always be said that the dream was unconsciously distorted, in the dozens of ways, including complete reversals.

Even more important is the fact that the same symbolism is applied to all behavior and disorders. Everything the neurotic does may thus represent a disguised, very different unconscious intent or idea. As Eysenck shows virtually everything we do can be "discovered" to have hidden sexual meaning.[25]

Curiously enough, Freud demonstrated extensively how dream contents originate from accidental associations, as when he dreamed of Pope while church bells were ringing outside. Other Freudians have accepted similar explanations by such association.[21] Still Freud postulated that the rest of the dream — difficult to trace to its endlessly multiple sources — has a deep symbolic meaning. In truth, dreams are the most haphazard, meaningless, nightmarish misinterpretations, by half-wakened, confused mind, of external or inner physiologic stimuli. Experiments with REM sleep show that dreams are such confused conscious interpretations, by wakening mind, of physiologic brain reactions that are regular and necessary counterprocesses of previous day's mental work. Freud's discovery that dreams reveal wish fulfillment explains nothing: all experience, in dream or wake, derives from striving for satisfaction. There may be dreams about incest as there are about other functional incongruities, when the physiology of the sexual or other function is disturbed.

But the Freudian *symbolism is the most convenient invention.* It makes any desired explanation possible, as anything can be claimed to stand for, or causally be, anything else the psychoanalyst needs for explanation.

The central problem to be explained is of course why and how man brings on himself the feelings and behavior he tries to avoid most — *why he works against himself.* Freud had to claim inherently absurd, unnatural constant strife between the instincts or agencies inside the organism. The person is claimed to be constantly at war with himself, as the Superego acts against the Id and Ego, or the death instinct Thanatos fights the Eros. Conflict between parts of self, the "war theory" was the ultimate explanation for Freud.[19] All the mechanisms and instincts that he invented served to explain how the person punishes, torments or deceives himself because of opposing drives inside him.

Scientifically this is completely wrong. The most certain scientific fact is the virtually miraculous coordination and harmony with which every mechanism, drive or instinct is integrated in the organism. In reality the "war" by the person against himself is the *simple, mechanistic result of the opposite causation,* of overenjoyment of the central drive, the pleasure. But Freud invented biologically useless, unpleasant new instincts just to have disruptive forces inside organism. Thus he created the Instinct of Repetition, "more primitive, more elementary, more instinctual than the pleasure principle which it sets aside".[20] This instinct has been accepted as a primary principle by other psychologists.[37] It serves to explain the cyclic improvement-worsening repetitions of the vicious circle in the unsuspected opposite causation.

One of Freud's greatest inventions is the *Death Instinct,* which can certainly explain anything negative that happens to the person. Of course the death instinct is an impossibility. An instinct controls all mechanisms and tendencies, but even a momentary interruption of a basic mechanism causes death. We would have hundreds of opportunities to get killed every day if we had the slightest tendency for it. The idea of Death Instinct is strikingly dramatic or impressive, because it represents the exception from the most universal rule, of self-preservation.

The *Freudianism is pure alchemy causally.* By its very definition *the unconscious life is not felt* by the person. Even the repressions or conflicts are unconscious.[21] As I. Hendrick explains "the impulse may be unconscious, the occasion for the punishment may be unconscious and rationally trivial",[23] while they cause grave disorders. Freud had a special theory about the

Omnipotence of Thought.[20] As if by magic, mere ideas, not reality, become causally determining. Especially all kinds of unconscious "phantasies" are accepted by Freudians as grave causes of disorders. Such phantasies and unconscious ideas are assumed to have arisen mostly in the early childhood, to be forgotten and ridiculously meaningless for the grown-up person, yet to be decisive for his whole life.[15]

It is the basic assumption of the Freudian theory that causes of disorders are in terms of real feelings — which have always to be conscious — so trivial that years of analysis are required before the person can remember them. Also, gravest emotions are assumed to arise from a mere switch in their sign or direction. The "forbidden impulse changes its sign, so to speak; that is, its sign is replaced by its contrary; pleasure is changed into disinclination, aversion, shame, disgust, etc."[20] Freudians have a special theory of Ambivalence, of emotions changing into their opposites through mere switch in the unconscious ideas.

Particularly obnoxious are the Freudian beliefs that *tiny acts,* specifically in early childhood, may warp personality for life. The result has been a "mass phobia", of parents being scared that "even the most innocent appearing act or carelessly spoken word may harm the child or damage his future happiness" (M. Clark).[37] By restricting the infant from sucking his toe "his whole life may be warped"; or by pulling a loose button from a boy's shirt you may arouse in him unconscious castration anxiety for life.[37] "If the mother pleads with child to have bowel movement" this leads in later life to generosity, charity and philanthropy; but too much emphasis on feces results in parsimony or thriftiness; and reaction-formation to retention of stool may lead to heedless dealing with money in "expulsive manner" (C. S. Hall).[22] Significantly, Freudians themselves have been puzzled that the education they have found as best has produced unfortunate results.[3] Freud sought explanations in a mixup of child's phantasies and in erroneous identification, with parents' superegos.[3]

The most dangerous practical fallacy of Freudianism is *its teaching that repression is the cause of disorders.* It compounds the blunder of the modern "scientific" logic in the most insidious way, by scaring people with insanity. Restrictions *are* part of "disease", as pressures back to normalcy; but for Freudians restrictions or repressions are the very source of all evil. According to Freud "repression is the pillar on which the edifice of psychoanalysis rests, and resistance, which is the same thing in analysis".[20]

Repression is an unmatched source of easy explanations. If anybody refuses to recognize the unconscious agencies, he is assumed to suffer from repression. When other scientists reject the Freudian theory, this is seen as the main proof of the repression.[23] The very discovery of repression was made by Freud when he encountered "resistance" by his patients to his cures. Psychoanalysis had to fail, but it seemed to Freud "as if the patient actively resisted his own cure. It was on this observation of such resistance that Freud built his theory of repression" (R. W. White).[7]

What is even more remarkable, *Freud later rejected the whole theory of repression,* though it had to and did remain the basis of psychoanalysis. He then replaced repression with simple nongratification as cause, in one of the last of his many revisions of his theory. As White explains, Freud's new theory stressed "increase in tension arising from nongratification of child's needs" and the fact that "the child appraises as danger a situation that is not gratified".[7] This final explanation by Freud, after forty years of theorizing, is pointless. Nongratifications constitute half of everybody's experiences. But Freud had finally discovered that "what was repression appears later as gratification", or that the mentally disturbed patients suffer from "pathological absence of repression".[23,37]

The important fact is that Freudians *scare modern men with dangers of repressions* as causes of insanity. Particularly sexual restrictions are blamed, though a statistical study, by R. B. Cattell and I. H. Sheier, shows that priests and even prisoners suffer less than other groups from anxiety. If Freudians were right, the psychopaths would be people living in saintliness, whereas the reverse is true (O. H. Mowrer).[24] The licentious beat generation is a living proof all around us. A special study by Stekel, who started as a follower of Freud, showed that disorders supervened during periods of sexual license and disappeared after periods of abstinence.[24]

But in spite of everything, Freudianism has been enormously successful, in becoming *the most influential theory* in psychology and psychiatry. This is due to the fact that, as we saw, the personified Unconscious offers unlimited, complete even "scientifically" or clinically provable explanations, where psychologists are desperately looking for any logical explanation. An additional, practically even more important fact is the enormous appeal that the Freudian lore of sex, dreams, magic and mystery has for everybody. We are not different mentally from our ancestors who believed in astrology, magic or witchcraft. The present revival of interest in such cults confirms this. We merely reject what science has clearly proved as unfounded. But in psychology, science has no accepted explanations, particularly none on the problem of how and why man brings on himself reactions he does not want. It has to be emphasized that *the general, mass appeal* is what makes an idea extensively known and can elevate it, through fixation, into a place of sanctity, while even the most important idea that is not popular and is rarely discussed is easily lost. The Freudian theory offers virtually everything people crave to hear about.

Besides, doctors are glad to find a theory that finally offers complete and easy explanations. Doctors as narrow, though highly skilled professionals are not bothered by the method of personification used in the theory. To see how the personification amounts to a prescientific ghost story a different kind of insight is required, from fields of philosophy of science, theoretics, the humanities and their criticism. Yet psychoanalysis has gained respectability exactly because *doctors with their medical authority have stood behind it.* Analysis could be started as a serious treatment because Freud and his disciples were doctors (B. Inglis). If they had not been doctors, the Freudian lore would be rather regarded as a joke.

But psychoanalysis *has failed in its real test, in providing cures.* Of course the analysis convinces patients of its accuracy. This is due to the peculiarity of men to relate anything as fitting their case.[25] Experimenters found that, in ninety percent of cases, every subject recognized the same statement, randomly taken from an astrologer's book, as perfectly fitting his particular case.[25] When it comes to cures, the failure of psychoanalysis is complete. The American Psychoanalytic Association itself has found that only one third of completed cases were cured. Other studies have shown that a mere 25 percent were cured.[26] More than half of patients derive no benefit from psychoanalysis and for 60 percent of these patients it is harmful.[37] At the same time it is generally known that two thirds of all neurotics recover without any treatment whatever (H. J. Eysenck).[25] Furthermore, psychoanalysts take only the lightest cases, as the theory prescribes. We are therefore not surprised to find the APA admitting that "no claims regarding the therapeutic usefulness of analytic treatment are made".[26]

It has been always known that psychoanalysis "is not regarded even by psychoanalysts themselves as providing a cure in the usual medical sense" (R. S. Woodworth).[15] Freud saw analysis more as an educational than a medical treatment.[15] The "father" of psychoanalysis in this country, Dr. A. A. Brill, felt "rather pessimistic" about curing patients with it.[21] The leading psychoanalyst in Great Britain, Dr. Ernest Jones, concluded from a survey of cases in that country that the success was mostly "analytic", analysts learning of "major unconscious factors".[37] What the patient gets from psychoanalysis is a relief that only delays his natural, hard recovery, for years that analysis may take.

Freudianism is an enormous success because it is an unlimited source of explanations. If the opposite causation is not understood, then for most psychic and behavioral phenomena the real cause is not seen. *Freud had the genius of demonstrating this invisibility of the cause* in most fields — folklore, myths, legends, literature, customs, taboos, swearing, wit and speech, as well as mental disorders. He saw the Unconscious as the missing cause. "For Freud what is unconscious is what is unknown" (C. S. Hall).[22] Man does feel and behave, with intense "ingenuity", in all fields, contrary to what he wants, intends, professes, or knows as true. The simple and mechanistic opposite causation explains how this happens. Even the notorious errors of speech can be explained by the simple fact of exaggeration.

A friend may react or say something in a way exactly contrary to what he feels and wants to feel, because he had exaggerated his friendliness, and the opposite reactions had to break out. He still feels friendly, though not as friendly as he exaggeratedly wanted to feel; and there is no reason to assume hidden, hostile, agencies inside him. The same applies to the idealistic politician who may momentarily react and say something contrary to what he really feels; or to any person genuinely feeling one way but for a moment reacting in opposite ways simply because of an exaggeration of his feelings. But Freud had to assume hidden, strangely evil agencies inside the person, to have an explanation.

Freud had neither a scientific way of thinking nor the intuitive psychological insights, which are even more important as long as there is no real psychological science. He was notorious for changing the very fundamentals of his theory, constantly inventing new ones, by way of imagination and admittedly pseudo-historical or pseudo-biological assumptions.[37] In a real scientific theory the fundamental principle never changes. If it does, the theory is not valid any more. *Freud abandoned the basis itself of his theory, the repression* — as well as the very "attempt to find a specific etiological source of neuroses" (R. S. Woodworth).[15] But psychoanalysis remained unaffected, because its basis and appeal never were scientific. Freud was not even interested in psychology. As Jones says, he "was ill-informed in the field of contemporary psychology and seems to have derived only from hearsay any knowledge he had of it".

More importantly, Freud lacked the practical intuitive insight in psychological causation. His whole personality was distinguished by practical psychologic ignorance — excellent for a literary genius as Freud probably was. He suffered from phobias, anxiety, mood swings, fatigue and obsessions.[27] He not only used drugs, notably cocaine, but was unaware of their connection

with the aftereffects and advocated their use among his friends.[27]
He was "inclined to self-torment and superstition", seriously believed in mystical numbers, feared that 51 was the number of
years he was destined to live, and suffered from hypochondriac
obsessions, notably that he had become poisoned by the food he
ate during his short stay in America in 1909.[27] Freud had the
genius of imagination and observation of human drama. *Psychoanalysis is a creation of such genius, not a scientific discipline.*

The unconscious agencies in the rich Freudian lore are prescientific personifications that can explain everything, as ghosts
and mythical spirits do. *But modern psychology is incapable to
offer anything better.* The theories of learning and conditioning
imply that man somehow, unwittingly learns or is conditioned
to torment himself without use of reason. Freudianism is pure
alchemy in the sense that the weightiest feelings and potentials
are assumed to originate from unconscious experiences, that have
never been felt. Moreover, enrichment of potentials is expected
from removal of restrictions — from direct increase in releases or
satisfactions, as the logic of the modern alchemistic scientism
requires.

Deepening Confusion

The effort, in psychology, of finding the causal explanations
has been enormous. There is probably more of speculative
theories in psychology than in all other sciences taken together.
On any subject, like learning or personality, a book may be
filled just describing existing theories. On some subjects, like
abnormal, social or educational psychology, nobody could de·
scribe the existing theories in one volume. Even one single theory
or concept may have thousands of variations. On the Rorschach
ink blots alone the works written can be counted in the thousands.
Yet the goal of all this effort is, or should be, to arrive at general causal laws or principles which as natural laws can be only
elementarily simple. It is generally understood that such laws
will be the basis of psychology as a science, that they exist, and
must be discovered.[14]

The reason why so much effort and intelligence have not brought us closer to discovering the simplest truths is that the very direction of the effort or the logic of thinking behind it is completely wrong. The main effect of not understanding the factual, relative causation, with its opposite logic, is that all explanations are reversedly wrong causally, or equally untrue. Consequently any theory, however esoteric, is as good or creditable as any other. Theories multiply as the unawareness that every gain requires equal hard effort encourages countless exciting alchemistic inventions and discoveries. Every active psychologist rushes to explain in new ways the never-ceasing discovery that positive reactions are pleasant as well as most beneficial.

The lately emerging Humanistic Psychology[36] is a good example of added confusion. It appears to be the strongest psychological movement of the last decade.[18,36] It stresses the "human fulfillment, growth and happiness". According to it, psychology should be related "to love and hate, to growing and regressing, to happiness and pain, to courage and anxiety" (A. H. Maslow).[13,28] This brings to psychology the humanistic value delusions and the ultimate alchemy of positive reactions deriving from positive value sources. The similarly alchemistic belief in free will is part of the humanistic psychology. Man is to be viewed as a purposive and striving creature who freely chooses, judges and organizes; reference to the moralistic enthusiasm of Harry Emerson Fosdick is found appropriate enough.[13] Even subjectivity is found to be acceptable under the newly expanding existential and phenomenological psychologies,[18] as well as under the uncertainties of the modern theory of physics.[13] The humanistic value delusions are being compounded by recourse to philosophies, Eastern or Western[13] — which have always been sources of endless, value-bound confusion. It may be noted that the human enthusiasm or the great free capacity of man to choose and plan should be extolled least in psychology. The very cause of functional disorders is man's enthusiasm and capacity to plan his improvements, value enjoyments or overadjustments. Animals, lacking such capacities, do not suffer from functional diseases.

All in all, the new humanistic, existential, phenomenological[36] and subjective value approaches have brought to psychology the endless *humanistic and philosophical delusions and fallacies*. These have been the traditional obstacles to positivistic or new, revolutionary causal discoveries and have produced the vastest amount of self-defeating philosophical theorization. Modern psychology is, evidently, embarking on a similar road of endless and futile, value-bound and subjective confusion.

At this point we may mention the glaring difference between real sciences, like physics, and modern psychology. If somebody discovered a new force or law in physics, this would cause a world-wide upheaval among physicists. In psychology as well, the real, natural causal laws or fundamental forces can be only few, simple and general. But here *scores of new laws, forces, causal principles and factors are "discovered" daily*; and psychologists, resignedly, see no point in contesting the conflicting discoveries.

As we saw, volumes are required just to list the causal theories, principles and concepts proposed by various psychologists. There are hundreds of laws and countless irreducible Gestalts in the Gestalt psychology; or as numerous drives, instincts, mechanisms and agencies in the dynamic psychologies. In the humanistic and existential approaches new causal principles and concepts are postulated by the dozen in every new book, even by the same author. One finds in limitless profusion fundamentally decisive causal concepts like Being, Self, Autonomy, Encounter, Freedom, Growth, Transcendence, Actualization, Logos, Concern, Angst, Non-Becoming, Un-Form, or Anti-Eidos.[37] Most of such concepts like Ego, Self, Identity or Personality, require multiplicity of other principles and mechanisms, sufficient to fill more volumes. A single theory on personality postulates 13 viscerogenic and 28 psychogenic needs, besides various functions and regnant processes.[37] And there are scores of personality theories.

One of the richest sources of confusion, in most theories, is the use of concepts of mechanisms like Identification, Projection, Substitution or Displacement. Many such mechanisms are generally accepted as explanations, even by conservative psychologists.[37] The central confusion here results from the fact that such concepts are derived from usual behavior, like one's identification with a hero, which the person adopts in pursuit of satisfactions or *pleasure*; but then the concepts of the mechanisms are applied to explain the most *unpleasant*, tormenting negative reactions and disorders. This is a distorting fallacy. It rests on *a logic that because man is uncannily ingenious in pursuing his pleasures he will as ingeniously seek ways for tormenting himself.*

Identification is probably the most frequently invoked mechanism. It is inferred from the common, pleasure-dominated forms of behavior, such as wanting to be like somebody else or to do as somebody else.[37] Identification with things is inferred from a person's boasting about his car or clothes.[8] But then Identification is used to explain how the manic-depressive suffers because he identified himself with a dead person; how the paranoiac has identified himself with a persecuted group; or how the sick person has adopted "the characteristics of a sick and handicapped person as though they were his own."[37] Similarly identification with multiple persons is blamed for multiple personality; with aggressor, for aggression; with mother, for homosexuality.[8]

Particularly lack of models for identification is blamed for maladjustments. Surely a person growing up among criminals will become a criminal. The day-by-day value experiences are decisive. But no amount of reflective, cognitive or ideational experience, as Identification is assumed to be, can make any difference. Everybody gladly identifies himself with the greatest men and best capacities, which would make a person great in any environment. When a person follows the evil leader or bad habits of environment he does so in pursuit of his pleasures; the real problems lie in the field of pleasure or release economy, not ideational concepts.

Projection is another often invoked mechanism. Again, it is inferred from usual, pleasurable behavior patterns, of people assigning their own faults or undesirable qualities to others (E. R. Hilgard).[29] But then the projection concept is used to explain the most unpleasurable, tormenting reactions, particularly the paranoiac fears. It is argued that by projecting his own hostility onto others the person, logically, starts seeing them as hostile.[31] In truth, no logic or reason can induce us to feel one way or another, still less to create for ourselves the torments of psychotic fears. Certainly the person who eagerly resorts to "projection", who overenjoys his own superiority and sense of power over others, is bound to suffer from as excessive opposite feelings and reactions, including irrational fear of the power of others over him. Thus the disorder here, as in all cases, is caused by the striving for pleasure, the naturally strongest drive.

Displacement is very frequently claimed as psychic cause. It is equally inferred from all kinds of usual pleasure-dominated behavior, like rationalizations, illogical distortions or false convictions. But after Displacement is thus proven it is viewed as explanation for a wide range of most unpleasant maladjustments and disorders. A person may continue "torturing himself with neurosis and mismanaged life" because he displaced his hostility onto himself.[9] Similarly a neurotic may suffer an unexplainable animal phobia or obsession because he displaced the fear of his inner, unconscious, horrible drives. It is accepted that anything can be displaced onto anything else (P. Symonds).[37] Thus explanation of even the hardest cases becomes speciously easy, particularly since displacement is assumed to be directed at unconscious distortion and disguise of real causes.

Many more mechanisms, like Dissociation, Substitution, Symbolization, Compensation, Reaction-Formation, Regression, Introjection, Isolation, Denial or Negation are claimed as explanations. They can be always easily established or proved from all kinds of usual behavior patterns, governed by the search for pleasures and satisfaction or usefulness. But then they are applied to explain the most unpleasant, unsatisfactory and useless reactions or behavior disorders and maladjustments. The reason for this widely perpetuated blunder is that psychology can offer no explanation of how and why people striving for satisfactions and pleasures alone bring on themselves all the negative feelings and reactions. Here as elsewhere the enormously complex sophistry and mystery would become unnecessary if the simple, mechanistic opposite causation was understood.

The most typical effort to explain this central mystery are the theories that due to hidden drives or instincts within the person he deliberately works against himself. Often the Freudian Death Instinct is invoked for support. A classical, authoritative work on the subject is Menninger's *Man Against Himself*. Menninger shows how almost every maladjustment or disorder, from failures in life or alcoholism to mental and organic diseases, is a form of suicide.

The *self-punishment* is probably the most popular theory, accepted by the best, classic authorities. Alexander explains by it a wide variety of maladjustments including professional failures, eccentricity, repeated marriages, delinquency and recidivism. He holds that criminals unconsciously leave clues so that they can be caught and receive the desired punishment; or that alcoholics drink because the "adverse consequences of drinking replace admirably other forms of self-punishment".[37] The best theory on self-punishment through crime is that of Reik, who contends that punishment of crime may become the main incentive for criminals to commit crimes.

Other authorities have accepted self-punishment as explanation for various puzzling problems. It is viewed by L. J. Saul as a drive that may dominate the person's whole life, yet "may operate very subtly, as when little slips or certain tastes or decisions which seem to be reasonable, lead regularly to unhappiness or even disaster." Unconscious conflicts are assumed as causes. J. C. Coleman attributes the self-punishment drive to repressed hostility toward love objects and the resulting feeling of guilt. But as Menninger admits, "the extraordinary fact that a person should prefer pain to pleasure cannot be easily explained."[19] Men do "punish" themselves, and *the most natural striving for pleasure, to excess, is the cause.*

Psychologists are puzzled and may claim that the person suffers from concrete acts of guilt. Mowrer explains that there is a "real palpable, indisputable guilt" in the disturbed person's past.[24] Other psychologists hold similar views (Menninger, May).[37] Actually the disturbed neurotics and psychotics only feel or imagine their crimes, and are rather perfectionists who have lived in the most sheltered, innocent overprotection. But the *assumption of some hidden inner evil may seem to be the only fitting expla-nation.* Why, for instance, does the logically ideal parent-child relationship of greatest natural love, observed in over-protection or pampering, contribute to most disorders? The proposed ex-planation is that the great love hides deep hate by the loving parent. This is now one of the most generally used explanations, accepted by best authorities (K. Menninger, J. Dollard, N. E. Miller, O. H. Mowrer, O. S. English, R. May).[37] The paradox is certainly there — if the opposite causation is not understood. The mother who wants to give her children deepest love at every moment starts feeling that she might kill them.[37] Excess or over-use of a mechanism in one direction here creates the opposite excess.

But logically the *facts are misleading*: exactly where the over-enjoying person wants the greatest success or most positive emo-tions, he meets with particular motivational failure or opposite emotions. The result is added confusion, as all kinds of theories are advanced, convincingly claiming that people somehow secret-ly want what they clearly try to avoid, are mysteriously set to defeat themselves, strive unknowingly for absurd goals, lead their lives in serving ideals that they secretly want to destroy, or are most evil where they are cultivating highest love.

Expectedly, the hidden drives and wishes are assumed to be of horrible nature. A girl developing anxiety about going to a camp "is afraid that if she is away from parents she will act like a wild animal and tear and devour other people, probably chil-dren".[3] The theory that anxiety and disorders arise from fear of repressed *horrible inner drives* is now generally accepted as a great discovery.[31] Factually, all hidden drives are only pleasant to the person himself, and should be particularly so to the un-conscious self — however shameful or horrible they may become when discovered by others. And no psychologist has yet blamed the difficulty of concealment, or conscious or unconscious en-joyment.

As the explanations become more confusing, psychologists tend toward mystification. They rather seek insights from dreams, nightmares or incoherent talk. Delirium or senseless muttering during anesthesia is preferred to conscious statements.[32] Loose "analyses" of legends, customs, art and literature are popular because they permit arcane sophistications about the most "remarkable" — therefore causally least revealing — inventions of mind. Mythical revelations are to be sought from archetypal unconscious experiences and "memories", of the prehistoric man or the fetus in the womb[32] — as postulated by Jung, Freud or Rank. Though inheritance or existence of such experiences and memories is scientifically clearly impossible, the esoteric theories are respectfully accepted and applied. They are a natural part of modern psychology, and nobody bothers to consider that they are glaringly unscientific.

Metaphysical and ontological explanations are as generally accepted, particularly in the newest humanistic and existential approaches. Cognition of Being or attainment of knowledge of the ontological self is viewed as the purpose of psychological guidance and therapy, in various theories (A. H. Maslow, V. E. Frankl).[28] Such cognition is expected to be ecstatic, much like the "peak-experiences", or "growth-through-delight", shown to be accepted as the royal road to Self by tens of psychologists.[28] One can only wonder why people have not rushed into discovering their ontological selves. Of course psychologists blame the fear of horrible inner instincts, or the still more mysterious ontological fear of knowing oneself.[28] Actually, the patients who resist such enticements to ecstatic "discoveries" of self know intuitively, through bitter experience, the disastrous aftereffects of overenjoyments. But the simple real causality is missed. Even the observation that deepest feelings of beauty, love or delight emerge upon survived threats of death is explained by metaphysical speculations (R. May, A. H. Maslow).[10]

We may note that all schools of psychology would have to resort to metaphysics, as Gestalt psychology did, if it was realized that an ultimate causal explanation has to be given for all the *multiple* concepts which the schools propose and which they cannot explain by a natural, simple causal law or source.

Most responsible for the increasing confusion is of course the virtually *alchemistic logic* that positive capacities come from positive, pleasant experiences. All the typical movements of modern psychology are directed at gaining positive potentials through more satisfaction, pleasure or other deepened release experiences, attained by stimulation, expanded consciousness, heightened sensitivity or performance of formulistic rituals, as well as by mere abstract gaining of insights and discoveries about the "self". The arcane practices of Yoga, Zen or similar Oriental and new-fangled modern movements are becoming increasingly popular, among the most educated groups. Maharishi Mahesh Yogi, promising easy transcendental regeneration, has 350,000 followers, from the best-informed people. Guru Maharaj Ji has attracted four million worshipers expecting similar enrichment.

A typical example is the wide Human Potential Movement, with its sensitivity training, encounter groups and the Esalen Institute treatment. It finds support in best theories— on Gestalt discoveries, Humanistic psychology or "operant conditioning" — expounded by foremost authorities, including Skinner, Maslow and Rogers.[33] The movement is based mostly on beliefs in rituals, symbolic performances, deepening of perception or "sensitivity", gaining of new insights, and finding better ways of release or of freedom from inhibitions and negatively felt experiences.[33] The training may consist of such performances as standing barefoot on a piece of paper, breaking out of a circle of persons, playing symbolic burial, imitation of giving birth, vomiting exercise, imaginary tug of war, dance improvisations or meditative rituals.[33]

The same lack of recognizing the requirement of the hard, negatively felt effort leads to acceptance of lightest, merely formal factors as important. *Mere enactment or "transaction" of roles* or states of mind is seen to be decisive — as has been dramatically presented in the best sellers *Games People Play* and *I'm O. K., You're O. K.* This would be so if adjustment was a play, instead of being a dead serious struggle for limited potentials. Yet even the best role theories stress as decisive the mere perception, understanding, skills in role enactment, or the cognitive organization of self[4] — all that is weightless in terms of emotions or releases by which man lives. No wonder that most readers accept psychological problems to be the results of mere play or misunderstandings. In truth, what may seem crazy, gratuitous or unnecessary game or state of mind may be the feelings and reactions the person compulsively suffers, wants least, and tries to avoid most, in exaggerated ways.

But dealing with really serious, weighty factors in modern psychology is outright dangerous because of the direct "scientific" logic, as we saw before. When Congress wants a clear important opinion from a psychologist, he is bound to stress how beneficial are the things which provide more enjoyment, freedom or feeling of well-being. He may skillfully try to find the answers from analyses of minds of the people, and still come up with the same fallacies. For even in the deepest recesses of their minds people connect their positive reactions with positive background experiences and never suspect the real, opposite causal sources.

Of course specialists, like industrial or school psychologists, can be useful. They learn what to do from factual experience, by use of common-sense intelligence, not from any theory. How could they apply theories when there are hundreds of them on every subject? Nor does any general psychologic orientation help them; they hate to be associated with any psychological school.[15] In fact, the strongest objections against use of general psychology in the given field may come from a specialist in it (R. Reger).

For the modern psychologist, "at the present moment the conceptual schemes at his disposal are the equivalent of what chemists and physicists were using in the late eighteenth century" (J. B. Conant).[34] Maslow asks, "what cultivated man in his right mind would read a doctrinal dissertation, or an elementary text book of psychology".[13] John Cohen agrees with the conclusion that "when the text books of psychology pass from simpler to more elusive mental processes they become in almost every case entirely useless".[35]

A real science has unquestioned, clear fundamental causal principles. But in psychology every principle or concept is totally useless in terms of the hundreds of others invented daily. At the present, psychology is, or should be, only a preparatory stage of discovering the basic laws, after which it can be forgotten and the real science of working with those laws can begin. Moreover, the discovery of such laws should be simple and easy, since they as natural universal laws have to be simple and evident from all organic value reactions, which determine everything we experience, feel or do. That *the exact reverse of such clarity and simplicity is true in modern psychology* confirms the total fallacy of its very logic or way of thinking. Almost the only result of progress in psychology has been the added confusion, complexity and endless multiplicity of theories.

Conclusion

Psychology is the key science because everything in man's world depends on the capacities of his mind. These, as satisfaction or release potentials, can be increased or enriched only through increase in needs, which are nonsatisfactions, or in restrictions. But psychology proceeds by the ordinary humanistic and "scientific" logic, confirmed by experimental immediate proofs, that positive capacities come from direct increase in the satisfactions or releases. This amounts to the alchemy of getting the most precious human capital without effort, with the ease of just accumulating the satisfactions.

Psychologists then have merely to find the easiest methods and formulas of learning, thinking, ideas, habits, skill or understanding of how to increase, directly, the satisfactions or avoid nonsatisfactions. Faulty learning or ideas are blamed for disorders, as if man could learn, uselessly, to torment himself. In truth, nothing is easier for man than to find satisfactions or releases — when their potentials are accumulated through the hard needs, nonsatisfactions or restrictions.

The above alchemy and reversedly wrong causal logic, evidently, make everything in psychology insidiously untrue or contrary to causal facts. Also, without insight in the opposite causation the concepts of satisfaction or pleasure, by which we all live, become inapplicable. The strict experimental scientists in psychology refuse to look at the "mentalistic", conscious or the truly psychological life altogether; and reject the only, virtually miraculous possibility of understanding causally the living mental processes, namely, through what we feel. Modern psychologists are dealing with psychologically irrelevant factors: either with mere reflexes, in experiments, or with the ideational and cognitive ideas and reasons, discovered in the minds of people, by analyses. Such ideational factors are psychologically as weightless as are all rationalizations or "reasons" that people believe to be the causes of their behavior.

In this atmosphere of alchemy and confusion, the Freudianism is offering the only complete explanation of the central problem of how and why man brings on himself the reactions he wants least. The opposite causation would be the simple mechanistic explanation, but it has remained unthinkable. The Freudian theory resorts to virtually ghost-like personifications — which, certainly, can explain anything. Moreover, it perpetuates the alchemy of gravest psychic effects arising from weightless causes, from the unconscious experiences, that have no emotional weight at all. For to the extent anything is felt it has to be conscious. Of course the Freudians can demonstrate clinically that the unwanted negative reactions man brings on himself are truly "ingenious" or viciously persistent. The opposite vicious-circle effects of equally ingenious and intense overadjustments is the reason. But the Freudian personified agencies — the modern demons — thus seem to be proven.

The gravest Freudian fallacy, the theory of repressions, is as "scientifically" proved. Clinical or experimental observations always show that the immediate cause of disorders or negative reactions is repression or restriction — which is actually the organism's natural effort to restore normalcy, much as in drug withdrawal.

The progress in modern psychology amounts to a progress of added confusion, as the same inherently alchemistic and reversedly wrong causal logic is perpetuated through colossal increasing efforts. The newest humanistic and existential approaches bring into psychology the complete humanistic value delusions and philosophical confusion. Every attempt to explain logically the central problem of man-against-himself only adds to the absurd theorization that men can be unaware of tormenting themselves. Finally, the logic of obtaining the positive potentials through added positive experiences, without equal negative opposites, is turning the practical modern psychology into a virtual alchemy of pursuing rituals, meditations, exercises, roles, techniques of stimulation, or direct increase in releases and satisfactions. Restrictions and nonsatisfactions or needs, the very sources of the release and satisfaction potentials or capacities, become the main evils to be avoided.

IV

NEUROSES AND PSYCHOSES: PERFECT
CLUES — AND MYSTERIES

Neuroses and psychoses are perfect, endlessly recurring real-life examples of the relative or opposite causation in action. They are aftereffects of overadjustments or overenjoyments, much like the drug aftereffects, which they "strikingly" resemble. The neurotics are persons who strive excessively for satisfactions and perfection. Neuroses are therefore as excessive opposite, most unwanted, tormenting reactions. The psychotics, particularly the schizophrenics, live in a self-centered autistic world they create for themselves, in which they, naturally, enjoy every satisfaction they want or imagine. Consequently the aftereffect, the psychosis is a world of every negative reaction, impoverishment and immobility. The vicious circle of overadjustment drives here, as in all functional disorders, the negative reactions to their incredible extremes.

But neuroses and psychoses have remained virtual mysteries — as have all functional diseases. The mystery is best reflected in the Freudian prescientific theories about personified agencies, the modern devils. Other theories seek causes in learning or conditioning and in ideational distortions, ideas or perceptions, like those about self, identity and alienation. In truth, nobody learns or gets conditioned uselessly to torment himself; ideas have no psychological weight; and if there is any distortion, it inexorably gravitates toward overenjoyment of the most positive ideas or perceptions.

149

Further, no physiologic explanations, even of such clearly physiologic disorders as schizophrenia, have been found. The reason is the paradox of opposite causation. The same reaction, substance or process that produces an experimentally clear improvement results in the disease. Conversely, the restrictive reactions and processes that show as the "disease" are actually the efforts of organism to conserve, or return to, its normalcy. This relative or opposite causal logic applies to every detail dealt with by the psychiatrist or scientist, who uses the exactly contrary, direct causal logic and therefore only adds to the confusion.

The cause of the intensely as well as "ingeniously" evolving mental diseases is the strongest force in human nature, the striving for pleasure, permitted to become excessive by the psychologically weak neurotic or psychotic. As long as this paradoxical causation is not even suspected, psychiatry will remain a system of mysteries.

Overadjustment, Vicious Circle, Defense and Conflict

As we have repeatedly explained, the release potentials and reserves, by which man normally lives, are accumulated by restrictions. When they are depleted, by enjoyment, organism tries to restore them by imposing restrictions, which are harrowingly felt as slow death, anxiety, impoverishment or, in case of longer overenjoyment, as the disease. Normally a person lives through the distressing restrictions, the hangovers, and the normalcy is restored. But some persons cannot stand the restriction, either because they have not been conditioned to bear nongratifications or because they genetically require grosser release expenditures in their responses and motivations. Permissiveness and ease of life, naturally, encourage overenjoyments and looser expenditure of releases. That is why mental disorders increase together with the modern progress.

Of course difficulties of life, requiring new motivations as accumulated release potentials, may strain a person's release economy (the concept of release has been defined in the first chapter). But if one is well conditioned, he can bear any amount of restrictions and thus accumulate all the needed potentials. The same is true of critical physiologic difficulties or setbacks, that normally have to be met by great pain.

The *vicious circle,* which can deepen the impoverishment or negative reactions to any degree, starts running when the person seeks avoidance of the necessary restrictions. This can be viewed as the self-deepening of the defenses. As a restriction upon overadjustment is avoided by further increase in releases, more restriction becomes necessary and its pressure is avoided by still greater increase in releases. The overenjoyment tendency and "capacity" must be there. A small *additional* "improvement" must be enjoyed at every turn to keep the vicious circle running. This tendency is typical of the defensive, pleasure-seeking and perfectionistic personality of the neurotic. The psychotic, living in his mental world as if it were real, has particularly the "capacity" of enjoying satisfactions at will and, naturally, uses it at every turn. Everybody can become the overenjoyer, and the victim of the vicious circle, if changes in living conditions and moral or cultural standards leave him free to enjoy more fully what he wants. Man pursues nothing but pleasure whenever permitted to do so.

It has to be kept in mind that overenjoyment or *overadjustment is a pleasure only at its short initial stage.* After that it becomes a deepening impoverishment against which the person struggles by adding more improvements that yield less and less pleasure at every turn. Further, the overadjustment *cannot be abandoned* by the person even after it has resulted in the overwhelming negativeness and increasingly elaborate defense. We explained before that each release improvement, even if obtained by mere snapping of fingers, is for the psychotic as real as are releases obtained from drugs. Inevitably, abandonment of any of the added elaborations would amount to retreating a concrete step from the high overadjustment level, just as in drug withdrawal.

The *Defense,* as a universal mechanism in mental disorders, is a clear proof of the vicious-circle paradox of improvements. There are various explanations of the Defense.[1] It is held that the neurotic chooses the wrong ways for warding off anxiety which are ineffective and become a difficulty rather than help.[1] Such wrong choices are attributed either to unconscious, irrational and symbolic motivations or to faulty learning. But nobody ever makes a mistake as to what is pleasant or emotionally positive, particularly not on the unconscious level; and nobody ever learns what is uselessly unpleasant. On the contrary, the positively felt reactions are the simplest, easiest things for man. Because the psychotic constantly chooses them, without restraint, as easy immediate improvements, the vicious-circle impoverishment deepens at every turn. The generality of the theories of Defense merely proves that the excessive striving for improvements is the observed dominant feature in mental disorders.

Conflict as cause of disorders is generally recognized. The reason is that the opposite causation in mental disorders is as general. Conflict in disorders implies by its very nature an intense, even well-reasoned effort to solve them (K. Horney, R. W. White).[3,32] The *paradox of worsening through improvement* or of restriction upon excessive release is the reason for such "conflict". Without the paradox there never would be any conflict. The neurotic needs only the positive pleasure releases and these are the easiest things to choose — after they have been made available, through restrictions. The *paradox* turns every improvement attempt into its conflicting opposite.

Psychologists recognize the "self-perpetuating and self-defeating" nature of the conflict (O. H. Mowrer).[23] Logical theories, seeking explanations in difficulties of choice, are untenable. They may use various combinations of concepts of approach and avoidance, to show how one goal or desire may conflict with other goals or fears (C. T. Morgan, J. Dollard and N. E. Miller).[2,4] But all life consists of making such choices. We face every hour far more important conflicts of choice than are the silly preoccupations of the neurotic or psychotic. Exactly the idle person living without any real problems to solve suffers from the "conflicts" most extensively. The dominant fact in all disorders is the self-perpetuation of the deepening impoverishment, "the persistence and recurrence of abnormal psychological manifestations" (A. H. Maslow).[32] As if under an evil spell, the person worsens his plight by his very efforts to improve it. Only the paradox of overadjustment, which turns pleasure into its opposite, or improvement into a worsening, can explain this.

The very *personality of neurotics and psychotics* ensures that the overadjustment, with its vicious circle, perpetuates itself. The main characteristics of the neurotic are "over-driven striving" and "protective traits" (R. W. White).[3] Naturally the striving is for the pleasurable satisfactions; and the protection, against negative reactions and aftereffects. The neurotic strives to do everything perfectly, to be flawless, to impress everybody, to dominate, to relieve bodily urges and to protect himself against anxieties (A. H. Maslow).[32] In psychoanalytic terms, the neurotic is too much dependent on the pleasure principle (I. Hendrick).[32]

The psychotics have not only the tendency to overenjoy their experiences, but the full capacity to do so. Their self-created inner world, with every enjoyment naturally in it, replaces the reality (E. A. Strecker).[5] The psychotic "lives in a world of his own making", a world of "fantasy carried too far" (C. T. Morgan).[4] He "gives himself over to daydreaming", and has lost contact with reality (E. R. Hilgard).[5] Of course the dream reality that the psychotic creates contains every pleasure he wants. Incidentally, psychologists find that daydreaming is a "harmless device for satisfying needs" and therefore a positive factor.[4]

It has to be added that one can overenjoy doing or having something as well as not doing or not having something. Hypochondria is a typical reaction of the *overenjoyment of not having or of avoiding* a disease. As the opposite reactions, the feelings of having the disease accumulate, through the vicious-circle effect, it may seem that the hypochondriac deliberately invents them, as

if wanting them. Phobias are aftereffects of overenjoyed avoidances, therefore appear equally mysterious. Obsessions and compulsions grow from overenjoyments of avoidances as well as
from enjoyment of perfectionistic performances. There can be
various combinations of kinds of overenjoyments. But the simple
end-result is that a neurosis or psychosis, like an evil mimicry,
consists of everything the person least wants to feel or do.
Strange, new forms of such negative mimicry may evolve as
soon as people invent new overenjoyments. Recently, obsessive
reactions of loss of identity, or of alienation are being discovered[19]
— because search for enjoyment of identity or of avoidance of
alienation has become a fixational fashion.

Overadjustment or overenjoyment explains the complexity of
syndromes as well as the simplicity of the general cause of functional mental disorders. This cause is the extreme negativity of
feelings or impoverishment of releases. That is why *one simple
drug*, like chlorpromazine or cortisone, may "cure", temporarily,
almost every one of the functional diseases.[16] A mental disorder
never appears when there are plenty of positive feelings or
releases. The psychotic has his faculties intact,[8] and his only
plight is a desperate struggle with a deepening negativity of
unwanted, compulsive feelings and reactions.

But the only way an organic negativity can deepen beyond bounds is the *vicious-circle overadjustment*. Without it, a
person can suffer severest adversities and still adjust to them
normally, by suffering equally severe restrictions in the life flow
and thus accumulating the needed release reserves. Conversely,
one can enjoy every ease of well-being and still drive himself
into release impoverishment. This happens if one spends more
of the releases than the situation warrants — than is normal according to the incredibly complex but precise correspondence
between internal releases and external fact values, psychological
or physiologic, by which normal adjustment is maintained.

Neurotic Reactions, of Anxiety, Obsession-Compulsion, Phobia, Neurasthenia, Hypochondria and Depression

Neuroses are perfect illustrations of the *opposite causation in action* — of negative reactions originating, and deepening in a vicious-circle way, through overadjustments or overenjoyments. Because the opposite or relative causation is never even suspected in modern psychiatry, and is contrary to its "scientific" logic, neuroses have remained mysteries as to their very nature and causes. There are as many theories and explanations as there are psychologists and psychiatrists. The only agreements are, as we saw, the alchemistic assumptions about negative reactions coming from some negative experience; about gravest emotions originating from unconscious, weightless ideas; or about people learning to torment themselves. At the same time it is clear, even under any given psychiatric theory, that the fundamental mechanism or cause of neuroses is general or common to all of them. As such it must be deriving from a natural principle, which can be only elementarily simple — as is the overadjustment.

Anxiety Reactions. These reactions are the most frequent form of neurosis; and anxiety is a component in all other neuroses. This is so because most satisfactions are conditioned ultimately on the *feeling of security* or survival. Thus overenjoyment of any satisfaction or value in our life has to bring the *opposite feeling,* the anxiety. Since the enjoyment of the satisfactions of security is so general, it is never noticed as anything particular and is merely felt as a pleasure in whatever we do. Overenjoyment of this feeling is attained through every one of the improvements in life and is as unnoticed.

Therefore the anxiety — upon the overenjoyment — seems to appear from nowhere, as a ghost phenomenon, without cause. Hence the endless mystifications about anxiety and its causes. No explanation fits as long as the paradoxical logic of the relative causation is not understood. The theorists rather blame all kinds of negatively felt experiences, exactly contrary to the real cause, the overenjoyment through the satisfactions of security or of survival needs.

Actually the *opposite causes of anxiety* are evident from simplest facts. Use of drugs and intoxication lead, upon discontinuation, to a virtual anxiety neurosis, but are resorted to for overcoming of anxiety. The most general proof of the opposite causation of anxiety is our Age of Anxiety itself. Never have people enjoyed more of everything they have always wanted — of all the values and feelings ultimately rooted in the security and survival pleasures. But never have men suffered more from anxiety, which fifty years ago was not even known as a problem.[7] Some theorists specializing in anxiety have noted that "normal anxiety" has to be suffered in order to avoid anxiety disorders (R. May, V. E. Frankl).[7,9] But the explanations given for this seeming paradox are still based on logical speculations about growth, death, "existential vacuum" or philosophical meaning of existence.[9]

Anxiety has been analyzed in endless discussions, though as a uniform common phenomenon it can have only one natural, therefore simple principle as its cause. This cause is not seen because the logic of the relative or opposite causation has remained unthinkable. Confusion is increased by the fact that mostly the *ideas and ideational contents* appearing together with anxiety are studied to explain it. The real determining factor the economy of feelings, never becomes the object of study, because feelings make no sense if their reversed causal logic is not understood. Most forms of analysis and psychotherapy, as well as most theories, from psychoanalysis to existential psychology, deal only with the ideational causes. They have made such concepts as alienation, self or identity the centers of attention.

In truth, the ideas in anxiety are purely accidental. Everybody can see that an irritated or morbid person will blame as reason of his irritation or as explanation of his morbidity anything that happens to be in his way. The first thing he accidentally meets with may become, by fixation, the center and the seeming essence of his whole system of preoccupations.

It is not the psychologically weightless ideas or philosophic existential concerns, but grave and deep organic impoverishment that is the source of anxiety. Psychologists know that anxiety is as physically concrete as asphyxiation or drug withdrawal. It is actually a *slow death, as the opposite of the overenjoyment of the life flow* itself through its controlling feelings of security or survival. And it is as simple causally as is any uniform natural phenomenon, even death. The opposite causation would be easy to observe; one only needs to look at anxiety after any excessive or artificial enjoyment. But the causal logic that the most positively felt experiences can be causes of as negative reactions is still the last thing a psychiatrist or anybody is ready to accept.

Obsessive-Compulsive Reactions. The very essence of these reactions is that the person suffers from feelings and *reactions exactly opposite to those he wants or strives for most*. This is, as we saw, the universal way the opposite causation works. In a typical obsession the man who cultivates the most loving thoughts about his wife and children is suffering from ideas that he may do horrible things to them.[32] Under the compulsive reactions, the housewife who strives to enjoy perfect cleanliness of her home finds it so unclean that she has to dust it twice a day. In a typical overenjoyment of not doing something, a neurotic noticing a stone in the yard is striving so excessively not to be concerned about it that he ends by going out and turning the stone over.[32] The person excessively wanting not to say "hippopotamus" is compelled to pronounce the word.[10]

All theories on the obsessive-compulsive reactions try to find explanations for the observed *opposite* emotions and reactions. Oversolicitous love or idealistic perfectionism is assumed to be a disguise for aggressive inner wishes or hidden hostility.[3,11] Mechanisms of reaction-formation, displacement and symbolism are seen as devices for hiding or abreacting repressed opposite drives.[12,13] The child avoiding cracks in the pavement assumedly wants rather than fears to "break mother's back."[11]

Of course an obsession is only an aftereffect, a phantom, and has no real motivation in it. The mother obsessed with the idea that she may kill her children is furthest away from doing so.

She is like the man standing on a cliff who is gripped by the feeling that he may jump off, exactly because he exaggerates his feelings not to do so. Neurotics obsessed with the idea of suicide never commit it (E. A. Strecker).[6] In obsessions "the possibility of these thoughts being carried out in action is virtually nil" (E. R. Hilgard).[5]

An obsessive idea, however, can have a direct effect through a further automatic reaction. Schematically, the man on the cliff overstrains the muscles that keep him from leaning out, so much that they give in and he falls off. In reality complex combinations of such secondary reactions and primary aftereffects produce complex compulsions, tics and mannerisms — through a simple principle. Whether the neurotic overenjoys an act or avoidance, he ends by feeling and doing what he wants least, as if he were obsessed by an evil spirit. Every overdriven mechanism has to reverse.

The compulsive *preoccupation with nonsensical detail* is revealing. It may look like a mysterious "displacement on the smallest thing or ceremonialization of behavior".[32] The neurotic or psychotic starts with a tiny, meaningless thing or act because he does not have available important potentials. These can be accumulated only through restrictions, which the psychotic cannot bear. He uses the easiest acts, like cracking knuckles, tensing muscles or improving breathing, which are found to give some release.[5] But the very capacity of the psychotic to obtain releases through the smallest, easiest thing becomes his trap. The tiny acts, so easy and pleasant at beginning, become through the vicious-circle aftereffects sources of as great distress as were the first enjoyments. Every distressing aftereffect then has to be compensated, by further additions of the easy, tiny performances, so that a complex ritual results. Evidently, such additions only deepen the distress, but none of them can be abandoned, as we have explained before.

Obsessive-compulsive reactions are perfectionistic desperate attempts to improve a situation that is becoming worse at every turn. There is a progressively increasing elaboration of improvements on one side, and a malignantly self-deepening negativity in all the aspired feelings and reactions, on the other. Clearly the overadjustment with its vicious-circle effects is the cause. This would not be difficult to understand, considering that every positively-felt excess has to bring a negative reverse. But the relative, opposite causal logic remains unthinkable.

Instead, explanations are sought through theories about person-like hidden agencies that scheme, deceive, conceal, choose symbolic performances or otherwise act against the person's will. Of course the *"ingeniousness" of reactions* here is particularly glaring, because the improvements are added in as ingenious ways by the perfectionistic neurotic. The obsessive-compulsive reactions are the clearest examples of how a person brings on himself through overadjustment the feelings and reactions he excessively starts to combat or wants least.

Phobic Reactions. *Overenjoyment of avoidances* is the cause of phobias. It is only logical that enjoyments can consist of enjoying the positive as well as avoiding the negative. The neurotic overenjoys, in perfectionistic ways, the avoidance of what can be feared or loathed. The decisive factor is not actual danger from the thing feared but opportunity to avoid it repeatedly, so that the vicious circle continues working. The most ordinary things one meets with *constantly,* like closed spaces, crowds, streets, insects, germs, cats, cars or bridges, become objects of phobias. They may be ridiculously innocent in comparison with really dangerous things. The neurotic may fear a dangerous thing, but he does not develop phobia about it, if there is no opportunity for avoiding it repeatedly, through constant encounters.

It is the vicious-circle accumulation of overenjoyments of the repeated avoidances that deepens the fear to incredible degree.

Everybody knows that the overprotected child starts fearing, unreasonably, smallest dangers. Such overprotection is intensified by the neurotic many times over, and produces so much greater unreasonable fear. He may start with enjoyment of safety and comforts of home, which is natural. But as such safety is overenjoyed, the unsafety of street becomes more felt, as a contrast. If this unsafety is then avoided by even stronger enjoyments of home, it becomes still more felt and the safety of home is sought and overenjoyed even more. The point is that any, incredible degree of negativity can be reached by nothing more than constant accumulation of positively felt overenjoyments. The mystery here is complete, because nobody can ever accept that by securing and enjoying more safety he gets more of the opposite feeling of unsafety — as the overprotected child does. What applies here to the feeling of safety applies to all the varied and interwoven feelings and reactions the neurotic lives with.

Not surprisingly, psychologists find that phobias are the most difficult reactions to explain — that they "do not seem to have rational basis".[11] Mystery is compounded as separate causes are sought for each of the endless kinds of phobias. According to an often invoked explanation, a woman fears the street because she is afraid to become a streetwalker. Or a man fears "high" places because they symbolize the "superiority of father". Even the "fear to be eaten by father" may be claimed as cause.[12] Also it may be concluded that the person evolves a phobia to obtain love, dominate other people, or prevent himself from going places.[32]

Even learning or conditioning have been assumed as causes, though the prominent authorities on the learning theory, J. Dollard and N. E. Miller, admit that "further research is needed".[2] Phobias are totally *unpleasant* and *useless*. But one learns something or develops a habit for it only if it is *pleasant*; and conditioning is a hard process evolved for some *useful* purpose. Nobody in the world learns something that is unpleasant and useless.

The extreme force of the unfounded fears or aversions in phobias is mystifying. From where could it come? It cannot be explained in logical natural ways, because it is so unreasonable, useless and unwanted. The mystery will persist as long as it is not realized that the strongest human drive, the striving for pleasure, in its excessive form of overadjustment, becomes a vicious-circle source of the opposite, strangely unrecognizable, negative reactions here as in other disorders.

Neurasthenia. The tiredness, irritability and feeling of pain in neurasthenia are easily understandable as the deepening opposite effects of excitement, gratification and avoidance of pain. Whereas hard work gives pleasant rest, overenjoyed activity has to lead to stressful, irritating fatigue. It is noted that neurotics can be very energetic but that fatigue takes over (R. W. White).[3] Typically neurasthenia has been called "American disease" (C. T. Morgan).[4] This country offers the best opportunities for excitement and pleasure, which are opposites of neurasthenic reactions. Expectedly, theories of unconscious intents and conflicts have been used to explain neurasthenia. They are here clearly incongruous, because neurasthenia is a physiologically concrete impoverishment, requiring as concrete physiologic causes.

Hypochondria. Not having diseases is a satisfaction, which for the neurotic easily becomes a source of overenjoyment. Then the vicious circle starts its endless course. As the opposite reaction, the feeling of having disease arises, it is compensated by even stronger satisfaction of not having it. Of course the progressively deepened feeling of disease soon becomes the dominant emotion, while the satisfaction potential has become exhausted.

Then it may seem that the hypochondriac has no other wishes than to feel the symptoms of his imagined disease — *that he wants to have them* (K. A. Menninger). This is now a generally accepted view.[8] In truth the hypochondriac, like anybody else, is deeply disturbed by the disease he feels. That is why he goes to the extensive trouble in seeking the relief. He cannot help feeling as concrete and painful reactions and symptoms of disease as were his *exaggerated* enjoyments of not feeling the disease and not having its symptoms.

Depression. The intensified enjoyment of excitement in moddern life inevitably produces equally intense and frequent reactions of depression. The neurotic, incapable of bearing such negative reactions, fends them off with increased improvements and thus starts the vicious-circle deepening of the depression. The excessive striving for gratifications and avoidance of all negative feelings by the neurotic is generally noted.[32] Ambivalence of emotions and hostility turned against oneself are sought as explanations for the dual and opposite nature of the reactions.[11] The progressively deepening depression, however, soon becomes the dominant reaction. Then it may seem again that the neurotic somehow wants or insists on having the negative reactions, that he is "happier with his psychoneurosis than he would be without it" (W. S. Taylor).[32]

Some other forms of neurotic reactions, like the "Christmas Blues" or Sunday and Vacation neuroses, are equally typical of the interdependence of excitement and depression.

All the neuroses we have looked at arise through the opposite causation, that is, excessive enjoyments and as deep negative aftereffects. There is *nothing unconscious* about them. Surely the aftereffects are "ingenious" and persistent, as if some person-like agency invented and enforced them against the neurotic's will. But as we have repeatedly explained, this is so because the neurotic strives for his oversatisfactions as ingeniously and intensively. Now we may turn to the neuroses that are unconsciously caused.

The Only Unconscious Neuroses: Hysteric and Dissociative Reactions

The hysteric and dissociative reactions are the only neuroses that are unconsciously caused. It is natural that there be two different kinds of neuroses. For *there are two different ways of how man adjusts, and overadjusts* — always under the pleasure drive. The one way is by active striving, with full conscious use of capacities; the other, by passivity, abandonment, or self-paralyzing "freezing", which is instinctive in animals in face of danger. This second way is, understandably, much rarer. But a neurotic facing an unbearable or horrifying situation may resort to a kind of self-hypnosis in order to block out the experience, even if this may require paralysis of whole areas of functions.

We mentioned the monumental error started by Freud in interpreting the first case of psychoanalysis, the girl treated by him and Breuer. This error amounts to the assumption that *because horrible experiences are repressed* by man, in crippling unconscious ways, he will repress in similar ways his *pleasures or natural drives*. This is particularly impossible because the unconscious life is governed completely by pleasure. But this blunder has remained the basis of the Freudian theory and of modern psychiatry. Liberation of repressed pleasures like the libido has become the logical goal in psychiatry.

Actually the opposite, the forcing on the neurotic of the unpleasant emotions which he avoids is the way to cure all disorders, as it clearly is for curing the hysteric reactions. The negative emotions to be forced on the hysteric are often so intense that psychiatrists do not dare to induce the whole recall in a single session.[11] Naturally, after the unwanted and avoided experience is lived through in full the patient has nothing more to block and the hysteric paralysis disappears. Probably the most successful cures in the whole history of psychiatry have been obtained in this way, notably during the last World War. But even in this kind of treatment confusion is brought in, particularly because many reactions which are not hysteric are treated as such. Psychiatrists are not sure when and why the treatment works. As Menninger says, "it does not always work this way, but it does sometimes — often enough to make this treatment an extremely promising one."[32]

The hysteric reactions are *completely different* from the other neurotic reactions, with which they are often confused. First, they are wanted by the hysteric, as shown by the *belle indifference* with which he accepts them, whereas all other neurotic reactions are the most undesired things for the neurotic. Secondly, the hysteric reactions are mechanistically simple causally. They are mere omissions, failures to respond or gross blockings of an area of functions: amnesias, paralyses, anesthesias. In contrast, the other neurotic reactions are endlessly "ingenious". As Strecker points out, hysterias are simple, "complacent laissez-faire affairs" in comparison with the similarly physiological neurasthenic reactions.[6] If the hysteric reactions become complex, or rather extensive, it is because of the very grossness of the blocking in the nerve centers. Thirdly, these are the only neuroses that are cured, perfectly, by use of hypnosis[13] — because they are caused by a kind of self-hypnosis.

The unconscious process by which the hysteric reactions are induced is a *self-hypnosis,* as has long been recognized, since the time of Charcot and Janet. Hypnosis is amazingly effective in producing the amnesias, paralyses, anesthesias or the shrinking of peripheral sensations, that are typical of hysteric reactions. Obviously self-hypnosis is a difficult, tricky procedure. But the hysteria sufferers are exactly persons who have long previous practice in similar escape techniques (C. T. Morgan).[4] They are "experts" in devious avoidance practices (N. A. Cameron).[32]

The blocking of threat or horror, past, present or future can have most confusing effects because of the gross interference with the extremely delicate and complexly interwoven brain mechanisms and mental associations. In a typical shell shock case, a soldier suffered paralysis of an arm, because at the moment the shell exploded he was throwing a grenade. To block the recall of it all, the innervation centers for the arm movement had also to be blocked. Generally, the hysteric symptoms affect the "organic system that was highly active at the moment of acute crisis" (R. W. White).[3] Due to the grossness of blocking, a paralysis of leg, for instance, may also affect speech because of the closeness of the brain centers. Or the person may want a mere disability, but due to grossness of associations the whole system of previous illness or disorders may be adopted.

But psychologists are *assuming separate causes* for each one of the endless symptoms. This assumption is as general as is the name "conversion reactions", used for these neuroses. Supposedly, inner unconscious conflicts, ideas, phantasies or anxiety are converted into the hysteric reactions, mostly in symbolic disguise. However, it is generally known, from clinical observations, that the hysteric patient adeptly changes his symptoms according to his observations of what others say about similar reactions, what the doctor does during examination or what symptoms other patients around happen to have.[14] The causal confusion is increased by the fact that many reactions are, naturally, mixtures of the usual neurotic reactions, caused by overadjustment, with the hysteric reactions.

Thus the "mass hysterias" are mostly aftereffects of psychological overadjustments, often spreading in a chain-reaction way. As one person sees reactions of others, he overstrains those mechanisms which keep him from having such reactions and ends by having them. Even the "grand" hysteria may be an aftereffect of overadjustment. Freud pointed out that the reflexes and movements in this hysteria resembled those of sexual act. If sexual reactions have been excessively repressed they are bound to break out. But such excessive repression can accumulate only if it has become an enjoyment. The Victorian women were apt to *overenjoy* their virtuousness of sexual restrains, therefore suffered the aftereffects. The "dancing manias" of the 15th and 16th centuries may have originated in similar overenjoyments of restrictive virtuousness.

Typical true hysteric reactions are *Amnesia* and *Fugue*. Because of an unbearable situation, the person lapses into forgetting who he is, wanders off and lives for months indifferent to such fate. A fugue lasting three years has been recorded.[12] The mechanism here is a simple discontinuance, blocking or notdoing, requiring no complexity.

Double Personality has a similar simple explanation. Psychiatrists have observed that changes in levels of stress and release produce startling changes in personality.[6] All people have cyclic fluctuations in such levels. But the neurotic exaggerates the release periods, and thus brings on himself so much stronger restrictive periods. During the strong release period he may be liberal, outgoing, unrestrained immature or licentious; but during the restrictive period, moralistic, strict or overmature. As the two periods alternate repeatedly, each accumulates into a way of life, conflicting with the other. To avoid the conflict, the person induces amnesia of one period while living in the other. Double personality evolves gradually and is not so dramatic as popularly believed.[4] More than two personalities may be observed if fluctuations in different release functions occur at different periods.

The important fact about the hysteric reactions is that they are desired by the patient. They become expressions of pleasure mechanisms, which govern all our unconscious reactions. That is why they can perfectly operate unconsciously, once induced by the hypnotic autosuggestion. This is particularly easy because the hysteric reactions are elementarily simple blockings or omissions of functions.

In contrast, it is inconceivable how any mechanism working against pleasure drive could ever exist or operate on the unconscious level; or how any complex, reflective and ingenious mechanism could evolve unconsciously. But Freud assumed all this as possible, when he adopted the unconcious, hysteric causation as the basis for all psychiatry. This is a blunder contrary to the very first fact of psychic life, to the distinction between pleasure and displeasure. It amounts to *an assumption that men would seek the tortures of disorders or denial of pleasures as intensively as they seek avoidance of painful horrifying experiences.* And this is to take place, of all things, on the unconscious level where only primitive pleasure drives govern. Yet this blunder has become the basis of modern psychiatry, which has accepted the unconscious causation for all disorders.

Schizophrenia

In schizophrenia, the most frequent and typical psychosis, the *opposite causation* is clearly evident. It is generally known that drugs, particularly the mind-expanding and stimulant drugs produce aftereffects which are similar to schizophrenia.[15,16] As White says, the aftereffects are "clearly analogous to a moderately acute schizophrenic episode with considerable turmoil and confusion".[3] The theory is that the drugs "trigger the underlying, hidden psychosis or personality disturbance".[17]

Any theory can merely add to confusion if the opposite causal logic is not understood. The same stimulating, tranquilizing or mind-expanding drugs that cause such symptoms are used to cure schizophrenia because they provide immediate temporary improvements.[16] Such temporary cures can be induced by drugs as well as by organic stimulants like cortisone or even niacin (A. Hoffer). The opposite causation explains why the means which improves releases directly is also bound to lead to their exhaustion. It does not matter whether the "improvement" in releases is obtained by external means or by what already Kraepelin called "autointoxication".[14] The person wants the drug for nothing else but the inner pleasure release. Here we come to the core of schizophrenia.

The schizophrenic has the *unique capacity of enjoying his inner pleasure releases directly,* at will, without a need for real or justified stimulation. This is observable as his ability and tendency to live with his ideas as if they were realities.[4,14] He creates for himself an inner world in which he, naturally, permits himself the deepest gratifications,[6] in form of ideational constructs as well as simple primitive release reactions. It has to be kept in mind that even a slight "capacity" to increase the releases can lead, through *long* vicious-circle accumulation, to the deepest impoverishment or extreme negative reactions.

Also, nothing in that increasingly negative world can be abandoned even if it has become only a burden and a fantastic monstrosity. We explained that exactly a capacity to derive enjoyment from easiest, tiny acts leads to the weird world of endless mannerisms and "meaningless" preoccupations. Since the schizophrenic overenjoys everything he feels or does, he ends by suffering every reaction of anxiety, obsession, compulsion, "tic", phobia, hypochondria, depression or fear, to a progressively deepening, excessive degree.

The capacity and, naturally, the tenacious persistence of the schizophrenic to live in the "world of his own making" has been generally recognized (C. T. Morgan). His "capacity to make thoughts however fantastic seem real" is viewed as his main weapon of defense (E. A. Strecker). He transforms the world, by autistic phantasies, when it does not yield gratifications.[14] The schizophrenic lives "like one lost in his dreams" (W. S. Taylor).[32] Of course it has to remain a mystery, in modern psychiatry, how this world of most positive enjoyments can lead to the deep psychic impoverishment that is the direct cause of schizophrenia.

It is argued that while fantasy is a "harmless device for satisfying needs" for normal people, the schizophrenic carries it too far.[4] Also the fact is blamed that unreality becomes real for the schizophrenic.[6] But logically, the more real such world, the greater the satisfactions; and as long as one has enough satisfactions there can be no psychotic reactions. It is also argued that by giving himself over to daydreaming the schizophrenic becomes careless and neglects his practical life. The vicious-circle deepening of the reactions is explained as a result of using a withdrawal in compensation for failures which, in turn, increase with the withdrawal.[32] Or the withdrawal is seen as increasing because the person starts fearing what others would think if they knew his thoughts.[3] But the schizophrenic is least worried about his practical life, failures, or opinion of others.[14] He may remain indifferent to financial loss, death of intimates or imprisonment, while getting upset beyond reason by a trivial disturbance in his daily routine[14] — because this interrupts his fixational inner enjoyments.

The personality of the schizophrenic clearly reveals his excessive striving for inner enjoyments as well as his capacity to obtain them. His main characteristics are "defective inhibition"[8] and intense tenacity in holding to his inner world of his own making[6] — which is for him the ready source of releases. The absence of restrictions is apparent from his lack of shame, his exhibitionism, looseness in sex behavior, fantasies of grandeur and lowest personal habits or moral controls (J. C. Coleman).[32]

His persistence to live within his inner world is his strongest, permanent personality trait. Already as a child he lives in his dream world, is seclusive, shy, reserved, diffident and secretive.[6] He has low tolerance for unpleasant realities or hardships of life, for discomforts, pain or fear.[3]

The *immediate cause* of schizophrenia is clearly an extreme emotional impoverishment or negativity, with its incredibly strong, most unwanted, compulsive and weird feelings, and reactions of the evil mimicry, that the opposite causation always brings, through overadjustment. The schizophrenic has not lost his other mental capacities, as numerous studies show;[32] and a simple release-increasing drug can restore, temporarily, his normal reactions.[16,17] The opposite causation is mechanistically simple here, as elsewhere; but because its causal logic is the last thing psychiatrists would accept, they are bound to look in the completely wrong direction. They rather blame the restrictive behavior of the schizophrenic and his apparent refusal to enjoy or "free" himself.[1] Surely schizophrenia amounts to an extreme restriction: the organism imposes it to counteract the overexpenditure and depletion of releases.

The central point is that every functional disease, as a natural reaction, is the pressure by the organism toward normalcy. As Dr. R. D. Laing, writing from his own experiences explains, schizophrenia has to be let to run its course; and its madness is the very way back to normalcy.[19] In his numerous impressive writings he shows how completely misdirected and confused modern psychiatry has become in its effort to suppress psychoses directly.

It is truly amazing that schizophrenia has become an *increasing mystery* — in spite of enormous efforts to explain it — though it has a common uniform, therefore necessarily simple natural cause. The number of varied and controversial explanations for it has increased to the extent that a book would be required merely to describe them.[8] It is clear that schizophrenia consists of *physiologically concrete* effects — as all overadjustment aftereffects do. Yet the vast research, by numerous, best authorities, has not produced one acceptable explanation of what is causally happening. Psychiatrists themselves are puzzled by this lack of success.[8] Thus, probably the most clearly physiologic mental disorder seems to arise "without any known physiological basis"[4] and no accepted conclusions about the biochemical processes involved have been reached.[8]

The reason is the paradoxical causal logic of functional diseases. Everything that seems to improve the condition, through direct increase in releases, actually worsens it, and vice versa. This applies to every detail, in every function, process or biochemical reaction the psychiatrists are dealing with. At every step the research shows as cause of schizophrenia what is actually the only way toward recovery from it. Or it shows as means of remedy the very factors that increase it in the end. This reversed logic can lead to incredible confusion because of the endless complexity and multiplicity of the biochemical processes involved, particularly since the "scientific" methods are centered on such processes alone, instead of the integrated, causally revealing pleasure economy.

In the absence of causal understanding, the *mysteries of unconscious causation* are sought as explanations. Symbolism is accepted even by sober psychologists, notwithstanding the deeply physiologic nature of the reactions.[3] Similarly, ulterior unconscious motives are invoked. The schizophrenic, supposedly, wants to punish himself, impress others or escape blame.[32] His necessarily restrictive reactions are interpreted as fear to show emotions.[1] All kinds of unconscious, symbolic mechanisms are blamed and psychoanalysis is used to discover the hidden meanings of the various symptoms.[11] Symbolic or unconscious regression is often invoked. Factually the schizophrenic's "regression" to more primitive forms of functioning is due to the recession of psychic energy from the more refined, branched-out, later-conditioned pathways. His maladjustments are "retreats from the intricate adaptation required in dealing effectively with reality" (E. G. Boring).[32] It is an alchemistic mystery how the symbolic, never really felt unconscious intents and fantasies could produce the deep physiologic changes.

Surely the schizophrenic reactions are bizarre and irrational as well as intensely persistent, seeming to have a purposive meaning of their own. But we saw how incredibly intense, weird and "ingenious" the negative reactions become under the opposite causation and the vicious circle. The person ends by feeling and doing, compulsively, what he wants or intends least in the world, and the "ingenuity" of such reactions is as vast as were his efforts in obtaining the overenjoyments.

The intensity of any negative emotion can deepen, as we saw, through the vicious circle of overadjustment to a staggering degree, by nothing more than constant added "improvements". But under an extreme negative emotion, such as fear, suspicion or hypochondriac feeling, even an otherwise normal person would behave like a schizophrenic. The mind-expanding and stimulating drugs can create such negativity only partially. But even their aftereffects can become weird distortions of reality, hallucinations, stupor, "regression" or similar reactions resembling schizophrenia.[15]

The only main alternative to the mystifications of the unconscious causation is the *learning theories*.[5] They seem to be preferred by the more conservative psychiatrists and underlie the more sober, generally practiced psychiatry in the vein of the system of treatment established by Adolf Meyer.[13] It stresses the exploring and analyzing of the patient's past, of his previous faulty learning, then providing him with new ways of learning and insights.[18] This amounts to acceptance of the major fallacies of modern psychology, particularly of the alchemy of gravest reactions arising from mere ideas and their associations, which are the objects of the analysis and new insights. Such ideas and associations are purely accidental for the disorders. Further, the "scientific" causal logic, contrary to what is causally true, is used in such analyses and treatments. Above all, it is accepted that one can learn or be conditioned to torment himself with most unpleasant as well as useless reactions.

In conclusion it may be noted that the problem of schizophrenia, the gravest of all mental disorders, reveals the complete confusion of modern psychiatry. Schizophrenia is a simple and clear expression of deepest psychic impoverishment or negativity that results, as clearly, from equally deep overadjustments or overenjoyments by the unrestrained or psychically weak and autistic schizophrenic. But the modern psychiatry proceeds only by the direct "scientific" logic of more positivism from more satisfactions or releases. Thus everything is seen in *ways contrary to what is causally true*. A simple look at the overenjoyments through drugs and their aftereffects, which so strikingly resemble schizophrenia, could have helped.

As the general simple cause is missed, endless explanations are sought for each of the countless reactions, through the analysis and study of ideational associations and learning, which are purely accidental or causally weightless. Thus *all the alchemy of unconscious and symbolic causation, and the learning of self-torture*, are brought in. Moreover, the extensive researches in the biochemically concrete reactions only deepen the confusion as the reversedly wrong causal logic is applied at every step. In schizophrenia the intensity and "ingenuity" of the reversals reach extremes, as every positive, excessive striving results in its "ghostly", unrecognizable and malignantly self-deepening opposite. The relative or opposite causation offers a simple and mechanistic explanation of it hall. But the modern psychiatry moves into increasing confusion as it proceeds by the exactly contrary, "scientific" logic and way of thinking.

Paranoia

Opposite reactions clearly dominate the paranoid personality. The paranoiac's excessive feelings of his own power or grandeur turn into as excessive *opposite feelings* of helpless danger or persecution. It is generally known that "delusions of grandeur are, indeed, almost invariably accompanied by delusions of persecution".[14] The generally accepted explanation of paranoia includes the opposites. It is held that the paranoiac infers his grandeur from his "observation" that he is so much persecuted and talked about. Thus mere logical inferences are accepted as causes of grave reactions.

A correlate set of *opposites* in paranoia is a great attachment or love and trust on one side, and the fear, hateful mistrust or feeling of being persecuted by the best friends on the other.[12] This attachment or "love" is so marked in paranoia that it has been repeatedly mistaken for homosexuality, by Freudians as well as other psychiatrists.[12] Of course the "love" here is the enjoyment of the most important emotion for man as a social being, namely, the sense of security in facing other men. This emotion is the basis of social conditioning, and is little noticed exactly because it is so general. Paranoia is the psychosis that afflicts the highly conditioned, intellectual person, who has high goals and broad interests as well as the tendency to be superior.[5,6]

However, we have to keep in mind that here, as in other disorders, the positive overenjoyment part in the causation is not always clearly noticed. The exaggerated positive background, whether it lies in the past or runs parallel to the disorder, always appears as a very normal, positive adjustment. It may not be noticed also because it is continuously there as the tenaciously sustained permanent overadjustment. But the unexpectedly emerging contrasting negative opposite is sharply felt. Its appearance may begin when the overall releases, spent in the overadjustment, start failing due to a general, often physiologic setback. It is known that paranoiac reactions appear with age, upon exhaustive illness, use of drugs, or other exhaustion, which as we saw, can deepen only through overadjustment.

Typically, the aftereffects of stimulants are almost undistinguishable from paranoiac reactions. In the classical treatise on *Amphetamine Psychosis,* P. H. Connell concludes that "the clinical picture is primarily a paranoid psychosis with ideas of reference, delusions of persecution, auditory and visual hallucinations".

The vicious circle deepens the paranoiac reactions where the positive emotions of the grandeur and "love" continue to be enjoyed, as in paranoid schizophrenia. As the fantasy of self-greatness is being overenjoyed the opposite feeling deepens and requires still greater enjoyment of grandeur. The paranoiac thus may claim to be an emperor and still fear the charwoman. Since it all is emotionally deep, it is for him as real as life. He feels that he has reached the status of Napoleon, and he cannot renounce one bit in it without painful descent from that level, though it is already bringing him nothing but continuous distress. Actually even a real-life status of an emperor would bring to an overenjoying person only trouble in the end and he equally could not renounce it. By the way, the delusions of being Napoleon, Messiah or Lincoln are not due to any mysterious externalization of prototypes of society, as expounded in some theories.[21] The psychotic merely takes the first or more frequent object or idea in starting his vicious-circle fixation.

Since the real causes of paranoia, the opposite backgrounds of overadjustment, are not seen, the symptoms must seem like ghost phenomena coming from nowhere. The usual mystifications about unconscious causes are resorted to. According to a standard explanation, first used by Freud, the paranoiac under his homosexual conflict unconsciously reasons: "I do not love him, I hate him; no, he hates me". And as a result of such merely rationalized conclusion, the overwhelming fear or oppressive feeling, opposite to that of love from others, is assumed to arise. Another standard explanation is hostility turned against oneself. Supposedly, "among the most dramatic manifestations of hostility turned against the self are persecutory paranoia" (L. J. Saul).[20] Thus a pleasure, the hating of others that a person enjoys, is turned into a torment by mere switch of direction. The opposite causation, which does reverse the emotion, is not suspected.

Other unconscious mechanisms like projection, displacement or substitution may be invoked in explanation; persecutor is seen as substitute for missed lover.[32] All this amounts to *the alchemy of gravest emotions arising from mere reasonings,* ideas, or arbitrary switches of pleasures into tortures, of all things, on the unconscious level. But the only alternative to such mysteries of the Unconscious are the learning theories. Somehow *the paranoiac learns to scare himself out of his wits* or develops a habit for it or is conditioned to it without any need or reason.

In truth, the opposite emotions, the enjoyment of security or of the feeling of total, subservient love from others, would be strived for by the psychotic a thousand times more intensely than any feelings of fear or persecution. All the unconscious drives and mechanisms as well as all learning and conditioning would be used by him to gain such pleasant, and useful, positive feelings, to the highest degree. Which is exactly what happens. But only the opposite causation can explain how the excessive striving for the positive enjoyment brings as deep, unwanted and utterly unrecognizable opposite reactions. Modern psychiatrists as scientists can never accept this self-evidently simple but seemingly paradoxical and "scientifically" unthinkable causation. The result is continued addition to the mystifications and incongruity.

Manic-Depressive Reactions and Involutional Melancholia

The very essence of the manic-depressive reactions is the *change of one psychic state into its opposite.* Psychiatrists recognize that the "elation and depression may be the opposite extremes of the same basic disorder".[4] But they are puzzled by the "gross differences of symptomatology" of the two states and their "mutually exclusive nature".[14] In practical terms it is revealing that the recent lithium treatment prevents the depressive stage *by suppressing the manic stage.* This treatment has been generally recognized and expanded. Dr. W. H. Stewart, as U. S. Surgeon General, reported that "lithium appears to be the best specific agent yet found for the treatment of any mental disease". But lithium has no effect on depressions when they are already on. It prevents depression only by suppressing the manic stage.

The alternation of the opposite states would be even clearer if psychiatrists paid more attention to the real causal factors, the emotions, rather than to external reactions. It is clear that a person may appear "manic" — excited, overactive or eccentric — under an acute distress as well as strong pleasure release. As a result, the present classifications into hypomanias, manias, hypermanias and as varied depressions are misleading. Further, *the exaggerated positive states are often not noticed* because intense positivism may appear as very normal adjustment. Also the positive state rarely appears with suddenness, because its causal source, the negative background is accumulated only very slowly or reluctantly. But the depressive state always breaks out with cataclysmic suddenness, for the converse reason. This is why clinical observations and statistics show, misleadingly, that there is less of the manic, and regular cyclothymic cases, or that the manic states are milder.[5]

Mystery is increased by the *absence here, as in all psychoses, of logical experimentally correlatable physiologic changes.* The reason is the paradox of functional diseases. The processes that cause directly the negative, restrictive symptoms actually bring the accumulation of releases or the cure in the end. Also, a stimulant in organism has lesser effect as it has become increased. Thus the drug user or the psychotic may have more than usual amount of stimulants in his blood and still be understimulated. It is revealing that manic-depressive psychosis is found to resemble morphine withdrawal and that no *logically explainable* physiologic changes are found in either.[14] Psychiatrists cannot understand why no physiologic explanations have been found for the clearly physiologic manic-depressive reactions.[37]

Expectedly, explanations are sought in unconscious conflicts and defense mechanisms: self-punishment, aggression turned against oneself, expiation of hostility, identifications with a dead person, flight from oppressive Superego, or repressed cry for love. Under the direct experimental or "scientific" logic, restrictive attitudes of the person are blamed for the negative, depressive symptoms, which are never connected with the manic, overenjoyment attitudes. Of course no real enjoyment is possible without concurrent restrictions. Therefore even the manic hyperactivity soon becomes "superficial" and yields "little true enjoyment."[21] For the same reason, cheering up the depressive with social distractions, parties, trips or new amusements "only serves to deepen the patient's depression".[14] *An exactly contrary treatment brings cure* — and is most revealing.

Shock treatment cures depression for good and without exceptions (if confusions in classification are taken into account). This is unique in psychiatry. But shock is the most negative impact that can be nonfatally inflicted on organism, since it comes close to the experience of death physiologically.[32] Psychiatrists frankly admit that shock treatment is contrary to everything they hold as true.[1,3] The unique success of this treatment reveals how completely contrary to facts are the beliefs and insights of modern psychiatry.

Involutional Melancholia is found to be "not essentially different from the depression in manic-depressive reactions"[11] or "closely related symptomatically to depression".[14] It is often regarded merely as a type of manic-depressive psychosis.[6] The regular alternations of elation and depression may be lacking, though they may be observed. But as we saw, it is only natural that the phase of positive overenjoyment passes unnoticed or is seen as a very normal state. The reactions of Melancholia are pessimism, lack of humor, rigidity, perfectionism, excessive moralism, sensitiveness and selfishness. They are easily explainable by psychic impoverishment and excessive restriction, which are typical aftereffects of overadjustment.

Here we may note that no amount of restrictiveness in life can produce psychic impoverishment. The more restriction there is, the more accumulation of releases results from it. But when one has adjusted to a gross spending in releases, any lesser spending, however high in nonrelative terms, will have the effects of release impoverishment. A drug user reduced to a lesser dose that would be still high for a nonuser would feel low.

In brief, only a previous background of overadjustment can produce the reactions of involutional melancholia. This however obeys the logic of opposite causation, which psychiatrists as scientists can never accept. They rather seek solutions in freer, direct increase in releases, and accept as explanations the mysteries of hidden unconscious life of conflicts, schemings, "bribings", identifications, self-torment or anal and oral erotism.[32] Physiologic causes and explanations are found as little here as in other physiologically clear psychoses, because the logic of opposite causation, applying to every detail, is the last thing scientists would suspect.

The Reverse Logic of Psychic Treatment

Mental diseases, as all functional disorders, grow from over-adjustment or increase in direct release improvements, which leads to the exhaustion of releases or to worsening, in the malignant, vicious-circle way. It is all a matter of the paradoxical economy of the releases of pleasure as the flow of life itself. We saw how one simple drug—chlorpromazine, meprobamate, iproniazid, or cortisone — can cure, temporarily, a whole series of functional diseases.[16] It does so by merely increasing the release flow.

We have to stress the reversed logic of opposite causation. It governs all organic value reactions, everything that constitutes apparent improvements or cures as well as worsening or diseases. But modern medicine and psychiatry know only the "scientific" causal logic of *treatments through added direct improvements — which actually foster overadjustments* and thus deepen the disorders in the end. This is the blunder of our scientific age, in which the most important sciences, those dealing with man himself, are still glaringly unscientific.

The direct improvement logic is so general in modern psychiatry that every known psychiatrist could be quoted in illustration. Direct improvement of feelings, in all forms, is constantly urged. Particularly the improvement of the basic feelings, like sense of security or freedom from guilt, is seen as the goal. But exactly the increase in basic satisfactions, that control the other, subordinate releases, opens way to overadjustments. All treatments, whether by psychotherapy, drugs or other means, are aimed at direct improvements. The opposite causation has never yet been mentioned, in any form. Even the methods of learning and conditioning merely aim at improved, easier adjustments, though only imposition of negatively-felt, hard restrictions could really help.

Certainly all such treatments by increase in releases provide initial relief, because the simple release impoverishment is the cause of all functional disorders. But the paradox of exhaustion of releases through their direct increase is inexorable. In brief, psychiatry sees direct improvements in releases as its goal, while exactly such improvements are the sources of overadjustments and their vicious-circle effects, by which mental disorders grow.

Psychotherapy. The most popular, but practically useless psychic treatment is psychotherapy. It embodies the pure alchemy of modern psychology: belief in potentials without equal restrictions, and acceptance of ideational associations as causes. If the opposite causation is not understood, it must seem that the lack of enjoyment of the pleasant and healthy positive reactions is due to ignorance, mistake or confusion. This of course could be perfectly corrected by *providing new insights,* upon analysis of the confusion. Which is what psychotherapy is intended to do. Practically it amounts to *talk and reasoning.* Since this is useless, as anyone with minimal insight knows, it all is surrounded by "scientific" complexity — clinically structured techniques and involved theories.

But the talk and permissiveness in psychotherapy help the patient to continue with the overadjustment, in some changed form. He is more than willing to find new ways of the positively felt overenjoyments. This then is welcomed as relief by the patient and as success by the therapist, though it only delays recovery, which the organism tries to reach through the natural reactions of the functional "disease". As research has advanced, accumulated statistical proofs show that psychotherapy does not improve "a patient's chances of recovery beyond what they would be without any formal therapy whatsoever".[22] The best compilation of statistical studies is probably that by Eysenck.[22] It shows that two thirds of patients recover by themselves without treatment or with any kind of therapy; but only 64% recover with psychotherapy, and a mere 44% with psychoanalysis.[21,22] As Maher points out, we are thus "compelled to draw the conclusion that psychotherapy is associated with lower rate of recovery than no psychotherapy at all!"[8] Mowrer concludes on basis of studies by Ausubel, Cartwright, Dollard, Eysenck, Massermann, Moreno and Ubell that for all forms of psychotherapy "the accomplishment is, in fact, nil" and that in view of the self-recovery "untreated controls seem to fare as well as the treated groups".[23] Mowrer adds that "all this, of course, is well known in professional circles and is gradually leaking through to the general public".

Understandably psychotherapists are now stressing the sub-jective improvement in feelings of their patients as the main achievement (A. T. Jersild).[32] Improvement in sexual gratifica-tions, as the readiest ones, is stressed even by non-Freudian therapists. Other improvements are aimed at sense of security, freedom from guilt, and creation of a permissive gratifying situa-tion.[23] Motherly love may be lavished on the patient, as in the Direct Analysis, or his distorted crazy world may be shared by the therapist, as in the Experiential Therapy.[24] Generally, the encouragement of license, in sexual as well as other feelings, is cultivated by most therapists.[24]

No wonder that the *Transference,* as the attachment to the therapist, becomes the main practical product of psychotherapy, so much so that it is now considered as the core of most psy-chotherapies.[11] The treatment becomes an excellent way of avoiding the natural, restrictive reactions of the "disease". This amounts to delaying real recovery. To the extent that psycho-therapy is a success, the neurotic starts "acting out" his con-flict and develops a graver psychopathy.[23] The patient feels, tem-porarily, better but becomes more difficult to live with.[11]

Increasing confusion and complexity are the inevitable re-sults. There are scores of different kinds of therapies, and ac-cording to the trend-setting theory of Carl Rogers "diagnosis, professional knowledge, and other frequently emphasized char-acteristics . . . may indeed be obstructive".[24] Harper concludes his book on thirty-six main therapies with the statement that in historic perspective "what we now call psychotherapy will re-late to scientific treatment and prevention of behavioral disorders as astrology now relates to astronomy".[24]

Psychotherapists deal with what is accidental and causally meaningless, even apart from the reversedly wrong causal logic they are using. As we have seen, the disturbed person may find anything he accidentally encounters, as the cause and reason for his ills and reactions. He may turn it into a veritable, "unconscious" core of all his psychic life by fixational focusing on it. No amount of interpretation, however deep or symbolic, can yield causal insights from inherently accidental associations.

Exactly the ideas from the "free association" that analysts deal with are most accidental. When you trace back a freely floating thought you can see that it originated from a random association with some incidental idea in a previous thought, which originated in the same way. We may refer here to the vivid descriptions of this process by William James. In Rorschach test or dream, ideas come from what was thought of, heard, read or seen precedingly. Moreover, the ideas that surge forth strongest, like the indecent sexual ideas in free association, are rarest, most unusual or "sharpest", therefore causally least important. The really determining, emotional causal backgrounds are so general — like the atmospheric pressure — for the patient that he notices nothing particular about them. They are the last things to come to his mind, because they are the causal opposites of his reactions and feelings. Besides, the strong negative reactions of the patient are glaringly clear from everything he does or feels. But emotions could make any sense to the therapist only if he had some insight in the opposite causation.

The point is that the world of ideas and their associations is not intrinsically causally related to emotions or releases and is *psychologically weightless.* Particularly *because the real psychic causes are opposites of the impoverishment they produce, no ideas or associations about them ever come to the mind of the patient, or of the modern therapist.* Psychotherapy continues as a seemingly successful treatment because it delays the unpleasant restrictive natural reactions of the "disease", which are the pressures of the organism toward real recovery.

Drug Therapy. The worsening through improvement is typically illustrated in the drug therapy. Drugs that according to their first effects would be sufficient to wipe out all mental disease are invented every year. But mental disorders are increasing progressively with the advances in the means of such direct improvements, of which drugs are the mainstay. Every authority recognizes that drugs relieve symptoms, thus temporarily curing the disease, but that real, permanent cure is never to be expected from drugs.[4,5] The usual argument is that drugs are helpful adjuncts in making the patient available for psychotherapy.[4,26] The "cures" provided by all kinds of wonder drugs are spectacular.[5] Yet the end result is that drugs do not "offer a solution to the problems of emotional illness but rather add to them".[11]

What turns the *clear improvements by drugs into worsening or damage* that "far outweighs the good they intend"[17] is the drug aftereffects. It would be ridiculous to imagine that a drug can reorganize organically anything in the body which operates by billions of purposefully interwoven elements. But a drug can destroy, eliminate, stop or selectively paralyze a mechanism or reaction, by knocking out one element in the endless chains of organic processes. If a restrictive mechanism is stopped, release flow is increased: the result is stimulation. If a mechanism that provides for organic requirements, through stressful restrictions, is stopped, freer enjoyment of releases becomes available: the result is tranquilization. But since in neither case a purposeful organic reorganization has been achieved, the body returns to whatever organic normalcy it maintains. Even if such normalcy is faulty, it is still a million times superior in organization and purposeful complexity than anything a drug could organize or construct. In any event, the overspent releases are restored by exactly equal amount of reimposed restrictions. Or the neglected organic requirements are met by exactly equal additional stressful effort. Thus *the result is always the opposite effects.*

For all drugs, the story has been miraculous improvements or "cures" followed by equally disturbing aftereffects. One of the widest studies, by H. A. Dickel and H. H. Dixon,[32] has proved this for the most used drugs. For the particularly praised drug, reserpine, the opposite aftereffects have been discovered in various studies,[16] notably those by J. C. Muller and his co-workers.[32] The most popular, meprobamate drugs have been miraculously successful in their first effects but have failed in the end and are being abandoned, as mere super-placebos (G.

Johnson).[71] They have been dropped from the U. S. Pharmacopoeia and found, in hearings before the FDA, to be "addictive or worse".[32]

Dr. T. H. Greiner of the AMA Council on Drugs states that "tranquilizers have caused about as much trouble as they have abolished".[17] The story of stimulant drugs, particularly the amphetamines, has been even worse. They lead to "the insidious onset of psychic symptoms resembling those of schizophrenia".[17] The problems of the pep-pills and of the illegal traffic in the drugs are becoming acute. The highly desirable, almost miraculous stimulation that amphetamines provide ends as dangerous aftereffects that are "several times" worse than the initial benefits.[17] More than half of the amphetamines are sold illegally.

The newest mood-elevating and antidepressant group of drugs, the MAO inhibitors are probably the most dangerous. They interfere with definite body functions, and the aftereffects may be damage to brain or other organs, even death.[17] But the initial effects of MAO inhibitors are miraculous, as was evident from the use of iproniazid — which has been hastily dropped by most doctors, but is still accepted as an important psychic energizer by some psychiatrists (N. S. Kline).[17]

The simple rule, which scientists cannot accept, is that the *initial improvements induced by drugs are followed by exactly equal opposite aftereffects.* (We explained why the organs or functions involved in the opposite reactions may be, naturally, different.) Thus the "toxic effects of the drug may merely accentuate symptoms for which a patient originally took it" (C. K. Aldrich).[81] In the simplest case, "the same tranquilizing drugs now commonly used to relieve the so-called anxiety or violent restlessness of schizophrenic patients are capable of temporarily inducing identical symptoms of this common malady in normal patients".[26] The vicious-circle deepening of the disorder results, as more of the same drug or a stronger drug is used to avoid the aftereffects. The final effects of the increase in dosage may be "an almost incredible and alarming range of emotional disorders — hallucinations, delusions, hysteria, amnesia, and so on" (R. Mines).[32] Prolonged doses of tranquilizers "increase chances of unpredictable physical disorders" (M. Fishbein).

The disappearance of the initial improvements is often explained by the assumption that drugs act only as placebos, therefore have no real biochemical effects.[25] In truth, experimenters find that the biochemical changes drugs produce are astonishingly concrete.[5] Misapplication or abuse of drugs is blamed, though it is admitted that "very little is known of the causes of drug abuse".[17] The "abuse" consists of taking a too small or a too large dosage. It is not realized that exactly the overstimulation by the drug either makes the dosage too weak or requires a dosage so large that it leads to graver "side effects". Also complexity and multiplicity of drugs may be blamed (W. Modell).[25] But the striking fact about the "miracle" drugs is that they work as perfectly in every way at the beginning as they come to be "abused" later. Actually "in the beginning, every potential abuser comes to feel that the effects of the drug he is taking are desirable and/or necessary for his well-being" (G. Johnson).[17] Apparently, the fact that the direct improvements by drugs lead to equal worsening is unacceptable to the ordinary man as well as the scientist.

But this worsening through improvement is the cause of *the most universal phenomenon in the use of drugs, namely addiction.* The process is simple. As the worsening starts, the drug user tries to overcome it by using the same drug, in larger dosage, which leads to deeper worsening, requiring still larger dosage or a stronger drug. The addiction is so general — whether it is to cigarettes and coffee or to drugs and alcohol — that it alone would be sufficient to prove the opposite causation and the vicious circle of overadjustment.

Typically, modern scientists have no generally accepted explanation for this universal phenomenon, though it is so clearly uniform that it can have only a simple, natural principle as its cause. Even the common addictions to smoking or alcohol remain mysteries, to best authorities.[26] It is speculated that perhaps the liking of the fragrance, or the air of elegance, or the need to have something for the hands to do, may be the cause of the need to smoke (H. Burn).[16] Explanation of alcohol addiction is sought in such vague factors as "essentially a psychological compulsion" or "the circumstances under which it is consumed" (W. Modell).[25] How could this produce the inexorably concrete organic exhaustion and the physiologic pressures for more release?

The very meaning of what addiction is has led to confusions. Thus it is found that "by contrast with nicotine, the hemp drugs, the amphetamines and cocaine seldom if ever produce physical dependence — but they unquestionably produce addicts".[25] Other drug experts hold that "we can speak of heroin addict or barbiturate addict but not an alcohol addict or cocaine addict",[26] though the withdrawal suffering and addictive compulsion of the alcoholic or cocaine user are as real as life. For the drug experts there are only a few addictive drugs. But in reality every one of the artificial means we use for improvement of our feelings or reactions is addictive in the same way that heroin is. Does not the coffee drinker or smoker suffer withdrawal torments and addictive compulsion exactly to the extent he has derived positively pleasant feelings from his use of coffee or nicotine?

Expectedly the drug experts, as experimental scientists, recognize only the physiological addiction or dependence, but not the "psychological" addiction. The reason is that anything purely "psychological" or "mental" is experimentally unreal; so is life itself as a living process. Experiment simply never comes even close to dealing with the endless, infinitesimal living processes. These are fully accounted for only through the integrated feelings or pleasure reactions. And the reversed logic of relative causation governs such reactions. No wonder that *drug experts miss the general, "psychological" addiction,* while noticing only some gross, physiological effects of addictions.

Practical life shows that the general, "psychological" addiction is what really matters. The FDA and AMA are continuously adding more of the "nonnarcotic" drugs to the lists of addictive drugs,[17] and the number of addicts to such drugs is now estimated to be ten times larger than that of "narcotic" addicts.[17] New legislation is introduced, as the illicit traffic in these drugs is alarmingly increasing. The most used drugs, tranquilizers and stimulants, are now sold more through the black market than legally. The illicit traffic in these drugs is measured in billions of dollars annually.[17] Is not this an equally extensive, real-life proof of the worsening through improvement, that drives the drug users to such desperate, addictively compulsive efforts?

The drug experts, logically, *seek for "toxic effects"* as harmful accidental residues of drugs, to explain *why the clear improvements turn into worsening.* But the sickening, death-like withdrawal reactions, negative in every respect, appear exactly to the extent the body is cleaning itself of the narcotic, "toxic" substances. Placebos could not possibly leave any toxic residues. Yet "just as placebos have beneficial results, so may they produce toxic effects".[27] It should be kept in mind that any purely physiologic or experimental findings are bound to be misleading because of the billions of factors involved and the reversed logic of the *integrated* organ *reactions* which are the only relevant data obtained.

Scientists, believing that clearly positive effects cannot result in negative reactions, often claim that drugs trigger "an underlying hidden psychosis or personality disturbance", which supposedly lies just beneath the surface (T. Itl, N. S. Kline).[17] Actually the potential of all functional disorders is constantly present, inherent in the functions themselves, however normal these may be at the beginning, as the overadjustments show. Other scientists may blame "some accident of body chemistry", as when it was discovered that stimulation through increase in adrenalin produced agents like adrenochrome with opposite effects.[27] Typically, scientists having discovered a couple of such factors, like serotonin or norepinephrine, are ready to change them, without regard to the innumerable other, ungraspably complex but purposeful processes involved. Of course the organism manages to overcome such interferences, in ways "about which little is known", but the scientists are intensifying this line of attack.[16]

The confusion about drug effects is so general that it may seem as if "an unbelievable fraud has been perpetuated on the public" (G. Johnson).[17] The "passion and letdown that drugs inspire in one after another person"[17] look like results of a hoax. Without a causal understanding of the inherently paradoxical drug effects, it may seem that in some cases the drugs work wonderfully and in others fail (W. Alvarez).[17] It is found that such unpredictability "makes it more difficulty for any medical practitioner to help create a lasting better mental outlook with any particular drug" (M. Fishbein).[32]

The frequent *assertions about variance of drug effects* are due to this causal confusion. Because the paradox of the reversal of effects applies through all phases and details, scientists, unaware of it, may find the effects totally irregular. Particularly in the extremely complex higher mental processes the effects may become confusing. For instance LSD, affecting such processes, has been found unpredictable (S. Cohen). The "ferocity of debate over LSD's benefits and perils"[17] has been noted. The drug has been "much praised and damned".[25] In fact LSD was highly praised at the beginning, when its mind-expanding effects were first observed. The damnation has come afterward, upon the discovery of its equally impressive negative aftereffects.

The variance in drug effects may be due merely to variance in capacities of persons and in conditions affecting the paradoxical release economy. In the classic experiments by Kolb and Lasagna it was found that only the person who derives pleasure from the drug suffers the negative aftereffects, which bring him "as far below his normal emotional plane as the first exaltation carried him above it".[26] For each person such "capacity" to enjoy or to learn to enjoy the releases may be different. Also the availability of releases may vary under varied conditions and thus influence the effects as well as aftereffects. Previous overenjoyment may decrease positive response, but also may bring on sooner the negative aftereffects. Moreover, external observations may be deceptive if their emotional quality is missed: one may scowl, complain or play a sufferer while enjoying it.

Endless variations in such factors may lead to endless confusion, if the paradoxical causation is not understood. Everybody knows what varied effects alcohol produces on different persons with varied enjoyment tendencies, drinking experience, history of previous drinking, or particular body condition. But we all know how inexorably uniform the general effects of alcohol are, in producing the opposite states, of sense of well-being and hell, as well as in leading to addiction, because of the opposite after-effects. However simple or complex the means used, the natural law that governs the releases of pleasure or life flow, in the inexorably limited organism, remains the same. Even in the use of LSD, the *opposites* of ecstasy and inferno, beauty and horror are the inevitable general results, however confusing their ideational contents or phases of development.

Those who are enthusiastic about drugs are pointing to the decrease of patients in public mental hospitals, though the more sober researchers find that the drugs have not helped and that hospitals are "crowded more than ever with chronic patients" (J. Dubos). Actually the number in which the decrease is noted is the former half million patients in *public mental hospitals*.[17] But such patients now constitute only one fourth of mental inpatients.[28] In the general hospitals alone the mental patients now occupy more than a half million beds.[28] The NIMH itself has pointed out the movement of patients away from mental hospitals, and "the increased use of psychiatric beds in general hospitals and of outpatient clinics and other community facilities such as nursing homes, half-way homes and sheltered workshops".[32] Further, the number of regular outpatients has reached two million.[28]

With the increased use of drugs since 1955, when the most popular "wonder" drugs went to market, the number of mental patients has increased from 1.6 million to four and half million.[28] Most of these patients are under outpatient care. The reason is that their disorders are due not to genetic, deep or irreparable problems, but to artificially created overadjustments, deepened as well as induced by the use of drugs. But even the number of inpatients has increased, by 25%, since 1955, if the above care in general hospitals and other facilities is taken into account.[28]

It has to be noted that among the scores of drugs used some may happen to produce permanent beneficial results because they may, on the whole, have the eventual effect of anti-stimulation or anti-tranquilization. They may be continued to be used upon incidental discovery of their practical success, though their action may not be understood and may be counteracted by the rest of the treatment, much as in the case of the shock therapy.

In conclusion, we may emphasize the paradox of our era of "wonder" drugs invented by the dozen every year. According to the direct, initial improvements that these drugs bring, each one of them could wipe out mental disorders. But the number of mental patients is increasing progressively, as the use of the wondrously effective drugs expands. Though the experimental proofs of the curing effects of the drugs are most impressive, there is hardly any authority now who believes that drugs can cure. The reason of the paradox is the opposite causation, which is perhaps most evident from the addiction and withdrawal effects of drugs, stimulants, alcohol, nicotine, coffee or other means of overadjustments, all around us.

Shock Therapy. The converse effect of opposite causation, namely *improvement through worsening,* is perfectly illustrated by the shock therapy. The shock amounts to intensification of the "disease" or of reactions that are like those of psychosis. The "disease" is thus helped to attain its natural effect and the cure. Psychiatrists have observed that "psychotic manifestations become outspoken" during the shock; and that all kinds of excessively negative influences, from febrile diseases to severe psychological crisis, can effect a cure.[32]

Shock therapy is the only treatment in modern psychiatry that cures definitely and without aftereffects, if used for disorders to which it is applicable in its present form. Here we have to emphasize that presently the shock therapy is primitive and limited, because there is no causal understanding of why or how it works and its use is purely accidental — a "blind stab in the dark".[3]

Shock therapy has been recognized as "the most promising method and the foremost achievement of psychiatric research". The "shock treatments are now the most widely used", so much so that they are, incongruously, seen as applicable to all psychic disorders.[4] The effects of shock therapy have been described as "miraculous" and "dramatic".[29] Its rate of cure for the depressive psychoses has been given as 80-90% and 90%.[32] Taking into account the confusion in the classification of depressive psychoses, we can say that the affective psychotic depressions are cured by the shock therapy without exceptions. It is because of the sheer success of the shock therapy that it is being increasingly used for "practically all psychoses and psychoneuroses",[6] and has become "far too common in practice".[11] The reason is not any enthusiasm. Usually a therapy is successful or is claimed to be a success when the therapists are enthusiastic about it. Nobody is enthusiastic about shock therapy in itself, for it is contrary to everything doctors believe, expect or practice.

We have to understand that a gross physiologic shock, the only one presently used, can remedy only gross physiologic disorders, the affective psychotic depressions. To the extent that a disorder originates in psychological, conscious overadjustments, as all neuroses and most of the psychotic reactions, do, it can be remedied only by equally psychological, consciously felt "shock". The natural simple rule of equal value opposites applies here as everywhere else.

Causal understanding of the shock therapy would show that all mental disorders could be as perfectly cured as now the depressions are, if the "shock" was made adaptable. Shock is an extremely strong restriction or depression, of the overextended release mechanisms, toward the zero or death level. Thus room is gained or potentials reestablished for new rise or the normal play of "ups" and "downs" in the releases. Death and rebirth similarity as well as the need for "retrenchment" have been emphasized in explanations of shock therapy.[11] But a strong restriction or depression of release levels can also be imposed through drugs and other means, even by psychological "shock" The lithium treatment shows how a drug can help by preventing excess releases or mania.

The point is that once the seemingly paradoxical causal logic of the shock therapy is understood, all possible combinations of drugs and of other means can be adaptively perfected to cure every psychic disorder as completely as now the depressions are cured by the present shock therapy. Of course such treatment would require totally new approaches, exactly contrary to the present ways of thinking. We might call it *antistimulation treatment*; we shall return to it later.

It is significant that shock therapy and its success are contrary to everything modern psychiatrists believe and practice. As White says "physicians and ordinary men alike wonder how such rough treatment can be beneficial when everything that we have learned about psychological disorders seems to indicate that kindness and interested understanding are essential to the therapeutic process".[3] He concludes that "we are truly without a theory" of the shock treatment. Menninger finds that "we have no definite knowledge as to why it has a therapeutic effect". Some fifty, controversial theories have been advanced but the reason why and how a shock can bring cure has remained a mystery.[29] As Aldrich concludes "none of the many theories which have been proposed to account for the success of either insulin or electric shock has been substantiated and the reason for their success remains obscure".[18] Most theories seem to be inclined toward the explanations claiming need for punishment or self-punishment (O. H. Mowrer).[23] As we have seen, theories of man acting against himself are the only way to explain "logically" the paradoxical effects of opposite causation.

Before we conclude, we may emphasize that *the shock treatment is the only one in modern psychiatry that cures fully and definitely; and that it is completely contrary to the very logic of modern psychiatric theory.* In its present, primitive form, it provides complete cure for the disorders it can be properly applied to. It could cure as fully and concretely all disorders if it was adapted to their treatment — if it was causally understood. The imposition of restrictions as source of releases, that the relative causation requires, is attained in shock therapy, though presently this is done in a crude form of an extreme one-stab shock.

In brief, the only psychic treatment that concretely works, and is causally congruous, is contrary to everything held as true or practiced in modern psychiatry, and is admittedly beyond causal understanding of modern psychiatrists.

Other Forms of Treatment. Hospital treatment of mental patients is undergoing big changes, a *practical turnaround, as various out-of-hospital forms of treatment* are being adopted. Psychiatric clinics, day-time units, "drop-in" clinics and community mental health centers are rapidly expanding. The traditional mental hospital treatment is being abandoned. The most advanced, British plan provides for closing of all mental hospitals in twenty-five years. In a similar move in this country a "revolution in the mental hospitals" is being brought about,[29] as the life of patients is being changed to resemble real life outside, with its tasks and ambitions.

This of course brings to the patients all the stresses and worries of responsibility, ambition and competition, with equally wider satisfactions or potentials of release. The popular "experts" then look at these more positive aftereffects and claim that the success of the "revolution" is due to a more relaxing pleasant or socially entertaining atmosphere in the hospitals. In truth, *if merely more relaxation or satisfactions were the source of the improvements, total success would have come by itself,* long ago. Everybody, the patients as well as the staff, would have gravitated into it eagerly and with ease, pleased and relaxed. The "revolution" is hard on patients as well as the staff. For instance, the "total push" treatment, the most typical innovation, has been criticized because of its hardships.[11]

The real-life conditions, brought to patients either in the hospitals or through the outside forms of treatment, work because only the real life with its subtle and contradictory ways can impose restrictions or stresses, in the name of satisfactions. The new, real-life or out-of-hospital factors are accepted much against the logical theory, which has offered here only scant and contradictory explanations. Logically patients are best protected against stresses and provided with all the relaxing or improving means in the seclusion of hospitals. Theory always advocates the protection or relaxation from stresses. Thus the half-day treatment is seen as beneficial because of its protective, relaxing part during the stay in hospital. It is overlooked that if you make such benefits complete, by keeping the patient all the time in the hospital, he will become a problem like other patients.

It can be said that the new approaches of moving mental patients back into conditions of real life with all its stresses are practiced contrary to theory, because of their practical success, much like the shock therapy is.

Psychosurgery. Various forms of lobotomy, lobectomy, leucotomy, or thalamotomy provide, temporarily, great relief. Exclusion of brain activity, through intoxication or even brain illness, can induce elation or increase in releases, because restriction is the evolutionary function of the brain. Naturally, removal of restrictions soon leads to exhaustion or release impoverishment. The first effects of uninhibited exuberance revert into depression and immobility of a "vegetable kingdom" (R. Linder). Psychosurgery was hailed as one of the greatest breakthroughs when its practice began, and it is impressive in its immediate effects after each operation. But it has been found disappointing, and debilitating, in its end-results; it is characterized by repeated enthusiasm and disuse.

Group Therapy. All kinds of group therapies are becoming popular. The psychopath loves to be heard and to attract attention. He indulges in his arguments and in proving once more how right he has been. This provides immediate improvement — and more overenjoyment, that can only deepen the disorder.

But group therapy can have corrective effect for very different reasons. In any social interaction the individual meets with a curious rebound effect. As the psychopath observes in others their loathsome, stupid, negative traits, he hates it all with great delight. But this very loathing will make him fear the same traits when he encounters them later in himself. For similar reasons the Alcoholics Anonymous, the Synanon and similar groups attain unexplained success.

There are *too many other used or suggested therapies* or ways of treatment to be listed here. Researchers have counted 2934 of them.[32] Apparently, in psychiatry the rule "everything works and nothing works"[29] applies perfectly. Anything can be turned into a means of immediate improvement because anything can be made an object of enjoyment. Modern life and psychiatry are providing and encouraging the widest range of such enjoyments or overadjustments. The result is as widely increasing mental disorders and admitted inability to understand or deal with them, strange but typical in our progressive age.

The confusion is reflected in the newest approaches underemphasizing professionalism, as in the nondirective psychotherapy; or turning to philosophy, the perennial source of mysteries, as in the existential and humanistic psychotherapies. The "intangibles" in psychic treatment are being stressed, and the knowledge of truth as source of freedom is accepted to be one of them (K. A. Menninger).[1] Treatments in which psychiatrists are not to be more authoritative than the patients are being practiced and expounded, particularly by the new leading authority R. D. Laing. Evil effect of the whole system of professional psychic treatment seems to become more plausible, as can be seen from the works of T. S. Szasz.

Only one thing is certain and generally accepted in modern psychiatry: *the logic of direct improvements.* Increase or addition in releases always shows under experimental or clinical observation as clear improvement. This is the only "scientific" logic modern psychiatry knows. In truth, direct increase in the releases of the life flow, without their opposites, the restrictions, leads to their exhaustion or impoverishment and disorder. But this universal, opposite causation has never yet been thought of in modern psychiatry, in any way. For instance, the best authorities may stress the direct increase in such emotions as love, faith or hope,[1] which are positive satisfactions or pleasures. Certainly the availability of such satisfactions is the panacea for all ills. But we can never have them without living through their stressfully hard, unrecognizable, negative opposites. If we could, there would not be one mental disorder in the world; for nothing is simpler or easier than enjoyment of positive reactions or satisfactions.

The point is that the *modern psychic treatments amount to fostering the overadjustments or the direct increase in releases, which is the very cause of mental disorders.*

The deeper reason for this is the same that has prevented all human sciences from becoming scientific: the "impossible" logic of organic value causation. The paradox of functional diseases belongs here. A functional disease as a natural reaction is the organism's endeavor to restore normalcy or the normal release reserves, through restrictions. This is, certainly, felt as a negative, sickly worsening or disease. Modern psychic treatments are combatting rather than helping such pressures by the organism toward its normalcy. That is why mental diseases are increasing, not decreasing, with the advance of modern psychiatry and the implementation of its spirit, made possible by the unique resourcefulness, plenty and liberalism of modern life.

The Trend Can Be Reversed

The present trend of disastrously increasing mental disorders can be reversed. This could be done in scientifically or causally simple ways, though the practical difficulties would be enormous. Mental disorders can be cured and, particularly, prevented as simply as they are caused. Their cause, as we saw, is the impoverishment resulting from excessive releases. Restriction of such overadjustment is all that is needed. It could be attained by the anti-stimulation treatment, including the use of anti-release drugs, like the lithium compounds, in countless possible adapted combinations, as we saw under shock therapy. But in addition to being contrary to everything now believed or practiced in psychiatry, such treatments would be resisted by the psychopath to the utmost. He is prone to mental disorders exactly because he cannot bear restrictions in pleasure releases.

We saw that shock therapy uniquely cures all cases to which it is properly applicable in its present form and that similar therapy could be adapted for all mental disorders. *Psychological* "shock" would be best for most disorders. Unbelievable sudden recoveries, even from chronic schizophrenia have been seen to occur in patients who have been just told of danger of fatal disease or coming grave operation.[12] (After the danger was over the patients relapsed.) Apparently, psychologíc containment, stress or restriction in the rate of pleasure releases is sufficient to counteract gravest psychosis.

But the same strong restrictive effect could be attained by prolonged, adapted restrictions, instead of the one-hit shock. People can live under strongest restrictions without feeling them if the restrictions have become universal like an atmosphere. Thus the general level of restrictions in a society determines what restrictions can be imposed on anybody. This is very important. The psychotic would have to be kept normal by stronger restrictions. But any restriction imposed above the existing general, "normal" level is felt as an excess and merely evokes opposite reactions. That is why the average amount of mental illness depends on *the general level of restrictive moral strength of the whole society*. Common intuition as well as history show general moral license and mental disorders as interrelated.[23]

Our present era is the best example. The unique modern affluence and progress permit us to live for enjoyments and to be carefree or permissive to a degree never attained before. With this has come the rejection of restrictions by the modern science and modern thought. In all other times the learned authorities were the main supporters of the restrictive morals. The modern medicine and psychiatry have followed the "science" totally in its experimental logic of improvements through direct release increases. Modern man has all the means to put these new ideas in practice. The result is the scourge of functional diseases.

Now "it is estimated that one out of every ten babies born today will spend some time in a mental hospital; community studies have shown as many as 30 percent of the population as having clinical symptoms of personality disturbance" (E. R. Hilgard).[5] The ten-in-one ratio is now generally accepted. It represents a doubling in estimates of even some thirty years ago.[32] At the beginning of this century there were 130,000 patients in mental institutions in this country. Now there are a million and a half inpatients, besides three million outpatients.[28] The accelerated increase in mental diseases has become the number one health problem, in the most progressive, affluent countries like ours. Mental patients now occupy more beds in hospitals than all other patients taken together.

It should not be overlooked that the lower classes, particularly of the *urban population,* have been affected most by such progress and permissiveness. Higher and middle classes, having always enjoyed some affluence and freedom, have evolved cultural, social and moral norms for coping with them. This is the source of the "middle class values" which are so strange and difficult for the lower class children that, we are now told, such values should not be forced on them. The lower classes have been formerly held under the necessarily superstitious religious and repressive social restrictions. These are now gone, particularly in the urban centers, without being replaced by other restrictions.

Man reverts to unlimited pursuit of pleasures and license at the first opportunity if he is not held back by conditioned, inbred restraints, which the lower classes do not have. The lower a social class, the more it has the "tendency toward impulse gratification", utmost and immediate enjoyment, hostility toward all authority, and contempt for moral standards.[30] Also the material stresses have lessened among the lower classes most, in relative terms, which alone count. This is reflected in the expensive drug habits, unconcern about jobs or material survival, and frequent extravagant spending.[30] In brief, license for overenjoyments here is complete — and the results are showing.

It has been found that in urban centers one fourth of population suffers from mental disorders. In some such centers, studies have shown only 14% of the population free of indications of psychopathology.[32] As Mowrer points out there is "direct connection between the paralysis with respect to the specter of mental illness and the confusion and apathy in the matter of moral values".[23]

Whatever last hold on sanity the affected one-fourth of the population may have, it can be destroyed by the methods of modern psychiatry. All modern treatments support as unlimited as possible direct improvements in feelings or releases, with liberation from stresses, guilt or repressions. One can easily see how use of *release-increasing drugs can turn the pathologically affected people into psychotics.* But the newest most popular out-patient as well as the routine hospital treatments rely on inten-sified use of all kinds of "improvement" drugs. Dr. S. Kellam, of the NIMH, has said that the "major effort in psychiatry to-day is to reduce the degree to which the physician and mental hospital stand in the way of the patients' own capacity to get better".[29]

The failure of modern psychiatry is well known among psy-chiatrists themselves. A report on *Progress in Psychiatry* by the American Psychiatric Association states that "psychiatry is to-day in a state of disarray almost exactly as it was two hundred years ago". The Joint Commission on Mental Illness and Health finds that the "twentieth-century psychiatry can add little to Pinel's principles for the moral treatment of psychotics, pub-lished in 1801". The modern psychiatrist cannot help even him-self. The suicide rate among psychiatrists is four times higher than among other people, as a study by Dr. D. E. De Sole shows. According to Mowrer, some authorities have decided that if a breakthrough does not follow soon, new ways outside the psy-chiatric profession are to be sought; and pilot studies for doing so have been started.[23]

The evident solution lies in making the psychotic live through the feelings he avoids most (much as the phobic is forced to do and is cured in the behavior therapy). The psychotic suffers the disorder exactly because he has avoided displeasures, stresses and restrictions. Balance is restored by forcing them on him. In more primitive life continuous restrictions are imposed by difficulties or stresses of life, and functional diseases do not develop. In a classical study, the rate of mental illness in Kenya was found to be only 2 percent of what it was in Massachusetts. But we cannot return to more primitive conditions. The modern progress is too fast to be met by the selectively evolving restric-tive traditions. *Now science based on causal understanding has to provide the restrictive guidance,* just as the present scientific attitudes have created the disastrous trend.

The system of restrictions to be complete has to be imposed culturally, psychologically, and medically or by drugs. Cultural or social restrictions, as we saw, have to be as general as the atmosphere we live in. Science and learning have changed this general atmosphere. Change back toward greater restrictions would be more difficult, but the influence of science is increasing and it can affect even emotional attitudes of men.

Psychological controls, made unreversing by the general atmosphere, could be very important. Mind is miraculously capable of evoking the appropriate reactions. A belief of being poisoned can produce the right elimination, sweating and circulation reactions, involving endless processes; just as a hypnotic suggestion of a burn can produce a real blister. If the potential psychotic became convinced that he will suffer madness unless he lives restrictively, this could induce all the needed organic effects. We saw how fear of fatal illness can counteract even chronic schizophrenia, and men fear madness more than any other illness. Of course such conviction and fear, as well as the accepted restrictions, can have real force only if they are conditioned throughout one's life, within the general restrictive atmosphere.

Finally *drugs* and similar means can be used where the disorder has purely physiologic causes. Depressions are such disorders and they are perfectly controlled by suppression of the manic stages through the lithium treatment. Drugs are, certainly, crude means. But even crude interference with release mechanisms or with influences from outside stimulants can stop them. Drugs, "shock" or other means can be made adaptively refined and continuous, through numberless possible combinations, if their causal logic is understood.

Anyway, *the system can be made complete* by use of cultural, psychological and medical means for imposing the restrictions. It is clear that the psychopath sinks into his disorder because he is too weak and unwilling to accept the hard, unpleasant experiences or to renounce pleasures. In other words, he exhausts the releases, which can be restored only by restrictions. Besides, it does not matter much how the restrictions are imposed. Once they make the release potentials available these can be used in any form. The hungry man has good appetite for any food, and a man having lived under hardships finds any normal effort satisfactory.

Beneficial effects of even indiscriminately imposed hardships have been confirmed in psychiatry, but as could be expected, only through admittedly mystifying chance observations. Menninger writes about unexpected recoveries by patients upon their placement under harder conditions, worse treatment, or upon "most unlikely" event, including intercurrent illness.[1] He concludes that "worse added to worse often works", and that this may explain the cruel treatments in the ages past. He finds this to be the very antithesis of our present views about the nature and complexity of mental illness.[1]

In their study on men in disaster, G. W. Baker and D. W. Chapman find that conditions of disaster have effects contrary to logical expectations. Thus according to British statistics from the last World War "mental illness actually declined in incidence during protracted periods of bombing and threat of destruction".[31] Also hospital observations show that "severe threat cooperatively encountered may inspire healthy behavior" and that realistic work schedules, or pressures of group coping have beneficial effects.[31] Of course logical interpretations are sought for the seeming paradox. M. H. Hunt contends that the hospitals applying treatments of long hours, dull chores and unfriendliness instead of kindness provide the patient with symbolic means of self-punishment and expiation of guilt.[29] However, the most "unsymbolic" threat can be surprisingly effective. In a well known case, 153 incurable mental patients fled, under the fear of advancing Germans in 1940, from the hospital La Charite sur Loire. A special commission found, after the War, that 57 percent of them had established themselves, in various communities, as fully recovered.

Evidently, *even the seemingly incurable psychotics can gain sufficient mental resources for recovery.* In mental disorders, even more than in the other functional diseases, the paradox of "disease" as the natural pressure toward normalcy is clearly evident. That is why two thirds of mentally ill persons recover by themselves — by living through the "disease". Psychiatrists have viewed this as encouragement for continuing with their present therapies.[1] But statistics show that the percentage of recovery is higher among those not undergoing the modern psychic treatments.[8] The incomparably lower rate of mental illness among more primitive people is rightly seen as due to the absence of facilities of psychic treatment — as it certainly is due to the absence of all the modern improvements.

In any event, nowhere has man greater opportunity than in dealing with his mental disorders to attain success by using only his own powers of mind. Yet the modern men suffer from mental disease at the unique, increasing rate of one in ten. Apparently, modern man and psychiatry, in their enormous efforts and successes, are proceeding in the completely wrong direction.

The reason is the natural delusory human belief as well as the "scientific" logic that direct increase in positive reactions or releases, felt as improvements, is the goal of best adjustment. Modern life and science provide richest means and encouragement for such "improvements", which thus are enjoyed to excess. It is self-evident that such excess has to lead to opposite reactions or exhaustion, and that *restrictive, negatively-felt reactions should be imposed as the necessary counter measures.* The key would be the reversal of the causal logic or of the very way of thinking in psychiatry. The technical means could be found and worked out to perfection, with the enormous efficiency of modern science. In other words, the present trend of increasing mental illness could be reversed through the simple but all-important insight in the "impossible" causal logic of the universal organic, relative causation.

Conclusion

Functional mental disorders are perfect clues for understanding the causal principle of value reactions, which determine all human behavior. The vicious-circle increase of negative reactions upon excessive enjoyment of positive releases or satisfactions is clear here. In all neuroses and psychoses the patient suffers from reactions and feelings that he wants least and that he is excessively combatting. This is evident also in the general mechanisms, like defense or conflict, observed in all disorders. The excessive indulgence of releases or avoidance of restrictions is the clearest personality trait of the mentally weak psychotic and neurotic.

As the psychotic uses all his skill and power in obtaining the positive overadjustments, the opposite, negative reactions or disorder has to arise with the same "ingenuity" and intensity. It may seem that a skillful agent inside him is working against him. Modern explanations of mental disorders resort to the mystifications about unconscious, scheming personified agents inside the person. The only main alternative to such mysteries is the theories about man learning or being conditioned to torment himself, without any use or reason. Which is equally untenable.

The central fallacy of modern psychiatry is the "scientific" logic of direct improvements. Experimentally a direct increase in releases always shows as logical, immediate improvement. Actually, it leads to exhaustion and disorder, because within the limited organic sameness only restrictions, the opposites of releases, can make these available. Every means or therapy in modern psychiatry aims at the direct logical improvement or increase in releases or satisfactions. Of course if such direct increase was possible, there would not be one mental disorder in the world. For there is nothing simpler or easier for man than enjoyment or addition of satisfactions or releases.

Thus the modern psychiatry helps to foster the direct improvements which are the very source of the vicious-circle overadjustments ending as disorders. Modern man having attained the highest satisfactions, all serving to relieve him from stresses as the greatest displeasures, suffers from mental disorders, as the malignantly self-deepening stresses, at the increasing rate of one-in-ten. Modern psychiatry more than anything else has helped modern man in this vicious-circle self-defeat.

The trend could be reversed, by reversing the very logic of the way nearly everything is understood and done in modern psychiatry. Man as a conscious planning being is bound to strive excessively for the pleasures or direct release improvements. The first task of psychiatry, as of all medicine and science, should be to counteract, not help, these excessive strivings by man for what he clearly, even insightfully, feels as logical, direct improvements in his well-being. The deeper reason here is the contradiction of the restrictive organic, relative adjustment, that man is not to understand — and that ultimately derives from the principle of opposition in evolution, or in all existence.

V

MEDICINE, MODERN DISEASES AND THE BLUNDER OF OUR AGE

Medicine is a very important field in the sciences of man both because it determines practically how man lives and because it can reveal theoretically the causal principles that govern organic life. Particularly revealing is the problem of functional diseases, which are becoming almost the only pathologic causes of deaths of modern men. The cause of these diseases is overadjustment, as overenjoyment of the physiologic releases or of the feeling of well-being. The blunder of our age, in the sciences of man, is the belief that we can improve or increase the organic functions which provide us with such enjoyments or feelings of well-being. In view of the unfathomable complexity and inexorable limitedness or sameness of organism, not the tiniest process or form in its functions can be *organically* or constitutionally changed or increased. But any nonorganic change or improvement merely evokes opposite processes or worsening, which deepens, in a vicious circle, as it is covered up by further "improvements".

The enormously expanding modern attempts to change, improve or increase the organic functions, particularly upon their vicious-circle worsening, virtually become massive ways of destruction of organic normalcy, mostly of its restrictive mechanisms. The result is an as wide increase in functional diseases, and disorders of unrestricted malignant growth — that causally have remained mysteries.

Functional, Modern Diseases, Overadjustment, Psychosomatics

All those diseases are to be treated as functional which are caused not by an organic defect or failure but by a way of living, actually by overadjustment. They are often named the "diseases of civilization". They can certainly be called modern diseases, in the sense that they are the scourge of modern man and may become virtually the only diseases from which men will die without remedy. The other, infectious diseases, and organic ills or failures, have been almost eliminated as causes of death, by the spectacular progress of modern medicine. In contrast, *the functional diseases have increased as spectacularly with the advance of medicine, which admittedly does not even understand their cause.* Thus in a period of the last sixty years, deaths from heart disease increased by 300 percent and from cancer by more than 400 percent.[1,2] It may be noted that even the nonfunctional diseases and defects become fatal mostly because of functional difficulties that plague modern men.

The usual argument that deaths from diseases like cancer or heart disease have increased because now people live longer is not true. Numerous studies among various peoples — Bantu, Chinese, Japanese, Italians, Swiss, Scandinavians — have shown that all through their lives the civilized, richer people accumulate more of the changes like increase in cholesterol, growth of "plaques" in arteries, rise in blood pressure, or strain in various organs, which finally cause the deaths. The differences here between the more advanced and primitive peoples are found to be striking.[11]

Also, specific modern enjoyments that account for the functional diseases are in many cases too evident to be missed, however confused the causal explanations. Overeating, smoking, preference for richer foods, the most direct, effortless enjoyment of leisure, and other too evident overindulgences, are recognized as causes of the functional diseases. Modern medicine, though, does not see the most important, insidious overadjustments — the stimulating modern improvements everywhere, from use of all kinds of drugs and stimulants to *directly increased satisfactions of life and work,* in avoidance of all negative reactions. In any event, the "increase in degenerative diseases is occurring faster than can be explained by longer expectancy of life" (R. Dubos).[3] The real old age that could be the assumed cause of deaths from functional diseases is not reached more often by the more advanced people. Rather the contrary is true. It is the average length of life that is low among less advanced peoples, because of numerous deaths of infants and younger persons. But the real old age, particularly of 70 or over is reached by more people in the less advanced countries, as is evident also from the *U. N. Demographic Yearbook.*[4]

Modern medicine has succeeded tremendously where the causes are clear and logical, as in dealing with infectious diseases or problems of surgery and technical improvements. Significantly, by far the greatest successes have been attained through inoculation, which already uses the paradoxical way of imposing rather than avoiding disease. In truth, even greater spectacular success could be attained in dealing with the functional diseases, if their causal logic was understood. For it is technically — though not motivationally — easier to deal with one's own reactions and drives or way of life than with myriads of germs or complexities of surgery.

The etiology of functional diseases shows that not their complexity but their causal logic prevents medicine from understanding them. It is generally recognized that these diseases are due to one or few common causes rooted in the modern way of life or its assumed stress. Revealingly, these diseases can be *cured, temporarily, by one simple stress-controlling drug or hormone,*[6] like cortisone, which is so simple that it can be produced synthetically. The "variety of human diseases that are eased by cortisone is astounding".[5] "What confounded and baffled doctors was that these afflictions have no cause common to all of them, yet cortisone affected them all as if it attacked some unknown common cause".[5] It is even believed that "the astonishing ability of cortisone apparently to turn disease off and on at will marks the opening of a new era in medicine".[6]

The cortisone action is only a more typical example. All controlling hormones can act in the same way, "as if they affected something that is fundamental to almost all disease".[6] The same is true of drugs. We saw before that drugs, like the MAO inhibitors, chlorpromazine, meprobamate, iproniazid, or even simple aspirin, can "cure" series of both psychological and physical disorders. The best logical conclusion is that such cures are attained by "protection against stress".[6] Certainly, by dealing with stress we can deal with every functional disease. This has been amply proven by numerous experiments and theories, particularly those of Hans Selye. "Stress" of course is a logical, nonrelative, therefore misleading concept that actually stands for scarcity of releases or of organic potentials of life. Release is the opposite of stress.

What it all proves is that the functional diseases are caused by a general *release impoverishment, which appears as the stress.* When a new spurt in releases is made possible, by a hormone or drug, the disease disappears. But a malignantly deepening stress or impoverishment in releases *can result only from overadjustment,* with its "impossible" logic of worsening through improvements, that keeps its vicious circle running. Continued use of cortisone or of the above drugs leads to extreme stress.[5,6]

Overadjustment. We have repeatedly explained why only the vicious-circle overadjustment can deepen the organic impoverishment to incredible degree, by nothing more than constantly added improvements. Primitive peoples, who cannot or do not know how to meet the painful restrictive organic reactions with further improvements, do not incur functional diseases, though they easily succumb to them when they start enjoying the modern improvements (P. D. White).[7] They may suffer from severest stresses, in their primitive conditions, but the results are not functional diseases. The idea that primitive life brings less of stresses is "cooked up out of our heads" (M. Mead).[7] Animals are free of functional diseases because they do not know how to improve their reactions.

Arguments about the increasing stresses of modern life have

been endless. Surely *stress* or emotional impoverishment meets modern man everywhere, because of his overadjustments or over-enjoyments in everything he does. This causal connection of course is never even suspected. But you can be sure that *modern man overenjoys first of all everything that provides freedom from stress* which is the most unpleasant feeling for him. He has all the power and skills to do so, and it is unreasonable to think that he is so stupid as to miss or miscalculate what he really wants. There is nothing simpler than gravitating into what is pleasant or desired. Naturally, the *overadjustments in avoidance of stress result in the vicious-circle, malignant stress.*

We have to mention the work of Hans Selye, the foremost authority on stress. He has shown that almost every functional disease can be caused by reactions of stress. General impoverishment of releases certainly can become cause of any functional disorder. Dr. Selye's theory does recognize two opposite phases in the stress syndrome: increased "resistance", and exhaustion. In experiments by Dr. Selye and others, hormones like corti-costeroids were used to bring out the "resistance" phase. As such stimulation was intensified, the exhaustion could, expectedly, be driven to the point it caused even death in the animals. Sig-nificantly, the control animals not receiving the hormone but subjected to the same stresses ended by having no harmful effects.

The opposites of overadjustment excesses here are clear, but the "scientific" logic did not permit the experimenters to accept that the same factor which provided the "resistance" improve-ment brought opposite effects in the end. Rather the theory was evolved by Dr. Selye that a prolonged stress induces poisoning of the body by its own products. In truth, exactly a prolonged stress eliminates functional disorders. People in concentration camps were "singularly" free of any symptoms of coronary di-sease[8] or of other functional disorders they had before.[37] The assumption that organism may turn against itself in a general, natural way is contrary to everything we know about the won-drous purposefulness of the body. But here, as in psychology, self-destruction seems the only logical explanation of the effects of opposite causation. This shows how reversedly wrong becomes the way of thinking even by best scientists about the organic causation.

That is why doctors cannot find the causes of functional diseases. Actually *the person does already what the doctors see as remedy*: he resorts to the means that in their direct effects lessen the "disease". For he feels and knows better than anybody what brings him immediate pleasurable relief from the reactions he is suffering. The vicious circle of overadjustment has to be kept in mind. It explains the imperceptible accumulation, to abysmal depths, as well as the malignant self-perpetuation, of the functional impoverishment. Also, overadjustment is possible without felt enjoyment, where the organism is "improved" up to a "normal" feeling of well-being when it actually is in a crisis or in conditions that require painful, restrictive adjustment.

It is important to note that the malignant overadjustment becomes almost inevitable as soon as man attains means rich and powerful enough to increase his feelings of well-being or greater "normalcy", and to overcome the worsening, resulting from such increase, by further improvements. Modern life, medicine and science are providing man with exactly such means and are upholding, without hesitation, the "scientific" logic of direct improvements.

Psychosomatics. Ultimately the source of all overadjustment and therefore of all functional diseases is psychological. For it is the conscious, planned search for increased satisfactions or pleasure releases that determines why and how the overadjustments are incurred. Consequently the functional diseases can be explained and controlled under the concepts of pleasure or general release, particularly of its relative or opposite causation. Dealing with involved biochemical products and processes may appear very scientific. But no amount of experimentally manageable factors can cover the myriad complexity of organic causation — which is perfectly accounted for, and governed, by the simple feelings or pleasure.

Psychosomatics approached in this way can be helpful. But the present psychosomatics proceeding by the direct, nonrelative causal logic is a dangerous fallacy, exactly because it deals with causally decisive factors. Psychosomatic approaches are now followed everywhere, by doctors and non-doctors, because the dependence of functional diseases on psychological factors or emotions is clearly evident. But dealing with emotions or general releases under the "scientific", direct-improvement logic amounts to supporting unlimited overadjustments, which could turn us all into patients. Mystery becomes inevitable, and psychosomaticists have fully espoused the Freudian alchemy of personified agencies, symbolism, hidden complexes and self-punishment.

Mere unconscious ideas and symbolism as causes reach widest acceptance in psychosomatics. The "organ language" may be viewed as explanation for almost every functional disease.[10] A mere idea "he makes me sick" brings a disease; "load on my chest" becomes a physical symptom; or "I cannot stomach him" causes gastric disorders.[9] Arthritis may mean a conflict over the use of extremities for sexual or aggressive purposes.[37] Shoulder pain arises from the idea of having "chip on the shoulder".[9] Dr. F. Dunbar shows in a comprehensive compilation how symbolism has been accepted by doctors as explanation for almost every disease.[10]

Further, patients supposedly act against themselves because of unconscious ulterior motives. A person may "consciously want to be cured, but his needs are often better served by illness".[37] Or one "may consciously want to reduce but unconsciously cheat on his resolve".[9] Even if a patient "may consciously want desperately to be well" he may unconsciously derive a satisfaction from having the disease.[37] Theories of self-punishment or masochism are popular in psychosomatics, as can be seen from the compilation by Dunbar.[10] The reason here is the same as in psychology: the person does bring on himself the functional impoverishment — because of the opposite causation. Recovery upon real trouble is noted, but is attributed to appeasement of vengeful Superego.[10] Restrictions are seen as the main evil. Typically, it does not make a difference whether pleasure, like libido, or displeasure, like fear, is repressed. It is only "clear that when emotions are not permitted direct expression they tend to become chronic and may find indirect expression through physical symptoms".[9]

The over-all result is that the now widely accepted psychosomatic approaches or thinking and methods are *extending to the field of physical health the dangerous fallacies and alchemy* perpetuated in modern psychology. The dangers here are greater, because physical overadjustments are more fundamental and we are less protected against them. Psychological overadjustments are biologically more superficial and are checked or corrected by pressures from the deeper normalcy below. Moreover, men are used to them and have evolved traditions for avoiding them. In contrast, physical overadjustments may distort the deepest bases of normalcy, and men have no tradition of guarding against them, because such overadjustments have become fully possible only with the most recent attainments of medicine, science and modern progress.

Before we conclude, we may note that a *functional disease as the system of natural restrictive reactions is actually the organism's pressure back toward normalcy.* Any overdriven mechanism has to return to its normalcy by opposite processes. It is evident that most organic functions can be "improved" or made efficient and pleasant beyond normalcy. Opposite reactions then become inevitable, and if they are further overcome, the result is the vicious-circle overadjustment and malignantly deepening impoverishment or "disease". Doctors know that all functional diseases have a common cause or mechanism by which they grow. As such it has to obey one natural principle, which can be only simple. But *in spite of colossal effort the causes of the functional diseases have not been found.* The reason is the unacceptability of the logic of the organic, opposite causation, which has prevented the simple causal understanding everywhere, from addictions and problems of anxiety to heart disease and cancer.

To illustrate it all the more concretely, we shall look briefly at the main functional, modern diseases. We have nothing to say or add in regard to the awe-inspiring professional and technical knowledge of modern medicine. There we can only refer to, and quote, the authorities, for whom we have deepest respect. But we shall, definitely, try to explain why in the field of functional diseases modern medicine is a danger rather than help. There the modern medicine is not even a science: it cannot explain the causation of these diseases. We offer a simple, though unthinkable fundamental causal law, which can serve as the basis in dealing with functional diseases, as it does in all sciences of man.

Heart Disease, Hypertension, Arteriosclerosis, Cholesterol

Modern men die of functional heart disease more than of any other cause. The reason is that the heart as the "seat of the emotions"[9] is affected most by all the efforts of overadjustments of modern life. The increase in the feeling of well-being is attained by modern man through the most resourceful and extensive means, from drugs, cigarettes, coffee, enriched foods and vitamins to the hedonistic drive for unrestricted satisfactions.

Stress of course can always be shown to be the direct cause of heart disease. But *stress can accumulate to a malignant degree only through the vicious-circle overadjustment.* The process is like that of taking stimulants to exclude fatigue and increasing their dosage to overcome the increasing need for rest, until final collapse. Of course the general need for rest as the opposite of hard exertion is pleasant, relaxing and healthy. Conversely, the aftereffects of the overadjustments in stimulation of heart are unpleasant, stressful and sickly reactions. As these are overcome, in the vicious-circle way, by all the resourceful modern means of improvements, a collapse of the heart function is the result.

Nature has no protection against such direct, planned "improvement" attacks on the heart. The unprotected mechanisms, ungraspably complex and delicate, are therefore extremely vulnerable when directly reached by the modern very efficient and incomparably grosser means of "improvements". Think of how a tiny clot formed by a chemically hardly noticeable imbalance can kill the person, while a drug can change that balance immensely either way.

The efficiency and determination of modern man in overcoming the naturally sickly feelings of strained or aging heart are decisive. Nature uses exactly such sickly feelings to protect the heart. In a natural state, animal or man becomes unable and painfully unwilling to exert or enjoy himself upon organic exhaustion. Life continues as a slowed down, weakened, unexciting or aged living. This may be sufficient for monotonous work and even advantageous for intellectual life, freed from natural drives. In any event, left to a natural adjustment man would never die of sudden functional heart failure, of which half of all modern people die now. Animals never die of it, and it is "strikingly" absent in underdeveloped countries.[11] In the most developed countries increasingly younger people are dying of heart disease in their thirties and forties (P. D. White).[7,11] About 35 percent of cardiac deaths are now in the 25-64 age group.[1]

The *overadjustment nature* of heart disease is clearly evident. Things that people enjoy most, like overeating or smoking, have also been most clearly proven to be causes of heart disease. In the Farmingham research project by the NHI on 5,127 people, it was found that overweight of 20 percent or smoking of more than a pack of cigarettes a day doubled the risk of fatal coronary. However, the more insidious "improvements", like those from alcohol, coffee, or other stimulating means are not connected with the disease. In fact the initially relaxing effects of alcohol have been found as beneficial by numerous doctors (P. J. Steincrohn).[12] This can be considered as one of the great discoveries of modern medicine.[8,13] In the same way coffee, or even the immediate effects of smoking, are found to be beneficial.[12,21] But according to a report in *Lancet* by a research team from Boston University, people who drink more than five cups of coffee a day are twice as likely to suffer heart attacks as people who drink no coffee.

The role of exertion and physical stress similarly point to overadjustment as cause of heart disease. Nothing seems more damaging to heart than hard work, which clearly burdens and disturbs it. Logically, not long ago, the medically minded people avoided strenuous physical exertion. Stair climbing, bicycle riding or running would have appeared as potentially dangerous.[15] But finally the doctors most familiar with heart disease, including such authority as Dr. P. D. White, have found exactly such activities to be protective.[15] Rather, relaxation and idleness have been found to be damaging to heart. The reversal of medical opinion here has been complete.[15,37] Controversies arise because stimulating or exhilarating exercise is dangerous, though "improvement" of exercise through added excitement and interest has been, logically, recommended by the AHA.[37]

People with good common sense have always known that hard monotonous work and restrictive unexciting food are best for long life. This has been confirmed by fact-finding investigations and statistics.[35] But the modern view is different: everything is valued for its direct invigorating or satisfying effect. Thus sex enjoyments, which could be most damaging — nature tends to sacrifice body for sake of reproduction — are viewed as beneficial,[8] because they provide feelings of vitality and satisfaction.[14] Under the same logic we are advised to enjoy fabulous food,[18] not to abandon relaxing drink or smoking,[14] to "live to heart's content",[8] or to use soporific and tranquilizing drugs.[14] The use of drugs for cardiac relief has been enthusiastically advocated, but also condemned, as "everything has been tried and nothing has worked very well".[16] Digitalis, the best known drug, is accepted as a "most valuable" means, to be prescribed in large dosages;[13] but also, its use is seen as a definite "blunder".[9] Some doctors may recommend nitroglycerin even if 100 tablets have to be taken daily;[13] and some may find heart drugs fatally dangerous.[17]

Stress, of course, is blamed for the functional heart disorders. But as we have repeatedly explained, *modern man is attaining his highest value, the freedom from stress, in all the conditions and ways of life he enjoys. The end result of this overenjoyment is its opposite, the malignant stress.* A further paradox of overadjustment has to be kept in mind. The negative, even fatal effect is always caused by some negative, often minor, final cause. This explains why observations show all kinds of stressful situations as the direct causes of heart disorders but why the inverse relationship between heart disease and difficulties or stresses of life and work generally applies.[8,15] Studies show that *emotional attitudes and not factual conditions* are decisive (J. Stamler, G. Blomquist). But emotional reactions are totally *governed by the opposite causation and the logic of overadjustments.*

The presently widest study on heart disease and stress, conducted by M. Friedman and R. H. Rosenman, on 3,500 subjects, shows that not any particular conditions but the personality is decisive. Two personality types, A and B, have been established, though the final causes of the typical behavior have admittedly not been discovered. The *emotional attitudes* of the types A and B are found to be the sole determining factors. This again means the effects are governed by the causality of emotions or general releases, with its paradoxical logic. Here, as in mental disorders, the seemingly restrictive, stressful, or "hard-driving" behavior actually originates in overenjoyments, perfectionism or lack of restraint. Conversely the person who has plenty of satisfactions for what he is doing, therefore seems to be "easy-going" or capable of enjoyment, has actually accumulated such potentials through restrictions. That is why the numerous logically scientific studies on stress have produced more confusion than simple explanation.

But the very fact that *emotions and stress* are the determining factors in heart disease leads to the conclusion that *overadjustment, as overenjoyment,* is the only possible cause of the disease. The dependence of heart disease on emotions has been one of the best established medical facts.[9,12] Particularly the psychosomaticists have demonstrated the decisive importance of emotions in heart disease.[13] The best proof of the unthinkable, opposite causation here is that medicine, proceeding by its direct "scientific" logic, has *admittedly no causal explanation* for the functional heart disease.[13,15]

The effort here has been unique, and the cause of this general uniform natural phenomenon should be simple. Apparently medicine has been looking in the completely wrong direction. No wonder that doctors die from heart disease four times as often as the general public.[11,14] We do not need to repeat that with its direct improvement logic *medicine here can do more harm than good,* since overadjustments are deepened by direct improvements.

Hypertension. High blood pressure is part of the functional heart disease. Its understanding or control would require the same insight in the paradox of overadjustment, of the worsening through improvement. Typically "the cause of hypertension cannot be determined"[2] or has "not yet been discovered"[18] and no generally acceptable explanation of it has been reached.[19] Also the confusion about seemingly beneficial effects of factors which in the end deepen the disease is general. Even such authority on hypertension as Dr. I. H. Page finds that tobacco, coffee or alcohol have no appreciable bad effect on the disease and may be even beneficial as sources of feeling of warmth and well-being.[12,21]

Certainly alcohol as well as coffee have beneficial immediate effects on hypertension,[20] because they are vasodilators. But it is well known that their aftereffects, during the hangover, lead to restriction of blood vessels. The vicious-circle deepening of such aftereffects explains why the user of alcohol or coffee is the one who suffers from high blood pressure most. Still, the peculiar great discovery of modern medicine that alcohol is good for circulation rests mostly on the experimental proofs that it acts as a vasodilator.[12] Smoking is seen as helpful because it has similar effects, and stimulates release of adrenalin which initially strengthens heart beat.[19]

Particularly the use of numerous drugs is based on the experimentally "scientific" observation that drugs easily relieve high blood pressure. In fact a doctor can lower the blood pressure any time he wants, and "scarcely a month passes" without appearance of a new drug for doing so.[5] But doctors know equally well that no really effective drug for hypertension exists. The improvement is only temporary, and the opposite reactions, the "side" effects can be disastrous (W. Evans).[17] Rather, conditions that have the effect of "shock" or excessive restriction offer relief. Here belong bouts of infection, fevers, injection of pyrogens or other disturbing substances, highly restrictive and "starvation" diets or even any grave operation.[21] One can see why the "whole subject has been surrounded by so much controversy".[21] It all points to overadjustment as a cause. Revealingly, "the early symptoms of hypertension are often exactly those of a neurosis".[13] Psychosomaticists have demonstrated that hypertension is caused emotionally and is governed by ambivalent emotions.[9]

Hypertension is a result of increased vasodilating stimulation and of tranquilization. The overstimulated circulation becomes constrictive or exhausted, but has to meet increased work load because tranquilization has left organic needs unattended. As the increased circulation requirements have to be carried out by a restricted or exhausted system, the tension results. Any *added stimulation or tranquilization can, naturally, lessen the tension — to make it worse in the end.*

The usual logic is misleading in understanding or dealing with the disorder. What the hypertension patient needs is to suffer through the symptoms, upon discontinuation of the improvements, whatever these may be in his case. The "disease" here, as the natural reaction, is already the pressure toward normalcy. Some authorities find that hypertension is compatible with normal life (R. Platt).[19] Japanese have the "highest frequency of hypertensive disease [but] only one-fourth to one-twentieth the rate of heart attacks in the United States".[2,15] Apparently, if the overadjustment improvements cannot be progressively increased, the malignant vicious-circle effects cannot deepen to a critical degree.

The right way to help is to find out what are the stimulating means that the person is using to make himself feel more "normal" but that are excessive under the specific conditions of his organism. This may not be easy. But the enormous skills of modern medicine would be more than sufficient, if the right causal logic was used. Even a general elimination of stimulants can help. The person knows that if only he could abstain from things like rich foods, drinks or cigarettes, he would be well, though experimentally such stimulating or vasodilating means appear beneficial, and are similar to the drugs or remedies the doctor may prescribe. The above gross effects of "shock" or excessive restriction can help because they counteract overadjustments.

Arteriosclerosis. The most clearly evident physical syndrome of coronary disease is the arteriosclerosis, with atherosclerosis as its main form. Expectedly, in its nature and etiology, arteriosclerosis *has remained an enigma.*[12] A foremost authority, I. H. Page, says that "surprising is how little we know about it".[21] He thinks that "it will be a long time before its inner nature will be known so that it can be prevented and cured". Presently there is only disagreement among scientists, who find atherosclerosis one of the unsolvable, complex problems.[16] "The causes of atherosclerosis, and of its strategic localization in the coronary arteries, are unknown" (G. R. Herrmann).[13] Equally the "complicated relationships between high blood pressure and hardening of arteries is not understood".[2] It is noted that the arterial degeneration disease is "rarely if ever reached in the normal wild state of animals".[19]

Overadjustment as cause in arteriosclerosis is evident from the fact that the arterial degeneration appears "wherever people lead a more luxurious life" or as soon as a less advanced people reach living standards enjoyed in richer countries (P. D. White).[7] Of course stresses and strains of modern life are blamed. And the relaxing alcohol is found to be "of considerable assistance in the management and control or arteriosclerotic change in elderly persons" (E. J. Stieglitz).[12] In general, persons suffering from emotional difficulties or stress also suffer from excess fats, lipids, fatty deposits and cholesterol that accompany arteriosclerosis.[2,19] This agrees with overadjustment as cause.

We saw repeatedly that malignantly deepening stress can grow only through overadjustment or overenjoyments. The same applies to all the functional excessive changes and products that come together with the stress. It is revealing that people living under all kinds of stressful conditions suffer from arterial degeneration least. This has been shown by studies on people under war conditions,[19] in concentration camps,[8] under the apartheid conditions in South Africa"[14] or generally in the underdeveloped countries struggling with every kind of difficulty.[19]

We may add that for arteriosclerosis as well one could give more involved physiologic descriptions of how the overenjoyed suppleness and unimpeded action of arteries change into their opposites, hardening and clogging. It could be shown how the increased protoplasmic vigor and efficiency of tissues revert into their exhaustion and saturation with metaplasmic, inert material, as in all aging. Still more detailed opposite effects could be found on the level of cells. But the deeper one goes into dealing with separate biophysical elements, the more factors he inevitably misses, in the myriad world of organic causation. The same is true for understanding or dealing with the endlessly varied means that the person uses for obtaining the overadjustments in as endlessly complex functions. He attains them by simply seeking the pleasure, by enjoying what improves his circulation. As simply by preventing the overenjoyments of such pleasures we can prevent all the ungraspably complex initial "improvement" effects and the negative aftereffects.

Cholesterol. We may look at the much discussed subject of cholesterol. It is a typical problem of the "scientific" approach to cardiovascular disorders. There is only confusion and controversy about cholesterol as cause of such disorders. The best doctors and scientists hold "diametrically opposed views" in the matter (A. M. Master).[22] On the one hand it has been shown, as in the Farmingham project, that cholesterol is the most decisive factor. The Farmingham subjects with blood-cholesterol level above a 260 mark incurred four times greater risk of heart attack than those with a reading of 220 or less. On the other hand, it is held that cholesterol is vital to life;[8] that it increases body's resistance to other, infectious diseases;[14] that the rise of blood cholesterol may indicate body's need for more of it;[16] and that reduction of cholesterol in blood, by drugs or other means, would not only fail to provide greater protection[19] but "would be potentially very dangerous" (I. H. Page). [21,13] Some authorities find the preoccupation with cholesterol a mere "fad" and relation of cholesterol to heart disease unproven (A. M. Master, H. L. Jaffe).[22]

The "scientifically" logical approach of seeking direct reduction of cholesterol has been abandoned, as more knowledge has accumulated. Experiments have shown that reduction of cholesterol in the food only increases its production by the body;[18] or that a direct increase or decrease of cholesterol in blood is counteracted organically by equal compensatory changes.[13] In fact the cholesterol we ingest has "little or no effect on cholesterol concentration in the blood" (A. Keys).[13] Drugs for reduction of cholesterol in blood are available, but are not used, because the results are disappointing.[13] Rabbits limited to foods with excessive cholesterol content did not develop coronary disorders (H. Burn).[19]

Cholesterol increase, like other restrictive, "negative" reactions, may be *part of the functional "disease" as pressure back to normalcy.* Of particular interest here is the connection of cholesterol levels with stress. In clinical observations, by Dr. Stewart Wolf and his colleagues, cholesterol level of patients increased dramatically when they were exposed to stress, disturbance and unpleasant or anger-evoking situations. In experiments at NIH, "volunteers when told they were to receive a painful injection showed rapid rise in blood fats".[11] In other experiments "exposure to socially charged situations increased blood lipids in but a few minutes".[11] Cholesterol is "manufactured by body during unrelieved stress", in animals as well as humans.[3] Many observers have noted such rise in cholesterol together with increase in clotting capacity and viscosity of blood during periods of stress.[13]

Evidently cholesterol, as all stress, restriction or functional "disease", serves here to prepare the organism for emergency or to restrain releases in order to restore their reserves. Surely it creates a "diseased" condition, a feeling contrary to pleasures of well-being, and it may turn the person into a weakling or partial invalid. But so do healthy reactions to danger that actually prepare and ultimately strengthen the organism. All the person has to do is to live through such "diseased" reactions in full.

The danger lies in the efforts to overcome such reactions by *further "improvements"*, which the organism has to meet with still stronger opposite processes. Such vicious circle can drive the production of cholesterol as the restrictive mechanism to excessive levels while *the whole disorder is deepened to the limits of organic collapse.* Of course physiologic interactions of cholesterol are as complexly involved as are all organic processes. That is why integrated pleasure reactions rather than biochemical processes should be dealt with.

The improvement paradox then would become apparent, in practical terms. Cholesterol is a tasteless fatty substance most richly found in bile, gallstones or nerve tissues. It would be the last thing anybody would like to consume. Similarly, tasteless unsaturated fats, that nobody likes to eat either, reduce cholesterol in blood. The tastiest, protein-rich foods are freest of cholesterol. But exactly the people who can afford such foods, or the stress-free conditions, that are valued above everything else, suffer most from cholesterol and its psychological counterpart, the stress. This can be seen from numerous studies on rich, and primitive peoples — Americans or Britons, and Eskimos or Bantus — living under varied conditions, of peace and war.[19]

To conclude, *improvements beyond normalcy* of any function are organically met by opposite "worsening", and if this is overcome by further improvements, the abnormalcy deepens, in a vicious circle. It thus can reach any, incredible degree by nothing more than continuously added experimentally clear improvements. That is why modern medicine never finds the cause of functional diseases and can only deepen them, by proceeding with the nonrelative, "scientific" logic of direct improvements. Now, the functions of heart, as the "seat of emotions", can be always improved, above normalcy. Of course natural adjustment has definite limits for such improvements. But the awesome skills and means of modern progress and medicine can make the improvements unlimited. Which is being done with deadly efficiency.

The result is the 300 percent increase in the deaths from coronary disorders,[1] as well as the total, admitted, inability to understand their causes.[2] This is typical, yet unbelievable, considering that these disorders are recognizedly uniform, therefore must be governed by one natural principle, which has to be simple, as overadjustment is.

Authorities know that discovering the cause of these disorders would be the first step in making their cure possible. No effort is being spared. In a recent project 40,000 subjects are to be studied and put on special diets for ten years. If the study is pursued with the same "scientific" logic, that is the only one now known in medicine, it will only increase the confusion. The paradox of the relative or opposite causation applies to every detail, in diet or physiologic process, through its every phase. For all of them the experimental *observations will again show the direct improvements as beneficial and the restrictive "diseased" reactions as the logical causes* of the disorders. This can only compound the same ingenious, extensive and "scientific" ways that have helped to increase the disease and the confusion. The limitedness of the organism, to its sameness, is inexorable and any improvement above its normalcy has to lead to opposite processes or worsening.

The Functional Causes of Cancer

Cancer, as all malignant growth, exhibits almost every characteristic of functional overadjustment. We find in it the unrestrained increase in releases, in their most fundamental form, of biological growth, concurrently with exhaustion of the normal, restrictive potential of growth. The paradox of worsening through improvement is confirmed by the fact that the same carcinogenic agents which cause malignant growth also provide temporary relief from it. Overadjustment as cause is confirmed by the causal connection of cancer with overactivity of the hormones that serve pleasure releases or emotional enjoyments. Cancer is a typical product of functional improvements strived for by man: it increases in direct proportion with the attainment of such improvements. Deaths from cancer have increased more than fourfold in a period of last sixty years in this country.[1]

We may look at some of the factors which cause cancer but also seem to relieve it, temporarily. Sex hormones are used in alleviating cancer, "but double dose may stir up the cells".[5] Most hormones act in the same way, causing cancer upon "prolonged exposure".[23] They are found "not only to cause cancers but also to cure them". "Many of the agents which are used in the treatment of cancer are themselves liable to produce cancer under certain conditions" (H. Burn).[6] Among such ambivalent causal agents belong steroids, "wonder" hormones, tars, enzymes, mineral-enriched preparations, X-rays, ultraviolet rays, the folic acid and various carbon compounds. (A. Haddow).[17]

As D. C. Huggins has observed in explaining the 3-methyl-cholanthrene treatment, almost every chemical used to alleviate cancer can itself cause the disorder. No explanation for this "paradoxical fact" is found, and doctors may merely state that "there is often a very delicate balance between normal and malignant growth" (J. Ewing). In truth, the difference between the two is that of black and white, positive and negative. In all overadjustments the same factor that provides direct improvement also leads to the final exhaustion of the function. This explains why cancers appear only a considerable time after the influence that causes them has started.

Overadjustment as cause of cancer is further revealed by the fact that cancer attacks mostly the organs and functions which regulate our pleasure releases, through the activity of hormones as the "liquid nerves". Thus cancer tends to occur in organs strongly affected by the steroid hormones[5] which regulate the most sought after pleasure releases, of sexual gratifications and of growth. Also, "there is growing evidence that disordered activity of the endocrine glands is a principal cause of cancer".[5] Hormone activity — which controls emotions — has been linked with cancer by various authorities.[19] Overproduction of hormones, particularly those of adrenal glands, pituatary and insulin-producing cells, has been observed (S. C. Sommers).

The rare cures attained in cancer cases have been those where removal of testes, ovaries and adrenal glands has been resorted to, notably by Dr. C. Huggins.[19] Neutralization of sex hormone activity by administration of hormones of the opposite sex has given similar results.[19] Cortisone, the most studied hormone, has shown to have affinity with cancer. Injected in rats which are resisting sarcoma tumors, cortisone causes them to develop the tumors and die quickly.[19] Increase of stress upon such injections is blamed, although cortisone is the best known protector against stress.

Generally, stress and emotional negativeness have been pointed out as causal factors, in the frequently adopted psychological etiology of cancer (J. Cohen). At the conference on Psychophysiological Aspects of Cancer, various negative emotions were emphasized as possible causes of cancer. Doctors have observed that persons exhibiting particular emotional negativity often become cancer patients — as is interestingly told by Sir Heneage Ogilvie.[17] Actually, if excessive stress and emotional negativeness can be related to cancer, this particularly confirms overadjustment as cause. For only through excessive overenjoyment can malignantly deepening negative emotional reactions be incurred.

Overenjoyment as a cause is practically clear when we consider that such indulgences as smoking and overeating have been clearly, statistically related with cancer. Restriction of food, in experiments with animals, reduced the incidence of cancer markedly.[37] Malignant growth afflicts more readily "well fed than ill-nourished animals", and various restrictive diets have been shown to inhibit cancers.[19] The most pleasant, affluent diet, of beef correlates statistically with the most frequent cancer, of the bowel. Smoking as cause of lung cancer has been widely documented, because use of nicotine is readily seen as not normal for man, and the link between smoking and lung cancer is too directly evident to be missed. The Seventh-Day Adventists, who do not smoke, showed a ten times lower incidence of lung cancer even while living in the air-polluted Los Angeles and its adjacent counties. Typically, mice forced to inhale tobacco smoke did not develop cancer;[37] but dogs did, evidently because they acquired taste for smoking and became addicted to it, as the experiments of W. G. Cahan and O. Amerbach showed.

Cancer is an abnormality of growth, its functional failure, or exhaustion of its normal, restrictive potentials. All growth is governed by the paradoxical law of the limited normalcy: adding to life brings closer its exhaustion or death. The paradox of the rate of growth shows in the fact that cancer is a disorder of the exhausted, slow, old age, but also of intensified accelerated modern living. To take the most general stimulator of growth, the folic acid, its effects have been found to be paradoxical. Early experiments on it, by Lewisohn, Laszlo and Leuchtenberg, showed it to be strikingly positive in relieving cancers. But later researches have led to opposite conclusions, and anti-folic agents have been found to offer the best definite treatment.[5] Methotrexate, recognized as the only drug that cures cancer, though only three minor forms of it, is an antifolic acid. Also aminopterin and other folic acid antagonists have been found to be helpful in childhood leukemia cases.[5]

Paradoxically, influences that are organically strongly adverse or alarming may have positive effect. In the presently most promising research, on immunotherapy, eminently promoted by Robert A. Good, the best results are obtained by injections of strong bacteria, viruses, or extracts from tumors similar to those of the patient. The BCG, a vaccine from live TB bacteria, has been used by the NCI and scientists in a dozen of countries. Similar effects of the TB bacteria and of strong infections have been long observed.[37] The cancer immunotherapy, not unlike inoculation, has to use organically alarming agents to evoke organic readjustment.

The bacterial toxins in form of polysacharides have typically shown to produce "a very strong shocklike reaction in human beings which is often alarming".[6] One may think here of shock therapy, which is an admitted mystery in psychiatry and exactly contrary to the beliefs held in modern medicine, but offers definite cure as no other psychiatric treatment does. We saw the vast possibilities that lie in a *causally understood,* adaptable "shock" or anti-release treatment. The discovery of interferon and studies on stimulation of its production point to similar possibilities. Interferon is a protein appearing upon destruction of cells by viruses and serving as an alarm agent in protection of other cells. Research by Dr. M. R. Hilleman and associates has shown that interferon production can be stimulated by injection of RNA or some forms of viruses and that this gives remarkable protection. Such cellular "shock" treatment may offer protection where merely physiologic overadjustment may be the cause of cancer.

This kind of overadjustment may be frequent, because every cell lives by the same striving for release, while complying with the restrictions. These may be overcome whenever the tissue comes under some unusual influence — ultraviolet rays, X-rays, atomic, mineral and biochemical concentration — against which the tissue has no evolutionary protection. Then the vicious circle of overadjustment starts, on the purely physiologic level. As abnormal releases are obtained, the resulting abnormalcy increases stress in the tissue and even more releases become necessary. The result is a chain reaction that spreads like a fire. In any event, control, or at least prevention, of overadjustments as causes of cancer could be made complete by adding the control over physiologic overadjustment to the control over the usual, consciously sought overadjustments.

This of course would require the use of the paradoxical relative causal logic at every step. We hardly can expect modern medicine, based on the contrary, "scientific" logic and methods, to be of much help. We can rather expect the perpetuation of the logic of direct improvements which are the very causes of malignancy. Doctors will expand treatments and drugs that provide the direct improvements, and will claim that, because the state of the patients becomes clearly better, they live longer, though nobody knows how much longer they would have lived without the improvements. Real benefits may accrue only accidentally, as the treatments expand and become drastic, therefore indirectly interrupt overadjustments.

However, counteracting the overadjustment only after cancer has started may be too late. Malignant growth is the end result of overadjustments affecting the deepest levels of growth and living process, where the constant "improvements" have finally removed the last standards of normalcy. In other functional diseases, particularly in mental disorders, pressure back to normalcy may constitute the whole "disease", as the deeper requirements of normalcy reassert themselves. In malignant growth none of the standards may be left to serve as the guide. That is why it would be important for medicine to use all its enormous skills — and a new logic — in discovering the overadjustments at their beginning. It is generally recognized that cancer is not unavoidable, or accidental like catching an infection. Rather a proneness to cancer is found as decisive (D. L. Morton, G. J. Todaro). This is typical of all functional disorders, since they depend on the overadjustment tendency of the person.

Yet modern medicine promotes rather than prevents the "improvements". Every drug or means used is selected for its direct improvement effect. Only occasionally, where the drug aftereffects are too evident, is attention paid to the deeper influences of drugs. Then it is discovered that chromosomal changes may be the result. It is typical that exactly those means which are used for obtaining artificially more pleasure or added satisfaction — from LSD and amphetamines to saccharin and glue sniffing — are found to produce the chromosomal changes. Pleasure is biologically the central, key mechanism, of the life flow itself. Its perversion has to affect directly the function of life and growth.

Scientists recognize that malignant growth is a disorder of the nucleus of the cell or of its chromosomes, which are the genetically determinant inheritable factors. The chromosomal changes from overadjustments thus can accumulate through generations. The drugs and "improvements" sought and enjoyed by the latest modern generations may be destroying the normalcy of the cells. The experimental conception of inheritance, of never-changing genes is only half true, particularly in view of the discoveries that the RNA can pass inheritable information "backwards" through the so-called "RNA dependent DNA polymerase". This enzyme is found together with six viruses that cause cancer in lower animals.

Because of such genetically accumulated overadjustments a person may be prone toward further overadjustments as well as closer to the final malignant exhaustion of normal restrictive potentials of growth. Variations in normalcy may be due to other factors, such as differences in foods, life conditions and customary, unnoticed backgrounds, of peoples and individuals. Enabling such people to attain general normalcy may amount to driving them into overadjustments. In a simplest case, people may compensate for lack of stimulation from their food — good in itself — by using strong, spicy additives. In more complex cases, people may learn to manipulate their releases in various special ways to compensate for hardships of life. Then it may seem that rather poor foods or hard life are the contributing causes of later disorders. Moreover, in all overadjustments the precipitating factor is always some negative event or trauma, however tiny, while the real cause is a long previous positive overenjoyment, which may seem as a very normal, satisfactory adjustment.

The overadjustment explanation of cancer is not contradicted by the virus theories. Viruses are always present in the body, in the form of "orphan viruses". Recent studies have shown that viruses with cancer-causing potential are generally inherited (R. Huebner), and that there are constant pressures on us to develop cancers (R. Good). It has been long known that every cell may contain viruses in a latent form (A. Lwoff).[37] Viruses become virulent only under certain conditions, as do most germs. Significantly, cortisone administration can "transform into antagonists certain normal innocuous viruses" (B. Inglis).[17] Thus only when cells have exhausted their normal potentials do viruses take over.

But what about the researchers who have contracted cancer while working on it? The explanation may be that they constantly handle chemicals which "cure" or alleviate cancer, and induce it for reasons we explained above. The virus theories have been used to explain why cancer medication usually provides improvement at beginning but makes the disorder worse in the end. It is reasoned that viruses become more virulent under medication by way of selection. If medication really annihilated viruses, it would cure in most cases, since selection is a very rare occurrence; and the selected, extremely strong viruses would be contagious. None of this is true.

Modern medicine, in spite of colossal efforts and skills, has not even begun to understand the causation of cancer, which as a general uniform natural phenomenon can be governed only by a simple causal principle. Such principle should be evident at any level, of detailed processes as well as of integrated reactions, feelings or pleasure. Overadjustment, with its opposite effects and vicious circle is such principle, evident throughout the causation of cancer. But it can never be understood in modern medicine, because it is exactly contrary to the "scientific" logic and everything believed, thought of or done in modern medicine. We can only agree with scientists that understanding of the cause of cancer would be a breakthrough in dealing with it. But to reach it, medicine would have to move in a direction that it presently cannot even think of.

Arthritis, Diabetes, Peptic Ulcers

The major functional diseases, after heart disease and cancer, expectedly originate in the major organic functions that can be improved by man beyond their normalcy in their rendering of feelings of well-being, vigor or pleasure. Modern man attaining the best means and ways for overenjoying such improvements suffers progressively from these diseases, whereas animals, unable to plan the pleasantness of their functions, are free of them.

Arthritis. Ease, suppleness and vigor of movement can be constant sources of pleasure. The various reactions of arthritis and rheumatism are the malignant opposites, unrecognizable as always, of such overenjoyed ease and vigor. Here again the biological processes involved both in the disease and overadjustment, are ungraspably complex, but the most inclusive, general integrated reactions or feelings are sufficient concepts for causal understanding and control. Typically medicine, in its staggering scientific efforts, has *not been able to discover the cause of arthritis*.[2,24]

Doctors frankly admit that "the cause or causes of arthritis escape us", or that "little is known about the subject" (W. Boyd).[23] Simply stated, "the cause of rheumatoid arthritis is unknown" (J. H. Bland).[25] Doctors are hopefully expecting the discovery of the causes of arthritis in the future, while noting that presently "this field of medicine is chiefly notable for its eager ignorance" (J. W. Brooke).[24] Many factors have been blamed as contributory causes, but experimental observations have shown that none of them — diet, climate, exertion, job, illness, heredity or traumas — are causally determining.[24,25]

The *paradox of opposite causation* is revealed in the curious effects of cortisone on arthritis. When the cortisone treatment was first applied the results were miraculous. "Lame and crippled arthritics climbed steps, did little jigs, swung arms and legs that had been cruelly stiffened".[5] But soon the cures reversed, patients became worse unless the doses were progressively increased,[6] and the end result was a host of "side" effects that were worse than the disease.[15] Disappointing reversals became the "usual pattern".[25] It had to be admitted that the cortisone, as other "wonder" hormones, did not cure anything, that the patients were only "holding a bear by the tail",[5] and that the various aftereffects, including "acute symptoms of mental disorder", made such treatments dangerous.[6,24] Generally, the initial effects of cortisone, ACTH, other steroids and similar drugs are an increase in physical and mental protection and performance, but the aftereffects are a dangerous decrease in protection against disease, infection or stress, and a psychosomatic exhaustion (H. Burn).[6]

Psychological etiology in arthritis is revealing. Arthritis has been viewed as "a muscular manifestation of mind", and stress has been blamed for it.[24] "Emotional injury or very difficult or impossible life situations frequently precede onset of rheumatoid arthritis" (J. H. Bland).[25] "Psychological factors, such as stress, operating perhaps through the adrenal cortex, seem to play a part" in arthritis (W. Boyd).[23] When emotional state improves arthritis becomes less painful and symptoms decrease.[9] Opposite fluctuations of symptoms are typical for arthritis.[25] Doctors are puzzled by "curious remissions and exacerbations",[23] as arthritis "waxes and wanes in severity for reasons as yet unknown" (J. W. Brooke).[24]

This confirms that overadjustment is the cause of arthritis. Only through overadjustment can stress or functional exhaustion reach malignant proportions; and the alternation of opposite effects is typical of overadjustment. It is revealing that a clearly nonspecific release-improving drug like aspirin can alleviate arthritis, temporarily. Doctors find here that "the most important drug remains simple aspirin";[23] that its "benefit is greater and more complicated than a simple matter of pain relief"; and that the reason "why this should be so is not yet clearly understood".[24] On the other hand, real relief of arthritis comes from a "friendly fever" or some other disease like a "good bout of jaundice", though nobody knows why the other disease helps.[37] Painful treatments, by use of injections, of milk, sulfur or even sea water, may have similar effects. Evidently they counteract overadjustments.

Probably the most interesting observations — which point to overadjustment as cause — have been made by Dr. P. S. Hench, the Nobel prize winner and foremost authority on the cortisone treatment. He found that it is not the simple deficit of adrenal hormones that causes the arthritic reactions, but a change in the circulating hydrocortisone from abnormally high to low levels. He observed that the disease flares up when the cortisone tide ebbs, and that the letdown in long-term cortisone treatment is due to the same phenomenon; understandably, continuous increase in the cortisone level is impossible.

Dr. Hench found that his observations required a theory so new that he did not expect other doctors to accept it. In truth the relative descent, not any actual level, in any release factor, causes the functional negative reactions in all overadjustment. Reaching higher levels of release leads to the opposite effects because descent becomes inevitable — as the use of narcotics shows.

The subtleties of overadjustment have to be kept in mind. The oversatisfactions may be as varied and unnoticed as are one's "normal" ways of life, and soon may not even be felt as yielding any satisfaction. It can be only generally noticed that the arthritics are people who enjoy physical activity.[9] Further, the opposite, positive and negative reactions in overadjustments never seem to have anything in common and may come through different organs or parts of the body. Moreover, there can be overadjustment even while the person lives through unpleasant hardships and merely attains more "normal" reactions under abnormal conditions. This explains why people who work hard or are exposed to climatic hardships suffer more from arthritis. But a hardship met in full, with all the natural restrictive painful reactions, causes no ill. No wonder that modern medicine has not found any logical relationship between arthritis and any factor (J. W. Brooke, J. H. Bland).[24,25]

Diabetes. All overadjustment characteristics are evident in diabetes. Logically it is assumed that diabetes is due to lack of insulin. But closer studies, namely by Dr. G. Reaven, and Dr. L. Power, have shown that the "insulin-like" activity is actually higher in the blood of diabetics. Thus a high insulin stimulation produces the understimulation effects of diabetes, as is also evident from studies by Dr. M. Linder and Dr. C. Weller.[28] It is known that sometimes insulin becomes inefficient while the patient is increasing its dosage which further lowers its efficiency (T. S. Danowski).[26] Diabetes improves or worsens together with emotions — which follow the paradoxical logic of opposite causation.

Typically, "the true cause of diabetes is still unknown" (A. M. Sindoni).[27] Doctors find diabetes a highly complicated, still imperfectly understood disorder.[15] They link it to "some unknown undetectable defect of the pancreas",[28] of which they "do not know the essential cause".[23] Simple lack of insulin does not explain diabetes and a "pluriglandular concept of diabetes" is being sought.[27] In 80 percent of cases diabetes is due not to insufficiency of insulin but to inability of body to use it effectively (C. Weller).[28] Changes in the Langerhans islet cells "are probably more often secondary rather than primary factors",[27] and diabetes "may also occur in the presence of normal islet cells, when the pancreas does not function properly because of over-stimulation by the pituitary gland".[27]

The dependence of diabetes on emotions, i.e., on general releases makes it *explainable by overadjustment.* Diabetes "is associated with almost every type of psychiatric disorder".[9] Stress or conflicts are found to be its determining factors, and anxiety or depression its accompanying symptoms.[9] Psychosomaticists have no difficulty in demonstrating emotional causes of diabetes. Logically, direct improvement of emotions is favored and strict enforcement of diets therefore seen as having negative effects.[37] But it is also found that diabetics are persons spoiled in childhood and reluctant to abdicate their pleasures or to change their diets.[10] Most doctors know that control of diet is the best way to deal with diabetes.[15]

In general, diabetics are found to be physically better off than most patients, but to have neurotics among their ancestors.[37] A "definite parallel between schizophrenic tendencies and diabetes" is noted.[10] Negative emotions as causes of diabetes have been proved in various experiments, notably by Drs. Hinkle and Wolf[9] as well as Dr. J. Walker and Dr. D. O'Neill.[17] Under "scientific" logic this means that direct improvement of emotions should be the goal of diabetes treatment. Actually overadjustment is the cause of diabetes. The disorder seems to "smolder in the body for months or years before it becomes severe".[27] This is typical of all "improvement" disorders. Confusing remissions and exacerbations of symptoms are also observed.[23] As typically, an "infection or other forms of stress may temporarily lower the insulin requirements".[28] Also the adrenal cortex, which controls all stress, seems to play a part in diabetes;[23] we saw how general is the reversal of effects of adrenal hormones. Hypoglycemia, the functional opposite of diabetes, often precedes it.[28] Above all, restrictions in foods are sufficient to control diabetes,[15] in more than 80 percent of cases.[28]

Insulin and drugs are of course very effective at the beginning, but on the whole are not found to offer definite remedy (B. F. Miller).[2] The most used drug, tolbutamide, prescribed for decades in most diabetes cases, is now found by FDA, AMA and ADA to be no more effective than diet alone and to contribute to heart disease. This has, understandably, caused vast discussion and controversy. Insulin is necessary in cases of organic, not functional, abnormalcy. Such cases — which may be ultimately due to overadjustment in previous generation — would be less than the 15 percent that cannot be treated by diet alone.[28]

Insulin in itself is not decisive: even if the pancreas is removed the body can still use sugar (T. S. Danowski).[26] Statistics from various countries and from the two World Wars[19] have shown that diabetes almost never afflicts people who suffer from scarcity of food, which inevitably means preponderance of starches and carbohydrates that are blamed for the diabetic reactions. Also the inheritance of *acquired* diabetic reactions is proved, as the benefits from such restricted diets extend to the next generation. The best study here is probably that by Dr. D. Brunner, on the Yemen Jews and their descendants deriving benefits from foods that are considered as worst by diabetes experts.[37]

In this country where people eat the most stimulating foods, which experimentally show as best for diabetes, we have five million diabetics, and the Diabetes Drive is discovering as many more potential diabetics who supposedly have the disease without knowing it. These persons can, certainly, be turned into regular diabetics by the "improvements" of treatment, while they could live normally, though restrictively, without the stimulating nutritional and medical improvements. But such programs as the Diabetes Drive can prove statistically their success. If so many people who do not have innate diabetic disease are made regular, statistical diabetics, the proportional rates of mortality from diabetes have to go down. Moreover, the great "improvement" treatments of such diseases as diabetes lead to deeper functional disorders, cancer and heart disease, which have become the typical great killers. Heart disease is now the main threat to diabetics.[2]

Diabetes is a typical overadjustment disorder. Studies from various countries[19] show that *diets which would shock diabetes experts keep people who eat them free of diabetes,* while in countries, like ours, where people can afford the most stimulating foods, diabetes is rampant. In their direct effects such foods offer great improvement. That is why the diabetic cannot renounce them. *He knows better than anybody what gives him relief* from the reactions that oppress him. Expectedly the general release improving drugs — aspirin, estrogens, antihistamines, general sulfa compounds or vasodilating drugs — can relieve diabetes. Even smoking and alcohol can be shown to be immediately beneficial.[27] No wonder that diabetes increases together with medical progress.

Peptic Ulcer. The functional overadjustment nature of peptic ulcer is evident from the increase of ulcer incidence together with increased improvements, and from its dependence on emotional or hormonal factors. Doctors, who have every skill and means to improve their physical well-being, suffer from peptic ulcers most, while poor people, in underdeveloped countries, have it least.[29] Peptic ulcer is said to be the disease of executives. Thus the people who can do most in attaining release improvements or satisfactions suffer from the ulcer most. Typically, the "executive" monkey who can avoid electric shocks develops ulcer, while the one who cannot avoid them does not.

It is revealing that stress and negative emotions can always be shown as causes of ulcer.[29] Of course any emotional stress can malignantly accumulate only through overadjustment. Relaxed attitudes and peace of mind are found to be best safeguards against ulcers.[30] The whole problem is one of management of his mind by the person.[30] But emotional management has to follow the paradoxical logic of opposite causation, contrary to the present medical logic of improvements.

That is why *modern medicine is confused and mystified* in its etiology of peptic ulcer. Many factors are considered, but it is admitted that nothing definite can be said.[19] "The cause of ulcer is not yet fully understood" (B. F. Miller).[2] Various tranquilizing and release improving drugs are recommended.[30,31] Even alcohol and smoking are found as permissible because they provide immediate relaxation. Their prohibition is seen as a misunderstanding.[31] Naturally, controversy continues and where the drug or relaxant is used so frequently that its role cannot be missed, the opposite effects are discovered. Thus it is recognized that smoking can be a cause of stomach ulcer;[30] that coffee is "productive of more ulcers than any other item of food";[30] or that "the most common ulcerogenic drug is plain or buffered aspirin".[31]

The mystery is inevitable because the ulcer is determined by emotions, which obey *the paradoxical relative causal logic*. Ulcer patients are found to be "high-strung, restless, irritable, prone to worry and upset by strain" (W. Boyd).[23] Psychosomaticists have extensively demonstrated the dependence of the peptic ulcer on emotional factors[9] — which can become malignant only through overadjustment. The increase in releases is here sought by the person through increase in the acidity of the stomach. This acidity is a sign of vigor or youth; and doctors who accept this simple logic recommend its increase by all means.[37] In general, it has been repeatedly proven, by direct observations, that acidity of gastric juices increases, within minutes, upon emotional stress,[31] requiring extra releases. Thus a person with tendency of overadjustment will respond with increase in the stomach acidity upon any stress or demand for more releases, which grows through overadjustment.

Normally there is a balance between the acidity and the stomach wall. But if the stomach functions have become exhausted, through overadjustment, its tissue growth and vigor decrease. Then the overproduced acidity erodes the stomach wall and causes the ulcer.[31] Necrosis of the stomach wall is generally recognized as the precondition of ulcer, though its causes remain a mystery.[23] Overadjustment would offer simple explanation; and it is indicated by the suspected overactivity of adrenal cortex (H. Burn).[6] Such overstimulation usually leaves tissues and their resistance exhausted. Interesting is the observation that aspirin, which acts through prostaglandins, causes the mucuous lining in the stomach to shed and replace cells at an abnormal rate, which results in gastric bleeding (R. B. Menguy).

Thus peptic ulcer results from a conflict between the specific striving for increase in releases and general resistance or rather inability of organism to live up to it. This conflict is reflected in the emotional attitudes of the ulcer patient. He is found to be a generally dependent, passive, retiring or submissive person forced to play independent, active, self-assertive or aggressive role.[9] The conflict nature of peptic ulcer explains its curiously changing syndrome. Ulcer symptoms oscillate in severity during periods of day and night, and during seasons.

When general overadjustment is enjoyed, e.g., during the months of summer, symptoms disappear, because there is no conflict, as the whole organism yields to the overadjustment. Symptoms start appearing during the months of September and October; and the September to January period "is now recognized as the high ulcer-hemorrhage period".[31] But during such periods the overadjustments are overcome, by painful readjustment. "Ulcers tend to heal quickly after a severe hemorrhage".[31] As the specific overadjustment starts again in early spring the symptoms reappear.[29] The oscillations during the periods of day and night are explainable by similar relationships between the overadjustment and the resistance of the body. Further, it is noticed that while ulcer continues there is no danger of cancer — because there is no continuous general overadjustment. Conversely, the cancer-prone, easy-going, obese people do not have ulcers, because with general overadjustment there is no conflict. Also the type A cardiac personality has ulcers rarely, for the same reason.

Treatments that increase general overadjustment may therefore bring relief. An ulcer patient resuming the rich eating and drinking he enjoyed before the ulcer appeared may find it beneficial.[17] For the same reason drugs, sedatives and nerve paralyzers, as well as more permissive diets, may be prescribed. Relaxation is the goal doctors are recommending, and direct means for enjoying it, drugs, alcohol or smoking, are approved.[30,31] The opposite effects that follow the use of such means are as inevitable here as in causation of all stress. Over-improvements create both the malignant stress and the ulcer. The very masters of the improvements, the modern doctors, have the highest incidence rate of peptic ulcers.

In conclusion we may repeat, for emphasis, that in spite of enormous efforts medicine has not discovered the uniform natural, therefore necessarily simple causes of diabetes, peptic ulcer or arthritis; and that these diseases are increasingly suffered by the more progressive, resourceful and affluent people, who know how to "improve" their functions. Animals, which do not know how to do this are free of them. *Man is uncannily skillful in choosing the pleasant means that relieve* him best from the reactions like those of diabetes, arthritic hormonal slack or ulcer-creating stress, that oppress him. Thus the patient is already doing what seems best for his disorder. Understandably medicine, proceeding by the same direct-improvement logic, can only help deepen these disorders and never discover their cause, however vast and precise its efforts.

Other Functional Disorders, Overweight, Longevity

Evidently, functional disorders can be as varied as are the organic functions that can yield excess improvements in reactions or feelings of well-being and pleasure. Because of the inexorable limitation or sameness of organic normalcy, every excess in a function or mechanism has to result in exactly opposite processes, felt as disease or slow death. This *paradox of worsening through improvement* is contrary to the very way of thinking and procedure of medicine, modern life and "scientific" progress. Consequently the same mystery and dangerous fallacy reign in the etiology and treatment of all functional disorders. Their causes are not known, and they increase together with the progress of modern life and medicine.

Respiratory Functional Disorders. The function of breathing, though open to man's direct control, is biologically too ingrown to yield to manipulations. When breathing is used in general overadjustment, as in smoking, the lungs are, obviously, too much part of it to remain free of overadjustment aftereffects. Smoking as cause of lung cancer has been extensively documented. A more specific, frequent disorder of respiration proper is emphysema, though it too may be a "complication from excessive smoking",[32] of progressive nature. Distention or inflation of the lungs is its main syndrome.[15,23] This points to overadjustment, if it is recognized that excess in breathing and in consumption of oxygen has to bring opposite effects, requiring more extensive use of the lungs, together with a decrease in their efficiency.

Overbreathing has been identified as the cause of a disturbing lack of breath[12] (F. D. Johnston). It has been found that 10 percent of all patients visiting the doctor suffer from shortness of breath due to overbreathing or "hyperventilation" that comes from abnormally prolonged, rapid and deep breathing (T. H. Noehren). This may give some idea of how a person chronically overenjoying his breathing function, by use of external means or internal stimulation, is bound to suffer from progressively worsening lack of breath as well as overworked lungs — which constitutes emphysema.

More "logical" explanations of causes of respiratory disorders are advanced. Mainly the *air pollution* is blamed — as the fashion requires. Air pollution is a major distortion of nature and thus a potential danger. But it is doubtful whether air pollution causes the diseases attributed to it. Even experts find that there may be more "hysteria" than evidence that it causes any disease.[37] The widest study so far, on 65,000 residents of Los Angeles and its adjacent counties, proved no connection between air pollution and respiratory or other diseases. Air pollution would rather prevent functional overbreathing and its disturbing aftereffects, which result from initial abnormally high absorption of oxygen in the blood (P. J. Steincrohn).[12] A study at Hazelton Laboratories showed that guinea pigs exposed to a higher sulphur dioxide pollution, which is blamed most, had rather a lower incidence of lung disease; the study was sponsored by utilities.

Here we have to make a general observation. An organ or tissue exposed to straight difficulty or injury grows stronger and more resourceful. Even the heart strengthens under physical burden or "disturbance". This should be true for any living tissue or function. In his famous experiments Carrel found, to his surprise, that poisonous substances in nonlethal amounts, had the effect of strengthening the organism in the end and extending the life of animals. Poisons in nonlethal amounts have no lasting bad effects.[4] In all living or growth, what restricts, slows down or hinders a function can rather conserve it — though everybody blames it as harmful. Real harm comes from insidious effects of pleasant factors, influences and products that everybody seeks, enjoys to excess and hails as beneficial.

Of course it can be statistically proven that periods of sudden strong air pollution increase deaths. But the paradox of the organic, relative causation has to be kept in mind. Though a difficulty is always the final factor that precipitates a functional crisis, it is the ease, or lack of difficulties and of adaptation to them that creates the conditions ripe for the crises. The widest studies on climatic conditions have shown that increase in illness is greatest immediately after periods of ideal weather.[37] It is fairly well known that not any climatic factor per se but sudden changes in atmosphere exacerbate pathological states.[3]

The paradox of worsening through improvement is evident in *asthma*, the cause of which is, equally, unknown. Hyperventilation as an excessive removal of carbon dioxide from blood is discovered in asthma (H. J. Berglund).[34] Typically, not improving the air but making it less rich, as by rebreathing the same air, helps the asthma sufferer.[34] Asthma disappears upon real emotional stress. The Nazi deportees lost their asthma, as well as their other functional diseases.[37] Trying to improve asthma only aggravates it; that is why doctors find it advisable to leave asthma alone.[17] Dependence of asthma on emotions is generally recognized. One of the best studies on asthma, by Drs. Rogerson, Hardcastle and Duguid, shows that overprotection by fussy parents is frequent in asthma cases. Strong restriction, caused by danger, threat or any overriding concern, can help here as in all overadjustment. Thus, organizing asthmatic boys into ambitious football teams cures them,[34] though footfall is anathema to asthma.

Allergy. Overadjustment is the cause of allergy in the sense that excessive repeated avoidance of a negative reaction deepens the reaction to an excessive degree. We saw how similar avoidance creates phobia as a mysterious overwhelming fear or disgust.

People who live with pollen or dust and cannot avoid it never suffer from allergies, while in this country, where people can choose and avoid everything they want to, 40 percent of them suffer from allergies. Also, much as in phobia, the most ordinary and frequent substances in air or food become allergens, because they can be repeatedly avoided, which keeps the vicious circle running. Desensitization as a deliberate enforcement on the body of the offending substance is the only successful treatment,[33] because it breaks the avoidance.

Yet the allergy specialists still proceed in the logical way of recommending more perfectionism in the avoidances. You are to build a special house, with hermetic walls permitting no seepage from outside; wear a mask, wash your bed, dust the ceiling, keep children away from toys; or avoid grass, trees, fruit, dust, humidity and heat.[33,34] At the same time, it is recognized that a "macroshock", from a massive dose of allergen, is the best treatment (H. J. Berglund).[34] Allergies disappear when organism lives through real trouble, acute infection or serious trauma (J. Feinberg). Dependence of allergy on emotions is noticed,[9] but remains paradoxical, as emotional improvements seem to alleviate allergies but real help comes from facing emotional troubles, or even from a shock. The mystifications about unconscious conflicts, disguises and symbolism are accepted as explanations.[9]

Headache. Modern men suffer increasingly from headaches. According to a study, probably the most extensive, at the Louisiana State University, on 5,000 persons, 60 percent of people in this country suffer from headaches. The results of the study, reported by Dr. Henry Ogden, show that the higher the educational or professional status of a group, the higher the rate of headaches. It should be clear that headache serves as the necessary pain reaction for functions like circulation, respiration or, partly, digestion in which the pain is not felt locally but is more centrally integrated. Apparently, those people who have more time, know-how and means for improving their general functions or feelings of well-being suffer here the opposite aftereffects of the improvements.

The *paradox of improvements* is clearly evident in headaches. A drink, cigarette, coffee, drug or pleasant excitement are the best means for chasing away headache, but also the clearest causes of headaches. Drugs that relieve headaches "cause a headache as a secondary effect".[34] Logical explanations are offered but are hardly helpful. A foremost research, by H. G. Wolff, showed a link between headaches and dilation of blood vessels. But here as elsewhere the same physiologic action may accompany completely different, even opposite, body conditions. Blood vessels may be dilated to cope with a stress as well as during enjoyment of stimulation. High as well as low metabolism may accompany headaches, which presents "puzzling and contradictory symptoms".[32] Alcohol dilates blood vessels, while relieving headache, though afterwards they become sealed off tighter than before. But blood vessels may also contract while stress is relieved, through tranquilization which works by abandoning peripheral needs. Then the headache as the aftereffect may, indeed, be accompanied by dilation of the vessels.

Stress can be always proven to be a cause of headache. This only confirms overadjustment as cause. People who avoid all stress suffer from it most. Stress is felt when there is critical restriction of releases; but abnormal restriction becomes necessary only when release reserves have not been accumulated by normal restrictions, therefore become exhausted at first emergency. *Relaxation, during a holiday or weekend, brings heaviest stress or "blues" headaches,* for which hidden depression is blamed.[9] All the mysteries of unconscious hidden conflicts, self-punishment, symbolic acts, or subconscious desire to have headache are invoked to account for the contradictions.[9,37]

But those doctors who are searching for less mysterious logical explanations do not find much. Most frequently blame is put on straining of muscles, blood vessels or nerves in the skull, neck, teeth, jaws, or shoulders[15] by maintaining tense, fixed postures, during work, driving, or sitting in office. Supposedly tension causes headache because the tension victims assume such strained postures as they "symbolically carry a great weight on their shoulders" (C. D. Aring).

The leading authority on headaches, Dr. A. P. Friedman, has blamed both hidden mental conflicts and physical stress from such contorted postures of head, neck and shoulders. In truth, all such stressful, distorting postures and conditions could be easily and simply discontinued, with great sense of relief, by the leisurely, professional people. But exactly these people suffer from headaches most, and the physical workers or farmers least.

Gastrointestinal disorders may be mentioned. Their dependence on emotions is amply documented; and hidden unconscious causation is widely accepted.[3] Emotional factors are blamed even for gall-tract and gallstone disease or for pancreatic disorders.[9] Doctors may accept the symbolic etiology of "organ language", of "retentive and giving trends"[37] or of the other unconscious conflicts.[43] All this confirms that stresses in reactions are the causes here, in ways unexplainable logically — that overadjustment with its paradoxical logic is the source of the disorders. Even in plain common sense, the more people fuss about their digestive and excretory functions, the more trouble they have. A typical instance is the use of laxatives. Reportedly some 100 million people use laxatives in this country. Laxatives can, certainly, be very effective at the beginning; and addiction[30] to them becomes inevitable as the opposite aftereffects deepen. The end result is that they "perpetuate the ill they purport to cure".[12] Similar worsening through aftereffects results from any drug, stimulant or gastroenteric added improvement.

Functional Factors in Infectious Diseases. It is being increasingly realized that infections become virulent to the extent the organism is functionally weakened or disordered. The belief that infectious disease starts upon mere catching of germs belongs in the previous century (R. Dubos). Stress as a necessary precondition of infection is often emphasized, though it is admitted that the mechanism involved is little understood.[3] Malignant stress is the most typical product of the paradox of overadjustment. Increase in cortisone or ACTH provides upsurge of protection against infection, as well as relief from stress, but the aftereffect is an increased chance of infection and deepened stress.[3,6]

Organisms reacting normally can resist almost any infection. This has been proven even by injection of dreadful microbes by experimenters in themselves. Less dramatic, extensive experiments have shown, that there is no sure way of deliberately infecting anybody with a cold. As long as organism does not overadjust and meets the condition in its full, there is no infection. Even inoculation, which accounts for most of the success of modern medicine, works by making the organism meet the disease rather than avoid it.

The *dependence of infectious diseases on emotional factors* or general releases has been extensively demonstrated. Tuberculosis is a typical, widely studied example. In the classic studies, by J. Wittkower, G. A. Day and D. M. Kissen, it was found that TB patients suffered from inordinate need for affection, or from emotional crises, and were the emotionally pampered individuals.[37] In tuberculosis as in cancer "the patient has lost the ability to have his mind maintain control over his body" (F. Dunbar).[10] For all infectious diseases psychological causes are being discovered, and their paradoxical logic has led to the usual mysteries about unconscious conflicts and self-punishing tendencies.[9] Unconscious yielding by patients to various infectious diseases has been accepted as true in modern medicine (K. Menninger). Whatever the role of emotional perversions, they can accumulate to a malignant degree only through overadjustment —through "overexcitement of mind and body" (B. Inglis).

The overadjustment paradox applies to improvements of releases as well as to an increase in the *general organic reactivity* which can protect the body against almost any infection. Such reactivity is the determining factor. But increasing the organic reactivity or sensitivity directly amounts to *overstimulation, which leads to its exhaustion* and understimulation, whatever the function or mechanism involved. Thus the fallacy of "scientific" medicine may become a practical danger even in treatment of infectious diseases. Antibiotics are subject to this paradox and misuse to the extent they work by arousing the general reactivity of the body, which seems to be the case. All antibiotics sensitize the body and often produce toxic effects.[5] They may be acting by acceleration of growth, which is the source of all organic dynamics. They are even used as growth accelerators in breeding of chicken, hogs or calves.[5,23] Antibiotics do not kill the microbes but only stop their growth,[6] apparently by arousing a basal growth activity by the body stronger than that of the microbes. Antibiotics like penicillin may have this strong arousal or sensitization effect by being products of living forms so strong that they kill off bacteria even in test tube.[5]

Significantly, antibiotics become ineffectual upon repeated use. This is typical of stimulation and sensitization. Stronger and stronger antibiotics, particularly the "mycins", are being sought, in soils all over the world, to keep up with the decrease in their effectiveness. Varied explanations are proposed for such self-defeat; it is even claimed that bacteria — altruistically or foresightedly — transfer or learn from each other their acquired resistance. Typically penicillin has been found to be ineffective with older people, in pneumonia cases (R. Austrian). The person must have reaction capacities before they can be effectively stimulated.

But all excessive stimulation exhausts or dulls reaction capacities. Fortunately there is no vicious-circle overstimulation with antibiotics, because they do not yield conscious pleasure release, therefore are not overindulged. But doctors should at least be aware of the opposite effects from increased stimulation, or of exhaustion through direct increase of organic reactions, including those evoked by antibiotics.

Overweight. The most prevalent physical health problem of modern man is overweight. It is a glaring embodiment of nutritional overadjustment or, simply, overenjoyment of food. In experiments by Drs. S. Hashim and T. Van Italie, food received in the form of bland liquid, by pushing a button, was consumed little by overweight subjects and led to extensive weight reduction, while it was consumed normally by other subjects. Because overweight is a product of overadjustment, it becomes a puzzling, *paradoxical problem.* Hundreds of means for reducing weight have been proven effective, often spectacularly so, but have failed or made the problem worse in the end (P. Wyden).[22] Scores of diets, hailed as miraculous at first have been tried, to end in failure and oblivion.[22]

The central paradox of overweight is that any means which provides stimulation or accelerated rate of living and is weight reducing at first, leads to understimulation, slowed down metabolism and overweight. Modern life itself is the best example. People in this country enjoy the tastiest foods, which are pleasant because they invigorate, accelerate the metabolism and therefore reduce weight, at first. But the end result is the "overweight society".[22] Of course fats in diet are logically blamed, because experimentally they do cause slower metabolism.

The experts here talk as if they had never seen an affluent modern diet. The kind of fats that could be associated with the excess fats in the body are totally excluded from such diet, because they are unbearably tasteless. Only the poor people, Eskimos, Indians, Blacks, or similar groups studied, eat such fats, and suffer from overweight least.[22] The equally unstimulating or tasteless polyunsaturated fats are also weight-reducing.[22]

Yet the great diet experts, like Dr. Ancel Keys, the author of *Eat Well and Stay Well,* still see solutions in stimulating, and experimentally weight-reducing, tasty diets, even in direct stimulation from food or drink.[12] Typically, alcohol is the best means for burning of fats in the body and thus for initial reducing, but also for incurring overweight. The confused experts blame the clearly insignificant calorie amounts in the drinks. The paradoxical reversal of stimulation effects is never understood. In the confusion, doctors seek explanations in wrong choices of diets. Dr. Jean Mayer, as the Chairman of the White House Conference on Foods, blamed advertising for the wrong choices. Actually nothing in the world can deceive man about what is invigorating or stimulating, therefore pleasant. The confusion is confirmed by the psychosomatic "explanations" — about overweight's symbolic meaning of impregnation, or about various oral symbolic tendencies.[9]

Metabolic sluggishness from overstimulation is the central cause of overweight. Overstimulation is particularly dangerous for individuals suffering from innate metabolic weakness or incapacity to derive enough stimulation from foods; this may be due to overstimulation in a previous generation. Such individuals are bound to suffer additionally strong sluggishness upon overstimulation, requiring increasingly more stimulation, more food. The result can be a particularly insidious vicious circle. But exactly for such individuals the expert is trying to provide more stimulation through diets and drugs, to make them act more "normal". Doctors are often surprised to find that a person eats little and still accumulates weight. The reason is that the stimulation he derives from food is not sufficient to make him exert, move or work enough to expend the calories consumed. In brief, the problem is one of economy of stimulation; and that is governed by the paradoxical logic of opposite causation.

Longevity. It is almost axiomatic that a *slower rate of living makes a longer life possible.* Any living function lasts longer at a slower rate.[12] Raymond Pearl, the classic expert on longevity, concluded that "the length of life is generally in inverse proportion to the rate of living", and that the people who live longest lead tranquil, serene lives. A Gallup poll confirms that people living longest lead "unexciting existence", take all things in moderation, are not choosy and live on diets that would horrify modern dietitians.[35] Dr. C. M. McCay, and Dr. C. A. Hochwelt, in experiments on retardation of growth of animals, by limitation of foods, extended their lives by the period of retardation, which did not impede their normal development. In experiments by Dr. D. Harman and Dr. A. S. Tappel, feeding of antioxidants to mice extended their lives, by as much as 50 percent;[36] the antioxidants slow down biologic reactions.

The easiest way to slow down living processes is to supply less food. Underfeeding of rats and other animals has been proven to increase greatly their longevity, in experiments by McCay and Hochwelt, mentioned above, as well as by B. N. Berg, G. E. Burch, J. H. Northrop, H. S. Simms, and others.[36]

These experiments show that particularly the foods that the animals love and gorge on, as rats do on lards and sugars, cause shortening of life, as well as tumors, heart lesions and kidney damage. Men love and overeat richer foods, which are their basic source of stimulation and enjoyment. Men shorten their lives at the rate of 25 percent for each 25 pounds of overweight".[19] Whatever the ways the life is intensified or stimulated, it is shortened by such improvements, which accelerate it.

Yet every medical effort or idea to extend life *has been directed at such stimulating and enjoyable, life-accelerating improvements*. The more popular and practically influential such efforts, the more the stimulation and enjoyments are stressed (E. L. Bortz, A. Aslan). Heightening of every enjoyable reaction, through "happiness and self-fulfillment", may be seen as the goal (M. Maltz). Even when controversy and mystery about old age are noted, the positive effects of "enthusiasm for life" are still stressed.[2]

Typical is the story of rejuvenation efforts. The early rejuvenators, Lejeune, Claude Bernard, Brown-Sequard, Voronoff, tried to intensify hormonal activity, particularly that of sex glands. They could produce great initial improvements, but the end results were deterring. Experiments show that testosterone injections in old horses produce temporary great spurts of vigor but disastrous changes.[4] In all times the "scientific" men have observed that increase in sexual activity rejuvenates men. But longer, common sense observations show that those who lead intense sexual lives age sooner. Women live longer because their active sex life ends earlier biologically and socially.

Science could increase longevity, by applying the principle of restriction, by which evolution has produced longer-living species. Animals with larger brains live longer,[4] and brain is primarily a system of restrictions. General restriction or retardation, which extends life when imposed in the primitive form of food limitations, could be engineered in unlimited scientific ways. Sense of restriction is always relative; and restrictions enrich human capacities.

Nature has produced longevity not by any inventive mechanism or complex formula, but in a simple, restrictive, arduous way. Scientists are finally abandoning the view that longevity is determined by some particular organic process, favorable life conditions, or special diets.[4] Solution lies *not in any lucky formulas but in the most difficult effort, of accepting restrictions* as limitations on life itself. One can think here of how plants like spinach or sisal when trimmed down constantly or prevented from flowering grow for years and years; or how insects prevented from reaching mature stage live many times longer than they normally would.[4] But restrictions are contrary to the experimentally "scientific" efforts of trying to extend life, by the pleasant stimulating direct improvements. Modern progress has extended only the average life expectancy, while the diseases that fatally affect health at old age are increasing. More people are now older than their age, and senile disorders have doubled in twenty-five years.[37]

Longevity is a good example of the paradox of all functional adjustment. *Direct increase in a function, "scientifically" showing as clear improvement, and felt as such, decreases or exhausts its strength.* Restriction or opposition is the way evolutionary and cultural selection has produced the higher forms and capacities. Medicine should proceed by the same method — even by infliction of difficulties, in the way it does in inoculation, which is its greatest success.

Instead, modern medicine is generally doing the reverse and promoting progressive increase in the direct improvements. The result is an equal increase in functional diseases, which are becoming the only unremedied, and causally not understood causes of death of modern man. Medicine is admittedly mystified by the causation of these diseases, therefore cannot even begin to help. In fact it promotes the very sources of these diseases, under its logic of direct improvements.

The Medical Blunder of Our Age

In all ages and cultures people have lived with peculiar medical blunders, crudely primitive as well as sophisticated. When Charles II was dying, 43 cures, like bloodletting and cupping, were used, which rather hastened his death. The people who eagerly sought such cures were as intelligent as we are and as anxious to follow the science of their time. The only protection against such blunders is a true scientism, which cannot begin without causal understanding. But as we saw, *there is admittedly no such understanding in modern medicine in the field of functional diseases,* which are becoming almost the only pathologic causes of deaths of the most advanced people.

The *direct improvement logic* is the central fallacy of modern medicine, and it is best illustrated in the treatment of pain or any negatively-felt reaction. If we did not feel pain, upon being hurt or infected, we would not last for long. But man avoids the feeling of pain more than anything else, and the goal of logically "scientific" treatments becomes the prevention of all pain or negative reactions, which are organic restrictions. The enormous medical effort is directed at increasing the positively-felt improvements, which man already overenjoys through most ingenious means. Medicine thus combats that side in adjustment which needs most support, and *helps the side which has to be counteracted above everything else.*

We have to emphasize here the *total difference between artificial and natural removal of pain* or negative reactions. Under natural adjustment pain has to be removed. This is the very purpose of pain as the guide in counteraction and removal of any ill, through complex readjustments. But when pain is removed artificially or nonorganically, by the medical means or drugs, it is like blinding a man or getting him drunk when he has to face a complex, dangerous situation. Yet everybody feels that he is improving and safe when pain is stopped, or that he is worsening and in danger when pain starts returning. The doctor thinks the same way and is always ready to eliminate the pain.

Two misconceptions have to be emphasized here. First, it is universally assumed that the doctor treating a functional disease removes or counteracts its cause. In truth even when the doctor makes detailed analyses and tests of body products and processes, he only gets reactions of organs, cells and tissues. All these act as integrated wholes reacting to stimuli, disturbances and restrictions. They show improvement upon increased stimulation, that may lead to exhaustion; and show worsening or restriction, upon meeting disturbances, that actually serves to sustain normalcy. Thus *the doctor deals only with organic reactions, which actually follow the paradoxical logic of opposite causation.* The doctor could properly use the direct scientific logic and deal with the *causes* of the functional diseases if he could analyze the biochemical factors, in their myriad multiplicity, at every point and instant — and if he understood the principle of life in the first place. Of course no genius in the world, and no human mind, can make such analysis.

Second, it is as generally assumed that organic processes can be improved, changed or added to by the advanced medical means. In truth, all the doctors in the world using every skill *could not create or change a tiniest bit organically in a living tissue or process,* except by destroying something in it or evoking its reactions, which are governed by the paradoxical logic of reversals. Yet greatest successes of science are expected from improvements of organic capacities by artificial means. Numerous means have been tried, from ascorbic acid to the MAO inhibitors. The first effects are usually wondrous, but no wonder drug has yet been found that works permanently or does not reverse in its effects.

None of such means changes anything organically, and the *organism responds with opposite reactions to all nonorganic changes,* as it restores the normalcy or sameness it inexorably maintains. Even if such normalcy may occasionally look deficient by usual standards, it is still billions of times superior to anything man-made compounds or artificial intervention could create; even the lowest living form is ungraspably miraculous in its complexity of multiple details. If the use of artificial means is particularly ingenious and the first aftereffects are overcome by further increase in releases or by effacement of deeper restrictions, functional disease and malignancy are the results.

The best illustration here is the expanding *drug treatments.* Drugs are preposterously crude compounds in comparison with organic forms. Yet they provide miraculous improvements, because they work by eliminating restrictions and thus increasing the releases. No complex skill is necessary to destroy, stop or paralyze anything living. Knocking out one element in the endless organic chain processes can produce selective effect. Then in restoring the normalcy or release reserves that the organism maintains, it imposes above-normal restrictions, which are felt as worsening or disease. As Dr. R. Dubos states, "it is a painfully but richly documented paradox that each and every drug proven worth in the treatment of disease can itself become a cause of disease even when used with understanding, skill and moderation".[3] He points out that these effects are "extremely indirect and delayed" and may follow from penicillin or cortisone as well as from tranquilizers and aspirin.

The whole modern medicine with its allopathic logic, of remedies by direct improvements, is being questioned. "To sum up", says Dr. B. Inglis, "it can now be asserted with depressing confidence that allopathic remedies are ipso facto a danger to man . . . the public does not have any conception of how many lives have been unnecessarily sacrificed, and how many disorders unnecessarily caused, by drugs."[17] He thinks that "the reaction of the life force against the drugs will in time be recognized as the basic cause of side effects; the body is regarding the drugs as interlopers".[17] The "side" effects are, indeed, the countermeasures by the body against the distortions or the excessive releases induced by drugs or any artificial means.

Drugs, hormones, vitamins or other medical means are used to provide added stimulation that body may seem to lack. They cannot and are not even intended to help the body rebuild its tissues or cells, which grow and adjust in ungraspably complex multiple ways. Even when a means like iron or iodine preparation is used, its effect is only stimulation. The organism builds by the use of foods which it finds and assimilates with inventiveness that no scientist can understand or control. Children may start eating strange things like bits of soil, dirt, stones or worms,[15] and pregnant women may sneak out at night to eat pieces of coal, because they may need something that doctors cannot explain.

If organism needs a hormone it can produce more of it than is necessary. Hormones are sufficient in incredibly minute amounts. The pituitary hormone can evoke physiologic responses even if diluted to one part in 100 million. Adrenalin can act in dilution of one part in 300 million. The estrogen produced by a woman in 200 days weighs less than a postage stamp. Moreover, the dominant hormones that determine all other reactions consist of steroids, made of elements most plentiful in the body, and are so simple that they can be produced or substituted even synthetically. Evidently hormones are only signaling devices or triggering switches operated by the whole unfathomably complex organic system. It would be a *sheer folly to start managing the signals or switches in such a system,* of living processes, that no genius can causally understand, create or direct.

Expectedly, controversies about drugs are endless. The "scientific" enthusiasm is matched by sober recognition of total failure, as we have seen before. Dr. J. B. Conant has blamed such failure on the dominant, misleading "empiricism"; we should call it the fallacy of the experimental direct improvement logic. Of course drug treatment can be helpful where it supplies some simple elements that body lacks, as in the few diseases like phenylketonuria, galactosemia or sickle-cell anemia. However, these are organic, not functional diseases, and their constant, inborn, directly logical causes are clear. None of the general health problems of modern man belong here, or are solved by drugs.

But is it not beneficial to calm the body with drugs so that it can recuperate in peace? Actually when the body needs peace it maintains it to a more than necessary degree. When a limb or organ is even slightly injured, the whole body is immobilized. And it is the pain, not its removal, that achieves this. Restlessness, when organically permitted, is the best way of how organism can find the new necessary readjustments, through intense search on all levels of integration. True, the body still functions, on the lower levels, even while consciousness that carries pain is excluded. But gravest *general risks lie in the exclusion of this very center of human organic control* from participation in important readjustments.

As we saw, it is the person's general conscious attitudes that determine whether he turns any, even ordinary, adjustments into overadjustments, which are the causes of all functional and malignant disorders. If one faces fully every difficulty, he "learns" that a temporary restriction or pain brings relief or normal readjustment whereas avoidance of pain deepens the disorder. Such learning may consist only of vaguely general, as if intuitive or emotional attitudes. But control of feelings is all that is needed for the simple but hard management of pleasure releases or organic potentials.

The disappointments with drugs and similar means are convincing many doctors that nature itself should be permitted to do its subtle curative work. It is pointed out that mere removal of *"symptoms"* does not bring cure. But such views still imply that some negative reactions as the symptoms are causally insignificant while others are the causes of the disease and should be allopathically or directly dealt with or removed. In truth, all *"symptoms" as the negative reactions are equally, decisively important and are the only things the doctor can deal with,* in functional diseases. Nothing is irrelevant in the organic reactions. The "symptoms" can be perfect guides — the only ones available — if the real, paradoxical causal logic of reactions is understood and followed. A functional "disease" acts as a natural pressure by the organism toward restoration of normalcy. Accordingly, the "symptoms" are to be kept alive or strengthened, rather than eliminated, in the functional diseases. They disappear when they have fulfilled their paradoxical role.

Sometimes it may be difficult to distinguish between a logically real disease like an organic deficiency, to be remedied by an improvement, and a functional "disease", which is only deepened by direct improvements. But modern medicine is phenomenally successful in solving such technical difficulties, once causal understanding is there. Of course it would have to use the paradoxical logic of reactions and overadjustments, as well as methods of relative comparison. The task is not impossible. People recognize when they see overadjustments, like an intoxication; or their aftereffects, like a hangover. Medicine can be here as much more effective as is a microscope in comparison with the naked eye.

The decisive point *would be the recognition in medicine, for the first time, that experimentally clear direct improvements can be sources of the diseases modern man suffers from most.* Then the awe-inspiring skill and power of modern medicine would go into a causally understood combating of these diseases, and not into the enormous "improvement" efforts that create them or make them worse. Even the vastly expanding use of drugs could play an important role, in new, different treatments. As we saw in discussing the possibilities of anti-stimulation or anti-release treatments in psychiatry, drugs can prevent overadjustments in the same way they induce them.

It is clear, particularly from such "less natural" overadjustments as use of narcotics, that overenjoyment of feelings of well-being has to lead to equally strong diseased reactions, during return to normalcy. Now the modern medical and general progress has provided man with means to *overenjoy his every organic function to similar extent,* in prodigiously inventive ways. This is unique for our age. Technical and material limitations of the past, as well as its restrictive traditions and wisdoms are outrun by the affluence, power of science and our liberal "scientific" attitudes. Modern medicine simply does not know any other logic than that of experimentally direct improvements; or of unlimited normalcy, even though the person has to live subnormally upon overadjustment or under any organic weakness that he may particularly have.

Actually *modern medicine does everything that can deepen overadjustments to their extremes.* If left to themselves, as in primitive or animal adjustment, occasional overadjustments are counteracted by immediate aftereffects, the diseased aftermaths; the result is absence of functional diseases. But modern medicine and its supported improvements of modern life enable man to meet every negatively felt afterreaction with still further increases in releases. Such overriding of aftereffects can deepen the vicious-circle exhaustion of the function to any, malignant degree.

Yet one of the main medical efforts has become the removal

of drug aftereffects, the "side" effects, since drugs that temporarily "cure" have already been found for almost every ill. The drugs against "side" effects are particularly aimed at mere continuation of overadjustments or increase in releases, rather than at rebuilding anything. They act merely through neural and hormonal controls, and only supress the restrictions, so that deeper sources of releases or potentials of growth can be overspent.

It is truly *ominous that modern medicine uses its staggering resourcefulness and influence for increasing the "improvements" that are the very sources of functional diseases.* If the direct improvements were the solution, doctors would have merely to prescribe everything the person does already while he deepens his disorder. For he knows better than anybody what gives him best, most pleasant relief from the reactions and stress that he is fighting against. The most insidious fact about overadjustments as causes of functional diseases is that the disease is deepened to extreme by means and ways of adjustment that *seem satisfactory, beneficial or positive in every logical or experimentally verifiable way.* This is the main practical reason why nobody, in medical sciences, or in other fields, has ever suspected the real causes of the functional diseases and disorders.

Conclusion

Modern medicine is not a science in the field of functional diseases, which are becoming almost the only unremedied causes of death and sickness for the advanced modern people. In this field medicine has, admittedly, no understanding of the generally uniform natural, therefore necessarily simple causes of the diseases. In fact the functional diseases are epidemically increasing together with the progress of modern medicine. The reason for this failure is the same that has prevented all sciences of man from becoming scientific. It is the unthinkable relative or opposite causal logic of the organic "value" reactions, which determine all organic adjustments.

Because of the never-yielding limitation of the organism to its sameness or normalcy, any increase in releases of life flow or pleasure, felt as improvement, has to lead to equal opposite processes, felt as worsening or disease. If man attains means strong or rich enough to overcome such worsening by still further "improvements", the result is a vicious circle that can drive the diseased worsening or exhaustion of the overenjoyed function to any, incomprehensible, malignant degree. The use of drugs is the simplest, general example. But every function is equally overenjoyed by man as soon as he is enabled to do so.

Modern medicine proceeds only by the "scientific" logic, which experimentally shows all increase in releases as clear improvement, though its end result is the exact opposite. Consequently modern medicine provides man with every possible means of functional overenjoyment and turns his every health effort into an unlimited striving for the direct "improvements". The result has been a threefold increase in the functional diseases as well as a complete confusion and mystery about their causes.

The greatest danger for man as a conscious planning being is his now enormously increasing power to remove the painful, restrictive side of his adjustment, in an effort to live solely by pleasures or constantly increased releases, felt as improvements. Every function is now being overenjoyed in this way, and every functional disease is increasingly afflicting modern man. When the restrictions are overcome on the deepest levels the malignant growth is the inevitable result. Primitive men or animals, unable or not knowing how to improve their functions, are free of these diseases. But man feels and "knows" that he is getting healthier, further away from the disease, every time his reactions are improved, by the removal of pain or restrictions. Modern medicine proceeds by the same way of thinking. It thus helps man, in his virtually suicidal most eager efforts, where he needs least help and should be most restricted.

We saw for all functional diseases their overadjustment nature, their increase together with direct improvements, and the avowed mystery about their necessarily simple causes. The incapacity of modern medicine to understand or deal with functional diseases will remain as complete as is its adherence to the direct improvement logic. We saw that even in their clearest, laboratory findings and analyses doctors are, actually, dealing only with reactions of organs or tissues. But reactions are always governed by the opposite causation, exactly contrary to the direct-improvement logic that the doctors follow in the field of the functional diseases. Besides, even an organic disease, disturbance, or injury may be met by restrictive, "negative" reactions, as the limited organism tries to establish resources or new adjustments. Such negative reactions, by the organs, cells or tissues, then may show in the tests and analyses as the causes of the disease. Thus life-saving reactions may be treated as ills to be removed, under the most advanced, experimental, laboratory methods. Or, richly wasting, experimentally positive reactions, that worsen the ill, may be favored in the experimental modern medicine, unaware of the paradox of reactions, that is due to the limitedness of organism.

THE UNSEEN CAUSAL SOURCES IN EDUCATION, ADJUSTMENT AND MOTIVATION

All interests, positive motivations and capacities are satisfactions or releases. Consequently, under the "scientific" logic, direct increase in satisfactions is seen as the goal of all education and better adjustment. In truth, satisfaction cannot arise without equal need or nonsatisfaction, its value opposite; and increase in releases requires equal increase in restrictions, because of the organic limitedness. But this logic, of the relative or opposite causation, remains unthinkable — which is the reason why the sciences of man have not evolved. Under the direct scientific logic, the theorists never recognize the real causes, the negatively felt opposites of the positive effects, in education, adjustment or motivation.

The practical all-important result is that there is no science of education and that the well intended extensive theorization in this field becomes a dangerous confusion. In thousands of books and discussions our best known authorities ardently urge the direct increase and enjoyment of the positive, pleasant satisfactions or interests in education, learning, adjustment and motivation. They blame educators for repressing these experimentally clear satisfactions or pleasures. They never realize that first one has to create the needs or nonsatisfactions and restrictions, all that is hard and furthest away from the satisfactions, before the pleasures or releases of interests, motivations and capacities can arise.

Education as an Art and as Science

Education, at home or school, reaches its goals in spite of the erroneous theories, because it has remained a subtle art, performed under the simplest rule. The educator or parent simply wants his children to be as he is: they are to find happiness or pleasure where he finds it, and see dangers where he sees them. The organic unity between parent and child is the deepest, instinctive basis on which all education rests. The Love as the panacea of all education is the result. By *treating the children as he would treat himself* the educator imposes on them all the restrictions, fears and nonsatisfactions or needs, as the sources of releases and satisfactions, just as he imposes them on himself.

Of course the restrictions or nonsatisfactions have to be imposed in the name of pleasure, in the subtle, contradictory ways cultural conditioning works. These pleasures are mostly the satisfactions of the deepest needs for security and growth — assurance of parental love or promise of future success — together with progressively strengthening fixational moral habits and values. The child simply fears what will happen to him if he loses parental love or never becomes a "man" or does something "abnormal". Avoidance of such threats becomes the source of satisfactions, derived through culturally desirable, conditioned performances.

An important fact here is the *"neurotically" deepening perfectionism* in such satisfactions. As the child overenjoys the security of love and own goodness, slightest disturbance in such enjoyment is strongly felt. To avoid such trauma the parents or educators intuitively lavish more of refined love on the child, which only deepens his fear of losing the love if he does not comply or is not good enough.

Thus the *perfect refined love, not punishment,* becomes the most effective means of conditioning. But a really unlimited, unconditioned love, as a complete satisfaction, destroys all motivation. If one uses methods of refined love on youths from rough environment, it can only increase their criminality. They are used to so much stronger experiences that such childish refinements mean nothing to them except more freedom to do as they please. But the enlightened educators see only the excellent results of the refined, "free", permissive, affectionate education, and try to use it as a panacea for all youth. The result is a tragic parody: the exquisite love is reciprocated by increased delinquency, as several experiments have shown (F. Redl).[46]

Naturally the "neurotic" refinement can grow only in an *artificially secluded atmosphere*. It succeeds to the extent that the child can be raised like a tender plant in a greenhouse. That is why close family life or the subtly enslaving love is the panacea in all education; or why the home determines, from one generation to another, what the children become; and why influences of the unsupervised neighborhood have to be shut out. Gangs have the worst influence on youth, though they offer all the satisfactions theorists praise — feelings of belonging, adventure, guiltless freedom, self-assertion, courage, pride and other genuine natural satisfactions.[2] Under the experimental or behavioristic logic the restrictive and limiting nature of family and home makes them unsuited for raising children, as Skinner makes clear in *Walden Two*.[1] In truth, no child can become culturally motivated without parental love which forces, limits and deceives him into accepting all the restrictions, that parents impose on him while wanting him just to have the same highest happiness and freedom that they believe to be living for themselves.

The tightly closeted conditioning is not noticed, either by the child or educational theorists. The very fact that *such conditioning is so tight or omnipresent makes it unnoticeable.* Theorists know that some kind of conditioning is necessary to create the motives so remote from natural drives. But the only conditioning modern educators as scientists know is the behaviorist kind of conditioning, illustrated by child's responses during feeding, toilet training, learning to avoid hot stove, being frightened upon touching a furry object, or saying "Please" when hungry.[3,4] Understandably educators conclude that not much of conditioning or of scientific methods can be used in education.[4] Any reasonable man would find the behavioristic, Pavlovian kind of conditioning in education ridiculous. As Razran states "to say that one's learning is no more than mere conditioning is more an insult than a theory".

But conditioning is the very basis of all education, or "learning". Only, the real conditioning goes on unnoticed, at every moment, on the levels of the "mentalistic" values and feelings by which we live, mostly those of security, growth and superiority. These also remain unrecognized, in the theory of conditioning, exactly to the extent of their universal importance. Thus educators, as well as the humanists outraged about ideas of conditioning in education, are missing what is most universal and decisive in it. The basal needs and satisfactions the same as their conditioning are like the atmosphere in which we live and therefore notice it least.

The present theories of education see *direct satisfactions* as the sources of motivations and interests.[5,6,7,8] Particularly the "progressive" educators and the radical reformers of education stress satisfactions or pleasures of natural interests as the motivational sources, that should be let free to be enjoyed instead of being restricted by the traditional education.[18] Many educators recognize that the satisfactions relate to the needs of the child.[6,9] But no modern theory considers the necessity of first creating the needs, because this would immediately require the acceptance of the paradox that nonsatisfactions or frustrations are the sources of satisfactions. For causally a need is never anything else than nonsatisfaction, created by opposition or restrictions. The actual creation of needs is overlooked because the accumulation of the restrictions or nonsatisfactions, during organic growth or cultural conditioning, is so universal and continuous.

Anyway, the present *educational theories aim only at satisfactions,* as the experimentally direct sources of motivations, never at creation of their opposites, the needs. According to a generally accepted theory, best explained by A. H. Maslow and C. Rogers, the higher satisfactions, of self-actualization or of need to know, arise after all lower needs have been satisfied.[5] Thus only satisfactions are to be cultivated. It is rightly pointed out that the theories of Maslow and Rogers assume motivations as already naturally given, so that there is not any "need to 'motivate' the pupil. The motivation is already there".[7]

The reality is completely different. Children do not become culturally motivated without hard effort or constant restrictive environmental conditioning. In those rare cases where children have grown up outside human community, without human conditioning, they have remained complete animals. One of the two girls of Mandalay who lived longer, after being taken from a den of wolves at the age of ten, required eight years to learn the first response of kindness or of human communication by speech. Such children imitated the animals they lived with, wolves, sheep, squirrels. The imitation is an elaboration of the need of growth; the child strives to attain the higher strength or skill he sees in others.

The natural drives of man, though they can be refined into the cultural capacities, are humanly as unacceptable as those of animals. If not conditioned, the person would strive only for physical security, food, sexual satisfactions or animal power and skills to "actualize" himself. The much hailed natural interests and curiosity of man if unconditioned would be actualized through breaking things, crude play, like splashing water, dirt or paint, and destroying everything breakable, as can be observed in the play of less conditioned slum children. The rough Western is preferred by the less cultural people because it expresses their natural interest in rough force and crude physical domination over other men or environment. Without hard conditioning, through restrictions or nonsatisfactions, we would not have any of the "human" satisfactions, values or interests.

The great humanistic idealists, admiring man's noble urge for knowledge and values or extolling the self-fulfillment of his nature, are merely blind to the omnipresent conditioning, which imposes the nonsatisfactions as the sources of satisfactions or values. Modern educators are as blind to this causal fact, and their delusion becomes practically dangerous. The old humanists at least did not hesitate to suppress and transform the noble, God-created nature of man by thoroughly restrictive education. The modern educators urge the fullest satisfaction of the natural, basic drives, and condemn restrictions. Aldous Huxley could conclude that the only real education in the world was provided by some of the savages of New Guinea, who had been praised by Margaret Mead as being most permissive with their children. Actually the lower most basic needs, like those of security, are the sources of the higher, cultural needs. This is the axiomatic way natural functions evolve. But a *need that is satisfied ceases to be operative,* as the theorists of education themselves have often recognized (H. J. Klausmeier, H. Sorenson).[4,9]

Some misunderstandings have to be explained. Because the theorists do not see the most general omnipresent drives, they accept such needs as that for food to be the basic needs. Actually an animal will not accept the food unless everything is safe around. Hunger has not been used for conditioning by men because its operation is too obviously clear. Its conditioning would be seen as cruel. The cultural conditioning evolves imperceptibly, by cultural selection, around the unseen most universal needs of survival and growth. Of course the specific needs, of food or shelter, have to be satisfied first, as far as they are not part of the conditioning system. Otherwise they would overrule the conditioned motivations, which are always weaker, more refined than natural needs.

The Opposite Causal Sources. The central task of education is the creation of lasting motivations and interests. We may repeat, for emphasis, that satisfactions surely are the only immediate sources of motivations and interests, but that any satisfaction or release can arise only upon previous nonsatisfaction as need or restriction. The only task of education is to create the accumulation of the varied needs or nonsatisfactions and restrictions. For when this is done the satisfactions and releases break out by themselves, without any help. Yet every modern theory or book on education stresses direct cultivation of satisfactions and releases, enjoyments and freedoms, in their endlessly varied forms, while deploring nonsatisfactions, frustrations or restrictions.

Pleasant feelings, successes and rewards are seen as the self-evident sources of positive, favorable interests and attitudes,[7,4] without noting that the pleasure of any reward or success is equal to previous painfully accumulated need for it. The same applies to the extolled cultivation of pleasures of hope rather than anxieties of fear,[5] or to creation of similar desirable emotional experiences[11] (A. N. Frandsen, S. L. Pressey). The educator may point out as glaringly evident that "joy, happiness, contentment and the like have a positive educational value, whereas such emotions as sorrow, fear, worry, anxiety, rage and the like are detrimental" (G. W. Frasier).[12] Pleasant emotions are shown to stimulate the maximum use of interest (H. W. Bernard).[13] Satisfaction of needs is repeatedly stressed, without even considering the fact that *first the needs have to be painfully created and accumulated* (L. J. Cronbach).[5] Even in the experimental, behaviorist conditioning the satisfactions as the only usable factors are stressed (B. F. Skinner).[15] Particularly the humanistic thought views with horror any idea that enjoyment of values, like love or freedom, should be limited by any conditioning (A. Montague).[16]

No wonder that the radical school reformers, from Paul Goodman to Charles Silberman,[17] have only to describe the practical traditional education to demonstrate how shockingly education suppresses all pleasures and values[18] that every enlightened man sees as the sources of interests and motivations. The enraged reformers — N. S. Neill, Jules Henry, Reston Wilcox, Ronald and Beatrice Gross, Sylvia Ashton Warner, Edgard Z. Friedenberg, Kenneth Clark, Herbert Kohl, Jonathan Kozol — prove how every natural or real interest, desire, curiosity, self-respect and freedom is repressed in schools.[18] It seems that absolutely everything has been done in the worst possible ways. Schools are shown to have proceeded by creating "essential nightmares" or fears as motivations while not using the love of knowledge for its own sake and not showing children how learning can be fun (J. Henry).[19] Moreover, the reformers have the testimony of the children themselves to confirm their conclusions.[18]

Evidently the whole practical tradition or the practical wisdoms of all men cannot be so absolutely wrong. The truth is that the selective practical tradition and wisdoms have to cope with the human contradictions, under which no inner value can arise without its opposite. Satisfaction requires need as nonsatisfaction; and any other positive potential, motivation or interest, as satisfaction, requires its unrecognizable value opposite. But men have to live by the belief in satisfactions without their opposites, though if this was true there would not be one human difficulty in the world. The children as well see only the pleasant satisfactions as the sources of their positive interests and hail the events that permit the releases, while hating the restrictions, which actually make the releases possible.

The irony is that the permissive, "free" educator reaps all the praise, though he actually degrades the education, whereas the restrictive educator, who upholds it, earns hate. In the simplest case, the permissive mother is loved and followed, while the stern father is "hated" and resisted, though without the for-biddances by the father there would be nothing for the mother to permit. The "free" schools show great initial success, but fail quickly. [20,21,2] More than 2,000 such schools have failed since 1969; some 900 are tried now, but are expected to last, in the average, only eighteen months.[47]

Typical are the achievements by practical enthusiasts of the "progressive" methods. J. Kozol tells how his closest three pupils ended in reformatory schools; but he, naturally, blames the other educators who had to discontinue his way of teaching.[23] If the teacher starts by permitting freer choice of interests he may be followed enthusiastically, but the education is bound to end by "running wild"[20] as more and more freedoms have to be granted. Similarly, H. Kohl admits that most of the students who enjoyed his "progressive" teaching later lost interest in school or became dropouts.[24] But again the other, later edu-cators are blamed for the failure. The "free" methods, as all enjoyments, make the later less enjoyable work unbearable, whereas the ultimate goal of education is to create potentials of pleasure or interest for any later learning.

Modern educational theory, with its emphasis on direct satis-factions, is pointless in addition to being obnoxious. For if the freedoms or release of natural interests was the right way, it would come by itself as a pure relief both for the pupils and teachers. The central, difficult and only problem in education is "to develop the motivation to study, but the student must some-how supply this himself" (C. T. Morgan). The famous study by Christopher Jencks[25] shows that our schools add nothing to the motivations and abilities that the students bring in from their homes. Fortunately, the restrictive, non-"progressive", middle-class, tradition still dominates most of our homes.

Confusion is inevitable and theories on education are innumerable. Alchemistic sophistry dominates the theories here as in psychology, for the same reasons. Mere ideas, learning, attitudes, principles, concepts, "sets", ideals or other *ideational cognitive* constructs, like Self or Identity, are assumed as sources of weighty motivations.[8,9,14] Theorists see interests and attitudes as ideationally learned principles, sets or methods, to be taught much like other courses, in rational ways.[14,26] Attitudes are viewed as meanings associated with certain objects or ideas; and values, principles or ideas of good conduct are to be learned through understanding.[1,14] Motivation is, consequently, compared to a vision, and perception is accepted as decisive for behavior.[7,8] Behaviorism, the main source of conditioning theories, rejects as "mental" the emotional factors and sees conditioning as a matter of mere method or skill. In Skinner's *Walden Two*, children acquire protection against negative emotions through a conditioning that is compared to inoculation.[1] Finally, the purely alchemistic, unconscious and psychoanalytic concepts, particularly of the mechanisms like the unconscious Sublimation, Identification, Regression or Defense, are widely applied in educational psychology.[5,8]

When educational theories do deal with the decisive, emotional factors, they invariably perpetuate the fallacy of positive emotions growing out of positively felt experiences. They stress "happy daily living",[13] rewards, praise, hope, sense of success,[4,14] self-esteem, feeling of competence,[5] confidence, high aspirations, satisfying experiences,[11,12] and a happy environment.[8] The educator is to convert the work of the pupil into a constant success and a joyful adventure. It is true that promise of happiness and success, or rewards, praise and sense of relief from stress and guilt have always been used as inducements of motivation in good education. But they all *have value only to the extent they are badly needed or lacking.*

A good word may give chokingly intense joy, or may mean nothing, depending from past accumulation of need or anxious expectation of approval. Feeling of freedom or relief as satisfaction is, evidently, only as great as was the previous feeling of stress or guilt. Educators who want to transform learning into an exciting adventure should note that even in a novel the degree of adventure depends on dangers to the hero. The joys of success derive from needing it desperately, with all the tensions and anxieties this involves. Success as full satisfaction extinguishes further motivations. Aspirations or hopes that are merely enjoyed in advance bring depressing disappointments.

Self-esteem[5] and self-understanding[8,14] have been prescribed as ways of better adjustment. Surely self-esteem or pride is part of positive motivations. But the normal satisfactions of self-esteem come from previous stressful needs to be good, and from fears to fail, which are the opposites of the positively felt self-esteem that theorists are talking about. Enjoyment of *this gratifying self-esteem* or pride can only exhaust sources of releases, so that the person has to resort to praising himself even for his worst conduct.

Self-understanding or self-discovery as mere satisfaction may amount to exploitation of inner pleasure releases, which is essentially the same whether one uses drugs or inner stimulation. In the modern theory the *self-discovery is, indeed, viewed as a process of attaining more complete satisfactions.* The great authority on Identity, E. H. Erikson,[27] sees only satisfactions, like trust, pride, freedom, sense of adequacy, self-acceptance, enjoyed intimacy or rejection of despair, as requirements of successful development through his "eight ages" of man.[27] If satisfactions or inner fulfillment is what is needed, why not attain it most directly by use of drugs?

Frustrations and repressions are, particularly, viewed as evils in modern educational theory. Needs, the sources of satisfactions, are always nonsatisfactions induced by restrictions which are the practical frustrations or repressions. But modern educators find it abhorrent that the child hears Don'ts many times more often than Do's. They do not realize that restrictions become unnoticed and separate Don'ts unnecessary to the extent the restrictive conditioning has become a general atmosphere.

The Freudian theory of repressions has been influential in education. According to it a slightest repression can warp one's personality for life, though in practice Freudians themselves can be "extremely authoritarian".[21] Freudians scare people particularly about restrictions of biological or instinctive functions during infancy. There is a glaringly simple proof against this theory. People all over the world have practiced extreme restrictions of infants, particularly under the swaddling and headbanding customs. A swaddled infant, looking like a "mouse choked in a trap",[46] would be a perfect case for proving the theory. Yet no ill effects resulted even from such extreme restraints.[46] The people might have intuitively known the value of early restrictions. In any event, the infants reacted to the restraints only after they had been freed from them for a time. The Freudian theories, applied in the "best" homes, have led to disastrous results (O. H. Mowrer).[46] Freudians themselves are discovering that the permissive education has produced children who lack interest in anything except "immediate gratifications" (O. S. English and G. H. Pearson).[46] As usual in such cases, "misapplication" of the Freudian theory is blamed for the disastrous results.

But the modern theorists stress permissiveness and repeat whatever proofs they find for it. Hence the popularity of studies like that by Margaret Mead on Arapesh and Mundugumor tribes, which tends to show that permissive education produces better people. Such studies, conducted without insight in the paradox of values and adjustment, are as far from being scientific as are presently all fields dealing with man. The result is rather a confusion. In fact, other studies, on Navajo and Hopi Indians[28] and on Kaska and Haitian personalities[29] as well as on other tribal customs,[28] have led to contrary conclusions.

Most of the modern best known authorities on child education, from Spock to Ginott, have been rightly characterized as liberal and permissive in their theories. But the same authorities have shown, particularly in their later books, to be conservative when it comes to practical discipline and morals. Then it is argued, with the "scientific" logic, that discipline or punishment provides a kind of gratification for the child and a more relaxed attitude for parents (Spock); or that lack of discipline causes anxiety (Senn). Supposedly the child reasons that the parents who punish him love him. In truth children live by their emotions, therefore find any discipline a frustration that creates anxieties, and any punishment an unjust hostility. If parents derive relaxation from disciplining the child they are sick. The healthy parent when he disciplines the children feels as badly as when he has to restrict himself.

A practical evidence against the permissiveness or the logically best, unrestricted love is the spoilt child. He is the one who is loved unconditionally, as required by great humanists, and is permitted to enjoy all satisfactions, particularly the natural, instinctive drives that are seen as so important by Freudians and scientific educators. But the spoilt child suffers from every educational problem. The theory is here so flagrantly contradicted by life that the theorists have had to resort to a reversal of meanings, with a help from the mysteries of the Unconscious. It is argued that the clearly unlimited love here is a hidden, unconscious hate. This is probably one of the most cited modern explanations of the parent-child relationship problems.[46]

The confusion in educational theory is complete. This is witnessed by the endless, controversial philosophies on education,[21] which agree only that its ingredients are bipolar and opposed to each other: free and authoritative, empirical and intellectual, progressive and conservative, ideal and real (J. S. Brubacher).[30] In practice educators may admit that anything, even frustrations,[20] anxieties, authoritarian teachers,[9] and methods of punishment[20] may work. It is recognized that "creative teachers with novel solutions are presently still unknown"[4] and that not one of the new methods or media makes much difference[31] (H. J. Klausmeier, J. M. Stephens). The extensive study by Christopher Jencks shows that none of the expectations from the vast and expensive modern school reforms have come true.[25] This agrees with the equally unexpected findings in the celebrated Coleman's report.

Without causal insights, education is merely perpetuating the fixational humanistic value delusions. The greatest educational authorities stress the *learning* of universal values, through philosophies, great books or appreciation of cultural "treasures",[32,34] and *enjoyment* of arts and literature.[33,35] In truth, no amount of knowledge of values or of philosophical wisdoms can have a practical effect; and any enjoyment, whether it is induced by artistic, cultural or more direct natural gratifications, can only deplete organic potentials. The pathetic dictum "knowledge will make you free" is as frequently cited as it is inane. In practice hardly anybody is morally more obnoxious than a rationalist, particularly one asserting his freedoms in the name of reason or knowledge. Educators have to resort to doubletalk. It is proclaimed that "the discipline that is identical with trained power is also identical with freedom" (Dewey), or that mind "is free if it is enslaved to what is good" (Hutchins).

Modern educational theories are scientifically or causally as totally wrong as is the modern psychological theory, built on the logic of direct, free increase in releases or satisfactions. The restrictive, often superstitious, and disparaged "middle-class" values are presently the only, practical basis of education. Practice shows that only integrated schools, where the general restrictive "middle-class" atmosphere can prevail, offer solutions. Of course such atmosphere is debased in a school to the extent pupils from less conditioned groups are admitted; but this is the inevitable price that has to be paid.

Education presently works in spite of its theories, because it remains a subtle art, as contradictory as all human existence. Children, as all men, can pursue only satisfactions or releases, which require their opposites as causal sources. The educators have to deceive the child, as unwittingly as they deceive themselves, in the sincere effort to give him the happiness they value. Even the freest educator imposes the cultural restrictions on his pupils, by merely trying to make them as cultural as he is. In fact, the "free" educators are usually the more refined idealists, who would tolerate least any really free, naturally crude behavior.

Education as a science is still nowhere in sight. We are, supposedly, another millenium away from finding answers to the educational questions raised by Socrates.[32] Hardly anybody even expects to have a science of education,[4,5,11] though human progress from it would be greater than from any other science. And all that is required is a causal understanding of the natural, therefore simple laws that govern the economy of organic potentials. But the very logic of humanistic thought is contrary to such laws. Is it not typical that the greatest pioneer of rational humanistic education, Socrates, had to be condemned for corruption of youth?

Abstract Learning. The interests in all learning are satisfactions, which can derive only from needs. In abstract learning the need to know or to understand comes from hard and continuous conditioning of the need of growth, superiority or survival. A culturally conditioned man actualizes himself, grows, gains status and ensures his survival through knowledge and understanding. You feel conditioned anxiety, setback or inferiority if you do not know or cannot understand something.

The animal "curiosity" results from evolutionary conditioning, apparently of the need for security. But it cannot serve as a direct basis for processes of abstract learning, because abstract thinking proceeds in a way completely different from the ways nature works. Intellect proceeds by reducing experiences to the simplest generalized "ones", whereas in natural reactions or feelings billions of our organic mechanisms respond to as innumerable factors in nature. That is why intellectual work can be only disturbed by direct natural experiences, or why best scientific work is achieved in barren isolation. Mathematics as a typical intellectual discipline and the queen of sciences shows how absolutely bland or "poor" the intellectual work is in comparison with directly natural experiences. Learning is hard work because the natural needs have to be conditioned into the intellectual or abstract needs so remote from the natural ways of reacting.

But educators have advocated direct, logical promotion of more pleasant experiences that are, necessarily, freer or closer to natural reactions, in thousands of ways. This has been the great cause of the enthusiastic "free" educators and educational reformers. Rousseau, Pestalozzi, Montessori, Dewey, or Silberman, all have tried to make the educational experience more *directly* interesting. This can be done only by bringing the experiences closer to the natural or already established interests. It amounts to regression toward the natural, seemingly much richer, but educationally more primitive sources of interests. The very gist of education, though, is to evolve the completely different, abstract interests. Once such interests for the abstract ways of thinking are there, everything else comes by itself.

Typically, the radical reformers, like S. Ashton Warner or H. Kohl, have used the natural interests of their pupils in the subjects of fighting, mugging, stabbings, drinking, drug use or street crime as themes in their compositions and reading. The next step in upholding such interests would be to enact, not merely write about, such themes. On the path of making the interests more naturally enjoyable the "progressive" teacher has to go down, closer to the crude biological drives. The radical reformers have demonstrated that learning can be made pleasurable if every present educational practice is reversed.[18] Yet when we have a practical task of teaching or learning, we find that the same hard, unpleasant work is the only way to do it. Even the easier methods of "learning by doing", visual techniques or the new mechanized media are of little help. They have been hailed with great optimism, but have made little difference in practical results (H. J. Klausmeier, H. C. Lindgren, J. M. Stephens);[4,20,31] the studies by Jencks, and Coleman confirm this.

Naturally, here as elsewhere educators have to use pleasant inducements for attaining difficult new adjustments, particularly with pupils to whom the more refined or abstract interests are strange. Montessori methods may be good for children of early age or from culturally deprived environments. The teacher may have to start with the more primitive, natural interests. But his goal should be to get away from them. Yet modern educators see such naturally richer more primitive interests, which certainly bring great initial success, as sources to be cultivated in themselves.

The great simple truth about learning is that the interests and acts of understanding or knowing are *pleasures,* but that they do not come without *equally hard effort.* Evidently the causal dependence of the pleasures here on opposite value experiences is the central fact. But not even the best theories on education, by Dewey, Whitehead, Russell or Hutchins, ever mention this fact in any form. Of course if learning is a pleasure in itself, then why not lead the young minds straight into this land of pure enjoyments?

As Whitehead argued, the subject to be learned is to be brought to the students in all its sensuous attraction and freshness. A history professor finding the period he teaches to be as interesting as life itself may want to reveal it to his students in all its excitement. Actually a subject becomes as real and interesting as life only after enough value experiences, needs and satisfactions, are worked into it. This means hard restrictive conditioning of innumerable detailed needs — while the corresponding satisfactions then come by themselves.

It all amounts to the unpleasant effort of hard work or seemingly unnecessary "drilling" in of detail. This requires enforcement, by inner stresses or external pressures, like grading and competition. Such negatively felt enforcements are, expectedly, condemned as horrible, unnecessary obstacles in the process of learning.[18,19] After a subject has been covered by the innumerous accumulations of needs and satisfactions, it surely is a genuine source of value experiences. Then every educator can point out how the most efficient learning results where it is pursued for the sake of its own pleasures.[5,8,9] In truth, *no education would be necessary for finding pleasures or satisfactions. It is necessary for creating their sources, the nonsatisfactions, needs, stresses or restrictions.*

Choice of Subjects. An important problem is the choice of subjects that are to be taught at schools and universities. Mostly the humanistic tradition and blind value fixations determine what is considered as the true general learning. The medieval educators were as intelligent as we are, but because they equally lived by their fixations and traditions, they limited all true learning to the study of Latin, rhetoric, philosophical points of discussion, a few, known classics and the Bible. Because of our fixations we have added arts, literature and the "treasures" of thought, in their historical or philosophical accumulation. They all could be eliminated today or replaced by completely different, contrary subjects or "treasures" and there would be no loss educationally or culturally. In these areas, the various cultures and religions offer *sharply opposing* value cults, "treasures", philosophical truths or cultural experiences, and it makes no difference educationally.

In our present general education the final goals are the *acquisition of ideas,* truths or reasons and *enjoyment* of "higher" inner values by the students. The study and enjoyment of "treasures" of thought and art may constitute ninety percent of our general education, in the liberal arts, that is to make us cultural before we learn professional skills. In effect, as the humanistic thought becomes more logical and efficient in promoting its ideas in practice, the choice of *art and treasures of thought* as main subjects is becoming exclusive. A review of college programs shows three trends: emphasis on great issues or great books; study of civilizations in their aesthetic or spiritual rather than factual aspects; and orienting of students toward study and appreciation of art.[33]

The authoritative view is that education should consist of study of "masterpieces of wise thought and art" (H. M. Jones).[34] The Great-Books method has been promoted by best authorities, notably by R. M. Hutchins and M. J. Adler. Pure philosophy is accepted as educational guide, since "the humanities, rightly understood, are philosophical discourse, not training".[34] The main task becomes to teach the students "how to think".[32] "A university, then, is a kind of continuing Socratic conversation on the highest level".[32] Clarification, *definition and choosing of values* is proposed as the most important subject.[14]

Equally strong is the emphasis on the artistic education, development of aesthetic taste or appreciation, and enjoyment of the different forms of art.[10] The arts together with literature and philosophy are accepted as the highest, life-enhancing values, to be cultivated through education.[34] The educational trend is toward practical appreciation and enjoyment of works of art, as through listening to music or artistic creation, painting and composition, in the "humanities laboratories".[33] This is so clearly the logical choice under the value theories that "mastering and consumption" of art are held to be primary goals of education.[33] Fine arts and literature are to provide moral formation, enrich human spirit, and reveal truths in the way science or medicine does.[35] Aesthetics becomes like a cult, replacing religion. The authenticity — the real "sacredness" — of art objects is stressed: only the original, authentic masterpieces are to be used in teaching, not imitations, spurious art, reproductions or incompletely copied works.[32,34]

Thus the educational goals become *enjoyment* of positively felt aesthetic or other value experiences, and *ideational or cognitive* acceptance of values, as well as the rational and philosophical reasoning, discussion and study of treasures of thought. In reality, any enjoyment or positively felt inner value experience, whether it is derived from authentic art or from physiologic stimulation, can only deplete human, organic release capacities. And learning to reason or philosophize rather weakens such capacities, which are accumulated through hard needs or stresses that the person cannot rationalize away. Rationalism has always bred morally impoverished, disruptive rebels and cultural misfits, in its logical rejection of restrictions.

We admit education may have to use the fame and glamour of great works and names to attract the young minds. But through fixations, growing under the unquestioning humanistic value beliefs, even worthless, boring works become sacred, and art degenerates into the travesty of depending on absurd sensationalism or mere fame of styles and names. Fixational self-entrapment becomes the dominant factor. Any subject, name, work or idea may acquire a value sacred beyond all reason because of mere additions of valuations or elaborations, through decades, by eager teachers and students. The subjects become so vast in meaningless elaboration that they *lose genuine attraction value.*

If it were not for the humanistic fixations and value delusions, education could be planned with practical efficiency. Cultivation of self-restriction, and learning of scientific skills is all that is needed. Of course moral preaching is ineffective, particularly because it appears hypocritical and backward under the liberal humanistic views and "scientific" theories. But once it becomes scientifically clear to everybody except morons that restriction is the only way of enrichment of capacities, then restrictive moral conditioning will be turned into the central interest most worthy of intelligent mind. Since hard practice is how such conditioning can be achieved, practical morals, not the Learning by discourse, should become the goal. There is plenty of what students can practically do, for themselves and others, particularly for the deprived groups. The abstract learning and interests, which are enormously important, should be developed through studies of science and professional knowledge, instead of the philosophical, literary or other "learned" disciplines, which have never supplied coherent answers. Literature is good for enjoyments that we cannot forsake, not for creation of the ultimate educational, moral, and abstract interests.

But we have to remember, again, that education is a practical art, in which the more enjoyable interests of art, literature and philosophy may have to be used as inducements on the way to the hard abstract interests and practical morals. Yet even here the present education renders a disservice. It tends to turn the study of these subjects into a *compulsory drudgery* by requiring detailed learning of all the fixational, actually *meaningless, elaborations.* In any event, educators should have a causal insight in what is practically happening. But the modern educational theory has never yet mentioned, in any way, that the satisfactions or releases, as the sources of capacities, derive from their opposites, the needs, nonsatisfactions or restrictions.

On the contrary, all the great modern theories, discussions or thousands of books, excitedly urge us to increase directly the satisfactions, inner values, positive feelings, natural interests, gratifications, releases and freedoms, in their endlessly varied forms. Since when has man needed encouragement to enjoy himself?

Education is a subtle art, performed under the simplest principle of the unity between parent and child, which brings imposition of needs or nonsatisfactions through the pursuit of satisfactions or happiness. At every step of moral conditioning, and abstract learning, inducements of pleasures are used to impose on the child greater restrictions and more elaborate conditioned needs or nonsatisfactions as sources of satisfactions and interests.

The educator deceives the child as unwittingly as he deceives himself, about the contradiction of existence or the value causation.

Can education ever be a science? Man could not live by the truth that his satisfactions result from their opposites. The deceit therefore has to continue. How can it after it is exposed? Actually we live not by truths or insights but by drives. These can be conditioned in scientific ways a thousand times better than by blind, necessarily contradictory and superstitious tradition. Man only has to continue wanting the enrichment of his potentials, whatever the ultimate goals or meanings of his existence.

The Unseen Causal Sources in Adjustment and Motivation

Only needs, which are nonsatisfactions, can make satisfactions possible. Because of the inexorable limitation of organism to its sameness, any increase in releases is possible only upon previous increase in restrictions. Thus all the inner values or satisfaction, that man lives for, can be attained only by living through their unwanted opposites. Consequently, what look like maladjustments under the direct logic are the real sources of positive adjustments and motivations. The "best" adjustment, with every need satisfied to its fullest, becomes a state of immobility. Because this is unbearable to the person, he resorts to overadjustments, excessive use of release reserves, which causes impoverishment and disorders.

But man cannot accept these truths of his inherent limitedness, of his role of a squirrel running its treadmill in the cage.

Nor can he accept the fact of the opposite causation, under which progress and enrichment of capacities *are* possible, without limits, even within the organic limitedness. Any amount of positive capacities, satisfactions or releases can be obtained through accumulation of equal amount of their opposites, nonsatisfactions or restrictions. Hence the contradictions of man's existence, in his culture as well as everyday adjustments. We do not need to repeat the explanation of satisfactions, motivations or releases deriving causally from their opposites or restrictions. We shall now look only at those instances which may seem like *exceptions* from such causation.

For example, a person living through a period of enjoyments or greater license, as during a vacation or a day of freer education, may return to his tasks with a greater rather than lesser motivation, or sense of duty. One can understand this better by thinking of the boy who feels greater conscience after having done a wrong. The reason of such reactions is still the opposite causation. A culturally conditioned person lives with a certain artificial sense of normalcy, to which he tends to return by opposite reactions. But this artificial normalcy, like the "conscience", is easily effaced by repeated violation of it. The conscience is lost, not strengthened, by repeated wrongdoings; people do not become more diligent by enjoying long vacations; and children do not develop higher sense of discipline by being left undisciplined.

A converse instance may be illustrated by cases in which children brought up very restrictively may later strongly reject the restrictions. Children forced to go to church every Sunday may become vocal atheists as adults. Such opposite reactions prove the opposite causation, which works here to the extent that the education of the children has not been thorough enough to change their natural normalcy. If children are conditioned or restricted thoroughly enough, and are excluded from contrary influences, then any amount of restrictions or discipline may become their normalcy, felt as little in particular as an atmosphere. Then they will act by opposing any transgressions against such moral normalcy, not in opposition to the restriction or discipline. This is important for explaining the vast confusion about early restrictions leading to later rebellion.

The child may smear walls, or the student may rebel, in plain reactions against the restrictions. It then may be argued that any restriction should be avoided as counterproductive. All conditioning produces resistance or opposition at first, but as it is further enforced and assimilated, compliance becomes permanent. On the social level, people may start revolutions, wars, persecutions or witch-hunts after attempting too much restriction or self-sacrifice but being unable to assimilate it at once. In general, unwanted, irrational reactions of hate are so frequent because people are urged and attempt to live with too much self-denying love while actually being unable or unprepared to bear the difficult restrictions this requires.

Other seeming exceptions from the opposite causation are due to various compensations and economizations in satisfactions or releases. A person having lived through a hard period of restrictions may still suffer from psychic impoverishment, because he might have overcompensated for the hardships of restrictions by anticipated enjoyment of future delights. Such enjoyment, as a release, leads inexorably to equal restriction or difficulty. A drug addict suffering through his treatment, or a delinquent bearing restrictive punishment, may enjoy by anticipation future pleasures or freedoms, which he then must get, through drugs or "anti-social" behavior. Conversely, a person living through a very happy event may be able for some time to be positively minded. This is so because we all try to accept as many restrictions and self-restraints as possible, and we can do more of this while we can compensate for it by enjoyments from the happy event. The negative aftereffects set in much later, when all other events start appearing less pleasant after the enjoyments of the particularly pleasant period.

But even after a past pleasure has created its unpleasant aftereffects, it is still remembered and judged by the person as pleasant. The delicious meal, the opera, or the love affair one has enjoyed are still remembered as pleasures. It is the other meals or later everyday experiences that diminish in pleasure. But the person never makes the causal connection, particularly not between an artistic enjoyment like opera and the later prosaic displeasures. Only in cases of unmistakably direct, grave experiences, as when a love affair ends, people learn, intuitively, that past pleasures bring pain not satisfaction.

One should always keep in mind the paradox that even while

you are experiencing a value you are heading for the opposite value experience. While you are enjoying the food you are decreasing the pleasure from it, while you sleep you become more wakeful, or while you add vigor in your action you get tired. This is true of all value reactions, from visual aftereffects, to the functional heart disease. Overprotection is the surest way of bringing up a fear-ridden individual. Modern men having the means and freedoms to cultivate every positive feeling end by suffering from all the negative reactions of anxiety, "alienation" or malignant impoverishment and stress, mental, social, or physical.

The opposite causal connections are difficult to see also because of the multiplicity of natural value reactions, their combinations and constant reversals. For instance, a reversal of a reversal may take place unnoticed. An overprotected boy finds the world full of dangers, but by reacting to them he develops special, higher capacities of self-confidence. Then the logical observer may conclude that the early protection was the source of later confidence.

But the simple, inexorable rule is that any value experience, as a release, however derived, has to be "paid" for or compensated by equal opposite value experiences or restrictions, sooner or later. Any exaggeration has to lead to equal opposite, unwanted, exaggerated reactions. And *strict reality or rather its assessments in exact terms of inner values* are the criteria for what constitutes exaggeration. To maintain his mental stability the person has to keep such assessments stable, which amounts to accepting undistorted reality. If a person enjoys a present or future event more than it is or will be of value in reality, he has to "pay" in equal displeasure or opposite feelings. Retirement neuroses, originating in such previous enjoyments, are the simplest examples.

Conversely, if under exaggerated restrictions or stress, excess of releases is created, then you get "paid" in enjoyment. If reality comes out less threatening than was anticipated, there is source of enjoyment. People who eagerly recount their past calamities are not masochists. They won't seek to recount past threats that were real and were less feared than they should have been. Even a very pleasant past experience that was overenjoyed is not remembered with pleasure. Every overvaluation, at any period, brings opposite feelings. A sure heir to an office, having anticipated its pleasures, may find it unbearable when he occupies it; or a movie director having enjoyed the beauty of a star finds the reality unexciting when he marries her; or a famous author having attained everything he has wanted and anticipated commits suicide, as did Yukio Mishima.

The central and almost the only problem of adjustment and motivation is the economy of satisfactions or releases. If one has plenty of release or satisfaction potentials for doing what he wants to achieve, everything comes out perfect. Nobody ever lacks perfectly good, reasonable intentions or plans. But every satisfaction or release requires equal need as nonsatisfaction, or restriction, which is the hardship itself. It is boring to repeat this, yet exactly the lack of understanding of this simple, seemingly paradoxical fact makes all theory on adjustment inane. Every one of the thousands of writers and reformers claiming new insights or discoveries, often attracting wide popular following, extol the direct increase in all kinds of positive emotions or potentials without ever mentioning the requirement of the opposite, negatively felt value experience or effort.

Such "discoveries" vary in sophistication but not in their direct value logic. The most popular, do-it-yourself practically direct ones stress all kinds of "positive thinking", enthusiasm, confidence, hope, faith, fulfillment, satisfying interests, freedom from negative emotions and the endless forms of the positively felt deeply gratifying Love. The theorists here range from Norman Vincent Peale or Harry Emerson Fosdick to Karl Menninger or Abraham Maslow. The "scientifically" structured theories may use more technical terms in urging the increase in positive experiences and adjustments, through finding continuous satisfactions or a better understanding of one's useless, rationally unnecessary conflicts (F. McKinney).[22] The theories on personality may stress development of insights, attitudes, roles, learning, perceptions, "balanced perspective", and self-understanding (D.

B. Klein).[29] The generally accepted concepts of Self, Roles, Identification or Alienation are seen as determined by perceptions, insights, ideas, or ideational conflicts, often of so little emotional weight as to be unconscious.[22]

In brief we find here, as in general psychology, the same confused alchemy of accepting the direct *increase in satisfactions* or releases and the *ideational* insights or *learning* as the sources of positive capacities. If this alchemy was true, we all would attain perfect adjustment with pleasure and ease. Reality shows how false and dangerous such alchemistic approaches are. The presently increasing emotional and functional impoverishment, disorders, anxiety, stress, disease, hate and strife between individuals and groups grow from the attempts of modern man to enjoy the easy positive motivations and adjustments without "paying" for them by the negatively felt restrictions or nonsatisfactions as the sources of needs that bring normal satisfactions.

Now we may look at specific problems of adjustment, to see in detail their seemingly paradoxical causality and the failure of modern science to understand it.

Drug Addiction and Juvenile Delinquency

Probably the most typical modern problems of adjustment are drug addiction and juvenile delinquency. Youth is plagued by these problems because youth is more exposed and more responsive to the newest modern attitudes of freedoms and gratification. In the hedonistic atmosphere of modern life the drug use becomes inevitable. This has to be emphasized. People living for satisfactions are bound to end by suffering emotional exhaustion or immobility which becomes as unbearable as physical pain. Narcotics offer the perfect remedy, and the modern man, practicing the cult of overenjoyments, knows this intuitively, upon slightest contact with drugs. As to the juvenile delinquency, one has to agree that "a juvenile delinquent is a youth who takes literally the progressive-educational stress on self-expression and freedom" (J. Burnham).

Drug addiction clearly illustrates the paradoxical causation of worsening through improvement. That is why it, strangely, remains unexplainable by modern science. In objective experimental terms narcotic drugs rather expand our capacities — as increase in releases always does. The best authorities find that drugs actually improve our functioning, make us feel more at ease or free to do what we intend to, thus increasing our ability for useful work (R. W. Rasor).[36] People in trouble are found to make a better adjustment and to return to normalcy through use of drugs.[36] As long as the drug user is given enough drugs to avoid withdrawal pain he remains a normal and positively minded individual (W. G. Karr).[36] Many prominent people are shown to have led productive lives while using drugs (L.Kolb).[36] Deviations from normal physiological behavior are seen as minor under steady use of drugs (N. B. Eddy).[36]

Conversely, drug withdrawal seems like infliction of "pointless suffering", since there is no impairment of productivity as long as the drug is continued (L. Lasagna).[37] Addicts are found to be "dangerous without drugs not with them" (H. S. Howe).[46] Even heroin is shown to be a "strikingly effective tranquilizer for people who suffer from acute anxiety, tension, despair, bewilderment" (W. C. Bier).[46] It is also found that "paradoxically drugs make possible some adjustment to reality" (K. W. Chapman).[46] Thus drugs seem to improve adjustment in every way that really matters; and the direct scientific logic permits no different insights — into the opposite causation and long-range after-effects.

The absence of scientific, which means, causal understanding of addiction is admittedly the main obstacle in dealing with the alarmingly increasing drug problem. From the Presidential and Congressional committees to educators and scientists themselves, everybody recognizes that the problem is unsolvable as long as such understanding is missing.[36,37] It is found "surprising" that there is so little insight about drugs, used by men for thousands of years.[36] Psychology and psychiatry have failed to help, for the same reason —lack of real explanations of the addictive process and its genesis (D. M. Wilner).[37]

At the same time, the universal addiction, that accompanies use of all pleasure inducing means, can only be governed by a simple natural law. This law derives from the fact that excess increase in pleasure releases is followed by their equally excessive restriction. Yet amazingly, though predictably, the narcotics specialists have used any other concept but pleasure in their explanations. Conditioning is most often blamed as cause of addiction; this permits "scientific" explanations. Such authorities as A. R. Lindesmith, L. Kolb and A. Wikler have accepted the conditioning concept.[37] Thus mere associations of stimuli or of environmental, "instrumental" situations are seen as the decisive factors.[37] Moreover, cognitive and linguistic associations are stressed: if the drug user has not conceptually or linguistically associated his reactions with the drug he supposedly cannot become addicted.[36,37]

Besides conditioning, unconscious and symbolic motivations are blamed for addiction.[36,37] This becomes necessary, here as in general psychology, to explain why the person so stubbornly or "irrationally" persists in his negative reactions and self-defeating efforts. It is argued that pleasure seeking is not the motive behind drug use, because the addict suffers miserably rather than enjoys his life and because there is no directly logical reason why he could not drop the drug (A. Wikler).[37] As confusedly, it is explained that the drug user wants to get hooked so that he can have new needs to be gratified or that the hustling and seeking for drugs is the main attraction.[37]

The consequences of the confusion are practically grave, as well as scientifically crippling. All efforts must inevitably fail, because the very logic or way of thinking behind them is reversedly wrong. Thus authorities in the field view drug addiction as an illness,[36] while admitting that the only effective remedy for such illness is administration of the same or similar, addictive drug.[37] Under the direct "improvement" logic the real effects of drugs may remain subtly hidden even upon exhaustive investigation, because the "improvements" show as such in every separate process. Consequently, doctors and scientists testify, as did Margaret Mead, that there are no bad effects from drugs like marijuana which have not yet been tested by life and tradition as to their practical, long-range aftereffects. Medically the common-sense beliefs about damage from drugs seem "misconceptions", since steady drug use is clinically shown to be consistent with good health and high efficiency.[36]

The paradoxical truth of the opposite aftereffects is lost in the sea of medical physiologic facts. The quantitative measurements of drug in the body offer no explanations,[36] because of the complete relativity and reversal of the effects. Similarly the emotional opposite aftereffects obscure the real cause, the excessive search for pleasure. Thus the prevailing theory, probably best presented by Anthony F. Philip, and Sidney Cohen of the NIMH, holds that the addicts are not seeking the pleasure, though they say they do, but are suffering from deep-seated depression, boredom and resentfulness growing from unconscious, early conflicts. In truth, if there is any depression or negative reactions, there must have been equal overenjoyments. But these start with innocently "normal", positive enjoyments. Marijuana with its seemingly benign effect is a good example.

Whether marijuana leads to general addiction may be an unsolvable problem for "scientists", but it should be clear from the simple fact that it is a means of special enjoyment. This is witnessed by its vast illegal traffic and 80,000 yearly law violations. The Congress and practical educators do not have to wait for scientific findings, which add more confusion. They can decide from merely observing the amount of traffic in marijuana, LSD, pep pills, tranquilizers, or other means of affectively sought improvements. Modern science and medicine can only compound the confusion — because they have never yet doubted the improvement logic.

Since the same overenjoyment effects govern all use of drugs, the more accessible drugs like marijuana or pills are sure steps to stronger narcotics. The New York Narcotics Squad reports that 95 percent of arrested addicts said they started with marijuana. Contrary to the medical view, addiction is not an illness. It is closer to crime, because it comes from seeking for easy enjoyment, in the most direct way of all. Why should this illness affect New Yorkers fifty times more often than others. New York City had, at one time, 380,000 addicts, two thirds of all addicts in this country, because it is the easiest place to bring in drugs and organize their traffic. Drug environment or imitation of other drug users is the cause of drug addiction. In repeated studies, most addicts attributed their addiction to having met other addicts.[38] Generally, environmental difficulties are blamed for addiction. Environment and background conditioning are also to be blamed for crime. Yet we cannot treat criminals as victims of illness.

There would be as many ways to help the addiction problem if it was causally understood as there are now ways that have made it worse through the erroneous, improvement-oriented, "scientific" attitudes. If science established — as certainly as it has established, say, the movement of earth — that there is no satisfaction gain from use of stimulants or drugs, this could create a different general atmosphere, which is the determining factor. Then a drug user would be viewed as a superstitious moron and all the present striving for increased satisfactions as a backward stupidity or inability to contain oneself.

Certainly a mere scientific declaration cannot stop pleasure seeking. But in our scientific age science can change the attitudes of people, just as it has helped to create the hedonistic liberal atmosphere we now live in. Expectation of pleasure is decisive. Presently 90 percent of addicts treated return to drugs,[39] because their anticipation, during treatment, of later pleasure gain makes the return to drugs compulsive. Youth does not believe that drugs bring misery and rather thinks that adults tell lies.[39] Science is now the general unquestioned authority, and its reversedly wrong logic inevitably contributes to the problem.

The present views that addiction is much like illness favor its treatment with drugs. The methadone programs are expanding and the immediate results are, of course, proven to be good (V. P. Dole, M. Nyswander, L. Bear). But such treatments amount to mere continuation of the addiction. Illegal traffic in methadone is becoming a grave problem; a majority of deaths from drugs in New York City are now caused by methadone. The arguments in favor of treatment with drugs rest on the "scientific" findings which show, as we saw above, that continued use of drugs is consistent with efficiency and good health. Smokers are also efficient and in good health, experimentally, as long as the nicotine intake is not decreased. The problem is one of longer range effects.

The final issue is whether we want a society of addicts. In view of the enormous efficiency of drugs they would be used much more "effectively" than tobacco. The health hazards would become as incomparably greater. The deaths from cancer and heart disease caused by smoking have become apparent; and worse effects are anticipated from drugs (A. Ochsner). According to NIMH statistics narcotic drugs shorten life by 15 to 20 years. Methadone is a particularly strong narcotic, worse to get rid of than heroin and has to be taken for life. One can visualize a free drug society as one of malignantly ill and prematurely dying people. It is almost impossible to discontinue a narcotic *once it has been culturally accepted,* because the immediate value reactions from narcotics are inherently positive and attractive. Tobacco or alcohol are good examples. The arguments that some drugs are better than alcohol would favor *cultural acceptance, for ever, of new* dangerous narcotics.

The control of drug use through law enforcement has not been successful in countries where the system is geared to alleviate the suffering of the addicts. Different methods were adopted in Japan, and its heroin epidemic was eliminated completely. But such methods are deemed unworkable in this country where doctors want to relieve, not increase, the pain of drug withdrawal (V. P. Dole). Perhaps it is better to permit the people who cannot contain themselves to die from drugs than let them victimize others and die in jails, since they have to that he is to ravage his health and die early without any gain in the pleasure he seeks.

Again, this certainty can have a force of practical conviction only after the science has turned it into a rule that could govern our scientifically minded society. This would require a reversal of the very logic by which science now proceeds.

Juvenile Delinquency. The logical humanistic and "scientific" theory, advocating more freedoms and direct positive satisfactions is as misleading in the field of delinquency as everywhere else. Freedom and direct, natural satisfactions are what the delinquents live by, more than others do. Particularly the youth lives with the easy modern attitudes, while the older people become steeped, with years, in the still persisting more difficult, restrictive tradition. The increase in juvenile delinquency is skyrocketing and has become one of our gravest social problems. Delinquency in general has more than doubled within ten years, increasing many times faster than our population, and the juvenile delinquency is accounting for most of the increase.

Juvenile delinquents have everything that in the modern theory is considered best for satisfactory adjustment. They are "vivacious, extroverted, less self-controlled, more manly inclined, more aggressive, less fearful of failure and defeat, more independent, more initiating, less submissive", as Paul Goodman concludes on basis of the authoritative research by Sheldon and Eleanor Glueck.[38] They are also more sociable, spend more time in play, are physically stronger, and suffer less from fears, inferiority, insecurity, conflicts or turmoils.[2,38] Various modern humanists, from Tillich to J. W. Krutch, have blamed nonsatisfaction of "basic natural" interests for deviant behavior. This is theoretically logical, but could not be more wrong in practice. The above qualities and adjustments of delinquents are products of satisfactions of the most "basic natural" interests, best provided for by gangs.[38]

All youth that is not restricted joins gangs eagerly. Gangs offer the best natural "actualization of self", "satisfactory roles", sense of belonging, adventure, and freedom from tensions, guilt or inferiority.[2,38] Such youths, naturally, pride themselves of being "tough" or independent, and have "terrific fear of dependence on adults" (F. Redl).[46] They know instinctively how effeminating and enslaving the cultural conditioning is. Of course gangs foster crime, which is always naturally satisfying.[2] The degree to which gangs create delinquents is amazing. More than 80 percent of juvenile delinquents are formed by gangs and peer groups. According to one research, "of 1313 gangs studied only 52 did not have some demoralizing effect" (M. H. Neumeyer).[38]

Scientists are misled by the paradoxical effects of the satisfactions. They do find that the delinquent suffers from feelings of nonsatisfaction, hostility by others, neglect, deprivation and harsh restrictions. This is so because he has overenjoyed the opposite feelings and suffers the aftereffects, as in all disorders. In fact, absence of restrictions, which are the central factor, is typical of delinquent background. "Laxness, which is more frequent among mothers than among fathers, is more prevalent in the most delinquent group than strictness".[38] In the lower classes, which have more delinquents, "restraint is often conspicuous by its absence".[38] The frequently invoked theory that overindulgence is hidden hate is typical of the logical explanations here, as elsewhere. But even such practical authorities as the Gluecks are adopting the "logical" formulations and are blaming assumed negative factors like "unsound discipline" or "unfair punishment" — as if reasons determined what the child feels.

Generally, theorists have blamed faulty identification, cultural conflicts, wrong role definitions, unconscious repressed tendencies, feelings of guilt and even self-punishment.[38] It amounts to the usual modern alchemy. The real determining factor is unavailability of positive capacities, which are gained by hard restrictions not by the alchemistic ease of satisfactions. Delinquents have the same final goals as nondelinquents,[2,38] but lack the power to delay present satisfactions for remoter, future goals. Delinquency is not so different from other maladjustments or disorders, together with which it often grows.[38] It has a common cause with them: the impoverishment of capacities or releases. Delinquency is thus governed by the general, paradoxical law of adjustment — which is contrary to the way of thinking of modern theory and science.

The result is a lack of understanding of the causes of delinquency. Even most extensive studies and research, like that conducted by the Gluecks for decades, have provided no causal understanding.[10] The Gluecks themselves have recognized that presently there is so little understanding of delinquency that no branch of science or methodology is of much help.[2] Causal criteria used by the Gluecks, e.g., understanding, affection, stability or moral fibre of parents, are common-sense notions that characterize traditional, well disciplined families. But such common-sense criteria are useless in scientific, strict causal terms.

For instance, "understanding" can causally mean anything, from overindulgence to the strictest discipline that the parent imposes on himself and his child whom he loves as much as himself. The same is true of "moral fibre", stability or "affection". Moreover, value experiences are felt and reported in causally paradoxical ways. The overindulged youth feels least loved. Or exercise of discipline may be seen as particularly strong where it is generally lacking most.

Presently science is of no help. Psychologists have praised themselves on their achievements in helping delinquents, but objective evaluations show that the actual results have been practically nil (B. Berelson and G. A. Steiner).[46] Probably the most frequent argument has been that poverty accompanied by hopelessness and loss of pride are causes of delinquency. But statistics show that poverty or economic difficulties reduce crime and that delinquency increases during periods of prosperity.[38] Pride, expectation or hope creates potentials of satisfactions when it amounts to tense accumulation of needs to attain something or be somebody. Only impoverishment, hate and disappointments are created by pride or hope that is merely enjoyed as the positive emotion, which is what the theorists are talking about.

The scientific and humanistic theory stresses positive satisfactions and freedoms. But delinquency is rising together with the unprecedented increase in freedoms and satisfactions. It has to be kept in mind that in relative terms — which are the only ones that are causally relevant — the minority groups have advanced most in the enjoyment of such freedoms and satisfactions. They have progressed from existence under life-threatening economic and social yoke to what must seem to them a life without any serious concern. Of course the common-sense theories about increased freedoms as causes of delinquency are equally undefendable, because they still miss the real, paradoxical causal insights.

The logical, satisfaction theory seems to be confirmed by experimental observations. Delinquents, as all people, live by the direct value beliefs. They never suspect the causal opposite, the restriction, need or nonsatisfaction as the source of the release or satisfaction. Thus the delinquents will always report, and their behavior will show, that whenever they do something positive it is because of some satisfactory inducement or increased freedom. This delusion may fool not only the amateur observer but also a scientific expert, prison reformer or a Congressional committee. In the simplest case, when greater freedoms are introduced in prisons, the immediate results are almost miraculous,[46] as long as the change is a relief from harsher conditions. Many such reforms have been tried[46] — to end as failures when the effect of relief from harsher conditions waned.

But here as in general education, pleasures or freedoms have to be used to induce the young delinquents to accept the restrictions. Also group interaction among delinquents themselves may be useful — as it is for patients in group therapies or for the Alcoholics Anonymous — because of the "rebound" effect. One is inevitably compelled to accept restrictions after he has enjoyed his superiority in observing the detestable effects of lack of restrictions in behavior of others.

Sexual Maladjustments, Social Complexes, Worries, Suicide

Sex is a most important constant source of pleasures, second only to the needs of security and food. It underlies our enjoyments of art, music and literature, most of our ethics, rooted in family, and many cultural values, growing from sense of beauty, order and love of nature. That this richest source of satisfactions is so strongly restricted in all cultures, proves the paradox of releases and restrictions. Exactly to the extent the direct enjoyment of sex is restricted, it becomes the "sublimated" force behind the above values.

If sex was not restricted, it would make all these more refined values and conditioned interests vanish under the overwhelming strength of direct sex drive. Then crude sex would appear as the only genuine interest, and all other values would be clearly seen as pretentious, stuffy hypocrisies sustained by moralistic lies, just as the radicals or hippies prove it. We saw how cultures like that of the Free Brethren, based on free sex, collapse by degeneration. Thus the simple cultural selection enforces the restriction of sex.

Without restrictions even the direct pleasures of sex would turn into sources of disaster, as they do already in modern life. Any natural *satisfaction disappears upon fulfillment,* and if one tries to extend it beyond natural limits the opposite hangover inevitably follows. Modern emphasis on freer sex is leading to disappearance of sex as pleasure. *Sex has become a matter of distress,* and experts like Maxine Davis or Albert Ellis are calling for help through more encouragement, new forms of stimulation and greater effort in making it pleasurable again. The most frequent argument is that sex has become a mere "fun" (E. Fromm). Blame is placed on excessive controls or cultural tyranny. Man is to be rescued from this prison so that he can enjoy "erotic exhuberance", or "love simple, dumbly, clumsily and without reproach" (J. Barzun).[40] The new prophets, like N. O. Brown, who see salvation in unrestrained enjoyment of sex, are taken seriously.[40] The simple fact is that exactly the full, unrestricted enjoyment of a natural pleasure turns it into a shallow monotony or mere "fun".

Sex as a richest source of pleasure, when overenjoyed has to create as "rich" disturbances. Scientists find that sex is becoming an increasing cause of disorders. Not surprisingly, the traditional restrictions, cultural taboos or feelings of shame and guilt are blamed, though the people who live with such traditions, like the Hutterites, are particularly free of disorders. The scientists are here so straightforward in the direct logic that they turn against clear healthy intuition. They want to promote "the psychic energy which would energize and sensitize the pelvic organs for sexual pleasure"; or to train children in use of genitals and in deriving pleasure from sexuality.[46] Even the instructions for using better lovemaking techniques are found praiseworthy (K. Menninger). Sex education in schools is intended to remove the negatively felt feelings of shame, modesty or guilt. The clinical and do-it-yourself advisers on marital and adult sex always aim at direct increase in the sex pleasures.

Here we have to emphasize the simple central fact about sex: its pleasures or satisfactions cannot exist without equal need as accumulated nonsatisfactions or restrictions. It is amazing how this simple fact, evident from every natural need and satisfaction, is overlooked. Everybody in the field, from medical experts, like W. H. Masters and V. Johnson, to the popular authors of the perennial best sellers on sex, proceeds under the assumption that the sexual pleasure is always there, not limited in itself. Then it can be enjoyed without limitations if it is set completely free and you have learned how to deepen it. This fallacy underlies the "revolutionary discoveries" of all sex liberators, beginning with Freud, Havelock Ellis, Krafft-Ebing or Marie Stopes. No wonder that the sex-related disorders have increased and their explanations become endlessly confused.

Fortunately the cultural tradition and healthy intuition sustain the wisdom of restrictions of sex and make normal sexual development possible. The sexual, as all restrictions are not felt while they remain constant, but serve as accumulated potentials. Particularly in the early years of puberty the releases have to be accumulated, by restrictions, to provide the later sex pleasures. Also, the strong natural drives of sex have to be kept out of play if the more refined cultural interests are to be assimilated. The traditional, intuitive wisdom is here as strong as are the logical and "scientific" endeavors to liberate sex from its restrictive, negative feelings. The two opposing views have led to extensive struggle, particularly in the field of sex education in schools. This is witnessed by the activity of wide organizations — SOS, CHIDE, POSSE, PAUSE, SIECUS and related institutions — fighting for and against sex education.

The *sex education, fortunately, never achieves what it in-tends.* Teachers, as all of us, are dominated by taboos on sex, because cultural conditioning has to be and is emotional, not merely ideational. It is these feelings, the taboos, that are further conveyed to the pupils in class, whatever the ideas taught. This is constantly found to be so, as a great obstacle, by the reformers themselves. Most objectives of sex education, such as the removal of the feelings of shame and guilt are, moreover, causally self-defeating. Shame and guilt are inevitable exactly to the extent that feelings of pride and merit are enjoyed; and sex education rather fosters enjoyment of these, or other positive feelings.

Surely the traditional feelings of shame and guilt can become disturbingly excessive, but only if the feelings of pride and merit have been overenjoyed, as unrealistically. Other feelings about sex, if overenjoyed, can create similar negative reactions or complexes. But it is precisely the sex education that is to make possible greater enjoyment of the various feelings about sex.

The ideal search for pure continuous sexual enjoyments ends in confusion or moralizing sophistry. Thus it is argued that free sexual enjoyment, like premarital intercourse, is right if the person is really in love. But one finds easily this, as any other perfect reason, under a strong drive that is let free or thought right, as sex is in modern life. In the same logical, idealistic way, *sexual enjoyment and "compatibility" in marriage* are stressed, even by our spiritual leaders. Actually enjoyment of sex in the best, most "compatible" ways is comparable to over-eating because of availability of luxurious or spicy foods. That is why an expert may find that "the better a marriage is, the worse its partners will sometimes feel" (R. Farson). Particularly *because marriage is many more things than sex,* the overenjoyments and overvaluations coming from sexual relations lead to weariness and undervaluation between spouses in the wider whole of their marital life. The "beautiful people", movie stars and millionaires, who can choose the sexually most "compatible" partners have least of happy marital life, though they want it as much as everybody else.

The practical results of the increased modern enjoyments and freedoms of sex are ominous. Besides the loss of real pleasure and the upsurge of disorders, one finds the general unhappiness of married couples and mounting rate of divorce, as well as of illegitimate children.[46] Understandably the very desirability of the traditional, naturally normal family is being challenged. Such family has been, unquestionably, the basis of our culture, but now its loosening is sought through new forms of family, as in the community, "lib", and hippie cultures.

Even the *sexual deviations* may be due to sexual overenjoyments. Some of such deviations may be genetic — because overadjustments in one generation do not remain without effect on the next. The point is that the working of *sex mechanisms can be radically "improved"*, by circumventing their very restrictive conditional requirements such as having a highly select partner of opposite sex and special, refined, natural or cultural stimulation. If partners of opposite sex are not available, masturbation or homosexual intercourse may be resorted to, and once a way for release is found it strengthens by itself. Or when the more conditional, refined mechanisms become exhausted, then more primitive, excessive direct stimulations may be sought, as in sadism, pederasty or other sexual deviations. *Modern experts favor, in principle, the direct improvements.* Masturbation is a good example. The young person is ashamed of masturbation because he instinctively senses how wrong it is for his normal natural development. But now the experts in the field are trying to remove this feeling of shame.[46]

The modern attitudes of freedoms and satisfactions lead to particularly intense overenjoyments or overadjustments in the field of sex. The resulting opposite reactions, impoverishment, loss of pleasure, exhaustion, disorders and abnormalcy or deviations are therefore equally strong.

Complexes. Typical complexes are those of inferiority, excessive shyness, shame and guilt. The person suffering from inferiority complex is usually one having superior qualities. He may know very well that he is superior, but may still suffer from the complex (F. McKinney).[22] In truth, exactly the person who enjoys his superiority is the one affected. This is confirmed by the best known study of inferiority complex, namely, by Alfred Adler. He observed, as his case studies show,[46] that the person developed his complexes of inferiority exactly on those lines where he aspired to particular superiority. His patients showed all kinds of incapacities, dissatisfaction, avoidances and sense of failure where they had particularly tried to enjoy the opposite feelings of superiority or success. To explain how a person reaches the opposite of what he wants and enjoys most, Adler developed his theory that the person unconsciously, but deliberately, wants to fail because of conflicts between his aspirations of superiority and sense of inferiority forced on him by social conditions, culture and education.

Inferiority complex is so frequent because overenjoyment of superiority is almost a necessity in our competitive mass society, where one's success depends on how superior he can show himself to be. The only way to play this role successfully is to feel genuinely and aggressively one's own superiority. Such exaggeration in feelings and reactions is inevitably followed by equally strong, unwanted, totally dissimilar, therefore causally unrecognized opposite feelings.

Excessive shyness results from similar overenjoyment, except that the overenjoyed feelings are those of social grace or urbanity. The shy person is one who aspires most to have, and often has to a high degree, these qualities. Moreover, he is the individual who lives in a rich inner world, where he enjoys at will the feelings of these desired qualities. Logically it would seem that he would have a particularly strong feeling of having such qualities, since he has so richly accumulated it. But here as in all overenjoyments the result is an opposite hangover or complex. The boy secretly in love with a girl dreams of her and enjoys feeling himself attractive, intelligent or suave in the imagined situations with her. Then upon meeting the girl in reality he feels much like a man having lived in warmth and being exposed to outside air.

The overenjoyed feelings revert in all their richness into as "rich" unwanted or compulsive opposite reactions. Excessive shyness is suffered in matters like romantic love, personal appearance or social graces, where inner overenjoyments are easy and not stopped by reality. In matters like career, school or job, complexes do not arise, though the person has to be and is much more concerned about them. In these matters deviation from reality is too dangerous to be cultivated as enjoyment. Of course the beautiful as well as the ugly girl can be excessively shy, to the extent she lives, innerly, above reality. The exaggeration in the inner life is not particularly noticed by the person, because it has become an atmosphere he lives in.

Guilt feelings and complexes have been blamed for a great many maladjustments. Surely guilt in itself is a negative feeling. But it fulfills the function of need that makes satisfactions like positive motivations of pride possible. Enjoyment of pride originating not from sense of need, guilt, duty or responsibility becomes a baseless conceit that requires more of egotistic enjoyments. Conversely guilt, as value opposite, comes with the enjoyment of the feeling of pride or merit. You cannot become guilty or ashamed in matters you have never cared about or been proud of. The causal inter-dependence of opposite values here is particularly clear, in plain common sense. But it is as unacceptable in "scientific" thought as is the relative or opposite causation generally.

Unproductive or unrealistic feelings of guilt are possible and frequent. Where one enjoys the sense of own merit or achievement that actually is not his, he has to suffer equal guilt upon failing even if it was not his fault. No amount of reasoning can help here, because inner values as releases and their loss are involved. You cannot cherish or be proud of something greatly, and then decide to forget about it when it becomes unattainable or disappointing.

There can be as many kinds of complexes or "irrational" compulsions as there are forms of value enjoyments. A complex starts with seemingly very normal satisfactory, often innocently small enjoyments. It grows in the vicious-circle way as more releases are resorted to when opposite reactions start emerging upon the enjoyments. The mere quantity of accumulated excess releases or value feelings is decisive. This explains why innocently small avoidances enjoyed for a long time in regard to something slightly unsafe or unpleasant result in terrifying or utterly loathsome feelings, as in taboos, cultural customs, or in personal phobic complexes and superstitions. In a simple case, a soldier wearing an amulet may not even believe in it but may enjoy, in fun, the good luck it brings, every day. Then if the amulet is suddenly lost he will feel very strongly the difference in what has become for him a normal state of security.

All complexes are products of overenjoyments or of attempts to distort the strict value meanings of reality, much as are neuroses. We have to stress the paradox that by avoiding a negative feeling, like inferiority, the complex, of inferiority, is incurred. The feeling of inferiority if it corresponds to reality is strictly necessary in normal adjustment. By avoiding it, by enjoying its opposite, the person creates the complex of inferiority. Modern theory and science are nuisances here, because *they try to help us to avoid the negative feelings, which is exactly what creates the complexes.* A professional best seller advising people to be their "own best friends", to avoid negative feelings, may help them to extend temporarily their enjoyments; but this can only deepen the underlying sources of their complexes.

Worries. Why do people worry when a difficulty lies ahead? Why not forget about it until it has to be dealt with? Sure enough, the "discoverers" of the negative effects of negative feelings have suggested various ways of shelving the worries. This, again, amounts to overlooking the necessity of the negative feelings in meeting reality; or of nonsatisfactions, needs and restrictions in obtaining satisfactions, releases or capacities. Living organism does not work against itself and is miraculously purposeful in its management of reactions and releases. That is why the worry returns, even with greater strength, if one tries to avoid it. This has induced some educators to recommend that worry should be faced squarely — and that the underlying conflict be solved through "understanding".[22]

Worry is a general, purposeful natural function. Even animals prepare for fight or danger by hormonal accumulation of release potentials. The way organism does this is complex but purposeful, beyond our understanding. Such preparations are shown to be negative emotions, in human, conscious terms. This confirms that the resources of human release potentials are created through negatively felt restrictions which constitute all displeasures. The worry amounts to counteracting the general human pleasure seeking by which we become lazy, conceited, over-optimistic, careless, complacent or unrealistic. All this has to be replaced by its opposites, through the release-accumulating restrictions, displeasures or worry, when heavy work, threat, danger of losing status, or meeting of a more difficult future is anticipated.

The forms of such readjustments, consequently, can be varied and subtle. The actor suffering stage fright prepares for the possibility that he may lose some of his cherished glamour or fame: he goes down, by anticipation, from his overenjoyed overly high status. The moment is terrifying because it has to equal a long past overenjoyment. The terror is thus quantitatively explained, and there is no need for mysteries claimed by psychologists who look for horrifying hidden sexual, anal, genital or destructive unconscious conflicts and ideas (D. M. Kaplan).

The phenomenon of worry illustrates how displeasure or restrictions work as the sources of enrichment of potentials and how general as well as subtly varied are man's strivings for pleasure which render him unprepared for full reality.

Suicide. People kill themselves when they are utterly unhappy or have nothing to live for. But the way this happens is paradoxical. Suicides are committed less by the miserable wretches, whose every hour of life would be a torture to us, and more by the lucky, rich, beautiful, successful stardom people. Suicides increase together with better living conditions (P. A. Sorokin), are more frequent among higher classes or professionals and decline during periods of wars or disasters (L. I. Dublin).[41] Economic suicides are committed more by men who are successful and "have nothing more to scramble for" than by those who are failing; and more during prosperous times than during depressions (T. A. Malone). Studies by Dr. H. A. Rusk, Dr. R. A. Kern, and the Harvard School of Public Health have confirmed that suicides are committed more by richer and professionally higher people, and that worries, even illness, help to prevent suicides.[46]

Typically, suicides are committed most during the brightest months of spring, May and June. Also they are committed by "persons who up to that point were generally associated with high degrees of personal security feelings . . . such cases have included suicides of professional psychotherapists" (A. Lauterbach). We saw that psychiatrists commit suicides four times more often than other people.

Actually the paradox is causally simple. Overenjoyment, in whatever form, is bound to bring its opposite, the excess displeasure. Then as the person sees nothing but torment ahead, what reason is there to continue living? In economic suicides "the change from affluence and prestige to lower conditions" has this effect (L. I. Dublin).[41] In other suicides the overenjoyment background may be that of fame, happiness or status. Marilyn Monroe had everything a woman could want; so did Brigitte Bardot when she attempted suicide. When a star has enjoyed a progressively increasing fame, then even a lesser increase in it is a decline that brings her displeasure — without relief, since her usual high position has become a normalcy that provides as little pleasure as breathing. Then she has nothing but unhappiness or more struggle ahead. She may as well quit, by suicide, or by exile from life as did Greta Garbo.

In suicide, as in all forms of overadjustment aftermath, the immediate, precipitating cause is some negative event. As long as the overenjoyment can be expanded, the person would not think of suicide. But while it is expanded, the pressure of opposite reactions, ready to break through, progressively increases. Then any negative event can precipitate the aftermath. However, the negative event has to be a somewhat bigger and sudden trouble. For otherwise it becomes fully a part of background, offering positive relief, before the suicide intent is carried out.

We should also note that suicide is always a miscalculation which the person discovers too late, probably in the last moments of organic or brain disintegration. For as long as organism functions fairly normally it still has wide potentials of releases, greater than the person can see. That is why time heals all sorrows.

It is significant that suicide, the most pronounced maladjustment, is so little understood.[42] Theories on suicide are inconclusive and controversial, based mostly on arcane ideological concepts, in the vein of those expounded by Durkheim,[42] or on the Freudian mysteries[42] about the unconscious vengeance or urge to kill turned against oneself, motivation by forbidden impulse, genital defeat, switching of identity, self-punishment or aggression (A. Alvarez). When it comes to practical problems, the confusion is hopeless, as J. A. Wechsler shows in his book *In a Darkness*. The confusion breeds mystery. If suicides are frequent during Christmas time, which "cannot create per se a state of unbearable anxiety", the cause must be a symbolic regression to "long winter sleep" or "Silent Night".[46]

Work and Leisure

Work is the panacea for better adjustment of every kind, physical or mental, because it amounts to application of the universal principles of evolutionary and cultural progress. Work requires enrichment and elaboration of releases by restriction of preexisting releases, within the organic limitedness, because there are no natural releases for doing work. That is why work is difficult. The decisive factor is the restriction which makes releases available, and renders the organism more elaborate, resourceful, skilled and longer-living. This has been attained through evolution and can be added to by work.

Certainly work can be a source of difficulties; but only if the releases are insufficiently accumulated or are spent in disregard of the requirement of restrictions. For instance, to make the hardship of work more bearable the person may overenjoy how well he is doing it, how superior he is, or how glorious will be the rewards. Then later when his superiority is not recognized or the rewards are not so great, he has to hate and blame somebody or something. He may have so overvaluated his work that he gets irrationally disturbed over the slightest change or criticism of it. There are innumerable, even undefinable forms of such overenjoyments, and of equal irrational aftereffects during return to normalcy or reality.

But to the extent that people bear the hardships of work without escape overenjoyments, they can enjoy equal pleasures of rest or leisure, and have all the higher, enriching capacities of better adjustment and health. Life of hard work is ideal for men, without being unhappier, or happier, than any other life.

Much discussed problems are the boredom and inhumanity of the *automatic assembly-line forms of work*. Theories and movements have perennially appeared blaming many ills of modern times on this kind of work. It is not realized that the interests, "self-expression", initiative, pride or "responsibility", which can make work exciting, require investment of exactly equal tensions, needs or nonsatisfactions, worry, study, tense anticipation and effort. Nobody wants this vexatious side of the interesting or responsible work. Even intellectual workers are "scared to death" when asked "to think up problems of their own", and prefer to take orders (P. Obler). The tense extra effort would not be accepted by the ordinary modern workers, who generally view work only as a means of living or a necessary evil (D. Bell).[43] That is why modern industry has adapted itself to the use of the assembly-line methods.

Leisure as rest from work should be the main pleasure in men's lives. But the modern man is trying to make leisure in itself, without the hardships of work, a source of pleasures. This is as impossible as it would be to derive continuous pleasures from eating or drinking, without having hunger or thirst. Leisure

then becomes an immobility that people try to relieve by re-
sorting to overenjoyments. The inevitable results are psychic and
somatic impoverishment and disorders. Leisure is becoming a
disturbing national problem, and great effort has been initiated
to solve it. But the solutions are, logically, sought in making
leisure even more enjoyable. Typically the first Chairman and
founder of the Committee on Study of Leisure, at the APA, Dr.
P. Haun, stated that pursuit of pleasure should be made a virtue
and enjoyments intensified. According to him "as long as man
is enjoying himself to the hilt, I don't give a damn what he is
doing; he's got it made".[46]

All present efforts to solve the problems of leisure follow the
same logic. The solutions offered merely stress more means of
enjoyment, freeing sexual play from its limitations, attracting
more enthusiasm, increasing consumption, even cultivation of
idleness, "spleen and sloth"[44] — *everything that is directly pleasant.* True to the usual direct logic, satisfactory attitudes and interests are to be promoted by addition of satisfying and interesting "settings" and facilities. Expressions like "meaningful activity" or "fulfillment" of life may be used rather to emphasize
the more deeply gratifying inner value experiences,[44] without
ever considering the causal necessity of the opposite, unpleasant
feelings. The authorities in the field are against any kind of
hardships, even the traditional "humanistic conscience".[44] Rather
cultivation of pure leisure, through "training in leisure skills"
and intensified consumption, is seen as the solution (D. Riesman).[45]

Play and games have to be mentioned in connection with
leisure. Play is a curious activity. It is imitation of life, of the
struggles and victories of life, but without the seriously unpleasant negative side of real-life struggles. In play or game you
can fully enjoy the victories but you can dismiss the defeats and
worries, because it is just a game. Thus the universal rule that
there can be no pleasures without equal displeasures seems to
be overcome. That is why play and games are highly favored
by psychologists and experts recommending easy sources of better adjustment, particularly for the enjoyers of leisure, who can

select only the pleasant diversions of life. "The Play's the Thing!" in the scheme of seeking man's salvation through leisure (D. Riesman).[45] Of course the rule of pleasure and displeasure equality is not overcome. To the extent that play or game is enjoyed, the rest of life becomes less exciting, less interesting. The empty immobility of leisure then drives the person toward overadjustments.

The only way to avoid the emptiness and maladjustments of leisure is to continue accepting hardships and tensions that a life of work requires. People should continue working forever, in one way or another. The opportunity for this has uniquely increased, since most of work now requires only mental effort and expert knowledge, rather than physical force. The only thing needed is change of attitudes. The older people should not expect to enjoy life, however absurd this may sound to the affluent modern men working all their lives just for that.

Rather, the older people should be ready for more unpleasant and subservient work, requiring pooling of effort and flexibility of adjustments. They would be able to do so; but only if they lived their whole lives in expectation not of pleasure but of continuous work and opportunity to serve. This in its turn requires general scientific understanding that the only sources of pleasure and enrichment of life are restrictions or hardships, best accepted through the traditionally evolved necessity of work.

Conclusion

Positive capacities and motivations are releases or satisfactions. But because of the organic limitedness, no satisfaction or release is possible without equal need as nonsatisfaction, or restriction. This simple truth is, however, contrary not only to the natural convictions of man but to the very logic of the modern humanistic and "scientific" thought. Experimentally, direct increase in releases or satisfactions always shows as immediate increase in positive motivations or capacities. But the reality of the contradictory human existence shows that greatest direct increase of releases or pleasures leads to deepest impoverishment. This is evident from all overenjoyments or overadjustments, including their most concrete form, the use of drugs.

Yet the "scientific" and modern humanistic theorists know only the direct logic of positive reactions or satisfactions deriving from positive experiences. And they are constantly discovering that positive capacities, motivations and interests are satisfactions or releases. Consequently they are zealously advocating direct increase in satisfactions and freedoms as the panacea for better adjustment and education in all their various forms, in the name of science and reason.

It is truly amazing how almost everything written or said by the most vocal and most authoritative, self-righteously incensed reformers amounts to such advocacy of more satisfactions, naturally pleasant interests, gratifying motivations and freedoms, in rejection of the whole cultural, restrictive tradition. If, in fact, direct satisfactions and freedoms were the real sources of the positive motivations and capacities we would irresistibly become supermen overnight.

Particularly in education, as the system by which capacities are created, the onslaught by the "scientific" and rationally logical, liberal reformers or the free educators is intense. Fortunately education remains a subtle art, by which parents and educators condition their children to be as tightly restricted as they are themselves, by simply loving them or treating them, instinctively, as parts of themselves. Of course the restrictions have to be imposed in the name of pleasures, in the contradictory ways all human existence and culture work. The other problems, drug addiction, juvenile delinquency, sexual maladjustments, complexes, work and leisure, reveal the same universal paradox of adjustment. They are immediately improved by increase in satisfactions or releases; but the modern hedonistic emphasis on satisfactions and freedoms becomes the very cause of these increasing problems.

The simple, all-important, though humanly unacceptable truth of adjustment is that you cannot have satisfactions without equal needs as nonsatisfactions; releases without equal restrictions;

pleasures without equal displeasures; or inner values, which derive from satisfactions or releases, without equal inner disvalues. Practically this means that you never get something for free and that anything of real, unreversing values has to be paid for in hardship and displeasure or what logically seems to be maladjustment.

VII

SOCIAL SCIENCES: MORE ALCHEMY, CONFUSION AND COMPLEXITY

How could such a sophisticated vast field of learning as social sciences not be scientific? The only criterion of scientism is, however, simple causal understanding; and social sciences, apparently, do not have it. Social behavior of peoples is determined by what men want to and are able to do. Laws of psychology, human potentials and adjustment could explain this. But as we saw the very logic of "scientism" in these fields is contrary to actual causality and has rather prevented the development of sciences of man. The result has been a virtual modern alchemy and confusion.

In effect, the social sciences are perpetuating this alchemy and confusion more extensively than the other fields, for two main reasons. First, social sciences have to deal with vast series of phenomena and do not go down to the basic causes, the potentials and motivations of man as individual. Psychology is dealing with these and it has at least discovered the wide inconsistencies in the universally held beliefs — though the result has been a world of mystery, hidden forces, irrationality, and endless contradictions. This realization of inconsistencies has not been directly reached by social scientists. They still proceed, fundamentally, only by the direct logic of positive potentials deriving from positive causal backgrounds and of rational or ideational factors determining the behavior. This logic is of course hopelessly alchemistic.

Secondly, social sciences are ideological or philosophical to a higher degree than other fields. The philosophical tradition goes here back to the theories of Plato; and every citizen wanting

311

to improve the world or to blame the system, as everybody does, has a political or social philosophy or theory. The deeper reason here is the vastness of a subject of great concern to everybody. The factors of social interaction are too many to be understood, but everybody has to have an explanation or "reason". Because of the ideological and philosophical nature of social sciences, they are dominated by the humanistic value delusions and belief in ideas as causes, characteristic of ideologies and philosophies.

Ideas, Ideologies, Doctrines, Symbols, and Myths as Causes

The real simple causes of human behavior are the pleasure drives, releases or satisfactions by which men live every minute of their lives. But as we have seen repeatedly, these causes are too commonplace as well as incomprehensible, actually paradoxical, to be recognized in any "scientific" or humanly acceptable thinking. This precludes a true causal understanding of why and how men tick. But since perfect "reasons" or "explanations" are found in the minds of people and behind their every action, such reasons or ideologies become the subject of study by social scientists and experts.

Ideas, ideologies, philosophies and reasoned beliefs are universally accepted in social sciences as causally decisive. A book on government or social theories may read much like a compilation of philosophies. Social philosophy may have changed in its form; modern theorists may not prescribe utopian forms of government. But modern social scientists accept equally radical underlying philosophical theories. Thus, all social life may be viewed as determined by the Superorganic,[1] a "kind of vast cultural entity or cultural system, or civilization, which lives and functions as a real unity" that causally determines everything else (P. A. Sorokin). The causality by social macrounits is, in fact, one of the few generally accepted concepts among modern social theorists.[1,8] Such approach becomes metaphysical, as we shall see later, and can be radically misleading, because it stresses higher values, like the "ultimate value", "major premise", or "prime symbol" of each civilization or supersystem. We saw that a sense of a value rather reveals prevalence of opposite value backgrounds or lack of the factual value.

In social psychology the *ideational and cognitive factors* are seen as decisive. The concepts of Self, Role, Identity, Identification or Alienation are accepted as most important, and as determined by perceptions, comparisons, differentiations and understanding. "One's self has its origin in perceived relationships to others [and] ego is a more restricted kind of self-perception".[5] Role, Identity, Identification and the related Alienation are equally assumed to be products of perceptions, learning, information, communication, comparisons, conclusions, and "strategic considerations" (T. M. Newcomb).[5] Attitudes and outlooks are seen as determined by the same cognitive processes; "a given attitude may be a conclusion of several syllogisms" (E. E. Jones and H. B. Gerard).

In all social psychology such cognitive factors are considered as determining.[1] In addition, the same main theories that dominate general psychology are accepted in social psychology: the classical conditioning and psychoanalytic theories, as well as the Behaviorist, Field, Role and Learning theories.[5,8] Above all, the direct "scientific" logic is never doubted and the actual, opposite causation never noticed. In reality the most important social problems arise from psychic stress and impoverishment, as products of opposite causation, *contrary to what people want, learn, reason or should feel according* to the direct logic.

The strongest, "irrational" social drives are emotional, opposite excesses from overenjoyed social feelings. Yet social psychology tries to explain social attitudes as logical products of perceptions, ways of viewing the world, cognitive habits of mind, or too narrow ideologies (E. S. Bogardus).[41] The only accepted alternative to the directly logical and ideational causation is the alchemy of the unconscious drives.

Ideas, concepts and symbols, in forms of ideologies, political philosophies, doctrines, constitutions, or national symbols are considered important causes. Ideologies like democracy, socialism, communism, freedom, capitalism, nationalism, sovereignty, or internationalism are the most discussed issues in social sciences. The conviction behind the discussions is that explanation and acceptance of the right ideology can improve or change social life.

In truth the ideologies and doctrines are only rationalizations or slogans for what people are doing because of their drives for daily self-interests, value enjoyments or pleasure, and their compulsions or psychic overadjustments. Marxist revolutions are revolts of masses who are least capable of understanding Marx. The more pragmatic social scientists see ideologies and doctrines as practically powerless theorizations, while others view them as all-important.

Thus it is found that *ideas are much discussed, blamed or praised, but also recognized as having no more power than abstractions* (E. M. Burns).[8] On the one hand, ideas are seen as the "empires of mind" that will determine the empires of the future (C. G. Friedrich).[4] On the other, it is shown that political ideologies become irrelevant, even in the Soviet Union (G. J. Holton). Generally the "importance of the role that ideologies serve and the power of ideas are stressed by most theorists.[11] Robert MacIver has called the power attributed to dogmas and ideologies a myth.[8] The belief in ideas fits within the philosophical orientation of political sciences.[3,7] Ideas are often assumed to be directly effective instruments in political struggles, as is shown in M. Lerner's book *Ideas Are Weapons*. Abstract understanding of ideas is thought important.[2] Communism has turned totalitarian supposedly because proletariat does not read Marx (F. Williams).[3] But it is also found that no amount of instruction can change political attitudes of peoples (W. G. Runciman).[3]

Doctrines are assumed to have powers of "most frightful tyrants".[10] The *doctrines of sovereignty and nationalism* are blamed as causes of wars and as obstacles to world government. It is argued that these doctrines have been misunderstood, that nationalism was not intended and does not have to mean fanatical attachments and hatreds; or that the sovereignty is now being wrongly interpreted to exclude the real will of the peoples of the world.[8] Scientists as well as lawyers—Einstein, W. O. Douglas, R. M. Hutchins, R. G. Tugwell, N. Cousins, C. Streit and E.

Reaves — have fought against such interpretation of sovereignty.[8] The real forces and paradoxical compulsions that make people resort to excesses of nationalism or of rights of sovereignty are not understood.

The *idea of freedom* has been extolled and discussed more than anything else by political and social scientists and leaders.[2,8] But freedom has no meaning without its opposites. Freedoms are most persistently proclaimed and strongly felt by the culturally advanced people who live under strongest restrictions. The theorists, however, fail to see the paradox and advocate freedoms as sources of progress and highest goals. Their gullible followers then lead peoples to chaos and misery. Some scientists do notice that paradoxically "liberty becomes possible only in the same conditions which give rise to likely restrictions upon it" or that liberty and restraints are always related.[10] It is obvious that "freedom is a concept that has meaning only in a subjective sense [and] can develop only in those cases where there are conflicts between the individual and the culture in which he lives" (F. Boas).[15]

Democracy is equally a foremost object of political and social doctrines and theories.[2] The logical theorists view democracy as a system of ideas or a wisely constructed invention that has changed the world and ensured freedoms.[8] In truth democracies evolve, selectively, where people live under tight self-imposed restrictions. Democracy is neither rational nor efficient, and can work only if its very basis, freedom and representation, are compromised.[16] Indeed "the drive for certain aspects of democracy itself, momentarily, makes the attempt to install and operate democratic government at best a hazardous adventure".[12] If the public participation or direct representation of opinions is too active, orderly government as well as international cooperation becomes impossible (H. J. Morgenthau).[6,10]

Democracies are dangerous and corruptive in practice. The new developing countries have become dictatorial after enthusiastic but disastrous attempts to have democracies. As Hayek says, by quoting Keynes, "dangerous acts can be done safely in a community which thinks and feels rightly, which would be the way to hell if they were executed by those who think and feel wrongly".[9] Feelings, motivations and potentials, ultimately depending on the simple pleasure economy, determine the social realities and can turn any ideology into a farce, or success.

Symbols, in various forms of national emblems, traditions, *rituals and myths,* are also believed to be important causes. Symbols, myths and rituals are considered so important that, supposedly, the political order depends on them; some new countries fail because they lack a founder's myth.[4] The necessity to have myths in every culture, notably expounded by Joseph Campbell, is now taken earnestly. Ritualism is considered important because rituals assumedly reflect social values and purposes.[11,32] It is seriously believed, and regretted, that people are guided by mere symbols, signs and rituals.[11,15] The real, paradoxical *value or pleasure causation, that creates the causally senseless strong fixations* of myths, rituals and symbols, is missed. Scientists may argue that men are lured even to death by their myths (R. C. Snyder).[11] It is held that adoption of more inclusive social symbols could lessen strife among people (G. W. Allport).[8]

Particularly the scientists emphasizing cultural primacy, like Kroeber, Benedict or Toynbee, see symbols and myths as determining causal sources. According to a typical theory, by Cassirer, the myth of the sorcerer or right man is responsible for totalitarian regimes. Symbolism as explanation is strong in modern sociology, as is witnessed by the theories of Levi-Strauss. Peoples are assumed to live by reasons expressed in myths and symbols serving a "scientific allegories" and "charters of belief" (K. Young).[15] Some scientists hold that even such modern phenomena as national solidarity or rise of technology are mere vehicles of new myths (D. Bidney). Apparently, you can change society by changing its myths and symbols.

In reality symbols, rituals, flags, myths and even constitutions are as meaningless causally as are all fixations, slogans, rationalizations and "reasons". The real causal forces are the paradoxical value reactions or feelings. People, though, see their strong "reasons", the rationalizations as decisive; and social scientists, the same as psychologists, deal only with such ideational content, in their analyses.

The Illogic of Values, Reasons and Factual Conditions

When social scientists consider *values,* which are decisive though paradoxical as affective reactions, they perpetuate the humanistic value delusions. The *values are viewed as directly logical, socially expressed ideologies.* In truth, people find the greatest values where the needs for the conditions valued are most desperate — where the actual values are lacking. Conversely disvalues, like anxiety, show strongest where values, like security, are enjoyed most.

Values of freedom, reason, equality and justice, or of various institutions and ways of life are considered as the central factors by highest authorities. C. Wright Mills stresses reason and freedom as the most relevant categories in social analysis.[17] Karl Jaspers views the great, classical values, including freedom, reason, beauty and faith, as the goals of political and social life and science. C. J. Friedrich states, with reference to Myrdal and Lynd, that any science of politics has to be value oriented and regrets that many theorists are abandoning value criteria as arbitrary or relative.[4] R. A. Dahl recognizes the "core values", of freedom, equality, progress and rationality, as the ultimate, still viable criteria.[9] Differences in value concepts are blamed for social conflicts;[15,11] and "objective values", or "one's theory of social values" is considered as decisive.[15] In truth the concepts and theories of values are weightless abstractions.

Values as logical causal concepts are most misleading, because the real causal sources of values are their opposites. Freedom and reason are values to the extent they are badly wanted or missing. We do not need to repeat that the objective values, like love, are most necessary, but are attained through nonsatisfactions felt as disvalues. Logical, direct cultivation or enjoyment of the above advocated inner values would lead to negative reactions, and to value fixations about institutions, beliefs or ways of life. Such, long felt fixations, as well as the reactions from value overenjoyments, are the real causes of social and political strife.

Reasons, intents, and reactions to factual conditions are treated in social sciences with the nonrelative, direct or "scientific" logic, as in all human sciences. In individual behavior practical observations show that reasons or intents are futile and that the most positive factual conditions have negative effects. But such observations are difficult in regard to societies; and social scientists proceed totally in the "logical" ways. Frustrations or nonsatisfactions are blamed for social disorders;[12] and logical incidence of events, even kairos or luck, is thought important.[4]

Most theories in social and political sciences are built on assumptions of rational decision making, logical pursuit of interests and nonrelative effects of factual conditions.[1] The game theory, quantification methods, system analyses, and the various analytic, positivistic or field theories are relying on the usual scientific, direct logic.[1,8] Theorists build on the logical assumption that people have a "crude understanding of their interests".[12] The extensively discussed "theory of action" of Talcott Parsons is a "voluntaristic" theory based on assumptions of intended choices.[1,18]

In reality the important social problems, requiring scientific understanding most, arise from *reactions that people never want or intend*. These reactions are the opposites of intensely wanted and overenjoyed experiences. The positive enjoyments of fulfillment and love during intense nationalism lead to stress and hate. But here, as in psychology, the actual, opposite causation is never suspected and explanations for the irrational, unwanted reactions are sought in the Unconscious.

Irrationality: More Confusion

Irrationalism due to unconscious causes is increasingly accepted as an alternative explanation in social sciences, and the Freudian or Neo-Freudian interpretations of it are the most common.[2] Mistrust of intellect and upsurge of Freudianism seem to be the trends in social sciences.[8,15] Rational views of social or political behavior are declining, in a "horror" toward rational thinking about social problems.[4] Thus "in a few decades we have abandoned the assumption of rationality" in political or social theories (D. B. Truman),[11] and turned to the "cult of the irrational" (E. H. Carr).[19] It seems that our atomic age is confronted here with a "basic streak of irrationality".[10] The Neo-Freudians, best represented by H. D. Lasswell, are gaining recognition in social sciences.[13] The traditional rational thinking is challenged by other theories, like Marxism, which "deny the reliability of consciousness of ourselves" and show that "things natural and social are not what they seem to be" (H. J. Morgenthau).[6] Thus "human beings may say that they want one thing and really want its opposite" (R. C. Snyder).[11] The irrationality of social behavior is also part of the theories of social macrounits and "systems", which exclude rational, purposeful behavior (A. Rapoport).[03] Such theories underlie the modern sociological thinking. The widely accepted concepts of the Superorganic or of cultures as causal determinants belong here.

Theories about the unconscious irrational behavior originate from misunderstanding. Social behavior is, indeed, often contrary to what people see as reasonable and desirable. But *the real sources of such "irrationality" are the consciously rational, voluntary and ingeniously planned efforts* of men to improve social feelings, reactions and cooperation. Exactly because such efforts are too successful and permit overenjoyment of exaggerated feelings, the opposite, disruptive, least wanted reactions break out, as aftereffects.

In sum, social scientists, proceeding by the usual direct "scientific" logic, perpetuate all the fallacies and delusions of psychology, human sciences and humanistic beliefs. Thus they accept the ideational as well as unconscious causation and the logic of positive reactions deriving from positive conditions or experiences. This, as we have repeatedly explained, amounts to a modern alchemy, which can only increase the confusion, and becomes a practical danger. In social behavior as well, direct improvements in satisfactions lead to impoverishment and stress.

Social Motivations, Intellect, Emotional "Improvements", and Restrictions

The factors that determine social behavior are the same drives for pleasure, release or satisfactions that determine all behavior. The down-to-earth striving for satisfactions or pleasure constitute all human motivations. Cultural values are conditioned pleasures, and accumulated satisfactions or releases are the sources of all potentials; we defined before the concepts of release, and of restrictions that create such potentials. Of course man's use of intellect, his most powerful tool, has to be considered. But man uses this tool for attainment of what his feelings and pleasure drives, or conditioned needs and values dictate. *Intellect* applied to improve such feelings or values directly and extensively *becomes the cause of equally intense negative or disturbing reactions.* Social motivations are myriad, but they all are value reactions — which turn through *excessive enjoyment* into anxiety, alienation or stress, as well as schizophrenia or heart disease.

The central problem is the extreme difficulty of man to restrict his pleasures. He not only overenjoys his social feelings, through the use of intellect, but also needs pleasure as inducement for accepting restrictions as sources of potentials and of conditioned social sacrifices. Social educators and leaders have to use the feelings of people about their own worth, security or success, to induce them to bear sacrifices for the nation. As such feelings are overenjoyed, the opposite reactions of inferiority, insecurity or disappointment become inevitable and the various disorders or complexes intensify. Thus the exaggerations of the positive feelings and the resulting disorders often are the inevitable price of national progress.

More positive emotions, and freedom from negative, irrational or unwanted reactions would be all that is needed for perfect social order. It may seem as if people merely lack insight or confidence for accepting the reactions that would be most beneficial as well as pleasant for everybody. The best social theorists may remain unaware of the alchemy of such "discoveries". In his book *The Recovery of Confidence* John Gardner demonstrates how all we need now to overcome our difficulties is to summon up our will, faith and determination, without even a need to change our tradition or values. Similarly Philip Slater, in his book *The Pursuit of Loneliness,* shows that our central problem is the poor emotional quality of our lives or our refusal to enjoy ourselves, in our mindless concentration on productivity and technology.

Positive emotions are the panacea for all problems, but they can certainly not be created through their logical addition, through mere increase in their enjoyment. That is why the logical scientism is helpless here as in all human sciences. R. A. Dahl explains, in his book on political and economic planning,[9] that the most important goals would be creation of "personalities capable of joy, love, friendship, spontaneity, kindness, respect, dignity and solidarity"; and that this "may well dwarf anything that is attainable by action through the larger politico-economic process discussed in this book". But he admits that "painfully little is known about the requirements of rational social action in such critical matters as these". He points out the paradoxes of the process of creating such positive emotions: "if one deliberately tries to manipulate them, their value declines"; and they are created through controls that are invisible yet ubiquitous.[9] Reversal of emotions and the unnoticeability of universal restrictions are certainly the central factors in creation of human potentials.

The general quality of emotions and capacities is reflected in the *"character" of peoples,* which has been often recognized as the determining factor. Gunnar Myrdal attributes the failure of development of Asian nations to the character traits of their people.[21] There can be no doubt of the decisive importance of national character. But the explanations by social scientists are confusing, because the only, simple determining factor, the capacity for restrictions as sources of potentials or releases, is lost amidst vast sophistications about logical factors, reasons, ideational values, ideas or cultural ideals, which may be mere rationalizations or fixations.

The external character traits, of rationality, efficiency, order-liness, self-reliance, dignity, face-saving, superstition, or rigidity[22] may work out in two, opposite ways, depending on the above capacity to enrich potentials through restrictions. Men can be rationalistic, efficient, self-relying, proud or superstitious in pursuing cheap, fixational and unproductive indulgences as well as in attaining enrichment of capacities. Moreover, the *fixational* traits and values are always the most salient and elaborate. The beliefs of the Chinese in Yin and Yang, the Confucian teachings, the five virtues or triagrams of laws have been found as their prominent cultural traits, while in fact they are mere fixations and rationalizations, that are repeated by communists as they were by mandarins.

External expressions or factual conditions are not decisive. The inner feelings are, but because of their strange causal logic they are not accessible in scientific analysis. A scientist may note that the external authority of father is equally strong in the German and the Chinese culture, but that the resulting character traits of the two peoples are different.[23] Social scientists rather become fascinated with prominent, "characteristic" historical events of a nation, say, a Mayflower, or Bismarck "tradition", which are only abstractly learned facts, not even thought of in the practical world of management of inner feelings. Or scientists may conclude that mental states, even psychoses, are generated culturally, as when the psychotics from Weimar may declaim their symptoms in styles of Goethe or Schiller, their home poets.[23] Similar observations have been made in regard to other peoples (O. Klineberg).[23]

In truth, any object or event can serve as the center of a cultural fixation, or of individual obsession, and it is usually the one that is most frequently encountered or mentioned in the locality. But such fixational or obsessional, accidental object or event, in itself, reveals nothing about the real forces in formation of character. Still the historical, anecdotal and superficially fixational or "cultural" explanations have been used in most studies of national character, of peoples of West and East (C. N. Parkinson).[22] The real *source of capacities, the ability to bear restrictions, is missed.*

The Compulsive Unwanted Reactions

The central, unanswered question is *why are people rejecting the positive attitudes* that are so beneficial and gratifying. Or why are they adopting the stressful, clearly irrational, damaging and even highly unpleasant behavior. The problem here is the same as in all compulsive negative reactions. All disorders, mental or physical, grow from excessive enjoyment of pleasures, of what is most wanted, and positively felt. Because this paradox is not understood, the negative, irrational unpleasant behavior is blamed on insufficient insights, faulty ideologies, wrong intents or mere lack of will. In the words of Gilbert Murray "we have the power and we know the course. Almost every element necessary to success has been put into the hands of those now governing the world", who merely lack a "resolute and sincere will".[24]

In comparison with the tremendous success of technology, it is argued that "the selection of social problems lags behind technology because we have not organized the same sharp search for ideas to deal with them" (J. R. Platt).[25] The same progress that now provides better houses and hospitals is expected to offer better choices of forms of society.[3] The insidious effects of direct "improvements" are not suspected. Logically there is nothing that would be impossible or against human nature in organizing the best world order.[4] It is argued that only the "failure to apply available and often self-evident knowledge to our social relationships" leads to social and political disturbances (N. Angell).[2]

Scientists may realize that "neither the lack of knowledge nor of skills is the main problem, but careless attitudes or highly ego-centered attitudes";[14] or that "skills may be taught but the changing of attitudes comes harder".[12] Individual and national self-interest may be recognized as the reason why best ideas fail.[7] Such observations still imply intents — albeit selfish or careless — and voluntary, strongly desired attitudes. Actually here as in all disorders the stress or extreme egotism that causes the strife or war is *a reaction least wanted by the people*. It is the opposite of the attitudes of national cooperation or mutual love that the people badly want and exaggerate. The *exaggerated* feelings of love reverse, and create the hate of "others".

Expectedly, *unconscious social drives* are accepted as the only possible explanation. According to Karl Mannheim the collective unconscious obscures the real conditions.[3] The Neo-Freudians can easily demonstrate how people work against themselves, therefore must be acting for hidden, strange, symbolic reasons. Lasswell holds that "the individual is a poor judge of his own interests. The individual who chooses a political policy as a symbol of his wants is usually trying to relieve his own disorders by irrelevant palliatives".[13] All strife and tension assumedly result from using political remedies for unconscious conflicts, and thus creating "another set of equally irrelevant symbols". Lasswell proposes psychoanalytocracy as the solution. Psychoanalysis is to make people free and ready to enjoy themselves to highest limits, through "maximization of Indulgences".[13] The blunderous Freudian alchemy is thus compounded.

The Metaphysics of "Social" Causality

The most important approaches in social sciences, namely those emphasizing the *society as the causal unit,* equally derive from the confusion about people doing what they clearly do not want. It is assumed that the "mind", "organic state" or the "unconscious" of the social unit is the causal source.[3] This seems logical, since often a "collective behavior results that no single individual would have rationally preferred".[25] Apparently "there is something in the nature of historical events which twists the course of history in a direction that no man ever intended" (H. Butterfield).[19]

Similarly, cultures seem to evolve independently of individual minds. As Kroeber explains, cultures vary widely, while human organism and psychology are everywhere the same.[15] Thus culture is found to be superorganic or superpsychic and unexplainable by individual psychology.[15] Most cultural anthropologists and sociologists hold this view.[1,15] The theory that society or culture rather than individual is the causal unit has been the starting point in social sciences since Durkheim.[1] Hence the numerous efforts to establish a valid "system" concept. The social philosophy, from Plato, Hegel or Spencer to Durkheim, Weber, Spengler or Parsons, has stressed the cultural essence or "spirit" and social entities as the causal sources.[1] The whole theory of social sciences can be viewed as being centered around the social and cultural causation.[14,15]

The simple reality, however, is that society or group does not feel, think or act. It is the individuals who do. To believe in the will or spirit of a society amounts to metaphysical anthropomorphism. We have to emphasize that human motivations derive from heavy, down-to-earth realities, not from a play with ideas or from spiritual influences. People behave the way they do because they are moved by the pleasure drive or what they feel, and by the desperate need to restrict or condition it for more useful or remoter pleasures. Man is uncannily skillful in obtaining his pleasures or satisfactions, which are the goals of his every hour of life. *He would never surrender them to any collective unit,* or permit them to be changed by such unit, unless he himself effects the change.

Of course individuals acting in a group may behave more irrationally, in some respects. In social or crowd interaction, the generally desired emotions are heightened. Nationalistic overenjoyments of self-esteem or superiority can be driven to a frenzy collectively. Consequently the opposite, unwanted, irrational reactions have to break out with equal strength. Also important are the obvious quantitative differences between a reaction by one individual and that of millions of individuals acting together. More time is required to start a reaction by a group, or to stop it. Also the group action is, necessarily, less articulate, more primitive and more confused. A nation may require decades to reach a point of excitement or revolution, and more decades to live through the opposite reactions.

Here the question about *ideas and leaders* becomes interesting. In individual life one often gets excited by an idea and starts acting with a strong "will" to carry it out. But since this amounts to an exaggeration in terms of motivational realities, the opposite reactions set in and the person soon finds himself in the same state he was in before. But a nation may take decades in its endeavors to realize an exciting idea, before it settles back to where it would have been without the excitement. Leaders as the carriers of ideas have the same effect. Externally it may seem that leaders bring great changes, since external forms are upset during the efforts and setbacks. But actually the nations do not attain more, or less, because of leaders, than they would have attained without them, in the end. The real potentials of peoples grow at a set rate and produce slow gradual progress, in spite of grandiose ideas promoted even by most powerful leaders of masses. Of course a leader, idea or movement may cause so much disturbance, through the convulsions of hope and failure, that it may amount to a major difficulty, creating vast restrictions, which then serve as sources of potentials.

We have to say more about the "*system*" *theories* as important efforts to establish the causality by social units rather than by individuals. In all sciences, "systems" are the main bases for establishing causal laws. Because man exists and thinks as one organism, reduction of phenomena to one system or "organism" opens the best causal understanding. Anyway, social scientists have repeatedly tried to construe "systems", integrated much like organisms. Comprehensive system theories have been proposed by Easton, Lipset, Shils, Apter and Merton, among others.[1,29]

The question is, do such systems exist? Easton explains that natural systems in social sciences cannot be discovered, but that "systems" have to be constructed for theoretical convenience.[28] He argues that physicists have similarly constructed uniform concepts like "mass", that they attribute to all physical things.[28] Actually the uniform concepts, principles or causal laws can be discovered only where some, necessarily natural, phenomenon exists in the same way all men permanently exist: they therefore understand it with absolute simplicity or uniformity. Men understand mass with such uniformity because men consist of matter as everything in nature does. But *social phenomena are not of natural origin or created under such unchanging natural laws.* They are created by man with his *ever changing,* inventive strivings.

Consequently, no social "system" can be dealt with under any causal laws or principles, as science requires. The assumed variables and laws in the system theories are "no more than guesses", and have no predictive power (A. Rapoport).[29] In sociology the system theories are being abandoned because they offer no laws for self-maintenance, change or dysfunction in the systems.[1] The asserted central principles of self-maintenance and equilibrium of the systems cannot be demonstrated (W. G. Runciman).[3] To the contrary, social systems as human creations are governed by incessant inventive efforts toward *new, different, endlessly varied changes* and improvements.

Such efforts in the case of individuals become subject to laws, particularly to that of the opposite causation, because of the unchanging natural maintenance of sameness by the organism. No such unchanging principles exist for social systems. Only individuals can be dealt with scientifically or according to causal laws; and all social behavior, including the vast irrational reactions by whole nations, can be explained by individual psychology. The possibility of explaining social behavior psychologically is recognized as "exceedingly important".[3]

Unfortunately *social sciences are dominated by the emphasis on social entities* or macrounits as the causal sources.[1] The result is not only universal confusion, as no causal laws, scientific certainty or agreement is found, but also a defeatism. If social causation is determined by superorganic macroagencies, shrouded in theoretical controversies or acting as metaphysical forces, then nobody can do much to affect social progress. As W. F. Ogburn concludes, "The idea that a tremendous development like the superorganic can be controlled or even directed is a fantasy. Such dreams are incompatible with a scientific sociology".[26] The modern science, with its logic of direct increase in releases, may indeed hamper rather than help progress. The unlimited possibilities of progress, through real, causally understood human sciences, remain unrecognized.

Here we may say a word about *the present state of social sciences*. According to H. J. Morgenthau, they "are still awaiting their Newton, their Leibniz, their Faraday, and their Maxwell".

J. B. Conant finds that in the social sciences, "their whole area of investigation is in a state comparable with that of biological sciences, including medicine, a hundred or hundred fifty years ago". He predicts that "a hundred years hence historians will be able to separate out science from the empiricism and both from the charlatanism" of the present social sciences.[27] Similarly A. Rapoport holds that "what is said of mid-nineteenth century medicine can also be said of present-day psychiatry and also of much of what goes today under the name of social sciences", and that there is "ample justification to dismiss it as quackery".[29] C. Wright Mills characterizes the work of social scientists as a "ritual established by cliques, personalities and schools", or an endless "shuffling of cards — while the systematic work on conceptions should be only a formal moment".[17] Most of the social sciences can be fully proved to be only a deliberately complicated, useless mumbo-jumbo sophistry, as is demonstrated in the book *Social Sciences as Sorcery* by S. Andreski.

Sociology is rightly called "the science with the most methods and least results".[7] It is becoming practically useless, as the problems like crime, education or social work are taken over by practical specialists.[1] Similarly the political science is criticized as a "sterile exercise devoid of originality".[8] The new political science based on modern psychology, "has no protection whatever, except by surreptitious recourse to common sense, against losing itself in the study of irrelevancies" (L. Strauss).[13] The "political theory as an academic discipline has been intellectually sterile".[6] The extensive theorization rather "diminishes the 'scientific' status of political sciences" (W. G. Runciman).[3]

Social sciences, in general, are not possible even in principle, since there is no general theory, no "adequate logic of induction" (R. S. Rudner).[31] Typically, social scientists "do not even take the trouble to debate their various theories seriously" (J. G. Kemeny). The greatest scientific problem of our times is the fruitlessness of social sciences (P. A. Sorokin). Of course the amount of perfectly scientific effort has been enormous, but it has produced only "data flood",[28] "rage for quantitative results"[7] or wealth of sampling techniques, all of which is useless without a general theory.[31] Of the same nature are the social science breakthroughs, attained only in the quantitative areas like system analyses, cybernetics, ecosystem analysis, or structural linguistics (K. Deutsch).

Cultures and Customs as Fixations

Next we have to look at *fixation* as the source of insidiously irrational social and cultural forms and values. Fixation is a phenomenon of the relativity of value reactions, second in importance only to the opposite causation. We explained the fixation before and saw that it is strongest in the fields of values created by man himself, of the cultural or social values. Here man drives himself into obsessive value cults through blind turning in circles on his own tracks. As accident or mere coincidence brings an object to one's appreciation, this increases its value, and the object is sought after even more. Thus, due to the relativity of their value reactions, people become unsuspecting victims entrapped in their own backgrounds born in mere accidents.

Furthermore, as the value of the fixational habit increases, it becomes sacrosanct, "rational", "self-evident" or perfectly right in every way. Also the vicious-circle pursuit of fixational values leads to endlessly rich neurotic elaborations around them, as increase in value enjoyments becomes necessary at every step. Thus the most valued, richest, or most evident social and cultural patterns are much like the senseless elaborations, around accidental objects, by the obsessive-compulsive neurotic. Fixations grow from resourceless mentality that offers little of new, different value interests, which require hard previous accumulation of new restrictions, needs or nonsatisfactions.

But since the mechanism of fixation is not understood, social scientists are bound to *accept the most typical, senseless fixations as the expressions of the very soul of the culture.* For exactly the fixations, deepened and expanded in the vicious-circle way, become the most pronounced, vastly elaborate patterns of cultures. Here the real force behind fixations has to be emphasized.

It is the human drive for pleasure, for the easy value enjoyments without the effort of creating new backgrounds. This is the cause of neuroses as well as fixations.

Yet because the fixational values are so deep and elaborate they are seen as the culture itself, extending from rare "treasures" to the typical everyday customs.[15] The real, productive forces of culture, the general conditioning, acceptance of restrictions or the hard ordinary pleasure economy, are so bland, universal and unadorned that they are hardly noticed. The multitude of the fixational cultural elaborations is hailed in theories on culture as the expression of the richness of the cultural spirit,[8,15] while it actually proves a less resourceful mentality, that should be fought against rather than fostered.

Foremost authorities in the study of cultures accept such fixational cultural riches as the sources of social and political potentials.[32] Customs of peoples, particularly their richly elaborate rituals, are viewed as the expressions of the genius of the people, that are to be studied by practical politicians as decisive factors.[32] Even myths or folklore are to be dealt with seriously in understanding important political problems.[8] The determining spirit or mental powers of peoples are supposedly expressed in the typical patterns of their culture.[15]

This is part of the great tradition of cultural philosophy, expounded by Hegel, Spengler, or Toynbee, which sees culture as distinct from, or even opposed to the material civilization or technology. Thus the systems of fixations, that typically constitute the "culture", are to be elevated to a place of control over the concrete, tremendous achievements of human civilization. Culture is generally viewed as the body of ethnically typical customs, patterns of life and legends. Such customs and legends are nonsensically fixational. Yet social scientists may seek from them the ultimate answers about man and society.[15,32] The socio-cultural theories of Levi-Strauss are a good recent example. No social theory is free of attributing decisive role to institutionalized cultural patterns,[1,18] which are mostly fixational.

The *mysterious force of customs* is a problem that well illustrates the confusion in social theory. The force of fixations, similar to that of neuroses, is due to long accumulation of easy value enjoyments. But social scientists have always held to ideationally logical explanations. Since the time of Frazer scientists have tried to explain customs and native magic in rational and intellectual terms.[15] Assumedly, the same principles of rational association that rule all science rule customs, and force of customs derives from past utility.[14] Functionalism, typically represented by Malinowski or Radcliffe-Brown,[3] is viewed as the alternative to the symbolic, mythical and psychoanalytic theories, represented by Boas, Cassirer or Roheim,[15] as well as to Marxism and theories about the superorganic.[8] Functionalists may contend that even the cult of sacredness of cows serves economic function (A. Alland). The self-evident irrationality of customs thus remains a mystery no less in the functional than in the psychoanalytic and mythical theories.

Those scientists who do not espouse the Freudian, or the metaphysical mysteries have only rational or *cognitive explanations* to offer. Perception and "political preception" have been viewed as causes of the strength of even such customs as religious rituals.[5,37] When the Russian Orthodox church introduced a new ritual, of making the sign of the cross by three fingers instead of two, this caused a long political upheaval.[37] Factors of perception or cognitive reasoning may seem here as the cause.[37] Actually, if one has lived his whole life under the security of a cross made by two fingers, he cannot abandon the ritual overnight, whatever the cognitive reasons.

Cognition or knowledge may be viewed as cause in various ways. A person is, supposedly, "intolerant to what shakes his orientation, his sense of knowing where he stands [and] what offers competition to the guideposts of values" (A. H. Leighton).[11] Cognitive association of symbols is an often assumed cause of the "slavery to custom" (H. J. Muller).[7] Also "vested interests" have been blamed for resistance to cultural change,[26] though customs serve no rational interest. Force of ideals or of ideas about the customary values is quite frequently stressed. According to D. Bidney, intolerant ideologies about values may become even a problem of survival: "ideological and survival crises are closely bound together, since man is prepared to sacrifice his life, if need be, for the values and institutions which render his life meaningful".[15]

We hardly need to repeat that perceptions, *cognitive factors*, symbolic meanings, ideals or ideological values *have no motivational weight or are mere rationalizations* about deep feelings that culturally grow through long, senseless fixations. Of course, if customs are assumed to be determined by perceptions and cognition or ideas, their change must seem to be easy. Social scientists are, indeed, suggesting change of "habits" in easy ways, by mere manipulation of associations. Merely finding the right direction may be considered sufficient, since "any belief system is easier to change in some directions".[11] Even the value systems that keep nations united internally and separated externally can, supposedly, be easily changed, by merely finding the right new attachments between the right groups, like the coal and steel interests in the European cooperation.[12] Surely all planning works where interests are rational. Yet practical realization of best ideological plans for political unification has remained as difficult as ever.

In his book *Change and Habit* Toynbee's main argument is that national habits unlike instincts can be as easily changed as they are acquired, and that we readily give up even the strongest habits.[34] Actually value fixations are like behavior disorders: they are not instinctive and are acquired easier than anything else; but no reason or good intentions can change them. The key here is the simple logic of pleasure, the dominant human drive. We abandon habits with dangerous ease where they are unpleasant or restrictive, as are the cultural traditions that modern men gladly reject.

We have to emphasize the *pleasure as the dominant force in the formation of cultural fixations,* through the easy value enjoyments. Its effects are as insidiously powerful and paradoxical here as in all release economy. The great idealistic philosophers, writers and scientists, guided by the humanistic value beliefs, extol the cultural "treasures" and the deepest cultural value enjoyments, which are mostly fixational. This opens way to social stress and strife. Nations or social groups deepen their fixational value obsessions by seemingly reasonable, even noble value enjoyments. But the resulting value fixations are irrational, accidental in their origin and as compelling as neurotic obsessions. Moreover, they are felt as the truths themselves by the people who cultivate them. Evidently, differing values must be *felt* as equally untrue, however tolerant the abstract reasonings. Disruption and stress between cultural groups are inevitable results of fixational value enjoyments, deepened by lofty value beliefs.

The Compulsion of Social Disorders

Finally we have to mention in more detail *the social behavior disorders,* which find expression in wars, political strife, persecusecution of minorities, "witch-hunts" and rebellion. Social disorders are causally or scientifically as little understood as are all behavior disorders, because they grow in the paradoxical ways opposite causation works. To take the most important example, wars originate in hate, fear and emotional stress; but the surest way to war is nationalism which drives the feelings of love, self-assurance and positive enjoyment to their highest limits. Logically it may be argued that people resort to excessive nationalistic policies because they suffer from "starvation" for recognition, from humiliations and frustration.[12] What actually happens is completely different — and as inevitable as are the opposite processes after any excesses in organic functions, values or most detailed mechanisms.

The Nazi Germany is the most typical case, and in it the people enjoyed to ecstasy all the positive feelings of their success of rebirth as well as of love and pride of their country and countrymen. Nationalism always brings the experiences that are considered by social scientists as sources of best adjustment: love, faith, belonging, reassurance, pride, and every enjoyment of the sense of "self" or "identity". But the result is typical social disorder.

Exactly *because of the overenjoyment of the positive experi-*

ences, intense nationalism brings opposite, negative reactions, in the way all disorders grow. The relative causality also determines the forms of expression of nationalism. Since no value has meaning without its opposite, the exalted pride and love for "our" nation can arise only together with despise and hate for the inferior, vicious "others". In all feelings of patriotism "their counterparts are the negative views of enemy countries. . . It is perfectly obvious that patriotic enthusiasm and belief in a political system or cause depend not alone on the attitudes of affection and approach but also on their opposite attitudes of hatred, distrust, and avoidance" (K. Young).[33]

Social psychologists rightly find the "snowballing" reactions of fear, inferiority, or sense of humiliation and contempt by other nations as causes of nationalistic aggressiveness.[2] But such self-increasing excessive reactions cannot arise without eagerly pursued positive overenjoyments. To take the feeling of pride, as one *overenjoys* the sense of his own superiority and strength, the opposite reactions arise and he starts feeling that he is inferior or weak against the others. Then he seeks even higher reassurances, from his crowd or leader, and ends by feeling even more despised or fearful. On a national level the result is an irrational "expectation of violence" or the "myth of encirclement".[12]

But *nationalism is a dire emotional necessity, not a mere ideational conviction or ideology* as social scientists tend to view it. Consequently it cannot be manipulated in the way ideas can. Here as in most motivations men are facing a hard task of gaining potentials, and are increasing release debts they want least. Gunnar Myrdal shows how the new countries have to foment nationalism to gain cooperation by the people, and how "these strivings in the individual countries, in themselves good and rational, result in international disintegration". He logically argues that the highly positive nationalistic emotions are turned into hate by a "masochistic and perverse" tendency of the people to "revolt against their own innermost ideals".[21]

Modern scientists, not suspecting the opposite causation, cannot understand how the negative reactions, which lead to disorder or war, result from the exaggerated positive enjoyments, in forms of the nationalism, that the people desperately need as motivations. The scientists rather blame inept politicians, faulty diplomacy, wrong techniques or misinterpretation of concepts like sovereignty.

Sir Norman Angell, winner of the Nobel Peace Prize, argued that "we do not desire to create social and economic evils, to impose injustice and bring about war, but we apply policies in which those results are inherent because we fail to see the implications of the policies".[2] H. J. Morgenthau blames wrong "identification of national purposes and policies"; "burden of obsolescent tradition" in questions of nationalism or international law; and "not knowing the rules of international diplomacy".[6] He finds that "political imagination is indeed the Key word. If the West cannot think of something better than nationalism it may well lose the opportunity to think at all".[6] Thus everything seems to depend on intended ways of thinking, ideas and skills. Toynbee sees the causes of disruptive nationalism in similarly intended "fashionable Western liking for political disunity and dislike for political unity",[34] that should be corrected by rational, historic understanding. In reality *the disruptive nationalism or disunity is never liked or intended by anybody*. It comes as unwanted as psychotic reactions do.

But scientists adhere to the logic of intended social motivations or ideologies (unless they accept the Freudian lore). What seems to be required is merely a "degree of practical wisdom which is rarely found among political leaders",[15] or a willingness of diplomats "to engage intelligently in organizing the friendship of peoples".[14] If we can get along wonderfully with Russians as individuals why cannot we be plain friendly with Russia?

It is not realized that ideologically nationalism, sovereignty or similar ideas can be beautifully changed, while the realities they stand for remain stubborn, desperate motivational difficulties. We can be motivated to bear sacrifice for "us" as a beloved nation only if there are different, hateful "others", as Russia or other nations. Moreover, we know that all people as nations exist by the same unwanted hostility to others. It is a well known curious fact that nations cannot evolve without enemies. Nationalism emerged in Europe during the Hundred Year War[4] when enemies were plenty and sacrifice was needed for survival. The love of self had to be widened to include "us", who have no meaning without different others.

The greater the national effort, as sacrifice for the beloved "us", the more intense the hate of the "others". It is illogical why a people in difficulty or in need for extra sacrifice should burn the United States embassy. But it is causally inevitable. A feeling of loved or frustrated "us" has to arouse the feeling of hate or revenge against the "others" who may happen to be neighbors or a more widely known nation. People induced to bear sacrifice for their superior nation or for a glorious future have to feel viciously humiliated and wronged when their superiority is not acclaimed or the reality comes out less glorious.

Scientists may, confusedly, claim that there are two kinds of nationalism, peaceful and aggressive;[2] that imaginary dangers and scapegoats are deliberately invented; that people suffer from instinctive drive for domination; or that crises grow through a "vicious circle created by fear and mythological ideology".[15] But the negative reactions of fear, recrimination, aggression or domination are unproductive as well as unpleasant. Everybody knows this, particularly the national leaders; and *men are far too intelligent to follow useless unpleasant reactions, drives, myths or ideologies.* Of course the Freudians claim that people go to wars because of unconscious death wish, displacement of hate of father, sibling hostility, castration complex or real and invented childhood memories.[8,33] The only other explanation is that the negative reactions are due to learned or conditioned intentions.

Naturally, any *intended* learned, conditioned or ideological factors would be easy to change, by adopting new methods, ideas or directions. In a statement by American psychologists, 99 per cent of them agreed that wars are preventable if men "direct their aggression against those natural obstacles that thwart them in the attainment of their goals".[13] Creation of more inclusive symbols and ideas that would not destroy but rather include national loyalties has been advocated, particularly by Allport, who also refers to the studies by Piaget on the way children learn.

The fact however is that *people never intend or want the negative reactions,* which they cannot help feeling. If they were driven by death instinct, unconscious conflicts, learned or conditioned intents or aggressive drives, they would rush eagerly into the fighting of the war, instead of being "forced to fight".[23] Or if positive motivations could be attained by merely changing the direction of our drives, the world would be free of conflicts. Nor can the equally easy process of making symbols, ideas and learning more inclusive have any effect. Piaget's theories are increasingly used for explaining social behavior.[1] But his studies deal with ideational or cognitive ways of learning, which are weightless in creating motivations or potentials.

The very richness of theories on causes of war, which include everything "from trade restrictions to a decline in religion",[10] points to the confusion. The "basic streak of irrationality" and "instinct of aggression" explain little. Man's rationality or intelligence is prodigiously successful in changing instinctive, irrational adjustments, wherever the change brings pleasure or satisfactions. Exactly because such satisfactions are enormously improved, and overenjoyed, politically as well, the irrational, "instinctive" negative reactions break out. Socially as individually, trying to get something for nothing leads to abnormalities.

We may add a word about *creation of larger countries, unions or federations.* It would be politically very beneficial. But as the people have to be induced to bear sacrifice for a wider nation or more remote groups and "strangers", the positive efforts have to be intensified and the negative aftereffects become disruptive. Logically it may seem that the clearly beneficial wider political integration is prevented because of misuse of governmental power or ignorance of the benefits. Scientists show that, by uniting internationally, as in the Common Market, "by mutually giving with those around us, we begin to make a kind of local Utopia" (J. R. Platt).[25] Then it seems that people resist their own good and that even scientists abandon their sound ideas when they get political posts.[11]

The worst practical misunderstanding is the *rejection of nationalism or patriotism*. Nationalism is the first step in conditioning a people to bear sacrifice for a larger community. By extending such conditioning political federations can be created. European countries with long traditions of patriotism are able to cooperate, because they do not need any more to use excessive appeals for every common sacrifice. The paradoxical fact is that, in all emotional management or conditioning, negative feelings are necessary and have to be lived through. Even in a behavior disorder the negative reactions, if suffered through without compensations, bring about the cure. In nationalism as well the disturbances and difficulties lived through as soul-searching hardships finally make the cooperation and sacrifice possible. But internationally minded theorists or lawyers condemn the troublesome nationalism, and aim for logical international laws and constitutions — which are worthless without motivational reality behind them.

What we have said about nationalism applies to all kinds of social motivations, potentials and disorders. While internationally the "others" are the foreign countries, nationally they are the minorities or different political groups. Logically anxieties, insecurity or frustrations may be blamed for group persecutions.[7] But did not Germans under the Nazi movement start by enjoying to extremes the feelings of superiority, self-assurance and success as well as love for their own people? Internal social disorders are perhaps best illustrated by the "witch-hunts", old or new.

The people who burned witches were as intelligent as we are and their irrationality was not more strange than are our neurotic obsessions. Their reactions arose, in the way obsessions do, as inexorable opposites of their excessive, exaggerated feelings. Belief in evil witches, fear of their power, and infliction of cruelty are the opposites of sense of freedom from evil pagan spirits and of neighborly love. These positive emotions were intensively enjoyed by people turning to Christianity. This amounted to strong exaggerations because the pagan beliefs and neighborly hates were still strong in reality. The inevitable results of the exaggeration were the outbreaks of the strange, unrecognizable opposite reactions. Any exaggerated value, organic process or mechanism has to be met by equal opposite value process.

It is important to note that the *witch-hunts came together with the highest fervor for Christian virtues which are essentially opposite to them.* In all movements, whether it is patriotism, puritanism, or Catholicism at the time of the Inquisition, strange reactions opposite to the essential spirit of the movement may emerge. The reason is the *exaggerated* emotionally enjoyed zeal of the spirit of the movement. Evidently, if this paradox is not understood, any social or cultural movement may be condemned as evil while it essentially is the very opposite of the disturbing reactions arising from exaggerated or unreal enjoyment of its virtues.

Before we conclude we may add a word about *social prejudices.* Explanations of the prejudices are sought in directly logical factors such as ideational associations, past experiences, fear, suggestion, unfamiliarity with alternatives, prestige, conformity or recourse to stereotypes (G. W. Allport).[1,23] It is found, though, that prejudices work irrationally, contrary to logical explanations.[23] Still, prejudices are blamed on faulty thinking, "cognitive weakness or limitation in our intellectual processes" (R. C. Snyder).[11] Supposedly mere norms of group identification become social realities.[5] Eager proponents of such cognitive explanations may list scores of ways our cognition is distorted. Walter Lippmann demonstrates how different classes, groups, religions, cliques, national, provincial and urban groupings and parties create different mental images or inner cognitive "pseudoenvironments".[11]

Actually men are far too intelligent to burden themselves with a vast accumulation of misleading ideas, images or cognitive errors, on simplest matters. The cognitive or ideational contents of prejudices are only rationalizations of what people feel, which is the real causal source. Prejudices originate in value fixations and social "disorders" in the various ways we explained, much like neurotic feelings and beliefs do. Social conformity, public opinion and stereotypes are, as we saw, typical forms of fixations. The important fact, explained before, is that the fixations and "disorders", the sources of prejudices, *are governed by the all-powerful and paradoxical pleasure drive.* This is why prejudices are as difficult to change as neurotic convictions, and remain unexplained.

Here as elsewhere social scientists see as decisive the ideational, cognitive world, of rationalizations or reasons, which people adduce as causes. The real causal sources, the pleasure or satisfactions, remain meaningless to the scientist because they are paradoxical, too common to be "scientific" and too universal to be particularly noticed.

All in all, the social sciences are even more alchemistic than psychology and become a vast, obstructive learning without scientific, causal understanding. Mere ideas, reasons, philosophies, ideologies, myths, symbols or other ideational concepts and beliefs are accepted as causal sources. The alchemistic logic of positive potentials growing from positive value experiences is accepted even less critically than in psychology, in dealing with factual conditions or social reactions. This leaves unexplained how people, seeking only positive satisfactions, drive themselves into negative behavior they want least. As a result, the mysteries of the Freudian Unconscious and of man's irrationality are generally accepted, though men are extremely, efficiently rational in everything they plan, do, enjoy — and *overenjoy.* Also explanations are sought in complex concepts of superhuman, *social* macrounits or systems and the Superorganic as the determining agencies. This amounts to metaphysics, since only individuals feel, think and act.

Men do behave in ways they clearly never intend. The reason is their least wanted, "irrational" reactions or feelings, incurred through excessive striving for positive satisfactions, values or pleasure releases. The two main social phenomena, the fixations and disorders, are due to the paradoxical causation by such excessive overenjoyments. But this is not understood. The rich fixations are hailed as expressions of cultural genius, though they are accidental, "neurotic" elaborations. And social disorders are viewed with the alchemistic, reversedly wrong causal logic of expecting positive reactions from positive experiences or enjoyments. In short, social sciences remain a vast, virtually alchemistic system of learning *without causal understanding.* Such learning has always been the worst obstacle to real science.

The Paradoxical Course of History

In all human behavior, as we saw, enrichment of capacities and motivations comes through what is felt as maladjustments, whereas fullest satisfaction, felt as best adjustment, leads to immobility and disorders. But this paradox is contrary to the very logic of thinking of all men, including social scientists. Consequently, the way peoples succeed or fail in the course of history or in their practical, political adjustments is contrary to the usual and "scientific" assumptions and logic.

In history, *fullest satisfactions become the causes of decline,* but are not recognized as such, because satisfactions in their immediate effects show as enrichments of capacities. Rather the metaphysical theories of historical cycles are used to explain why periods of fullest bloom are followed by decay. Conversely, difficulties are deplored, and blamed as obstacles, rather than recognized as the challenges and sources of new motivations, by the contemporaries as well as the modern historians concentrating on the "spirit" or value atmosphere of historical periods. In political movements the paradox of "maladjustments" or restrictions and of satisfactions or freedoms makes the movements reverse their course and nature: the movements rise to fight the restrictions but end by accepting them because of requirements of practical, normal adjustments.

Whatever the controversies and confusion, the gross historical facts show that peoples rise under difficulties and decline under ease or fullest satisfactions. The *concept of challenge* as a difficulty belongs here. Toynbee could write the history of all civilizations in the terms of challenge and response. But without the insight in the relativity of value causation the explanation of progress through response to challenge amounts to description of how people progressed because they had a more progressive attitude. The causes of the response are missed. It is not realized that only previous wants or nonsatisfactions make the difficult benefits from a challenge appear worth while; and only higher capacities evolved under harder conditions can make the response profitable. Any people may be living right now amidst hundreds of challenges, which it does not see as being of value or cannot exploit.

Historians see the progress through challenge as depending on emergence of satisfactory challenges. In truth nonsatisfactions in previous backgrounds are the real sources of such progress. The positive response logically is a satisfaction, comparable to interest or love. It is therefore viewed as coming from similar, positively-felt value sources. Actually it comes from previous non-satisfactions, or dire wants, much like the pleasant interest or love derives from harrowing needs or nonsatisfactions.

Historical facts reveal the rule that hardier, *more capable people evolve under harsher conditions*. The relative causation accounts for this rule as well as for the seeming exceptions to it. If the harsher conditions people live in never change they become the normalcy for the people and are not reacted to or even felt. That is why peoples like Eskimos or isolated mountain and desert tribes do not progress. They have become adjusted so well that the conditions for them are fully satisfactory. To progress people have to be switched from better to worse conditions and then back again, so that they may evolve higher capacities and then use them for exploiting the better conditions.

This explains why people like the Nordic races have been originators of higher cultures, yet why the great civilizations have evolved in the more favorable regions like the river valleys of Mesopotamia, Nile, or Yellow and Ganges rivers. A similar development was, apparently, the evolution of the Mayan, Aztec and Inca civilizations. This seeming paradox is source of continuous controversies. One school of historians, particularly from Scandinavia and Germany, has proven — as has recently Colin Renfrew — that the North-European cultures have predated the Near-East civilizations. The other school insists on the clear proof of the superiority of the Egyptian and Near-East civilizations, claiming, in the words of Lord Raglan, that "savages never invent or discover anything".

We may add that the Northern men are more strongly motivated because they are more "maladjusted". The Nordic man is mentally more tense, worrisome, pensive, depressed or restricted; and physically deficient, like a pale, stretching plant growing in darkness. This maladjustment never becomes the normal adjustment because the climate that we are used to consider as temperate combines the severity of winter with very favorable conditions of summer. Since the winters are so harsh that man could not survive them in his natural state, he has started the industries and accumulation of reserves that have become the bases of higher civilizations.

The paradox of adjustment is more misleading in history than in study of individuals. Individual behavior luxuriously rich in external vigor, enjoyment, beauty and exuberance is easily recognized as overenjoyment or "sin" that brings disorders or degeneration. But in historical study of peoples their luxuriously rich, beautiful, exuberant enjoyments and elaborations are rather seen as proofs of vitality; and none of the historical or social "sins" are really recognized. This is particularly so under the modern view that enjoyments are sources of better adjustment or that artistic pleasures and luxurious cultural elaborations are the highest values. The result is general admitted confusion. Historians admit that we cannot learn from history,[35,36] though the past record of successes and failures of men should, evidently, offer the best insights for progress.

To take the most frequent evaluation of cultures, historians love to show how superior were the ancient Greeks to the "unimaginative" Romans. The Greeks enjoyed what we now view as highest cultural achievements, including art and philosophy as well as democracy. But exactly the highest period in this Greek culture was followed by decadence, cultural disintegration and political chaos. Even the art stagnated and the philosophy sank into skepticism that continued for the next three hundred years. The potentials, knowledge and skills, like crafts and use of writing, that made the "culture" of arts and philosophy possible, were acquired during the period when the Greeks were as "unimaginative" as the Romans.

By using such potentials and skills "unimaginatively", the Romans became the greatest organizers and builders in the world. We as Christians are the continuators of the Roman culture. It is naive to assume that Christianity was accepted because of revealing words in its teaching. It gained converts because it came together with an impressively advanced way of life, the Roman culture. Typically, even the political structure of Rome, in the form of the Holy Roman Empire, continued, though finally only in name, to 1806.

In all history, the periods of luxury and enjoyments are followed by decay and degeneration. The riches and capacities that such periods may display are accumulated during periods of "unimaginative" restrictions. Embellishments or the "rich" expressions of musing spirit come when people feel they have attained what there was to attain. The praised, backward-looking Renaissance is an example. It wasted the previously accumulated wealth and skills, thus delaying the industrial revolution which an uninterrupted accumulation of the resources and skills could have brought. That revolution was achieved by the "practical ascetics" of the bleak Puritan England.[46] Even the stories of historical heroes — Alexander the Great, Attila, Louis XIV, or Frederick the Great — extol their spectacular often reckless use of wealth or armies built by their *unnoticed* fathers.

But the decline of peoples upon their externally most vigorous, lavishly richest periods is so clearly evident that historians cannot miss it. Extinction of motivations upon fullest satisfaction is the cause of such decline. But seeking for *"logical"* *explanations* historians assume that peoples follow a regular pattern of bloom and decay because of *cyclic nature of cultures*. This is the reason why the cyclic theories are so popular, and the only ones used by the historians who want to offer a general, necessarily simple causal law of history. In Spengler's theory, which is still considered the best,[36] cultures follow an inexorable cycle of bloom and decay much as plants follow the seasons. Toynbee's theory is similar in explaining inevitable doom after flourish of civilizations. All expounders of cyclic theories, from Vico to Kroeber,[36] try to explain the decline of cultures upon their richest external flourish by a higher, superorganic, virtually metaphysical law.

Cultures or civilizations become metaphysical units, not unlike organisms, in the cyclic theories. They are to follow definite laws, phases or rhythms, like the three-and-half beat in Toynbee's theory. Such laws or destinies are not simple and not reducible to simple principles. A definite personality, like Napoleon in the Faustian culture or Alexander the Great in the Apollonian, is to appear at a definite point in the cycle. Or a definite movement, like that of the outside proletariat, is to appear in a similarly predestined pattern. Moreover, the civilization has to fulfill a mission, bear a new religion or pass through phases as predetermined as a chrysalis of a butterfly. Also each culture has a peculiar character, embodying ideal or symbolic meanings — like an ornament or a tune of a melody according to Spengler — that are impressed on everything within the culture.

It all *amounts to humanistic metaphysics* of supernatural complex causality. Natural causal laws can be only brutally simple. Nonsupernatural causality does not know complex prescriptions. (When organisms follow complex forms, the causal law is still the brutally simple maintenance of their selectively evolved sameness.) The very fact that the cyclic theories are humanly interesting or meaningful in value terms, purposefully revealing or pathetic, confirms that they are dominated by sense of values. We saw how totally misleading causally is the sense of values, since value appears highest where the needs for it or its objective absence is greatest. It may be justified to say that the "cyclic theory is a myth", with a "style that has become pompously prophetic and melodramatic".[36]

But the philosophy of history is dominated by the protagonists of the cyclic theory as well as of the humanistic value outlook — Dilthey, Croce, Spengler, Toynbee, Sorokin, Niebuhr, Dawson, Jaspers, Teilhard de Chardin, or Tillich.[36] We do not doubt the enormous erudition of such authorities. But vast self-perpetuating learning without causal understanding prevents real science. It is typical of the confusion in social sciences that a vast erudition, however unscientific, makes one an authority. That Toynbee is a metaphysician does not diminish him as historian, according to Dawson.

The real significance of the cyclic theories is the confirmation by the facts they adduce that in history as well fullest satisfactions, appearing as highest flourish, lead to impoverishment of adjustment. *This is the general simple law,* but it applies to individuals, and only through them to all groups, institutions, parties, movements, states or empires. The bigger the unit, the more diffused and slower the effects. Groups composing a state may rise and decline in reciprocally compensating combinations so that the state may remain steady. While the Western part of the Roman Empire succumbed, militarily, the Eastern continued for a thousand more years.

Or the factor that brings the satisfactions may be progressive in itself. The modern world is motivationally decadent because technology has brought unprecedented enjoyment of satisfactions. But technology in itself is the most progressive force. The doomsayers have to invent exceptions to explain why the West is not about to collapse.[36] On the widest level of the civilization, of the whole humanity, the progress is growing continuously, at exponential rate. This contradicts the metaphysical assumptions about predetermined phases or decline, and separateness of civilizations, in the cyclic theories. But the theorists easily disregard the reality. As one critic observes, the last seven hundred years since the fatal emergence of Frederick II are according to Toynbee's theory a mere aberration.

Another major source of confusion in history is the paradox of evaluations, due to their relativity. What is so typical of an era as to be universal is not noticed, whereas the exceptions to it are felt as most remarkable. To the extent that satisfactions increase, more dissatisfactions are recorded. In our era of greatest satisfactions and security, we express in our literature, philosophies or social movements sharpest feelings of dissatifaction and anxiety. The value paradox may subtly affect all historical records.

A people with few riches may talk more than others about its treasures which it is bound to find impressive because they are rare. Historians of small nations, like Jews or Greeks, wrote of enormous battles and great buildings, whereas the Roman historians rather dwelt on exotic refinements, feasts, luxury, effeminacy and Oriental cults. Nobody ever mentioned the everyday Roman life, which we would find remarkable in its primitivism and squalor, particularly in the city tenements without plumbing, heating, chimneys, or windows for light. In the Middle Ages the primitive conditions began to be noticed, but the barbarians concentrating on material improvements left record only of spirituality and chivalry.

The Industrial Revolution is known as the most squalid era, because the squalor was being noticed against the background of rising improvements. As H. J. Muller says, in quoting H. Heaton, "what was revolutionary was not the evils but the discovery that they were evils. It was not the ageless misery but the indignation over this misery".[7] The workers in large factories earned eight times as much as the other workers were used to getting.[7] Public support for large families was introduced for the first time. Prices did rise, due to shortage, though the amount of goods had greatly increased; and typically workers complained about shortage of beer and meat (L. Thorndike). This is similar to the modern inflation, caused by improved, excessive consumption. Of course one trained in the usual history may be indignant, as is Lewis Mumford, about people of that era writing of worse conditions in previous times.

To take a differently typical era, the Victorian age, it represents in fact the sharpest turn toward loosening of morals, at the beginning of the modern trend. That is why all closer studies of morals of that age disclose surprising immorality and hypocrisies. The Victorian age produced the greatest amount of record about puritanism and moralism because these started to be noticed as remarkable, special and discussable customs. The restrictive customs were unnoticed and beyond discussion when they were really universal. It is unrealistic to assume that the modern spirit of moral license emerged suddenly from nowhere. The Victorian age, appearing strongly moralistic, was the period of greatest change toward such license.

The point is that *value reactions, which determine all behavior, show under the nonrelative view as true the exact reverse of what is causally true.* Anxiety suffered by people enjoying unprecedented security is only one example. The same paradox applies to all value reactions recorded for history by everything people say or do in their writings, discussions, philosophies, literature, art, cults, customs or patterns of life. And historians have always looked for value expressions, interpreted with the usual direct value logic, in explaining historical facts and causes.[19,35] Particularly the present emphasis on absorbing the spirit or value ambience of an era, in the study of history, is bound to deepen the fallacies. The same is true of the emphasis on the intuitive, sensory or "direct" knowledge, by the increasingly numerous adherents of the superorganic or cultural explanations of history.[36]

Due to the adjustment paradox, people are reversedly wrong in blaming difficulties as causes of their failures and praising satisfactions as sources of their capacities or successes. Historians accept such interpretations, expressed and recorded by the peoples, with the same direct logic. The causal misunderstanding here is the same that applies to mental disorders and functional diseases originating equally in oversatisfactions. Interpretations by historians would rather support the attitudes by which people pursue the fullest satisfactions and thus rush to their own ruin, much as in the functional disorders.

The Contradictions of Political Movements

Political movements follow a paradoxical course because people try politically as well to gain more freedoms or satisfactions, but end by accepting restrictions in order to sustain the necessary positive motivations of normal social life. Here, as in education or other fields of adjustment, the theorists and leaders urge people to gain more of the logically positive, beneficial and liberating satisfactions or releases. Political movements are started, parties founded and revolutions or rebellions fought to remove the existing, traditional restrictions, which appear as plainly negative repressions under the humanistically logical or rationally liberal view.

But the movements and parties turn restrictive or reactionary as soon as they come to power, have to deal with practical problems responsibly or gain experience. All parties, liberal, socialist or communist have undergone this process. Also forms of government, like democracy, become in practice very different from theory, which stresses the "positive" aims of freedom, equality, true representation or individualism.

Revolutions as the strongest manifestations of political strivings are the most typical examples of the paradox of freedoms and restrictions. Movements of freedom degenerating into their opposites is a process as general as Michels' "iron law of oligarchy" which explains its external effects. Revolutions seem to pass through phases the last of which brings the restoration of the old cultural traits and ways of life.[4] Revolutions aim to destroy the past but in the end reveal a continuity with the past.[12] The great English and French revolutions led to exact political restoration. Revolutions "devour their children", and even the most radical ones finally establish, in a different form, the old system. Stalin became the Tzar, the Communist party the traditional autocratic bureaucracy, and kolkhoz the old village community, the mir. In a revolution "the old society, even the old regime, gradually begins to reassert itself from grave".[37]

The way revolutions originate is equally explained by the paradox of the relativity of value reactions. Clearly a revolution is an uprising against intolerably bad conditions. But improvement in conditions is necessary before a revolution can originate. "Revolutions are not made by downtrodden masses".[33] Conditions, however bad, that have been always there are felt as normal. All major revolutions, in France, America, Russia, Germany or China, started after conditions had improved (K. Young).[33] Revolutions originate mostly in countries where conditions are better than in other countries. Social scientists know that "it is not poverty per se that leads people to revolt" and that "social tensions are expressions of unfulfilled expectations" (D. Bell). Progress or rapid growth is the precondition for a revolution, as "people rise when their expectations have been satisfied for a prolonged period and are frustrated" (J. C. Davies).[37]

Forms of government, *like democracy or communism* are equally fought for because of freedoms and satisfactions expected from them, but in practice have to become systems of subordination and restrictions. Democracies work because people, let free, restrict or "oppress" each other in tense competition for economic improvements, security and superiority. The tensions and competitions are heightened by constant unsatisfaction of men due to the relativity of value feelings. But neither this relativity nor the reciprocally imposed tensions and restrictions are recognized as the sources of the progressive motivations. Rather the competition and tensions are condemned as a "rat race" that brings unhappy, negatively felt experiences, which seem disruptive. Marxism then is seen as a better system, for it promises the material satisfactions without the tensions and restraints.

It has to be emphasized that *Marxism* is a humanistic theory, advocating a *logical, "scientific" humanism.* Theorists of diverse convictions, including such authorities as Russell, Marcuse or Fromm, recognize that real humanism and human liberation are possible only through the Marxist socialism.[38] The main defense of communism, by most varied theorists, from the free world as well as the communist countries, is its promise of true humanism, even of real Christianity.[38] The communism promises, with its automatic equalization of wealth, the only freedom that really matters to most people, the material enjoyment without restraints from others. The drive for such enjoyment or simply for free distribution of wealth motivates the revolutionary masses which are the real force in carrying out communist revolutions.

The fallacy of the humanistic assumptions shows flagrantly in the communism as it becomes in practice the most repressive system. The root of the fallacy here is the humanist belief that the positive human potentials come from the positive satisfactions of "human nature". This is logical if the real, opposite causal sources of the potentials are not suspected. Marx was a humanist thinker, faithful to the deeply ingrown traditional, even bourgeois humanism of his time.[7] Under the belief in the human nature, he expected that once men are made really free, all restraints or government will "wither away" as unnecessary. This is the central promise of Marxism and it is glaringly contradicted by practical life: the compulsion and governmental control had to increase under communism to proportions never seen before.

Naturally, humanists are horrified by the results of Marxism in practice, though they are unable "to present a coherent, sensible and persuasive philosophy of democracy, whereas communism is very 'rational' " (H. M. Jones). Our thinkers are particularly appalled by the communist "brainwashing". Imposition of restrictions through conditioning is the way to create the necessary potentials, and we are far superior to communists in real brain washing. Communists proceed here in the obvious, therefore humanly offensive, direct ways. We attain the restrictive conditioning in the name of moral happiness and rewards, in ways so subtle and universal, endlessly interwoven in a thousand-year tradition, that it is not even noticed. Conditioning works best where it is subtly indirect, ubiquitous and invisible.[9]

Finally we have to look at the *authoritarian forms of government* — and recognize their inherent superiority, even if this may amount to a sacrilege. All countries have resorted to some authoritarian forms of government whenever they have faced very difficult tasks. The less developed countries, even the young democracies in Europe after the World War I, have done so. Such countries have struggled for relatively enormous progess that they have learned to know from other countries. If we had a sharper vision we would realize how enormously great progress is awaiting us and we would equally resort to the more efficient, authoritarian forms of government.

The simple truth is that any complex organization, say, a company requires one person as the head who can make precisely planned, complexly envisioned and consistently thought-through policies and decisions without interference from others with varied, conflicting views or interests. Democracies, trying to represent interests of everybody have to be inefficient. They have been successful only "where extraneous or fortuitous factors have managed to keep a bungling and incompetent system afloat in spite of its defects" (H. B. Mayo).[39] Democracy does not permit scientific planning, is "most unscientific" and "not particularly committed to purposes".[39] It is incompetent, unsuited to the modern complex world and needs enemies or wars to maintain unity.[6,39]

Of course in practice democracies abandon their principles, compromise and resort to makeshifts. The paradoxes of democracy at work have been widely discussed (S. Hook).[16] Typically the executive power in democracies has increased enormously. The representation or government of the people and by the people is a myth: if all interests were to be represented, we all would be talking and fighting endlessly on every issue and nothing would be accomplished. Accurate representation is neither possible nor necessary.[39] The very essence of useful government is to disregard individual interests and to act on behalf of the country as a whole. A democracy requires an economy of plenty, a people of high moral character and a widespread education (R. A. Dahl, H. J. Muller).[9,7] This would make any government work perfectly, and achieve much more with an authoritarian rule.

It has to be noted that presently authoritarian governments are enormously handicapped and cannot even start working properly. For now everybody who has more of the modern, "enlightened" education, therefore everybody of importance, sees fight against authoritarianism as his sacred duty. Evidently, authoritarian rulers now can prevail only by ruthless oppression; and no morally refined or intelligent person wants to be such a ruler or take part in his government. The field is left to reckless adventurers, lacking intelligence. The situation would change totally if the modern liberal trend was reversed. Even the selection of leaders in authoritarian governments could be coped with, by some central body like an independent court or the Party (C. J. Friedrich).[4]

But far more important is the fact that *authoritarian government does not have to be a dictatorship.* All that is needed is change in attitudes. Any government can become a unified, incomparably more efficient authoritarian system if people permit it to do so in its various acts. During the last World War democratic governments could act "dictatorially" and accomplish extraordinary feats. This cannot be done regularly because modern people have lapsed into the easy attitudes growing from the fallacies of the humanistic, logically rational liberalism. People are deprived of the vision of the extraordinary progress awaiting man that deserves an effort as efficient as was that of the War.

Returning to the *reversal of the nature of political or social movements,* we have to note the confusions it creates. A student of a historical movement may accept the ideals and theories under which it arose as its essence, while in practice it has become completely different. Or he may accept the later, restrictive attitude of a movement as the spirit in which it arose. Probably the most prominent example here is the Christianity. As we know it now, it is a restrictive, antilibertarian, conservative, tolerant, nonviolent, refined, nonmaterialistic, almost "ascetic" religion. As such it serves best the practical moral and even economic progress. This spirit of Christianity then is imputed to the early Christians.

Actually the early Christians could have been only crude, intolerant, aggressive, materialistic or unspiritual, though rationalistic revolutionaries, as are all rebels who succeed in their revolutions. The rationalistic and materialistic communist revolutions are probably closest in nature to the early Christian movement. Both have fought against existing restrictions and for material equality. It is naive, indeed, to think that the lowest Roman masses were spiritually minded, materially unconcerned, tolerant, refined people. Understandably the aggressiveness and materialistic bitterness of early Christians had to take the forms of martyrdom and condemnation of worldly riches. For in their era direct aggression against authority or open grab for power and material equality was unthinkable. All revolutionaries love martyrdom almost as much as violence. The martyr feels that the wrong inflicted on him proves how bad his superior adversary is. The bitterness about material inequality was vengefully met by the belief that everybody will be equally rewarded and punished in the other Kingdom.

But this is only one example of how the nature and causal forces of historical movements appear in ways contrary to facts if one does not account for the reversal, in practice, of aspired freedoms or enjoyments. Particularly the modern study of history, concentrating on inherent essences of historical eras and movements, is bound to perpetuate this kind of causal distortion.

In sum, the central fallacy in the study of history and of historical movements is the nonrelative view of the value reactions. It shows as true what is least so for any given period of history. Particularly, it accepts as best adjustment what is in fact the opposite, for any people, including ourselves. People praise and rush to enjoy fullest satisfactions, which actually lead them to ruin, much as in functional diseases. Conversely, they avoid and blame for all their difficulties the "maladjustments", which are sources of increased capacities. And the nonrelative views by historians are bound to show such judgments and value reactions as causally true in the same way the people have expressed them, as the very essence of their period — in the way *exactly contrary to the real causes,* the value opposites of the reactions.

Science of Economic Adjustment

Economics is an "inexact science",[40] because in economy, as in all adjustment, the motivations and progress follow a paradoxical rule contrary to the direct scientific logic. Satisfactions of "normal" economy are its experimentally clear motivational factors, but restriction of satisfactions, and "abnormalcy" are the real causal sources of economic progress. Thus consumption as satisfaction is experimentally the central economic motive, though restriction of consumption as accumulation of capital is the real source of economic expansion. The satisfactions of normal or balanced economy are the motivations that economists deal with; but abnormal, unsatisfactory or disturbing conditions are the ones that determine economic advance. There is no industry or economics in regard to things like air or water where it is plenty; and disturbances like competition, wars, or psychological unsatisfactions create new economic levels.

Here as in all progress, new more resourceful forms are developed after the normal adjustment or satisfactions are obstructed by opposition, restriction or difficulties.

Capital, accumulated by restriction of consumption, is the first requirement of economic development. This is particularly evident from the modern problems of the developing countries. The production factors are labor, capital and management. But labor is available more than needed; unemployment is the big problem. Management is important as the source of inventive, enterprising drive or adventure. But the invention and adventure are possible and fruitful only when capital as surplus means has been accumulated. Particularly in modern economy the research and the exploitation of invention are exclusively dependent on availability of capital. Adventurous entrepreneurship is now a function of the vast industrial resources.[41] All economic skills and learning are made possible and necessary by capital accumulation, whether it is training of labor or building of schools.

Invention or discovery are primary sources of progress but inventions can be exploited only when a certain level of industry, raised by capital investment, is reached. The notorious "Yankee ingenuity" in the car industry consisted of application of foreign inventions,[40] that was possible because of our higher level of capital accumulation. In modern industry invention or discovery comes through enormous investment in research. Even a general higher level of facilities and skills, roads and schools, is necessary before inventions can be exploited. And this requires equally vast capital investment. Human capacities are given, and can be increased only through a system of facilities and of instruction, which is made possible and profitably useful by capital accumulation.

Capital is best thought of as machines and we know that the utopian progress will come when man will have or do anything he wants by push-button operation of machines. That will be attained through investments thousands of times greater than we now have. But such *progress is clearly illogical. It requires production of machines for production of more machines,* in disregard of the logic that only consumption can be the motivation for production. A man from an underdeveloped country would prove that restriction of consumption, for accumulation of capital, would disrupt the existing industry and economy. Our economists know that excess savings are necessary for underdeveloped economy.[40,41] But they do not see how our own economy is equally underdeveloped in view of the progress awaiting us. The economist is scared of "excess" savings, and accepts them as normal only after they have, seemingly absurdly, created new, higher levels of investment — which inevitably brings higher consumption as well.

Thus all economic advance seems illogical or contrary to balanced, normal economy that economists deal with. The progress requires renouncement of immediate exercise of potentials, during capital accumulation and learning, for "temporarily remoter ends", as is excellently explained in Boehm-Bawerk's theory of "roundabout" production.[43] But logical theorists, particularly Marxists, see restriction of consumption for the masses as the doom of all production. For them capital is merely an accidental factor of a mere "scarcity value".[1] Actually no modern economist sees the real, unique yet paradoxical role of capital. Restriction of consumption is the source of capital *but stimulation of consumption is seen as the goal, in modern economics.* The paradox of economic adjustment is the reason why economics is not scientific.

In spite of its enormous effort and highly scientific sophistications, *economics has not become a science.* It does not have generally accepted simple laws. At the same time, economies are fairly uniform in their development, potentials and motivations, particularly the effects of capital investments and expansion. Apparently they follow some general law of adjustment, which as a natural law can be only simple. Yet the economic theories are endlessly varied and controversial.

Most of the great predictions and explanations by economists have been shown to be wrong (S. Chase).[44] Economists themselves recognize that they may give several answers to a question and various quite different recommendations to a problem or that they are not accurate in their forecasts (P. A. Samuelson).[44] On the most important problem, on the prediction of recessions and expansions, the forecasting had become "a modest profession in which reason, divination, incantation and elements of witchcraft had been combined in a manner not elsewhere seen, save in the primitive religion" (J. K. Galbraith).[41]

The more critical economists therefore have abandoned theorization and turned to statistical indicators.[40] But such indicators, in their direct logic, are the worst means for predicting the decisive economic changes. A recession comes when least indicated, when the boom economy is at its highest most characteristic levels. Unindicated reversal of trends is the very essence of recessions and expansions. If a recession is anticipated, it does not develop. This supposedly happened with the incipient recessions of 1947 and 1952.[44]

Economists know that they must have a theory, and that economy does follow general laws — which have to be simple. But the enormous effort of economists to establish such laws has led to almost as many theories as there are leading economists. Ninety-five percent of economic theories of the past have been discarded as wrong, but they continued in their time to guide economists.[8] The same can be said of the present theories, since modern economics has not attained any breakthrough in establishing generally acceptable theory or principles. The only principles that economists agree upon are the psychologic "axioms" like the human rationality and self-interest, which are used as the bases in establishing economic laws. But all psychologic behavior is illogically relative or paradoxical.

The Role of Capital, Consumption and Savings

The central cause of fallacies in economics is however *the paradox of enrichment of adjustment,* through opposition or restriction. It is best illustrated by the main economic factors, consumption and capital formation. Consumption is the only, logical and direct economic motivation in its various forms and phases. But economy guided by a strongest consumption drive would end as a hand-to-mouth economy. Man has to restrict the direct economic drive if he is to attain higher economy. Savings as economic "abstinence" has been the source of economic progress in all industrial countries, England, United States, Germany, Japan, and particularly the Soviet Union, which has "compressed a century or two of abstinence" into a few decades (G. Piel).[42]

As M. Harrington points out, "the capitalist West was built in R. H. Tawney's phrase, by 'practical ascetics' . . . indeed, in the past five centuries, it was precisely this practical ascetism that drove the West to the most extraordinary material achievement".[45] Calvinism and Puritanism, the most restrictive, even other-worldly ways of life, have been found, since Max Weber, to be the sources of the capitalist and industrial revolutions.[45] Of course the explanations of this paradox have been confusing. Historians of economics have often discussed, yet not causally explained the curious fact that the industrial revolution grew in the restrictive, puritanic England and not in Venice or Florence.[46]

Europeans started on their higher economic and industrial development about 500 years ago,[45] at the time of the highest Medieval spirituality and other-worldliness. Spirituality is the restrictive way of life, therefore best for all progress. But the *paradox* of economic progress through restriction is not understood and everybody attributes material progress to direct materialistic drives. Consequently spirituality and material progress are seen as opposed worlds, while they are causally of the same nature and purpose. This misunderstanding is so wide that all progress, which ultimately has to be material, is theoretically stymied by it.

Even the everyday simplest facts show that economic progress follows from restriction of immediate economic enjoyments. To the extent that you save enough to invest you can live without hardships or toil. This is not exploitation of others, though Marxists may cry that it is. All people can live in ease, leaving the work to "machines" — which embody capital — to the extent there are the savings. Each bit of saved capital is a step toward the utopian future progress when men will live by merely commanding the machines. Probably the most convincing proof of this role of capital is the interest paid on it. You can be sure that the producer paying the interest knows with exact, practically tested precision the production gain he is getting from the capital.

We all know that the future progress will be attained with such additions to the capital until it reaches gigantic proportions, and that all "machines" or capital goods are created only by savings.[41] It is clear that "savings is the first step on the way toward improvement of material well-being and toward every progress on this way" (L. von Mises).[43] Moreover, no socialized governmental intervention is necessary to promote such progress. All that is needed is that everybody save more, just as the Puritans did in creating the new industrial era. But the modern, "scientific" economists are scaring us with the dangers of saving.

The only problems could arise if savings exceeded possibilities of investment. This is the last thing to worry about, since lack of capital is the greatest perennial problem. Above all, the slumps, which temporarily disrupt investments as everything else, are caused by insufficiency of capital accumulation, as we shall see in a moment. Demand for capital increases together with economic progress. Lack of capital is the number one difficulty for the "less developed" countries, which actually include every country, in view of the future progress. Even the everyday simple facts show how much we lose because of lack of capital. We hear everywhere justified complaints how people suffer great losses because necessary improvements or projects that would bring great gains cannot be carried out due to "lack of money".

The argument that special knowledge or skills are necessary

before capital can be invested does not hold. Simplest things, like building of dams, roads and schools or opening and improving of land or natural resources, require much capital that can bring great profits to all. The more sophisticated investments require and follow inevitably such basic improvements. The real difficulty in the backward countries is that people spend their incomes immediately or on items of prestige, luxury and unproductive fixational customs instead of investing for later, "capitalist" profits. The savings and investments for profit perform their role whether the profits or interest is received from government realizing advantageous, badly needed projects, or from a capitalist enterprise.

Economic *recessions and inflation* are the foremost, continuous problems of modern economy. Inflation clearly grows from lack of savings or from excess consumption and is devastating in its effects on economic motivation and planning.[40] Even more importantly, recessions are equally caused by lack of savings or excess consumption. Without recessions economies would expand progressively and provide unlimited employment, profits and progress. Logically such expansion would be automatic, since everybody wants to produce more and work more. The *economic reason why the expansion stops is the shortages of capital or of savings.*

Whatever the theory, it is clear that economic expansion stops because of increasing difficulties, which economically are always the increasing costs, since in economy money buys everything. Such increasing costs are those of credit, equipment, capital goods, expenses, and particularly of wages of labor suffering under inflation.[1] Evidently, *every one of these increased costs is due to excess of demand over supply,* in capital and goods, or simply to excessive consumption and lack of capital accumulation, in their various forms. The human factors, of discovery or skills, are all there, but the material means have become exhausted. The seeming vigor generated by increased consumption of the expansion has led to opposite effects.

Of course after the recession has started, causing the interdependent panic or a paralyzing slump, investment possibilities collapse, as everything else does. Then savings can be blamed for making the situation worse, just as everything else can be and has been blamed, in the dozens of theories on recession. It is generally recognized that over-savings have their seemingly logical adverse effect only when the "national income is at a depressed level", after the depression has already brought unemployment and "insufficiency of demand", which makes everything "go into reverse" (P. A. Samuelson).[40] Savings have their normal multiplier effect when employment remains unchanged.[40] Even Keynes recognized, particularly under his "multiplier" theory, that more investment, through more savings, multiplies the possibilities of employment and incomes. His logical solution for recessions amounted to the failproof remedy of more consumption and more savings.

Economists derive their theories about savings as cause of depression from observations during depression, which is what "scientific" observers should do, as did Keynes. But since depression is governed by negative reactions contrary to what men really want or normally feel, the theories are contrary to reality. Attitudes exactly opposite to such reactions of doom govern economy, which always tends to grow and expand, therefore suffers reverses only when means for expansion, to be accumulated by savings, are lacking.

But the most influential modern economists, particularly the Keynesians, see savings as danger and increased consumption as the goal. "Not the shortage of savings but a recession resulting from the failure to use all available savings is the specter that haunts all policy makers" (J. K. Galbraith).[41] The wisdom of less consumption or of being economical has been reversed; all Presidential advisers have urged people that their duty is to consume (M. Harrington). Thus the economic expansion that has been attained has "happened accidentally".[45] Training people for consumption is viewed as a primary task.[42] Nonproductive spending is promoted, in the belief that savings will cause unemployment, and now constitutes sixty percent of all spending (G. Piel).[42] The fear of savings has the effect of "terror" for modern economists.[40]

The leading economists do not dare to suggest support for savings. On the contrary, they rather want to stimulate consumption. During the recent, 1969 recession, instead of urging increase of interest on the main savings, in the savings banks, they worried about "consumer confidence". The natural forces of economy had to pull it out of recession, against the plans of economists. Interest rates rose, in various indirect ways, people underconsumed and oversaved under the sobering mood of recession, and this brought about the renewed, though hampered expansion. In all recessions the direct, planned measures of stimulation rather interfere with the necessary hard readjustments. That is why recoveries come with long delays, after the difficulties have imposed tightening of expenses, greater economizing or savings everywhere.

The increase in consumption or the "consumer confidence", about which the economists are always so concerned, never needs any help or stimulation. The consuming masses are always ready to start spending at crazy speed, using every possible form of credit, as soon as they are sure of employment. But possibilities of employment are directly proportional to the amount of capital invested, as even the Keynesian theory recognizes; and consumption is what decreases capital. Fortunately there always are savings, by the industrialist producers, as they "exploit" the consumers, and labor. The industrialists already supply three fourths of the capital needed.[41] Thus economy grows in spite of the concerns of economists and through the strongly combatted exploitation of people instead of their active participation. Econmy goes through convulsions because the inherently self-exhausting consumption economy is, in addition, dependent on the emotional, necessarily reverting, enthusiasm of the masses.

Advertising becomes an important factor, recognized as necessary by economists.[41] It costs now some 20 billion dollars yearly, an amount sufficient to support a program of renewal of inner cities. It becomes a reciprocally self-defeating effort by the competitors to outshout each other. Where it succeeds it creates, by deceit, wasteful fixational distortions in consumption.

Stimulation of economy, through heightened consumption and consumer confidence, is part of the general modern use of stimulation in all fields as the great remedy. It has been made professional in economics by Keynes and his followers. We saw how in all fields of adjustment the stimulation leads to malignant, vicious-circle exhaustion and mystifying disorders. In economic adjustment the seemingly invigorating increase in consumption decreases the capital accumulation which is the real source of economic vigor. If economic expansion derived from the "scientifically" clearly invigorating effects of increased consumption, we would instantly have a utopian continuous economic expansion. For *there is nothing easier and more self-enforcing than consumption.* People with good common sense know this, but the economists can always prove that increase in consumption is the way to stimulate economy. Hence the perennial controversies, on the highest levels of our economic policy making.

One of the most used logical arguments in economics has been that underconsumption destroys production. Marx argued that if workers are not permitted to consume what they produce, production will come to a standstill, capital will become unusable, and mass unemployment will follow.[1] This argument is still strong, in various forms, among the vast socialist following of Marx and among the "progressive" theorists.[1] But life has proven that just the reverse is true. Capitalists have attained hundredfold increase in capital, which is possible only by not permitting the masses to consume what they produce, and the result has been an equally vast expansion of employment, consumption, production and demand for more capital. *Consumption cannot help rising with economic progress. But the source of the progress is the opposite of consumption. It is capital accumulation,* possible only through underconsumption.

The stingy capitalist whom we detest increases improved means of production in the most productive way, planned with ingenious care, and leaves them to others to continue producing. The benefit goes to the general public, for whom the stingy capitalists ultimately produce, since they themselves spend little. Revolutionaries fighting to redistribute the wealth of the capitalists would destroy the perfect source of their own employment and consumption. They are fighting for scraps while not visualizing an incomparably richer future. Certainly capitalists and particularly their jet-setting descendents, whom we admire, can also be as unimaginative and unproductive, in their waste of wealth. For that they would deserve to be treated as unimaginative morons and dregs of society.

Post-mortem Economics of "Normal" Economy

Abnormality of conditions, actual or psychologically felt, is the source of progress. Under threats of war people can produce at levels they never thought possible. The two World Wars brought more inventions and their applications than any period in history. One may think here of atomic energy, aviation, telecommunications, radar, computers, automation, and finally space missiles, invented during the War and perfected under the pressures of the cold war. The countries that suffer most from a war, as did Germany and Japan, progress most. Fortunately people constantly live under some feelings of abnormalcy, because they become dissatisfied with what they have, due to the relativity of sense of values. Progress by virtue of abnormality reveals the paradox inherent in all economic adjustment. Opposition or restriction of potentials and means, for their vaster accumulation and refinement, is the way economic adjustment is enriched. This paradox is contrary to the very logic of the modern, experimentally scientific economics.

The logical view is true for a "normal", balanced economy in which production equals consumption and the laws are derived from past observation. Such logical economy constitutes the subject of scientific economics. But all economy is abnormal, unbalanced and future-oriented. People always strive to produce more for the future than they have now, therefore have to accumulate capital, produce machines for more machines, diregard the consumption balance and proceed as if under abnormal conditions. Even with all this, little progress results, because the natural adversities, the hostile world of deterioration and accidents, sets us constantly back. The *abnormal* saving is required whether you have education, build a business or buy insurance.

The *logically normal or balanced economy would turn into a more and more primitive hand-to-mouth economy* — suffering under the "gravitational pull of stagnation" that acts like a trap.[1] The "scientific" observations from the past are post-mortems, untrue for the living, future-directed economic adjustment which is abnormal or higher-aimed even where it seems to stay on the same level.

Thus *the scientific economics has nothing to offer for the only economic adjustment that matters or is real* — the abnormal, unbalanced economic future of what ought to be, that everyone lives for. Economists themselves recognize that economics is a science only of what is, not of what ought to be, and that it has little to say on economic change.[40,43] Economics provides no guidance for what should be done beyond the mere static equilibrium (J. G. Kemeny). It is argued that economics avoids principles of change because it needs the stable platform that every science requires.[41] We can only agree that the present, static, logical economics would be unfeasible if the dimension of the constant unbalanced change was added. Predictions by laws of the present economics, even those of marginal productivity, value, utility or demand, become untrue as the level of economy changes or exceeds itself, which is the very essence of living economic development.

Now we may look at the *psychological "axioms" which become the bases for economic laws,* and which seem to be the only truths economists agree upon. All economic theories, laws, formulas or calculations are based on logical psychologic assumptions about what people do under certain economic circumstances. Such assumptions are used even while economists recognize that the classic psychological axioms are not true.[43] Actually the logical assumptions here are totally misleading, because of the relative or opposite causation of value reactions. The rationality of man determines as little here as in all human behavior.

The logical assumptions may be true for some of the static, "normal" aspects of economy but not for the economic behavior, like recessions or expansions, that is relevant in economics as a science of policies. Such behavior is determined by value reactions, and it is illogical or paradoxical exactly to the extent it is causally important. For values have the decisive *opposite* effect where they are strongest; reverse where they have been excessive; decrease relatively upon increase in factual values; become irrationally fixational when continuously enjoyed; and are noticed least where they are omnipresent.

For instance, the excessive loss of confidence of the slump results from excessive optimism of the boom. Or, the propensity to save does not increase logically with increase in income, as Keynes assumed in establishing one of the main assumptions of his theory. Statistics show that people with rising incomes borrowed most (G. Katona).[44] Similarly demand, as needs, does not decrease logically with supply, as satisfactions. The more people have the more they want, in various ways of economic adjustment. It is not that people want to stir the devil or run the treadmill, as Galbraith observes in discussing the problem for our affluent society. The logical theory assuming a saturation point in demand or buying is not true of what actually happens. The value relativity is indirectly admitted by the more advanced theories on the subtleties of the "marginal", actually relative factors, of the marginal value, demand, utility, or even marginal productivity. These theories are becoming of dominant central importance in economic thinking;[1] but the paradoxical causal logic, of the values and value reactions that such theories deal with, is never suspected.

In one way or another *value reactions determine economic behavior. But value causation is totally misleading* if its relative or opposite logic is not understood. Whether it is economic value, expectations, competition or "reasoning", people behave illogically. They become unsatisfied upon fullest satisfaction, lose faith because of excessive optimism, continue competing when they logically would not have to, and "reason" in ways contrary to facts because of opposite value reactions. The confusion is reflected in the endless variety and controversy of theories on the practically decisive economic problems. We may look at the most important problem, of the economic recessions and expansions. Here both the economic and psychological factors reveal themselves in full.

Business cycles

Business cycles are a general phenomenon of economic life.[40] Economy apparently has to go through periods of opposite reactions. Moreover, such opposite reactions are inherently dependent on each other. This clearly reveals their paradoxical causal logic. Vigorous expansion and intense optimism produce sudden depression and excessive pessimism. Conversely, the restrictions and gloom of depression become the sources of renewed strength and optimism. That is why depression has to be permitted to run its full course, so that it can "digest the maladjustment", according to the foremost authorities on business cycles, W. C. Mitchell and J. A. Schumpeter.[41] The paradoxical logic of economic adjustment makes the business cycles causally confusing, though as general, uniform and nonsupranatural phenomena they can be only simple. The multiplicity and variety of theories here reflect the causal confusion. Dozens of theories on a single factor, like the income schedule shifts, may be advanced;[40] and no practical predictions are attained.

The paradoxical *causal logic of opposites* is inherent in both the causes of slumps and booms: in the economic, and the psychological cause. The economic cause, as we saw, is the exhaustion of economic means, through increased consumption or spending which has the immediate effect of seeming invigoration of economy. As the boom and increased consumption advance, everything becomes more inflationary, costly or difficult. This in itself would not, however, create the precipitous collapse or irrational, paralyzing pessimism and panic that cause the slump. Economy could gradually adjust itself to its decreased means of production. Evidently, the final cause is psychologic.

Such cause is the paradoxical reversal of excessive optimism or confidence into its equally excessive opposite, gloom or apprehension, which results in a general panic and stampede because of the economic interdependence of business enterprises. The negative reactions here are as unwanted and irrational as in all disorders. Actually people want and exaggerate to excess the optimism, which is so beneficial, in bringing the boom, as well as pleasant. The negative reactions may come with cataclysmic suddenness exactly because the optimism is accumulated to the last possible, precipitous limit. For converse reasons the recovery from slump is slow, as the necessary, negatively felt background is accumulated only reluctantly.

The *oscillation or ambivalence in confidence* and in related reactions, that comes together with booms and slumps, has often been considered as their cause (A. Lauterbach).[46] But it is admitted that there is little understanding of this variable and no "specific explanation either of the reasons for its oscillation or of its exact frame of reference".[46] According to Samuelson, one explanation of business cycles would be people becoming "alternately optimistic and pessimistic, each stage leading as inevitably to the next as the manic stage of disturbed people leads to the depressive stage".[40] As we know this is exactly what happens in all forms of behavior overadjustments. We have to agree with Samuelson that one cannot, however, be presently satisfied with the above explanation "as it stands, for it says and explains little".

Psychology has indeed little to say or to explain about opposite value reactions leading to each other. Psychologists would not even start thinking about such phenomena as the business cycles, governed by the logic of opposite causation which makes no rhyme or reason for them. Thus psychologists are missing the unique opportunity to explain or help control this practically most important modern problem.

Occasional conjectures by psychologists about business cycles remain unnoticed, for good reason. The "symbolic meaning of specific commodities to individuals, groups or entire populations" is thought important, and explanations are sought in distortion of "perception"[46] — which could be easily straightened out by mere information. Expectedly the irrationality and excess of the fears or pessimism of recessions are attributed to unconscious conflicts, even to castration complex or to unconscious association of the success during the boom with guilt.[8] Thus it is explained that making a "killing" on the stock market may be identified with an unconscious wish to kill (H. Krystal). In truth, negative feelings, of conflict, guilt or anxiety never come directly, with the success. They come through the opposite causation, as unwanted, weird aftereffects, of the success. Scientists have occasionally recognized the "feedback" process in the causation of business cycles;[44] but it can hardly explain them if the opposite causality is missed.

The *economic interdependence of enterprises* is what turns the reversal of emotions into a general panic and stampede. It is clear that you can prosper if you expand your business when the boom is on; if you buy stock when its prices are climbing; invest when companies are expanding; or share otherwise in the expanding economy. Also when production increases, employment and consumption increase, creating demand for even more production. The whole expansion becomes interdependent. Boom creates more boom. Even if one realizes that rationally he should stop expanding his business, he may still expand it in reliance that others will continue with the boom.

Because such interdependence is nation-wide the movement is slow and acquires enormous inertial weight. Logically it should never stop; but increases in human emotions have the most illogical, reversal effect. When the continued enjoyment of the optimism becomes excessive, even normal conditions must start appearing, in contrast, as intolerably depressing. The economic interpendence then creates the stampede. Everybody knows that his overexpanded enterprise will collapse if others start receding. Moreover he feels that, after the continuously exaggerated conditions, this will happen and that others will think and feel in the same way. Evidently, everybody then starts limiting his business to avoid ruin before it is too late, and the recession degenerates precipitously into a self-increasing stampede.

The business interactions are myriad, but they are governed by one simple consideration, of gains or losses; by the positive or negative expectation. And since the whole economic community is interdependent in such evaluations, the booms and slumps follow the single law of value reactions, the law of opposite causation. In words of Keynes, "the opposite error of optimism", particularly by the speculating public, causes the slump. Such dependence on the mood of the public is strongest where economy concentrates on the consumption or the consumer confidence of the masses as the source of economic growth.

The pessimism during the slump is as excessive as was the optimism during the boom. It is unwanted and obsessive, like a psychotic compulsion. The economic community is paralyzed by it and resists the rational remedy of fearing "nothing but fear itself", that would make everything work perfectly. Stimulation does not help because the very cause of the slump is excess of optimistic stimulation. The great recession of the 1930s, as any other, had to run its full course and was not stopped by all the stimulation measures tried. Recessions can be made milder by governmental infusion of funds. But such funds have to be accumulated, through a central reserve system, during the expansions, thus lessening them to the same extent. Of course one frightening crash like that of 1929 may be sufficient to hold down reckless optimism for decades. Then neither the booms nor slumps become excessive. Economists then may argue that the controls work and that great depressions will not occur any more, "although nothing is impossible in an inexact science like economics".[40]

Recessions can be prevented only by preventing the booms, in an economy relying on consumption or the consumer confidence for its growth. During the boom the consuming masses exhaust the economic means, as well as overenjoy the confidence. Particularly the action by the masses of unionized labor can be disruptive, because it is not controlled by the natural, competitive, free forces of economy. But other tendencies, like the domination of politics by masses, or the hedonism of rich and poor, have the same effect. Evidently, if economic expansion could continue without recessions, we could reach incomparably higher economic levels, in few decades, with unprecedented overemployment and prosperity for everybody. Booms bring extraordinary progress because new, daring projects become realities. Even after the slump later takes its terrible toll the gain from a boom is still considerable.[1]

A continuous economic boom could make every dream true. Just before the big crash of 1929 the economic progress was seen as bringing a visionary "new era".[40] *Continuous boom is possible.* There is no reason why people wanting and capable to produce more should be hit by the paralyzing inability to do so. The only condition is that the boom be fed by real expansion in means of production instead of enthusiasm and consumption stimulation that reverse, and exhaust such means. The key is savings. They provide the capital, and prevent inflation which makes everything more expensive or difficult.

Savings vs. Consumption

In the end, savings are the source of all economic progress. If this sounds too simple the reason is that enrichment of economic, as of any other adjustment is simple, yet extremely hard. The past progress has not required, or been helped by, much inventiveness in the theory of economic policy, but has been slow in coming because it is very hard to save or restrict consumption and very easy to consume. It is the ease of consumption that makes it spectacularly effective in seemingly invigorating the economy. This has misled the experimental scientists into *the alchemy of expecting riches from skillful increase in consumption, which is most pleasant for men,* and would have rushed them into the highest economic progress at once. Saving is as hard as has been the progress, attained in spite of economic theory. It is almost self-evident that *economic progress has come and will come with enormous increase in capital,* in the "machines" that work for man. Such capital can be created only by savings or *restriction in consumption.*

Normally even hoarding can help expansion, though the modern economists have blamed hoarding as the worst of evils of saving. Hoarding merely increases the value of money held by others. This has the effect of an interest-free loan to the others and lower prices for everybody. Evidently, this makes invest-ment more profitable and production easier because of lower costs and wages. Any oversaving, with its lower interest rates and prices, has the same effect. The worst that oversavings could do would be creating conditions requiring more consumption which comes automatically at the slightest intention.

But *savings has remained the "specter" and "terror" for mod-ern economists.*[40,41] Stimulation of consumption and consumer confidence are seen as the primary goals. The paradox of self-exhaustion of economy through its directly apparent invigoration by increased consumption is not understood in the experimentally scientific economics. The fallacy has led to the confusion of endless, controversial theories, that cannot predict or help any-thing in practice.

We admit that practical life may require compromises, and consumption may be the best lure, in our hedonistic age, to get people "exploited" so that industry can sell more and thus provide the necessary savings for investment. The consuming masses may not be able to save, themselves, though standards of consumption are completely relative and savings could al-ways be made. Motivations of consumption, satisfaction and "normalcy" may have to be used to attain the real, opposite goals of economic progress. But economists should at least be aware of the real factors of expansion and should try to promote rather than prevent them.

Conclusion

Social sciences are even more misleading than the other sciences of man. The alchemy of accepting ideas as causal factors or positive experiences as sources of positive behavior is here more complete than in psychology, which at least is not so sure any more of the direct, rational logic. Social sciences have produced, with this alchemy, more confusing complexity than any other field — particularly because there are as many social ideas and philosophies as there are thinkers, philosophers and people having social solutions, which includes everybody.

Social scientists deal not with the simple pleasure, release factors or what men feel and live by, but with ideologies, ideas, doctrines, philosophies, beliefs, symbols, myths, perceptions, cognitive concepts, like the Self and Identity, logical truths and other forms of ideational or cognitive experience. All this certainly constitutes what people think and accept as their motives and reasons. But it is causally as meaningless as all "reasons" or rationalizations. Then, as social sciences encounter contradictions, they blame the irrationality of man and accept the mystifications about the Unconscious. In truth the rationality of man is supreme, and exactly because he is so successful in enjoying his perfectly improved social emotions, he incurs the "irrational", weird, negative reactions he wants least. Any excessive value reaction, social or physiologic, has to reverse, because of the limitedness of organism.

The real causal sources of social life are simple strivings for satisfactions, value enjoyments or positive motivations. Fixation is the easiest way to value enjoyments, and fixations constitute almost everything that appears as the external culture or the most cherished, elaborate, richest and "truest" values of a people. This spectacular external culture is the one scientists accept as expressing the soul and genius of the people. Actually these fixations are causally as meaningless as neurotic elaborations. They originate from accidental, low-mentality satisfaction factors, much like neuroses.

Social disorders, wars, witch-hunts and social strife grow from excessive enjoyment of social positive emotions, often required for national motivations. Nationalism offers the highest satisfactions of love, identity, belonging, self-assurance, security and deepest positive feelings. The result is as excessive opposite emotions of hate, insecurity, humiliation, fear and suspicion, that are turned against the "others", without which there can be no sense of "we". But this opposite causation is never suspected.

History and political movements follow a paradoxical course, because men avoid difficulties or restrictions, which are the sources of capacities; and pursue fullest satisfactions or freedoms which lead to impoverishment of motivations and of potentials. People decline upon attaining their highest satisfactions. The cyclic theories of history, the only ones that offer generally accepted causal laws, confirm the decline of civilizations upon highest bloom. But the involved. humanly meaningful laws in such theories can be only metaphysical, not scientific. Political movements always start with strivings for more freedoms or satisfactions, but end by turning restrictive and "reactionary", as the need to sustain motivations and capacities becomes imperative in practice. Yet the paradox is not understood, and a wisdom, for our modern era of liberalism and of free satisfactions, is lost.

Economic adjustment as well is enriched because of nonsatisfactions, opposition or abnormal conditions; industry is largest for the things we lack most. Such enrichment by virtue of opposition is embodied in capital, accumulated by restriction of consumption. The logical economics dealing with normal, balanced economy is a post-mortem science offering nothing for the living economy that aims at what ought to be, at the enormous unbalanced increase in capital.

Consumption, as all release or the pleasant part in adjustment, has the immediate effect of invigorating the economy; and economists see its increase as the primary goal. Actually, increased consumption exhausts the means of expansion, creates inflation and increases wages, thus makes everything more costly or difficult and brings recession. Evidently savings do the reverse. They can provide capital for continuous expansion, and will bring the future of giant capital as "machines" doing everything for man. But economists see savings as the greatest danger. Of course if consumption was the source of progress, men would gravitate into the highest progress instantly, by just enjoying themselves.

VIII

THE UNSEEN CAUSES IN PHYSICS, THEORY OF LIFE AND GENETICS

Because of the nonrelative human view of the world, man tends to see only the positive value, never its negative, opposite causal sources, particularly where these are universal or the value is really essential. No value is more essential or universal for man than the Reality, the sense of our physical world. Consequently the nothingness, the opposite of matter is never a reality for man, though anything is knowable or exists for us only in its differentiation from nothingness.

Physicists have always been compelled to recognize that the "nothingness", as Ether, fields, space, "structural" space or curvature of space, is as real as matter. What has not been realized is that the "nothingness" as the causal opposite of matter can be millions of times denser or stronger than any substance and still not be felt, known or registrable in any way, because of its absolute universality. The atmospheric pressure remained unknown and unregistrable to scientists for a long time, and is still nonexistent for man. Such "nonexistence" is total in regard to the absolute medium or causal source of absolutely all effects of matter.

The relative view reveals the "nothingness" as the universal causal source as surely and simply as the usual view reveals a blackboard when we see white signs on it, or a field of sand when we see imprints in it. We can establish the causal source of matter, its opposite, from nothing more mysterious than the effects of matter. But once such causal source is established, this makes possible a causal understanding and prediction of all physical phenomena. Even the process of life, or principles of biology and genetics then can be causally understood. For it is the interaction of matter with its causal opposite that creates life and living forms, much as it makes atoms "alive" with activity.

Matter and Field as Causal Opposites

We shall use the term Field for designating the "nothingness" as the causal opposite of matter. The two opposites are causally equal. Whatever effects matter or the Field has, each derives them from the other. We know matter only as a differentiation against the Field or "nothingness". If everything was matter, we could not know what matter is: it would not exist for us. In common-sense terms the Field is, certainly, nonmaterial or non-existent — because it is the opposite of matter.

Of course it may seem in the common-sense view that we could not move freely or see through empty space if there was a dense medium, like the Field, everywhere around us. Such objections should not bother scientists. Not a molecule can move or act, in or around us, even to the tiniest extent, unless compelled by equal force — the unseen and unregistrable source, characterized by requirement of opposition. Nor do we see through empty space. Precisely the seeing requires the Field as the medium that carries the light waves.

All physical effects, from light and electricity to movement and gravitation, are brought about by a medium, mostly in the form of waves. *Every great physicist who has made discoveries or offered causal explanations has done so by recognizing a medium,* an Ether, or "fields" and "space" which are only different names for the same medium[3] performing the same functions.[2] This is true of the work and theories of Boyle, Huygens, Newton, Faraday, Maxwell, Fresnel, Kelvin, Lorentz, Hertz, Lodge, Einstein and other, more modern physicists, as we shall see later. Particularly in the relativity theory of Einstein the concrete reality of the "field" is stressed. Einstein recognized that "we have two realities: matter and field"; that the "field became more and more real", though "we have not yet succeeded in formulating a pure field physics"; or that the "field is, for the modern physicist, as real as the chair on which he sits."[1] Einstein continued working on the Unified Field theory as the final solution.

But the way physicists have thought about such medium or Ether makes it clearly incongruous. Physicists, from Newton to Einstein, have argued that such medium would "resist the motion of material bodies" and create friction, drag or similar effects.[1] Experiments on Ether drag or "wind" were performed by authoritative physicists — Fizeau, Fresnel, Hertz, Stokes, Lodge, Miller, Kennedy, and Michelson and Morley. Their negative results were finally accepted as definite proof that the Ether does not exist.[4]

This shows *how even the best physicists are bound by the usual thinking.* They were ready to accept the Ether as the universal causal source that carries light and produces other effects. But they did not realize that a universal causal source would not be experimentally registrable exactly because of its universality. A piece of wood carried by a stream would not experience any drag or friction with the stream. Since it is the Field itself that moves or causes everything, including the performance by instruments and conditions of the experiment, the experimenter can never observe anything beyond the usual, already known effects of matter. By the way, all physical effects ultimately consist of movements or shifts between the Field and matter, in forms of waves. P. W. Bridgman, a Nobel laureate in physics, explains that an instrument can never discover whether the medium exists, because the instrument itself is part of the conditions affected by the medium.[2]

The modern, quantum physics, founding its explanations on "wave mechanics", shows that physical effects are waves in motion and that matter itself consists of "individual and periodic material waves" (M. Planck).[4,5] Even the practical view shows that the "nothingness" around us is full of waves, of light, electromagnetism, radio, television or cosmic radiation. But waves can exist only in a medium and have no meaning without it. As Einstein has pointed out the wave must be *in* something.[1]

Actually the most compelling reason for accepting the existence of the Field is so general that it is not even noticed. The Field, as we shall see, creates all forms and effects of matter by its simple uniform force of pressure. The forms and effects of matter are uniform throughout the universe. Only the "nothingness", the Field, is there throughout the universe. Without the Field as the universal creating force we would have to assume miracles — of angels manufacturing and repairing everywhere precisely in the same way each one of the clockwork particles and effects.

The properties of the Field are evident from the forms and effects of matter, its causal opposite, much like the shape or properties of a matrix or mold are evident from the forms it casts. The enormous pressure or density of the Field is evident from the compression by which atoms are held together and created, or from the propagation of radiation with enormous speed. The absolute homogeneousness and fluidity of the Field are evident from the fact that the physical effects are uniform and take the form of waves.

In effect, the Field is simply Force in its simplest form of a medium consisting as if of mere points of force, from which then all the above properties derive. The Field is so simple because for man matter as the ultimate reality is equally simple — also just mere points of substance — and the two relate as mold and cast. Matter, in its turn, is so simple for man because he exists as matter. This is the same kind of reason that makes all laws of nature simple. Of course the properties of the Field as the opposites of man's ultimate, physical values are utterly strange or unthinkable for him — more "contrary to common sense" than Francis Bacon found the Copernican theory to be.[6]

Einstein avoided insulting the common sense, by proceeding only in terms of mathematics. He recognized the reality of a medium, as established by Maxwell. But he replaced the old Ether with "space" or "space-time" and the old lines of force with the "curvature" or the "structural" properties of space. Any structure, field or curvature can be only of, or in, something.

Bridgman states that the modern physicist "thinks of the field as expressing action through a medium by the bonding on of an action through contiguous parts".[2] Bronowski finds that "the true causes are now imbedded in the nature of space and the way in which matter distorts space; and they have no resemblance to the causes in which we believed for nearly three hundred years".[11] The field equations established by Maxwell are generally recognized as yielding complete answers,[1,2] but Maxwell's concepts of Ether are most concrete. They are quantitative representations of Faraday's Ether with all its "lines" and "tubes" of force as "states of stress in an elastic extended body". Equally concrete are the models of Ether in other theories, of Lord Kelvin or Sir George Stokes.[7]

In modern physics "ether has been junked and physicists talk about warped space, the fourth dimension and relativity . . . so they feel happier".[8] But "when we endow space itself with properties such as curvature, we are making it play the part of an ether".[3] Sir Edmund Whittaker has used the term "interphenomena" to explain the properties of space which "seem to imply that however extreme the vacuity, there is always still something there".[3] The most recent theory on the properties of empty space is, probably, that of J. A. Wheeler, who sees it filled with infinitesimal electromagnetic fluctuations of "stupendous" energy.

On the other hand, physicists are reluctant to accept the concrete properties of empty space. As Bridgman says, "it is in any event a bit shocking, I think, to realize that the concept of empty space, which appears unavoidable and a necessity of thought, can have no guarantee that it is anything more than an artifact of our thinking".[2] Margenau finds that everything falls in line with the theory of Ether of Faraday and Maxwell, but he notes "the jolt one receives from the idea that the universe is filled with invisible solid matter of extreme rigidity".[7]

Scientists sometimes recognize that a universal medium could not be measured, just as water could not be measured by fish. Sir Oliver Lodge has used this argument to support the view that a dense Ether could well exist without anybody noticing it. Einstein has said, in a context of a personal remark, that fish cannot know the water they live in. Actually, a being limited to life in water or air still could measure or know it, by creating vacuums or pressure differences in it, as fish do in swimming or we do in flying. Only when the medium is *the absolutely universal causal opposite of matter*, as the Field is, are we unable to register it by any instrument or in any way except as the ordinary effects of matter already known. For then a "vacuum" in the medium is matter and a pressure difference or loosening in it is an effect of matter or its quantum, in the form of a wave. But physicists have, logically, sought causal relations between any Ether or fields and matter in the same, not opposite, terms. Even when Einstein recognizes the importance of the field, he tries to view matter as "regions in space where the field is extremely strong"[1] — which could only deepen the incongruity.

No wonder physics becomes a mystery as soon as it looks at the causes of its phenomena with deeper precision made possible by modern research. Then it appears that the causal source in every physical phenomenon is missing, that "nature does not present us with a single instance . . . of a causal connection" (M. Planck).[4] The very idea that physics should seek for mechanistic explanations, as it always did, is to be abandoned. The "metaphysical vision is on the increase in recent researches".[7] Now in physics "the question whether the outer world really exists, not only cannot be answered but cannot even be expressed".[6] Modern physicists see causality as a misleading habit of thought, not to be accepted in physics, where causally nothing is true or false.[5]

Physics is "abandoning the mechanistic and materialistic scheme" and becoming idealistic.[10] The great authority Sir Arthur Eddington found that "reality, the unknown something which underlies the worlds both of sense and science . . . is spiritual in nature", and that the world is the result of a process of mental construction.[10,6] The equally distinguished Sir James Jeans held that the physical world can be interpreted only in mathematical terms, rather than physically explained — that its "Creator is mathematical, and since mathematics are formulas of symbols, the world is also only symbolic".[10] According to Jeans "the universe begins to look more like a great thought than like a great machine".[10]

Significantly, another great authority, Erwin Schroedinger finds that "the ether in which all events of the universe take place could reduce to a mathematical abstraction".[5] Thus generally the theory of modern physics is turning into a metaphysical mystery. For modern scientists the "physical 'being' has lost its ultimate permanence".[4] As the founder of the quantum physics Max Planck points out, "it is impossible to demonstrate the existence of the real world by purely rational methods".[4] Uncertainty, indeterminacy, mere probability, acausality and the double-truth complementarity are accepted as the fundamental principles in modern physics.[16] The difficulties of visualizing the atom are compared to those men have in visualizing God.[8] We can have only "probable knowledge" in modern physics.[2] "Individual events are no longer related in causal fashion" and causal uniformity reveals itself only statistically as an aggregate probability.[5] No causal prediction is possible and "the only kind of law in nature is statistical".[4,6] Apparently there is a cause behind the statistical effects, which governs them uniformly. But because the physicist does not see what it is or how it works, he can only register statistically the uniform effects.

The confusion is confirmed by the fact that the greatest physicists such as Einstein or Planck do not accept the absence of causality as a final explanation.[4] Einstein's remark that God could not be playing dice with the world, has been often quoted. But as it is now, modern physics can offer no causality, knowledge of reality, or certainty of anything.

The principle of complementarity, enounced by Bohr, is typical. It permits a yes and no answer to the same question. Electrons and other "particles" are, in truth, wave systems, which appear as mass quanta or particles when isolated and statistically measured. The Field action, its power to create and re-create the waves and "particles", is the explanation, as we shall see later. But if the Field is not recognized, physicists have to view the "particles" as waves in some ways and as particles in others. Practically this is "equivalent to saying a box is both full and

empty".[16] Bohr expressly proclaimed a new double-truth logic
for modern science, to the extent that any concept, even that of
justice or love, can have two complementary, different meanings
(P. Bridgman).[2]

The end result is that the "conclusions reached by modern
physics seem almost like a declaration of the bankruptcy of
science".[7] Scientists admit that presently "physics can never be
certain of its postulates"; that the "modern physics is, admittedly, in a state of uncertainty and confusion"; or that it is passing through a "period of storm".[4,16] The admitted mystery, confusion and double-truths in physics as the most exact science
have encouraged mystifications in all fields. Men love mystery, and
now every metaphysical sophistry, humanistic delusion or philosophical double-talk can be justified. Scientists can rest un-
bothered, by merely repeating the accepted dogmas of acausality
and uncertainty. Of course without discovery of causes there
can be no knowledge why anything happens, no science and no
coherent thought.

This is not the first time that a vast, sophisticated field of
learning has sunk into complex mystifying confusion, because
a simple causal truth has remained unthinkable. The Field is
unthinkable under the natural, nonrelative, humanly prejudiced
view. But it is as self-evident under the relative view as is light
from existence of shadows. It requires no assumptions of new
forces or hypotheses but only abandonment of an old, naturally
prejudiced world view.

The various above arguments that the physical reality may
be incomprehensible to man, only reveal the extent of the confusion. Nothing is clearer or simpler for man than the physical
reality, matter or substance. This is so because man exists as
matter — and thinks the way he exists. All that is simple, like
logic or natural laws, is so for man only because it coincides
with the way he exists. That the universal cause and effects of
the physical world are simple is confirmed by the fact that
mathematics can be used in accounting for them, as modern
physics excellently shows. Mathematics can be used only where
absolute uniformity and simplicity prevails, without exceptions.

Even a minimal irregularity or complexity, like an irregular or additional factor in the study of air and water waves, makes mathematics inapplicable or too complex to be formulated. Mathematics, in its turn, rests on concepts like "one" and quantity, which are simple because man exists as one quantitatively material being. The absolute, mathematical simplicity of the fundamental physical phenomena would be impossible if they did not exist or work in the same way man exists and thinks. In brief, there is no valid reason for the mysteries of modern physics. The "impossible" relative view, revealing the Field, provides simple explanations.

Causal Explanations of the Dilemmas of Modern Physics

The practical proof of the reality of the Field lies in the causal explanations it offers where modern physics has reached only mystery and dilemmas. The Field makes possible simple, automatic explanations in all parts of physics, from the particle-wave dilemma to the mysteries of gravitation or of astrophysics. Generally, the Field explains why and how the forms of matter and laws of nature are exactly the same throughout the universe that has only the "nothingness" everywhere. It also explains how the physical phenomena, ultimately all of them, interact at distance, without "contact", and why they do so mostly by way of waves or why most of them are waves.

The Particle-Wave Dilemma. All the fundamental units of matter — atoms, nucleons, electrons and photons — have been discovered to be systems of waves, as well as particles.[3,4,5] The quantum mechanics explains all effects and forms of matter in terms of waves. Schroedinger and de Broglie have offered explanations of all "particles" as wave systems, and Born and Heisenberg have worked out formulas for dealing with them both as with particles and waves. But how could a "corpuscle have anything to do with a wave", in the words of Einstein. The duality seems to imply that something is there and is not there at the same time.[16]

The explanation is automatic if the Field-matter opposition is recognized. A wave in any medium is the effect of a loosening or emptiness in the medium. *But an "emptiness" in the Field is automatically a quantum of matter,* its opposite. In its static state a "particle" is compressed by the Field on all sides equally, therefore acts as a spherical wave system because both matter and the Field are fluid pressure opposites. The enormous force that compresses atoms is the great mystery of physics. It is automatic, if we consider that the Field as the cosmically vast force opposed to matter surrounds it and acts against it on all sides.

All matter "particles" are equal because the Field pressure is uniform; it is inherent in any fluid medium to equalize pressures within itself. The standard, initial "particle", the hydrogen atom is an inevitable product of the Field pressure. Any larger piece of matter is automatically broken up and reduced to the limits of hydrogen atom, at which it can resist further breaking up. Conversely, smaller pieces of matter, like photons, can accumulate to the same limit, the hydrogen atom. Thus hydrogen, as the primary source of all elements, is continuously created — to be burned up later in the stars. The universal presence of hydrogen atoms in the interstellar space is well known; they may constitute half of all matter in the universe. Such creation of new atoms is not possible on earth because here the generally impoverished matter absorbs all loose bits or quanta of matter.

Larger atoms are created by the same Field pressure, under the special conditions of large concentration and pressures of mass during the creation of stars and planets. The Field compresses two primary atoms because that permits a gain by the Field as the dominant opposite. Each atom as an elastic spherical wave system within an elastic compressing medium has a margin of compression by which it exerts its normal counter-pressure or balance against the Field. If two such full atoms are compressed into one, they can maintain the same balance with only one margin of compression, abandoning the other to the compressing Field. The new multi-unit atoms can be further compressed in the same way. Schematically, several balls have reduced their aggregate surface by forming one ball. The well known "packing loss" in the formation of larger atoms is explained by the compression of primary atoms by the Field. Of course the fluid mass within the new larger atom becomes a system of concentric waves under the Field pressure. Moreover, these waves have to be *standing waves*, since they travel in opposite ways within the fixed sphere.

The *standing or stationary* wave is the key for explaining the properties of atoms. The waves within the atom are like concentric layers that are of exactly equal thickness because they are stationary waves. They are also of equal mass. The inner layers are denser or more compressed exactly to the extent they are smaller, because the lines of the concentric pressure become denser as they converge toward the center. Mass, in all its effects, is only a function of pressure and counter-pressure between the Field and matter. Such equal spherical waves, the nucleons, are the same in all elements and correspond to the merged primary atoms, because the *uniform* Field pressure creates and maintains all of them.

All phenomena of physics, particularly as revealed by the quantum physics, are explained by "standing waves, represented mathematically by the surface harmonics of a hypersphere".[3] Einstein praised de Broglie's explanation of "particles" as *standing waves*, which measure only in integral numbers and can change only by jumps, as the quantum theory requires. But he pointed out that such a system cannot exist without a medium.[1] Einstein found that a radiating atom acted like a system of stationary waves comparable to those of an oscillating cord or the membrane of a drum. Matter as "vortex rings in a perfect fluid" has been explained already by Lord Kelvin.[3]

The usual explanations of matter as consisting of particles do not correspond to reality — so much so that "explanation and particle thus seem in a sense incompatible".[2] "The particle as imagined in the classical picture *does not exist*,"[3] according to Sir Edmund Whittaker. Only phenomena of spherical waves are observed in modern physics. Typically, the Nobel Prize for work on the structure of the atom has been awarded to E. P. Wigner, J. H. Jensen and M. G. Mayer, who established the "shell model" with protons and neutrons arranged like onion shells, with nothing in the center.

When the nucleons — actually spherical waves — are compressed and lose a margin of expansion or electron for each compression, they can be viewed, "with certain difficulties",[7] as protons and neutrons joined together. A nucleon minus an electron then is calculated in as the proton. Any such combination tends to regain the electron, therefore is positively charged. Anyway, when energy or quanta of matter pour into atoms, the compressed nucleons tend to regain the lost margins of expansion. But the Field is always there to recompress them, when definite limits under given conditions are reached, and thus to squeeze off photons and electrons. The mysterious ghost nature of electrons is explained by this temporary regaining and subsequent loss or release of the margins of expansion: *the electron is a mere potential.*

The Impossible Electron. The electron has no "local position", "whereness" or "ubiety", in the atom.[5] This in simpler words means that the electron is not there. As Bridgman states "we should not talk about 'electrons' as such but rather say: 'Under such and such conditions the apparatus electrons'".[2] Electron as a particle can appear only outside the atom. Typically, Sir James Jeans has said that while a "hard sphere takes up a very definite amount of room . . . it is as meaningless to discuss how much room an electron takes up as it is to discuss how much room a fear, an anxiety or an uncertainty takes up". In the formulation by de Broglie, electron as any "particle cannot be observed so long as it forms part of the system, and the system is impaired once the particle has been identified".[5] This fact has led to the conclusion that "perhaps all the particles are generated in the disintegration process rather than existing preformed in the nucleus of the atom".[16] The famous uncertainty theory of Heisenberg has been generally accepted because it is the best way to concede the mystery.

Electrons, as all "particles", have the mysterious dual nature of particle and wave. Electron has been clearly observed and measured as a particle in various experiments, notably by Thomson and Millikan. But as conclusive experiments, beginning with those of Davisson and Germer, and comprehensive theories, particularly by de Broglie, Schroedinger and Heisenberg, have shown the electron to be a wave.[7] Electron even passes through two pinholes at once as only a wave can do, and forms typical wave patterns, showing in the electron interference experiments.[7] The dichotomous theory of complementarity by Bohr was postulated to account for the dual nature of electron.

The mystery is explained by the simple fact that electron in the atom is *only a potential of expansion of spherical waves,* which creates and releases the quanta of matter. But outside the atom the released quantum of matter can be measured and observed, or even assume a spherical form in its stationary state under compression by the Field. Generally, electrons as such potentials yield the only changes atoms can have, since the nucleons are formed and held compressed by full forces of the Field, too strong to be ordinarily affected. Electrons, therefore, are the cause of all ordinary activity and properties of elements, particularly their participation in chemical bonds, through the "sharing" of electrons.

If electrons were particles inside the atom they would, necessarily, be all uniform and behave in the same way. But as has been established, under the exclusion principle of Pauli, there can not be in an atom two electrons having the same set of quantum numbers or the same behavior status. This is what has to happen with the spherical waves or layers in the atom, since there can be only one of them at each distance.

Two neutron-proton compressions can be further compressed within the atom by the Field, leaving only one margin of expansion for all four; and such a four-nucleon formation can be doubled with another. Atoms having numbers of nucleons that do not double up evenly have more actual electrons and are chemically more active, while the even doubling, and redoubling, confers particular stability. This explains the properties of elements as listed in the element table, governed by even-number patterns and particularly the octets of electrons. Physicists have construed an admitted fiction about electrons combining in shells that accommodate only certain numbers of electrons. No causal explanation for the complex rules is even offered. It is not realized that all the electrons are not actually present. This is why an element having 18 or 54 electrons is as inactive as one having only 2, though the "sharing" of electrons would make elements with more electrons exceedingly active. Elements are also stabler to the extent their nucleon numbers can double up into square numbers like 16 — plus the basic combination of 2. This is due to the combining of the nucleon waves into superwaves which as spherical and standing waves are governed, in their formation, stability and pressures, by square relations and integral numbers.

, Compression by the Field is the cause of the "sharing" of electrons in chemical bonds, just as it is in the above formation of elements. By compressing two atoms the Field can squeeze off looser electrons and still leave the molecule with sufficient, balanced margins of expansion. The "sharing" of looser electrons is generally recognized as the way chemical bonds are formed. The Field pressure *offers the missing causal explanation.*

The central fiction in physics is the picture of ball-like nucleons with smaller ball-like electrons orbiting around them. Bohr's theory is the main, last support for the concept of orbiting electrons, and he had to admit its wave nature as well. In Bohr's theory the electron is, miraculously, held in orbits having only the radiuses of square integrals 1, 4, 9, 16, 25; and all its effects are products of its jumps from one orbit to another. The process "is indeed a miracle, for when the jump occurs another entity is born or dies".[7] There is no causal nor even physically comprehensible relation of such jumps with real emission and absorption of energy or matter quanta.

At the same time, absorptions and emissions by spherical stationary waves can explain the miracle of the square integrals[11] as well as of the other quantum effects, governed by wave mechanics, since "all frequencies emitted and absorbed by atoms correspond to transition from one quantum state to another[11] or to "superimposition of two stationary states".[3] Bohr's complementarity was unnecessary: the "electron wave picture fits all facts".[11]

The Nonexistent Particles. Other theories have been construed, particularly before the era of quantum physics, about electrons and nucleons as particles. Einstein's explanation of photoelectric effects, Compton's experiments with X-ray scattering, and Rutherford's discovery of "empty" matter have to be mentioned. Einstein and Compton assumed that not only electrons but also photons were particles, though photons are clearly waves. They found that impacts and scatterings by photons and electrons complied with mathematics of particle interaction and angles of collision. If they had assumed that wave systems were interacting, they would have found equally good agreements. For ultimately particle movements are reducible to wave movements, because all movement is "joint effect of all kinds of periodic material waves".[4] Photons and X-rays as units of impact could not have possibly acted as particles, though they can and did produce phenomena of "particles" as wave systems.

Rutherford's discovery of "empty" matter has been widely accepted, because matter does appear empty and "fuzzy"[2] if physicists continue looking for particles in it. This discovery was made from experiments in which alpha particles were shot through metal foil. Here, as above, the calculations were made under the assumption of particles, while they could have given equal results under the assumption of wave systems. Actually these experiments confirm that alpha particles are wave systems. While mostly passing unhindered through the Field in which all matter floats, they may sometimes collide with other "particles" as wave systems and consequently be absorbed and re-emitted by them. Rutherford's conclusions were derived from the fact that the alpha particles passed through the metal foil unhindered to the extent of only one particle in a half-million being deflected; and that the deflected particles shot back at very narrow angles. It was assumed that matter was empty, with very hard small particles sparsely distributed in it. The general effect was, according to Rutherford, like that of shooting bullets through tissue paper and then seeing some of the bullets shoot back.

Actually, such shooting back could never result from mere collision of ball-like particles. The alpha particles "shoot back" with a delay ten billion times longer than mere collision of particles would permit. In similar experiments, first performed by Juliot-Curies, alpha particles could be observed radiating out of the foil half an hour after the experiment. Absorption and re-emission of "particles" as wave systems is the explanation here as in most phenomena of moving matter quanta.

A beam of rapidly moving nuclei, as well as of electrons, behaves in the same way as a light beam of photons,[16] which are waves that are absorbed and re-emitted. In view of the wave nature of matter "the 'path' of mass point loses inherent significance and becomes fictitious as light ray".[5] Electrons or photons are matter quanta that can be measured or behave as particles in their stationary form. But it is incongruous to assume that a photon runs as a particle from the sun or that electrons run all the way through the wire, though the amount of electrons supplied at one end of the wire does appear at the other. Local oscillations, that is, absorptions and reemissions, are the way matter quanta as wave systems travel. Even in the Wilson chamber, particles passing as mere physical balls could never create the tracks. A process similar to ionization, to absorption and re-emission, produces the straight tracks in the *uniform* bubble chamber, as ionization produces the path of lightning in nature.

There is "no real existence for either Bohr's or Rutherford's atom model",[5] but modern physics can still offer nothing better than such constructs, worthy of Ptolemaic inventiveness. It is held that, if you imagined an atom having the radius of a football field, the orbiting electrons would be as tiny as bees and the nucleons as small as softballs. Why should not such atoms collapse into each other, under the intermolecular attraction. The argument that the electrons circle so fast as to form a shield is untenable, because the electrons of other atoms would be moving equally fast, therefore would penetrate the "shield" and enmesh the atoms instantly.

All said, the explanation of the dilemmas of the forms of matter lies in the fact that the Field, in its simple automatic action, works as the invisible creator that creates, transforms and re-creates "particles", waves and wave systems. A wave is always caused by a loosening or emptiness in a medium. But an emptiness in the Field is automatically a quantum of matter as its opposite. *Hence the otherwise inconceivable sameness of wave and particle.* Under the concentric pressure by the Field, a static accumulated matter particle automatically becomes a harmonic system of stationary spherical waves. Modern physicists are ready to recognize that the "particles" are spherical wave systems. But without the Field as the compressing medium such systems and their action are utterly inconceivable.

Mysteries of Light and Radiation

A mystery that physicists have most extensively discussed is how can light be waves as well as quanta of matter or particles.[7] Light is matter quanta while it is being emitted and received, but waves while it is being transmitted. The same applies to electrons and even to a beam of rapidly moving nuclei.[11] The explanation is simple, and the same here as in the wave-particle dilemma. Any wave results from a quantitative difference or emptiness in a medium, but such emptiness in the Field is automatically a quantum of matter as its opposite.

Another mystery is the absence of loss of energy in the transmission of radiation. Sir William Bragg has said, it is as if a wave, created by dropping a plank 100 feet, having traveled 1000 miles makes a plank, out of another ship, fly 100 feet high. The reason is the role of the absolute density of the Field in transmission of its pressure difference or waves. The simplest transmission of pressure differences is through pushing; and if you push a metal rod or a column of mercury at one end you get an equal almost instantaneous push at the other end of it. The Field, of course, is much more compact than any matter.

Radiation is created when the Field squeezes off surplus matter quanta from an atom or "thrusts" into it, to the same extent. As it does so it leaves a loosening behind, which is then filled by further Field thrust-in, creating further loosening, and so on, as in all waves. But unlike in other waves, there is no dispersion or loss in such wave. The enormous pressure of the Field holds the quantum together; and as the opposite of matter the Field can never absorb it. Of course enormous pressure, of billions of pounds per square inch,[7] is required to propagate the waves at the speed of light. But as science shows, cosmic factors are of such magnitudes. This merely means that the measurements of man's world are enormously tiny, which is clear anyway.

The enormous pressure of the Field is confirmed by the fact that only a medium of such pressure or density can produce the transverse waves that constitute radiation.[3,7] An "elastic solid" transmits such waves. Solids may have also longitudinal waves but these decrease as the medium gets softer and more elastic. Here it should be understood that, as Asimov notes, the usual properties of molecular matter make "no sense whatsoever when applied to an absolutely continuous substance such as that which light ether is considered to be".[11] The Field can have all the properties of solidity while being perfectly fluid, because there are never any particles or divisions in it to interrupt its solidity.

The enormous pressure of the Field also explains why radiation goes in a straight line. In the above process of the Field thrusting in to form the wave, the thrusts come, automatically, from the closest, most "economic" or shortest distance, that is, from directly behind every loosening. This follows with inexorable precision because of the enormous Field pressure. An absolutely straight wave path is the result.

The *quantum mechanics,* and the mysteries that arise from it, are explainable by the wave nature of radiation as well as of matter. The strange discontinuity of quantum effects is due to the fact that any "particle", as a *stationary wave* system, can change only by jumps measuring in integral numbers. The surplus of matter that is pressed off the atom by the Field has to accumulate to a certain limit before it yields to the Field. Two elastic, opposing or counteracting media act, automatically, by way of oscillations between extreme limits, for the same reasons that an elastic ball, musical cord or surface of a drum oscillates between opposite extremes.

The spherical wave of matter when it starts gaining matter enrichment continues expanding to the extreme at which it cannot further resist the pressure of the Field. When that extreme is reached, the opposite process starts and the Field compresses the matter wave to the extreme where it cannot press further into it. These oscillations are the universal, uniform and automatic ways of interacting between the two universal, uniform, elastic opposites. Each wave or quantum resulting from such oscillations is the universal "quantum of action", known as the Planck's constant, which is the last, indivisible quantum of all radiation and energy, or the ultimate grain of the universe.

The curious universal inverse relationship between the length of a light wave and its energy level is explainable by the fact that each spherical wave inside an atom has the same mass, but that the total volume of a more external wave is larger. Absorption of such more external wave by the Field therefore yields the same mass or quantum of energy but takes a longer time, therefore creates a longer radiation wave. A reverse process takes place in absorption of radiation by atoms it encounters. Only those waves are absorbed which find corresponding vacancies or potentials of expansion of the same volume or length. The process here is the same as in all resonance between systems producing similar harmonic waves. The principle of resonance, even comparison of atom radiation with waves from musical instruments, has been generally accepted.[1] But only the omnipresent absolutely dense Field can make the resonance between systems at enormous distances perform as if there was no distance at all between them.

Finally, the relationships of squared integrals in radiation frequencies, as revealed in spectra series, are explainable by the fact that atoms are and act as systems of spherical and stationary waves — which only the compressing Field can create and operate.

The most obvious proof of the existence of the Field as the universal medium is the uniformity of the speed of light. *Only a transmitting medium can make light move always at the same speed.* Otherwise the speed of light emitted from an approaching system would be increased and from a receding system decreased by the speed of the movement. When physicists could not discover the Ether as the medium, they were faced with an unsolvable mystery and welcomed the Relativity Theory of Einstein as the only explanation.[7] Einstein was "so foolish as to assume that light moves at constant velocity" in spite of any movement by its source.[8] According to Einstein, "we must accept the concept of relative time in every coordinate system, because it is the best way out of our difficulties".[1]

Einstein's theory derives from a very simple fact, as all great discoveries do. This simple fact is the uniform speed of light. A mathematical genius can derive predictions by using one correct formula, without necessarily revealing or visualizing what the reality he is dealing with actually is. A medium is the only possible explanation of the uniform speed of light, but Einstein as a mathematician did not have to bother about the unthinkable reality of such medium. Of course explanations in terms of reality were also sought for Einstein's relativity of time on different coordinate systems. The curious Lorentz-Fitzgerald theory of contraction of moving systems was proposed. On a fast moving system everything, including clocks and measuring sticks, was assumed to shorten and time to slow down.

In truth, the contraction has neither been proven, e.g., by experiments on double refraction that should have shown it,[3] nor has ever been intended to represent reality.[7] The contraction as a reality would not be helpful anyway — in plain reason, free of double-talk. Two, opposite changes would be required to explain how the approaching as well as retreating systems compensate for the change in the speed of light. Both contraction and lengthening of distances, or both slowing down and speeding up of time, on moving systems, would be required. Of course a mathematical formula can give both plus and minus at the same time, with a factor like the square root, used in the equations of the speed of light. In the world of reality, however, the same factor or cause cannot be bigger and smaller or have positive and negative effect. Nor can a system at one moment be assumed to be standing, at the next to be moving.

But here as elsewhere men love mystery. Particularly popular are speculations about astronauts becoming younger when traveling at speeds of light. Surely, such astronauts could catch a ray of light that passed us a time ago, and thus recapture a tiny past effect. Fliers of supersonic planes can do the same with sounds, which are a bit more substantial. Yet they do not regress in time. Rays of light or sounds are only tiny facets of reality while the whole universe, with every atom in it, would have to be changed back, to attain regression into the past. Time is merely the relationship of changes, which are infinitely many. Moreover, as we saw, one of two, opposite effects, acceleration of time or its slowing down, would have to be assumed, depending on whether the system or spaceship is approaching or retreating. For more confusion, in the relative world of the Relativity Theory the same system can be considered to be approaching as well as retreating, under the argument that every reference point in the space is as good as any other.

Mystifications have been perpetuated also around Einstein's concepts of the Fourth dimension and Curvature of space. Einstein himself was careful to point out that there is "nothing mysterious" about the application of the fourth-dimension time coordinate and that the same method is used in timetables of trains or graphs of weather reports.[1] The curvature of space was Einstein's geometrical explanation of the "structural" or "metric" field properties around gravitational bodies.[1] But it has induced speculations of how a strange different geometry curves all space, so that a system traveling away into space would ultimately return to its starting point. This is an imitation of the past discovery of the roundness of earth. That discovery, however, did not imply any new geometry. Our ancestors were in error only about the fact that earth is round. They always knew that a path around a sphere curves back. If a geometry or logic of curved space governed the world, the curved line would be the "straight" one in everything. Also, there is a total curvature around the earth, as its gravitation shows; yet if we travel in a straight line away from earth we do not return back, within such curvature.

The Relativity Theory is built on the mathematics of a uniform speed of light, but such speed is possible only if light is carried by a medium. Sound has a uniform speed, however the emitting system moves, and no contraction, or slowing down of time has to be postulated. Only the frequency of sound changes with the movement of, say, an airplane, much in the same way that frequency of light from moving stars changes, as is well known in modern physics and astronomy.

All the phenomena revealed and predicted by the Relativity Theory require the medium as soon as they have to be explained as realities. The bending of light rays in a gravitational field and the red spectrum shift from heavy stars are explainable by the weaker Field pressure in gravitational fields, as we shall see later. The abnormal revolutions of the perihelion of Mercury were explained by Einstein by use of structural properties of gravitational space instead of the old Newtonian attraction. Such properties, as spherical gradations around a gravitational body, are identical with the concrete gradations in pressures of the Field around the body.

Before we conclude, it may be mentioned that not only radiation but all *movement* results from quantum interaction of "periodic material waves".[4] Radiation ensues only when movement is stopped and the wave quantum has to be given off to the Field. Otherwise an energy-enriched atom or molecule moves endlessly, and the surplus never leaves it. As the Field begins to "squeeze" off the surplus, the free moving particle moves toward the separating quantum wave, because the Field pressure from that side is less. But as they start reuniting the Field repeats its pressure of separation, on the same side, where the surplus hovers; and the movement by the particle is repeated. In brief, movement results from oscillation between the Field and matter around a surplus quantum, which becomes a wave of matter that never completely separates from the particle.

The Avowed Mystery of Gravitation

Modern physicists admit unreservedly that the force of gravitation is a mystery. It is evident that something in the space or in the nothingness around matter creates the gravitation. One may think here of the physics professor who started his course by showing his students a falling ball and telling them this was the greatest miracle. Newton himself recognized that attraction between bodies without anything between them "is to me so great an absurdity . . . that no man can fall into it".[3] But he could not decide what the medium between bodies was, though he speculated about the particles of Ether being finer in the vicinity of bodies.[3] He admitted the mystery by attributing the cause of the force of gravitation to God.

The generally accepted modern explanation of gravitation by the "curvature of space" amounts to an equal mystery. Curvature has to be in or of something. Einstein's final explanation, which served as the basis for his theory of General Relativity, was the assimilation of gravitation to inertia. From his descriptions, illustrated by accelerating elevators, one can only conclude that we or gravitating objects must be accelerating away from earth — which is not true or conceivable for gravitation on earth or on any other system.

Maxwell, whose equations are generally accepted in the Relativity Theory,[1] construed a gravitational formula from the forces in the space around matter. He found that this space or medium possesses "an enormous positive intrinsic energy, and that the presence of dense bodies influences the medium so as to diminish this energy".[3] He abandoned the explanation because he was "unable to understand in what way a medium can possess such properties" — though the quantum mechanics is now using the concept of such energy.[3]

The explanation of *gravitation becomes almost self-evident if the existence of the universal Field pressure is recognized.* A body compressed from all sides has to slide toward another body of matter, because from that side the pressure is less, as the matter shields off the pressures coming from behind it. Where matter particles are very close the pressure is almost completely one-sided, which explains the strong intermolecular attraction. Matter that is more compact, or of larger molecules, provides better shielding, therefore has stronger gravitational effect.

A very large mass of matter is required to provide any noticeable gravitational effect, because the Field is all around matter and inside it, therefore renders the shielding effect always very incomplete. That is why gravitation is such a weak, shadowy force, in comparison with the pressures that compress atoms or propagate radiation at enormous speeds. There is never anything more than a slight one-sidedness in the Field pressures, like a slight shadow around bodies, which quickly decreases with distance. But since the Field, in its cosmic vastness, maintains its pressures through enormous distances, any less enormous distance is "close" enough for the one-sidedness to have some effect.

Here we may mention the theory of Le Sage, who assumed that gravitation results from shielding off, by matter, of impacts by ultramundane particles that move from all sides with enormous velocity.[3] Apparently this would have the same effect as the shielding off by matter of the Field pressures. Computations by Le Sage showed that the effects would be exactly those of gravitation, measuring in the inverse square relation to distance. Other scientists have calculated that gravitation obeys the rule that governs shadows, which are typical effects of shielding off. The only fault with such theories is that the assumed ultramundane particles, or the rays of gravitation have remained mere assumptions.

Since gravitation means lessened Field pressure, all other physical effects, being products of the same pressure, are affected by gravitation. Thus radiation, propagated by the pressures of the Field, bends slightly when passing near a star, because the Field pressure from that side is less. An atom expands, however slightly, in a strong gravitational area, therefore emits slightly longer waves — which produces the red spectrum shift. All movement, as product of the Field pressures, is hindered when it goes against gravitation and is accelerated when it goes with it. This is sufficient to explain the centripetal and centrifugal effects without the requirement of the "strings" of attraction. The spherical gradations of the Field pressures around the body constitute perfect curvature of the "structural" space, which has made possible more precise explanations than the Newtonian attraction.

The speed of light is decreased in areas of gravitation, because the Field pressure there is weaker. The speed of light may be greater in the parts of space that are further away from galaxies with their various gravitational areas. Matter and energy become "softer" and weaker, at least in principle, under the weaker pressures of the Field. But practically nothing changes, because the "softer" matter acts in an equally weaker Field.

The curious difference between the usual and the gravitational acceleration is a problem, raised by Einstein in his theory of General Relativity. Whereas a big or heavy body requires more force to be accelerated, all bodies big or small, heavy or light, fall with the same acceleration. Evidently the force that makes bodies fall is already inside all matter, therefore does not need to be added or accumulated from outside before the body starts moving or accelerating. This inherent force is the Field pressure which compresses all matter exactly equally therefore makes all matter move uniformly in the direction of lesser pressure. Denser matter embodies more of the Field pressures, on its more numerous or massive particles, therefore is heavier.

Einstein explained gravitation by a structural or curved space which he found to be *as concrete as are depressions on a bowling green*.[3] Obviously, the structure or curvature, in the space, must be of or in a concrete, though experimentally unregistrable medium or continuum, that the Field is, with its pressure gradations around a body of matter.

The Unseen Cause of Electromagnetism

What is electricity or its causal source? Scientists have never been able to find it out and finally have given up the search, by accepting mere mathematical concepts as the irreducible fundamentals. They know that the "energy of electric charges and currents is not situated in the conductors with which they are most obviously associated, but is diffused throughout the surrounding medium".[3] The explanation is simple if the existence of the Field is recognized. Electricity is the effects of the *automatic equalization of pressures within the Field*. Self-equalization of pressures is automatic in any fluid medium. Many of the phenomena of electricity have been shown to resemble those of hydrodynamics.[3]

The equalization starts when inequalities in enrichment of matter are created. When matter is enriched by addition of electrons it is more easily compressible. The Field presses in, thus forcing the electrons along the conductor until the pressures, and matter enrichment, are equalized throughout the Field around and in the conductor. This explains the current and the electromagnetic forces around it.

As Field presses into the conductor it leaves instantaneous loosenings behind. Naturally, if other matter is passed through this area its atoms expand or accrue because of the loosenings. It thus becomes enriched, therefore compressible by the Field and capable of creating current. Thus the inductance, as well as the creation of electromagnetic transmissions and fields, is explained. If matter is left free in the space where such loosenings in the Field become saturated, it naturally moves into the area of loosenings, because the Field pressures from that side are less. This explains the principle by which electric motors work or matter "gravitates" in electromagnetic fields.

It has to be understood that in all these phenomena of electric flow, inductance or fields, the unit or "grain" of action is the electron. Therefore only the kinds of matter that can respond to this grain, like metals and ferromagnetic substances produce electromagnetic effects. Such kinds of matter permit free flow of electrons by merely passing them on, through instantaneous re-emissions after absorptions, thus creating the current. Other substances may have no aptitude at all to respond to the electron "grain"; still others may break down electrons upon absorption and thus create heat or light.

The automatic self-equalization in the Field pressures also explains the attraction of opposite charges, and repulsion of charges of the same pole, at distance. When direct equalization of differences in electron enrichment is impossible because the bodies with the different enrichment or charge are apart, the Field automatically tends to bring them together, through its omnipresent pressures tending to equalize themselves out everywhere. Uncharged bodies are attracted by charged ones because that offers at least a partial or half equalization. Conversely, by pushing apart equally charged bodies the Field diffuses the pressure inequality in that area. We have to keep in mind that all matter and charges in the bodies are ultimately products of the Field, and that the omnipresent Field controls all effects as if everything were in contact, except that the electron equalization or current is delayed as long as the bodies are apart.

These effects may not be very different from what happens in every homogeneous liquid, automatically tending toward equalization of pressures within itself. Experiments have shown that moving bodies with cavities through which liquid can flow, and bodies pulsating in unison, when immersed in a liquid, exert mutual forces on each other similar to electromagnetic attraction.[3]

Electrostatic induction, generally illustrated by capacitators, Leyden jar, electrophorus or other electrostatic generators, is a product of the same automatic equalization of pressures within the Field. As we saw, the Field pushes separated oppositely charged bodies together and identically charged ones apart. If the Field cannot move bodies to attain equalizations in charges, it dislocates, at least, the charges within the bodies. One effect is that a neutral body acquires, in its parts facing a charged body, a charge that is opposite to that of the charged body. By its automatic equalization of the pressures the Field thus matches any inequality, that a charge constitutes, with an equal opposite inequality, within the area closest to the charge. Naturally, if one side of a neutral body gathers all the positive charges then the other side is left negatively charged, or vice versa.

Charges created by electrostatic as well as by electromagnetic induction can be accumulated to create current. But force has to be used to do so. For otherwise all the equalizations of pressures reestablish themselves instantly and there are no more inequalities for a current to arise. To create further induction, the initial inequality conditions have to be reimposed; and force is needed to do so, because the self-establishing equalization or equilibrium has to be broken. The mechanical application of this principle may require complex electric generators, particularly if current has to be created on a large scale.

Modern physicists recognize that the force which creates electromagnetic phenomena is distributed *in the space around the conductors* and magnets.[3] What is more, this force comes from the vastness of the space all around the conductor. If the conductor is hollow, no electric effects arise in the hollow space inside it. Apparently the Field pressures accumulating throughout the vast space determine overwhelmingly all effects.

Magnets are metals that are deformed by the electricity-creating Field pressure passing through them. If a metal lies in the path through which the Field passes as it presses into the conductor, the metal is eroded to make the passage easier. Some metals retain this deformation even after the current stops. Natural magnets are created by the perennial, slight Field pressures that constantly circle the earth. These pressures may result from equalization by the Field of matter-enrichment inequalities arising from the varying exposure of the earth to the sun, due to earth's rotation. Magnets align themselves in an electric field in the same way they stood when they were "eroded", because this offers easier passage for the Field pressures which constitute the electric field.

One can visualize it better if he thinks in terms of "West-East" rather than the usual North-South magnetic alignments. The natural magnets are created by West-East Field pressures. Therefore the "West-East" direction of a magnet placed close to a conductor indicates better how the Field pressures move — *straight into the conductor.* The North-South direction confuses because it shows as if the pressures or forces moved around the conductor. Surely the magnetic needle aligns itself in this North-South direction. It does so because it was "eroded" in this position by the pressures moving in the West-East direction. It is made in the form elongated along the North-South alignment because in this form it catches more of the pressure lines, going West-East, and therefore is a more stable indicator. That the

"West-East" direction corresponds to the forces or pressures is shown by the structure and effects of magnets. The force of a magnet does not depend on its length, in the North-South direction, but on its thickness, in the "West-East" direction. A magnet can be sliced along this direction into thin slices and each of them exhibits the full force of the magnet.

Physicists agree that magnets result from deformation of the metal within its submicroscopic "domains". This is logical, since dislocations on any larger scale within the metal would be impossible. We can imagine that matter may become eroded by the Field pressures in such a way that components which can be easier dislocated are moved further ahead, within the domains. Anyway, asymmetry is bound to be created by the eroding stream of the pressures. An asymmetry of opposite direction, naturally, offers a more balanced state or more equalized Field pressures. Consequently, magnets of opposite poles cling together, and since the Field pressures prevail inside matter as well as in the space around it, the "clinging" together starts even at distance, thus producing the magnetic attraction.

Nonmagnetized ferromagnetic matter is attracted because it offers at least a half equalization of the asymmetry. Then such matter becomes half-asymmetrical in opposite way, which makes it act as a magnet of opposite pole, after each asymmetry close to the magnet becomes automatically transferred further and further on.

What we have said on electricity and magnetism agrees with the more detailed descriptions of complex lines of forces and numerous other effects physicists have observed. The greatest authorities, Faraday, Maxwell or Lord Kelvin, had to assume existence of very complex lines, vortex filaments, tubes, whirls, spheres, or wheels of Ether, to have some explanation.[3] It is even worse not to see any causal source for all these electromagnetic effects. Then skillful and intelligent creation and maintenance for each one of the complex and varied phenomena remains the only explanation.

But because the universal, dense, yet "nonexistent" compressing medium is utterly inconceivable under the nonrelative view, physicists have never even started to think of the real simple cause behind the complex phenomena. *Physicists could explain incomparably better* what we have here indicated only in principle — if they recognized the clearly existing forces in the space as deriving from an *absolutely omnipresent therefore unnoticeable* medium, that we have tried to explain by the concept of the Field.

The Mysteries of Cosmic Creation, Planets, Formation of Elements, Nuclear Reactions, Negative Matter

It is humanly congenial to think that the material universe originated in one dramatic event. The theory of the "big-bang" and expanding universe is generally accepted. The longer wave lengths of the radiation coming from further galaxies are assumed as proof. Actually waves in any medium lengthen while traveling long distances; and if physicists visualized the Field in action they would think of such less dramatic explanations. Matter, as we saw, is created in the interstellar space, from bits of matter, photons or radiation quanta, coming from stars on which matter is being burned up. Thus a never-ending loss and gain, entropy and regeneration, sustains the symmetry that physicists know should exist.

Stars grow by the simple process of matter happening to accumulate and thus acquiring greater gravitational attraction that makes it accumulate even more matter, in a chain-reaction way. Stars become denser in a similar chain-reaction way, as density increases their force of gravitation which in its turn increases their density. Naturally, opposite chain reactions are inevitable. If due to local conditions the accumulation or condensation rate decreases, the chain reaction collapses, because it has created an abnormal condition sustained only by further increase in the process. Then the opposite chain reaction begins. As the Field pressures start dispelling the accumulation or condensation of matter, this increases their effectiveness which dispels matter even more. Such *opposite chain reactions* can explain the pulsars, the pulsing action of quasars and galaxies, as well as the novae and supernovae, by way of which stars disintegrate. Since the Field is the dominant opposite the distintegration may take explosive forms.

According to the present theories stars disintegrate or explode by crushing themselves with their own immensely increasing gravitation. This is untenable, because a tendency, in itself, cannot create an opposite tendency. All opposite reactions that we encounter in the physical world are due to the opposition between the Field and matter, which gives the world its symmetry and balance. The present theories also hold that under the enormous pressure of gravitation matter reaches fantastic temperatures, to 100 billion degrees. Actually matter compressed to extremes would behave as if it were totally cold or immobile.

The Field *pressure* also explains why everything rotates, spins, whirls or spirals in the space. The simplest examples are the whirls, twists and cyclic movements in streams, storms, tornadoes and cyclones, created and operated by material universal *pressures*. A pressure that tries to dispel a formation while at the same time confining it from all sides, has to create the whirls, spins, and spirals.

Another effect of the Field pressures is the **creation of planets**. Any movement in the Field as a fluid medium creates counter-movements. Movements in water do so, and this can be easily observed when it happens on the surface. A drop falling into water creates splashes upward. As matter "drops" into the forming sun, it also creates the outward "splashes". Only, this happens on enormous scale, in uniform ways and under the immense Field pressures. The result is uniform spherical storms or outward radiation of matter of enormous dimensions. Because of the opposite directions of the uniform mass movements the whole region may act as a system of standing waves. This helps to explain the regularities of the planetary system, revealed in the laws of Kepler, as well as the creation itself of such a system.

A planet begins to form, within its wave region, by accumulation of matter, which increases its gravitational power to accumulate more matter. Thus the same process by which suns grow takes place, including emergence of "planets" or moons around the planet. It merely all happens within the spherical gravitationally "structured" wave region, which becomes for the planet-forming mass its only, normal or "straight" space of action. The energy of matter in the spherical region determines the rest. All matter having surplus energy moves, under the Field pressure. But the direction of the movement is not pre-determined. In the planet-forming mass, any one movement may precipitate more movement in the same direction, which then precipitates even more movement in that direction, until the forces of movement of the whole mass are consolidated into one orbital and rotational movement of the planet. The simplest il-lustration here may be a slippery ball compressed by fingers, which shoots off with all its force in one direction upon slightest push. Naturally, all kinds of movements may conflict and delay the process. Rotation of planets or suns results when there are loosely moving masses around or within them, and the force of movement of such masses is similarly consolidated.

The existing hypotheses about the origin of planets have either been found untenable, like the nebular, Kant-Laplace and the binary-star hypotheses, or imply that planets are due to ex-traordinary occurrences. According to the close-encounter hypo-thesis only one star in a billion may happen to have planets. This is contradicted by the stark fact that in our solar system six out of nine planets have moons or planets of their own.

Larger atoms, of the heavier elements, are created by the Field pressure, from the primordial, hydrogen atoms after these have accumulated to form a star. In such enormous concentration, the atoms inside the star are more protected against the Field pres-sure, therefore expand, fuse and become highly enriched. Then they are often pushed outside, probably in the form of plasma, under increasing pressures; plasma is found to consist of fusing atoms of great energy.[11] Such "softer", enriched matter cannot withstand the normal Field pressures. As the Field starts com-pressing it, a chain-reaction excess of strength is developed by it, which produces special, *above-normal or implosive* compres-sions of the atoms.

Here we may note that all fundamental processes in the universe are chain reactions. Two equal opposites remain locked in immobility or balance, unless one side gains an advantage that sustains itself. We saw that the universal "quantum of action" is the result of oscillations in which the one opposing elastic medium accumulates advantage to highest limit before the opposite reaction starts and reaches its highest limit. What happens there on extremely small scale, under ordinary energy changes, is similar to the colossal chain reactions in the creation and annihilation of stars. The *chain-reaction principle* governs all fundamental phenomena, from fire and chemical changes to living processes and nuclear reactions, including the creation of elements.

The important fact about a chain reaction is that through it *one opposite gains a force stronger than its normal force,* and that this happens after the other opposite had reached its highest limit of strength. Schematically, in a balanced state, disturbances or events take the form of opposite swings that gain above-normal force. Anyway, when the above-normal or implosive compression by the Field acts on the atoms in the plasma, its forces are stronger than those in creation of the standard, hydrogen atoms. It "packs" atoms together while gaining from them the margins of compression or the "packing loss". Thus matter becomes slightly impoverished or is being "burned", and the more complex elements are the residue or "ashes" of such burning. This automatic tendency to "pack" together more of the atoms meets, however, with the general tendency of the Field pressures to break up larger pieces of matter. Where the two tendencies reach their full impact a middle ground is met and the more stable elements, of the middle of the element table, are created.

Nuclear reactions are started by re-creating the conditions under which the creation of the more stable elements was not completed. Matter that can be further split has to be accumulated so that the chain reaction by the Field can start. A chain-reaction "burning", whether it is fire or chemical reaction, is started by accumulation of enriched matter, though the result sought is its opposite, the violent loss of the enrichment, which then creates the heat or the desired chemical bond. Besides accumulation of enriched matter, the starting of chain reactions, in fire or chemical process, is enhanced by purification of such matter and by isolation or protection of it. In the case of nuclear reactions this is achieved by the purification of the fissionable material and by the neutron-enriched shielding. In brief, conditions of excessive matter enrichment and expansion are accumulated so that the opposite chain reaction bringing loss and compression of matter can start.

Of course this is inherently contradictory, though the same is true of creating simple fire. Expectedly, physicists seek more logical explanations. It is assumed that nucleons coming from the neutron shielding shatter nuclei and thus release more nucleons. But the first thing one learns about nuclear fission is that the neutrons should be slowed down, not accelerated. Moreover, it is hardly conceivable that a mere physical impact of any "particle" can split an atom. Why does not this happen everywhere else? Rather it is clearly evident that an intense accumulation of conditions comparable to enrichment of matter in starting a fire, is here the cause of the chain reaction as an intense opposite effect not unlike fire.

Negative particles are being increasingly discovered, as experiments on atom and nucleon shattering and "shooting" are intensified. Physicists now speculate about negative galaxies and stars, or negative matter in the "black bodies". Actually the negative "particles" are only the necessary opposite effects, in the Field, of the positive effects of matter. They are as real in their action as are matter "particles"; because the Field is as real as matter. If physicists see most effects in matter as particles, they have to find their opposites in the Field also to be particles. The "pair production", as appearance of a negative particle upon creation of a positive one, is a well-known fact and is noted as the only form of creation physicists presently know of (W. A. Fowler).[11]

Each new, more powerful cyclotron or atom smasher may

produce a new series of such effects, which have to be uniform under the same conditions or degree of force applied. Thus some two hundred new uniform particles, with their negative counterparts in most cases, have been discovered. One thinking of such effects as particles — precisely formed and regulated — has here a miracle, of nature creating and maintaining a vast array of uniform clockwork systems. Yet the Field-matter interaction is all that is needed to explain various uniform, quite complex effects, under various uniform conditions, as we saw in discussing particles.

Negative radiation is also explainable by the Field-matter interaction, under unusual conditions — opposite to those of the usual, positive radiation. Usually it is the Field as the dominant opposite that thrusts into enriched atoms and thus creates the positive radiation. But under reversed conditions, as when atoms are created, out of smaller bits of radiation quanta, the negative wave may arise. Physicists have connected negative rays with creation of new atoms. A particle springing into existence thrusts into the Field, and such thrust is carried by the absolutely "solid" yet fluid Field, which transfers the thrust further and further on, as in all radiation. Naturally, such negative rays can pass through matter much like positive rays pass through the Field. A molecule yields to the thrust of the negative ray, momentarily loses a matter quantum and compensates for it by absorbing a matter quantum from the next molecule, which does the same. Thus the negative ray is carried by matter much like the positive ray is carried by way of the "loosenings" or waves in the Field.

Whether it is "particles", radiation or other phenomena, the reality of the Field reveals itself in the symmetry of positive and negative effects, that physicists have always known to be the order of nature. Physicists are using the concepts of electromagnetism or gravitation to have some explanation for the forces, movements or other strange phenomena in galaxies or on our sun, moon and planets. This amounts to substituting one mystery for others. That is why there is so much controversy and guessing about phenomena that can be governed only by natural universal, therefore elementarily simple principles; nature does not know complex laws.

The Unseen Causes in the Living Process

Living process is a "negative fire", the opposite of the ordinary fire. It is a chain reaction by matter against the Field, just as the ordinary fire is a chain reaction by the Field against matter. In living process matter expands against the Field, by increasing in energy and richness, whereas in fire the Field expands against matter and destroys its enrichment. Scientists see that living processes resemble fire or flames, which "not only reproduce, by means of sparks, but also show metabolism and growth".[12] But scientists also recognize that life proceeds by "negative entropy", which is the exact opposite of what happens in fire. If scientists saw the Field, they would automatically recognize that, under the requirement of symmetry, evident everywhere in nature, the living process and fire are the necessary opposites.

The properties of life, as negative fire, are automatically evident from the Field-matter interaction. The Field as the dominant opposite destroys matter through fire with explosive suddenness and ease, requiring no involvement. But the living matter as the dominated, "oppressed" opposite, can proceed with its chain reactions only by circumventing the Field, in "surreptitious", *involved, endlessly delayed and extended ways.* This is what makes life enormously complex, long-lasting, extensive in all its forms, and endlessly "inventive". At the same time, life as the chain reaction expansion against the Field is ultimately of the same cosmic strength as the Field.

What is the causal source of the chain reaction of life? It is the factor that is scientifically *most evident in every living process, namely, the giant size of a living molecule.* A giant molecule can start the chain reaction against the Field, just as a spark can start fire. We shall try to explain later how a giant molecule could have arisen, but once it is there it offers protection against the pressures of the Field so that in its "shadow" other matter and energy can accumulate. This increases its power, which in turn attracts more matter and energy, in a chain-reaction way. Absorbable matter, and energy, mostly coming from the sun, is required to sustain such reaction and keep it from collapsing.

Atoms always absorb energy or matter enrichment, but under the Field pressure they immediately give up the enrichment. They can keep and accumulate the enrichment in the protective "shadow" of the giant molecule. Such enormous accumulation of enriched atoms then can evolve all kinds of forms and grow into rich formations. The "large numbers of electric charges" as well as the large size of the living molecules enable them to form "liquid crystals" that living forms are (H. Shapley).[13] Living processes realize themselves through formation of "energy-rich bonds" that are "aperiodic crystals" or protein crystals (A. I. Oparin).[14]

The difference between the nonliving molecules, forming the usual crystals or bonds, and the giant living molecule is so enormous that it amounts to a difference in their very nature. The nonliving molecules may have dozens of atoms, with a couple of electrons that can be shared, in forming bonds, whereas living molecules may have hundreds of thousands of energy-rich atoms. The DNA polymers which are considered to be the organizers of living forms may have millions of atoms. Genes may consist of single DNA and RNA polymers, and viruses are compared to incomplete genes. Yet even virus molecules may have millions of atoms; the atomic weight of tobacco mosaic virus has been found to be 17 million, and of psittacosis or parrot disease, 3.5 billion. Proteins, which are the most important, universal forms of living matter, are macromolecules that can have atomic weight of up to 10 million.[15] One can imagine what an astronomic number of combinations of bonds or "crystals" living molecules can form. The effect of this can be as inconceivably far-reaching, since millions of facets of each such "crystal" determine in their turn further formations of bonds and crystals — to the tiniest details of the whole organism.

It is clear that *the field forces of the giant, living molecules* are the source of all organic products and forms. Enzyme is a typical illustration. Scientists know that its mere presence enables the organic compounds to form — that it "merely offers a surface upon which a reaction can take place" (I. Asimov). Actually the living giant molecules offer protective fields, within which matter can accumulate, enrich itself and form the vast bonds or "crystals". Enzymes, in their turn, are formed by proteins in the same way,[15] while proteins are similarly created by the RNA and DNA polymers according to the present theories. (Proteins may have a higher role.) [15] But whatever the hierarchy, it is the protective field forces of the giant molecules that are the sources of all living processes.

Ultimately the pressures of the Field determine, with their inexorable presence, the *exact formations, as if according to strict, predetermined laws,* of all the innumerable possible combinations of atoms and molecules. The shape and force of each formation depends on the kind and number of atoms constituting it. The dominating principle is that each molecule or form "gravitates" or falls in automatically, under all the forces and counterforces, into a position where it is least exposed to the Field pressures — which offers the best equilibrium. Crystals are always formed by such automatic gravitations or adjustments under the pressures of the Field. Scientists have difficulties in understanding the dynamics of all crystallization[5] — because the pressures of the Field, which scientists never suspect, are here the causes.

But scientists see the *similarities between living forms and crystals.*[15] Sponges ground down to powder, if left in water recombine themselves into formations similar to their original forms, in the way crystals form themselves.[11] Crystals are "self-propagating" much like living matter is (P. Handler).[12]

Crystallization can explain how living matter seeks to have definite as if predetermined or planned forms. A seed of crystal immersed in a liquid selects out of it and forms into predetermined growing shapes the corresponding material in it. The living matter can do this millions of times better and more extensively, because of the giant size of its molecules and the endless far-reaching richness of their combinations. Crystallization in the usual sense is however only part of the process of predetermined orderliness of living matter. In effect, all kinds of formations and bonds of living matter grow in similar strictly ordered, "predetermined" ways because of the intense vast interaction between the pressures of the Field and the protective field forces of the living molecules, with their millions of combinations.

Thus predetermined growth and selective search for material or "food", incomparably richer than in usual crystallization, can be explained as being inherent in living matter. The evolutionary selection determines which of the forms thus evolving are more suitable for survival or more resourceful. Such selection is chaotically wasteful and requires a vast supply of new forms. But life proliferates explosively, like a veritable fire, in all kinds of forms and ways. It expands to every possible condition where energy and matter can be absorbed. This selective expansion works by the reproduction, the other main function of life besides the growth and the selective search for food.

Reproduction of living forms is an automatic outcome of the pressures of the Field acting on the accumulation of living matter. Scientists know that "a growing colloid particle may reach a point at which it becomes unstable and breaks down into smaller particles, each of which grows and reproduces".[13] Actually the unseen pressures and tendencies of the Field and living matter are the causes. The Field tries to break down any matter accumulation, but matter accumulating within the protective fields of the giant molecules tends to hold together. Under such two opposing tendencies a living formation breaks up at one point of its growth but does so by keeping as much mass together as possible.

The result is division into only two units, that hover within each other's field forces until each grows to its own full size. During such growth the two units become exactly equal, because if one is smaller it attracts more matter from the other with which it is joined. Any other dissimilarity may be equalized in the same way, between the two competing yet joint units, under the same pressures and forces. (The double helix construct offers an atomistic explanation of the reproduction by joined elements.) Further, the selection promotes only those formations that reproduce exact copies of themselves.

Here we may repeat that living forms, as nature in general, work with a multiplicity which is beyond human grasp. If we understand the above principles of growth, search for "food" and reproduction, as well as of the selection, that is all we can or need to know; we cannot understand, control or deal with the infinitely interrelated myriad complexity anyway.

The present theories about the nature and origin of life are not less conjectural than our explanations, but reveal no basic principle and are contrary to what is known about life. All the theories assume that the complexity and the principal properties of living compounds resulted from specific chance combinations, without any singular driving force or principle behind them. Even those theorists who see living process as qualitatively different from nonliving phenomena or as a "special form of motion of matter", still seek explanations in gradual evolution through various chance formations (A. I. Oparin).[14,15] A look at theories old and recent shows a mere repetition of *the belief that life evolved cumulatively and gradually by complex specific chance combinations* of the usual, nonliving matter. At the same time scientists find that life is a unique process contrary to general laws of entropy;[14] a special kind of yet undiscovered charge or potency;[11] and a singular phenomenon that remains everywhere the same.[15]

The simple clear facts we all know about life show that it is not due to merely complex, unique combinations of elements. Every one of the myriads of living forms would require such uniquely rare combination. But living forms evolve and grow in ordinary conditions, from elements found everywhere — under the cosmic force of living matter. Without a special force or principle behind it, accumulation of multiplicity and corresponding complexity of all living forms would be impossible in our physical universe governed by inexorable destruction and dispersion of any accumulated organization or enrichment of matter. The principle of selection has been used, particularly by Oparin, to hold that gradual accumulation of chance improvements could work in evolving life. In truth, any form of matter increasing in size and multiple complexity would be least fit to survive in

the world tending toward entropy and minimal organization —
unless a special force or principle promotes it.

The Field as the dominant opposite restricts the "inventive",
expanding fire of life at every step, with ubiquitous cosmic force.
This amounts to imposition of countless inexorable laws, predictable, at least theoretically, or full of predetermined, exact
"purposes", for every living form or function. Biologists have,
hopefully, turned to concepts like tropism to explain how, for
instance, roots turn downward under gravitation. But such forces,
or laws attributable to them, are only few, while the laws governing living phenomena are endless. The control by the Field
of the living matter at every point is the simple unseen source
of such endless laws or "purposes" for every minutest thing in
the living world, which otherwise has to appear a metaphysical
miracle.

Finally we have to try to explain *the origin of the spark of life,
of the giant molecule,* always found at the root of the organizing
living processes. Under ordinary conditions the Field precludes
or destroys any essential increase in particles of matter. But we
can imagine different conditions during the latest cooling off
periods of our planet. First, such cooling off is still a continuation of intense burning or yielding to the pressures of the Field.
But yielding to the Field also produces in it the momentary
loosenings, that constitute radiation. Thus the saturation of cooling off also creates saturation of loosenings in the Field. In such
saturation it may happen that the loosenings may accidentally
concentrate, at one crosspoint, to the extent of creating a spot in
which the Field pressures are momentarily absent and a giant
molecule can instantaneously accumulate. Second, a cooling off
period in its latest stages is not dominated by totally universal
burning by the Field, which would destroy any incipient living
formation. Thus there is enough ambivalence, in the slackening
chain reaction of the Field, for the opposite chain reaction
to arise.

Experiments on creation of compounds resembling living products confirm such conjectures. The apparently most efficient
recent experiments, performed by Akiba and Nurit Bar-Nun,

at the University of Cornell, are interesting; according to Carl
Sagan they open the possibility of producing amino acids on an industrial scale. Temperatures of several thousand degrees were
created, in these experiments, by shock waves, for periods so
brief that the newly formed nucleic acids were not broken up
or burned. Also interesting are probably the most advanced experiments, conducted by Gerhard Schramm, at the Max Planck
Institute in Tuebingen, in which complex nucleic acids were
produced. High heat was used in these experiments, but in such
ways that it was prevented from burning or breaking up the
new compounds.

In the frequently mentioned experiments by Dr. Sidney W.
Fox, temperatures of up to 1,900 degrees, under similar conditions, were used. Other experimenters — Oparin, Urey, Miller
and MacNevin, to mention the best known — have used electric
sparks or charges similar to lightning. This can, naturally, produce conditions of saturated loosenings in the Field, for periods
short enough to prevent burning or breaking up of the new
compounds; electric current, as we saw, always creates loosenings in the Field.

Scientists know that giant molecules are at the root of all
living processes, or that life resembles fire. But only the unseen
Field-matter interaction can explain life as the negative fire
and the giant molecule as the spark that sustains it.

Genetics: Half-Truths, "Scientism", The Unseen Causes, and the Inner Selection

Causal understanding of genetics is next in importance to
that of life itself. Modern genetics is based on the theory of unchanging hereditary characters or traits carried by unchanging
genes. This theory is half true. Maintenance of its sameness by
organism is the first law of the organic world. The relative or
opposite causation is due to the law of organic unchangeability.
Mendel's law, on which modern genetics is built, equally
derives from the unchangeability of traits or characters. In relative causation organism returns to its sameness by opposite pro-

cesses upon interference. In genetic continuance, the characters reverse back to their identity upon an interference such as cross breeding. How the unchanging or reverting characters combine in all later generations after the cross breeding is determined by an as simple probability as that of drawing combinations of white and black balls from a bag. Only because organic traits are innumerable, geneticists have to write thick books to explain by Mendel's law even remotely what happens in real inheritance.

But the organic unchangeability does not preclude possibilities of adaptive change. Only, such change is experimentally imperceptible and "scientifically" unmanageable, even illogical. It is the change induced by conditioning or by learning in its widest sense. Conditioning is an *imperceptibly gradual, "deceitful"* turning of release mechanisms away from their pathways under inducements of *general* organic drives. Conditioning can be dealt with only in such terms of *organic wholes* as drive, "pleasure", or release economy, never in terms of experimentally registrable or isolated factors separate from the whole organism. The usual "scientific" methods dealing with isolated factors, like the genes, are in general futile because of the humanly ungraspable myriad interdependence of all organic factors. This "scientism" is particularly incongruous here because *only the whole organism "learns"* or becomes conditioned — and thus adaptively changes through generations.

Furthermore, *conditioning is contradictory in its immediate experimentally registrable effects.* These effects show rather a resistance or moving away from what is being attained by conditioning. Whether it is a child being morally trained or an animal being conditioned to a food, the immediate or directly observable effect is such resistance or opposition. If one is being brought up on a diet of, let us say, beans he will reject them on every single occasion in favor of other foods. But he will end by preferring them in general, as his usual food.

The resistance or opposition is total and final if a change is imposed directly, without the "deceitful" gradual organic integration. Organism compensates by opposite adjustments for any distortion, difficulty or deprivation. Lamarckism was found disproved by Weissmanians because experiments like those on cutting off tails of mice to produce a hereditary change failed.[17] Actually, mice with cut off tails would rather produce stronger tails, if anything, in the next generation. A release flow under straight opposition breaks out a wider, stronger channel. The hybrid vigor, which has remained a mystery to biologists,[17] can be explained by such self-strengthening of organic mechanisms under reciprocal opposition between characters.

To be inherited, a character must have become a part of the whole organism, through the "deceitful" conditioning. Pavlov and McDougall, two great authorities, found in their experiments that conditioning and learning *was* transferred by inheritance. This is feasible, at least in principle, though learning by brain processes is biologically so superficial or shallow that it could hardly have any permanent effect. What can be transferred in such inheritance are deeper mechanisms deriving from essential drives changed by the conditioning.

The central issue is the *inheritance of acquired concrete, general traits* or characters It is clear to everybody that organisms acquire, through conditioning, various concrete adaptive traits in their lifetime. Organs, tissues and functions are expanded, or decreased, to cope with environment better or more purposefully. Such purposeful adaptations are maintained even through several renewals of cells and of almost everything else in the organism. Apparently, deeper organizing mechanisms have changed. There is no reason why such change could not go as deep as the very centers of organization, which reproduce themselves and determine inheritance. In the organic hierarchical integration, influences always proceed through all levels, except that they become *imperceptibly slight on the deepest levels.* Evolution reveals exactly such exceedingly minute, experimentally unregistrable adaptive changes; and their inheritance is required by the genial theory of Darwin.

But modern science is dominated by experimentalism, and experiments can show only the above reversals and unchangeability of isolated traits, which is the basis of the modern, Mendelian genetics. A modern scientist would have to be crazy to oppose evidence from experiments. The tyranny of a discipline of half-truths thus perpetuates itself.

In effect, to see the other half of the causal facts the recognition of the unseen interaction between the Field and matter would be required. As we saw, living forms, comparable to crystals, are determined by the fields of forces of living matter which is the center and source of such fields. Thus there is always the center-and-field interaction, even if it is ungraspably complex. Viewed as one whole the organism is determined by a genetic center of matter through its fields, however complex or dispersed such center may be. The stronger the center in some facet, the more effective the corresponding organic function or form organized by its field of forces.

What is more, *the center-and-field interaction is reciprocal.* The strength of a field of forces if it happens to be increased, by advantages in environment, correspondingly increases the strength of the center. Generally, a greater accumulation of living matter increases its field of forces; but a stronger or wider field permits larger accumulation of matter. Such two-way influences can be observed in any interaction between matter as center and its field forces. In electromagnetism, increased charge in a body strengthens the field around it; but strengthened field around body increases its charge. In burning, a greater initial size of fire at a given spot intensifies the conditions of combustion there; but, also, more intense conditions of combustion, like heat, dry air or burnable material increase the size of the fire.

For an organism the strengthening or advantages of the field are ultimately those of the external environment or conditioning. But they reach the determining center of the organism only through innumerous levels. For each such level the "environment" or conditioning medium is the next more external level. That is how the acquired traits reach the genetic center that determines the whole organism. Because this center is so deeply hidden under the uncountable levels of millions of years of the evolution of the given species, the changes induced in it by the environment or conditioning can be only imperceptibly slight. Yet however infinitesimal or humanly imperceptible the changes, absolutely every one of the endless environmental influences leaves its corresponding effect.

This is how the adaptation to environment can be so gradual as well as purposeful to every tiniest, humanly inconceivable detail. It is attained by myriad additions, through millions of years, of repetitive influences that leave their averagely streamlining infinitesimal effects, like sandstorms polishing the cliffs. All purposefulness in such environment-to-center influences is automatic because the influences proceed on exactly the same lines both ways, and strict purposefulness of every line of influence from the center toward environment is established by selective adaptation. Schematically, the complex organs of vision of a crab, evolved purposively under stimulations of light, weaken or strengthen correspondingly in response to simple decrease or increase in such stimulations.

The possibility of this *"backward" action or reverse transcription* agrees with recent experimental findings, e.g., on the "reverse transcriptase", particularly by Howard Temin, who proved that RNA can organize DNA; and by Sol Spiegelman, who demonstrated similar reverse action for a dozen viruses. Two-way influence between nucleus and cytoplasm has always been viewed as a central principle.[15] But any form of reverse transcription is totally impossible according to modern genetics, which recognizes only the unchanging genes as bearers of traits. Of course there are disagreements. Scientists may find that cytoplasmic inheritance is equally significant,[18] or that bacterial adaptation to abnormal and again back to normal environment points to adaptive inheritance[12] and "makes possible the mechanism of evolution" in the only way it makes sense.[16] The Darwinian evolution is by far the greatest, simple discovery in biological sciences and their only possible basis, but it makes no sense without the inheritance of acquired characters.[16,19,20]

Unfortunately Darwin chose to explain the inheritance of acquired characters in the atomistic or usual "scientific" way. In his theory of pangenesis, he reasoned that each cell in the organism releases gemmules that form the reproductive cells.[17] Surely the whole organism forms the reproductive cells. *Anything that happens in an organism is a product by everything else in it as a whole.* This is what makes the "scientism", dealing only with distinct separate units, useless in study of organisms. Evidently the reproductive cells are the centers of organization of the future organisms; they are replicas of the center of organization of the parent organism.

But *such center can be, and is, present in the organism everywhere, dispersed and involved in every mechanism. Yet it can still act as a true, single center* to which every influence flows and from which all organization emanates, including its own reproduction in millions of replicas. The principles by which nature works here, as elsewhere, are simple: the interaction between the center and the organism as elaboration of the field forces; and the mere replication. But because nature does its simple work, in organism, with *interdependent astronomic* multiplicity, the atomistic scientism can never explain what really happens.

The glaring proof of adaptive inheritance is the whole body of findings of biological history. Every living form has evolved gradually and has been *shaped by nothing else but environment* so as to suit it. Gradually transitional adaptive forms, with all the incipient rudiments and persisting vestiges, constitute everything that is found in biological history. Selection merely eliminates the forms which do not adapt. It is absolutely impossible that the *disruptive* and *sudden* genetic changes through gene mutations could produce this adaptive gradualness. The whale, with its vestiges of a land mammal, is only one example of how environment has shaped organisms. Many mammals, porpoises, seals, manatees, various reptiles, and even penguins to a degree, have been shaped into "fishes" by the sea. The wings of birds, bats and butterflies have been shaped by the flying, into best adapted almost uniquely similar shapes in spite of total genetic dissimilarity of the species.

Purposive adaptation and gradualness of development govern every observable living form and every known instance of evolution. It is always the way a foot, flipper, hand, eye or any organ is used that determines how it is shaped, to serve the purpose with admirable perfection. This is well illustrated by the evolutionary transition of forms, everywhere, from crude, rudimentary beginnings, of older geologically recorded samples, to skillful adaptive purposefulness in every minutest detail, gradually accumulated through millions of years. One might compare the adaptive gradualness of evolutionary forms with the gradual shaping of a kneeling stone by its use or the purposeful age-long "engineering" of a river valley. Scientists may characterize the genetic evolution as a change with "definite direction or consistent 'upward' trend".[20] We saw that the cause of such minutely gradual, streamlined adaptation, comparable to sandstorms shaping a cliff, is the simple "backward" action of environmental influences through the reverse transcription.

The gradualness of adaptation as a mere elaboration of the previous mechanisms is the only way the miracles of nature can be explained. Only by absolute conservation, at every step, of the previous purposes, ultimately going back to growth and division, can the astronomic final purposefulness be explained. The organism or the beehive *can be so complex yet so purposeful because each of its endless million-year elaborations is only an expansion of some previous purposeful mechanism.* The gradualness or continuity is so inherent in organic development that evolutionary forms are even repeated during embryo growth. Anyway, the whole adaptive and gradual evolution, that scientists have always known, is a complete proof against the tenets of modern genetics.

Such purposive adaptation and gradualness of evolution are *exactly contrary to the disruptive and sudden mutations* that are the only assumed factors of change in modern genetics. The mutations are totally accidental disruptions of genes, by radiation, heat, shock or other physical and chemical abnormal conditions. Geneticists themselves recognize that mutations are destructive rather than constructive.[18] The only constructive factor, for the modern geneticist, is then a disruption that might happen to be adaptive. Here we have to emphasize how impossible such theory is and how the geneticists, in their atomistic "scientism", have overlooked glaring facts about it.

Organisms consist of trillions of cells and molecules, and every one of them is in a unique arrangement with the rest, in the one-and-only way of purposive integration—each to be governed by a corresponding "gene". To be purposive, every change in one of the cells, molecules or "genes" would have to be coordinated with the trillions of the rest of them. Therefore the probability of this happening by pure chance would be one in trillions of times. But even if we assume that there could be one adaptive chance mutation in every thousand, this still would produce only a total chaos in organic forms, if they depended on such mutations.

A look at the streamlined smoothness of a hand, eye, heart or any living form shows that all the billions of cells and molecules in it are arranged adaptively *without any* nonstreamlined, unadaptive, or out-of-place formations. The same applies to any organic function, and necessarily to the genetic factors which determine the organic forms and functions. Now, if there were a thousand unadaptive mutant changes for every adaptive one, *they would inevitably accumulate in every organic form and function, even while the one adaptive gene change was added.* If the gene mutations were the way evolution worked, it would amass deformations or deteriorations at least at the rate of billions for every one improvement. Even at a rate of thousand to one, complete deterioration would take over, since any abnormal mutant change sticks out like a sore thumb among all possible amounts of improvements.[20] The way evolution must be working is a selective total exclusion of any chance mutations in genetic factors.

Geneticists resort to speculations about selection to save the theory of chance mutations. Selection does work by chance influences, that promote the fittest forms — ultimately conditioned, gradual adaptations, even in the cases of sudden organic changes. But there is never any fitter form to be promoted if massive deterioration is heaped on for every one possible improvement. Selection can prevent total destruction of species rather by promoting organic forms that are immune to such ways of "improvements" as the gene mutations. The fallacy of geneticists lies in their "scientific" attitude of ignoring the virtually infinite interdependent multiplicity of organic factors. Definite numbers of possible improvements are speculated about while the endless numbers of possible deteriorations are not thought of.

The atomistic scientific methods of geneticists are misleading in every respect because *organic forms work only as wholes of reciprocally dependent myriads of factors*. Thus geneticists, pursuing single genes, do not realize that absolutely every one of the myriads of cells and processes has to find its purposeful adjustment. Taking this purposefulness for granted is equal to missing the very core of the problem. There are, supposedly, seven octillion atoms and ten trillion cells in man;[18] and genes are recognized as the regulators of everything in organism.[18] Consequently, there should be at least as many genes in man, because every atom will fall chaotically rather than purposefully in place unless a gene — or, necessarily, more than one gene — determines its exact action.

In modern genetics, governed by experimentalism, genes are assumed only for those characters which can be experimentally shown to follow the Mendel's law. This can happen only with the characters that exist in allelic forms or can undergo the Mendelian mutations. If all men had blue eyes there would be no Mendelian gene of eye color.[18] Nor can there be such a gene for a character like the backbone in vertebrates, which never mutates. But exactly such characters, infinitely many, gross or submicroscopic, are decisively important. The characters, simply, *turn infinite in number* if one starts separating them, as a correct experimental method would require; and each of them must be determined by genes, in its one and only possible purposeful performance.

Who, what or how, created the trillions or octillions of genes in the first place? Nature can create astronomic purposeful multiplicity, but then it must have a purposeful principle, however simple, to work by. Such principle is the "backward" action of environmental influences, that we explained above. We admit, geneticists have discovered a few phenomena, like the chromosome rearrangements, breakages, polyploidy, genetic drifts and other kinds of genetic interactions, which seem to permit selective evolution in ways explainable by the theory of unchanging genes.[17,18] But in all these phenomena the adaptive characters are already there and the changes involve their mere recombinations. As to the original evolution of the innumerable characters, the "mutations are the ultimate source of all variability",[17] according to modern genetics; and mutations are chaotic disruptions that can only destroy adaptation.

The main, typical fallacy of "scientism" in modern genetics is *the concept of the gene itself* as a separate unchanging atom of inheritance. The present "scientific" methods permit dealing only with analytically clearly delineated units or atoms. Unfortunately, in the organic world nothing but the wholes determine what happens, while their constituting units can explain as little as dead atoms. That is why organic causation can be understood only through concepts of organically integrated phenomena like over-all drives or pleasures, conditioning, adaptation, release, overadjustments, opposite reactions or return to previous traits, and preservation of the genetic self.

What scientists have discovered about genes, like the gene maps or enzyme effects of assumed genes, is fully explainable by the natural fact that a *major part of a genetic material* connectable with a character or process may be, expectedly, located on one spot in the chromosome or in one strand of DNA. This is causally very different from existence of separate genes. In a chromosome as in an organism, factors for a certain process, like eating, may be centered around one spot, like the mouth. But mouth as an isolated unit cannot organically exist and would be causally incomprehensible.

Geneticists themselves recognize that "talking about traits as though they were independent entities is responsible for much confusion" (T. Dobzhansky).[18] Modern genetics is, however, built on the separation of traits or characters as units determined by genes as separate atoms. If, instead, the wholes of genetic traits, and of "genes", were seen as determining, then the over-all drives, conditioning, adaptation, or the return of the genetic self to its sameness would be the concepts used. This could make genetics more than a discipline of half-truths, and explain the Mendel's law as well.

The all-important *practical fallacy of modern genetics* is that according to its theory it does not matter genetically how generations live, adjust, overadjust, "sin", become conditioned, "learn", improve or degenerate. The "genes" are never affected by life influences and change only through the mutations caused by physical and chemical accidents. This experimentally established half-truth is, of course, contrary to practical facts, common sense wisdom and tradition, as well as to scientific knowledge about evolution, practical breeding and the newest findings on the reverse transcription.

If the whole organism can be determined to its tiniest details by the reproductive cell, it is much more conceivable that the vast organic system and its influences can affect the genetic core. Scientifically, the genetic self which acts as the core or center of the organism continues through generations, by reproducing itself in the reproductive cells. The generations are periods in the life of the genetic self and necessarily leave their influences, particularly from overadjustments or degenerative life-long enjoyments, eagerly increased by man.

Functional, degenerative diseases, like cancer, have been traced to inheritable chromosomal or gene abnormalcies, which can be acquired during life, especially through chemical and artificial life-long "improvements". It is significant that scientists working on cancer research have seen the importance of environmental influences on inheritance and their "backward" action, through the reverse transcription. Practically important problems, in the promotion of the health and potentials of our next generations, will depend on management of genetic changes. But modern geneticists have renounced here, in principle, any control or planning. They only can wait for the disruptive accidents, like the mutations from cosmic rays, to become the sources of change, though geneticists also fear increase in such mutations, more than anything else. Even the enthusiasts of modern genetics admit that it has remained "a pure rather than applied science".[21]

Modern geneticists cannot do much more than dwell on the combinations of existing genes, or "explain", after the fact, how the genes supposedly mutated, which by definition is unpredictable and uncontrollable. Genetics has become a vast science, as it continues to demonstrate the law of the permanence of characters in their naturally endless multiplicity. But such law, deriving from the *permanence of organic sameness, needs neither proof nor demonstration.* The rest of genetics consists of patching up its own assumptions, since the half truths become less and less sufficient when final explanations have to be found. Complexity increases, as the geneticists have to resort to postulating all kinds of special causal factors, like suppressors, inhibitors, modifying, complementary, supplementary or "certain elusive" factors, and unpredictable, multiple effects or genes.[21]

Of course when scientists have to obtain practical results or to explain why and how a species has evolved its characters, they proceed as practical breeders and evolutionists have always done. They try to obtain new, better, *changed traits;* and they accept *adaptations to the needs of environment as the explanations* of any observed trait or capacity of a species. In practical breeding, and in evolution, the combination of traits by cross-breeding, as by all sexual reproduction, is the primary, easy way of improving the stock. But mere recombination of characters cannot create the new, completely different permanent traits, that evolution and practical breeders obtain and use besides the mere combinations of existing characters.

The classical experiments by Johannsen,[18] the inventor of the gene concept, are accepted as proving that "artificial selection can do nothing but disentangle a mixture of variations and that a continual elaboration of a character as it was postulated by Darwin is impossible".[13] But new permanent improved characters do evolve, actually in myriads, on all, even tiniest levels, and with the gradual or continual adaptive "upward" trend that the Darwinian evolution requires. Mere recombination of genes could not bring this about. Nature could have only few and crude genes. If they can merely combine and have to segregate, forever unchanged, this can never result in new better characters — particularly since the mutations can bring only more deterioration.

Now we may explain what we have called the **Inner Selection**. The evolutionary selection as usually conceived is so grossly incomplete that people with good common sense may see in it only possibilities of chaos. It implies that at every improvement in a species all its members perish except the one who has the improvement, and his progenes. But as we saw, *virtually infinite* numbers of tiny changes have to accumulate with such multiplicity that they seem continuous; and each of them can evolve only through selection. Members of species could not be perishing all but one at every one of such *infinitely numerous* changes. Gross, sudden changes can play part in selection, in the all-but-one way. Still, even such changes require infinite, tiny adaptations, to become viable. Darwin rightly saw that evolution is not determined by "sports" or sudden deviations, but is a gradual product of mass selection.

The endless improvements, on all levels, with infinite forms of transition, can be provided only by the Inner Selection, in which *every tiniest form inside the organism improves automatically by the same principle of selection*. Schematically, every mechanism or release follows and deepens, automatically, the channel that offers better, stronger flow. The only additional principle needed, to integrate such tendencies organically, is that of subordination. The lower processes, though they automatically self-increase, must stop doing so whenever this does not increase the higher process they are subordinated to. As we saw such a principle of subordination can work in simple, natural ways. It certainly is an observable fact in the organism. Only because of the multiplicity of levels in organism we cannot visualize or "understand" how it works in detail.

We can be sure, however, that if every mechanism automatically self-improves, in such a way as to permit the equally automatic self-improvement of higher mechanisms and thus of the whole, then integrated adaptive progress is inevitable. The automatism of the self-improvement is insured by the principle of selection, the Inner Selection, as the processes which find or deepen better channels of release or growth expand, eliminating the others. Of course restrictive processes soon become dominant because they offer richer release potentials on the whole. *Nature, working with astronomic multiplicity, can create astronomically complex, seemingly miraculous purposefulness if the simple principles by which it works are purposeful or adaptive.* The "backward" action of the environmental influences and the Inner Selection are such principles. They are sufficient to create the virtual miracles of nature, by way of blind, chaotic selection or opposition.

The ultimate fallacy of modern genetics is its experimentally "scientific" attitude. Experiments can reveal only the permanence of genetic traits, as predicted by Mendel's law. The cause of this permanence is the maintenance of its sameness by every organic form. All organic laws, including the relative causation, derive from this maintenance of sameness. But this principle does not preclude adaptive changes. Only such changes are imperceptible and paradoxical. They affect *endlessly gradually the organism as a whole; show initially as opposite reactions; and "require "deceitful" conditioning of over-all drives, like pleasure, of the organism as the whole.* The atomistic and directly logical experimental approaches can never reveal such changes.

Thus genetics is left with one half of the insights and misses the other which is the only one that offers possibilities of genetic change, control or planning, in preventing degenerative influences, or in finding guidance for our genetic future.

Conclusion

The relative view reveals everywhere the never recognized negative causal sources of positive values. A physicist adopting a relative view would see at once that the "nothingness", which alone can make matter knowable or existent for man, is the causal source of matter and its effects. As the ultimate source of all effects of matter, and as its opposite, the "nothingness" or the Field cannot be known or even experimentally registered, otherwise than through the ordinary effects of matter, even if it is a million times stronger or denser than any substance. An object moved by a medium experiences no resistance or drag against it; and all effects of matter are moves or "shifts" of it by the Field — in forms of waves which cannot exist without a medium. No assumption of new forces or hypotheses, but merely an objective, relative view is required to see the reality of the Field.

Physicists have always recognized the concrete reality of the causal medium, in the forms of Ether, fields or "space". Such concepts, though, are incongruous without the above relative insight that the medium can be so enormously dense or strong yet experimentally unregistrable. This insight is the simple contribution of our relative approach, but expert physicists could reach revolutionary explanations — far superior to those we attempted — with a concept of such a medium. The present physics, missing the very cause of its phenomena, has resorted to a philosophy of a world without causes or certainty, even without reality, governed by indeterminacy, the double-truth complementarity and merely mathematical or mental causes. This philosophy of physics as the most certain science has been readily accepted in all fields. The modern sciences, thought and learning thus are sinking deeper into metaphysical sophistry, mystery and esoteric self-justifications, permitting all the eagerly sought humanistic or philosophical delusions and mystifications.

Once the real causal sources of matter and its effects are recognized, the dilemmas and mysteries become explainable for all material phenomena, in physics, theory of life or genetics. Similarity between life and fire has been observed in science as well as in common knowledge. All properties of life as negative fire become automatically clear if the Field is recognized. Life as "fire" or chain reaction by matter against the Field, the dominant opposite, becomes a delayed or extended and refined process, "inventively" complex and resourceful in its selective expansion amidst obstacles.

Further, the action of living matter through its field forces explains how the genetic matter as the center, and the environment or conditioning as the modifier of its field forces, interact both ways. This makes possible the "backward" action, through reverse transcriptions, of influences from environment or from acquired adaptive traits toward the genetic self — which is the only way the astronomically multiple and detailed, miraculous natural purposefulness can evolve.

In dealing with the Field, we have extended the "impossible" relative view to the very first value of man's world, the physical Reality itself. We therefore expect the causal world we discovered to be contrary to the common sense we all share. The Field is still a "nothingness", if only because it is the opposite of matter. But scientifically or objectively the Field is real and universally revealing, as the causal source of the physical reality.

IX

HUMANISTIC DELUSIONS IN PHILOSOPHY, ARTS AND CULTURE

The humanistic value delusions dominate all learned thinking, artistic cults and cultural fixations. These delusions are inevitable as long as it is not understood that the real sources of value experiences are their opposites, their negative backgrounds which are felt as disvalues. Even thinking or knowledge is a value process, however refined and complex its forms. It is governed by the dependence of the cognitive values or satisfactions on opposite backgrounds or needs. Philosophy as pursuit of pure and complete cognitive satisfactions, without their opposites, becomes a futile, self-defeating perfectionism, comparable to what neuroses are on emotional level.

Artistic enjoyments become superstitious cults, adoration of smears of paint or religion of names and true originals, because the delusory and fixational nature of such value enjoyments is not suspected. For the same reasons cultures become vast fixational systems, governed by accidental, inherently worthless fixations, while the real, paradoxical, and universal, therefore unremarkable causal sources of culture are missed. We admit that *nothing is simple, or attainable in logically reasoned ways in culture and cultural conditioning.* The philosophical, artistic and cultural delusions and fixations often are a necessary, intricate part of the superstitions and deceit by which we are culturally conditioned. But the danger from the totally wrong causal beliefs increases as the humanists themselves turn away from the restrictive, necessarily deceitful, cultural tradition and toward a scientific, logical application of their beliefs.

431

Philosophy as Self-Defeating Perfectionism

Philosophy is a pursuit of perfect, pure and complete knowledge or of understanding of things in themselves. This is what distinguishes philosophy from other knowledge. In practical or scientific knowledge we merely have problems or needs for solutions, under given premises, and we find the corresponding, delimited satisfactions. The philosophical method of searching for complete cognitive satisfactions in themselves is what makes philosophy inherently impossible and turns it into a cognitive "neurosis". The satisfaction here, much as in a neurosis, seems to lie just ahead. But without further negative, opposite backgrounds or premises and needs to know, no real satisfaction or knowledge is reached. As the futile effort is intensified, it leads to endless complexity, which has become the main attainment of philosophy and resembles the endless elaborations in neuroses.

All cognition is a value process, rooted in the mechanisms of need-satisfaction or of disturbance and restoration of normalcy. It could be viewed as a matching of innumerable minute needs or disturbances with corresponding satisfactions and organic standards; or as evaluation of countless tiny changes in previously established extensive sets of values. Change is the source of all values or valuations, but change must be relevant or correspond to the organic, always relative values, from which it derives its conscious meaning. Thus cognition as all evaluation can be only a process of relating — *a relative comparison or differentiation.*

Against this, we have the *philosophical method* of striving for pure and perfect cognition, complete in itself, without dependence on any different, opposite, negative backgrounds or premises. We may best discuss this method under three main qualities of knowledge that philosophy seeks, namely, perfection, highest value and finality. The perfection is attained when everything can be explained by one term and in itself, without a need to refer to anything else. The highest truths or values have to be explained and justified in philosophy as a pursuit of perfect cognitive satisfaction. Finality is required because complete cognitive satisfaction is not gained if knowledge is unfinished or relative.

Search for Perfect Knowledge in Philosophy. All philosophies have tried to explain everything by some one essence, or by terms reducible to one essence. This is inevitable in the search for perfect cognitive satisfaction. Man exists as one organism, and he thinks the way he exists. He tries to reduce everything to terms of "ones" or to generalized "things". The ultimate, most satisfactory reduction or generalization would be reached if everything was explained by one term, one essence, in itself, without a need to refer to further, multiple terms. Consequently philosophers have tried *to explain the whole world by some one essence like the Being; or by concepts like Atoms or Forms, that are mere multiplications of one essence.*

Thus at the very beginnings of Western philosophy, Thales proclaimed water as the stuff of which everything is made; Anaximander postulated the Boundless; and Anaximenes held that air, vapor or mist is the source of everything. To solve the problem of change Heraclitus declared constant flux as the essence of things and fire as the stuff of which everything consists. Eleatics postulated one Being as the essence of all reality; Plato, the world of Forms; Aristotle, the Substance; Pythagoreans, the Number; Neoplatonists and Medieval philosophers, one God; Descartes, God as source of Mind and Matter; Spinoza, Substance; Leibniz, the world of Monads; Kant, the world of Things-in-themselves; Fichte, a self-determining Ego; Schelling, an Absolute; Hegel, the Idea; Schopenhauer, the Will; Hartmann, the Unconscious; Green, the Universal Consciousness; Bergson, Elan Vital; Alexander, Space-Time.[1,3]

But reduction of everything to one single unchanging essence leads to patent impossibility. In a typical case, Eleatics postulated that everything is one Being, therefore there could be no variety, change, origin, causation or motion. Variety would exclude the oneness of being; change or origin would imply degrees of being, or the nonbeing which is impossible; and motion would require empty space, which too is a nonbeing, therefore unthinkable. To account for multiplicity of phenomena philosophers have postulated some one essence in multiple forms: Atoms (Democritus), Roots (Empedocles), Seeds (Anaxagoras), Ideas or Forms (Plato), Monads (Leibniz), Reals (Herbart), Presentations (Renouvier), Ideas-Forces (Boutroux).[1,3]

Particularly the use of the Universals is frequent in philosophies. Such universals as the Platonic Ideas or Forms are often resorted to, even in modern philosophies, because this offers an easy way out of difficulties. The real, ever changing and multiple world does not comply with the world of ideas of philosophers. The solution is to accept the ideas or generalizations themselves as the realities. Anyway, even modern philosophers have postulated universals, Forms or Ideas as explanations. Whitehead assumed eternal objects as the Forms for the actual entities of the real world. Russell had universal "data" inherent in objects, and value universals like goodness or beauty. Santayana had a theory of essences that represent general characteristics and qualities of objects. Husserl, the founder of modern phenomenology, assumed essences, like roundness, existing apart from individual minds. The point is that the reduction of reality to some one essence, idea or universal is the inevitable part of philosophy. Universals have been long proven, by nominalists, to be only constructs of mind, yet have been resorted to throughout philosophy.[3]

In the end, the perfect philosophical explanations are short-sighted delusions. Nothing can be known in itself, and understanding or knowledge is gained only through relation or differentiation of something with something else. The philosopher gets away with his explanations because he makes his last terms so sublime, eternal, or holy that further questioning is precluded. But explaining the reality by, say, Idea only leads to a further problem of explaining the Idea; and if it is explained by, say, Spirit, then this has to be explained in its turn.

Surely, in all knowledge we explain and know the world by reducing it to "ones" or "things". We have such things as "life" or "thought". But we know that the "things" are only abbreviations or signs and that no such concrete thing as life or thought exists. Yet for philosophers exactly such inherently fictitious things, like Being, Idea, Mind, Consciousness, Reason, Beauty, Spirit, or Space-Time, become the ultimate essences. And such concepts are accepted in their direct logical meanings, whereas they derive causally from their value opposites.

In any event, the static "things", the essences, forms or universals can never account for the endless multiplicity and flux of reality. It may seem very satisfactory to explain all horses as copies of the Platonic form for a horse. But every horse is different in its molecular details, and these are as real as the horse itself, therefore must have forms of their own. Moreover, every real thing changing, moving, persisting in time, is different at every moment. The Aristotelian potentialities may seem to offer nice explanations: acorn becomes oak tree, or stone a statue, by virtue of its potentiality. But at every stage or moment the tree or statue is different yet as real as at the stage the philosopher had in mind. Typically, philosophers may have forms or monads for lions, mountains or temples, but not for vermin, garbage or mousetraps, though these are equally real.

Even the most ambitious philosophical efforts help little. To explain the reality we experience, Whitehead had to invest his actual entities with prehension and feeling,[2] turning them into organisms with higher, even super-human qualities.[3] Similarly Leibniz invested each monad with capacities to comprehend all other monads in all their destinies to the end of time. But even such a fantastic world of superhuman capacities for every fly or grain of sand leads to no explanation. Absolutely every detail or change in our world would have to be covered by a monad, or actual entity and eternal object. This amounts to postulating an as complex causal source of monads as is our world they determine; and such source requires a still further equally complex source.

In brief, the perfect knowledge in itself that philosophy strives for is inherently impossible. Knowledge is a value process of differentiating or relating something with something else, actually opposite to it. From Aristotle's explanations of logic to Goedel's theorem of knowledge, it has been known that every proposition or set of premises contains its own contradictions or paradox, requiring a further set of premises.[5] In the words of Whitehead, "natural knowledge is exclusively concerned with relatedness [and] there is always the background of presuppositions which defies analysis by reason of infinitude".[2] No knowledge, as satisfaction or value, is possible in itself, without its opposite. In the end, "certainty is an illegitimate concept"[5] and "exactness is a fake",[2] in philosophical terms.

Search for Values in Philosophy. Philosophy as the quest for perfect satisfaction, on the cognitive level, has to find and justify the highest human values. The most frequently invoked philosophical essences like Beauty, Love, Harmony, Reason, Mind, Universal Consciousness, Intelligence or Purpose are value concepts. Of course philosophers, particularly of the early periods, have rationalized that they have arrived at the values as the highest essences by way of strict reasoning. Philosophy is the most exalted of human rationalizations.

The Greek and Roman philosophers argued that virtues were the essence of human soul, therefore could give men true happiness.[4] Socrates, supposedly, taught everybody the truths of reason to make men virtuous. Plato had highest Forms for values and virtues, like Justice or Courage, with the Form of the Good at the top. He demonstrated that the souls of men possess all the virtuous insights, and that men do not follow them only because of a blindness due to life in darkness, like that of men living in a cave. Plato, who created the image of Socrates for us, thus shared his naivete. Life showed that the light of reason, offered by Socrates, corrupted the youth instead of making them virtuous. Athenians were very tolerant in matters of ideas, but a stubborn rationalist can become a morally dangerous pest. (Heinous crimes and hateful violence have been committed in the name of reason and "universal" values.) The general Aristotelian doctrine, of the golden mean, amounts to an equally naive value theory: whatever the Athenians considered as right, as not being extreme, was to become a universal truth. Most of the early philosophies, Epicureanism, Stoicism, or even cynicism and skepticism, were primarily concerned with values of life, or with absence of values.[1]

Finally the Neoplatonists, though followers of Plato and Aristotle, established the beliefs that were to become the system of the Christian values. St. Augustine said that Plotinus would have had to change only a few words to become a Christian.[3] Even the doctrines of trinity and of the supremacy of faith are already found in the Neo-Platonism.[1,3] This confirms that even the teachings claimed to be new sacred revelations grow from the general value beliefs of their era. Of course in the Middle Ages philosophies only served to support the Christian value system.

Probably the clearest evidence of the dominance of value outlook in philosophy is the unfailing acceptance by philosophers of the beliefs or cultural values of their time, though the simplest observer, coming from a different culture, could have seen the fixational distortions. Aristotle found that slavery was not only normal but was required by the essence of ultimate potentialities. Plato earnestly discussed and accepted ghosts and human-like gods. Sophists and cynics who tried to break out of the cultural and subjective preconceptions were never taken seriously. The medieval and early modern philosophers always managed to find ultimate truths consistent with the Christian beliefs. Even the early British empiricists did not dare to leave out God as the source of certainty in their uncertain world. Finally, in our times nonconformism has become the fashion — a new value attitude. The modern, nonconformist and existential philosophies are value-oriented to the point of becoming emotionally determined.

Openly admitted abandonment of reason in favor of value insights began early in modern philosophy. The monumental criticism of reason by Kant marked the new modern era. He turned to practical reason or morals, which are exclusively governed by conditioned value feelings. After Kant, values became increasingly the criteria of truth. Fichte and Schelling saw the ultimate truths in the feelings of ethical self and sense of beauty.[4] The rising romanticism and idealism turned to similar emotional and value concepts. Post-Kantian philosophies, of Eucken, Lotze,

Windelband or Rickert, stressed ethical, religious, and other pure value experiences.[4] Schopenhauer's Will, Nietzsche's Will to Power, Bergson's Elan Vital or Croce's Spirit are emotionally or intuitively discovered realities.

The most modern philosophical trends — pragmatism, logical empiricism, positivism or existentialism — and the eclectic modern approaches, by philosophers like William James, Dewey, Santayana, Whitehead, Russell or Hocking, have accepted practical success, common logic, science, literature, esthetics, emotion, intuition, instinct, or any experience as equally good sources of truth. Reason, on which all philosophy should be naturally based, has been found insufficient and been supplanted by intuition (Bergson), immediacy of feeling (Bradley), "loyalty" (Royce) or even "animal faith" (Santayana).[3,4]

In brief, values and value experiences have always been accepted as sources of truths in philosophy, rather increasingly so in modern philosophies. We do not need to repeat that value convictions show as causally true the exact opposite of what is so in reality. Particularly forms of knowledge like intuition or immediacy of feeling are misleading. They are closest to natural satisfactions which can arise only from their opposites, the needs.

The worst are the increasingly prevalent modern philosophical approaches like existentialism which seek truths in emotional, "existential", literary, religious or other direct value experiences. Existentialism is the strongest modern philosophical movement. The central themes of existentialists are anxiety, dread, despair, abandonment, futility or senselessness. These preoccupations only reveal that existentialists are the typical, pampered modern individuals. Such excessive sense of the negative emotions cannot arise without as excessive opposite emotional backgrounds or expectations. Overprotected children find the world full of dread and anxiety. Existentialism is more interesting for psychological case study than for discovering ultimate truths.

All men feel deeply that there must be some sense in our existence, that it all can not be a senseless absurdity, a pointless joke. Absurdity or pointlessness would, certainly, be unexplainable. Its very presence would imply requirement of sense and purpose. But the problem would not even arise if thinking was free of value feelings. The central fact is that values are contradictions in themselves, arising from their opposites and the contradictory part of human existence. Man should have learned by now that in value terms his world is a meaningless speck of dust in the universe. True, the consciousness or intellect may be of a different order of greatness. But the value delusions and value feelings are obstacles and lowest forms in the work and evolution of intellect.

A series of philosophical fallacies results from the fact that value approaches show phenomena in their *last "purposefully" adjusted phases.* Particularly the *mind* has gradually evolved vast systems of purposeful adjustments. In his struggle to comprehend and deal with the adverse aspects of the world, man has accumulated, through ages, the learning, ideas, concepts, language, mathematics, disciplines of thought and ways of thinking, that constitute an ungraspably vast yet purposeful world of mind. Such elaborations, seen as reflecting perfection and values, are not evolved in the really perfect adjustments, like our never-failing instinctive drives. Also, the functioning of the mind is unfathomable in its multiple complexity, as all living processes are. Moreover, mind cannot understand itself, much as the hand cannot grasp itself. The final reality of consciousness or the ultimate meaning of meaning has to remain inherent mystery because last terms that cannot be related to something else can, simply, not be understood.

For all these reasons, the world of *mind when viewed at any given last stage* of its adjustment looks like a transcendental, incomprehensible and purposeful miracle. Here man first adjusts everything purposefully, through ages, then turns around as a philosopher and wonders that everything is so miraculously adjusted. However sophisticated the philosopher, he cannot help falling into this error, inherent in the value outlook, which inevitably impresses the last-phase purposefulness.

Thus the seemingly miraculous — selectively evolved — capacity of mind to grasp the world is seen as proof that nature and

mind have the same matrix, therefore emanate from a higher
Mind. This has become the basis of quite modern idealistic philosophies. For the old philosophers such an ordinary fact as our
capacity to understand the world did not seem worth deep
thoughts. Also, the incomprehensible, complex mind was simply
accepted as a supernatural entity or soul; even quite modern
philosophers, like Lotze, Fechner or Wundt, have postulated a
soul.[4] The more sophisticated speculations, by Neo-Hegelians or
Neo-Idealistis, stress the affinity between mind and nature inferred from the above capacity of mind to understand nature.
Universal consciousness was postulated by Green because he
found that knowledge of nature would be impossible without a
unifying spiritual principle. Bradley demonstrated that mere
phenomena are contradictory and that a unifying transcendental
principle is required as the ultimate source of cognition. Royce
held that an all-inclusive consciousness was necessary in a world
that he found to be "rational, orderly and in essence intelligible".[3,4]

This delusion of seemingly inherent affinity between mind and
nature underlies the systems of the best known modern philosophers — Croce, Gentile, Renouvier, James, Santayana or Whitehead — as well as of all idealists including Hegel. According to
Hegel the Absolute, Nature and man's mind work in the same
way.[3] In the naive, early, Platonic idealism, the concepts taken
from the mental activity became the eternal Ideas or Forms of
the supranatural, and natural world. All universals are such concepts viewed as eternal realities.

The argument that the reality may be only in our minds is
the most general defense of philosophizing. Even solipsism cannot be disproved.[1] We see the world only by seeing. But an
awful lot of intervention from Somebody or Something would
be required to make the worlds in individual minds coincide, so
precisely, or to make the visual world appear and disappear every
time one opens or closes his eyes. However unreal or subjective
the world is assumed to be, it still continues without slightest
interruptions and with strictest causality, as a perfect reality
in itself.

Merely adding the qualification that the world is unreal, subjective or phenomenal does not change anything. If nothing is real

then everything is equally real; for this is the only world we have. Yet the subjectivism has been always strong in modern philosophy, in most diverse systems, of Descartes, Berkeley, Kant, Fichte, or Mill. By the way, the famous Cartesian dictum "I think, therefore I am" amounts to saying "I exist therefore I am". For thinking is merely a derivative form of existence which is the only real, ultimate mystery.

The idealism and subjectivism, whether in the Hegelian Pan-idealism or in solipsism, would be defendable only if the seeming world of mind was causally at least equal to the world of matter. Yet even Hegel did not claim that ideas or thoughts can affect matter. The stark fact is that material factors and forces determine all thought, have even created the mind, through evolution, whereas the most grandiose thought cannot make the tiniest object move. The belief in Mind, Self, or Soul is humanly compelling, though the life that animates even an insect is as incomprehensible or spirit-like. Similarly, the beliefs in free will are still strong, though it is clear that nothing happens without material — genetic or environmental — causes, ultimately independent from the imagined self. The seeming mental causation is always seen as real. Supposedly, Lincoln's hand writing the Emancipation Proclamation was moved by something completely different than what moves a stone.[4] In truth, the causes are the same, though psychology would have to explain the ungraspable multiplicity of living processes by concepts like drive or pleasure to make this evident.

The belief in Mind as a distinct reality leads to one of the patent incongruities in philosophy, namely, dualism or parallelism. If Mind is an essence different from the physical world, then a cut in your finger and conscious feeling of it cannot have a causal connection. Modern philosophers do not repeat the explanations of occasionalists like Geulincx or of parallelists like Berkeley, about God arranging our every mental act to occur at the same moment that the physical events do. But the incongruous parallelism has to be accepted even by modern philosophers, as long as most of them recognize a nonmaterial Mind,[3,4] which evidently cannot move or be moved by matter. Only the terminology has been modernized. The early modernists and empiricists, Descartes, Leibniz or Locke, invoked God to explain the parallel causation, whereas James and Russell have postulated a higher unifying "stuff".[5]

Not only the Mind itself, but the products of mind become delusory essences. For instance, men have evolved mathematics — from simplest general or uniform organic terms like "one" and quantity — to measure and record most things around them. Then viewing the result in its last phase the philosopher proclaims that mathematics reveals intelligence inherent in the world. Pythagoreans proclaimed Number as the essence of reality; they noted occasional regularities while overlooking the infinite irregularities. Empiricists, like Locke or Hume, contrasted the uncertain empirical knowledge with the certainty of mathematics and logic,[1] though these are as empirical, while being merely uniform for all men. Finally in the modern philosophy of physics the Creator is assumed to be a mathematician and the universe a mathematical, idealistic reality. One might as well argue that the universe is the expression of inches and miles, because we know it in these terms.

Similarly morals, law, conscience, culture or other systems of mind seem, in their last-phase adjustments, to be purposeful miracles transcendentally bestowed on man. There are thousands of things or relationships that make no sense or have no value for every one that does. But man sees only his tiny island of sense in the ocean of non-sense, and this tiny world becomes his evidence of Reason or Intellect governing the universe. Exactly where the order or actual values are rare or lacking man invests his greatest efforts and derives his deepest, hard won satisfactions or sense of values. Philosophy has been the worst guide in understanding the universe and man, because its value outlook has precluded the insight in the opposition, difficulties and disharmony as the real sources of universal causation, evolution and progress, as well as of value. The most important causal truth, the dependence of values on their opposites, has remained repugnant to philosophical thinking.

Search for Finality in Knowledge. Since philosophy is a pursuit of full cognitive satisfaction, it strives for knowledge that is to be final, so that there be no need to seek further. But all knowledge is relative. It is a value process, consisting of evaluations or differentiations of something against something else, ultimately of relating tiny complex needs, disturbances or changes to their opposites, satisfactions, normalcy and organic standards. As pragmatists have shown, knowledge or meaning is fulfillment of a purpose or need,[5] "inquiry" being the essence of logic, and meaning a form of adjustment.[1]

The result is that the sense of knowing something for good or with finality is never reached. It extinguishes itself, as any satisfaction does, upon being attained. Further relating, on and on, has to be continued as final knowledge is being sought. According to pragmatists, a God who knew everything, in His complete ways, would have nothing to think about.[5] We have final knowledge in science or practical life because such knowledge is limited by definite problems, questions, background of premises or needs. The simplest illustration of the impossibility of final knowledge is the cognitive infinity of time and space, which are the clearest or simplest categories of thought. Scientifically or practically we know what time or space is. It is relations between changes or things, and we reflect merely on a limited number of such relations. But when we start thinking philosophically what time or space really or completely is, we have to go on and on relating infinitely. What is true of these clearest forms of thought shows to apply, upon closer look, everywhere.

Any category of thought, or knowledge of any individual thing is subject to the same infinity of relations. Causality, movement, substance, quality, magnitude, value or any meaning of anything derives from relation to something else, which can be known in its turn only by being related further on. If one goes into analyzing something in depth, he has to recognize smaller and smaller universes inside the atom. The endlessness is equally true for what is small or nonsensical as it is for what is great or noble.

Philosophers admit that cognition is a process of mere relating, therefore relative or endlessly non-final, though they may exempt "essential relationships" from this rule.[2] In the often quoted antinomies of Kant, he recognizes that reason permits equally well a world without an end and a limited world; division downward without end and limits to such division; endless chain of causality and break in it by freedom; reality without an ultimate Being as the beginning and necessity of such Being. Kant admits that it is the Practical Reason which requires the second alternatives or a limited world with the absolute Being in it. The Practical Reason, though, is a pure value approach, therefore shows as true the reverse of what is so in fact. Only the first alternatives, revealing the endlessness in cognition, are true.

The ultimate Being as God in the beliefs of common people can be a source of mystery and humble awe. But when philosophers postulate some anthropomorphic first cause, to stop the endlessness, they are adding a contradiction. They profess to be proceeding by reason; but reason cannot stop at any "first" cause, still less accept an anthropomorphic one. The First Mover of Aristotle or St. Thomas rather leads us to asking, by reason, how did He originate or derive His force to move. Surely everything must have a cause. But we always observe that the only, material reality men can know comes from reality of the same nature, which in its turn originates in the same way. Of course such endlessness is not satisfactory. But perfect satisfaction in cognition precludes knowing, just as perfect functioning of the body provides no feeling.

Men become concerned and build philosophies about infinity when they think of humanly great things, man's destiny or the great Creation. In truth, the same infinity is inherent in all knowledge. A concept of an ordinary object like a book seems final enough, because such concept serves its definite, limited functions. But if you start thinking of what a book really is, you find that it consists of other things which are known through their qualities, like shape, substance or color. These are values, however varied, relative as always and determined by your past background of endless value experiences, since infancy.

The empiricists, who pay most attention to the problems of knowledge, have long established that we know only the qualities or values of objects, their color or form, heat or shade (Hume),[1] or that we can have only ideas about objects (Locke),[1] without ever knowing things in themselves or having more than a relative knowledge (Mill).[3] It was easily demonstrated by Hume that one never finds any real causes but only connections of events assumed as causes by habit of thinking. If one tries to deal with the infinite connections or relations of reality, he gets easily lost.

The famous paradoxes of Zeno illustrate this. He argued that a moving arrow must be at some definite place, therefore at rest, at any of the infinite points of its trajectory. But since zero movements can never give any magnitude of movement, the arrow cannot be moving. Or, in race between Achilles and tortoise, Achilles can never win if the tortoise starts, say, ten feet ahead. For when he has moved the ten feet, the tortoise has moved some distance, and when he has moved that distance, the tortoise has moved another small distance, and so on, to infinity. Of course these paradoxes can be solved, by mathematics and logic, which are only other languages for common sense. One meets with the impossible paradox only when he tries to know or think of something in its philosophically final, "real" or nonrelative terms.

We may mention here the categories, like time, space, quality, quantity or causation, that philosophers like to establish. Each philosopher has a different system of categories which he logically demonstrates as central forms of thought. All knowledge is a system of relationships, like a net of meshes, in which anything can be traced to anything else, if one takes the effort. A philosopher not fearing ridicule could as well start with his beard and demonstrate how everything in the world relates to it as the center that determines all other concepts. Some ways of relating, in cognition, are so common to all men that they become the uniform or "logical" forms of thinking. Space and time are such ways, deriving from the way all men exist. But any, even totally arbitrary starting point can serve for building a system of knowledge. The non-Euclidean geometries, of Saccheri, Lobachevsky, or Bolyai, are good examples of systems of knowledge built on deliberately false or noncommon assumptions. The relationships alone make a system complete.

Particularly when it comes to changes, movements or processes, the infinity of relationships or phases makes final knowledge impossible. Cognition itself is a good example. It is a process extending from external stimuli to the final organic and brain responses. Any phase in this process can be viewed as decisive. Thus each philosopher stresses his own central concept, like "data of sense" (Santayana), "sensibles" (Moore) "sensations" (Russell), "initial data" vs. "objective datum" (Whitehead), or "ideas" (Lovejoy).[4,5] Also, any one phase in the process can be viewed as standing between the world and mind therefore as excluding direct or true cognition of reality.

Philosophers know that final answers to their questions are impossible,[1,5] because knowledge is "intrinsically imperfect"[4] and analytically endless.[2] Actually all knowledge, even of the most insignificant, smallest things or events is equally nonfinal or relative. If we know something perfectly or with finality, to the extent it needs no relating or differentiation, we do not "know" it. Existence is the reality we know perfectly, but in its last terms, or without disturbances in it, existence means nothing. Ultimate unrelatable meanings of consciousness or cognition are equally unknowable or incomprehensible. Finally the higher, necessarily *perfect* realities, God, Ultimate Ground, Higher Reason or Soul, cannot be known, because they are beyond our *nonsatisfactions,* disturbances or differentiations — our sources of values and cognition. Speculations about such realities are simply incongruous, founded in sense of values deriving from the *nonsatisfactions.* Hence the unlimited diversity and confusion of philosophies about the higher realities.

Philosophical Criticism and Self-Defeat. Diversity of theories and complexity are the main, almost only achievements of philosophy. There would be no reason for philosophy to be diverse or complex. It has to deal only with necessarily few fundamental principles, not with the multiple complexity of facts. The philosophical issues are a few "eternal" questions. Even the various movements in philosophy, like idealism, realism or positivism, merely expound the same few basic differences of belief. Yet in repeating the same few beliefs, each philosopher arrives at a vast different system, shrouded in mysterious complexity. There is only one way to do something right but unlimited ways to do it wrong.

In sciences or practical knowledge progress brings uniform, principally simple certainties or laws. In philosophy the progress has led to loss of all certainty, even of the hope that philosophy can provide it. Modern philosophy mostly turns against itself, showing that its very bases, the use of reason and metaphysical inquiry, are inherently impossible.

The founder of modern philosophy, Descartes, started with doubt and distinction between faith and limited knowledge. The first truly modern philosophical movement, the empiricism, represented by Locke or Hume, established that nothing is certain, that we deal only with our own sense perceptions and ideas. This led to the total skepticism of Hume, or to the "esse est percipi" theory of Berkeley, which practically means the world does not exist when you close your eyes. In the later empiricism of Mill, the reality we know was shown to be mere phenomena. But the idea that all knowledge has to be uncertain was unthinkable to empiricists as philosophers. They, consequently, sought for certainty of knowledge in disciplines like logic and mathematics (Locke, Hume),[1] or relegated the true reality to the world of things-in-themselves (Mill).[3] We saw that logic and mathematics are as empirical or "uncertain" as all other knowledge; and the reference to transcendental realities amounts to admission of mystery.

The next decisive advance in modern philosophy was the criticism of reason by Kant. It clearly proved that reason cannot be the basis for discovering the ultimate, philosophical truths. This of course means that all philosophy is futile. Kant turned to a value outlook, accepting the Practical Reason or morals and values as the sources of truths. After Kant philosophers have increasingly built their systems on various value convictions. We do not need to repeat that this is the worst possible way of discovering what is actually, causally true. Kant's speculations about Things-in-themselves, that he justified on basis of Practical Reason, are merely incongruous. It is a contradiction to talk in any terms of "things" or being about something that does not exist in the terms of being, space and time.

Finally, in the most recent modern philosophies nobody is so naive as to expect any rational solutions from philosophy. Modern philosophers are not even attempting to build comprehensive philosophical systems.[4,5] Typical modern philosophies like the logical positivism or empiricism hold that knowledge can never be anything more than statements of facts and tautological expressions. Now philosophical reasoning is increasingly abandoned in favor of aesthetic and emotional experiences — often verging on antirationalism, as in the works of Unamuno, Ortega y Gasset, Croce, or existentialists. Also, rationally different or opposing explanations may be recognized as equally valid.[2] Philosophy should, evidently, rest on reason or strict reasoning. Modern philosophy is, as evidently, abdicating it.

Modern philosophy has rather turned to various beliefs in intuitive or "immediate" knowledge, which is closest to natural needs, instincts and emotions, therefore totally depends on value opposites. The founder of the philosophy of intuition, Bergson, saw it as a feeling of sympathy or liking[3] and as "the instinct at its best".[1] (Bergson extolled the miracle of instinctive life — which is ungraspable merely because of its multiplicity.) Modern philosophical movements like the phenomenology, which stress direct insights and viewing of phenomena in their immediate essence, perpetuate the one-sided causal blindness of value delusions on the most general levels of knowledge.

Philosophy is turning against itself as it is attaining, in our age of sciences, higher precision and freedom from mystery. Modern philosophers, it appears, are realizing that philosophy is inherently impossible. The most widely followed modern philosophical approach is the *Analytic Philosophy*.[5] It has become part of the main schools of modern philosophy — logical positivism or empiricism, language philosophy, notably its Cambridge and Oxford schools, and the latest systems of pragmatism and operationism.[5]

With the analytic approach these schools seem to be coming to the conclusion that the final task of philosophy is to end the usual philosophizing. Wittgenstein, the leader of the language philosophy, states that the goal of philosophy is "not a body of propositions, but to make propositions clear".[5] The logical positivists are looking forward to the time when "there would be no books written on philosophy, but all books would be philosophically written".[5] Phenomena of language and logic have become almost the exclusive concerns of Analytic Philosophy, as the failures of all philosophizing are being discovered.

Actually the reason for the failure is deeper than incorrect use of language or logic; it is the relativity of all knowledge. If problems merely of logic or language were the difficulties, then the attainment of ultimate truths and agreements among philosophers would be a simple matter of gradual progress, increasing with effort. The few simplest, most fundamental problems could be resolved right away. Yet the increased effort and precision, particularly by use of logic and mathematics, have only revealed more difficulties, failure and impasse.[3] Logic or mathematics merely express in uniform, unvariable, therefore more limited ways what is known in common sense. Russell in particular struggled with the problem and came to the conclusion that "mathematics is only the art of saying the same thing in different words".

In substance the modern philosophy is dominated by two general movements: *positivism and existentialism.* Both reject the philosophy as it has always been known. Modern positivists limit knowledge to that of empirically verifiable facts and to tautological statements of logic and mathematics, or practically to the scientific methods. The founders of the logical positivism or empiricism, from the famous Vienna Circle, were scientists, not philosophers. Yet positivism is the only seriously considered approach in modern philosophy.[5] Similar positivistic views are held by other modern philosophers. Pragmatists recognize the scientific and practical methods as the only possible ways of knowledge. The same limitation of knowledge to facts and to relative conventions or fictions underlies the presently influential phenomenology, conventionalism formulated by Mach and Poincare, fictionalism, instrumentalism and operationism.

The *existentialism* dominates the rest, the nonpositivistic part, of modern philosophy. It is recognized as the most relevant modern movement even by conventional philosophers.[3,4] The expanding literary, artistic, experiential, "direct" or generally emotional quest for philosophical truths is existential.[5] Yet, as we saw, the central, *emotional* "truths" of existentialism reveal the misunderstood psychological problems of existentialists rather than philosophical truths. It can be said that the strongest modern philosophical movement originates in misunderstood pathology.

Various other philosophical movements, naturally, exist. But they are found to be "trivial" or "doomed to failure".[4] Uncertainty and problems of cognition, which have to be solved before a philosophy can be built, are the dominant preoccupations of modern philosophers, even of such giants as Whitehead or Russell. Uncertainty of truths and relativity of knowledge are repeatedly stressed by Whitehead.[2] Mathematics and logic — the different languages — were tried as ways to certainty by Russell and Whitehead. Mathematics now has an aura of authority that Latin had in the Middle Ages. A typical problem, posed by Russell, was that of the being of nonexistent things like a golden mountain. Philosophically such being is as true as are the other philosophical essences, like Being, Idea or Mind. Russell's explanation by way of logic that the golden mountain has no being amounts to repeating the common sense truths in the language of logic, while the clearly contradictory philosophical problem remains unexplained.

The Limits of Cognition and Language. Ultimately the philosophical contradictions and self-defeat are due to the relativity of knowledge. Just as satisfaction without need is impossible, so is a valid idea or question without a real background of premises, or of concrete need to know. Here as elsewhere in mental economy, you can obtain only as much as you have made preparations for. Children ask pointless Whys because they have not realized this sobering everyday truth. There can be no cognition without previously established conditions or opposite backgrounds for differentiation. In the analytic or positivistic explanation this is stated by the rather unconvincing dictum that "when an answer cannot be expressed, neither can the question be expressed". The relativity of knowledge is, certainly, unsatisfactory. But whether it is cognition, or more direct, emotional value experiences, the very precondition of satisfaction is nonsatisfaction. If we reached in cognition the fully satisfactory state of knowing perfectly everything, we would have nothing to know or think about.

Insight in the limiting relativity of knowledge should make men humble. We can neither deny the higher Unknown, nor say anything about it, because cognition is limited to that narrow, ultimately organic, adjustment that is exposed to disturbances or needs, as the sources of values. All knowledge is confined to the mere terms of man's existence. There may be millions of worlds passing in different dimensions through the room you are sitting in. But it is incongruous to use any terms like "be", "world", "dimension" or anything for what does not exist in the limited terms of our cognition deriving from those of our existence.

Also, because of the relativity of cognition, any knowledge that explains most or satisfies best seems meaninglessly simple or blank. Science shows that the laws which offer widest explanations are simplest. Conversely, cognition seems richest where it is deficient, or acutely busy, where the nonknowledge, needs to know or questions are most extensive. Sciences dealing with numerous factors — under simplest principles — present such "rich" knowledge. In imitation, philosophers may look for complex explanations as ways to provide similar enrichment of knowledge, though philosophy never has to deal with multiplicity of facts. Actually the *deepest, most "philosophical" and fruitful truths are those which are so simple, or commonplace* that they are never seen by philosophers as being worthy of their attention. We saw this everywhere, from the sameness and oneness of organism to the simplicity of existence and its conscious counterpart, the pleasure.

Now we may look at the most important simple fact about knowledge or thought — reflected in languages — namely its absolute, incredible limitation to the terms of our organic existence, that is, matter, space and time, as we shall see in a moment. Ways of thought are embodied in the ways of language, and *all languages have the same parts of speech*: nouns, verbs, adjectives, adverbs. Language can be improved to express thought quite closely, but it never goes beyond the same parts of speech and never creates new ones. It is a virtual miracle that peoples who never even heard of each other maintain the same laws in their languages without failing once. Even simple practical work with languages — I have done translations from 14 languages, at one time or another — makes one sure of the generality of the laws of language. But there is an absolute proof for it. All the philosophers, scientists and linguists of the world, laboring together, *could not invent one word that would not be a noun, verb or other part of speech* and would still have a meaning.

If there was a language having even a single different part of speech, it would be incomprehensible, to any man, and untranslatable. Yet all languages can be understood and translated. Of course there is no lack of sophistications about great differences in languages.[6] But a closer look shows that such differences still always comply with the same parts of speech.[6] In English also the same word can have different meanings, yet none beyond the parts of speech. We say, the "light", to "light," "light" weight, or to tread "light". Also a word spelled the same way can have different meanings, still within the parts of speech. Or in a primitive language an abbreviated sentence may stand for one noun or verb;[6] yet each such sentence complies with the parts of speech.[6]

It is true that the parts of speech, and their modifications, are only few. But this exactly confirms that they represent laws of nature. *The simpler or less "rich" in its terms a natural law is, the wider the world of phenomena it governs and explains.*

As could be expected, philosophers and theorists do not find these simple rules, taught in elementary grammar, worthy of their attention. Anthropologists, and sociologists like Levi-Strauss, recognize language as a key in studying the miraculous similarties of thinking of various peoples. Theorists, from Descartes to Chomsky, have demonstrated that men follow *complex rules* in their languages without knowing it. Of course, a simple principle or natural law can produce numerous *complex regular patterns* under the numerous factors of nature or living adjustments it applies to. But the theorists have not "discovered" that simple principle, evident from the rule of parts of speech. Hence the confusing complexity of theories, implying mysterious, metaphysical capacities of mind.

The principle or natural law of the parts of speech results from the fact that man exists as a material being seeking *persistence or permanence.* Thus permanence or stability becomes the value of all values for man, the primary form of his relations with everything else around him: he grasps the world in terms or relations of material stableness. This leads, in his thinking, to "things" or nouns, under his other organic tendency to reduce everything to "ones". Since space is nothing more than the continuum of actual or potential relationships of such "things", it can be said that *nouns represent relationships of matter in space.*

But the world is not all stableness, however much man may want it to be so. The change and movement around him have to be recognized in his coping with the world. Actually the stableness derives its felt value from the change, its value opposite. Anyway, the necessary complement of the stableness is the change expressed through verbs. Again, because time is only the continuum of relationships of changes, it can be said that *verbs represent relationships of matter in time.*

Further, *relationships of matter to matter,* not fitting the terms of "things" are expressed by adjectives; and such relationships thought of in terms of time are expressed by adverbs. There can be other added combinations of relationships of matter in space, time, or to different matter, leading to such forms as gerunds, participles, nouns derived from adjectives or verbs, and vice versa. But there can never be any more combinations than those of the relationships of matter, space and time, whatever the language. Such parts of speech as prepositions or conjunctions merely serve to relate the other relationships, the words or sentences; and a part of speech like pronoun is merely an abbreviation or substitute for a primary part of speech like noun.

This inexorable limitation of language to relationships of matter, space and time proves that men can never think, either, in other terms. For as we saw, not one of the myriads of improvements in languages for better expression of thought goes beyond the parts of speech, and no genius in the world can invent a single word beyond them. All limits of the capacity of thought are reached in full in the simplest thought, of a child, that the red ball rolls away. Since philosophers do not have to deal with multiplicity of factors, their ideas do not have to be more involved than such simplest terms, which they cannot exceed anyway. Their attempts to deepen thought are futile, and lead only to increasingly complex elaborations, as renewed efforts end in failure.

Complexity has been almost the only distinctive achievement of philosophy. As we saw, and as science proves, the greatest, most extensive truths are simplest, and philosophy seeks only the great truths. Apparently it does not have them. We may note that one does not need to go into the complexities of philosophies to see them as futile. Think of the great philosophical sophistications of the Ptolemaic system. If you tried to refute them in their own, complex terms, you would probably fail. But it all became obsolete, without anybody bothering to disprove it, after the discovery of the simple though seemingly impossible fact that earth spins and orbits.

In all fields, complex systems of philosophical learning and sophistication have collapsed by themselves after simple, undignifying causal explanations were found. Philosophy has withdrawn from such sciences, but clings to the fields dealing with human mind, knowledge and values, where causal explanations are still completely lacking. The relative insight provides here the simple, understandably "impossible", causal explanation, whatever the deficiencies in our presentation of it.

The relativity of knowledge, and the feasibility of philosophy can be viewed as alternatives. If knowledge is relative, philosophy is impossible — which modern philosophy itself is increasingly discovering, in its criticism and self-defeat. The "mystery of knowledge"[4] or the fact that "nothing can be known totally or perfectly"[3] is admitted even by conventional modern philosophers, though this, evidently, renders philosophy impossible. It is sometimes argued that relativists contradict themselves because they still assert nonrelative certainty of their concepts. We have explained that all cognition, without exceptions, is relative; therefore there is no different, either "relative" or "absolute", knowledge. We had to call the normal knowledge "relative" only because we had to distinguish it from the assumed absolute, actually nonexisting knowledge.

All in all, the goals of philosophy are inherently unattainable, because the very condition of cognition is nonsatisfaction, incompleteness, nonfinality, dependence of everything on something else, and origin of values from their causal opposites. Philosophy becomes, on the cognitive level, what neurosis is on the emotional. Satisfactions are possible, cognitively as well as emotionally, when their opposites are there. But man pursues satisfactions without ever suspecting the requirement of their opposite causal sources. If cognitive satisfaction is attainable, why not have it in full, perfect or pure form? As every effort fails, the elaborations become endlessly complex, much as in the neurotic perfectionism.

However, the cognitive "neurosis" is rather beneficial, because it deepens intellectual preoccupations. Moreover, philosophy as search for the ultimate generalizations or laws will always be part of the effort to understand the universe and man. But to be of use, philosophy would have to reverse its very logic and abandon its philosophical methods.

Art as the Modern Cult

People, as intelligent as we are, have been enslaving themselves in irrational cults everywhere and in all times. The main cause of this is the mechanism of *fixation*. As some value object happens to be more frequently appreciated, it acquires more value, due to the relativity of values, and is being appreciated even more. By such vicious circle, any object can gradually acquire a supreme value, excessive and sacred beyond any rational limits. Obviously the modern man would not start a cult of a sacred stone or prayer wheel. But the *insidious effect of fixation is as little understood* by the modern man as it was by savages worshipping totem animals.

All that is needed for a people to entrap themselves in fixations of a cult is that the value object bring some satisfaction and that its use be frequent, encouraged or permitted. The satisfaction can be an avoidance of threat, as in religious cults, or a permitted enjoyment, as is art for modern man. Art offers natural pleasures, but in such a remote way that they are less harmful than the direct pleasures. Further, science provides no insights either on the fixation or on the nature of beauty which is paradoxical as all values. Hence the permissiveness and confused fixational overvaluation of art enjoyments.

Of course culture is never simple or logical. Art may be useful in luring people away from the grosser, more direct natural pleasures. But the senseless entrapment in fixations has to be understood. Otherwise we shall sink deeper into veneration of smears and junk or spending millions for sacredly adored originals, that have no other value than fixational fame. Best intellectual capacities may be wasted on merely cultic preoccupations.

The modern aesthetic cult is superstitious because art is viewed as a highest value *without anybody even questioning why it is so, or knowing what art is,* in the first place. Art objects or their creators, when they become sanctified through the fixation, are not valued because of anything objectively valuable in them. The old masters as well as the modern ones — Picasso, Matisse, Modigliani, Braque, Klee, Miro or Chagall — can be imitated to perfection. Objectively, all of them, particularly the old masters, could be improved in every respect. A forger, like David Stein or Elmyr de Hory, can imitate a series of masters, and do it so well that not even experienced art collectors can discover the fake.

Experts have to use special techniques, analyses and X-rays, to distinguish originals, and only a half-dozen specialists for each master or period can safely tell an imitation. Thus as regards everybody except rare experts museums should offer us enjoyment from widest choices of imitated or improved masterpieces. Such an idea is a sacrilege because modern aesthetics is a religion in which only the true or holy objects, much like the real bone or a hair from a saint or prophet, are held sacred. An imitation, even if it improves the oiginal, is sacrilegious. Five million dollars were paid for the Ginevra because a few experts could tell it was an original by da Vinci. Nobody even doubts that a more beautiful, natural, true or aesthetic face could be drawn by a modern third-rate painter. The most adored face, of Mona Lisa, would be sickening on a real woman. But the sacred, fixational enjoyment by the millions of spectators is genuine here, as in all cults.

Any activity involving repeated valuation of an object can become an irrational cult. All kinds of collector crazes are good examples. Even the collectors of cartoon characters and ball-player cards from bubble-gum packs may create cults stronger than all their other interests and values. Art has additional attraction because it has come together with the greater culture of the higher classes who can afford such leisurely occupations. Christianity in Middle Ages also came with the higher Roman civilization and everybody was scared to be viewed as uncivilized if he did not confess to such religion.

Fixation creates the religion of the true, holy names and styles in art. Nobody is so naive as not to know that a famous name makes a painting — or a mere scrawl — worth thousands of dollars, while the greatest work by an unknown or "undiscovered" artist is worthless. Moreover, it is the meaningless fixations that make names famous. When the sensation-hungry media mention an "original" artist this attracts evaluation of his work, which increases its value, that attracts still more appreciation. Of course everybody knows, from practice, that fame grows this way, and attraction of attention becomes the great race. The result is that the more outrageously sensational an artist is, the more chance he has to gain the status of a sacred genius. That is why *modern art turns into a deliberate travesty or sensation-arousing absurdity.*

The travesty is helped by the need for contrast in art, which leads to reversal of values. Originality serves this need. But art critics and followers of the aesthetic cult never understand the causal mechanics of contrast, and originality becomes confused with the sensational travesty. The sensationalism then is all that matters. The fixations it starts can lead automatically to the fame and cultic veneration of the artist. The key factor is that he be there first and gain the attention for repeated evaluation of his work.

Picasso has risen to the top of the fixational holiness because he was the first in being totally nonsensical, by painting eyes in stomachs, double noses or disjointed arms and legs. As the fixation grew, his style acquired unique value. Surely Picasso had a typical way of drawing. Everybody has his style, in handwriting, or in walking; and it is preserved best by those who are least skillful. Typically, the art of Picasso has been best compared to the primitive art or to the cave paintings.[8,9] Fashions, "crazes" or mass opinions, which grow by the same fixation, seldom have much to do with real value. The absurd thing is that the followers of the aesthetic cult have elevated Picasso to the status of a transcendental genius, piously adored and discussed by the most learned men. Of course there are accidentally interesting bits in Picasso's work; they had to occur during his deliberately accidental play with painting or "sculpture" for years and years.

The fixations are heightened to extremes by the competition between followers of art fashions or between collectors. They know that values in art, much like fashions, grow irrationally and that a style or an artist can become sanctified by merely being noticed first and continuing to be repeatedly evaluated. Antique things in particular have this advantage of having been there first and having enjoyed continuous, nostalgic appreciation. The competitors, knowing intuitively how the cult works and realizing that others know it too, rush into buying almost anything that is antique. Thus value fixations as cults about names and styles, old or new, may grow by a kind of competitive mass hysteria.

Now we may look at the *need for contrast in aesthetics,* which is the ultimate reason why art can easily turn into a travesty. The need for contrast, the same as fixation, is one of the principal phenomena of relative causation. Every value experience needs contrast. In aesthetics contrast becomes all-important, because art tries to heighten values. The simplest example is the use of very dark colors, as in paintings by Rembrandt, to achieve brilliance of light. As we saw in discussing opposite causation and Gestalt phenomena, contrast can make us perceive something that is not there at all. The uses of contrast in art are varied, subtle, causally hardly understood and inevitably paradoxical. They easily lead to reversal of the very first values in art, of beauty, care, skill and meaning.

Search for contrast in the form of originality or spontaneity is the highest goal in art. It is best attained by a creation strongly different from or opposed to the old. Genius in art has always been identified with such originality. As the artists seek to oppose the old forms, they may end by a reversal of everything the art stood for. The Modern artists have reached this end result in its logical completeness. Beauty has been replaced by deliberate ugliness; sense by absurdity; meaning by abstract meaninglessness; and artistic care or skill by intended carelessness, primitivism and travesty.

For a true artist who creates against a background of masterpieces and traditions, his ugly, abstract distortions may constitute a genuine experience of extreme originality. That is why the various kinds of travesty and absurdity in modern art may still be significant artistic expression. But most of the followers of the art cult, and the critics, never understand the paradoxical function of the need for contrast. They merely see the external absurdity as the new fashion or style, that they rush to accept, and may start genuinely admiring by way of fixations. The proofs of the absurd results are all around us. Think of the abstract art, pop art, op art, sop art, plop-plop art, or the other "abstract" forms of art in painting as well as in other fields of art. A bed mattress streaked with paint is a famous work of art. So is a six-by-six-by-six-foot cube that the artist ordered by phone. The notorious Brillo boxes are made to look exactly like Brillo boxes. Identical squares of white canvas representing nothing except pencilled-in words River, Mountain and Spring, are accepted as works of art.

Paintings by chimpanzees are found indistinguishable from those of abstract artists, or even to be superior to them.[10] The art of Paul Klee or Joan Miro is compared, in all earnestness, with "paintings" by four-year-olds; and further recession of art, to the level of ape "artists", may be viewed as the trend of modern progress in art.[11] A painting by orangutan Djakarta Jim, sneaked into a regional art exhibition in Kansas, won the first prize. In Sweden, art critics, deceived about the fact that a painting was by a chimpanzee, praised it as revealing "powerful", "determined", "fastidious" talent and "delicacy of a ballet dancer". There is no doubt that any "painting" — by ape's finger smears or donkey's swings of tail — could be foisted on critics as a work of art, if enough effort was made to conceal the deception.

Primitive "art" is being accepted as deeply revealing, because of similar confusion. The primitive artifacts are queer or distorted due to lack of skill or to the intent of making them extraordinarily strange for greater impact in rituals. They are, thus, unnatural or distorted for nonaesthetic, practical reasons. Abstract art is also distorted, but the reason is its reference to beauty, to previous aesthetic tradition that is opposed.

Here we may mention the generally held theory that art expresses directly the nature of the people who create it. In truth, people admire most and try to reproduce what is unusual or rare to them, while the value atmosphere they live in is for them a nothingness. The glass beads or dance masks are valued because they are contrary to the usual or the natural. Peoples of nature may never even mention the beauty of nature. This beauty became an object of adoration, at the time of Rousseau, when the intellectuals had lived long enough in the cities.

The need for contrast is well illustrated by the history of styles. Each style arises as an outrageous opposition to the previous style. To take the prototype of all styles, the impressionism, it was at first met with outraged disbelief. The very name Impressionism, "was given by a journalist in a spirit of derision".[12] But the impressionism acquired its haunting brilliance through the very opposition to the previous styles. It replaced the natural shaded colors with divided pure colors not found in nature; and the studied, serene meaningfulness of mood or form with momentariness of impression and casualness of form. The spirit itself of art was changed, to a degree that the impressionists were seen as immoral decadents. Postimpressionism, in its turn, acquired status of a new style by opposition to impressionism, through the subdued colors of Cezanne, mystic vision of Gauguin or inner intensity of van Gogh. In all fields, styles arise as opposites: realism against romanticism; irrationalism against rationalism. Finally, the modern art reaches the most complete opposition, to the very fundamentals of art — to beauty, harmony, skill, care and meaning.

Evidently, the need for contrast works in ways conflicting with those of fixation; conflict is inherent in art. An art object acquires sharper effect by contrasting with the existing forms. But traditional repetition of form gives the work its "true", important value. This dichotomy is typically illustrated in styles, fashions and peculiarities of artifacts. Traditional art objects become "stylized": the previous, rigidly conserved form becomes crowded with contrasting detail. Theorists are puzzled by the strange effect and seek for unconscious or archetypal explanations.[8] The fixational dependence of values on the traditional form explains why styles change only by gradual steps. Abstractionism, primitivism, cubism or surrealism would have been unthinkable in the periods of classicism, romanticism or naturalism.

A general source of mystery in aesthetics is the *confusion about the nature and causal sources of the sense of beauty*. The value of beauty derives from natural needs, which are negatively felt, base nonsatisfactions or restrictions. If this were understood, the sublime idealistic philosophies of which aesthetics consists would collapse. The feeling of beauty is clearly a biological satisfaction or release — which "scientifically" or analytically remains a miracle because of its myriad complexity. Only things that affect us biologically trigger such release: light, seasons, luxuriant growth, richness of nature, moods of weather, blue sky, other general functional qualities like orderliness, clarity, smoothness, easiness or freedom, and above all, the functional perfection of human body.

The concept of the triggering of organic releases offers explanations without mystery. Sublimest, divine experiences and insights are, subjectively, released by LSD or some other drug, and nobody will contend that a divine formula is contained in the drug. But in humanistic thought, and modern science, all feelings have to remain, causally, virtual mysteries, because they are explainable only through their value opposites, and by concepts like pleasure which accounts for myriads of factors from million-year evolution — that can never be covered "scientifically". In short, the feelings of beauty are organic, most often general sexual releases. But all organic releases derive from equal restrictions, their value opposites.

Art can present the natural qualities of beauty in a richness that nature can never match. A painting can show together rainbows and sunshine, waterfalls and mirroring waters. In the most direct enrichment, human body can be painted as absolutely, or subtly, perfect or supreme. In music, the sounds from an orchestra are hundred times richer than the natural human love song. This is a wider form of pornography, too indirect to be noticed as such. Above all, paradoxically involved use of contrasts as originality may be highly effective, though confusing. Thus underemphasis becomes the highest achievement, because it offers a sophisticated originality or contrast against ordinary emphasis or previous contrast.

Expectedly, one finds in the *theories of aesthetics* all possible speculations but no causal certainty or agreement. Every modern "civilized" man of course extols art; but it is a religious praise without causal understanding. Art is viewed as revelation of God,[13] manifestation of secret laws of nature,[14] "inkling of God's beneficient creation",[7] or expression of inner transcendental knowledge, postulated by the great philosophers, Plato, Kant, Schelling, Hegel, Nietzsche, Croce, Dewey or Heidegger.[13] The greatest poets and writers, Goethe, Coleridge, Wordsworth or Tolstoy,[15] have proffered divine, and earthly, exaltations about art in richest variations. The more modern aesthetics expound similar beliefs through unconscious, symbolic and existential explanations.[7,8,15] The metaphysical nature of art may be reformulated in positivistic and existential concepts (P. Weiss),[16] or explained by hidden meanings of modern art, still as revelations of God (J. Maritain).[17,12] Art is claimed to be superior to science in providing insights, or to be an important guide in adjustment and adaptation.[18] The higher the authority, the more extensive the importance attributed to art. Sir Herbert Read holds that "our whole education should consist" of aesthetic training[7] which cultivates "primordial images", sensuous capacities and unconscious or symbolic insights, revealed in art of children, particularly in their finger paintings.[7]

Not surprisingly, opposite views are equally strong. The idea that art can help knowledge is rejected.[12] Even the great defenders of art are confused about its meaning and recognize its ambivalent, paradoxical nature (V. C. Aldrich, I. Jenkins).[14,18,19] Degeneration of art or distortion of its very purposes, of beauty and order, are found to be inherent in the progress of modern art (H. Read).[8] It is demonstrated that art rather satisfies man's "rage for chaos"[21] or his search for what is ugly, negative, displeasing and unreal.[19] The need for contrast is not understood. Modern artists are found to be unwilling, confused enemies of true aesthetics, "doing the work of dehumanizing they abhor" (J. Barzun).[20] Or violation of beauty is accepted as the prerogative of genius (E. Gilson).[9] Unconscious and symbolic causes are sought as explanations, particularly for the apparent absurdities in the works of artists like Klee or Picasso.[8,12]

Causal understanding would remove the mystery and confusion. It would reveal the simple, very prosaic, *opposite* sources of the mysterious sense of beauty. Insight into the mechanism of fixation would explain the compulsive, cultic nature of the genuinely felt sacred values in art. With such insight, intelligent people would, at least, stop adoring as sacred art mere paint smears, inflated plastic hamburgers or heaps of broken car parts just because of names and styles. Also, if the principle of contrast was understood, art would not sink into a mere travesty or confused sensationalism. Then we would require from the artist a truly genial, rare and difficult originality. The deepest, surprising originality or contrast is attained by being brought out against fullest reality, with rich, concrete points of reference. This should reveal the real artist, just as it distinguishes a gifted, natural comedian from a slapstick clown.

Art could serve as an excellent means of conditioning or as a lure for attracting people to more refined, cultural interests. It has done so in the past, particularly through religious art and architecture and music. But this becomes difficult as the modern art is turning into a nonsensical cult of mere license and travesty. No wonder that modern artists and the truly absorbed, total followers of modern art are, generally, cultural decadents living in moral degeneration, alcoholism, drug culture or sexual license.[20] Art in itself, as any pleasure, can only impoverish human potentials. Luxuries of art have been, historically, enjoyed most by degenerate rulers or by peoples moving toward decadence and decline of their powers.

Moral and sublime qualities are attributed to art because it has become a superstitious religion. The Nazis were great lovers of art at its best and of noblest music. They could find justification of genocide in genuine artistic admiration or in enjoyment of Wagnerian music. Men find every justification for, or in the name of, their sacred values; and artistic enjoyment creates such values by fixations, which are inherently as distorted as neuroses and the crazes of fashions. All cults grow by such fixations.

Music. We may look at music to illustrate two facts — the need for contrast and the element of "pornography" in art. The basis of music is the human love song, which is almost the only biological use of sound for release of pleasure. Man's love song, much like that of cat, dog or steer, originally consists of mere heightening of his specific call for love or attraction. But man learns to enrich and vary the effect by *using contrast,* the lowering of pitch. For in itself any pitch can be high or low depending on the preceding or following pitch; and its heightening is possible only after its lowering. Soon the lowering of pitch, for contrast or variation, acquires release effects or value meanings of its own — of anticipation, calm, resignation, serenity, sadness, preparation, gathering of force, expectation or anticipatory reserve. Above all *patterns of contrasts* to previous patterns of contrasts can *become melodies of increasing richness and originality* or surprise in every possible value meaning.

It may be added that the octave itself is a product of simple contrast, on three levels, of pitch variations between the natural high and low, of inhaling and exhaling. Equally, patterns of rhythm are produced by simple contrast. All rhythm has biological effects of heightening the releases, by providing an emphasis-and-rest order. Then various *patterns of contrasts in rhythm* may be used to enrich and elevate this primary effect. Thus in the end melodies as well as rhythms become complex systems, containing unexplainably rich, often conflicting patterns, yet obeying a strict hidden order. In the simplest patterns, as in rhythms or in octave series, such order can be even mathematically established. Transcendental mysteries are, expectedly, proffered as explanations.

Music is the most deeply enjoyable art because here the biological release can be increased hundredfold by artificial means. One can say that the degree of "pornography" here is extreme. It has remained permissible because the human love song serves only the preparatory courtship releases in the sexual drive, not the sexual act itself. Human love song is the basis of music and human voice is, evidently, the basis of the sound of musical instruments. But the instruments can substitute human voice with sounds hundred times stronger and more perfect in amplitude, precision, refinement, resonance, richness of timbre or any other quality. Think of the human voice chords and those of the piano; or of the sound of man's voice and that of an orchestra. Thus the effects of music can be compared to those of stimulating a nerve center with a hundred times stronger current than the natural stimulus. That is why music can produce very strong releases. These are invested by the person with equally profound sublime value meanings, as he seeks to "explain" his feelings.

Literature. We may say a few words about literature, to illustrate the power of fixation, and to see how educational or causally true literature is, or is not. Nobody dares to question the genial value of classics like *Odyssey, Divine Comedy, Don Quixote* or *Hamlet*. Such works are, certainly, literary monuments. But they are literarily so inferior, i.e., failing to render relivable experience, that nobody can read them with true interest. Any similar work by a modern author would be laughed at as unbelievable example of lack of talent.

The *Odyssey* is a collection of unreal, uninteresting and meaningless tales strung into an unimaginative ancient Western, without the slightest psychological rendering of true characters or genuine real-life interest. *Don Quixote* was intended as a hilarious story; but for modern readers it is a series of practical jokes so sad that it now serves as an example of the tragic sense of life. The *Divine Comedy* is a pretentious, unreadably boring collection of endless exaggerations worthy of its goal — to serve the readers who believed in the fires of hell. Learnedness and complexity, in content and form, were intended to impress the sinners.

People who praise these works as masterpieces of literary genius should first go through the boring task of reading them in full and in original. Such works are important and historically interesting. But they lack the only literary genius we can talk about, namely, the talent of making the story interesting. This is equal to *making it as relivable as life*. There simply is no other source of interests. The classics may be culturally better for the reader, because they lack natural interests which as pleasures serve us badly. But the feeling that the classics reveal higher genius of literary talent is due to mere fixation, growing through repeated valuations. A verse from *Hamlet* repeated through generations may reverberate in our ears like the very standard of truth and beauty. In the same way, distorted language or point-less tales in scriptures, repeated through ages, become deeply and truly touching.

Even the greatest literary genius, Shakespeare, stands below a third-rate modern author. One would be crazy to think that he could sell today a play written in the way Shakespeare wrote — as contortedly unnatural in form, and as unreal, exaggerated, unbelievable, artificial, merely bloody, unimaginative, pretentious, superstitiously silly, lacking perceptive characterizations or genuinely true simple interests. Such work could not sell today because it would not be interesting, which is the same as not being naturally real or as lacking literary talent. Our feelings about the genius of Shakespeare may be deeply genuine. Fixation can make them so beyond every reason. His works have been staged with exquisite effort for centuries, therefore had to become fixationally sacred. If a character like Hamlet is impossible, any interpretation that suits best the fashion is given to the role, which renders it universal.

The argument that Shakespeare or Homer wrote for different times is irrelevant as to their talent. People in all times have had similar intelligence, sense of humor or genuine interests. But the early writers considered as worthy subject matter only what was extraordinary, learnedly arcane or nobly superior. Even an intelligent man makes a fool of himself when he starts showing how learned he is or pretends to be worthier than men are. We find, though, in the works of Shakespeare already bits of what can be of real interest. After all, he had to manage a theater, at profit, therefore learned to collect material that was interesting to the public.

In modern literature the true talents and interests have prevailed because they have started to bring fame and money. Descent to unadorned life has even gone to extremes. The real life is the only source of thrills; there can be no real satisfactions without real needs. It took a long time for writers to get down to the simple life, because logically this meant abandonment of great, extraordinary interests and of true "literary", learned forms. In other arts, early cinema or television, the evolution from exaggerations and excesses to the interests of simple genuine life has also been slow. By the way, in all acting it is only gradually being learned that the true reaction by man to his emotions is an effort to counteract them rather than to express them directly as is taught in theory and done in poor acting.

It is *the fixation that makes us genuinely feel* to be standing before a genius when we enjoy an old master, while we would laugh and be bored if the same kind of talent was exhibited by a modern author. Our feelings here are genuine, as in all fixations; and when such value feelings are there we find every explanation or justification for them.

We may as well look at the general value of literature, old and new. Literature has promoted book reading, which is very important. But *the educational or causal truth value* of literature is worse than nil, except in the rare cases where a writer records facts without any opinion or arrangement. For as soon as an author starts creating characters and events he has to know the causal, paradoxical law or logic of values and behavior, which is the last thing writers would understand. That law is contrary to the deepest, most convincing human value beliefs or feelings, and the writers are the foremost, ardent expounders of such beliefs and feelings, in the name of freedoms and subjective experiences.

As a result, every causal fallacy of psychology and humanistic thought, that we have explained, is compounded in literature. Thus we find everywhere, in literature, the belief in positive reactions from positive enjoyments and in negative effects from restrictions or frustrations; as well as the alchemy of weightiest potentials, or ills, arising from mere ideas, thoughts, intents, coincidences or unconscious causes. In typical modern writing, by Sartre or Beckett, a person may be suffering a never ceasing anguish or despair. One may think here of the descriptions of Medieval saints as having grooves under their eyes from incessant weeping.

In a word, most everything in literary creation is causally misplaced or contrary to causal truths. It amounts to creation of monsters with mismatched parts. Our literature is causally not different from the former books on horrors and miracles, with descriptions of impossible beasts. It is true that all men live by similar convictions — without having a causal understanding of their behavior. But in practical life the ubiquitous, contradictory and illogical, selectively established ways lead men to the right behavior. In literary creation no such "absurd" limitations hinder the author. He creates a world that complies with the directly logical value convictions — exactly contrary to the real causality.

It is typical that writers are psychologically the least wholesome people. As Leslie Fiedler says, all great writers need a "charismic weakness", a psychological flaw, which drives them to alcoholism, drugs or psychic disturbances. Our greatest masters, O'Neill, Fitzgerald, Lewis, Faulkner or Hemingway were alcoholics, addicts and mental patients. The writers are mostly overenjoyers, who end by suffering the opposite reactions. They are psychologically least perceptive and mismanage their own lives, because they lack the intuitive powers normal people live by. They do perfectly as the sensitive, incensed prophets of the deepest, logically direct, generally held value convictions, that they see violated everywhere. But we could learn from them as little about life as from bankrupt spendthrifts about business. Literature deepens the universal value delusions which have kept men from discovering the causal truths in all fields of human sciences.

Culture by Value Fixations

Each people live in a culture that may look strange to others but seems only rational and right in every respect to themselves. We are no exception. Progress, affluence, freedoms and strong value attitudes intensify, in subtle ways, *value fixations, which can make our culture irrational to any degree* yet lead us to believe that it is absolutely right. This is true of our fashions and social "musts", which consume most of our surplus resources, as well as of our ideas of progress, value priorities and cultural or aesthetic convictions. A hundred years from now our culture will seem unbelievably strange and backward. We can even know in what direction the future progress will move. Yet we cannot help feeling that our present values are the only possible ones; the future may seem even ridiculous.

The objects and forms of fixations are as many as there are the values by which people live. In the simplest cases, of sacred and totem animals, a people may start noticing or valuing an animal more generally, due to its frequent presence or to an accident that brings attention to it. This automatically increases its value and it is valued or noticed even more frequently, which further increases its value. The vicious-circle fixation is thus started.

Because of their relativity, values can arise only to the extent there is a background or satisfaction channels through which they acquire their meaning. But *in cultural adjustment such backgrounds are created by previous cultural experience.* Thus any object in a culture can become sacred beyond all reason because some meaningless circumstance has brought it to attention first or keeps it constantly present.

It is necessary that the fixation object yield some pleasure or satisfaction. Otherwise the people would not repeatedly turn to it. Yet, inevitably, fixations create the most painful customs and disturbing beliefs. In fixation, much as in neuroses, the negative reactions grow from initial pursuit of satisfactions. People starting to connect good luck with appearance of an eagle or with throwing sand over the shoulder will cultivate such belief with great pleasure, as an easy insurance. But the greater such enjoyment, cultivated over long periods, the more frightening and obsessive the fears if the lucky sign does not appear or the ritual is not performed right. Power and perfection of cults and rituals thus self-increases automatically. As an improved reassurance or satisfaction from a cult is overenjoyed, the opposite reactions arise, requiring even stronger compliance.

Evidently, the fixations enslave mostly those people who seek easy satisfactions and avoid difficulties or restrictions which are sources of more varied, new interests. The modern affluent people indulging satisfactions, avoiding restrictions and free of difficulties are ready victims of cultural fixations. Their fixations merely are more general, extending to the fields of values, mental life, cultural attitudes or psychological and social problems. Here scientific, causal insights are still missing and the inherently superstitious fixations can flourish unhindered. Only the more primitive superstitions contrary to physical or natural sciences are avoided.

The simpler more primitive fixations grow, through repeated valuing, mostly because the value object is always there. The sacredness of cattle, cows, bulls or sacrificial sheep, is frequent for this reason in cults and legends. One finds it among varied peoples, including ancient Egyptians or Greeks as well as peoples of India. The "lamb of God" has come down as a term of Christian liturgy. But a rare animal or "miracle" may also become object of frequent valuations and fixation, if due to its spectacular or unusual appearance people start attaching to it their most frequent preoccupations.

However started, fixations may cripple cultural adjustment, mysteriously and often grotesquely, with increasing grip. The use of cow becomes limited, for its worshippers, though its holiness grew exactly from its general use. Observances of foods, like those of kosher, may start with accidental associations having, evidently, no general factual justification, but may acquire value so deep that nobody even dares to question the crippling enslavement to the "laws".

The overwhelming irrationality of cultures disproves the rational theories like those of Frazer or Sumner, as well as the explanations of functionalists and "scientifically" logical empiricists, like Malinowski, Radcliffe-Brown, Benedict or Mead. Understandably, unconscious, superorganic, symbolic and metaphysically historic explanations are accepted, by best authorities — Kroeber, Ogburn, Northrop, Levi-Strauss, Sorokin or Toynbee. We saw how absurd it is to view the neurotically senseless fixational customs as creations of the genius or higher powers of a people.[22] Quite a lot of modern sophistry is required to make it believable that higher, transcendental principles are embodied in the piercing of noses, ritual dances or acceptance of cows as Godly Mothers. Customs have no inherent value, though the cultural conditioning that is effected through them may be most important. People conditioned to be moral in fear of a two-headed god may lose moral discipline if such god is discredited. But the cult of two-headed god in itself has no significance: it could as well be that of a winged dragon or anything else.

Modern man lives under the same law of value causation as primitive men did, and the modern *humanistic emphasis on the inherent truth of values,* together with the lack of causal insight in the fixation, makes him rather more prone to fixational self-enslavement. Tendencies of fixation are strong in all adjustment, but nature has safeguards against them. Every organism tends to use previously used channels. Rats, in experiments, stick to the same food for long periods. But organic demands force them to vary the food. Similarly, higher organisms have innate demand for variability or novelty of stimulation. But modern man has advanced far beyond such natural safeguards as well as difficulties that would require abandonment of habitual satisfactions. In his natural reactions, like his choice of colors or forms, man does exhibit, in experiments, a preference for novelty. But such lowly natural reactions have lost all importance amidst the colossal elaborations by which civilized men enjoy their satisfactions.

The result is that everything in modern culture becomes fixational, as the only standards of value for modern man come to be his own previous elaborations in the satisfactions he seeks and the values he establishes. Equally important is the fact that this enormous fixational superstructure of elaborations *comprises almost everything we do with our surplus* in resources, time or effort. It is the surplus that makes progress possible, whereas a mere getting even in man's struggle with nature, or the depletion of the surplus, leaves him without means of ·advance.

Except for the prime necessities, all our resources and efforts are consecrated mostly to fixational values and interests. We spend our surplus resources on what fashions or other people say is "in", right, beautiful, enjoyable or new, though it may be less beautiful, less worthwhile and even less enjoyable than what we have already. The proverbial competition with Joneses that governs most of our lives consists of such efforts. For instance, in the garment industry more effort is spent on fashion, attraction, "beauty", or frills than on real usefulness, comfort or beauty. The expensive fashions of today will look ridiculous and ugly a couple of years from now. Whether it is the women's contorted gowns or men's ties, we are compelled by the fixational fashion. Without it we could have simple, comfortable, really beautiful clothes; for beautiful is what is naturally simple.

Fashions in clothes are only a more visible example. Every other surplus spending by modern man — on cars, homes, furnishings, or social "musts" — is similar. Billions of dollars are spent on advertising, selling and producing, as well as on discarding, what is merely fashionable. To take only the yearly change of cars because of new models, it has cost us hundreds of billions of dollars over the years —enough to bring progress to underdeveloped countries of the world. The extensive use of cars, in general, is mostly due to a value fixation. In all times carriages, chariots, coaches have been objects of fashion or social standing. The fixation here grows because of the natural pleasure of "riding", enjoyed by peoples in various forms, as well as by children riding sleighs, or ash can tops. If cars were merely means of transportation, they would have long been substituted by a more rational system of transportation.

Almost everything we do in our surplus spending is irrational, and costly. But we simply cannot see how it could be different. Only a look at irrational costly habits in some other culture reveals their fixational nature. The noblemen of two hundred years ago would have found life senseless without their castles, frilly clothes, carriages, social occasions, or the other forms of class entertainment and status. A nobleman spent more on a ridiculous bombasted suit of clothes than a village of peasants spent on their whole living. Higher economic and technological development would have been possible, but the noblemen wasted their resources on their culture.

We are not doing much better, though we can know for sure what the future possibilities are. The bourgeoisie imitated the wasteful habits of the noblemen as soon as it could afford them, and we are following suit. Our expenditures on competition for status and on "proper" observances are even more wasteful, because of mass following. The Christmas season alone determines the course of commerce and great part of industry for months while billions of dollars are wasted. Merely because we "must" or something is "in" we waste on appearances, fashionable living, social observances, "cultural" interests of the moment, conspicuous consumption, or pursuit of habits set by stardom people. Our whole material culture consists of such efforts. Marxists and rebels can easily demonstrate how every one of our cultural values amounts to a useless "bourgeois" aberration, though they themselves evolve even stronger fixational cults.

We never notice our fixations and rather can prove that *the interests are genuine.* Sports, like baseball or football, are good examples. An outsider would find it rather absurd that grownup men can chase a silly ball around a big field with such grim earnestness. Clearly the interest has grown here through custom: we find no interest in games people in other countries are crazy about. But our games have become institutions for us and may consume one third of our interests, as media coverage shows. Arguments that sports are healthy or educational are rationalizations. Not health but injuries are typical of the sports we follow most; and the primitive, destructive rage of sports fans can be great problem. Costly wreckage of trains by soccer fans in England is one example. In Latin America soccer fields are now protected by moats, after hundreds have been killed — three hundred in one explosion of fan rage.

Above all, the sports make our youth, even that capable of direct intellectual interests, imitate as their heroes men excelling merely through superior muscles and reflexes of animals. But our sports have become a national institution that one would hardly dare to question, though they consume tens of billions of dollars yearly, or more than a good war-on-poverty program.

All our *cultural institutions* are similar products of fixations. We saw this in the fields of arts and literature, as well as in education where fixational humanistic tradition determines what is accepted as learning and valuable education. Our national monuments or natural treasures have a genuine value for us, and none for an outsider. They can be important for patriotic conditioning. But the fiercest defenders of natural treasures are the liberal humanists who disparage patriotic education. They may fight construction of a dam or atomic plant to protect a hill or rock mentioned by a poet. They are unwitting victims of cultism under which any knoll or river bend can become a sacred monument, much as in the cults of Indians. Anything can acquire a genuinely sacred value for us once it comes to our special attention and is repeatedly valued.

We have to emphasize that *the most important fixations are those about general values,* like freedom, individuality, human nature, basic rights or constitutionality. Actually these values stand for *our established ways of life in their various forms.* We do not dare even to question them because fixation has made them sacred. Evidently, this is the greatest obstacle to progress in every field of life. Stagnation becomes sacred, whereas progress requires unthinkable changes. We shall see how the progress is being opposed because of abhorrence of "ant-hill" society and "brainwashing"; or how human race is being abominably degraded because of sacred protection of our primitive reproduction habits. In fact, eugenic controls could provide humanity with its greatest, concrete progress, and save unspeakable suffering for hundreds of millions of persons. But fixations are strongest in such most important areas, governed by the ways of life that have always been there.

Fixation is also strong in the formation of *social conformity* and public opinion. The fixation here reinforces itself because of social interaction. Everybody fears to be generally despised or left out, if he misses what the others value. And people know intuitively that a value can become excessively strong by way of "fashion", without reason — through the fixation. Consequently, once an opinion or value starts to become somewhat more general, everybody rushes to adopt it. Then as the value is being generally repeatedly experienced it may acquire the quality of genuinely felt sacredness.

Of course fixation can also serve cultural or moral conditioning. In our morals or restrictions as well we are stronger when we follow the trodden paths or used channels, that provide us with greater sense of values. Cultural conditioning is best built on the strong, sacred values as motivations. It all can become confusing, but the simple decisive fact is how much restriction is attained. If fixation proceeds merely by added satisfactions, as it does if left to itself, the result is impoverishment of potentials. That is why most cultures exhibiting enormous amount of moral elaborate customs and cults generate little of real morals as capacities to act unselfishly or "rationally" or to have the rich love, which everybody wants. Only the difficult accumulation of restrictions can provide the releases or capacities. This is exactly contrary to the hailed enjoyment of the positively-felt, satisfactory, divinely rich cults and values, that the humanistic theorists see as the direct source of culture.

In sum, our culture is as irrationally wasteful and backward as was that of the noblemen a few centuries ago. The future men will find it incredible how we could waste our surpluses on our culture without concern for the direly needed progress and really desirable goals. We will appear like the savages who spend their surplus efforts and time on neckbands and cults, without realizing how their life could be made completely different. The reason is the fixation, by which men become entrapped in accidentally started patterns of satisfactions, where these can be indulged without natural controls, external difficulties or inner restrictions. Such freedom has become almost total in our culture wherever we have attained surpluses in means and in possibilities for extension of value goals. These are the areas on which progress depends — and where our culture fails insidiously.

Conclusion

The fact that inner values causally derive from their opposites is contrary to humanistic thinking. But exactly the inner values are accepted as the sources of capacities and insights or as the highest goals, in the humanistic thought. Moreover, this thought has dominated all our learning, education, philosophy, aesthetics and cultural life. Thus we are governed by a thought that is contrary to causal facts.

Philosophy is a special cognitive endeavor, of striving for pure, complete and final knowledge as cognitive satisfaction. It seeks to know everything in itself, in its essence, and in its ultimate, final terms. But cognition is a value process, of differentiation or evaluation of changes against organic, relative values, or of meeting minute needs with satisfactions. Consequently knowledge is always relative and anything is known only by being related to something else, by way of value differentiations. Nothing can be known in itself or with finality. If knowledge is relative, philosophy is inherently impossible; and the progress of philosophy has shown that it does end in self-defeat. In its striving for the perfect, inherently impossible cognitive satisfactions philosophy resembles what neurosis is on emotional level, both leading merely to endless, futile, complex elaborations.

Moreover, philosophy in particular accepts the positive inner values as the direct highest insights and goals. This is what philosophy as pursuit of satisfactory knowledge requires. Thus the real causal sources, the value opposites, are never recognized and every humanistic value delusion is perpetuated. Philosophy, extolling the value-centered world of man, has been and remains the main obstacle to scientific, causal, unthinkably new discoveries and insights, particularly in the sciences of man.

In the field of aesthetics modern man has become a gullible victim of a cult, by way of fixations he never suspects. Much as in religion, in modern art only the sacred names and originals or the true styles are valued, though nobody but few experts can distinguish the originals from imitations. Because of the need for contrast, art has to end by opposing its previous values and forms of expression, including those of beauty and mastership. But since this is not understood, mere distortions are accepted as advanced art. And the more outrageous such distortions are, the more noticed the name of the artist becomes. This starts the fixation running; and the artist's work may soon be felt as genuinely sacred. Thus modern art becomes a competition in a deliberate sensationally nonsensical travesty.

In literature, old masterpieces become for us treasures of genius because of the fixation. Anybody trying today to create works in the same way, with the same amount of talent, would be laughed at. In general, almost all fictional literature produces only distortions, because writers are the most intensely involved expounders of the human value beliefs and their direct causal logic. Since such beliefs and logic are exactly contrary to factual causality, no fictional literary creation corresponds to what is true or causally real.

Our culture is a system of value fixations, particularly in our use of material surpluses and "surplus" possibilities for evolving new ideas and values. Progress depends exactly on the surplus means and possibilities. But almost everything we spend above prime necessities is wasted on our "bourgeois" culture, status, social musts, fashions, conspicuous consumption, fixational cults, habitual entertainments, or the competition with the Joneses. The fixational, excess cultivation of our values and ideas, particularly those about freedom and individuality, has invested them with irrational sacredness that blocks progress which requires unthinkable new insights.

X

THE SCIENCE OF MAN AND
HUMAN SELF-CREATION

As we have seen throughout this book, the law of relative causation offers a causal explanation of value reactions or releases,
which determine everything man feels, thinks or does, including
his health and knowledge of reality. This causal law can serve
as the basis for the sciences of man. It is also simple, almost
self-evident — as is the maintenance by organism of its sameness, from which it derives. But this law is contrary to the very
logic and beliefs by which men, as well as scientists proceed.
It shows that releases, satisfactions or inner values can be enriched only by their restriction, opposition or hard accumulation
of needs as nonsatisfactions or disvalues. The humanistic thought
and modern "scientism", however, perpetuate the virtually alchemistic logic that releases, satisfactions or values are enriched
by their direct increase — which would be the easiest thing for
man.

Consequently in the fields of human sciences there is only
endless confusion and controversy, but no science, causal law or
workable theory; this explains the wide present disappointment
with sciences. Man has progressed, up to now, in spite of his
logical or "scientific" beliefs, by mere social and cultural selection, which has promoted those people who follow traditions of
restriction. Cultural progress is a continuation of the evolutionary progress which too has worked by virtue of restrictions,
difficulties or opposition, in transforming simpler organic channels of releases into more complex, enriched forms. It can be
said that man, up to now, the same as animals, has progressed
blindly, by being exposed to selective restrictions against his will.

If the blind animal progress has produced man with his consciousness, then unimaginable miracles can be expected, in the

end, from a progress by plan. Such progress can proceed by mechanistic causality, under the simplest principle, just as the progress that brought the consciousness did. But the end result can be more miraculous than the consciousness is in comparison with life of animals, who don't even know that they exist. Exactly because we cannot imagine what suprahumanly different transformation the progress will bring, human effort can have meaning — however mechanistic or unidealistic it has to be. By understanding the principles of progress man will create men better than himself. Man as self-creator can exceed himself without limits and become more miraculous than any gods people have ever conceived. Such self-creation is, evidently, the destiny of man as a conscious being.

Opposition or Restriction as the Source of Progress

The ideas of Progress, and of the rational science that has brought it, may have become odious, for good reason. Every time men have started on some drive for progress they have ended by suffering more degradation. One can think here of rationalistic revolutionaries, who have killed millions in the name of progress, as well as of our attainments of affluence and "improvements" that have turned the life of modern man into a diseased emptiness. Failure and disorders from more progress and "science" are inevitable if the paradox of enrichment of releases or capacities through restrictions is not understood; we saw the disastrous effects from direct increase in releases, in every field.

But a truly scientific. causally understood promotion of progress is the only possible way for us to achieve what we practically want, as well as to make our tiny contribution to whatever may be the destiny of man. We all want the enriched capacities, mental or physical, and freedom from diseases or disorders, caused by impoverishment of such capacities. This is an obvious goal, for the present and the future, regardless of what theories or beliefs are adhered to. A truly scientific, causally understood progress in dealing with man would make this goal possible, as we have seen for all fields of human sciences. The present rejection of sciences is explainable; but nothing coherent can be done without scientific, causal understanding.

We want to emphasize how completely *contrary to the existing beliefs and theories* is the causal principle on which the human sciences and causally understood progress is to be founded. We can view it as a *principle of progress through opposition,* or through restrictions and difficulties that the opposition practically consists of. It implies that man will have to oppose or act against himself, by plan, if he is to progress in a consciously planned way or to have true sciences of man. Of course practically, by the selective cultural tradition, men already impose restrictions on themselves; and moral intuition tells us that "to progress man must fight himself", in the words of Lecomte du Nouy. But the point is that the contradictory and necessarily superstitious cultural tradition has to be replaced by causally or scientifically understood system in our era of sciences.

The principle of progress through opposition or restriction is embodied in the law of the relative or opposite causation, as well as in the contradictions of existence, as we have repeatedly explained. Evolution, the prototype of progress, works through the principle of opposition. It is *because of encountered opposition or difficulties* that the living forms "seek", selectively, *more circuitous and complex adjustments, which are richer,* in human terms. It can be said that the higher living forms are results of disasters imposed on the species by the opposition or difficulties. The primitive animal has been subjected to the tortures of living on dry land, suffering the rigors of climate, famishing from lack of its usual foods, or avoiding increased dangers, before it has become richly "endowed" to cope with the difficulties. Of course in viewing the higher animal in its last stage of adjustment it may seem that the more complex and resourceful forms have been purposefully created. Living on more varied foods, growing a furry coat, or adopting swifter movements for survival seem to be marvelous, more satisfactory choices.

But to assume such seemingly more satisfactory choosing is

to imply that the animal or the forces creating it know in advance or foresee what will be more satisfactory. For otherwise the only satisfactory or pleasant condition for the animal is the one he is suited for in his existing form. The change to new, more complex conditions can be only unpleasant and is resisted. A pleasant change that organism may seek is always a relapse to simpler, more primitive adjustments. Animal or man, when permitted fuller satisfactions, sinks into the immobility of ease and degeneration.

The evolution of higher forms requires compulsion; and there is only the irrational, chaotic struggle of forces in the universe. That is why selection through adversity becomes the method of progress. Every form that is not fit for the harder, complex conditions is eliminated. Thus the very irrationality opposition or difficulty becomes the source of limitless, humanly marvelous progress.

We saw how the *brain and consciousness* represent further stages of evolution through opposition or restriction. Consciousness amounts to a life within the organic life of the individual, as it delays and stores the lower brain reactions, thus providing memory, and foresight through it. Such life requires its own resources. They are provided by restriction on releases. This is not very different from what higher organisms do in all creation of their reserves, through restrictions. *The next stage of "evolution" will be a consciously planned opposition or restriction* of organic releases. The restriction that has created consciousness requires action by organism against itself, as if its own paralization. This is an extraordinarily unnatural, inherently abnormal procedure. That is why the consciousness has to be an exceedingly rare phenomenon, emerging from some extraordinary upheaval. It may be significant that man as a conscious being evolved during the ice ages, the hardest period for his species. We may also note that the larger brain of higher animals, working as a brake on their rate of living, has been correlated with their increased longevity.[5]

Generally opposition as the creative principle becomes more important as nature progresses, in human terms. On the nonliving level the opposition, between the Field and matter, provides the physical reality we know, with its simple laws. The variety or richness of phenomena and laws increases with the living process, where the opposition becomes a vastly extended struggle between the opposites. In the evolution of living forms, their seemingly ingenious enrichment is proportional to the amount of opposition or difficulty the species encounters and has to overcome by new adjustments. Finally, within the higher organisms their capacities, as the satisfaction or release potentials, are created by the opposition in the form of non-satisfactions as needs, and restrictions.

Without opposition there would be no reality, which man knows only by the differentiation; no richness of life or its forms; no "purposefulness" of the seemingly endless harmony of creation; and no enrichment of the higher organic potentials. In universal terms, forms of matter become exquisitely "resourceful", "inventive" and "purposefully" predetermined to the extent their "oppression" is equally extensive and pervasive — as we explained in the case of living matter.

The enrichment by restriction or opposition is causally true for all human behavior and adjustment, mental, physical, cultural and social. We saw this in all fields of human sciences. Here we may look at the *general course of human progress and culture*. Progress is, evidently, beneficial to man. Moreover its sources are not difficult to discover. Unselfish social and economic co-operation — love, and reason unhampered by short-sighted selfish interests — would be sufficient. This has been theoretically clear in the various utopian visions implied in most of the leading ideologies. All utopias are logically possible; people should just accept the clear rational requirements of the progress that brings the utopian benefits for all in the end. Furthermore, the progress would be automatic and immediate as the progressing people would notice the benefits that progress brings for all and would logically accept it to maximum extent. But the usable love or unselfish "reason" can be created only by *opposition of the fundamental,* selfish drive.

The opposition of this drive is attained by moral and social conditioning. *Morals have always been restrictions,* almost by their very definition. Everybody can see that a perfectly moral society would not need the half of our efforts that now go into protection, moral education, justice, distribution, commerce or administration. People could be twice as rich with the same effort. But such ideas belong in utopias, because nobody would dare to abdicate his selfish interests, knowing well that others would exploit him. Thus here as elsewhere men are prevented from reaching utopian benefits by their universal inherently anti-progressive nature.

Even after a person has acquired the moral virtues of inhibitions, shame or sense of guilt, he views them as unfortunate afflictions. Particularly the logically scientific, modern moralists condemn such negative, restrictive reactions.[9] Further, sins are directly pleasant, invigorating, satisfactory or liberating. Men have always loved intoxication, or forms of Bacchanalia, to get rid of moral restrictions. Modern life has added revolts, rationalistic enlightenment and liberalism, cultivated by the humanistic thought, education, literature, art and "scientific" theory. No wonder that the basal human resources of progress have hardly grown at all and are expected rather to decline if the modern trends continue[8,15] (R. L. Heilbroner, M. Harrington).

Similarly, *social cooperation,* which is the first source of progress, has been created by opposition or insurmountable difficulty. Without society there would be no specialization, industry, morals, organization or anything larger than a family group could build. But social cooperation has emerged only because of the gravest, insuperable threat to man — threat from other men. In the last few thousand years the human race has approached overpopulation at a progressive rate and the progress has increased at the same rate. The late homo sapiens, like the Cro-Magnon man, had as much brain as we have. But he did not progress at all, for a hundred thousand years, because his intelligence made him the ruler of nature, free of critical difficulties.

Only other men, with equal powers of intelligence could present a threat to him. This started happening when increasing populations brought people in contact. The primitive tribes, as extended families, faced destruction by larger tribes unless they also united in larger groups. For men only kill, enslave or eat other men not belonging to their tribe. Rare species do this. Evidently, societies had to become larger and closer integrated, in a reciprocally generated spiraling way. If men were social by nature, societies would not need the elaborate codes, morals, laws, institutions or the whole social "culture".

The inherent resistance of man to social progress is excellently proven by the attitudes of humanists themselves. The progress requires integration of society into a veritable organism and transformation of human drives — the "anthill" society and "brainwashing". But these are the most odious notions to every theorist, writer, philosopher, scientist or spiritual leader. The practical progress is moving in this "odious" direction, as is typically foreseen by writers like Orwell or Huxley, who are horrified by the prospect. Men will progress in spite of the individualistic and liberal ideas of humanists. An organically integrated and totally conditioned society will enjoy a hundredfold increase in efficiency, and the highest practical selfless love between its people — which will make the selfish individual freedoms meaningless. In brief, the highest progress will come through opposition of human natural drives.

Even the concrete forms of progress are determined by difficulties. Obviously men have industries and vast organization only for those things that are lacking or difficult to obtain. However, due to relativity *permanent* difficulties or advantages lose effect. Americans have created higher civilization because they came from Europe where scarcity of land and resources was a great difficulty. They compulsively exploited the new plentiful land more than they needed for living and thus created the surplus capital. Fortunately men constantly create difficulties for themselves. They "neurotically" want more, in compulsive competition, as they get more. Also the blunderous strivings for freedoms, equality or more satisfactions create revolts, disturbances, strikes, failures and progressive discontents. To cope with them, social efforts and cooperation have to be increased and production made more efficient. Spreading liberation and equality debase motivations, but also open the strenuous competition to more people, since slaves do not compete with masters.

Poverty is an interesting problem. The liberal reformers argue that the wretched problems of the poor would be solved by giving them enough money, as through the "negative income tax". But in our modern liberal atmosphere the best conditions fail to help the poor. Even exemplary housing, like the Pruitt-Igoe project in St. Louis, turns into an intolerable slum if left to the poor alone; the project is being torn down. Every inveterate poor, to be kept rehabilitated, now would require special guidance, psychiatric and other help costing tens of thousands of dollars yearly, as the Chicago study showed.

Before our modern, liberal era poverty was a scarcity of means which created increased motivations to work hard, out of it. Greatest men and most capable groups, in every nation, have been formed by such poverty. The main present problems of the urban poor are the exact reverse: use of drugs instead of lack of means, truancy from schools that are free, avoidance of hard work, lowest morals and dissolute family life. Instead of "liberation" these people need more difficulties and restrictions, even the harsh fears and taboos they have lived with before. But nothing of this can work in our liberal and scientific era, least of all in our cities. The result is motivational and mental deterioration, even worse than among other groups.

Poverty could be, as it has historically been, a source of greater motivations and capacities. Unfortunately the rational liberalism has turned the strong motivations of the poor toward easy solutions through revolutions and rejection or hate of existing order. Even so the movements of liberation, communism or revolutionary parties are so much better motivated that they win against larger forces. Throughout history, the poor classes, the plebeians, peasants, burghers and workers, as well as people living under harsher conditions, have come to power, through their stronger motivations and capacities.

In conclusion we may emphasize how completely contrary to the usual human value outlook is the causal principle on which

a scientific progress is to be built. It is the principle of enrichment of capacities through opposition or restriction — which
would amount to man acting against, or operating on, himself.
Actually, man would start *doing by plan what has been done
blindly.* Up to now men have adopted restrictions only in blind,
confused ways, imposed by cultural selection or superstitious,
seemingly backward morals. A causal understanding of the principle of opposition or restriction would be the humble starting
point for a scientifically understood progress by man — for his
conscious self-creation.

The Humanistic and Scientific Fallacies About Progress

The very logic or way of thinking in sciences and humanistic
thought is blunderously wrong in regard to the causation of
inner values or value reactions, which determine all human capacities and behavior. It is the logic that positive values originate
from positive value sources or from experiences of same value.
But the all-important fact is — however often we have to repeat
it — that men do not attain the highest inner values or capacities by endlessly enjoying themselves. The exact reverse is
causally true.

Yet the direct, perfect *enjoyment of inner values is stressed*
in the humanistic thought above everything else. Search for the
inner quality of feeling and deeper experience of values are
seen as the most important objectives of human progress (J.
Huxley, L. Mumford, E. Fromm). Deepening of inner value feelings, contrasted with the present emotional weariness, is viewed
as the promise of cultural rebirth and progress (A. J. Toynbee,
P. A. Sorokin).[8] The whole "humanistic tradition" rests on the
enjoyment of the emotionally most valued works of art, literature or religion.[7] The "saving experience" for man is the enjoyment of values — "stirred by music, poetry or moonlight" (H.
J. Muller).[4] Restrictions on enjoyments imposed by religion are
condemned as momentous obstacles to progress (V. Brome).[9]

Even scientists and science-fiction futurists accept the deepening of value feelings, or enjoyments of beauty and art as the ultimate gains for man (L. V. Berkner, A. C. Clarke).[10,11] The fact that value enjoyment, as every satisfaction, extinguishes itself, or leads to opposite reactions, has never been considered.

Particularly the recent cultural movements want to promote progress through *direct heightening of value experiences.* The most readily accepted works, like *The Greening of America,* by C. Reich, or *At the Edge of History,* by W. I. Thompson, are totally devoted to the widening of inner value enjoyments. According to Reich, the Consciousness III, centered on the grooving to inner pleasures by the modern youth, has already arrived as the beginning of the future progress. Thompson sees solutions in value enjoyments that border with the ecstatic experiences of mysticism, meditation, Yoga, Zen, Subud or Sufism, as well as in the practices of the counter-culture.

All most recent reformist movements and theories are aiming at the direct increase in value enjoyments[12] as the remedy against the emotional impoverishment suffered by modern man[15] — which grows exactly from his increased enjoyments. Even the traditional religions are welcoming the ecstatic Eastern mysticism and practices, that our most learned groups are rushing to indulge. The science of man itself is to be helped by abandon and ecstasy, in love or painting, revealing man's "self-relatedness" (R. May).[23] Theorists in various fields have accepted value experiences as sources even of scientific truths (B. Glass, G. R. Harrison, F. S. C. Northrop). Of course values show as causally true the exact opposite of what is so in fact.

The result is that modern man is progressing into the "improvements" which bring impoverishment and disease; is accepting mere fixations as most sacred values; or is pursuing the modern alchemy in science, even turning to esoteric ritualism. We saw the advance of these practically dangerous and confusing fallacies in every field. Understandably, the flight into deliberate irrationalism and mysticism of the value world is becoming the modern trend. Our learned groups are seeking their insights and world view from mystifications, by authors like Carlos Castaneda or Theodore Roszak, about sorcery, shamanism, drug trips, hallucinations or other irrational experiences.

Against this background of mounting afflictions and practically total confusion we may mention the noble philosophical arguments that only by recognizing the exalted nature of man we can conserve his progress. The doctrine that man has been created in the image of God is seen threatened. The issue is deemed decisive by greatest authorities, as is shown in the book *The Difference of Man and the Difference it Makes,* by Mortimer Adler. In truth, abstract knowledge is weightless motivationally and can never change our value attitudes. Scientists did not become bestial upon accepting Darwin's theory. Men will not lose motivations upon understanding the relative causation. Yet theorists love to speculate how ideas change life and history. Of course no two polemicists agree; and world-shaking new discoveries make no difference. It is only a game. If the great world view of individualism, of Emerson, Whitman or Henry James, is proven to be corruptive, as is shown in the book of Quentin Anderson *The Imperial Self,* nobody gets practically concerned.

Finally we have to repeat the all-important fact about the *qualitative promotion of inner values: the effort is as futile as chasing one's own shadow.* Value is always a feeling or organic experience, and as such it only can derive from, or lead to, opposite value experiences. Thus the qualitative gain that the humanists are stressing is never possible in value experiences. The only possible progress is the deplored quantitative one. The learning and knowledge, left as traces of the equal gains and losses of value experiences, can be endlessly rich. Also the inner values as quantitative satisfaction potentials, like the love, interest or morals, can be enriched and are the most needed psychic capital. But such value potentials are created by the accumulation of their opposites, needs or nonsatisfactions and restrictions, always felt as disvalues.

When we turn to *modern science* we find that it is becoming a menace rather than help to human progress. We have seen in every field how the logic of direct "improvements" has fostered the overadjustments as causes of vicious-circle exhaustion of mental and physical capacities. The deterioration is increasing everywhere, from "alienation" to the deaths from heart disease. In fact the present scientism is becoming so disastrous that the more sensitive learned groups now are turning against it, as we already mentioned. But the humanistic theorists are deploring our only successful, technical progress as the threat to inner values of modern man.

This is ironic. For exactly the humanistic emphasis on the direct most fundamental, free value enjoyments has led to the era of overenjoyments and "improvements" that cause the malignant impoverishment, disorders, weariness, negative reactions and functional diseases. The technical progress has been merely used by modern man to attain these overenjoyments and "improvements" to their full, malignant extent.

The unexpected, exactly opposite results of the unprecedented improvements are found to be near-catastrophic, uncontrollable and insidious. They have been labeled as "dehumanization" of man, collapse of traditional values, indifference to morals and deepening alienation amidst affluence (H. Kahn).[1] Scientists may note the insidious effects of overnutrition, overprotection, overpopulation, or atrophy from lack of effort (R. Dubos).[3] Many theorists blaming the "dehumanizing technology" are fearing that the machine has taken over our lives beyond recall.[15] The general pessimism has inspired the most recent speculations that the growth of material progress should be stopped, as has been advocated by the authoritative Club of Rome. All these arguments imply the absurdity that man does not notice what hurts him, what deprives him of the inner values, which are pleasures he seeks — *and overenjoys* — through the modern progress.

The great *schism between humanists and scientists* is blamed on scientists being ignorant in most value disciplines (C. P. Snow).[5] Scientists *have to* exclude the delusory verities of humanists, who therefore have to become the unemployable "natural Luddites"[6] of our scientific era. The humanists then feel that the uniquely successful "cause-tight" world of sciences is a "night" world without values and quality.[7] The contrast between the impoverishment of value experiences and the richness of quantitative progress is constantly noted.[15] Scientists may be shown not to be concerned with human values or inner value experiences — with the "quality" of life (R. Dubos).[3] But this rather proves that scientific success depends on freedom from the value delusions.

It is inane to urge the scientsts, or modern man, to be more concerned with the inner values or "qualitative" experiences. Everybody strives for such values and experiences to the utmost, and they are the simplest things to understand or to enjoy. Hence the overenjoyments, leading to the afflictions. Certainly the calamities of modern men can be construed as complex difficulties of too much change, novelty, acceleration or stimulation, having the effect of shock (A. Toffler).[14] But the point is that men seek and accept it all because they want it, in calculation of their "qualitative" inner values as true satisfactions or pleasures, which even animals "calculate" precisely.

The Modern "Alchemy", and Progress

The *alchemy of trying to gain potentials without equal difficulty* is the central fallacy. Mere discovery of new, lucky ways of increasing the positive reactions is accepted as a goal. New working methods and ideas, to be discovered by intensified research, or a few "seed" operations and devices could assumedly change the whole progress, as has been done by inventions of alphabet, coins, stamps, keys, tokens or cards (J. R. Platt).[16] Even a practical social observer may conclude that the evidently beneficial and pleasant human progress or change should come easily if only we could make this clear to the people on a large enough scale (G. Gallup).[17]

Similarly the ideas about cultural conditioning become alchemistic under the "scientific" logic. Conditioning surely is the main source of human progress. But it works by imposing conditioned restrictions, not by mere learning as in the animal conditioned learning. Even after conditioning becomes automatic, through value fixations and the "neurotic" perfectionism, it has to impose restrictions or nonsatisfactions every time it has to create the potentials. But the theorists of conditioning accept the logic of the behaviorist conditioning that amounts to the learning of new behavior through finding better satisfactions. In his famous book *Beyond Freedom and Dignity*, Skinner stresses the "positive reinforcers", total avoidance of negative reinforcement, and acquisition of a desired behavior not requiring later restrictions.[19]

Even the opponents of the conditioning accept the possibility that the satisfactions can be easily learned. They only reject such "posthuman animal happiness" or satisfactions of "cheerful robots" as humanly debasing.[13,23] Actually to the extent men have plenty of satisfaction potentials, however acquired, they are perfect humans. Here we have to make an important general observation. The dominant humanistic thought and education are condemning as horrible any conditioning or changing of human mind and values. It is argued that conditioning would turn men into inhuman robots without sense of values or reason who would be manipulated to hate and destroy. In truth, every man wants the most perfect values and reason, the deeply gratifying love, beauty, peace or harmony. The only thing men lack in order to have such value reactions is the satisfaction or motivation potentials. *If conditioning, however "inhuman", can provide these potentials, it can turn men into perfect, nobly "spiritual" beings.* Rather the direct value enjoyments, leading to overadjustments, turn men into inhuman, irrational haters and destroyers.

Typically alchemistic are the expectations by modern science to reach utopian progress through *improvement of human mind by artificial means* and molecular biology. Particularly drugs can be shown to have miraculous immediate effects on mind. Drugs may be expected to make people content, as described in the science fiction *Island* by Aldous Huxley; or to improve their intelligence, after we "succeed in stimulating the working of the brain, just as we do with other less exalted vital parts" (J. Rostand).[5] Since every capacity depends on increased releases, drugs as potential means of improvement seem acceptable to a strict scientist, like Skinner, or to a practical expert like J. O. Cole of the NIH. In the book *The Year 2000*, Herman Kahn predicts that people will be wearing pleasure consoles and using drugs for political control as well as mental improvement.[1]

In the future of man, drugs and artificial means are always expected to play a decisive role, in control of personality, improvement of intelligence or cure of disorders.[5,25] Similar benefits are expected from use of hormones or stimulation of their production.[5,21] Control of behavior by electrodes or electric fields applied to affect brain, as in experiments by R. Heath and W. Ross, also seems a clear possibility.[21]

The present research on improvements of mind and memory is concentrating on use of brain stimulants, "smart pills" and organic compounds, as well as transfer of "memory molecules". We may refer here to the studies by B. Arganoff, J. McConnell, J. McGaugh, K. Conners, S. Barondes or G. Ungar. Drugs for improvement of memory are expected to be applicable in near future (D. Krech). McConnell's experiments with flatworms and Ungar's with rats were to show that specific learning acquired by one animal can be transferred to another by feeding or injecting extracts from the first to the second. Similar experiments by other scientists have mostly failed. Anyway, the flatworms or rats receiving the extracts only learned more quickly some very primitive responses. Apparently some general release-controlling biochemicals, like the RNA and its proteins in brain neurons, that increase with learning, were transferred. General control of releases is possible and it affects, in its paradoxical ways, all organic functions, including brain processes. But it is preposterous to imagine that the myriad organic mechanisms could be built or changed in molecular ways.

We have to emphasize that any artificial change or improvement, by drug, electricity or other means of stimulation, only leads to exactly opposite counterchange or "worsening". The organism always returns to its normalcy, by opposite processes, after the artificial interference. Permanent organic change, requiring endless reorganization of myriads of interrelated processes, is unthinkable. Even if it was possible, the changed organism would again have to maintain its limited new normalcy and to reverse, further, all "increase" efforts. The organic normalcy, evolved through millions of years, in uncountable ways, can only be damaged by outside intervention. In this sense all "molecular" biology, physiology or genetics is a dangerous imitation of physical sciences, which at best can lead only to reversals of its own efforts.

However involved or sophisticated the nonorganic, outside interference or change, the equal opposite effects are inevitable. The recent *bio-feedback* studies, particularly by Neal E. Miller, have to be mentioned. They prove scientifically that organic processes, like heart beat or blood pressure can be controlled by mind. Apparently, all tensions and releases could be thus controlled, with some training; and increase in releases can improve almost every function. Why not expand such improvements attainable by mental control? In truth, there is no difference whether the immediate improvement is obtained by a drug or by mental suggestion. The mental control still cannot, and should not, create permanent integrated molecular changes in the organism, which always returns, by opposite processes, to whatever organic normalcy it maintains.

Unreversing improvements are obtained only to the extent they remove some abnormalcy or restore normalcy. Brain surgeries, like those performed by Drs. Vernon Mark, and William Sweet, can change personalities by removing some abnormal condition that had caused excessive reactions like aggression. Similarly aggression as a response by animal to frustration, need or other abnormal condition can be eliminated, by inner, neural simulation of normalcy. Thus in experiments by Jose Delgado, and Carmine Clemente, aggression in bulls and cats was controlled by electric impulses.

Surely, by controlling emotions or personalities other motivations, interests and potentials can be changed. But the only unreversing change is the one that restores normalcy. That is why the usable source of potentials is restriction or need as conditioned abnormalcy that provides motivations as ways of return to normalcy; even restrictions by drugs could increase potentials of releases. But this amounts to imposition of hardships, felt as disvalues, that nobody wants or recommends.

Another area of alchemistic scientism is the modern **ethology**. It holds that instincts, like those of aggression or territory, are the bases of human behavior. All higher reactions do derive from the lower drives, particularly from the needs of security, survival, growth or functional fulfillment. But ethologists see the specifically and permanently patterned animal instincts as the underlying drives. This is clear from such works as *On Aggression*, by Konrad Lorenz, *The Imperial Animal*, by Lionel Tiger and Robin Fox, *The Territorial Imperative*, by Robert Ardrey, *Human Aggression*, by Anthony Storr or *The Naked Ape*, by Desmond Morris. These and other ethologists advocate recognition of the instincts as the bases of behavior, to be dealt with in their specifically patterned ways. Thus the instinct of aggression or territory should be satisfied, released or sublimated, in symbolic, psychoanalytic, ritualistic or other formulistic ways, in work, play, education, social life or therapy. This adds to the useless alchemistic confusion or actually weightless formulism and ritualism.

Human behavior is determined by conscious pleasure, deriving directly from the basal survival drives, and not by any limitedly patterned automatic instincts (which serve the same survival drives). The ways and means men use in attaining their pleasures are colossal in comparison with man's incidental instinctive satisfactions. Our "aggressive" superiority or "territorial" security extends to thousands of material, social and cultural achievements, ambitions and enjoyments. In comparison with such values and pleasures the gratification one may derive from the instinctive kicking a man next to him or from the instinctive protection of the room around him is ridiculous.

If biological "instincts" or rather functions have pleasure value, then this pleasure, consciously and ingeniously enjoyed, *changed, manipulated and planned*, is determining. Exactly because man manages and manipulates the enjoyment of the pleasure so inventively, unhindered by any instincts, he drives himself into the aggressive, beastly, "instinctive" behavior.

Equally alchemistic are modern scientific ideas about the use of technologic achievements for human progress. The main fallacy here is of course the "scientific" logic which supports the direct improvements, that lead to the exhaustion of capacities, to disorders and diseases. We shall not repeat the explanations. The higher material progress could offer new superior, extensive ways for imposing the conditioned restrictions. But the modern theorists know only to blame the material progress for the calamities, which they themselves promote with the direct improvement methods. Or they expect the technology, improved communications, new media and other advances to bring progress by themselves, *without regard to the requirement of hard restrictions* of satisfactions or releases.

Thus the technical progress is expected to create a completely new environment permitting utopian possibilities. According to the synergistic views of R. Buckminster Fuller, the results of technological progress will be completely different, qualitatively superior to the means used in promoting it.[15] This amounts to *the alchemy of obtaining human potentials through mere techniques.* The same alchemy underlies the various cybernetic and system-analyses approaches. Particularly the communications, media, and information are expected to transform man.

According to Marshall McLuhan or Harold A. Innis, the form of communication or medium is more important than its contents. The "hot", electric form of the television medium, for instance, is viewed as decisive.[22] It is blamed for the "electric implosion" supposedly bringing the numbness of reactions of modern men. The real causes of such numbness, the enjoyments sought through the media, are not considered. Always the form of the medium, rather than the satisfactions or pleasures that men use it for, is shown as decisive in the various theories of McLuhan. This implies men are so imperceptive about their satisfactions that they use forms of medium which prevent satisfactions. For in McLuhan's theories as well, the positively felt satisfactions are seen as the positive factors.[22] If the form of communication was decisive, then blind and mute persons would have completely different personalities and psychologies. Think of Helen Keller, who received all her communications through pressures on her hand, which is totally weird in comparison with colors and sounds. Yet she had an as normal personality and reacted as adequately as the best of us.

All in all, the modern scientism becomes either a danger or a futile alchemy, in its efforts to promote human progress. Under the direct improvement logic science is enabling man to try to live by releases alone, and thus virtually to destroy his normalcy. The causal logic that positive value reactions or releases can be enriched by their direct addition turns human sciences into an alchemy. Human capacities, which are releases or satisfactions, then seem attainable with the ease of added enjoyments. Since this is exactly contrary to the real, opposite causation, human sciences have nothing useful or relevant to offer. Rather the fallacies of more satisfactions and freedoms are perpetuated. Restriction is the very source of potentials or releases, but science rejects it — and sees no use for restrictive morals in the future of man.[12,15]

Religion, Immortality and Man's own Redemption

All men have had, and must have, some kind of religion. The relative view is not only compatible. with the religious beliefs but is the only one that can *scientifically justify the religious restrictions as well as save religion from the demeaning value outlook.* It can bring religion out of the primitivism of value beliefs which are humanly selfish and degrading, since values derive from our tense needs as base disvalues. The relative view can at least make our beliefs consistent with the serene, above-human, universal "design", that is the progress through opposition in man's terms, and that may harbor a dazzlingly unimaginable future for men.

Theorists have not succeeded in defining religion. It is all things to all men. The reason is that religion constitutes the endless missing parts in the jig-saw puzzle that existence is for men because they lack so much in it emotionally and cognitively. The primitive man has gods and spirits as providers for what he needs, and as explanations for what he does not understand. The more civilized men equally believe in God as source of values and as the ultimate Reason or Intelligence where the values and understanding are wanted or missing most. When modern physicists, in their inability to see the omnipresent negative causal source, were faced with mystery, they postulated a mathematician God.

Modern men of course can see how absurd it is to believe in providential gods only where calamities, failures of crops and dangers reign, and not where things like air, light or the ground is always "providentially" there. Of such religions we can say that the *beliefs in god originate from the godlessness in the world*. But the same is true of our religion as long as it is dominated by value beliefs.

If we are to have a religion in human terms, then we should postulate a god of opposition, difficulty and disvalue, because these are the real causal sources of reality, evolution and value. The eternal question why did God create evil is part of the seeming paradox. The double-talk of value apostles is too transparent for modern man. The God-is-dead idea becomes far more convincing, and may be discussed even by theologians. Existential despair and defeatism are the result. There is no need for it, if we think of God as the source of creation and evolution — through the opposition — and if we understand the value delusions. In a religion governed by value convictions the love of God becomes strongest, most genuine where threat of death or calamity is gravest. Totally helpless victims of terrorism have similar love for their dictator when they willingly and sincerely confess their crimes. There as well the satisfaction of submission is genuine, because the need is oppressing.

Any human terms are demeaning in our thinking about God. Even viewing God as pure intellect is degrading. As we saw, intellect is a very clumsy capacity, of proceeding by "ones", while nature works with myriads of elements at every point and instant. The only advantage intellect has is that it can relive or remember the past, and project future from it. If one such simple advantage makes the whole difference, the world of human intellect must be limited indeed. The more learned a religion is, the more fatuous it becomes. Anything men can say or pretend to know about God is preposterous. Yet thousands of books are being written and uncountable words said every day, in explaining God, by millions of highly learned men. The plain waste of talent and effort is deplorable.

Moreover, the dogmas and doctrinaire issues become fixational — irrationally sacred and endlessly elaborate — in narrow, humanly value-bound ways. In fact the doctrines have remained so naively delusional, requiring a providential anthropomorphic creator, that religion is still in conflict with science.[24] Further, the logical and effective modern realization of the value outlook is making religion liberal and permissive. Freedom from guilt or restrictions, even from sense of sin is now to be provided by healthy religion.[9] Hippie culture has easily merged with religion; and a "progressive" church service may include rock music.

Nonridiculous and undemeaning religion, consistent with the universal law of reality and progress — the law of opposition or restriction in human terms — is possible. We can believe in a God as miraculously mysterious as is the progress that awaits man at the end of his destiny, while we work for that progress in following the above law. Acceptance of the humanly contradictory, indifferent, even coldly severe laws of the universe might be the truest recognition of God. The wisdom of opposition or restriction is embodied in the religious thousand-year practical tradition.

The simple men who live by this restrictive tradition and bow in awe before the severe will of a mysterious, incomprehensible God, are closer to a true religion than the learned theologians in their fatuous, endless "explanations" of a humanistic God. We may repeat that the relative insight provides the only scientific or causally understood explanation why the restriction has to be the goal of human effort — or the core of the truest religion men can have.

We may look at the belief in *immortality*, which is the strongest belief in all religions. This is so because continued life is the ultimate value but is denied by death. Religion is to supply here, as elsewhere, the missing satisfaction. Nobody could live with the certainty that his life is to end in nothing. But if the belief in immortality is the strongest for man, it is also the craziest. A minute organic change, sometimes produced by a grain of biochemicals, can distort our conscious life to unrecognition. How could such life continue after the whole body has disintegrated? Any soul we may have that does not participate in this organic life is as irrelevant to us as are the souls, lives and deaths of millions of men which have not been part of our organic lives. But organically death is the end of everything.

The humanists have argued that though immortality is impossible we have to sustain the belief in it because this satisfies the deepest need in us. This would be right if it were not for the inexorable causality of value experiences. By sustaining the belief in immortality *one only accumulates the horrors of death to the last moment* when such belief as unreality or exaggeration collapses and the opposite reactions all rush in at once.

Moreover, if we had immortality in the way we want it — or even a real belief in it — our existence would have no meaning. A true immortality would remove the fear of death; but every value, pleasure or satisfaction we have in life derives from the fear of death or need of survival. Also, if we were immortal we would not even bother to think about immortality. It would then have as little value as does the spatial continuity of matter in our body.

We could, rather, diminish the whole problem of immortality and the horrors of death by diminishing the enjoyment of inner values or pleasure releases. This would not necessarily affect our powers of motivations. In the world of values and mind minimal releases can have unlimited power to the extent all other drives are equally restricted. We saw that restricted life is a longer as well as richer life. By managing the emotional, opposite causal sources we could decrease the fear of death to the minimum even for the moment of dying. Emotions can be planned to occur in any way we want if their paradoxical causality is understood, though no value gain should be ever expected. By the way, even the sense of longevity is relative. If men normally lived one year, having necessarily sharper realizations of death and life, they would have as much of value experiences as if they lived a thousand years with necessarily remoter realizations of death and life. Mere living without excitements is often viewed as a misery, particularly by the young.

Above all, *even God could not give us immortality in those terms we want it,* namely, as a freedom from fear of death while we have joy of life. For even He cannot create for us mountains without valleys, or values without disvalues; and the *value or pleasures of life or survival derive from the fear of death.* It has to be kept in mind that immortality is sought by men not as any objective condition but as a subjective value and organic necessity. Objectively death is a return to nothingness, therefore should be something like falling asleep, suddenly being nothing, feeling nothing and knowing nothing. This would be almost a delight, similar to getting drunk or being drugged into unconsciousness.

The decisive fact is that death brings destruction of accumulated growth, or *equalization of all values by equal disvalues.* All pleasures or values are expressions of organic growth, therefore lead to opposite processes upon death; something that has not grown cannot cause pain or be destroyed. Of course growth is not the mere bulk of flesh but the release of the life flow. We have always shown this to be so. Accumulation of "reserves" is a restriction on the flow of life, so that potential of its release becomes available. Consequently a person restricting himself has great reserve potential for growth, and since this growth has not been realized, he does not suffer pain for it if he dies. Thus restriction enables one to live with least amounts of accumulated growth, therefore with least suffering in case of death, but also with greatest potentials for the motivations he needs.

In simplest terms, any previously not equalized joy or pleasure has to be repaid with equal displeasure or horror upon death. The repayment can be done gradually, before death, by suffering the restrictions of growth, through displeasure or anxiety, that resemble slow death. That is why a person who knows he has to die starts, instinctively, such repayment, by suffering the anxiety. Logically he should rush into enjoying life in its fullest while it lasts. He does the opposite, because his whole world of instincts and values tells him that death amounts to the equalization of his accumulated values with equal disvalues. Typically the suicides, who believe — erroneously as we saw — that death is easier than the seemingly unbearable life, do not think of immortality, though logically they should be interested more than others in the possibility of another, different life.

In sum, equalization of inner values with equal disvalues is the meaning of death which brings the biological self back to the zero level it started from. Nothing in the world or heavens can change this rule of equalization, just as nothing can make ascents of a plane more than its descents, if it has to land at the same level from which it started.

The anxiety and preoccupation about death and immortality will increase as men progress and their other concerns diminish. Psychopathy or neurotic reactions are bound to follow if the pleasant but unreal beliefs are sustained by increasing efforts. Men will have to choose between such inherently psychopathic efforts, and a causally understood restriction of the inner values or pleasures of life so that the horrors of death are equally reduced, to the level the person wants — without any value gain.

Here we come to the ultimate problem of the aspirations of man, the *redemption* of his existence. If our life cannot offer us any gains in value enjoyments or satisfactions what is it good for? Men asking the eternal question "What is it all about?", in their moments of insight into the futility of existence, have been struggling with the same problem. Nobody has found the answer, because there is no logical immediate purpose in our existence. Yet man will be redeemed by his unimaginable future which promises miracles greater than is the present human consciousness in comparison with the reactions of, say, a primeval crab. You participate in this redemption when you help the progress of man, even if you do not know what miracle awaits him at the end of it. Absolutely everything might well be justified and redeemed by that miracle. Thus our very uncertainty is the promise of our redemption.

Becoming his own Creator is the ultimate role of man as a conscious being. The self-creating man will plan his releases or value reactions, by accepting equal restrictions, so that he can have unlimited capacities, and reduce the horror of death to any level he wants. He will have everything men can want, except the *gain* in pleasures or inner values, which is unattainable anyway. He will also extend the length of his life almost at will by slowing down its rate by the restrictions. Such life will be filled with presently inconceivable amount of abstract thought, and determined by unlimitedly imaginative, truly "spiritual" ideas, in the absence of stronger, natural drives as qualitative values.

Serenity of thought will have replaced the brutish pursuit of inner value gains, that even God cannot give man. Serene, restricted life is always the mark of higher culture and mature mind. Logically or "scientifically", restrictive, resigned life may seem contrary to strong motivations or vigorous progress. But such humanly natural view is deceptive. A civilized, resignedly reflective and self-controlled person may seem like a weakling to primitive savages full of life, strong emotions, excitement and external vigor. Even in the world of the qualitative inner values like love or beauty, which are common to all men, the primitive man has deeper, stronger emotions. Human redemption lies not in the futile pursuit of qualitative values, as it seems to, but in serene, unlimited self-creation by man, through the principle of the universal reality and progress — the causal principle of opposition or restriction.

Man as his own Creator

Evidently the human self-creation, with its unimaginably miraculous goal, is the destiny, even the duty of man as the only conscious being. The possibilities are unlimited, and progressively self-increasing, since men can create, at each step, a man capable of creating far better men. Once the unthinkable logic of the organic value causation is understood, the human progress will reach presently unimagined colossal proportions, as all true sciences have done. Causal understanding has always been the only requirement for a science to start on its way to explosively cumulative success.

In human sciences the progress has been up to now insidiously self-defeating or seemingly impossible, because the present "scientific" and humanistic thought aim at direct increase in functional improvements and inner values, which inevitably leads to least wanted, baffling opposite effects. This has vitiated all modern progress and turned it into a calamity rather than a blessing.

Total, "impossible" *change of the way of thinking,* in abandonment of previous value beliefs, is evidently the key here, as in all cases when a new science begins. Change of attitudes is required even in dealing with the immediate, clear problems of human progress. A particularly clear, practical way of progress would be the use of eugenic methods, that are presently opposed or neglected because of humanistic value attitudes. Simple *eugenic techniques, like the artificial insemination,* would permit creation of superior men capable to improve all their capacities. But in the present culture dominated by emphasis on value enjoyments and freedoms or "natural rights", artificial insemination, and all human eugenics, are viewed as atrocious threats to human dignity and democratic liberties.

We admit that the feeling about "blood ties" and the desire to see oneself repeated in one's children can be strong. But cultural conditioning could change this. Having and bringing up children are essentially spiritual and educational rather than physical or sexual achievements. Culture had already made men ashamed of the more direct sexual aspects in reproduction. Couples who adopt or bring up children begin to love them as their own in a short time. The way we invest our emotions is decisive and it can be culturally determined. If we started to invest our aspirations and pride in how we make our children superior through education, this would become the central value, and the ideas about the physical relationship would fade. Then artificial insemination would naturally be chosen, as the surest way to have superior children.

An eugenic technique like the artificial insemination can make men progress in a couple of generations more than they have done during thousands of years. If the IQ, for instance, is increased in average from 100 to 130, it would be more than men could otherwise hope to achieve for ages. It is clear that this simple method can give all men, in few generations, the capacities that now only exceptional men and geniuses enjoy. Since everything else ultimately depends on such capacities, we have here a *key to a progress that all of us badly want.*

Of course in dealing with the IQ or other endowments, the capacity to bear restrictions should be the criterion. It comes usually, but not necessarily always, with a better brain or higher intelligence. The present science, generally deriving its positive criteria rather from capacities to obtain more release, can do here more harm than good. This is why presently men with good common sense may intuitively feel that scientific intervention in planning of human abilities is a menace. But methods like artificial insemination can be made reliable even now, and there is no reason why men should continue the blind, unplanned animal ways of reproduction instead.

Birth control and abortion, for prevention of undesired births, should have been used by any rational people. Typically these measures have come with the increasing difficulties of overpopulation and contrary to the strongest humanistic prejudices of thousands of years. Here again enormous advantages can be gained by simple further eugenic measures. *The vilest, unnoticed crime against man and humanity* is to bear children who are to live in misery and degradation as a burden to themselves and others, or who are to spread further within humanity their genetic scourge. Humanity can be saved from all undesired births of persons who are to become unloved and uneducated criminals and unemployable misfits, or whose low capacities are to bring them inhuman, shameful debasement. The steps for eliminating this crime against everything that is human in men and noble in humanity could be as simple and humane as the prejudices are overwhelming.

The main general prejudices are perpetuated under the slogans of the "sacredness of life" and individual rights. In truth, the sacred right and dignity of man require that he not live in degradation, therefore not be born in it. In evaluating anything that is human, the *consciousness or the feeling of pain and pleasure is decisive, not mere life.* Animals and germs also have life. But no animal feels anything, in the only sense we know feeling. Animals do not even realize that they are there. It is animistic to infer conscious feelings from the similarity of animal reactions with ours. People of good sense know this and use or slaughter animals without remorse. The idealist believing in the sacredness of life and still living peacefully in our world where meat is eaten and pelts or leather worn must have an unbelievably callous soul. Otherwise he should be struggling, in horror, to prevent the killing and exploitation of animals or the "genocide" of insects. If such idealist goes fishing he must be a sadist.

The prejudices, like that about the sacredness of an embryo's soul, are as deep as they are animistic. Surely the embryo is the beginning of the later man. But so is the ovum and sperm. Should we start crying about their destruction? The only thing that humanly matters is the conscious feeling, the suffering and pleasure. We could prevent *misery and degradation of hundreds of millions* of people by control of preconscious life, that would cause no suffering whatever. Not to use such control amounts to a cruel crime. The early infant knows less than a fish or animal that he or anything exists. It would have mattered absolutely nothing to me if I had been killed or even vivisected before I started to develop consciousness, which comes months after birth.

Humans should start distinguishing between what is instinctive animal love for the newborn infant and what should be the real, human love that should save him from suffering or inhuman degradation. Of course if parents start investing their love in the fetus, they suffer upon its loss. Cultural conditioning or change in attitudes could help here easily. Up to some twenty years ago abortion was universally considered a murder. Now it is accepted as an operation on the mother's body. Social trends are shown as indicating that "eugenic infanticide will be widely adopted before the year 2200 and will become universal before 2400".[25] We have to emphasize, however, that without the criterion of the consciousness and suffering any "infanticide" can become an atrocity.

Only as long as consciousness has not yet started, the infant can be put to final "sleep" without feeling or suffering. After that, the suffering cannot be prevented by any means, drugs, anesthetics, or by other manipulation of consciousness. Even a mentally completely deranged person suffers. Only the strictly preconscious life can be permitted to be controlled. With this in mind somebody has to start mentioning the unspeakable "infanticide" *where it is the most humane thing men can do.* Dr. James Watson, the discoverer of the DNA molecule, has urged legalization of infanticide, to "save a lot of misery and suffering", if the genetic engineering, with its possible mistakes, is to continue — as it has to in *human* progress, beyond animal ways of reproduction.

As science advances, selection of future men with only the best qualities would become possible by control of preconscious life. Intellectual capacities should be predictable from responses of neurons or brain in its earliest stages. The simple restrictive capacity alone may be revealing. Here the present science should start understanding the paradoxes of organic restrictions and releases. Presently even the IQ measurements are confusing. They may show fairly high IQ scores for persons or groups that later fail in life due to lack of capacities. The reason is that such measurements do not take into account the capability to bear restrictions, which mostly but not totally coincides with higher intelligence. Anyway, science could predict the capacities of human organisms before their birth or beginning of consciousness.

Thus *generations of perfect individuals could be chosen, with revolutionary consequences for all progress; and the tragedy of failures could be spared.* This can be done even before science advances toward the more involved methods of artificial incubation and insemination, transplants of ova, cloning or the unfeasible molecular genetics. All that men have to do is to be more truly human or sensible to human suffering and less superstitiously blind or prejudiced. We have to emphasize that the gravest crime against man and humanity is the perpetuation of genetic degradation. It is becoming ominous. Under our improved conditions and humanistic attitudes the world is being overpopulated with the lowest grade persons. Now the more intelligent families have only a couple of children, while the least intelligent have many. A couple of near morons may produce a half dozen children, uneducable, unemployable, potential criminals, cared for by welfare, who will produce more of the same.

The present indifference to this virtually gravest crime is unbelievable. The problem could be easily helped. The least intelligent parents of the great families are not the ones who love children more or are ready to care for them. They simply have them because of dissolute, irresponsible ways of living. They would have no children if governmental or welfare policies gave them benefits for not having children and made it easy and simple to avoid conceptions and births. Means and ways could be easily found, through increased effort, if the inertial prejudices were overcome. More improvements in providing easy and simple, costless contraceptives alone would help. Eugenic efforts, starting with subsidized, easy abortions, birth control education and artificial insemination, could do the rest.

Eugenics could and should be as enormously improved as it is now primitive. Everything else depends on what capacities men have. It is rightly conjectured that a nation promoting genetic selection would gain unique advantage, so that other countries would have to do the same.[21] The present eugenic efforts are negligent, as well as misdirected because of our "scientific" fallacies. Presently the main means of birth control is the pill, and its use is inherently dangerous. Interference with hormonal releases is bound to lead to opposite reactions. That is why discontinuation of the pill increases fertility and chances of multiple births. To keep the opposite or rebound effects off, the pill has to disrupt deeper levels of normalcy, which is always dangerous. Easier methods could be devised, since nature can be fooled even by a tiny switch in channels.

The genetic selection discussed here — and even now feasible through means like the artificial insemination — is not only free of racism, but is *contrary to racist attitudes*. It would enable every family, group or race to improve its children in disregard of race. The "purity" or conservation of one's own race is a selfish stupidity. Selective mixing of races is the best way to improve man; all progress requires change and variation, as we saw from the way peoples respond to challenges. Races surely are different in their capacities. But these are so multiple and subtle that each race can contribute something in the creation of the best men. Also, superior individuals are born in all races. All men know and want almost the same "ideal" qualities, except for minor details dictated by fixations which will disappear with the progress.

A man with a 30 point higher IQ will be recognized as superior and desired by any race. A beautiful girl of any race would be elected beauty queen, among ordinary girls, by men of all races. How we know the "ideal" qualities is as miraculous as is men's ability to recognize healthy foods or beautiful things. Geneticists may warn us not to destroy the richness of genetic variability. Such "richness" may be infinite when it consists of abnormalcies or defects, while each perfect quality is essentially one and the same for all men. If men are not enabled to become similar, closer to the intuitively known common ideal, then racial frictions will become the fundamental, increasing causes of wars between races and continents.

A frequent objection to the "quality control" of population is that through it destinies of men will be decided by authoritarian groups. Practically, once the prejudices are overcome, every family will want the best qualities for its children, and specialist doctors will help it, much as they do with other medical problems. Such specialists will need extensive amount of knowledge and consultation with other specialists. But this is hardly more authoritarian or risky than are other decisions by doctors, involving problems of life and death.

The real reason why the eugenic planning appears so unacceptable is the *age-long, fixational value prejudices* of humanists and scientists, for whom all eugenic control is "inherently repugnant", in the words of Bentley Glass. The value prejudices here are so deep because of immemorial value fixations. Men have always reproduced in the same ways and attached their value feelings to these ways. Most values relating to human body become strongly fixational, because the body is continuously valued in its same, permanent forms. Thus dissection of the body or operation on it remained sacrilegious for thousands of years. Abortion has been viewed as murder because of similar fixations. When such strong value fixations are there, men find every justification and reason for them, religious or ideologic, particularly in the absence of real science as well as of insight into the phenomenon of fixation.

Before we conclude, we may emphasize the *extension of human lives,* which should evidently be a major goal of the human self-creation. It is generally accepted, and obvious, that duration of life can be extended by restricting the rate of living. Studies and experiments show that life is extended by various restrictions that slow down the rate of living: by restriction of food, starvation diets, feeding of anti-oxidants, freezing or enforced hibernation.[5,20,21] Science has not advanced much here because it seeks for solutions in direct improvements, requiring removal of restrictions. The future sciences will develop means for imposition of the restrictions in ways thousandfold more effective than now can be thought of. As a result, life will be extended to last many times longer than at present. We have explained repeatedly that a restricted life is rather richer in motivations and capacities. In absence of stronger natural drives, the culturally conditioned moral, rational or "spiritual" motivations take over.

All capacities of man will be enriched by restrictions. Evidently, human capacities or potentials are the elaborations and reserves of satisfactions or releases. But satisfactions are equal to the needs or nonsatisfactions, and release reserves are accumulated by restrictions. Thus the limit for human capacities is the limit to which men can impose on themselves the nonsatisfactions or restrictions. This limit can be extended endlessly, once science starts concentrating on restrictions, educational and physiologic as its goals. The end result may well be that man's capacities as well as longevity will be increased thousandfold, in presently inconceivable richness, through causally understood, planned self-creation by men.

The Unimaginable Future of Man

What man and his world will be like at the end of his progress we can imagine as little as protozoa can think what conscious life is like. But the only possible progress is quantitative and mechanistic. The qualitative progress or direct increase in the inner values is self-defeating, for it leads to opposite value experiences or to functional exhaustion and psychic impoverishment. It may be sufficient here to think of the modern mind-expanding drugs inducing the deepest "transcendental" experiences, and their aftereffects. Value experiences do not reveal or lead to a miraculous world of God, as men conceitedly assume, in their natural delusion. Values only reveal the causal presence of their opposites or disvalues. Positive values do not grow from positive background sources. If they did men would long have found this blissful way to unlimited capacities or inner values. Rather, the modern, scientifically efficient direct pursuit of the concretely satisfying inner values has brought the era of their clear opposites.

We have to repeat this because the whole present thought about progress centers on the "qualitative" goals as opposed to "quantitative" achievements. We could quote here every noted work on human progress, from the books of the "greening" variety we have discussed before to the well-reasoned books like *A God Within* and *So Human an Animal*, by Rene Dubos. The dismal effects — of the present already too intense "qualitative" efforts — are attributed to modern man's mistakes or wrong intents. In truth, man knows better than anything what the deepest, most positive inner values are, and he seeks nothing else.

To the extent any goal is "qualitative" it is simply self-defeating.

The "quantitative" and mechanistic procedures (which, as we saw, require dealing with the pleasure concepts) are the only ones relevant in sciences; and sciences are the only possible ways as well as goals of progress. The now fashionable anti-scientism is an irrational confusion about the present fallacies of sciences. To have scientific, causal understanding is to know what is really happening, so that men can act coherently. When the human sciences become scientific — as the admirably successful technical sciences have done — man will change or create himself, in quantitative, mechanistic ways to attain the highest enrichment of the *inner values as quantitative capacities*. We may recall that consciousness of man has evolved in natural, therefore mechanistic ways.

The future man will have more of such quantitative values, the *unselfish love, spiritual interests or other positive motivations*, than we can imagine. But all values are increased and enriched by accumulation of their opposites, the needs or nonsatisfactions and restrictions, *felt as inner disvalues*. The human sciences will have to provide extensive means and ways for imposing the conditioned nonsatisfactions and restrictions, educationally, culturally and medically or physically. This will have to be done by dealing with organic values or pleasures because that is the only way to deal mechanistically with the otherwise ungraspable organic releases. Evidently, immense scientific, technologic and economic skills and resources will be required to achieve it all. Every person will have to be educated, conditioned and kept in artificial environment to an extent requiring far more numerous specialists and extensive resources than presently could be made available.

It is therefore imperative that the technological and economic growth continue at the highest possible rate. The recent *attacks on technologic and material growth reflect the total confusion* of the modern humanistic and scientific thought. The extensive material growth has, indeed, brought the human impoverishment and disorders. But this is happening because the progress is used for the direct increase in qualitative human "improvements", which inevitably leads to every form of exhaustion. Precisely the humanistic idealists who condemn the technological growth are most to blame for the direct "improvement" or overadjustment attitudes, which flourish in the atmosphere of value enjoyments and freedoms. The same material growth could be used to build a more restrictive culture that would insure unreversing enrichment of capacities as accumulated and refined releases or inner values.

The antigrowth prophets, like those of the prestigious Club of Rome, also predict a global cataclysm within 75 years through overpopulation, overproduction, exhaustion of resources and pollution. Their nearsightedness is astounding. To a medieval scholar, similarly, the age of power engines and electricity might have

looked devilishly cataclysmic. The very standards of future production will change, and it will increase thousandfold. Every
time a natural source has been exhausted, a better substitute has
been discovered. All resources or materials can be substituted,
if there is enough energy; and matter around us is concentrated
energy of inexhaustible immensity.

The sooner men face the shortage of oil and coal, the more
intense will be the development of sources like the thermonuclear
fusion, which can provide limitless energy. Such fusion is already
used in the hydrogen bomb, and merely its harnessed application has to be developed. Theoretically, lasers concentrating energy, concentrated in the same way on several levels, would be
sufficient to burn the heavy hydrogen, suspended in magnetic
field. Various solutions would be found if men were more desperate than we were to invent the atomic bomb.

Once the *problems of pollution* are really, inventively attacked
they will require less revolutionary changes than did the urban
canalization and plumbing. New methods would even yield materials and benefits from disposal of wastes or from thermal
pollution. We may add that our *most vocal environmentalists*
are naive victims of fixations and esthetic prejudices. Pollutions
that uncomfortably restrict enjoyment of life are far less harmful than the pleasures men seek through modern intensified improvements. The plaintive perfectionism about beauty of nature
is childish and humorless in a wider human perspective. Factories could become objects of beauty through a "new-gothic"
esthetic fashion. Extinction of a cute animal may be decried,
while it could as well be conserved in zoos and may be scientifically uninteresting. Far more interesting living forms, say,
strange bacteria or rare chromosomes may be perishing or
emerging with nobody bothering about it.

Overpopulation is of course the central problem. In truth,
it is a menace only to the extent humanity is overpopulated by
lower-grade persons. If the quality of people is improved, under-
population will become the real problem. People with higher
intelligence do not have many children. Moreover the world
needs as numerous high quality population as possible. The
strength, inventiveness and progress of humanity depends on

the number of people pooling their efforts and competing, through integrated societies.

The very difficulties of overpopulation will force people to be radically inventive and to integrate into the more efficient virtual social organisms, as all trends show. Experiments with animals cannot prove much here, but even they show that animals born overcrowded remain totally unaggressive.[21] It seems our earth can support 200 billion people even with our present technology;[21] an estimate of 400 billion has been mentioned.[12] One should not use the present standards of what can be done. According to calculations of Malthus we should be all dead from starvation. There are more people in the two Trade Center skyscrapers in New York than were in the ancient Rome.

Though we cannot imagine how the future man will live, we may go along with *the futurist vision of man functioning as a giant brain.* The organic functions serving stronger value experiences will be reduced to a minimum. Tiniest organic releases, as in abstract thought, are sufficient if all stronger drives are restricted; and the amount of releases is equal to the imposed restrictions. The peculiarity of brain is that it can function, as a peripheral biologically unessential outgrowth, with minimum of releases or flow of life; brain does not even cause pain when cut. Thus brain could well grow to any extent, without much aging by the organism. But brain is, evidently, the organ of thought and intellect. Thus the future man may well become an expanding brain or intellect with least of biologic life. Physically man is ridiculously small. But his intellect can conquer the universe.

We can envision the future man, living in biologic suspension, staying in a computerized room resembling a machine or laboratory, without even a need to move. In few decades men will study, work and socialize by tele-communications. In the end man will be able *to be "present", to see, or even "touch" things,* at any place he wants, even *on a planet or a star without moving from his room.* New radaring techniques permitting a focusing on objects at distance would be required. But in view of the rapid advances in such techniques, man will be able, in few centuries, to have all sensations he wants of things at any distance. The future man will find unlimited interest and beauty in the intricacies of what to us seem mere numbers and data; the quantitative, abstract interests are the only ones that do not reverse in value, and can serve progress.

Man is to conquer the universe around our tiny earth, and to discover other conscious beings. But he is *too puny physically* to do so by his bodily presence. The present scientific and science-fiction ideas about space travel are short-sighted. Future men will admire our space programs in the way we admire the pyramids, as wondrous efforts for humanly futile aspirations. To reach even a single closest star man would have to travel thousands of years. Tele-presence is the only possible way, and scientists should concentrate on it. The conquest of interstellar distances would still require major breakthroughs. We can hope that different forms of the Field might be discovered which can give higher transmission speeds. The universe seems to be limitless in possibilities, each of them relative, when we go into fundamental phenomena like the Field, which have not yet been even suspected by scientists.

A presently conceivable possibility would be the *control of time by man.* Since time is only relationships of changes, one could turn a hundred years into few days by suspending changes in himself and the immediate environment. Astronauts are pictured as being frozen into sleep and traveling without aging. Forms of freezing are considered as ways of controlling time.[12] We can be sure that various means for suspending the organic processes will be discovered and men will create for themselves as much time as they need. The control or creation of time is a too important matter for future man to miss. It will become as common as is our living by the watch, which would have seemed crazy to primitive man.

Evidently the future man will be capable and rich in his intellectual world by being *free of the biologic values like beauty, sexual interests or physical excellence.* Cultural values are always relative; and individuals preoccupied with values like physical beauty, masculinity or esthetic concerns will, conceivably, be viewed by future men as cases of mental retardation. They will be in fact relatively retarded, by having less undivided intellectual interests than the others. The future man will be finally free of the biological, animal drives, that underlie all value feelings, while his world will be rich in abstract intellectual or the truly spiritual interests, to a presently unimaginable extent.

The world of intellect or brain is the only one that provides unreversing values and enables man to create or to progress. The mere biologic body may well be sacrificed for the brain. A peculiar possibility would be to create preconscious bodies, as if without brain or soul, and use them to extend the life of the brain. One way to do so would be by the cloning that scientists have recently speculated about. Chromosomes taken from a person would produce an identical organism, which could be grown without permitting its consciousness to develop. Its parts then could be transplanted to renew the person, and there would be no rejection. This is not more absurd than are the deaths of people having full consciousness or life of the brain whose hearts or kidneys fail.

The present speculations about the future are either dominated by the delusory value outlook or limited by the incompleteness of our sciences. Scientists still do not see the most important side of the physical reality, the negative causal backgrounds like the Field. Evidently, nothing fundamentally new can be predicted without an insight in that causal world. Scientists and science-fiction writers cannot even speculate about different forms of forces and of matter, imaginable with *different kinds of Fields which almost certainly exist* in the evidently unlimited universe. They may instead speculate by mere projections from the past about some new force like that of antigravitation,[11] though such force can never be anything more than the counterpressure by the Field that we use already as the mechanical force. By missing the real causal sources of the world, the forces of the Field, scientists simply miss the possibilities inherent in the universe and all nature.

The living world is a good example. The living process is a negative fire, as a chain reaction "burning" against the Field. It is therefore an energy source potentially more powerful than are the other chain reactions like the ordinary fire or atomic reactions.

Science can amplify gigantically any haphazard forces of nature. It could create living processes of every form or intensity. All kinds of elements could be "burned" by living processes. The only condition would be the presence of energy, from sun, natural heat or other radiation. One could envision luxurious new kinds of growth "burning" forth on deserts or the moon, much like the "storms" on Mars, to serve as sources of energy. The present era, before the causally understood use of living processes, would be comparable to the era before men started using fire.

One could even speculate about a perpetual source of energy produced by using the inherent opposition between the living process and the Field forces. For instance, science could devise a living process capable of absorbing the energy from the usual earth environment, which is far above the minus 459 degrees or zero energy. The effects and products of such process would provide energy that men could use while the environment regains its equilibrium or the produced materials are burned.

The point is that once we learn to play out in controlled ways the Field and matter against each other, by the use of the chain reaction of life, we can harness the eternal energy of the universe in forms we can use. This energy never exhausts itself. It works all the time, infinitesimally, around the atoms. We only have to collect this energy of opposition between the Field and matter in usable amounts, through the specially designed living processes.

Under the general *value outlook* human progress should aim at spiritual transcendent fulfillment through the world of values. The ultimate attainment is expected to be some form of spiritualization, unanimization or etherealization of the humanity. The concept of the noogenesis by Teilhard de Chardin is a good example.[26] Miraculous fusion of humanity into one ecstatic consciousness is expected to emerge through deepening of inner values. We have to repeat that value experiences seem indeed to be miraculously transcendental but in fact only reveal preexistence of their opposites, the disvalues, or create them as aftereffects. Not the self-contradictory and self-defeating value experiences, but *mechanistic progress can bring unimagined possibilities, more miraculous than the humanists can think of.*

For instance, if consciousness — which has evolved mechanistic-ally — could be combined with the multiplicity of interaction of natural, living processes, we could have virtual miracles. A being capable to act consciously in the multiple ways of living processes could transform himself into any imaginable new form or create new living beings, just as man now can move his limbs or create tools. He would understand, predict, re-create, cure or perfect in himself anything as easily as we now understand, predict or control the working of machines. He could even predict the future or resurrect the past, just as man now can predict future changes or reconstruct past forms in his dealing with separate things in his environment.

Evidently, we have here capacities of unlimited creation of life, resurrection of the past or knowledge of future, that men consider as miraculous powers of gods. Of course such combination of consciousness with the multiplicity of nature would be difficult to achieve, though the workings of pleasure show it is conceivable. To enable the consciousness to deal with the multiple elements, these should be integrated in an organism or brain governed by the consciousness. Thus to resurrect a world, its elements should first become parts of the conscious organism. One cannot immagine how this could be done. But the point is that the humanistic thinkers speculating about the most sublime concepts, like the "noosphere" or earth transformed by conscious-ness, need only to think of simple mechanical principles like the multiplicity of living processes, to have greater miracles than they have dared to imagine. *The simple mechanical world is more essentially supreme* than are the complex philosophical concepts; *ultimate essences are simplest.*

Practically as well the future progress will be very different from the imagined humanist ideal. Future societies will become the "anthill" organisms, with individuals conditioned to such extent that everybody will strive only for the social good. Surely, men will not do physical or routinely mental work. Machines and computers will do it, better than men ever could. But everybody will be *strenuously competing* for tensely responsible roles of superiority and command, in a *society that will exist by subordination,* as every organism does. Drives, not ideals, are the forces that determine behavior. The power to command, though, will derive from greater knowledge or true spirituality; and the subordination will be expression of conditioned love for society or others.

The creation of such spirituality and love will require vast effort. Man is always born an animal. To transform him into what the future men will have to be will require numerous educators and specialists working on every person, as well as the vast restrictive environment that each person will live in *The worry that future men will have nothing to do*[1,15] *is shortsighted.* In addition, the conquest of the universe further and further out will keep the future men intensely busy.

It is futile to try to predict in detail what the future progress will be like. We can be sure however that the progress will be built in a scientific or causally understood way, leading to successes as progressively explosive as those of all true sciences. That is why *it is so important to establish the sciences of man,* through the presently unthinkable though simple causal insights, that we have tried to explain in this book. A true, causally understood science is the only way men can attain or do *what they really, coherently want.*

We may add that the *study of the future* should be made a prominent field of learning, to be taught at schools as a main subject. In everyday life men plan and think about their future more than anything else. Why should they be prevented from doing so in regard to the most important thing in human life, the future of humanity. If men start envisioning and needing a progressive future, they will have motivations for attaining it. The teaching of the past history rather than of a subject on the future, at schools, is due to fixational inertia.

Final Conclusions

Everything man feels, thinks, knows or does is determined by his value reactions, ultimately, organic releases, which are governed by the law of relative causation. This law is not humanly interesting at all. It shows that satisfactions, releases,

520 The Science of Man and Human Self-Creation

pleasures or inner values derive from equal needs, nonsatisfactions, restrictions or disvalues. Nobody can live with the conviction that there is never any gain in satisfactions, pleasures or values. The law of relativity therefore has to appear impossible or ridiculous. It is also too simple to seem worth knowing, where it is evident. Everybody knows that satisfactions cannot arise without needs as nonsatisfactions; that transition from pain brings pleasure; that overenjoyments lead to painful aftereffects; that things are evaluated by comparison; or that we have the greatest values, like morals, where the lack of actual values, therefore the need for them, is greatest.

Thus the relative insight can hardly be considered an interesting discovery, and we do not expect to convert anybody to relativistic beliefs. The only merit of the explanation of the law of relativity is that it can serve as the causal basis for the sciences of man, whose behavior is determined by value experiences. Simple, previously unthinkable causal truths have been bases of all new sciences. The key to the sciences of man is the "impossible" relativity governing all value reactions as the determining factors.

We may repeat here the universal simple fact from which the relativity derives. It is the maintenance by organism of its sameness, so universal and self-evident that it is never seen as worth knowing. Organism cannot become more than its normalcy in any of its forms, dynamics or reserves. Therefore the only way a release, satisfaction or inner value can be increased is by first increasing the corresponding restriction, need or inner disvalue.

If pleasure releases are overspent, the organism subsequently restores the normal release reserves by opposite processes or restrictions, felt as displeasures. If such restrictions, appearing as sickly reactions, are relieved by further increase in the releases, this starts the vicious circle of deepening impoverishment through increased "improvements". The organism can be driven to any degree of exhaustion, abnormalcy or malignant disease by such vicious-circle additions of experimentally clear improvements. Drug use offers the simplest illustration of the opposite aftereffects. In other cases, ingenious improvement efforts bring equally "ingenious" opposite reactions, attributed to the Unconscious.

The relative or opposite causation is exactly contrary to all humanistic and "scientific" logic or way of thinking. Positive value reactions, which constitute our positive capacities, are always assumed to derive from positive experiences. And all values are value reactions, deriving innerly or from qualities seen in value objects. Thus values like love, interest or beauty are satisfactions or releases, and are assumed to derive from positive background experiences. In truth they, as all satisfactions or releases, can derive only from their opposites, the needs or restrictions as tense, unpleasant conditioned nonsatisfactions of the drives for growth, security or other organic values. Thus love or interests are certainly satisfactions or pleasures, yet are so difficult to attain.

Theorists, not understanding the paradox of the opposite causation, logically urge people just to enjoy the values as the satisfactions or capacities. The whole modern thought has been deluged with the vast, righteously enraged advocacy, by reformers and liberals, of direct increase in the satisfactions of interests, love or other values, in the fields of education, behavior, health or social life. The resulting overenjoyments have led to exhaustion, impoverishment and disorders everywhere, from student riots and "alienation" to mental disorders and heart disease.

Scientism dominates our era. But present science becomes a menace rather than help in dealing with man, because it knows only the logic of direct improvements or increase in releases. Experimentally, positive motivations and capacities always seem to improve upon increase in releases, though the end result is the exhaustion. The experimental modern medicine, proceeding by the direct improvement logic, has to admit that it does not understand the causes of the functional diseases which now kill three fourths of the people best cared for. These diseases can be "cured", temporarily, by drugs which make them worse in the end.

In all fields modern science proceeds by the same logic of direct improvements, which bring similar unexplainable functional impoverishment. Life by the increased releases or pleasures alone becomes the goal, made possible by progress and the scientific attitudes that condemn restrictions or the old restrictive tradition. Hence the increasing human calamities in spite of the unique general progress.

The experimental logic that the positive reactions or capacities derive from positive experiences governs everything theorists write or say. But in human sciences this logic leads to a virtual alchemy by which the most precious human capital, the positive reactions, would be attainable with the ease of pleasures. The reality is totally different. Yet all theories about human capacities or value reactions, about everything men can and want to do, follow this "scientific" logic. They become alchemistic confusions, because they miss completely the real causal factors. The real causal sources of the positive reactions, the negatively felt, hard, even "diseased" restrictions and nonsatisfactions or needs are never suspected as such sources.

Similarly, in all fields of human knowledge, from philosophy to physics, the real causes remain unrecognized, because knowledge is a value process and most everything in man's world has a value meaning for him. We saw how in physics the fundamental causal source of its phenomena is not recognized because it is the negative opposite of man's primary value, the physical reality. In all knowledge and science, presently only the positive effects are seen, valued or eagerly advocated as the realities and values, while their real causal sources, their negative opposites remain unnoticed or are rejected. The relative insight reveals in man's world and mind this opposite causal side, more important and extensive than the side man sees and values.

Above all, this insight into the causality of value experiences, by which man lives, would make human sciences possible. These sciences have remained unscientific because their real causal logic is humanly unthinkable. Otherwise they would be easiest for man. The factual evidence of the unthinkable relative causation is everywhere. The millions of addicts to drugs, tobacco or other means of overadjustments are living experiments on the inevitability of the opposite effects. All the contradictions of human existence exacting restriction or displeasures from man striving only for release or pleasures, prove the same. The greatest authorities have discovered the facts, referred to throughout this book, which clearly warrant and require the explanation by the relative causation. Yet the law of that causation has remained unrecognized and human sciences virtually nonexistent.

We can be sure, however, that once the sciences of man begin they will gradually become more miraculous than even we of our stupendous scientific era can imagine. For then man will be creating himself, by "engineering" his own capacities as the very sources of increasing progress. Such capacities, including longevity, can be as unlimited as are the possibilities of conditioned restriction — the "damming" up — and refinement, of the releases of life flow. This will require, as we saw, a reversal of the present "scientific" and value convictions. Value feelings may seem transcendentally deep, but much like the drug-induced religious convictions, they merely lead to opposite reactions. Everything "qualitative" is self-defeating. Only the "quantitative" capacities or emotionally gainless values, like the selfless love, morals or interests, can be increased. They are satisfactions, as releases of flow of life, deriving from conditioned needs, as nonsatisfactions or restrictions, which can be increased without limits — and are felt as disvalues.

Thus the increase in human capacities can be limitless, and man as self-creator will end with a progress that we can imagine as little as a microbe can conceive conscious life. Our very incapacity to imagine this destiny of man is a promise that our existence may have a meaning and be redeemed.

REFERENCES

Chapter I (pp. 1-51)

1. Russell, Bertrand, *A History of Western Philosophy*, Simon & Schuster, New York, 1955, pp. 21, 239, 360, 611.
2. Whitehead, A. N., *Alfred North Whitehead* (ed. R. N. Anshen), Harper & Row, New York, 1961, pp. 57, 91, 157, 176, 177.
3. Berelson, B., and Steiner, G. A., *Human Behavior: An Inventory of Scientific Findings*, Harcourt Brace, New York, 1964, pp. 248, 276.
4. Norris, Louis W., *Polarity; a Philosophy of Tensions and Values*, Henry Regnery Co., Chicago, 1956, pp. 24, 115, 212.
5. Cohen, Morris, R., *Studies in Philosophy and Science*, Frederick Ungar Publ. Co., New York, 1959, pp. 198, 355.
6. Watts, Alan W., *The Way of Zen*, Pantheon Books, New York, 1963, pp. 63, 64, 163.
7. Nagel, Ernest, *The Structure of Science*, Harcourt Brace, New York, 1961, pp. 7, 8, 398, 401.
8. Dubos, Rene J., *The Dreams of Reason*, Columbia University Press, New York, 1961, pp. 105, 109, 218.
9. Munn, Norman, L., *Psychology; the Fundamentals of Human Adjustment*, Houghton Mifflin Co., Boston, 1966, pp. 188, 215, 286, 428.
10. Morgan, Clifford T., *Introduction to Psychology*, McGraw-Hill, 1961, pp. 221, 253, 272, 273.
11. Maslow, Abraham H., *New Knowledge in Human Values*, Harper & Row, New York, 1959, pp. 120, 136, 137, 214.
12. Wolman, Benjamin B., *Contemporary Theories and Systems in Psychology*, Harper & Row, New York, 1960, pp. 143, 403, 486, 487, 553.
13. Gallup, George, *The Miracle Ahead*, Harper & Row, New York, 1964, pp. 179, 181, 189.
14. Hocking, William Ernest, *Human Nature and its Remaking*, Yale University Press, New Haven, Conn., 1943, pp. 164, 168, 173.
15. James, William, *The Will to Believe and Other Essays*, Dover Publications, New York, 1956, pp. 42, 145, 168, 169.
16. Perry, Ralph Barton, *Realms of Value*, Harvard University Press, Cambridge, Mass., 1954, pp. 373, 426, 484.
17. Dixon, W. Macneile, *The Human Situation*, Edward Arnold & Co., London, 1950, pp. 145, 202, 210, 299, 415.

18. La Barre, Weston, *The Human Animal,* University of Chicago Press, Chicago, 1954, pp. 189, 203, 216.
19. Brome, Vincent, *The Problems of Progress,* Cassell, London, 1963, pp. 76, 103, 144, 145.
20. Robert, Marthe, *The Psychoanalytic Revolution,* Harcourt Brace Jovanovich, New York, 1966, pp. 110, 111, 248, 386.
21. Severin, Frank T., ed., *Humanistic Viewpoints in Psychology,* McGraw-Hill, New York, 1965, pp. 37, 237, 296, 301, 346, 347, 412.
22. Garan, D. G., *Relativity for Psychology,* Philosophical Library, New York, 1968, pp. 20, 23, 92.

Chapter II (pp. 53-95)

1. Huxley, Julian, *et. al., The Humanist Frame,* Harper & Row, New York, 1961, pp. 25, 29, 188, 196, 243, 445, 607.
2. Sorokin, Pitirim A., *The Way and Power of Love,* The Beacon Press, Boston, Mass., 1964, pp. 180, 229, 313, 314, 343, 465, 478.
3. Hazo, Robert G., *The Idea of Love,* Praeger Publ., New York, 1967, pp. 217, 326, 367, 422, 425.
4. Schneider, Isidor, ed., *The World of Love,* George Braziller, New York, 1964, pp. 219, 220, 489, 510, 511, 513.
5. Barzun, Jacques, *Science: The Glorious Entertainment,* Harper & Row, New York, 1964, pp. 227, 235, 254, 279, 290, 298, 305.
6. Perry, Ralph Barton *General Theory of Value* Harvard Unversity Press, Cambridge, Mass., 1950, pp. 145, 305, 351, 551, 553, 576, 693.
7. Jones, Howard Mumford, *One Great Society,* Harcourt Brace, New York, 1960, pp. 79, 98, 187, 192, 239.
8. Northrop, F. S. C., *Man, Nature and God,* Simon & Schuster, New York, 1962, pp. 106, 108, 254, 262.
9. Muller, Herbert J., *Freedom in the Modern World,* Harper & Row, New York, 1966, pp. 316, 338, 473, 542.
10. MacIver, Robert Morrison, *The Pursuit of Happiness,* Simon & Schuster, New York, 1955, pp. 72, 86, 118, 204.
11. Watts, Alan Wilson, *The Meaning of Happiness,* J. L. Delkin, Stanford, Cal., 1963, pp. 5, 20, 21, 136, 219.
12. Jones, Howard Mumford, *The Pursuit of Happiness,* Harvard Univ. Press, Cambridge, Mass., 1953, pp. 128, 153, 159, 160, 163, 164.
13. May, Rollo, *Love and Will,* W. W. Norton, 1970, pp. 104, 153, 201, 233, 283, 286, 307.
14. Blanton, Smiley, *Love or Perish,* Simon & Schuster, New York, 1956, p. 127, 157, 168, 240.

15. Harper, Ralph, *Human Love Existential and Mystical,* Johns Hopkins Univ. Press, Baltimore, Md., 1966, pp. 170, 172, 175.
16. Hodge, Marshall Bryant, *Your Fear of Love,* Doubleday & Co., Garden City, N. Y., 1967, pp. 66, 215, 258.
17. Mumford, Lewis, *The Human Prospect,* Southern Illinois Univ. Press, Carbondale, Ill., 1965, pp. 290, 301, 303, 305.
18. Reich, Charles, *The Greening of America,* Random House, New York 1970, pp. 152, 153, 235, 241, 258, 261, 263, 389.
19. Bell, Daniel, *The End of Ideology* Free Press, Glencoe, Ill., 1961, pp. 30, 33, 34, 112, 248.
20. Fromm Erich, *The Sane Society,* Holt, Rinehart & Winston, New York, 1955, pp. 206, 208, 310, 311, 356.
21. Marcuse, Herbert, *One Dimensional Man,* Beacon Press, Boston, Mass., 1964, pp. 73, 232, 237, 251.
22. Lamont, Corliss, *The Philosophy of Humanism,* F. Ungar Publ. Co., New York, 1965, pp. 79, 190, 191, 233, 277.
23. Hocking, William Ernest, *Human Nature and Its Remaking,* Harper Bros., New York, 1956, pp. 39, 140, 164, 184.
24. Kennan, George F. *Democracy and the Student Left,* Little, Brown, Boston, 1968, pp. 205, 212, 217, 237.
25. Roszak, Theodore, *The Making of Counter Culture,* Doubleday, Garden City, New York, 1970, pp. 64, 129, 155, 164, 178, 182, 184.
26. Jacobs, Paul, and Landau, Saul, *The New Radicals,* Random House, New York, 1966, pp. 4, 6, 82, 97.
27. Howe, Irving, ed., *The Radical Papers,* Doubleday & Co., New York, 1966, pp. 108, 120, 147, 173.
28. Keniston, Kenneth, *The Uncommitted Alienated Youth,* Harcourt Brace Jovanovich, New York, 1965, pp. 74, 240, 271, 352, 425, 447.
29. Goodman, Paul, *Growing Up Absurd,* Random House, New York, 1960, pp. 51, 70, 119, 131, 225, 240, 251.
30. Stein, Maurice, *et al., Identity and Anxiety,* Free Press, Glencoe, Ill., 1962, pp. 37, 289, 520, 581.
31. Sypher, Wylie, *Loss of Self in Modern Literature and Art,* Random House, New York, 1962, pp. 126, 127, 131, 149.
32. Braden, William, *The Private Sea: LSD and the Search for God,* Quadrangle Books, New York, 1970, pp. 83, 119, 120, 250, 252.
33. Holton, Gerald, ed., *Science and Culture* Houghton Mifflin, Boston, Mass., 1965, pp. 16, 102, 104, 284, 289.
34. Snow, C. P., *The Two Cultures: And a Second Look,* Cambridge University Press, Cambridge, Engl., 1964, pp. 152, 153, 161.
35. Bronowski, Jacob, *Science and Human Values,* Harper & Row, New York, 1965, pp. 112, 113, 152, 158, 177.
36. Perry, Ralph Barton, *The Humanity of Man,* George Braziller, New York, 1956, pp. 55, 73, 147, 166.

37. Pepper, Stephen C., *The Source of Value*, University of California Press, Berkeley, Cal., 1958, pp. 135, 150, 141 183.
38. Hall Everett W., *Modern Science and Human Values*, Van Nostrand, New York, 1956, pp. 383, 453, 473, 475.

Chapter III (pp. 97-148)

1. Menninger, Karl A., *Love Against Hate*, Harcourt Brace, New York, 1960, pp. 75, 89, 116, 122, 137.
2. Murphy, Gardner, *Human Potentialities*, Basic Books, New York, 1958, pp., 66, 91, 125, 171, 180.
3. English, O. Spurgeon, and Pearson, Gerald H., *Emotional Problems of Living*, W. W. Norton, New York, 1963, pp., 198, 204, 273.
4. Gordon, Chad, and Gergen, Kenneth J., eds., *The Self in Social Interaction*, John Wiley, New York, 1968, pp. 35, 88, 155, 275, 393.
5. Packard, Vance, *The Naked Society*, David McKay Co., New York, 1964, pp., 7, 239, 240, 289, 291.
6. Skinner, B. F., *Beyond Freedom and Dignity*, Alfred A. Knopf, New York, 1971, pp., 26, 47, 103, 168, 169, 194.
7. White, Robert W., *The Abnormal Personality* Ronald Press, Co., New York, 1956, pp., 83, 146, 171, 215, 248.
8. Kimble, George A., and Garmezy, Norman, *Principles of General Psychology*, Ronald Press Co., New York, 1963, pp., 23, 34, 137.
9. Saul, Leon J., *Emotional Maturity*, J. B. Lippincott, Philadelphia, Pa., 1960, pp. 54, 169, 172, 238, 253.
10. May, Rollo, *Love and Will*, W. W. Norton, New York, 1970, pp., 38, 39, 159, 192, 215, 224.
11. Dollard, John, and Miller, Neal E., *Personality and Psychotherapy*, McGraw-Hill, New York, 1956, pp., 246, 327, 347, 348.
12. Mowrer, O. Hobart, *Learning Theory of Behavior*, John Wiley, New York 1960, pp., 124, 245, 249, 342.
13. Severin, F. T., ed., *Humanist Viewpoints in Psychology*, McGraw-Hill, New York, 1965, pp., 37, 38, 189, 237, 296, 301, 347, 416.
14. Wolman, Benjamin B., *Contemporary Theories and Systems in Psychology*, Harper & Row, New York, 1960, pp., 143, 403, 486, 487, 553.
15. Woodworth, Robert S., *Psychology*, Holt Rinehart & Winston, New York, 1953, pp., 124, 133, 172, 232, 264, 269.
16. Koehler, Wolfgang, *The Place of Value in a World of Facts*, Meridian Books, Inc., New York, 1959, pp., 372, 399, 408, 413.

17. Murphy, Gardner, *An Introduction to Psychology,* Harper & Row, New York, 1951, pp., 35, 64, 90, 128, 164.

18. Misiak, H., and Sexton, V. S., *History of Psychology,* Grune & Stratton, New York, 1966, pp., 328, 378, 414, 454, 455.

19. Menninger, Karl A., *Man Against Himself,* Harcourt Brace, New York, 1958, pp., 40, 128, 162, 203, 216.

20. Freud, Sigmund, *The Basic Writings of Sigmund Freud* (ed. A. A. Brill), Modern Library, New York, 1938, pp., 62, 113, 245, 386, 377, 411.

21. Brill, A. A., *Basic Principles of Psychoanalysis,* Garden Books, New York, 1949, pp., 35, 36, 38, 206, 207, 235, 281.

22. Hall, Calvin, *A Primer of Freudian Psychology,* World Publ. Co., New York, 1954, pp., 248, 249, 270, 271, 284.

23. Hendrick, Ives, *Facts and Theories of Psychoanalysis,* Alfred A. Knopf, New York, 1958, pp., 134, 240, 241, 303, 306.

24. Mowrer, O. Hobart, *The Crisis in Psychiatry and Religion,* Van Nostrand, New York, 1961, pp., 126, 144, 167, 195, 202.

25. Eysenck, H. J., *Sense and Nonsense in Psychology,* Penguin Books, Baltimore, Md., 1957, pp., 210, 211, 319, 320.

26. Pinckney, Edward R., and Pinckney, Cathy, *The Fallacy of Freud and Psychoanalysis,* Prentice-Hall, Englewood, N. J. 1965, pp. 108, 109, 121.

27. Robert, Marthe, *The Psychoanalytic Revolution,* Harcourt Brace Jovanovich, New York, 1966, pp., 48, 68, 110, 111, 248, 249, 386.

28. Maslow, Abraham H., *Toward A Psychology of Being,* Van Nostrand, New York, 1968, pp., 48, 103, 169, 171, 173, 197.

29. Hilgard, Ernest R., *Introduction to Psychology* Harcourt Brace Jovanovich, New York, 1967, pp., 38, 42, 135, 150, 167, 232, 290.

30. Menninger, Karl A., *The Vital Balance,* The Viking Press, 1964, pp. 38, 69, 77, 117, 162, 264, 285.

31. Morgan, Clifford T., *Introduction to Psychology,* McGraw-Hill, New York, 1961, pp., 85, 167, 174, 253, 267.

32. Strecker, Edward A., *Basic Psychiatry,* Random House, New York, 1952, pp., 92, 137, 174, 215 231 287, 301.

33. Howard, Jane, . . . *Guided Tour of Human Potential Movement,* McGraw-Hill, 1970, pp., 18, 25, 53, 95, 115, 133, 199, 207, 237, 244.

34. Conant James B., *Modern Science and Modern Man,* Columbia University Press, New York, 1953, pp., 49, 194, 225, 318, 325, 342.

35. Cohen, John *Humanistic Psychology,* George Allen & Unwin, London, 1958, pp. 26, 119, 124, 163, 178, 180.

36. Schultz, Duane P., *A History of Modern Psychology,* Academic Press, New York, 1970, pp., 124, 136, 306, 325, 326.

37. Garan, D. G., *Relativity for Psychology,* Philosophical Library, New York, 1968, pp., 37, 41, 51, 72, 81, 88, 96, 109, 115.

Chapter IV (pp. 149-203)

1. Menninger, Karl A., *The Vital Balance,* The Viking Press, New York, 1964, pp., 162, 264, 285, 357, 385, 399.
2. Dollard, John, and Miller, Neal E., *Personality and Psychotherapy,* McGraw-Hill, New York, 1956, pp., 199, 246, 261, 318, 327.
3. White, Robert W., *The Abnormal Personality,* Ronald Press Co., New York, 1959, pp., 83, 146, 171, 215, 248.
4. Morgan, Clifford T., *Introduction to Psychology,* McGraw-Hill, New York, 1961, pp., 167, 184, 189, 205, 213, 225.
5. Hilgard, Ernest R., *Introduction to Psychology,* Harcourt Brace, New York, 1967, pp., 38, 150, 167, 232, 290, 529, 533, 547.
6. Strecker, Edward A., *Basic Psychiatry,* Random House, New York, 1962, pp., 92, 137, 174, 231, 287, 301, 302.
7. May, Rollo, *Love and Will,* W. W. Norton, New York, 1970, pp., 38, 93, 159, 192, 215, 224.
8. Maher, Brendan A., *Principles of Psychopathology,* McGraw-Hill, New York, 1966, 192, 235, 436, 472.
9. Frankl, Victor E., *Man's Search for Meaning,* Simon & Schuster, 1970, pp., 159, 169, 201, 241, 248, 270, 273.
10. Klein, D. B., *Mental Hygiene,* Holt, Rinehart & Winston, New York, 1965, pp., 327, 370, 403, 548, 625.
11. English, O. Spurgeon, and Finch, Stuart M., *Introduction to Psychiatry,* W. W. Norton, New York, 1957, pp., 62, 138, 197, 232, 276.
12. Brill, A. A., *Basic Principles of Psychoanalysis,* Garden Books, New York, 1949, pp., 35, 145, 146, 147, 206, 220, 235, 281.
13. Wolman, Benjamin B., *Contemporary Theories and Systems of Psychology,* Harper & Row, New York, 1966, pp., 143, 403, 486, 553.
14. O'Kelly, Lawrence I., and Muckler, Frederick A., *Introduction to Psychopathology,* Prentice-Hall, Englewood, N. J. 1955, pp., 148-169.
15. Ebin, David, ed., *The Drug Experience,* The Orion Press, New York, 1961, pp., 132, 174, 258, 369, 373.
16. Burn, Harold, *Drugs, Medicines and Man,* Charles Scribner's Sons, New York, 1968, pp., 41, 114, 129, 132, 148, 215, 224.
17. Johnson, G., *The Pill Conspiracy,* Sherbourne Press, Los Angeles, Cal., 1967, pp., 22, 45, 47, 52, 56, 86, 90, 95, 163, 164.
18. Aldrich, Clarence K., *Introduction to Dynamic Psychiatry,* McGraw-Hill, New York, 1966, pp., 141, 159, 186, 203, 247.
19. Laing, R. D., *The Divided Self,* Pantheon Books, New York, 1970, pp. 72, 85, 109, 132, 161, 194.
20. Saul, Leon J., *Emotional Maturity,* J. B. Lippincott, Philadelphia, Pa., 1960, pp., 44, 169, 172, 238, 253.

21. Eysenck, H. J., *Sense and Nonsense in Psychology,* Penguin Books, Inc., Baltimore, Md., 1957, pp., 210, 211, 237, 283, 319.
22. Berelson, Bernard, and Steiner, Gary A., *Human Behavior, An Inventory of Scientific Findings,* Harcourt Brace, New York, 1964, pp., 158-162.
23. Mowrer, O. Hobart, *The Crisis in Psychiatry and Religion,* Van Nostrand, New York, 1961, pp., 144, 167, 195, 202.
24. Harper, Robert A., *Psychoanalysis and Psychotherapy:* 36 *Systems,* Prentice-Hall, Englewood, N. J., 1960, pp., 127, 138, 141, 185.
25. Modell, Walter, and Lansing Alfred, and the Editor's of Life, *Drugs,* Time Inc., New York, 1970, pp., 7, 58, 150, 151, 163.
26. De Ropp, Robert S., *Drugs and the Mind,* St. Martin's Press, New York, 1967, pp. 63, 78, 109, 157, 174.
27. Talalay, Paul, ed., *Drugs in Our Society,* The Johns Hopkins Press, Baltimore, Md., 1964, pp., 205, 216, 222, 235, 273.
28. U. S. Bureau of the Census, *Statistical Abstract of the United States,* U. S. Government Printing Office, Washington, D. C., 1973.
29. Hunt, Morton M., *The Thinking Animal,* Little, Brown & Co., Boston, 1964, pp., 139, 172, 317, 397, 400.
30. Hollingshead, August B., and Redlich, F. C., *Social Class and Mental Illness,* John Wiley, New York, 1958, pp., 161, 252, 284.
31. Baker, George W., and Chapman, Dwight W., eds. *Man and Society in Disaster,* Basic Books, New York, 1962, pp., 19, 133.
32. Garan D. G., *Relativity for Psychology,* Philosophical Library, New York, 1968, pp., 136, 161, 164, 171, 173.

Chapter V (pp. 205-259)

1. U. S. President's Commission on Heart Disease, Cancer and Stroke, *Report to the President,* Govt. Printing Office, Washington, D. C., 1964, pp., 3, 4, 8, 12, 22, 29, 33, 48.
2. Miller, Benjamin F., *The Complete Medical Guide,* Simon & Schuster, New York, 1970, pp., 21, 420, 428, 435, 438, 443; 525.
3. Dubos, Rene, *Man Adapting,* Yale University Press, New Haven, Conn., 1965, pp., 32, 191, 192, 240, 340, 428.
4. Milne Lorus J., and Milne, Margery, *The Ages of Life,* Harcourt Brace, New York, 1968, pp., 187, 233, 237.
5. Cooley, Donald G., *The Science Book of Wonder Drugs,* Franklin Watts, New York, 1964, pp., 81, 97, 134, 140, 158, 184, 201, 202, 230.
6. Burn, Harold, *Drugs, Medicines and Man,* Charles Scribner's Sons, New York, 1966, pp., 17, 22, 115, 116, 184, 215.
7. Nelson, James, ed., *Wisdom for Our Times,* W. W. Norton, New York, 1961, pp., 45, 48, 49, 208.

8. Prinzmetal, Myron, and Winter, William, *Heart Attack: New Hope, New Knowledge, New Life,* Simon & Schuster, New York, 1965, pp., 8, 107, 119, 132, 140, 141.

9. Weiss, Edward, and English, O. Spurgeon, *Psychosomatic Medicine,* W. B. Saunders, Philadelphia, Pa., 1967, pp. 45, 85, 86, 181, 192, 226, 256, 316, 350, 430, 431, 522.

10. Dunbar, Flanders, *Mind and Body,* Random House, New York, 1955, pp., 46, 58, 141, 159, 207, 259, 297, 316.

11. Graham, M. F., *Prescription for Life,* David McKay, New York, 1966, pp., 26, 28, 38, 46, 154.

12. Steincrohn, Peter J., *You Can Increase Your Heart Power,* Doubleday, New York, 1958, pp., 30, 79, 140, 187, 237, 241, 290, 307.

13. Fishbein, Morris, ed., *Heart Care, an Authoritative Guide by Twenty Experts,* Hanover House, Garden City, N. Y., 1960, pp., 6, 51, 105, 150, 152, 166, 173, 179, 198, 208.

14. Speedby, Henry J., *The 20th Century and your Heart,* Associated Booksellers, Bridgeport, Conn., 1966, pp., 67, 110, 113, 128, 155, 173.

15. Dally, A. G., *A Reader's Guide to Modern Medicine,* Harper & Row, 1968, pp., 28, 46, 215, 220, 255, 263.

16. Needles, Robert J., *Your Heart and Common Sense,* Frederick Fell, New York, 1963, pp., 45, 60, 147, 234.

17. Inglis Brian, *The Case for Unorthodox Medicine,* G. P. Putnam's Sons, New York, 1965, pp., 21, 36, 37, 51, 183.

18. Zugibe, Frederick T., *Eat, Drink, and Lower Your Cholesterol,* McGraw-Hill, 1963, pp., 7, 14, 15, 23, 102, 157.

19. Burn, Harold, *Our Most Interesting Diseases,* Charles Scribner's Sons, New York, 1964, pp., 17, 25, 33, 35, 95, 115, 126, 173, 206.

20. Brams, William A., *Managing Your Coronary,* J. B. Lippincott Co., Philadelphia, Pa., 1960, pp. 80, 82, 118, 119, 132.

21. Page, Irvine H., *Hypertension,* Charles C. Thomas, Springfield, Ill., 1956, pp., 35, 72, 128, 155, 184, 230, 267.

22. Wyden, Peter, *The Overweight Society,* William Morrow & Co., New York, 1965, pp. 128, 151, 156, 161, 169, 311, 330.

23. Boyd, William, *An Introduction to the Study of Disease,* Lea & Febiger, Philadelphia, Pa., 1965, pp., 254, 267, 302, 438, 439, 454.

24. Brooke, James W., *Arthritis and You,* Harper Bros, New York, 1960, pp., 34, 55, 89, 103, 107, 109, 146.

25. Bland, John H., *Arthritis: Medical Treatment and Home Care,* The Macmillan Co., New York, 1960, pp., 23, 41, 53, 54, 61, 63, 126.

26. Danowski, T. S., *Diabetes as a Way of Life,* Coward, McCann, New York, 1967, pp., 67, 70, 138, 141.

27. Sindoni, A. M., *The Diabetic's Handbook,* Ronald Press, Co., New York, 1959, pp., 6, 57, 65, 108, 191.

28. Weller, Charles, and Boylan, Brian Richard, *The New Way to*

Live with Diabetes, Doubleday & Co., Garden City, N. Y., 1966, pp., 10, 28, 37, 41, 52, 73, 163, 182, 194.

29. Crohn, Burrill B., *Understand Your Ulcer,* Sheridan House, New York, 1957, pp. 104, 118, 161, 174.

30. Montague, Joseph F., *How to Conquer Nervous Stomach Trouble,* Argonaut Books, London, 1964, pp., 57, 58, 114, 195, 251, 275.

31. Serino, Girard Samuel, *Your Ulcer; Prevention, Control, Care,* J. B. Lippincott, Philadelphia, Pa., 1966, pp., 38, 55, 63, 73, 77, 94, 104.

32. Wassersug, Joseph D., *Understanding Your Symptoms,* Abelard Schuman, London, 1963, pp., 26, 146, 186, 188, 202, 218.

33. The Allergy Foundation of America, *Allergy Its Mysterious Causes and Modern Treatment,* Grosset & Dunlop, New York, 1967, pp., 13 14, 25, 63, 70, 87, 90, 144, 161, 199.

34. Berglund, H. J., and Nichols, H. L., *It's Not All in Your Head,* North Castle Books, Greenwich, Conn., 1963, pp., 111, 121, 132, 156, 180, 219.

35. Gallup, George, *The Miracle Ahead,* Harper & Row, New York, 1964, pp., 179, 180, 182.

36. Prehoda, Robert W., *Extended Youth, the Promise of Gerontology,* G. P. Putnam's Sons, New York, 1968, pp., 143, 185, 187, 193.

37. Garan, D. G., *Relativity for Psychology,* Philosophical Library, New York, 1968, pp., 213, 215, 218, 226, 230, 256, 257.

Chapter VI (pp. 261-309)

1. Skinner, B. F., *Walden Two,* The Macmillan Co., New York, 1963, pp., 80, 117, 352.

2. Hartley, E. L., and Hartley, R. E., *Fundamentals of Social Psychology,* Alfred Knopf, New York, 1962, pp., 357, 480, 541.

3. Carpenter, F. and Haddan, E. F., *Systematic Application of Psychology to Education,* The Macmillan Co., New York, 1964, pp., 50, 67, 83.

4. Klausmeier, H. J., and Goodwin, W., *Learning and Human Abilities,* Harper & Row, New York, 1966, pp., 20, 70, 91, 375, 425, 457.

5. Frandsen, A. N., *Educational Psychology,* McGraw-Hill, New York, 1967, pp., 33, 308, 311, 476, 589, 643.

6. Cronbach, L. J., *Educational Psychology,* Harcourt Brace, New York, 1963, pp., 41, 151, 326, 406, 515, 613.

7. Clayton, T. E., *Teaching and Learning,* Prentice-Hall, Englewood Cliffs, N. J., 1965, pp., 65, 74, 77, 82.

8. Blair G. M., *et al., Educational Psychology,* The Macmillan Co., New York, 1962, pp. 68, 97, 125, 208, 232, 302, 413.

9. Sorenson, H., *Psychology in Education,* McGraw-Hill, New York, 1964, pp., 310, 311, 347, 375, 430, 511.

10. Huxley, Julian, *et. al. The Humanist Frame*, Harper & Row, New York, 1961, pp., 35, 355, 418, 428.

11. Pressey, S. L. and Robinson, F. P., *Psychology in Education*, Harper & Row, New York, 1960, pp., 175, 189, 203, 317.

12. Frasier, G. W., *An Introduction to the Study of Education* Harper & Row, New York, 1959, pp., 138, 141, 166, 172, 200.

13. Bernard, H. W., *Psychology of Learning and Teaching*, McGraw-Hill, New York, 1965, pp., 144, 237, 291, 313.

14. Raths, L. E., *et al.*, *Values and Teaching*, Charles Merrill Co., Columbus, Ohio, 1966, pp., 38, 51, 204, 316.

15. Skinner, B. F., *Beyond Freedom and Dignity*, Alfred Knopf, New York, 1971, pp. 64, 131, 180, 209.

16. Montagu, Ashley, *The Humanization of Man*, The World Publishing Co., New York, 1962, pp., 187, 214, 310.

17. Silberman, Charles, *Crisis in the Classroom*, Random House, New York, 1970, pp., 124, 172, 196, 215.

18. Gross, R., and Gross, B., *Radical School Reform*, Simon & Schuster, New York, 1970, pp., 38, 187, 206, 211, 244.

19. Henry, Jules, *Culture Against Man*, Random House, New York, 1963, pp., 43, 319, 321.

20. Lindgren, H. C., *Educational Psychology in the Classroom*, John Wiley, New York, 1962, pp., 114, 260, 265, 352.

21. Reger, Roger, *School Psychology*, Charles C. Thomas Springfield, Ill., 1965, pp., 107, 108, 168, 170.

22. McKinney, Fred, *Psychology of Personality and Adjustment*, John Wiley, New York, 1960, pp., 69, 115, 152, 309, 416, 426, 461, 482.

23. Kozol, Jonathan, *Death at an Early Age*, Houghton Mifflin, Boston, 1967, pp., 112, 185, 231.

24. Kohl, Herbert, *Thirty-Six Children*, W. W. Norton, New York, 1968, pp., 163, 175, 192.

25. Jencks, Christopher, *Inequality: A Reassessment of the Effect of Family and Schooling in America*, Basic Books, Inc., New York, 1972.

26. Skinner, C. E., *Educational Psychology*, Prentice-Hall, Englewood Cliffs, N. J., 1960, pp., 93, 352, 392, 468.

27. Erikson, E. H., *Childhood and Society*, W. W. Norton, New York, 1968, pp., 132, 240, 256.

28. Klineberg, Otto, *Social Psychology*, Henry Holt, New York, 1954, pp., 310, 343, 345.

29. Klein, D. B., *Mental Hygiene*, Holt, Rinehart and Winston, New York, 1965, pp., 327, 370, 403, 625.

30. Brubacher, J. S., *Modern Philosophies of Education*, McGraw-Hill, New York, 1962, pp., 31, 98, 349, 352, 353, 362.

31. Stephens, J. M., *The Process of Schooling*, Holt, Rinehart & Winston, New York, 1967, pp., 72, 73, 568.
32. Cohen, Arthur A. ed., *Humanistic Education and Western Civilization*, Simon & Schuster, New York, 1964, pp., 10, 45, 91, 123, 227, 230.
33. Fisher, J. A., ed., *The Humanities in General Education*, Wm. C. Brown, Dubuque, Iowa, 1960, pp., 230, 232, 237, 338.
34. Jones, H. M., *One Great Society*, Harcourt Brace Jovanovich, New York, 1960, pp., 56, 79, 98, 187, 192.
35. Stevens, D. H., *The Changing Humanities*, Harper & Row, New York, 1953, pp., 74, 107, 122, 127.
36. The Joint Committee of ABA and AMA on Narcotic Drugs, *Drug Addiction*, Indiana Univ. Pr., Bloomington, Ind., 1968, pp., 37, 41, 47, 56, 87, 106, 125, 136.
37. Wilner, D. M., ed., *Narcotics*, Univ. of California Pr., Berkeley, Cal., 1965, pp. 17, 32, 40, 45, 56, 63, 88, 134, 189, 191.
38. Neumeyer, M. H., *Juvenile Delinquency in Modern Society*, Van Nostrand, Reinhold Co., New York, 1969, pp., 56, 87, 91, 97, 146, 173, 192, 287.
39. Jeffee, Saul, *Narcotics — An American Plan*, Paul S. Erikson, New York, 1966, pp., 23, 76, 91.
40. Barzun, Jacques, *Science: the Glorious Entertainment*, Harper & Row, New York, 1964, pp., 278, 279.
41. Dublin, L. I., *Suicide; a Sociological and Statistical Study*, Ronald Press, New York, 1963, pp., 56, 58, 67.
42. *International Encyclopedia of Social Sciences*, Volume XV, pp. 376-396, The Macmillan Co., New York, 1968.
43. Bell, Daniel, *The End of Ideology*, Free Press, Glencoe, Ill., 1964, pp. 275, 367, 368.
44. Larrabee, E. and Meyersohn, R., eds., *Mass Leisure*, Free Press, Glencoe, Ill., 1968, pp. 18, 105, 161, 340, 352, 363.
45. Riesman, David, *The Lonely Crowd*, Yale Univ. Press, New Haven, Conn., 1960, pp. 342, 343, 348, 372, 385.
46. Garan, D. G., *Relativity for Psychology*, Philosophical Library, New York, 1968, pp., 197, 243, 245, 251, 252, 253.
47. Newsweek, Vol. LXXXI, No. 17, p. 113 ff., April 23, 1973.

Chapter VII (pp. 311-374)

1. *International Encyclopedia of Social Sciences*, The Macmillan Co., New York, 1968

References

Vol. II — pp. 226-237, 239, 240, 241.
Vol. IV — pp. 410, 415, 423, 446, 457, 460.
Vol. XV — pp. 375-396.

2. Ebenstein, William, *Modern Political Thought*, Holt, Rinehart, New York, 1960, pp., 53, 55, 233, 268, 472, 625, 743, 778.

3. Runciman, W. C., *Social Science and Political Theory*, Cambridge University Press, Cambridge, Engl. 1963, pp., 117, 108, 123, 134, 156.

4. Friedrich, Carl Joachim, *Man and His Government*, McGraw-Hill, New York, 1963, pp., 22, 27, 99, 123, 125, 383, 523, 558, 469, 659.

5. Newcomb, Theodore M., *Social Psychology*, Dryden Press, New York, 1964, pp., 220, 274, 275, 595, 647.

6. Morgenthau, Hans J., *Dilemmas of Politics*, University of Chicago Press, Chicago Ill., 1958, pp., 52, 103, 183, 235, 284.

7. Muller, Herbert J., *Freedom in the Modern World*, Harper & Row, New York, 1966, pp., 45, 58, 155, 168, 212, 216, 362; 542.

8. Burns, Edward McNall, *Ideas in Conflict*, W. W. Norton, New York, 1960, pp., 6, 25, 83, 91, 181, 398, 450, 465, 497, 519, 551, 563, 572.

9. Dahl, Robert A., and Lindblom, Charles E., *Politics, Economics and Welfare*, Harper Bros., New York, 1958, pp., 102, 110, 287, 318, 521, 526.

10. Hitchner, Dell G., and Harbold, William H., *Modern Government*, Dodd, Mead & Co., New York, 1965, pp., 203, 205, 491, 560, 614, 615, 617.

11. Snyder, Richard C., ed., *Roots of Political Behavior*, American Book Co., New York, 1959, pp., 8, 9, 19, 44, 63, 231, 263, 506, 526, 544, 641.

12. Pennock, James R., and Smith, David G., *Political Science*, McMillan, New York, 1964, pp., 50, 85, 298, 376, 427, 598, 606, 641, 656.

13. Storing, Herbert J., ed., *Essays on Scientific Study of Politics*, Holt, Rinehart, New York, 1962, pp., 227, 272, 273, 295, 299, 303, 318.

14. Bogardus, Emory Stephen, *Fundamentals of Social Psychology*, Appleton-Century Crofts, 1959, pp., 80, 323, 336, 343, 525, 526.

15. Bidney, David, *Theoretical Anthropology*, Columbia University Press, New York, 1963, pp., 31, 112, 168, 297, 338, 385, 401, 437, 450, 451.

16. Hook, Sidney, *Reason, Social Myth, and Democracy*, Harper & Row, 1965, pp., 68, 274, 283, 288, 293, 296.

17. Mills, C. Wright, *The Social Imagination*, Oxford University Press, New York, 1959, pp., 49, 72, 107, 164, 166, 187, 194.

18. Black, Max, ed., *The Social Theories of Talcott Parsons*, Prentice-Hall, Englewood Cliffs, N. J., 1961, pp., 7, 13, 20, 63, 242.

19. Carr, Edward Hallett, *What is History?*, Alfred A. Knopf, New York, 1962, pp., 7, 64, 160, 185, 209.
20. Lasswell, Harold D., *Psychology in Politics*, Viking Press, New York, 1960, pp., 65, 68, 121, 157, 193, 206, 211.
21. Myrdal, Gunnar, *Asian Drama*, Pantheon Books, New York, 1969, pp., 47, 63, 225, 226, 378, 704, 706.
22. Parkinson, C. Northcote, *East and West*, Houghton Mifflin Co., Boston, 1963, pp., 21, 241, 245.
23. Klineberg, Otto, *Social Psychology*, Henry Holt, New York, 1954, pp., 99, 310, 343, 345, 383, 411, 513.
24. Murray, Gilbert, *Humanist Essays*, Unwin Books, London, Engl., 1964, pp., 132, 187.
25. Platt, John R., *The Step to Man*, John Wiley, 1966, pp., 132, 137, 181.
26. Ogburn, William F., and Nimkoff, Meyer F., *Sociology*, Houghton Mifflin Co., Boston, 1964, pp., 372, 464, 670, 742.
27. Conant, James B., *Modern Science and Modern Man*, Columbia University Press, New York, 1953, pp., 49, 194, 225, 318, 325, 342.
28. Easton, David, *A Framework for Political Analysis*, Prentice-Hall, Englewood Cliffs, N. J., 1965, pp., 22, 24, 27, 34, 134.
29. Rapoport, Anatol, *Science and the Goals of Man*, University of Michigan Press, Ann Arbor, Mich., 1950, pp., 246, 267, 268, 283.
30. Buehring, Edward H., ed., *Essays in Political Science*, Indiana University Press, Bloomington, Ind., 1966, pp., 10, 30, 34, 62.
31. Rudner, Richard S., *Philosophy of Social Sciences*, Prentice-Hall, Englewood Cliffs, N. J., 1966, pp., 46, 63, 108, 110.
32. Northrop, F. S. C., *Man, Nature and God*, Simon & Schuster, New York, 1962, pp. 45, 98, 108.
33. Young, Kimball, *Social Psychology*, Appleton-Century Crofts, 1956, pp., 571, 572, 615, 616, 617.
34. Toynbee, Arnold J., *Change and Habit; the Challenge of Our Time*, Oxford University Press, Oxford, Engl., 1966, pp., 100, 138, 149, 151.
35. White, Morton, *Foundations of Historical Knowledge*, Harper & Row, 1965, pp., 9, 109, 180, 225, 257, 271, 291.
36. Manuel, Frank E., *Shapes of Philosophical History*, Stanford University Press, Stanford, Cal., 1965, pp., 136, 157, 158, 161.
37. Davies, James C., *Human Nature in Politics*, John Wiley, New York, 1963, pp., 106, 116, 350, 358, 364.
38. Fromm, Erich, ed., *Socialist Humanism; an International Symposium*, Doubleday & Co., Garden City, N. Y., 1965, pp., 33, 53, 99, 130, 199, 210, 230, 278, 284, 303, 309, 315, 316.
39. Mayo, H. B., *An Introduction to Democratic Theory*, Oxford University Press, New York, 1960, pp., 136, 236, 259, 260, 282, 296.

40. Samuelson, Paul A., *Economics*, McGraw-Hill, 1970, pp., 2, 212, 224, 226, 232, 234, 241, 250, 251, 253, 756, 757; 758, 761.
41. Galbraith, John Kenneth, *The New Industrial State*, Houghton Mifflin Co., Boston, 1967, pp. 3, 33, 37, 44, 58, 205, 411.
42. Piel, Gerard, *Science in the Cause of Man*, Alfred A. Knopf, New York, 1962, pp., 262, 263, 264.
43. Von Mises, Ludwig, *Human Action; and Treatise on Economics*, Yale University Press, New Haven, Conn., 1963, pp., 13, 490, 684.
44. Lerner, Daniel, ed., *The Human Meaning of Social Sciences*, Meridian Books, New York, 1959, pp., 192, 193, 194, 196.
45. Harrington, Michael, *The Accidental Century*, The Macmillan Co., New York, 1965, pp., 39, 254, 255, 256, 263, 265, 271.
46. Lauterbach, Albert, *Man, Motives and Money*, Cornell University Press, 'Ithaca, N. Y., 1959, pp., 5, 114, 116, 238, 239.

Chapter VIII (pp. 375-430)

1. Einstein, Albert, and Infeld, Leopold, *The Evolution of Physics*, Simon & Schuster, New York, 1954, pp., 124, 148, 151, 158, 159, 196, 253, 256, 288, 303.
2. Bridgman, P. W., *The Way Things Are*, Harvard University Press, Cambridge, Mass, 1959, pp., 152, 157, 167, 173, 188, 191, 206, 207.
3. Whittaker, Sir Edmund, *From Euclid to Eddington*, Dover Publications, New York, 1960, pp., 53, 60, 82, 94, 118, 148, 155, 174, 178, 179, 201.
4. Planck, Max, *The New Science*, Meridian Books, New York, 1959, pp., 14, 97, 113, 170, 173, 174, 188, 205, 213, 215, 264, 268.
5. Schroedinger, Erwin, *Science, Theory and Man*, Dover Publications, New York, 1957, pp., 51, 59, 131, 141, 177, 195, 200.
6. Frank, Philipp, *Modern Science and Its Philosophy*, Harvard University Press, Cambridge, Mass., 1959, pp., 57, 98, 199, 129, 133, 289, 290.
7. Margenau, Henry, *Open Vistas*, Yale University Press, New Haven, Conn., 1961, pp., 50, 83, 97, 110, 112, 118, 127, 162, 199, 201, 233, 236.
8. Harrison, George Russell, *What Man May Be*, William Morrow, New York, 1956, pp., 17, 226, 241 252.
9. Gamow, George, *One, Two, Three . . . Infinity*, Viking Press, New York, 1961, pp., 91, 138, 144.
10. Joad, C. E. M., *Philosophical Aspects of Modern Science*, Allen & Unwin, London, Engl., 1963, pp., 24, 61, 148, 181, 265, 274.
11. American Foundation for Continuing Education *The Mystery of Matter*, Oxford University Press, New York, 1965, pp., 102, 106, 109, 117, 535, 539.

12. Handler Philip, *Biology and the Future Man*, Oxford University Press, New York, 1970, pp., 20, 21, 165, 166, 172, 175.
13. Shapley, Harlow, *et al.*, *The New Treasury of Science*, Harper & Row, 1965, pp., 378, 392, 403, 421, 423, 425, 468.
14. Oparin, Aleksander I., *Life, Its Nature, Origin and Development*, Academic Press, New York, 1962, pp., 7, 14, 55, 65, 111, 113, 159.
15. Scientific American Book, *The Physics and Chemistry of Life*, Simon & Schuster, New York, 1954, pp., 44, 45, 61, 73, 113, 119, 178, 180, 182.
16. Conant, James B., *Science and Common Sense*, Yale University Press, New Haven, Conn., 1961, pp., 41, 50, 57, 59, 293.
17. Phillips, Edwin A., *Basic Ideas in Biology*, The Macmillan Co., New York, 1971, pp., 609, 617, 618, 633.
18. Dobzhansky, Theodosius, *Genetics of the Evolutionary Process*, Columbia University Press, New York, 1970, pp., 1, 59, 60, 64, 79, 98, 136.
19. Dubos, Rene, *Man Adapting*, Yale University Press, New Haven, Conn., 1965, pp., 116, 121, 122, 126, 154, 159, 160.
20. Medawar, Peter Brian, *The Future Man*, Basic Books, New York, 1960, pp., 39, 43, 48, 52, 65, 98, 99, 125, 136, 174.
21. Papazian, Haig P., *Modern Genetics*, W. W. Norton, 1967, pp. 101, 165, 220, 265.

Chapter IX (pp. 431-478)

1. Russell, Bertrand, *A History of Western Philosophy*, Simon & Schuster, New York, 1945, pp., 21, 611, 668, 674, 793, 822, 823.
2. Whitehead, A. N., *Alfred North Whitehead* (ed. R. N. Anshen), Harper & Row, New York, 1961, pp., 6, 43, 54, 55, 91, 157, 176.
3. Stumpf, S. E., *Socrates to Sartre*, McGraw-Hill, New York, 1966, pp. 133, 143, 165, 335, 348, 398, 391, 400.
4. Trueblood, D. E., *General Philosophy*, Harper & Row, New York, 1963, pp., 28, 33, 45, 52, 60, 137, 146, 152, 318, 323, 326.
5. Caplan, Abraham, *The New World of Philosophy*, Random House, New York, 1961, pp., 19, 24, 28, 37, 59, 61, 117, 300, 303, 308, 351.
6. La Barre, Weston, *The Human Animal*, University of Chicago Press, Chicago, Ill., 1964, pp., 188, 189, 203, 204.
7. Read, Sir Herbert, *Education Through Art*, Pantheon Books, New York, 1956, pp., 70, 104, 108, 185, 283, 301, 308.
8. Read, Sir Herbert, *Icon and Idea*, Harvard University Press, Cambridge, Mass., 1955, pp. 25, 52, 128, 130, 134.
9. Gilson, Etiene, *Forms and Substances in the Arts*, Charles Scribner Sons, New York, 1966, pp., 81, 85, 98, 100, 105, 115.

10. Taubes, Frederick, *Abracadabra and Modern \ Art*, Dodd Mead, Boston, 1963, pp., 20, 26, 54.
11. Morris, Desmond, *The Biology of Art*, Alfred Knopf, New York, 1962, pp., 56, 151, 158, 172.
12. Philipson, M., *Aesthetics Today*, The World ,Publ. Co., New York, 1961, pp. 205, 212, 341, 346, 381, 448, 556, 649.
13. Hofstadter, A. and Kuhns R., *Philosophies of Art and Beauty*, The Modern Library, New York, 1964, pp., 27, 140, 205, 280, 381, 448, 556, 649.
14. Aldrich, V. C., *Philosophy of Art*, Prentice-Hall, Englewood, N. J., 1968, pp. 4, 33, 73, 75.
15. Garritt, E. F., *The Theory of Beauty*, Methuen & Co., London, 1960, pp. 31, 71, 80, 195, 197, 300.
16. Weiss, Paul, *The World of Art*, S. Illinois Univ. Press, Carbondale, Ill., 1961, pp., 61, 132, 136, 155, 167.
17. Maritain, Jacques, *The Responsibility of the Artist*, Charles Scribner, New York, 1960, pp. 57, 78, 108.
18. Jenkins, Iredell, *Art and Human Experience*, Harvard University Press, Cambridge, Mass, 1963, pp. 126, 129, 292, 294, 295, 301.
19. Ducasse, C. J., *The Philosophy of Art*, Dover Publications, New York, 1966, pp., 223, 225, 228.
20. Barzun, Jacques, *Science: the Glorious Entertainment*, Harper & Row, New York, 1964, pp., 229, 230, 235, 236.
21. Peckman, Morse, *Man's Rage for Chaos*, Chilton Book Co., Phila., Pa., 1965, pp., 314, 315.
22. Morris, Bertram, *Philosophical Aspects of Culture*, The Antioch Press, New York, 1961, pp., 17, 19, 30, 268, 274, 280, 281.

Chapter X (pp. 479-523)

1. Kahn, Herman, and Wiener, Anthony J., *The Year 2000*, The Macmillan Co., New York, 1968, pp., 110, 111, 193, 196, 198, 207: 348, 349, 351.
2. Huxley, Julian, *The Humanist Frame*, Harper Bros., New York, 1961, pp., 35, 39, 355, 418, 428.
3. Dubos, Rene, *Reason Awake*, Columbia University Press, New York, 1970, pp., 11, 17, 40, 63, 145, 239, 240, 246, 248, 249.
4. Muller, Herbert J., *Freedom in the Modern World*, Harper & Row, 1966, pp. 45, 58, 155, 168, 212, 216, 362, 372, 542.
5. Taylor Gordon R., *The Biological Time Bomb*, World Publishing Co., New York, 1968, pp., 109, 110, 143, 144, 186.
6. Snow, C. P., *The Two Cultures; and a Second Look*, Cambridge University Press, Cambridge, Engl., 1964, pp., 152, 153, 167.
7. Herndon, S., Beaver, J. R., and Davidson, R. F., *The Humanistic*

Tradition, Holt, Rinehart and Winston, New York, 1964, pp., 102, ff.

8. Sorokin, Pitirim A., *The Crisis of Our Age*, E. P. Dutton & Co., New York, 1965, pp., 105, 106, 125, 211, 247, 259, 263, 268, 320, 324.

9. Brome, V., *The Problem of Progress*, Cassell, London, Engl., 1963, pp. 139, 143, 153, 163, 223, 224.

10. Berkner, L. V., *The Scientific Age*, Yale University Press, New Haven, Conn., 1964, pp., 87, 88, 92, 146.

11. Clarke, Arthur C., *Profiles of the Future*, Harper & Row, New York, 1962, pp., 156, 162, 163, 209.

12. Kostelanetz, Richard, ed., *Social Speculations; Visions of our Time*, William Morrow, New York, 1971, pp., 64, 79, 107, 108, 216, 223, 224.

13. Glass, Bentley, *Science and Ethical Values*, University of North Carolina Press, Chapel Hill, N. C., 1968, pp., 81, 95, 261, 263, 302.

14. Toffler, Alvin, *Future Shock*, Bantam Book, Inc., New York, 1971, pp., 59, 95, 152, 166, 180, 263, 284, 314, 316, 323, 334, 358, 365, 446, 486.

15. Kuhns, William, *The Post-Industrial Prophets*, Weybright & Talley, New York, 1971, pp., 15, 65, 80, 82, 111, 138, 169, 181, 193, 217, 243, 259.

16. Platt, John R., *The Step to Man*, John Wiley, New York, 1966, pp., 25, 46, 128, 131, 137, 181.

17. Gallup, George, *The Miracle Ahead*, Harper & Row, New York, 1964, pp., 49, 60, 182, 184, 199, 203.

18. Riesman, David, *The Lonely Crowd*, Yale University Press, New Haven, Conn., 1960, pp., 325, 341, 348, 372, 385.

19. Skinner, B. F., *Beyond Freedom and Dignity*, Alfred A. Knopf, New York, 1971, pp., 24, 25, 43, 60, 61, 103, 121, 155, 168, 194.

20. Prehoda, Robert W., *Extended Youth: the Promise of Gerontology*, G. P. Putnam's Sons, New York, 1968, pp., 63, 143, 185, 187, 193.

21. Warshofsky, Fred, *The Control of Life: the 21st Century*, Viking Press, 1970, pp., 20, 21, 85, 88, 180, 181.

22. McLuhan, Marshall, *Understanding Media; the Extension of Man*, McGraw-Hill, New York, 1964, pp., 3, 4, 5, 20, 70, 139.

23. May, Rollo, *Love and Will*, W. W. Norton, New York, 1969, pp., 29, 194, 201, 233, 284, 286, 307.

24. Monsma, John, ed., *Science and Religion*, G. P. Putnam's Sons, New York, 1962, pp. 61, 140, 183, 208, 235, 331, 385.

25. Beckwith, Burnham P., *The Next 500 Years*, Exposition Press, New York, 1967, pp., 76, 78, 158.

26. Teilhard de Chardin, Pierre, *The Future of Man*, Harper & Row, New York, 1969, pp., 60, 96, 183, 270, 307.

INDEX

A

Adjustment: and the alchemy of enjoying only the "positive", 70, 261, 280, 284 (see also Alchemy, modern); onslaught by "positivistic" alchemists, re, 70, 94, 261, 284, 308; the opposite causation in, 280, 281; the satisfaction-need equivalence in, 261, 280.

Adler, Mortimer J., 489.

Alchemistic logic, the: contrary to the real, relative value causation, 46, 47, 522; experimental causal logic as, 50, 99, 100, 111, 146; the like-from-like logic of "sciences" and value beliefs, 46, 47, 50, 146; the logic of more satisfaction from satisfaction, 65-71; obstacle to sciences of man, 50, 86; of all "logical", non-relative causal concepts, 46, 50, 522; of behavioral scientism, 86, 144; of humanistic thought, 70, 71, 94; of psychology, 99-106; of the universal value-from-like-value beliefs, 70, 71, 94; of the weightless, ideational and unconscious, causality, 103, 105, 106; vs. the satisfaction-need and restriction-release equivalence, 46, 47, 261, 280.

Alchemy, modern: as all theory of values from like values, 46, 47, 94, 317, 318, 522; as the logic of enrichment

through positive enjoyment, 46, 47, 65-71, 94; in all "logical" modern science, 79, 83, 84, 280, 283, 479, 481; in behavioral "scientism", 54, 86, 522; in psychology, 97-147, 146; in social sciences, 311, 312, 319, 320; of all nonrelative thinking, 46, 47, 522; of unconscious and ideational causal theories, 105, 106, 312, 313, 317, 324, 340.

Alienation: as avoidance of anxiety and reality, 77, 104; as impoverishment through over-enjoyments, 76, 77, 82, 155; in the modern life and thought, 75, 76, 81, 156; its ideational alchemistic theories, 77, 104; its unsuspected opposite causes, 76, 156.

Allergy, 241-242.

Allport, Gordon W., 109, 316, 336, 337, 339.

Analyses: and the alchemy of their ideational causal theory, 105, 179, 181; in psychotherapy, 179-181; loose, of legends, folklore, etc., 143; never revealing the real, opposite causes, 181.

Angell, Sir Norman, 323, 335.

Antibiotics: functional aspects of, 245, 246; overstimulation danger in use of, 246.

Antistimulation treatment: as a unique future possibility, 190, 191; by adapted drugs, 195; by psychologic "shock", 195,

543

V

Value delusions, 53-95: about the last stage harmony, 87-88; the alchemistic like-from-like logic of, 52, 55, 65, 70, 94; as obstacles to progress, 64, 81-92; contrary to causal facts, 85, 86, 87, 90; in humanistic thought, 53-94; most important, universal factors recognized least, 83, 84, 112; the "negative", real sources of values not seen, 45, 50, 79, 85, 94; practically dangerous, 64, 71, 79, 81, 92, 93; rare, unessential factors seen as remarkable, 82, 83, 90, 91; their gullible victims, 71-80; their like-from-like logic contrary to causal facts, 54, 81, 94, 95; vs. the relative, opposite causation, 79, 94. *See also* Alchemy, modern; Humanistic value delusions.

Value enjoyments, 64-71: and the alchemy of positive reactions from, 52, 66, 70 (*see* Alchemistic logic, the); as the highest humanistic goals, 66, 67, 487, 488; insidious overadjustments and dangers through, 67, 68, 71, 80, 81, 92, 93, 94, 103, 104, 490; their self-defeat, 67, 68, 69, 71, 92, 487, 489, 491, 511; vs. the only possible, mechanistic progress, 489, 511, 512.

Value experiences: as sources of all behavior, 3, 53, 55, 64, 261, 492; as mechanisms of cognition, 7, 53, 432, 433; self-defeat of "qualitative"

deepening of, 79, 80, 489, 493, 523; their opposite, relative causation, 24, 55, 93, 261.

Value theories: as the necessary bases in humanistic thought, 91; no agreement or science yet in, 92.

Values: as the paradoxical sources all capacities, 3, 53, 64, 91, 261, 523; as satisfactions or releases deriving from needs or restrictions, 2, 5, 13, 54, 58, 75; the most important, universal values noticed least, 83, 84, 85, 94; showing as true the opposite of what is causally true, 84, 85, 87; their enrichment through relative causation, 55, 523; their opposite causal sources, 54, 55, 322, 510; vs. the relative view, 55, 65, 70, 94. *See also* Alchemy, modern; Relative causation.

Vicious circle, the: as a noose tightening with "improvements", 14-15; in all overadjustment, 14, 151, 210; in functional diseases and disorders, 210; in neuroses and psychoses, 151; the "ingeniousness" of opposite reactions through, 98, 121, 159.

W